THE ILLUSTRATED ENCYCLOPEDIA OF
WORLD MYTHOLOGY

THE ILLUSTRATED ENCYCLOPEDIA OF
WORLD
MYTHOLOGY

A COMPREHENSIVE A–Z OF THE MYTHS AND LEGENDS OF ANCIENT GREECE, ROME, EGYPT, PERSIA, INDIA, CHINA, AND THE NORSE AND CELTIC LANDS

ARTHUR COTTERELL & RACHEL STORM

HERMES
HOUSE

C O N

Publisher: Joanna Lorenz
Editorial Director: Helen Sudell
Editor: Emma Gray
Editorial Assistant: Helen Marsh
Designer: Artmedia
Illustrators: James Alexander, Nick Beale, Glenn Steward

ISBN 978-1-78214-337-6

Manufactured in China

2 4 6 8 10 9 7 5 3

NOTES
Although the information in this book is believed to be accurate and true at the time of going to press, neither the authors nor the copyright holder can accept any legal responsibility or liability for any errors or omissions that may have been made.

The entries in this encyclopedia are all listed alphabetically. When more than one name exists for a character the entry is listed under the name used in the original country of origin for that particular myth. Names in ITALIC CAPITAL letters indicate that that name has an individual entry. Special feature spreads examine specific mythological themes in more detail. If a character is included in a special feature spread it is noted at the end of their individual entry.

T E N T S

PREFACE

Every culture has evolved its own mythology, defining its character and offering a way to understand the world. This collection of myths contains stories drawn from the three outstanding traditions of Europe and from the great civilizations of Asia, some of the oldest, most powerful narratives in the world. Greek, Celtic and Norse legends form the core of European mythological thought. Myths from the Middle East include those of the Sumerians and Babylonians; the ancient Iranians; the Egyptians; the Canaanites and Hebrews. The section on South and Central Asia deals with the Hindu and Buddhist deities of India, Sri Lanka, Tibet and Nepal. Daoist and Buddhist myths; the folk religion of China; the Shinto deities of Japan; and animist and shamanistic religions practised from Siberia to the South-east Asian archipelago are included in the section on East Asia.

GILGAMESH was the Assyro-Babylonian hero of a great epic poem dating from the second millennium BC. Here, flanked by centaur-like figures wearing the horned crowns of the gods, Gilgamesh supports the winged disc which represents the Assyrian creator god, Ashur. (SYRIO-HITTITE STELE, 9TH CENTURY BC.)

From Mesopotamia, the cradle of Western civilization, come legends of which we are able to glimpse only fragments, while the belief systems of other ancient societies, such as the Egyptians and

A CELTIC DEITY, possibly Dagda, dangles two warriors high above his head, and thus reveals his awesome power, while the warriors in turn lift two boars, showing their supremacy over animals. (GUNDESTRUP CAULDRON, GILDED SILVER, C. 100 BC.)

Greeks, are far more readily accessible. The stories that have survived from these ancient civilizations describe gods that have long passed into history. Other deities, such as those of Hinduism and Buddhism, remain at the centre of living faiths, worshipped by millions of present-day devotees. But whether the myths recounted in this book belong to current or long-vanished cultures, they continue to exert their influence on the civilizations of the world, as their themes are explored in literature and the visual arts, and the archetypes they present help to deepen our understanding of human psychology.

All human societies recognize powers that are greater than themselves, such as light and dark; sun, storm and frost; flood and drought; and the growth of the plants on which their lives depend.

Investing such powers with spirits that have a recognizably human nature has allowed people to make greater sense of a random and threatening universe. Propitiating the spirits with offerings and prayers allows their worshippers to feel that they have a degree of control. At the same time, by seeking the protection of a deity, devotees are able to relinquish responsibility for their own lives to a higher authority. Myths concerning gods and goddesses help to give shape to the powers that are seen to preserve or endanger humanity.

Another strand of mythology recounts the experiences of human or semi-divine heroes, and touches upon the fundamental issues of existence. These stories deal with the large themes which underlie our present-day consciousness, expressing these profound ideas in terms of individual biographies and events comprehensible in human terms. The legends of heroes endure from age to age, and hold our attention because they dare to go to the extremes of human terror and delight. Myths of every culture reveal the power of love,

SIGURD, the great Norse hero, helps his mentor, Regin, re-forge his wondrous sword. With it, Sigurd slew the dragon, Fafnir. (WOOD CARVING, 12TH CENTURY.)

with its accompanying anxiety and jealousy; the conflict between the generations, the old and the new; the violence of men, especially on the battlefield or in hand-to-hand combat; the mischief of the trouble-maker, bored by the steady pace of everyday events; the sadness of illness or injury; the mystery of death; and the possibility of another life after it. Stories about individual heroes chart the effect of enchantment upon the mind and body; the horror of madness with its disruption of human relations; the incidence of good luck and misfortune, and the whole issue of fate; the challenge of the unknown, whether a voyage into uncharted waters or a quest for a sacred object; the personal danger of a contest with a monster, even a beheading game; and the sadness of betrayal and treachery by family or friends. Myths about the wider world try to explain its mysteries, dealing with the cycle of fertility in human beings, animals, and plants; the relationship between humankind and the gods; the creation of the world and the origins of society; and, last, but not least, the nature of the universe.

Different myths tackle these great questions in distinct ways. But the heroes and heroines of every civilization find themselves facing the same basic problems. The Athenian hero Theseus successfully confronts the Minotaur on Crete, but, full of his success against the bull-man, forgets the agreement made with his father about raising a white sail on his ship if he escapes death himself. As a result of this moment of carelessness, Theseus' father commits suicide by leaping from the Athenian acropolis when a black sail is sighted. Similarly, in Ireland, the inability of Cuchulainn to stop and think for a moment leads to his killing of Conlai, his own son by the Amazon Aoifa. The Hindu hero Arjuna, on the eve of the great battle of Kurukshetra against his enemies the villainous Kauravas, has a crisis of conscience when he realizes that he can only achieve victory at the cost

NESSUS, a wild Greek centaur, tries to abduct Heracles' new bride while ferrying her across the River Evenus. (THE RAPE OF DEIANIRA BY GUIDO RENI, CANVAS, 1621.)

made to slow down the operation of fate's decrees, sometimes to thwart them entirely, but they never work. The great hero Gilgamesh accomplishes feats beyond the strength of any other man. He even succeeds in reaching the underworld in his search for the secret of immortality. But the knowledge he ultimately returns with is that he cannot avoid his own death. The tangled web of difficulties which besets the Greek hero Theseus can be traced to a number of actions, but one stands out clearly: the refusal of King Minos of Crete to sacrifice the white bull from the sea to the god Poseidon, its real owner. Once this sacrilege has been committed, the fate of Minos and his family, intertwined with that of Theseus, is sealed.

The gods are equally subject to the workings of fate. Odin can do nothing about his future death at Ragnarok, the doom of the gods. The Celtic sun god Lugh cannot save his son Cuchulainn on the battlefield. And even immortal Zeus, the chief god of the Greeks, has a duty to see that fate takes its proper course. He cannot control events.

One of the most striking characteristics of myths is the way they have been adopted and adapted by successive cultures. The myths of Asia were carried by missionaries from one part of the continent to another, giving rise to subtle variations in archetypal legends, and different manifestations of important mythological figures. Buddhism, for instance, which arose with the teachings of Gautama Buddha in northern India around 500 BC, was introduced to China around the time of Christ and to Japan in the sixth century AD. The buddha Amitabha, whose cult may in turn have been influenced by Iranian religion, became the leading figure of Japanese Buddhism as Amida, who was more highly venerated in Japan than Gautama himself. Gautama, meanwhile, was accommodated in Hindu myth as an avatar of Vishnu. Similarly, when the Romans absorbed

of killing his own relatives, and is only saved from his loss of nerve by the encouragement of his close friend, the god, Krishna.

Such stories underline both the variety and the continuity of human nature. Though the great myths concern gods, heroes and monsters, much of their fascination lies in the human values they illuminate. It is easy to identify with the grief of the widowed Isis or the bereaved Orpheus; with the disgust of Amaterasu at the awful behaviour of Susano-Wo, and her consequent sulk in her cave; with the happy family life of Shiva and Parvati; or with the hopeless love of Guinevere and Lancelot.

Very many myths reveal an interwoven pattern of circumstances outside the control of both mortals and gods. Fate and destiny in mythology are almost beyond manipulation. Attempts may be

KRISHNA, *the divine hero and the most beguiling incarnation of the great Hindu god, Vishnu, is accompanied by musicians as he dances in the rain, holding a lotus flower, a Hindu symbol of life and consciousness. (MINIATURE, RAJASTHAN SCHOOL, 17TH CENTURY.)*

power of the gods to destroy humankind, and arising from a universal awareness of the precariousness of human existence. Thus do the myths peculiar to each culture and religion point to the essential truths common to all humanity.

The abiding interest of mythology is its frankness about basic human drives. It could almost be described as sacred literature undisturbed by theologians. The raw and ragged ends of existence are still visible in its tales of both men and gods.

BAAL, *which means "Lord", was the name given to the chief god of the Canaanites to conceal his true name, which could not be uttered and was known only to initiates. As a weather god, Baal wielded thunderbolts and dispensed rain. (BRONZE AND GOLD STATUETTE FROM RAS SHAMRA, UGARITIC, 1400–1200 BC.)*

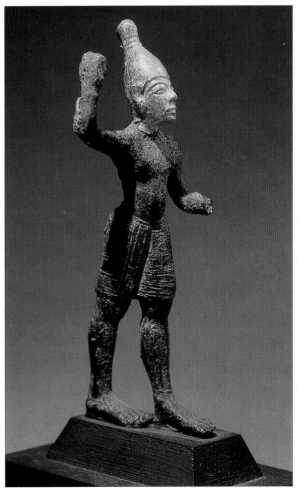

Greek mythology, they adopted figures such as Aphrodite – translated into the goddess Venus – who had evolved from older Mesopotamian deities including Inana, Ishtar and Astarte.

The themes of the great myths are universal. Creation myths have evolved in every culture, often with striking similarities – such as the limitless ocean from which the universe arises. A major preoccupation is that of life after death, which is explained in terms of parallel worlds: the underworld to which the dead descend to be judged; and the heavens to which the righteous aspire. Even within Hinduism and Buddhism, in which life is seen as a succession of reincarnations leading to the final release of nirvana, complex pictures of these unearthly realms have arisen. The idea of a catastrophic flood is another powerful and recurring theme, illustrating the potential

9

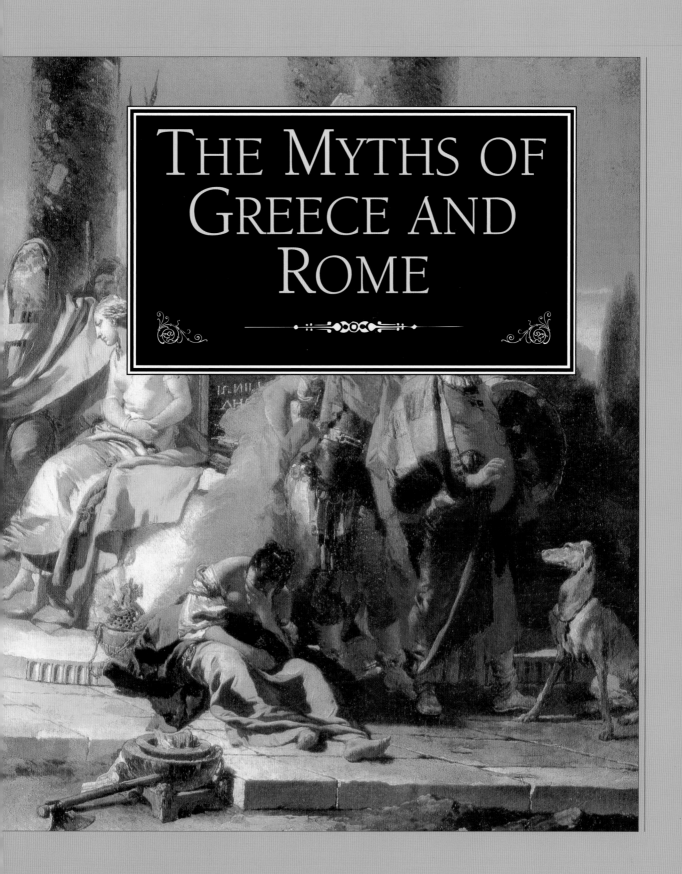

THE MYTHS OF
GREECE AND
ROME

INTRODUCTION

T HE ANCIENT GREEKS WERE THE great myth-makers of Europe. They even gave us the name by which we refer today to the amazing stories told about gods, heroes, men and animals. Around 400 BC the Athenian philosopher Plato coined the word *mythologia* in order to distinguish between imaginative accounts of divine actions and factual descriptions of events, supernatural or otherwise. Although he lived in an age that was increasingly scientific in outlook, and no longer inclined to believe every detail related about gods and goddesses, Plato recognized the power that resided in myth, and warned his followers to beware of its seductive charm.

The strength of Greek mythology, like all active traditions, lay in its collective nature. Unlike a story composed by a particular author, a myth always stood on its own, with a plot and a set of characters readily under-

MARS AND NEPTUNE, two gods of ancient Rome, ride over the Eternal City, guarding its military and maritime interests. At left, an airborne putto above Mars bears his horse's helmet, while Neptune's putto carries a seashell, symbol of the god's dominion over the waves. (MARS AND NEPTUNE BY PAOLO VERONESE, CANVAS, C.1575.)

ANCIENT GREECE

stood by those who listened to the story-teller or dramatist making use of it. When, for instance, the Athenians watched the great cycle of plays that Aeschylus staged about the murder of Agamemnon, they were already aware of the main characters and their actions. The audience knew how the House of Atreus, Agamemnon's father, was fated to endure a terrible period of domestic strife. Not only had Atreus and his brother Thyestes been cursed by their own father, Pelops, for killing his favourite child, their half-brother Chrysippus, but a bloody quarrel of their own had also added to the family misfortune. A dispute over the succession to Pelops' throne at Mycenae led Atreus to kill three of Thyestes' sons, although they had sought sanctuary in a temple dedicated to Zeus, the supreme god. Even worse, the murderer then served the bodies of his nephews up to his brother at a banquet, after which he dared to show Thyestes their feet and hands. Atreus paid for the outrage with his life at the hands of Thyestes' surviving son, Aegisthus, who later became the lover of Agamemnon's

wife Clytemnestra during his absence at the Trojan War.

All this would have been familiar to the Athenians before Aeschylus' treatment of the myth began with Agamemnon returning home from the Trojan War. Some of the audience doubtless recalled an even older curse laid on Pelops himself by the messenger god Hermes. Pelops had provoked the god by refusing a promised gift to one of his sons. Nothing that Aeschylus included in his plays was unexpected: neither the murder of Agamemnon, nor the revenge of his son Orestes, nor Orestes' pursuit by the Furies for shedding a mother's blood. What would have fascinated the audience was the dramatist's approach to these tangled incidents, his view of motive, guilt and expiation. For that reason another dramatist was able to tackle the same story later in Athens during the fifth century BC. It needs to be remembered that such drama remained very much part of ancient religion. Today we cannot expect to appreciate the full meaning of these performances, but we are fortunate in having the raw materials from which they were made, the myths themselves.

Myths retain much of their power, even when told in summary, as they are in this encyclopedia. Because Greek myths were fashioned and refashioned over so many generations, they acquired their essential form, a shape that had been collectively recognized for longer than anyone could remember. Even now, we continue to be fascinated by the stories of Oedipus, the man who murdered his father and married his mother; of the Athenian hero Theseus, slayer of the strange bull-headed man, the Minotaur; of the great voyager Jason, who sailed across the Black Sea to distant Colchis in order to fetch the Golden Fleece; of Agamemnon, the doomed leader of the Greek expedition against Troy; of cunning Odysseus, one of the bravest of the Greeks and the inventor of the Wooden Horse, the means by which Troy was taken; of the hapless Pentheus, victim of Dionysus' ecstatic worshippers, who included his own mother; of the unbeatable champion Achilles; of the labours of Heracles, Zeus' own son and the only hero to be granted immortality; and many others. As Greeks living before and after Plato evidently understood, myths were fictitious stories that illustrated truth.

The Romans were no less impressed by the range and interest of Greek mythology. Indeed, they adopted it wholesale and identified many of their own Italian deities with those in the Greek pantheon, even adopting others for whom they possessed no real equivalent. The unruly Dionysus gave Rome considerable trouble. This god of vegetation, wine and ecstasy was by no means a comfortable deity for the Greeks, but the Romans were more deeply disturbed by his orgiastic rites. In 186 BC the Roman Senate passed severe laws against the excesses of his worshippers. It is likely that several thousand

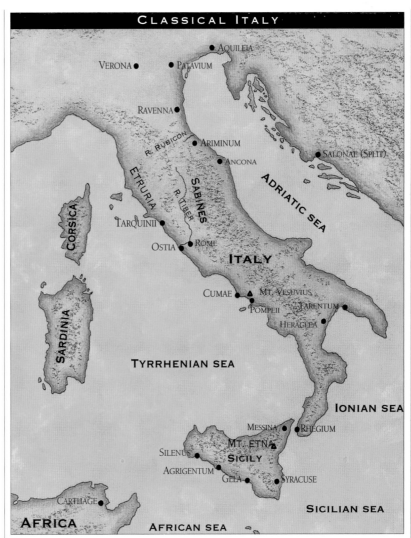

people were executed before the cult of the native wine god Bacchus discarded those aspects of Dionysus which met with official disproval. This taming of a Greek god, albeit Thracian in origin, could stand for the entire process by which Greek and Roman mythology merged in the second century BC. There were just too many myths for the Romans to resist, although they chose to impose a typical restraint on Greek extravagance.

Roman heroes could never compare with Heracles, Jason, Theseus, Perseus or Bellerophon. Something synthetic can be felt in the story of Aeneas, the leader of the refugees from Troy. His adoption as a founder-hero made him of particular concern to the first Roman emperor Augustus, but *The Aeneid*, the epic poem about Aeneas written by Virgil in the 20s BC, turned out to be a balanced celebration of Roman authority rather than an exciting heroic narrative. The hero heeded the call of duty and abandoned the woman he loved, as Roman heroes were expected to do in every myth.

A

ACHILLES was the son of King Peleus of Thessaly and the sea nymph *THETIS*. He was the greatest of the Greek warriors, although in comparison with *AGAMEMNON* and the other Greek kings who went on the expedition against Troy, he appears to have been something of a barbarian. His anger was as legendary as his prowess.

The uncertain nature of Achilles is apparent in the story of his birth. Both *ZEUS* and *POSEIDON* wanted to have a son by the beautiful Thetis, but *PROMETHEUS*, the fire god, had warned them that her offspring would be greater than his father. Anxious to avoid the emergence of a power superior to themselves, the gods carefully arranged the marriage of Thetis to a mortal. Because she was so attached to Achilles, Thetis tried to make him immortal by various means. The best known was dipping the new-born baby in the Styx, the river that ran through *HADES*, the world of the dead. Since Thetis had to hold him by the heel, this one spot was left vulnerable and at Troy brought about Achilles' death from a poisoned arrow shot from the bow of *PARIS*.

Achilles learned the skills of warfare from *CHIRON*, leader of the *CENTAURS*, who also fed him on wild game to increase his ferocity. Under Chiron's care Achilles became renowned as a courageous fighter, but his immortal mother knew that he was doomed to die at Troy if he went on the expedition. So Thetis arranged for him to be disguised as a girl and hidden among the women at the palace of King Lycomedes on the island of Scyros. The Greeks felt that without Achilles their chances of beating the Trojans were slim, but no one could identify the hidden hero. At last, cunning *ODYSSEUS* was sent to discover Achilles, which he did by means of a trick.

Having traced the young man to Scyros, Odysseus placed weapons among some jewellery in the palace. While Achilles' female companions were admiring the craftsmanship of the jewels, a call to arms was sounded and the warrior quickly reached for the weapons, giving himself away. Unmasked, Achilles had no choice but to sail for Troy.

There he bitterly quarrelled with Agamemnon, the leader of the Greeks. It may be that he was angered by Agamemnon's use of his name to bring *IPHIGENIA* to Aulis, for she had been told she was to marry Achilles, whereas Agamemnon intended to sacrifice

ACHILLES, relaxing beside his tent with his companion, Patroclus, welcomes his comrades, Odysseus (centre) and Ajax (right), who implore the moody hero to return to battle where he is sorely needed. (ACHILLES RECEIVES AGAMEMNON'S MESSENGERS, BY JEAN-AUGUST INGRES, CANVAS, 1801.)

her to the goddess *ARTEMIS*, to ensure a favourable wind for the Greek fleet. For a long time Achilles stayed in his tent and refused to fight the Trojans. He even persuaded his mother to use her influence with Zeus to let the tide of war go against the Greeks. But Achilles was roused to action by the death of Patroclus, his squire and lover, at the hands of the Trojan *HECTOR*. Patroclus had borrowed Achilles' armour, which had been forged by the smith god *HEPHAISTOS*, and entered the fray, but he came up against Hector who easily defeated him.

In brand-new armour Achilles sought out Hector, who asked for respect to be shown for his body if he was defeated. Achilles refused, slew Hector with his spear and dragged the Trojan hero round the tomb of Patroclus for twelve days. Only Thetis could persuade her son to let the Trojans recover the corpse and arrange a funeral, a serious obligation for the living.

Back in the fight, Achilles struck fear into the Trojans, of whom he killed hundreds. But his own life was coming to an end, which he

ACHILLES falls beneath the Trojan walls, shot by Paris. The sun god aims his arrow straight for Achilles' heel, the only mortal part of the hero's body. In some myths, Apollo guided Paris' bow; in others, the god shot the arrow, as seen here. (APOLLO SLAYS ACHILLES BY FRANZ STASSEN, WATERCOLOUR, 1869.)

ACTAEON was a young Greek hunter who unluckily chanced upon the pool where Artemis and her nymphs were bathing. In outrage, the virgin goddess turned him into a stag and he was torn apart by his own hounds. (ILLUSTRATION FROM DICTIONARY OF CLASSICAL ANTIQUITIES, 1891.)

had been warned about by his steed *XANTHUS*, before the *FURIES* struck the divine creature dumb. An arrow from the bow of Paris, guided by the god of prophecy *APOLLO*, gave Achilles a mortal wound. Heroic yet also arrogant, Achilles was the mythical figure most admired by Alexander the Great. At the commencement of his Asian campaign against the Persians, the youthful Alexander participated in funeral games that were held at Troy in memory of Achilles. (See also *HEROES*)

ACTAEON was the son of a minor royal god and Autonoe, daughter of *CADMUS*. A Greek hunter trained by *CHIRON*, he offended the goddess *ARTEMIS* and paid with his life. There are several reasons given for his terrible end. Actaeon may have boasted of his superior skill as a hunter, or annoyed the goddess by seeing her bathing naked. To stop his boasting, Artemis turned him into a stag and he was chased and devoured by his own hounds. But these faithful animals were broken-hearted at the loss of their master, until Chiron carved a statue of Actaeon so lifelike that they were satisfied.

AEGEUS was the son of King Pandion of Athens, and father of the hero *THESEUS*. Having twice married without begetting any children, Aegeus went to consult the Delphic Oracle but received only the ambiguous answer that he should not untie his wine skin until he reached home. When he sought advice from his friend Pittheus, another ruler, the latter realized that the oracle had foretold how Aegeus would father a heroic son. To secure the services of such a man, Pittheus made Aegeus drunk and let him sleep with his daughter Aethra. When Aegeus understood what had happened, he placed a sword and a pair of sandals beneath an enormous boulder. He told the princess that if she bore a son who could move the rock, he was to bring these tokens to him in Athens on reaching manhood. Thus it was that Theseus grew up and was eventually reunited with his father.

Meantime, Aegeus had married the sorceress *MEDEA*, whose magical powers had given him another son, Medus. It was for this reason that Medea did everything she could to thwart Theseus. At her

suggestion Theseus was sent to fight the wild bull of Marathon, which he captured alive. Once Aegeus recognized his son, Medea returned in disgust to her native Colchis on the Black Sea. But bad luck continued to dog Aegeus and eventually caused his death. For it was agreed that Theseus should travel to Crete with the seven girls and seven boys sent as tribute each year to feed the *MINOTAUR*, a bull-headed man. If Theseus was successful in his dangerous mission to kill the Minotaur, the ship bringing him home was to fly a white sail; if unsuccessful, a black sail would signal his death. Returning to Athens after an incredible adventure in the Labyrinth at Knossos, Theseus forgot the agreement to change his sail from black to white, with the result that, upon seeing the vessel with its black sail, Aegeus threw himself off the Athenian acropolis to certain death.

AEGEUS, looking out to sea, sees his son's ships returning home, all with black sails hoisted. Thinking that his son had died, Aegeus hurled himself into the sea, afterwards named the Aegean. (ILLUSTRATION BY NICK BEALE, 1995.)

AENEAS *gazes in wonder at the decorative temple in Carthage, while Dido, the queen, welcomes him to her exotic kingdom. Around them, pillars, doors and beams are made of bronze, while the fabulous walls are decorated with the famous tale of Aeneas and the Trojans.*
(ILLUSTRATION BY NICK BEALE, 1995.)

AENEAS was a Trojan hero and the son of Anchises and *VENUS*, the Roman goddess of love. He was the favourite of the Romans, who believed that some of their eminent families were descended from the Trojans who fled westwards with him from Asia Minor, after the Greek sack of their city. Upstart Rome was only too aware of its lack of tradition and history in comparison with Greece (there was a notable absence of a glorious past peopled with mythical heroes and gods), so the exploits of Aeneas conveniently provided a means of reasserting national pride. It was not a coincidence that the first Roman emperor, Augustus, took a personal interest in the myth.

During the Trojan War Anchises was unable to fight, having been rendered blind or lame for boasting about his relationship with Venus. But young Aeneas distinguished himself against the Greeks, who feared him second only to *HECTOR*, the Trojan champion. In gratitude *PRIAM* gave Aeneas his daughter Creusa to have as his wife, and a son was born named *ASCANIUS*. Although Venus warned him of the impending fall of Troy, Anchises refused to quit the city until two omens occurred: a small flame rose from the top of Ascanius' head and a meteor fell close by. So, carrying Anchises on his back, Aeneas managed to escape Troy with his father and his son. Somehow Creusa became separated from the party and disappeared. Later, Aeneas saw her ghost and learned from it that he would found a new Troy in distant Italy.

After sailing through the Aegean Sea, where the small fleet Aeneas commanded stopped at a number of islands, the fleet came to Epirus on the eastern Adriatic coast. From there it made for Sicily, but before reaching the Italian mainland it was diverted to North Africa during a sudden storm sent by the goddess *JUNO*, the Roman equivalent of *HERA*, who harassed Aeneas throughout the voyage. Only the timely help of *NEPTUNE*, the Roman sea god, saved the fleet from shipwreck. At the city of Carthage, the great trading port founded by the Phoenicians (which was located in present-day Tunisia), Venus ensured that Aeneas fell in love with its beautiful queen, the widow *DIDO*. Because of her own flight to Carthage, Dido welcomed the Trojan refugees with great kindness and unlimited hospitality.

Time passed pleasantly for the lovers, as Aeneas and Dido soon became, and it seemed as if Italy and the new state to be founded on its shores were both forgotten. But watchful *JUPITER*, the chief Roman god, dispatched *MERCURY* with a message to Aeneas, recalling him to his duty and commanding him to resume the voyage. Horrified by his intention to leave, Dido bitterly reproached Aeneas, but his deep sense of piety gave him strength enough to launch the fleet again. Then the weeping queen mounted a pyre which she had ordered to be prepared and, having run herself through with a sword, was consumed by the flames.

When the Trojans finally landed in Italy, near the city of Cumae, Aeneas went to consult the *SIBYL*, who was a renowned prophetess. She took him on a visit to the

AENEAS *and his comrades battle with a flock of raging harpies who hover above them in the sky, waiting to carry off the weak and wounded. Beside Aeneas shelter his family: his blind father Anchises, his wife Creusa and their two sons.* (AENEAS AND HIS COMPANIONS FIGHT THE HARPIES BY FRANCOIS PERRIER, CANVAS, 1646-47.)

underworld. There Aeneas met his father's ghost, who showed him the destiny of Rome. Anchises had died of old age during the stay in Sicily, but his enthusiastic outline of the future encouraged his son. Aeneas also saw Dido's ghost, but it did not speak to him and hurriedly turned away.

Afterwards, Aeneas steered for the mouth of the River Tiber, on whose river banks the city of Rome would be built centuries later. Conflict with the Latins, the local inhabitants, was bloody and prolonged. But peace was made when Aeneas married Lavinia, the daughter of King Latinus. It had been foretold that for the sake of the kingdom Lavinia must marry a man from abroad. The Trojans, in order to appease Juno, adopted the Latins' traditions and language. (See also *VOYAGERS*)

AGAMEMNON, according to Greek mythology, was the son of *ATREUS* and the brother of *MENELAUS*, king of Sparta. He was married to *CLYTEMNESTRA*. From his citadel at Mycenae, or nearby Argos, he sent out a summons to the Greeks to join the expedition against Troy. The cause of the war was the flight of Menelaus' wife, *HELEN*, to that city with *PARIS*.

However, the Greek fleet was delayed at Aulis by contrary winds. Agamemnon then realized that he would have to make a human sacrifice in order to appease *ARTEMIS*, the goddess of the forest and wild animals. His daughter *IPHIGENIA* was therefore sent to Aulis under the pretext that she was to be married to the Greek champion and hero *ACHILLES*. According to one tradition, Iphigenia was sacrificed, but according to another, she was saved by Artemis herself and taken to Taurus to become a priestess in the goddess's temple.

Clytemnestra never forgave Agamemnon for Iphigenia's loss, and she took Aegisthus for a lover during the ten-year siege of Troy. Aegisthus was the son of Thyestes, the brother and enemy of Atreus,

Agamemnon's father. On her husband's return, Clytemnestra at first pretended how pleased she was to see him. Thanking the gods for his safe return, Agamemnon crossed the threshold of his palace, ignoring the warning of his slave *CASSANDRA*, the prophetic daughter of *PRIAM*, the defeated Trojan king. He then retired to a bathroom in order to change his clothes. Clytemnestra quickly threw a large net over Agamemnon and twisted

it around his body, rendering him an easy target for Aegisthus' axe.

AJAX was the son of Telamon of Salamis and, like *ACHILLES*, was a powerful aid to the Greeks in their assault on Troy. After Achilles' death there was a contest for the armour of this great warrior, which had been forged by the smith god *HEPHAISTOS*. When *ODYSSEUS* was awarded the armour, Ajax became mad with jealousy. He planned a night attack on his comrades, but the goddess *ATHENA* deceived him into slaughtering a flock of sheep instead. In the light of dawn, Ajax was suddenly overwhelmed by a fear of his evil intentions, and fell on his sword and died.

ALCESTIS, according to Greek mythology, was the daughter of King Pelias of Thessaly. When she was of an age to marry, many suitors appeared and her father set a test to discover who would be the most suitable husband. Alcestis was to be the wife of the first man to yoke a lion and a boar (or, in some versions, a bear) to a chariot. With the aid of *APOLLO*, the god of prophecy, a neighbouring monarch named Admetus succeeded in this seemingly impossible task. But at the wedding he forgot to make the necessary sacrifice in gratitude to *ARTEMIS*, the goddess of the forest and wild animals, and so found his wedding bed full of snakes. Once again Apollo came to the king's assistance and, by making the *FATES* drunk, extracted from them a promise that if anyone else would die on Admetus' behalf, he might continue to live. As no one would volunteer, Alcestis gave her life for him. *PERSEPHONE*, the underworld goddess, was so impressed by this complete devotion that she restored Alcestis to Admetus, and they had two sons who later took part in the Greek expedition against the city of Troy.

ALCESTIS (below) welcomes her suitor, Admetus, who arrives in a chariot drawn by lions and bears, while Alcestis' father, Pelias, looks on in disbelief. Admetus was the only hero to yoke the beasts, so winning the hand of Alcestis. (ILLUSTRATION FROM STORIES FROM GREECE AND ROME, 1920.)

ALCMENE was the daughter of Electryon, son of *PERSEUS*, and the mother of *HERACLES*. She married Amphitryon, king of Tiryns, near Mycenae in the Peloponnese. Alcmene refused to consummate her marriage to Amphitryon until he had avenged the murder of her brothers. This king did, but when he returned he was amazed to learn from Alcmene that she believed she had already slept with him. Amphitryon was enraged until

ALCMENE (right) was one of the sky god Zeus' many lovers, but was punished for her infidelity by her angry husband, Amphitryon, who here is portrayed setting alight a pyre beneath her. She was saved by a heavenly downpour sent by Zeus. (ILLUSTRATION BY NICK BEALE, 1995.)

the seer *TIRESIAS* explained that *ZEUS* had come to Alcmene disguised as her husband in order to father a mortal who would aid the gods in their forthcoming battle against the *GIANTS*.

So Alcmene became pregnant with twins: Heracles, the son of Zeus, and Iphicles, the son of Amphitryon. Zeus could not hide his satisfaction from his wife *HERA* who realized what had happened. She sent the goddess of childbirth,

Eileithyia, to frustrate the delivery, but a trick saved Alcmene and her two sons. Hera then put snakes into Heracles' cradle, but the infant hero strangled them.

Zeus never let Hera fatally injure Heracles, and always protected Alcmene. Once Amphitryon tried to burn her for infidelity, but was stopped by a sudden downpour. When Alcmene died naturally of old age, Zeus sent *HERMES* to bring her body to the Elysian Fields.

THE AMAZONS (opposite), fierce and independent maiden warriors, fought with passion and skill. In early images, they appear in exotic Scythian leotards, bearing half-moon shields, but in later Greek art, they wore Dorian chitons, with one shoulder bare, as seen here. (THE BATTLE OF THE AMAZONS BY PETER PAUL RUBENS, WOOD, 1600.)

THE AMAZONS

THE AMAZONS were a tribe of female warriors, supposedly descended from *ARES*, the Greek war god, and the *NAIAD* Harmonia. Their home was situated beyond the Black Sea. It is thought that their name refers to their breastless condition, for Amazons voluntarily removed their right breasts in order that they might more easily draw a bow. The ancient Greeks believed these fierce warriors periodically mated with the men from another tribe, afterwards rearing their female children but discarding or maiming all the males.

During the Trojan War they fought against the Greeks. Although he killed the Amazon queen Penthesilea, *ACHILLES* never succeeded in shaking off the rumour that he had been in love with her. He even slew a comrade who mentioned it. Fascination with Amazon power affected other heroes besides Achilles. The adventures of both *HERACLES* and *THESEUS* involved battles with Amazons. One of Heracles' famous labours was the seizure of a girdle belonging to the Amazon queen Hippolyta, a theft that required considerable nerve.

AMULIUS, in Roman mythology, was a descendant of the Trojan hero *AENEAS*. He usurped the throne of Alba Longa from his younger brother Numitor and forced Numitor's daughter *RHEA SILVIA* to become a Vestal Virgin so as to deny her father an heir. When Rhea Silvia was raped by the war god MARS, Amulius imprisoned her and ordered that her twin sons, *REMUS AND ROMULUS*, be drowned in the Tiber. But the two boys escaped a watery death and grew up in the countryside. Once they realized their parentage, Romulus and Remus returned to Alba Longa and killed their uncle Amulius.

ANDROMACHE, the daughter of Eetion, a king of Mysia in Asia Minor, was the wife of *HECTOR*, the foremost Trojan warrior. Her entire family – parents, brothers, husband and son – was killed during the Trojan War. After the sack of Troy, Andromache was taken off into captivity by Neoptolemus, the son of the great Greek hero *ACHILLES*. Neoptolemus had shown the same

AMULIUS (left) casts out his nephews, Romulus and Remus, the twin sons of Rhea Silvia and the war god Mars, ordering that they be drowned in the river Tiber. But they are eventually found by a she-wolf who suckles them until a shepherd, Faustulus, takes them home. (ILLUSTRATION FROM STORIES FROM LIVY, 1885.)

violent and tempestuous temper as his father when he ruthlessly killed the Trojan king, *PRIAM*, at the altar of *ZEUS*' temple. Andromache bore Neoptolemus three sons, and in consequence suffered the hatred of his barren Greek wife. When Neoptolemus died, Andromache went on to marry Helenus who, like her, was a Trojan captive. Her final years were spent in Asia Minor at Pergamum, which was a new city founded by one of her sons.

ANDROMACHE, Hector's young wife, bows her head in captivity. One of the noblest but most ill-starred of heroines, she sees her husband, father and seven brothers killed by Achilles, and her son hurled from the city walls; while she falls as a prize of war to Achilles' son. (CAPTIVE ANDROMACHE BY LORD LEIGHTON, CANVAS, C. 1890.)

in an uprising against the new ruler *CREON*, and his body was condemned to rot unburied outside the city. Antigone refused to accept this impiety and sprinkled earth over the corpse as a token burial. For this she was walled up in a cave, where she hanged herself like her mother Jocasta. There are a number of different versions of the myth, but they all cast Antigone as the heroic victim of a family wrecked by a terrible deed.

ANTIOPE see *LOVERS OF ZEUS*

APHRODITE was the Greek goddess of love, beauty and fertility. Unlike her Roman counterpart *VENUS*, with whom she was identified, Aphrodite was not only a goddess of sexual love but also of the affection that sustains social life. The meaning of her name is uncertain, although the ancient Greeks came to believe it referred to foam. Quite possibly this belief arose from the story of Aphrodite's

ANDROMEDA was the daughter of Cassiope and Cepheus, king of the Ethiopians. When Cassiope boasted that Andromeda was more beautiful than the Nereids, the sea nymphs, they complained to the sea god *POSEIDON*. He avenged this insult by flooding the land and sending a sea monster to devastate Cepheus' kingdom. To avoid complete disaster it was decided to sacrifice Andromeda to the beast and she was chained to a rock at the foot of a cliff. There *PERSEUS* saw her as he flew past on winged

sandals carrying the head of the Gorgon Medusa. He fell in love with Andromeda, and obtained both her and her father's consent to marriage if he defeated the monster. This Perseus did by using Medusa's head, the sight of which turned all living things to stone. After some time, Perseus and Andromeda settled in Tiryns, which Perseus ruled. The constellation of Andromeda lies close to that of Pegasus, and both Cepheus and Cassiope were also commemorated in the stars.

ANTIGONE was the daughter of *OEDIPUS*, king of Thebes, and his wife and mother Jocasta. On learning of their unwitting incest, Oedipus tore out his eyes while Jocasta hanged herself. The penitent Oedipus was then guided by Antigone in his wanderings round Greece. She was with him at the sanctuary of Colonus, near Athens, when her distraught father gained some kind of peace just before his death. She returned to Thebes, but her troubles were not over. Her brother Polynices had been killed

APHRODITE, *goddess of love and beauty, was born from the foam of the sea; she rose from the waves on a seashell, stepping ashore on Cyprus. At her side, the west wind, Zephyrus, and Flora, the spring, blow her gently ashore in a shower of roses, her sacred flower.* (THE BIRTH OF VENUS BY SANDRO BOTTICELLI, TEMPERA, C. 1482.)

birth. When the Titan *CRONOS* cut off the penis of his father Ouranos with a sharp sickle, he cast the immortal member into the sea, where it floated amid white foam. Inside the penis Aphrodite grew and was then washed up at Paphos on Cyprus. There were in fact sanctuaries dedicated to her on many islands, which suggests that she was a West Asian goddess who was brought to Greece by sea-traders.

Once she arrived, the ancient Greeks married her in their mythology to the crippled smith god *HEPHAISTOS*. But Aphrodite was not content to be a faithful wife and she bore children by several other gods, including *DIONYSUS* and *ARES*. When Hephaistos found out about Aphrodite's passion for the war god Ares, the outraged smith god made a mesh of gold and caught the lovers in bed together. He called the other gods from Mount Olympus to see the pair, but they only laughed at his shame, and *POSEIDON*, the god of the sea, persuaded Hephaistos to release Aphrodite and Ares.

Perhaps Aphrodite's greatest love was for the handsome youth Adonis, another West Asian deity. Killed by a wild boar, Adonis became the object of admiration for both Aphrodite and *PERSEPHONE*, queen of the dead. Their bitter quarrel was only ended by *ZEUS*, who ruled that for a third of the year Adonis was to dwell with himself, for a third part with Persephone, and for a third part with Aphrodite. So it was that the ancient Greeks accommodated a West Asian mother goddess and her dying-and-rising husband. Indeed the Adonia, or annual festivals commemorating Adonis' death, were celebrated in many parts of the eastern Mediterranean.

Because of her unruly behaviour, Zeus caused Aphrodite to fall in love with Anchises, the father of *AENEAS*. In the Roman version of this myth Venus herself is deeply attracted to the Trojan, but warns him to keep the parentage of their son Aeneas a secret. This Anchises fails to do, and as a result suffers blindness or a disability of the limbs. While the Roman goddess provided, through the leadership of Aeneas, a means for some of the Trojans to escape and flourish anew in Italy, the Greek Aphrodite actually helped to cause the Trojan War. In order to ensure that he would name her as the most beautiful of the goddesses, Aphrodite promised *PARIS*, son of *PRIAM* the king of Troy, the hand of the most beautiful woman in the world. This fatefully turned out to be *HELEN*, wife of *MENELAUS*, king of Sparta.

APOLLO

APOLLO was the son of *ZEUS* and the Titaness *LETO*, and the twin brother of the goddess *ARTEMIS*, the virgin huntress. He was one of the most important deities of both the Greek and Roman religions, and was the god of prophecy, archery and music. The origin of his name is uncertain but it is probably non-European.

A fight with the gigantic earth-serpent Python at Delphi gave Apollo the seat of his famous oracle. Python was an offspring of *GAIA*, mother earth, which issued revelations through a fissure in the rock so that a priestess, the Pythia, could give answers to any questions that might be asked. After he slew the earth-serpent, Apollo took its place, though he had to do penance in Thessaly for the killing. Indeed, Zeus twice forced Apollo to be the slave of a mortal man to pay for his crime.

Apollo's interest in healing suggests an ancient association with the plague and its control. His son *ASCLEPIUS* was also identified with healing and connected with sites in northern Greece. Indeed, so accomplished was Asclepius in medicine that Zeus slew him with a thunderbolt for daring to bring a man back to life. (See also *FORCES OF NATURE*)

ARES

ARES, the son of *ZEUS* and *HERA*, was the Greek god of war, and was later identified with the Roman war god *MARS*. Although Ares had no wife of his own, he had three children by *APHRODITE*, the goddess of love. The twins, Phobos, "panic", and Deimos, "fear", always accompanied him on the battlefield. In Greek mythology, Ares is depicted as an instigator of violence, a tempestuous and passionate lover and an unscrupulous friend. The Roman god Mars, however, has nothing of Ares' fickleness.

APOLLO *(above), the sun god, urges the sun-chariot to rise in the sky. This unusual version of the myth has Apollo, rather than Helios, as rider, and lions, instead of horses, pull the chariot, recalling the link between Leo and the sun.* (PHOEBUS APOLLO BY BRITON RIVIERE, CANVAS, C. 1870.)

ARES *(below), in full armour, leads the gods into battle. However, in war, the gods were not impartial; Ares, Aphrodite (left), Poseidon and Apollo (centre) would often aid the Trojans, while Hera and Athena (right) supported the Greeks.* (ILLUSTRATION FROM STORIES FROM HOMER, 1885.)

LOVERS OF ZEUS

A STRIKING ASPECT OF GREEK MYTHOLOGY is the marital conflict between the two chief deities, Hera, an earth goddess, and her husband, Zeus, supreme power on Olympus. One of the most amorous gods in mythology, Zeus loved countless women and he courted them in as many forms, sometimes as a bull, as a satyr, as a swan, sometimes as a mortal man, and even in the form of a golden shower. Hera was notoriously jealous and vengeful, pursuing without mercy his lovers and their offspring. The antagonism between the two could be viewed as a clash between different religious traditions or local cults, each cult recognizing a different lover who was often regarded as the ancestor of a ruling family.

ANTIOPE (above), daughter of a river god, was loved by Zeus in the form of a satyr, a goat-like creature. She bore him twin sons, Amphion and Zethus. Here, Zeus, disguised as a youthful satyr, gently shades Antiope from the sun while she sleeps beside Eros, sweet god of love. (ANTIOPE SHADED BY ZEUS DISGUISED AS A SATYR BY ANTONIO CORREGGIO, CANVAS, 1523-25.)

CALLISTO (above), forest nymph and companion of Artemis in the chase, was loved by Zeus and bore him a son, Arcas. She was then changed into a bear either by Zeus, wishing to hide her from Hera, or by Hera herself. As a bear she was shot by Artemis in the forest and was placed among the stars as the She-Bear. Here, surrounded by the trophies of the chase, Artemis and her nymphs comfort Callisto possibly after her encounter with the overwhelming god, Zeus. (DIANA AND CALLISTO BY PETER PAUL RUBENS, CANVAS, 1636-40.)

EUROPA (right) was wooed by Zeus in the shape of a beautiful bull who emerged from the waves and carried her over the sea to Crete where she bore him three sons. The various stages of the drama are represented here: on the left, Europa mounts the bull encouraged by its tameness. On the right, she is borne sedately down to the sea, with many little Erotes (love spirits) hovering in the sky. Finally she floats happily away, waving to her maidens. (THE RAPE OF EUROPA BY PAOLO VERONESE, CANVAS, 1580.)

DIONYSUS (above), Zeus' child by Semele, appears here hugging his mother, while Apollo stands by with a bay tree. Once he became a god, Dionysus raised his mother to heaven and placed her among the stars as Thyone. This Etruscan mirror is bordered with ivy, which was Dionysus' sacred plant. (ILLUSTRATION FROM DR SMITH'S CLASSICAL DICTIONARY, 1895.)

DANAE (below) was confined in a brazen tower by her father who feared an oracle predicting that he would be killed by a grandson. In her tower she was visited by Zeus in the form of a golden shower, and bore him a son, Perseus. When her father discovered the baby, he cast both of them out to sea in a wooden chest, but they floated ashore on the Isle of Seriphos where they were rescued by Dictys. (ILLUSTRATION BY GEORGE SOPER FROM TANGLEWOOD TALES, C. 1920.)

SEMELE (left), encouraged by Hera, persuaded Zeus to show himself in all his splendour. When he appeared before her as the radiant god of thunder and lightning, Semele was consumed by the flames and, dying, gave birth prematurely to Dionysus, whom Zeus saved from the fire. In this powerful Symbolist version of the myth, the great god radiates fiery, blood-red lightning. A winged child hiding from the light could be Dionysus, while the dark, horned god seems to be a fusion of Hades and Pan. (JUPITER AND SEMELE, BY GUSTAVE MOREAU, CANVAS, 1896.)

THE ARGONAUTS were very early explorers, most likely the first Greek voyagers to the Black Sea. They sailed from Thessaly, where their leader, JASON, was the rightful king of Iolcus. According to the myth, Jason's father, Aeson, was deposed by his half-brother Pelias, who was warned at the time how he would in turn be overthrown by a man wearing only one sandal. In order to protect Jason from Pelias, Aeson had secretly sent his son to CHIRON to educate the young man, like many other heroes. On reaching manhood, Jason determined to return to Iolcus and reclaim the throne. During the journey, however, he was tested by the goddess HERA, who was disguised as an old woman. She begged him to carry her safely across a swollen river,

THE ARGONAUTS (top) commissioned Argus to build the Argo, a ship with twenty oars. Here he carves out the stern, while Athena makes sails. Behind her, perched on a pillar, her sacred creature, the owl, symbolizes her wisdom. (ILLUSTRATION FROM DICTIONARY OF CLASSICAL ANTIQUITIES, 1891.)

JASON (above left), helps Hera, disguised as an old woman, across the stream. In the current he loses a sandal, fulfilling part of an oracle that a half-shod man would take Pelias' throne. The peacock beside Hera denotes her all-seeing vision. (ILLUSTRATION FROM TANGLEWOOD TALES, C. 1920.)

JASON (above), with Medea's help – she anoints him with a salve to protect him from fire and steel – ploughs the fields with the bulls of Aietes. He was the first hero to yoke the wild and fiery creatures. (ILLUSTRATION FROM TANGLEWOOD TALES, C. 1920.)

which Jason did at the cost of one of his sandals. Thus the prophecy was fulfilled: a man wearing only one sandal arrived at Iolcus to challenge Pelias. Because Jason made his intentions known at the time of a religious festival, Pelias could not kill his nephew without the risk of suffering divine disfavour. So the king told Jason that he could have the throne provided he obtained the Golden Fleece, which was an apparently impossible task. This miraculous fleece belonged to a ram which had flown to Colchis, a distant land identified with modern Georgia. It hung from a tree there, guarded by an enormous snake that never slept.

The DELPHIC ORACLE encouraged Jason to undertake the quest. Hera inspired a group of Thessalian

ARIADNE (above) hands the vital skein to Theseus, which allows him to track his way through the Labyrinth. After killing the bull-like beast, the Minotaur, in the Labyrinth, he sailed away with her, but then deserted her on Dia, possibly believing that she was destined to marry a god. (ILLUSTRATION FROM TANGLEWOOD TALES, C. 1920.)

warriors to join his expedition and they became known as the Argonauts, the crew of the ship *Argo*. Among their number were Castor and Polydeuces, ORPHEUS the poet, Calais and Zetes the sons of BOREAS and the hero HERACLES. Together they crossed a sea of marvels, visited strange lands and overcame many obstacles before reaching Colchis, where Hera used the goddess of love APHRODITE to make MEDEA, the second daughter of King Aietes, fall in love with Jason. The king hated Greeks but he kept his feelings hidden from the Argonauts. He even consented to Jason's attempt to capture the Golden Fleece. But first Aietes set Jason a challenge that was intended to result in his death. The hero was required to yoke a team of fire-breathing bulls, plough and sow a field with dragon's teeth, and slay the armed men who would at once rise from the ground.

With the assistance of Medea's skills in the magic arts, Jason accomplished Aietes' task within a single day. But the king of Colchis was not prepared to give up the Golden Fleece so easily. He secretly planned to attack the Argonauts, who were warned by Medea, now Jason's lover. She employed her magic once again to deal with the unsleeping snake, and Jason seized the Golden Fleece. The Argonauts quickly rowed away from Colchis with the fleece and Medea, whom Jason had promised to marry once back in Thessaly.

The Colchian princess seems to have been associated with the rites of dismemberment as well as magic, for during the pursuit of the Argonauts across the Black Sea, Medea slowed the fleet of her father Aietes by killing and cutting up her own brother, Apsyrtus. Pieces of Apsyrtus' body were thrown overboard, forcing the Colchians to gather up the remains for a decent burial. Later, in Thessaly, Medea also persuaded the daughters of King Pelias to cut their father to pieces and boil him, so as to restore his youth. This they did, and in killing him avenged the disgrace of Jason's father Aeson.

Jason and Medea led an unsettled life in Greece. After a few years he deserted her for another woman, but Medea killed this rival and her own children by Jason. Jason died in Corinth as a result of a rotten piece of the *Argo* falling on his head. Afterwards the gods raised the ship to the sky and made

it into a constellation. The Golden Fleece also appears in the heavens as the first constellation of the Zodiac, Aries the ram.

ARIADNE, in Greek mythology, was the daughter of *PASIPHAE* and King *MINOS*, the ruler of Knossos on the island of Crete. When the Athenian hero *THESEUS* came to Knossos to pay the annual tribute of seven young men and seven girls, Ariadne gave him a sword and a skein of thread that allowed him to escape from Daedalus' Labyrinth after a bloody struggle with the dreaded bull-headed man, the *MINOTAUR*. Theseus and Ariadne then fled from Crete, but for some unknown reason the hero abandoned the princess on the nearby island of Dia. The deserted princess may then have become the wife of *DIONYSUS*, the god of ecstasy and wine. Local legend would suggest such a connection, although the whole story of the Minotaur was probably no more than a garbled

version of far older tales of the sport of bull-leaping, which dated from the pre-Greek era of Cretan history. Dionysus himself was known to the Greeks as "the roaring one", a "bull-horned god" who was full of power and fertility.

ARION see *VOYAGERS*

ARTEMIS was the daughter of the Titaness *LETO* and *ZEUS*, and the twin sister of *APOLLO*. She was in all likelihood a very ancient deity whom the Greeks adopted as goddess of the wild. Traces of human sacrifice could still be found in her worship. Most of all, Artemis liked to roam the mountains with a companion band of nymphs. Certainly the virgin goddess resented any kind of intrusion into her domain, or any harm done to her favourite animals. For killing a stag sacred to Artemis, the leader of the Greek expedition against Troy, King *AGAMEMNON* of Mycenae, found his fleet stranded by contrary winds

ARTEMIS, virgin goddess of the wild, always resisted the love or attentions of men. When the hunter Actaeon saw her in the nude, bathing with her nymphs, she indignantly turned him into a stag, which was set upon by his own hounds. (DIANA AND ACTAEON BY TITIAN, CANVAS, 1556-59.)

at Aulis. Only a promise to sacrifice his daughter *IPHIGENIA* was enough to appease the goddess, although there are differing accounts as to whether the girl was actually killed.

Another mortal punished by Artemis was *ACTAEON*. He had the misfortune while hunting to come upon the goddess as she was bathing. She changed him into a stag and he was chased and torn apart by his own hunting dogs. However, according to a different version, Actaeon actually tried to approach the naked goddess hidden beneath a stag's pelt.

To the Romans, Artemis was closely identified with their goddess Diana, who was also a goddess of light as well as of the wild.

ASCANIUS was the son of *AENEAS* and Creusa. According to the Romans, he founded the city of Alba Longa thirty-three years after the arrival of the Trojan refugees in Italy. An alternative tradition makes Ascanius' mother Lavinia, a Latin princess whose marriage to Aeneas brought peace and unity to the Latin and Trojan peoples. It was in her honour that Aeneas founded Lavinium within three years of landing. This would mean that Ascanius was king of Lavinium following Aeneas' death, and before he left to take up residence in a new city at Alba Longa. Early rivalry between the two cities probably explains the removal myth.

The family of Julius Caesar, the Julii, claimed descent from Aeneas through Ascanius, who was also called Iulus Ilus ("made of Ilium"), Ilium being the old name for Troy.

ASCLEPIUS, the Greek god of healing, was the son of *APOLLO*, god of prophecy, and the lake nymph Coronis. In mythology he is a somewhat shadowy figure, which suggests his late arrival as a major deity. Asclepius would seem to have been a Thessalian healer whose skills became known throughout Greece: his cult eventually took over the sanctuary at Epidauros in the Peloponnese. Sacred snakes resident there were believed to embody the god's healing power. The ancient association between snakes and medicine is probably due to the snake's apparent ability to renew its youth each year by sloughing off its own skin.

Only the stories of Asclepius' birth and death were ever well known to the Greeks and Romans. When Coronis dared to take in secret a mortal as a second lover, an enraged Apollo sent his sister *ARTEMIS* to kill the lake nymph with a disease. However, as the flames of the funeral pyre burned Coronis, Apollo felt sorry for his unborn son and removed him from the corpse. Thus was Asclepius born. He was taught medicine by the Centaur *CHIRON*, whose knowledge was so great that *ZEUS* himself feared that Asclepius might learn a way of overcoming death. When he did succeed in resurrecting one of his patients, Zeus decided that Asclepius should be punished for threatening the gods' monopoly over immortality. Asclepius was slain by a thunder-bolt, but at Apollo's request the god of medicine was placed among the stars, as Ophiuchus, the serpent-bearer.

So impressed were the Romans with Asclepius' cult that during a time of plague they requested aid from Epidauros and a sacred snake was duly shipped to Rome.

ATALANTA, in Greek mythology, was the daughter of Iasus of Arcadia and was known as a famous huntress. As an unwanted daughter she was exposed and left to die on a mountainside, but was suckled by a bear and later brought up by hunters. This experience may have inclined her to manly pursuits. She even tried to enlist with the *ARGONAUTS*, but *JASON* refused her because the presence of one woman on the ship might cause jealousies amongst them.

Atalanta's most famous myth concerns the lengths to which she went to avoid marriage. She said that her husband must first beat her in a race and any man who lost would be put to death. Despite the awful consequence of losing, there were many who admired Atalanta's beauty and paid the price against her speed. None could catch her, although they ran naked while she was fully clothed. Finally, the love goddess *APHRODITE* took pity on a young man named Melanion and provided him with a way to delay

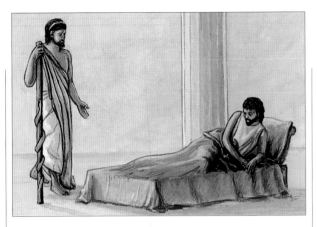

ASCLEPIUS, Greek god of healing, tends a man on his sickbed. A son of Apollo, the greatest healer, Asclepius was gifted with miraculous powers, once resurrecting a mortal from death. His attributes, staff and serpent, signify power and renewal of life. (ILLUSTRATION BY NICK BEALE, 1995.)

Atalanta. She gave him three golden apples, which he placed at different points on the course. Curiosity got the better of Atalanta, who stopped three times to pick up the apples. So Melanion won the race and Atalanta as a wife. But in his haste to make love to her, Melanion either forgot a vow to Aphrodite or consummated their union in a sacred place. To pay for the sacrilege both he and Atalanta were turned into lions.

ATALANTA, the gifted huntress and unusually athletic heroine, found her match in the equally resourceful and energetic Melanion. Here the heroic pair hunt and slay the monstrous wild boar which has been ravaging the plains of Calydon. (ILLUSTRATION FROM TANGLEWOOD TALES, C. 1920.)

ATHENA, sometimes Athene, the daughter of ZEUS and the Titaness Metis, was the Greek goddess of war and crafts. Although a fierce virgin like ARTEMIS, she did not shun men but on the contrary delighted in being a city-goddess, most notably at Athens. This city adopted her cult when an olive tree grew on its acropolis: the other divine rival for worship was the god POSEIDON, who produced only a spring of brackish water. Athena sprang into being fully grown and armed from the head of her father Zeus, after he had swallowed the pregnant Metis. The smith god HEPHAISTOS assisted the birth with a blow from his axe. Quite likely this intervention accounts for her title of Hephaistia, the companion of the smith god. Athena's symbol was the wise owl, which featured on Athenian coins. The Romans identified her with MINERVA, a goddess of wisdom and the arts.

An early myth relates how Hephaistos tried to rape Athena. To avoid losing her virginity, she

miraculously disappeared so that the semen of the smith god fell to the ground, where it grew into the serpent Erichthonius. The three daughters of Cecrops, the semi-serpent who first ruled Athens, were given a box by Athena and told not to look inside it. Ignoring this command, two of them looked inside, found themselves gazing upon Erichthonius, and went insane. However, Athena continued to protect Athens. Although the city fell into enemy hands during the Persian invasion of Greece in 480–479 BC, the Athenians later went on to achieve mastery of the sea and found their own empire. It was during this period that the Parthenon was built on the Athenian acropolis.

Athena was always regarded by the Greeks as an active goddess, involved in the affairs of men. She helped several heroes such as BELLEROPHON, JASON, HERACLES and PERSEUS. Also, it was she who eventually got ODYSSEUS back to the island of Ithaca, following his epic voyage home from the Trojan War. Perhaps Athena's most significant aid was given to the matricide ORESTES. Not only did she offer him protection, but she also arranged for him to be tried and acquitted of his terrible crime by the ancient court of the Areopagus, in Athens. The verdict meant an end to the blood-feud, not least because for the first time even the FURIES accepted Orestes' deliverance from guilt.

ATLAS was a TITAN, the son of Iapetus and the Oceanid Clymene. He was thought by the ancient Greeks to hold up the sky, and his name means "he who carries". His most famous encounter was with the hero HERACLES, one of whose labours was to obtain the golden apples of the HESPERIDES, female guardians of the fruit that mother earth, GAIA, presented to HERA at her marriage to ZEUS. Atlas offered to fetch them for Heracles if the

ATHENA, goddess of wisdom and crafts, guided and helped her favourites. Here she visits the hero Bellerophon with a gift – the bridle with which to tame and mount the winged horse, Pegasus. (ILLUSTRATION FROM STORIES FROM GREECE AND ROME, 1930.)

hero took over his job of holding up the sky. When Atlas returned with the apples he suggested that he should deliver them himself, as Heracles was doing so well. The hero pretended to agree and then asked if Atlas would take the world for a moment so that he could adjust the weight on his shoulder, so tricking Atlas into resuming his lonely duty. (See also GIANTS)

ATLAS, the great Titan giant, was condemned to shoulder the heavens forever, as punishment for fighting the sky god Zeus. (ILLUSTRATION FROM DICTIONARY OF CLASSICAL ANTIQUITIES, 1891.)

B

ATREUS was the son of *PELOPS*, an early king after whom the Peloponnese in southern Greece is named, and Hippodameia. The house of Atreus was infamous for the hereditary curse laid upon it by the son of *HERMES*, the messenger god. A terrible cycle of murder and revenge was ended only by the trial in Athens of Atreus' grandson *ORESTES* on a charge of matricide.

Family misfortune stemmed from the action of Pelops, the father of Atreus. He seems either to have brought about the death of Hermes' son Myrtilus, or to have caused him great grief by refusing to make a promised gift. Friction between the sons of Pelops, Atreus, Thyestes and Chrysippus, arose about the ownership of a golden ram, a wondrous animal placed in Atreus' flock by Hermes. First, Chrysippus was murdered by Atreus and Thyestes, then Thyestes seduced Aerope, the wife of Atreus, in order to gain her help in seizing the golden ram. An enraged Atreus slew Aerope and exiled Thyestes.

At a banquet supposedly for reconciliation, Atreus served his brother Thyestes with the flesh of his children. When Thyestes had

ATREUS, son of Pelops, cherished a golden ram, a double-edged gift of the god Hermes. The god gave the coveted treasure to Atreus, hoping to sow strife and discord in the house of Pelops, in revenge for the murder of his son, Myrtilus.
(ILLUSTRATION BY NICK BEALE, 1995.)

BELLEROPHON swoops down for the kill on his winged horse, Pegasus, diving through the smoke and flames of the fire-breathing Chimaera, a monster with the forepart of a lion, the hindpart of a dragon and its middle formed from a goat.
(ILLUSTRATION FROM TANGLEWOOD TALES, C. 1920.)

finished eating, Atreus showed his brother the hands and feet of his dead sons and told him what he had consumed. In horror the sun halted in its course. Thyestes' only surviving son, Aegisthus, may have slain Atreus in revenge for this outrage. Certainly he became the lover of *CLYTEMNESTRA*, whose husband *AGAMEMNON* was the eldest son of Atreus and his successor as king of Mycenae, or Argos. Not until Clytemnestra and Aegisthus had murdered Agamemnon, and were themselves killed by Agamemnon's son *ORESTES*, did the curse of Myrtilus come to an end.

BELLEROPHON was a Greek hero from the city of Corinth and the son of Glaucus. He possessed a wonderful winged horse named *PEGASUS*, which had sprung out of the *GORGON* Medusa's blood when she was beheaded by *PERSEUS*. The goddess *ATHENA* gave Bellerophon a special bridle in order to help him tame Pegasus.

Bellerophon's problems began, as his own name indicates, with a murder. He evidently killed an important Corinthian because in exile he changed his name from Hipponous to Bellerophon ("killer of Bellerus"). Although he was given refuge in Argos by King Proteus, the passion of the local queen Stheneboea for him caused further difficulties, and not least because he steadfastly rejected her advances. Stheneboea accused him of attempted rape and the enraged

BOREAS, one of the four winds, blew from the north, whistling through his conch. He often helped sailors with a friendly breeze. Along with his brother winds, Eurus, Zephyrus and Notus, he was depicted in the Temple of Winds. (ILLUSTRATION FROM DR SMITH'S CLASSICAL DICTIONARY, 1895.)

Proteus dispatched Bellerophon to southern Asia Minor, where he was supposed to meet his end, but service in the local king's forces saved his life. Mounted on Pegasus, the hero was able to overcome the monstrous Chimaera, defeat neighbouring peoples, including the Amazons, and even become the champion of Lycia. A constellation was named after his fabulous winged horse.

Two tales cast a certain shadow over Bellerophon's character. In the first he is credited with a brutal revenge on the false Argive queen. By pretending that he really loved her, Bellerophon persuaded the queen to elope with him on Pegasus, only to push her off the winged horse's back in mid-air. The second tale almost ends in the hero's death when he attempted to fly to Mount Olympus, the home of the gods. *ZEUS* in anger caused Pegasus to unseat Bellerophon, who was lamed for life.

BOREAS, the north wind, was the son of *EOS*, the goddess of dawn, and the Titan Astraeus. His home was thought to be Thrace, which is situated to the north of the Aegean Sea. In contrast to Zephyrus, the gentle west wind, Boreas was capable of great destruction. During the Persian invasion of Greece, he helped the Greek cause by damaging the Persian fleet at the battle of Artemisium in 480 BC.

Boreas abducted Orithyia, a daughter of King Erechtheus of Attica. Coming across Orithyia dancing near a stream, he then wrapped her up in a cloud and carried her off to Thrace. She bore Boreas twin sons, Calais and Zetes, who were known as the Boreades. At birth these boys were entirely human in appearance, but later they sprouted golden wings from their shoulders. They were killed by the great hero HERACLES.

Boreas was worshipped in the city of Athens, where an annual festival, known as the Boreasmi, was celebrated in his honour.

BRITOMARTIS fled from King Minos who pursued her for nine months, until at last, in despair, she leapt into the sea. Luckily, she became entangled in some fishing nets, and when Artemis changed her into a goddess she was known as Dictynna, which means "net".
(ILLUSTRATION BY NICK BEALE, 1995.)

BRITOMARTIS ("sweet maid") was said to be the daughter of ZEUS. She lived on the island of Crete, where she spent her time as a huntress. King MINOS of Knossos tried to make Britomartis his mistress. But she fled from him and in her desperation to preserve her virginity threw herself off a cliff into the sea. The king finally gave up the pursuit when the Cretan goddess sought sanctuary in the sacred grove of ARTEMIS, and became her close associate. The myth is almost certainly an account of the amalgamation of two ancient cults.

BRUTUS was said to be the son of Tarquinia, who was the sister of TARQUINIUS SUPERBUS. He was the founder of the Roman Republic. Like most Roman myths, the story of Lucius Junius Brutus lays emphasis on duty to the state, even though in this instance it involved the sacrifice of two sons. During the early part of his life Brutus was regarded as a simpleton, which his name implies. Indeed, he was something of a joke in the court of Tarquinius Superbus, the last Etruscan king to rule Rome. When a snake was found in the king's palace, two princes travelled to Delphi to ask the Oracle to explain this event and Brutus accompanied them almost in the role of a jester. The Oracle told the Romans that the first person in the delegation to kiss his mother would be the next ruler of Rome. The princes drew lots to decide who was to kiss their mother on their return home, but Brutus tripped and kissed the earth, much to their amusement.

BRUTUS, the first consul of the new republic of Rome, condemns his sons to death for rising against the government. Brutus, as his name implies, feigned idiocy but was no fool; wisely and dutifully, he led the trial against his rebel sons.
(ILLUSTRATION FROM STORIES FROM LIVY, 1885.)

Shortly after their return to Rome, the youngest prince raped LUCRETIA, a Roman matron. This act of violation was the last straw for the oppressed Roman aristocracy, especially when it was learned that Lucretia had stabbed herself to death. The outrage was cleverly used by Brutus as a means of overthrowing the monarchy and setting up a republic. The now eloquent Brutus was elected consul, one of the two highest offices of state. But this fulfilment of the Oracle was soon to cause him grief, when a conspiracy to restore Tarquinius Superbus to the throne was found to have the support of Titus and Tiberius, two of Brutus' own sons. As he was the chief magistrate, Brutus, with great dignity, oversaw their arrest, trial and execution. Thus, at the moment of the new Republic's triumph, the typically Roman idea of self-sacrifice appears as part of its foundation myth.

C

CERBERUS snarls and growls by the mouth of Hades. A three-headed hound with a snake for a tail, he allowed no shades to return from the dead, though a few slipped by with the help of the gods. His dark den opened onto the Styx along which Charon ferried the dead. (ILLUSTRATION BY GLENN STEWARD, 1995.)

CACUS see *GIANTS*

CADMUS was the son of Agenor, king of Phoenicia, and Telephassa, and the brother of *EUROPA*. When Europa was forcibly taken to Crete by *ZEUS*, disguised as a bull, Cadmus and his four brothers were sent after her, with instructions not to return home without her. Although the five Phoenician princes failed in their task, they seem to have had an impact on the places where they eventually settled. Cadmus himself was told by the Oracle at Delphi to forget about Europa and instead find a cow with a moon-shaped mark on its flank. He was to follow the animal and build a city on the spot where it chose to lie down and rest. Having found the cow and followed it eastwards to Boeotia, where at last it sank in exhaustion, Cadmus then sent some of his men for water so that they might sacrifice the animal to *ATHENA*. But these men were attacked by a serpent sprung from the war god *ARES*. After Cadmus had killed the monster, the goddess Athena advised him to remove its teeth and sow half of them in the ground. Immediately, armed men arose, but wily Cadmus threw stones among them so that, suspecting each other, they fell upon themselves. It was later believed

CADMUS sows the teeth of a dragon he has slain, and instantly the soil bristles with armed warriors, who spring up to attack each other. Only five survived, to become ancestors of the Thebans, whose city Cadmus founded on the site. (ILLUSTRATION BY NICK BEALE, 1995.)

that the Theban aristocracy was descended from the five warriors who survived the mutual slaughter.

After a period of penance for killing Ares' serpent, Zeus gave Cadmus a wife – none other than Harmonia, the daughter of Ares and *APHRODITE*, goddess of love. Since he was marrying a goddess, the gods themselves attended the wedding and gave wonderful gifts. The unusual union of mortal and immortal was not blessed by particularly successful offspring, however. One of their descendants, Pentheus, suffered a horrible fate. Having insulted *DIONYSUS*, he was torn to pieces by the god's female worshippers when he spied on their secret rites. Among the frenzied worshippers was Pentheus' own mother, Agave, the daughter of Cadmus and Harmonia.

The ancient Greeks always acknowledged the importance of Cadmus' reign, hence, his divine wife. He was credited with the introduction from Phoenicia of an alphabet of sixteen letters. There

are in fact a number of ancient accounts of Phoenician activity in the Aegean Sea. For instance, on the island of Cythera, which lies off the southern Peloponnese, a shrine to Aphrodite is known to have been erected based on the goddess's chief temple in Phoenicia.

CALCHAS see *ORACLES AND PROPHECIES*

CALLISTO see *LOVERS OF ZEUS*

CASSANDRA was the daughter of *PRIAM*, king of Troy, and his wife Hecuba. Her beauty was as remarkable as her power of prophecy, which was said to have been a gift from *APOLLO*, who loved her, but because she refused his advances he condemned her to prophesy the truth but never to be believed.

Cassandra foretold the Trojan War, the true purpose of the Wooden Horse and the murder of

CASSANDRA, frenzied seer, flees through burning Troy, aghast at the sight of her own predictions. Gifted with prophecy, she clearly foresaw the Trojan War and the trickery of the Wooden Horse, but no one believed her for she was fated to be ignored. (ILLUSTRATION BY NICK BEALE, 1995.)

AGAMEMNON, to whom she was awarded as part of his share of the spoils. But ultimately Cassandra had her revenge on the Greeks. When Troy fell, she had sought sanctuary in *ATHENA*'s temple but was raped, and so the goddess punished this sacrilege by killing many of the Greeks during their voyage home. However, Cassandra met her own end at the hands of Agamemnon's wife *CLYTEMNESTRA*. (See also *ORACLES AND PROPHECIES*)

CECROPS see *FOUNDERS*

CENTAURS, according to Greek mythology, were said to be the descendants of *IXION*, son of *ARES*. These strange creatures had the head, arms and chest of a man but the legs and lower half of a horse. They lived in Thessaly, fed on meat and were given to riotous behaviour. They were usually depicted as drunken followers of *DIONYSUS*, except for wise *CHIRON* who was the tutor to several heroes, including *ACHILLES*. (See also *MONSTERS AND FABULOUS BEASTS*)

CERBERUS was a three-headed hound, the offspring of two monsters, *TYPHON* and Echidna. He was the watchdog of the Greek underworld and stopped anyone trying to return to the land of the living. One of *HERACLES*' labours was to fetch Cerberus, a challenge the god of the dead, *HADES*, allowed him to

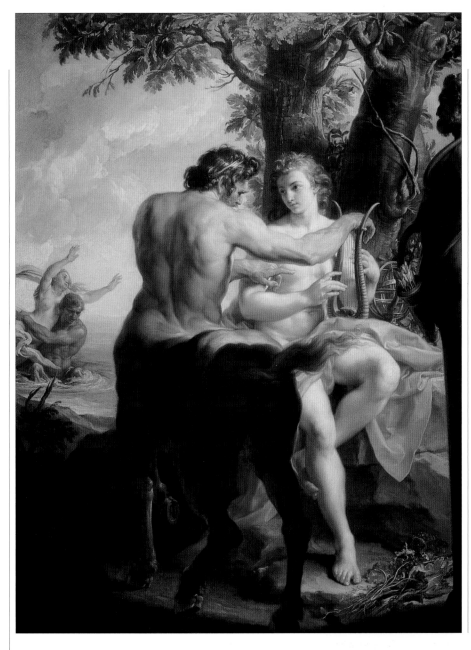

CHIRON (left) instructs the youthful Achilles in the arts of war, medicine, hunting, music and prophecy. Unlike his brother Centaurs, who indulged in riotous revelries, Chiron was noted for his wisdom and gentleness. (THE EDUCATION OF ACHILLES BY POMPEO BATONI, CANVAS, C. 1770.)

CINCINNATUS

CINCINNATUS was a Roman hero who was instrumental in saving the early Republic. In 458 BC, Rome was in danger of being destroyed by the Aequi, a neighbouring Italian tribe. To defeat this threat, the Senate voted to appoint Cincinnatus as dictator, a temporary office vested with unlimited powers. A deputation was sent to his small farm, which was the smallest landholding allowed to qualify for citizenship. The senators found Cincinnatus at work tending his crops. He was told of the Senate's decision and was saluted as dictator. However, the plebeians, the ordinary people, feared that Cincinnatus might abuse his position. Their fears proved groundless and, after the defeat of the Aequi, they voted Cincinnatus a golden wreath at the end of his sixty days of office. He then returned to his fields and was remembered as the perfect example of a virtuous and dutiful Roman citizen.

CINCINNATUS, one of the most modest of Roman heroes and a model of Roman integrity. After 60 days in office, he quietly returned to his farm. (ILLUSTRATION FROM STORIES FROM LIVY, 1885.)

undertake, but only on condition that he was unarmed. Like the *GORGONS*, Cerberus was so dreadful to behold that anyone who looked upon him was turned to stone. He was brother to the Hydra and the Chimaera.

CHIRON was the son of Philyra, daughter of *OCEANOS*, and the Titan *CRONOS*, who had adopted the form of a horse to hide from his wife *RHEA* his passion for Philyra, which is why Chiron had the appearance of a typical *CENTAUR*, with the body and legs of a horse, and the arms and head of a man.

His unusual parentage explains why Chiron was so wise, unlike other Centaurs, for he was learned in music, medicine, hunting and warfare. He was a friend of *APOLLO* and the tutor to several Greek heroes such as *ACHILLES, ASCLEPIUS* and *JASON*. He lived in a cave on Mount Pelion in Thessaly, and when he died *ZEUS* set him in the sky as the constellation Centaurus.

HEROES

T HE MYTHS OF ALL CULTURES contain inspiring individuals who express ideal traits and talents, such as the courage of Achilles, might of Heracles, wit of Odysseus and endurance of Oedipus. A classic hero is a champion in every sense, overcoming trials, ridding the world of troublemakers, blazing trails and winning through despite all the odds. Yet he is neither invulnerable nor immortal, though often helped, and sometimes hindered, by the gods. Greek mythology is unusually rich in heroes and heroines of every kind. Some, such as Achilles and Hector, are wartime champions; others, such as Odysseus or Theseus, are heroes for peacetime; some are positive and outgoing, such as Heracles or Perseus; still others are heroes of attitude rather than action, such as Oedipus, Antigone, or Hector, who, at the end, remained steadfast in the face of hopeless defeat.

HERACLES (below) shoots his poisoned arrows at his old foe, the Centaur Nessus, who raced away with his wife, Deianira, while ferrying her across the river Evenus. The dying Centaur offered Deianira the gift of his blood as a salve for preserving the love of Heracles. The love philtre proved to be a fatal trick by which Heracles died many years later, tragically, by the hands of his insecure but loving wife, Deianira, who in her sorrow killed herself. (HERCULES AND NESSUS BY FRANZ VON STUCK, CANVAS 1863-1928.)

HERACLES (above), best known for his mighty labours, was all his life a helper of gods and men, setting the earth free of many monsters and rascals. Worshipped as a hero and deity, he was invoked as a saviour; as the hero of labour and struggle, he was patron deity of the gymnasium. In art he appears as the ideal of manly strength, with massive muscles and grave expression. This celebrated Greek sculpture shows the hero in repose leaning on his club, draped with the famous lion's skin. (THE FARNESE HERCULES BY GLYCON, C. 200 BC.)

ACHILLES (above), godlike hero and peerless warrior was, paradoxically, disguised as a girl in his youth. His divine mother, Thetis, wishing to save him from the Trojan War, hid him amongst the daughters of Lycomedes on Scyros. There Odysseus went, disguised as a merchant, and showed the girls jewels, dresses and arms. Only Achilles seized the arms eagerly, suddenly realizing his true sex and role in life. He then accompanied Odysseus to Troy. (ODYSSEUS RECOGNISING ACHILLES AFTER FRANS FRANCKEN THE YOUNGER, CANVAS, C. 1570.)

PERSEUS, guided and guarded by the gods, was able to slay the mortal Gorgon, Medusa, one of three frightful sisters who dwelt on the farthest shore of the ocean, and whose looks turned men to stone. By viewing Medusa in his shining shield, Perseus was able to cut off her head as she slept. Hidden by the invisible helmet of Hades he flew to safety on winged sandals given him by the nymphs. Medusa's head was placed on Athena's breastplate – a paralysing power in battle. (ILLUSTRATION FROM TANGLEWOOD TALES, C. 1920.)

CLOELIA (above), Roman heroine, was given as a hostage to the Etruscan, Lars Porsenna, during his campaign against Rome. But she escaped from his camp and swam across the Tiber to Rome. When the Romans sent her back to Porsenna, he was so taken by her gallantry, that he set her free with some other hostages and gave her a splendid horse. Here she rides triumphantly to freedom with her companions. (ILLUSTRATION FROM STORIES FROM LIVY, 1885.)

JASON (above), the celebrated captain of the Argonauts, embarked on a great adventure to bring back the Golden Fleece, which was suspended from a branch of an oak tree in the grove of Ares in Colchis. It was greatly cherished by Aietes, the king of Colchis. With the help of a potion from the sorceress Medea, daughter of the king of Colchis, Jason charmed to sleep the ever-watchful dragon that guarded the Golden Fleece. (ILLUSTRATION FROM TANGLEWOOD TALES, C.1920.)

HORATIUS (above), brave Roman hero, held the Sublician Bridge with two comrades against the Etruscan army. While he held off the Etruscans, the Romans hacked the bridge behind him until it collapsed. Having sent back his comrades, Horatius stood alone until the bridge fell, then he swam to safety across the raging Tiber, amid enemy arrows. The state erected a statue to his honour in the Comitium. (ILLUSTRATION FROM LAYS OF ANCIENT ROME, 1891.)

CIRCE (left), *an enchanting nymph, invites Odysseus to drink from her magic cup, containing a potion which turns men into swine. But Odysseus has been forewarned and, immunized with the herb moly, he drinks without coming to harm.*
(ILLUSTRATION FROM TANGLEWOOD TALES, C.1920.)

CLYTEMNESTRA (above), *the estranged wife of Agamemnon, watches and waits for the ships from Troy, bringing her husband home. Yet no hero's welcome awaits the returning warrior, only betrayal and murder by his wife and her lover.*
(ILLUSTRATION BY NICK BEALE, 1995.)

CIRCE, daughter of *HELIOS*, the sun god, was a powerful witch who had poisoned her husband, king of the Sarmatians, before going to the fabulous island of Aeaea. Her magical powers turned *ODYSSEUS'* men into swine when they landed on Aeaea on their way home from Troy. Aided by *HERMES*, the messenger god, Odysseus was immune to Circe's magic and restored his crew to human form, and also gained the witch's aid for the next part of his journey. For a year he stayed as her lover, before she told him how to navigate through the waters of the Sirens and between Scylla, a monster, and Charybdis, a whirlpool. Scylla had been a rival of Circe, who had turned her into a monster when one of her many lovers had shown an interest in the unfortunate girl. In some accounts, Circe eventually married Odysseus' son Telemachus.

CLOELIA see *HEROES*

CLYTEMNESTRA was the daughter of *LEDA* and Tyndareos, king of Sparta, and the estranged wife of *AGAMEMNON*. Sometimes she is portrayed as a weak woman, easily persuaded by her lover Aegisthus to assist in the murder of her husband on his return from the Trojan War. Otherwise it is Clytemnestra who is the strong character, the instigator of the murder, while Aegisthus is little more than a weakling. Even before the the Greek force departed for Troy, Clytemnestra already had good reason to hate her husband. In order to gain a fair wind to Troy, he agreed to sacrifice her favourite child *IPHIGENIA*. Even though the champion *ACHILLES* had promised to defend the girl against all threats, the Greek host had its way and Iphigenia was offered to the god-

dess *ARTEMIS*, either as sacrificial victim or as priestess.

Like her sister *HELEN*, whose elopement with *PARIS* caused the Trojan War, Clytemnestra felt no loyalty towards her husband. She openly conducted an affair with Aegisthus, Agamemnon's cousin, and ruled Mycenae with him. The end of the war required desperate measures. When he returned home Agamemnon was butchered by Aegisthus, using a two-headed axe, while Clytemnestra had him entangled in a net. For this terrible crime, Clytemnestra was herself killed by her son *ORESTES*.

CORIOLANUS was a legendary Roman traitor of the fifth century BC. Conscious above all of his noble birth, Coriolanus objected to the Senate's wish to distribute free bread to poorer citizens, who were starving because of Rome's endless

wars. He said that unless the plebeians, the ordinary people, were willing to restore to the nobility its full ancient privileges they should expect no charity. Hounded from Rome for such an opinion, he joined the Volsci and eventually led a Volscian army against the city. All seemed lost until his mother Volumnia spoke to him, asking Coriolanus whether he saw her as his own mother or as a prisoner of war. As a result he quit the battlefield and went into exile.

CREON, in Greek mythology, was the brother of Jocasta and a reluctant ruler of Thebes. He was regent during the uncertain period after King *LAIUS*, Jocasta's husband, had been killed near the city. Creon offered the throne and the hand of Jocasta to any man who could solve the riddle of the *SPHINX* and thus rid Thebes of this bloodthirsty

CORIOLANUS, *a Roman exile, marched against his old city with an army of Volscians, encamping just outside Rome. There, he ignored all entreaties for peace until visited by his mother (centre), his wife and the Roman matrons, whose tears softened his stern heart.* (ILLUSTRATION FROM STORIES FROM LIVY, 1885.)

monster. *OEDIPUS* managed to achieve the apparently impossible task, then took over the kingdom, married Jocasta and raised a family. Not until a plague threatened Thebes and the Delphic Oracle was consulted about its cause, did it become known that Jocasta was Oedipus' mother and that he had killed Laïus. Oedipus blinded himself, Jocasta committed suicide and Creon became regent once more.

A quarrel between Oedipus' sons, Eteocles and Polynices, caused another period of dismay, eventually leaving both of them dead and Creon on the throne. Whereas Eteocles was regarded by Creon as a patriot and properly buried, the body of the rebel Polynices was thrown outside the city walls and forbidden burial. Such a situation was unacceptable to *ANTIGONE*, Oedipus' daughter and companion during his wanderings around Greece, and on her return to Thebes she sprinkled Polynices' corpse with earth, so as to give her brother a token burial.

As a result of this act of defiance, Creon had Antigone walled up in a cave. The seer *TIRESIAS* told Creon to bury the dead and disinter the living, but he refused. The result was personal grief, when his own son committed suicide on learning of Antigone's death, and his own wife soon followed suit.

Although Creon was well known to the ancient Greeks, his own character seems less important in myth than his role as regent in the troubled city of Thebes.

CRONOS, in Greek mythology, was the son of Ouranos, the sky god, and *GAIA*, the earth mother. With the help of Gaia, Cronos emasculated Ouranos and seized control of the universe. He then married his sister *RHEA* and followed the example of Ouranos in disposing of his children by swallowing them, because he had been warned that he would be displaced by one of his sons. Rhea, however, gave him a stone wrapped in swaddling clothes instead of the infant *ZEUS*, his youngest son, who was taken secretly to Crete in order to grow up safely on the island. When Zeus came of age, he forced Cronos to vomit up his brothers and sisters – *POSEIDON, HADES, HERA, HESTIA* and *DEMETER* – and to release his uncles and aunts, especially the Titans, whom Cronos had chosen

CREON, *reluctant king of Thebes, lost his son, wife and niece in a tragic cycle of suicides caused by his inflexible will. His crushing fate was to endure a life of solitary grief and remorse.* (ILLUSTRATION BY NICK BEALE, 1995.)

to keep chained up. In gratitude, the Cyclopes, the single-eyed giants, fashioned for Zeus his famous lightning and thunderbolts.

In a subsequent struggle for power, Zeus and his brothers successfully dealt with all the might and power that Cronos could direct against them. After his defeat, Cronos was either banished to a distant paradise, or he simply slowly faded away as an unimportant deity. The Romans equated Cronos with their *SATURN*, who

was a corn god whom they associated with the Golden Age.

CUPID was the Roman god of love and son of the love goddess *VENUS*. He was depicted as a beautiful but wanton boy, armed with a quiver full of "arrowed desires". Some of his arrows, however, would turn people away from those who fell in love with them.

According to one myth, Venus was jealous of *PSYCHE* ("the soul") and told Cupid to make her love the ugliest man alive. But Cupid fell in love with Psyche and, invisible, visited her every night. He told her not to try to see him, but, overcome by curiosity, she did try and he left her. Psyche searched the world for him, until the sky god *JUPITER* granted her immortality so that she could be Cupid's constant companion. The couple's daughter was named Voluptas ("pleasure").

CUPID *fishes playfully amongst the waves. He is usually portrayed as a cute, capricious child with wings and often with a quiver of arrows or a torch to inflame love in the hearts of gods and men.* (CUPID FISHING BY GEORGE FREDERICK WATTS, SEPIA C. 1890.)

D

CURTIUS leaps into the chasm in the Roman forum. The seers declared that the chasm could only be filled by Rome's greatest treasure, and so Curtius jumped in, declaring that there was no greater treasure than a gallant Roman citizen. (ILLUSTRATION FROM STORIES FROM LIVY, 1885.)

CURTIUS is the subject of a strange incident in Roman mythology. Around 362 BC a great chasm appeared in the Forum in Rome, which led straight down to the underworld. It had appeared because the Romans forgot to make an appropriate sacrifice to the dead. Marcus Curtius therefore plunged on horseback into the bottomless pit and was seen no more.

CYCLOPES see GIANTS

DAEDALUS, according to Greek mythology, was said by some to be the son of Alcippe, the daughter of the war god ARES, and by others to be the son of Merope. It is agreed, though, that he came from Athens. He was a gifted craftsman and was employed by King MINOS at his palace of Knossos in Crete. Daedalus designed and built the Labyrinth for the dreaded MINOTAUR. This was the offspring of PASIPHAE, Minos' wife, and a great bull. Daedalus had designed an artificial cow into which the queen could place herself and so be able to mate with the bull. Thus was the Minotaur conceived. Minos later imprisoned Daedalus for revealing the secret of the Labyrinth, but he managed to escape by constructing

DAPHNE, a river nymph, was loved by Apollo who pursued her until, on the banks of her father's river, she prayed for help and was at once changed into a laurel tree. Here, her father, the river god Peneius, weeps inconsolably, while Apollo strokes her leafy arms in wonder. (APOLLO AND DAPHNE BY NICOLAS POUSSIN, CANVAS, C.1627)

wings of wax and feathers for himself and his son Icarus. Despite his father's warning, Icarus flew too close to the sun, the wax of his wings melted and he fell into the sea and drowned. Daedalus managed to arrive safely in Sicily, where he amused the daughters of King Cocalos with his inventions. When Minos eventually caught up with the fugitive craftsman, a battle of wits ended in Daedalus' favour: Minos was killed by boiling water, or oil, which Daedalus persuaded Cocalos' daughters to pour down a pipe into the king's bath.

DANAE was the mother of the Greek hero PERSEUS and the daughter of Acrisius, king of Argos in the Peloponnese. It had been foretold that her son would cause the death of Acrisius, so he locked her in a bronze tower. But ZEUS visited her as a shower of golden rain and Perseus was conceived. The king banished the mother and her son, but after many adventures Perseus did accidentally kill Acrisius when throwing a discus. (See also LOVERS OF ZEUS)

DANAE (above) was imprisoned in a bronze tower by her father, because he feared a prophecy that he would be killed by his grandson. Yet even hidden away in her tower, she was still accessible to the god Zeus, who came to her as a golden shower. They had a son, Perseus. (DANAE AND THE GOLDEN RAIN BY TITIAN, CANVAS, 1554.)

DAEDALUS (right) crafted wings of feathers, held together by wax, to escape from Crete, and taught his son, Icarus, how to fly, warning him that he must not fly too close to the sun. But Icarus was drawn to the light of the sun, so his wings melted and he fell into the sea, now named the Icarian. (DAEDALUS AND ICARUS BY CHARLES LANDON, 1799.)

DAPHNE, in Greek mythology, was the daughter of the river god Peneius. She was similar in many ways to the goddess ARTEMIS, in that she was also a virgin huntress who happily roamed the wilderness. One day, the love god EROS shot a flurry of arrows in response to taunts from APOLLO, the god of prophecy. The first of Eros' arrows was a gold-tipped shaft and when it struck Apollo it made him fall immediately in love with Daphne. The second one, however, had a lead tip and caused Daphne to become even more indifferent than she already had been to any lover. Apollo, however, pursued Daphne relentlessly until, in desperation, she turned herself into a laurel tree.

DELPHIC ORACLE see
ORACLES AND PROPHECIES

DEMETER, (left) goddess of the earth, and her daughter, Persephone, holding a mystic torch, consecrate the young Triptolemus, the first man to sow corn. This relief was found at Eleusis, site of the Eleusian mysteries which centred on Demeter and her worship. (MARBLE RELIEF, C. 490 BC.)

dead she pined and refused to eat any food, while in the world of the living her mother lost all interest in fertility, so that plants languished, animals ceased to multiply and people feared for their future. Eventually, Zeus had to intervene and rule that Hades must give up Persephone if she would not consent to stay with him. As she had by then eaten something in his realm, it was deemed that she had not completely rejected Hades, so henceforth Persephone would divide the year equally between her mother and her husband.

DIDO (below), exotic queen of Carthage, tragically stabbed herself when her lover Aeneas deserted her to fulfil his destiny, and lead his people to Rome. The heroine is portrayed by Virgil as a noble and generous soul who, in the classic tradition, endures her tragic fate alone.
(ILLUSTRATION BY NICK BEALE, 1995.)

DEMETER, the Greek goddess of vegetation and fruitfulness, was the daughter of CRONOS and RHEA. Like her Roman equivalent, Ceres, she was especially associated with corn. Demeter possessed mysterious powers of growth and even resurrection. She was the focus of an important cult at Eleusis, just south of Athens, where rites were celebrated annually in the autumn when, through music and dancing, her worshippers recalled the loss and rediscovery of her daughter PERSEPHONE. Demeter means "mother earth" – the abundant soil as well as the resting-place of the dead (which were known by the Athenians as "Demeter's people").

Her myth turns on the disappearance of Persephone. When the girl was a child, her father, ZEUS, without even consulting Demeter, agreed to his brother HADES' request that Persephone should be his bride and rule the underworld with him. Hades was impatient and rose from the earth and abducted Persephone as she plucked flowers in a field. But in the world of the

The story of Demeter and Persephone is clearly ancient. It has parallels in the mythology of West Asia, where growth and decay were closely associated with a dying and reviving deity. For the Greeks, Persephone as Kore ("the maiden"), was identified as the power within the corn itself, which was a natural extension of her mother the corn goddess Demeter.

DIONYSUS, the vital and beautiful Greek god of wine, whirls in a state of blissful euphoria induced by his own fruit, the grape. Entwined in his hair is a wreath of vine, and covering his shoulders the skin of a lynx, one of the creatures sacred to him.
(RED-FIGURE VASE, C. 400 BC.)

DIONYSUS was the son of ZEUS and SEMELE, who was a Theban princess. In Greek mythology, he is a youthful god of vegetation, wine and ecstasy, known as the "bull-horned god" because he often adopted the form of this powerful beast. In Roman mythology he is represented by the god Bacchus. Originally, he may have had a mythological role somewhat similar to that of the goddess DEMETER ("mother earth"). His cult in later times, however, developed into one of personal salvation, particularly for women worshippers who were known as maenads.

From the beginning, the ancient Greeks were well aware of the strange character of Dionysus, and in some city-states his wild, orgiastic rites were outlawed. The most famous attempt to prohibit his worship was by King Pentheus of Thebes. The king even tried to imprison Dionysus, but the chains fell off him and the prison doors could not be closed. Dionysus then told Pentheus that he could observe at first hand the secret rituals performed on a mountain close to the city, but only if he disguised himself as a woman. The king readily took the bait and spied on the maenads from a hiding-place in a tree. However, the maenads soon discovered him and, in their ecstatic frenzy, thought that he was a lion and tore him limb from limb. Afterwards his mother, Agave, who was also one of the leading maenads, realized to her horror that they had dismembered not a lion but her son. After his burial, Agave, together with her parents, CADMUS and Harmonia, left Thebes and went into exile. (See also LOVERS OF ZEUS)

DIDO, originally a princess of Tyre, in Phoenicia, became the tragic queen of Carthage and the abandoned love of AENEAS. Her husband had been murdered by her brother, when the latter ascended the throne of Tyre. Dido escaped from Phoenicia with a small band of followers and settled in present-day Tunisia, where she purchased enough land to found the city of Carthage. The local ruler agreed to sell her as much ground as a bull's hide might contain, so Dido cut the skin into strips in order to obtain an adequate plot.

When the Trojan hero Aeneas arrived in Carthage, having been blown off course on his way to Italy from Troy, Dido welcomed him and his fellow refugees with great understanding. Aeneas and Dido soon fell in love, but the Roman god JUPITER sent MERCURY with a message reminding Aeneas of his destiny to found a new Troy in Italy and ordering him to resume his voyage at once. When Aeneas sailed away, Dido became so overwhelmed by the loss of her lover that she stabbed herself and then leapt into the flames of a pyre. (See also FOUNDERS)

E

THE DIOSCURI, the mysterious twin sons of *LEDA*, queen of Sparta, were known to the Greeks as Castor and Polydeuces, and to the Romans as Castor and Pollux. They were brothers of *HELEN* and *CLYTEMNESTRA*. Around all these children, except Clytemnestra, there hung a definite sense of divine parentage, and it may well be that they were ancient deities whose worship had declined so that their exploits could be told as the mythological actions of mortal rulers. Castor and Polydeuces ("the heavenly twins whom the corn-bearing earth holds") were regarded as being both dead and alive. In one story, Polydeuces was the immortal son of *ZEUS* while Castor was the mortal son of King Tyndareos. At Polydeuces' request the twins shared the divinity between them, living half the year beneath the earth with the dead, and the other half on Mount Olympus with the gods. They are shown together in the constellation of Gemini.

In their youth the Dioscuri ("the sons of Zeus") were *ARGONAUTS*. During the expedition to retrieve the Golden Fleece, Polydeuces killed with his bare hands Amycus, king of the savage Bebryces, who were a people living in Asia Minor. On another occasion the twins were ranged against the Athenian hero *THESEUS*, who carried off the twelve-year-old Helen prior to her marriage to King *MENELAUS*. They brought their sister safely home to Sparta, and even set up a rival to Theseus on the throne of Athens.

THE DIOSCURI (above), twins Castor and Pollux, returned to earth to help the Roman ranks against the Latins in the fabled Battle of Lake Regillus. Adorned with gleaming armour, and mounted on snow-white steeds, they led the Romans to victory. (ILLUSTRATION FROM LAYS OF ANCIENT ROME, 1881.)

The Dioscuri were revered by the Spartans and the Romans in particular. Roman soldiers swore that the presence of Castor and Pollux on a battlefield secured for them victories against all the odds.

ELECTRA was the daughter of *AGAMEMNON*, king of Mycenae, and *CLYTEMNESTRA*, and the sister of the matricide *ORESTES*. Her name (which once may have meant "fire" or "spark") refers to amber. When Agamemnon returned from the Trojan War and was murdered by his wife and her lover Aegisthus, Electra rescued her young brother Orestes and ensured that he escaped Aegisthus' evil intentions. Years later, Orestes returned to Mycenae as a grown man. Electra met him at the tomb of their murdered father and gave him advice and encouragement. In at least one version of the myth Electra is portrayed as being so consumed by hatred for Clytemnestra that she participates in the act of revenge herself. Later she was overwhelmed by remorse, while her distraught brother fled before the *FURIES*, the deities who wreaked vengeance on murderers.

ENDYMION was the king of a small city-state in the Peloponnese,

ELECTRA (above), heroic daughter of Agamemnon and Clytemnestra, meets her exiled brother Orestes outside Agamemnon's tomb. It was Electra who rescued her brother from the evil intentions of Aegisthus by helping him escape. Having thought that she would never see him again, she is seen here rejoicing in his return. (ORESTE AND ELECTRA, MARBLE, C. AD 100.)

EOS (below), Greek goddess of the dawn, rises early each day to announce the coming of the sun. She was the daughter of Hyperion and Theia and sister to the sun god Helios. In works of art, she is often depicted hovering in the sky, her rosy form adorned in a golden mantle. She is accompanied here by her starry daughters. (ILLUSTRATION FROM STORIES FROM HOMER, 1885.)

ENDYMION (above) was loved by Selene who visited him in his eternal sleep. Here, the lovers part at dawn. In the sky, the goddess sprinkles dew before the sun-chariot, while on earth Nyx draws a curtain of darkness about her. (SELENE AND ENDYMION BY NICOLAS POUSSIN, CANVAS, C. 1594-1665.)

EUROPA (right) was a Phoenician princess borne away by Zeus, who assumed the form of a great white bull. He swam to the island of Crete with Europa riding on his back. She eventually married Asterius, the ruler of Crete. (ILLUSTRATION FROM DR SMITH'S CLASSICAL DICTIONARY, 1895.)

in all likelihood Elis. According to Greek mythology, he became the lover of the moon goddess Selene (frequently identified with Diana), who bore him fifty daughters. Because she could not endure the thought that Endymion would eventually die, Selene put her youthful lover into an everlasting, deep sleep. However, in another version of the myth, it is said that ZEUS granted Endymion his wish that he might be allowed to sleep forever in a cave without ageing

EOS was the Greek, winged goddess of the dawn and the third child of the TITANS Hyperion and

Theia. She was seen as a charioteer riding across the sky just before sunrise, pulled by her horses Shiner and Bright. Her brother, the sun god HELIOS, had a four-horse chariot to indicate his greater status. The Romans called her Aurora.

Eos had a reputation for passion and fell in love with a large number of young men, including the particularly handsome Tithonus, son of Laomedon, king of Troy. When Eos asked ZEUS to make Tithonus immortal, she forgot about eternal youth and ended with a lover made helpless with age. Thereupon, according to different versions of the myth, she

locked him in a bedchamber or he became the cicada (an insect noted for its complaining sound).

ERINYES see FURIES

EROS, according to some Greek traditions, was the son of Erebos and the Night, while in others he was the son of ARES, god of war. As the youngest of the gods and the companion of APHRODITE, he appeared to enjoy making as much mischief as he could by firing his arrows of passion into the hearts of gods and humans alike. His connection with homosexual love may have derived from his supposed

relationship to Ares, for he was the patron divinity of the Sacred Band of Thebes, which was a group of one hundred and fifty pairs of lovers who were all killed by the Macedonian army at the battle of Chaeronia in 338 BC. After the battle King Philip of Macedon granted them a special burial.

EUROPA, in Greek mythology, was the daughter of Telephassa and of King Agenor of Tyre, a city in Phoenicia. Agenor's five sons, including CADMUS, were sent out to look for their sister after ZEUS, disguised as a white bull, swam to the island of Crete with Europa on his back. There she bore the god three sons, MINOS, RHADAMANTHYS and SARPEDON, before marrying the local ruler Asterius. By way of compensation for Europa's virginity, Zeus gave Asterius a mighty bronze man, Talos, to defend his realm. (See also LOVERS OF ZEUS)

ORACLES AND PROPHECIES

I N THE ANCIENT WORLD, a man's life was thought to be determined by fate or destiny. Even the gods themselves were, to a large extent, subject to fate, although it was Zeus who saw to it that fate took its proper course. As people believed that the future could be revealed, they frequently consulted oracles of every kind for personal and political purposes. The most famous was the Delphic Oracle where Apollo, the seer-god, spoke through a priestess. The future was also revealed by oracular signs, such as the fall of dice, lots, or burnt offerings. Dreams afforded another type of oracle, usually inspired by the gods, sometimes to mislead. Prophecies were also sought from seers, both living and dead. Although the Romans consulted lots (or sortes) for personal problems, they rarely, if ever, prophesied for political purposes.

DREAMS (below) could sometimes reveal the future and were often inspired by the gods, usually to guide a favourite mortal in distress. Here, Penelope is visited in her dream by Athena in the form of her sister Iphthime. The vision consoled Penelope in her troubles and predicted that her son, Telemachus, though in grave danger, would nonetheless return home safely. (ILLUSTRATION FROM STORIES FROM HOMER, 1885.)

CASSANDRA (above), fairest daughter of Priam and Hecuba, was a gifted but tragic seer, who was doomed to be ignored. She was endowed with prophecy by Apollo, in exchange for the promise of her love. When she broke her word, he punished her by decreeing that her prophecies, however true, would always be ignored. This powerful portrayal of Cassandra reveals the solitary, all-seeing world of the sorrowful seer, who accurately predicted the fall of Troy. (CASSANDRA BY MAX KLINGER, MARBLE, 1886-95.)

THE DELPHIC ORACLE (left), ancient and fabled seat of prophecy at Delphi, was described as the "navel of the earth". The oracle itself was a cleft in the ground which emitted cold vapours, inducing ecstasy. Over the chasm the seer sat on a gilded tripod inhaling the vapours and uttering enigmatic words which were recorded by a priest and interpreted as the revelations of Apollo. (ILLUSTRATION FROM TANGLEWOOD TALES, C. 1920.)

THE FATES (above), or Moerae, spun out a child's destiny at birth, symbolized by a thread which was drawn, measured and cut off. Although Greek portrayals of the spinners reveal grave, busy maidens, the Romantic Fatae can seem mean, denying humans their hopes and desires. Here they appear as frightful old hags: Clotho, on the left, unravels a spindle in the shape of a helpless child, while Lachesis squints through her glass and Atropos manically waves her scissors. The fourth figure possibly symbolizes the general concept of destiny. (THE FATES BY FRANCISCO DE GOYA, CANVAS, 1819-23.)

SIGNS OR OMENS (below) foretold the future in a variety of ways. Sometimes lots or dice were thrown; sometimes burnt offerings were inspected at the altar. In some sacred precincts, the sound of a rustling oak or the clash of cymbals signified a response to the seeker's question. Here, offerings are burnt at the altar, and examined for signs of the future. (ILLUSTRATION FROM STORIES FROM HOMER, 1885.)

CALCHAS (above), celebrated seer, accompanied the Greeks on their expedition against Troy, correctly predicting that the Trojan war would last ten years. It was prophesied that he would die when he met a seer wiser than himself, and when the soothsayer, Mopsus, beat him in a match of guessing riddles, Calchas died of grief. A temple was erected to him in Apulia where the votaries received oracles in their sleep. (THE SACRIFICE OF IPHIGENIA BY GIOVANNI BATTISTA, TEMPERA, 1770.)

G

THE FATES, from the Roman, Fatae, were three goddesses known to the Greeks as the Moerae. Their origins are uncertain, although some called them daughters of night. It is clear, however, that at a certain period they ceased to be concerned with death and became instead those powers which decided what must happen to individuals. The Greeks knew them as Clotho ("the spinner"), Lachesis ("the apportioner") and Atropos ("the inevitable"). A late idea was that the Fates spun a length of yarn which represented the allotted span for each mortal.

Although *ZEUS* was the chief Greek god, he was still subject to the decisions of the Fates, and thus the executor of destiny rather than its source. Hence the great importance to both gods and humans of oracles which indicated the inevitable drift of events. In mythology, however, the Fates played little direct part. (See also *ORACLES AND PROPHECIES*)

FAUNUS was the Roman god of the countryside and identified with the Greek *PAN*, god of the mountainside. Faunus was said to be the grandson of *SATURN* and was credited with prophetic powers, which on occasion inspired the Romans to renew efforts on the battlefield in the face of defeat. Perhaps this is the reason for Faunus sometimes

FAUNUS, a spirit of the plains and fields, frolics along with a friendly goat. Faunus' children, known as Fauni, half-men, half-goats, were delightful but capricious creatures, who sometimes plagued men's sleep with nightmares. (ILLUSTRATION FROM DR SMITH'S CLASSICAL DICTIONARY, 1895.)

being seen as a descendant of the war god *MARS*. His mortal son, Latinus, was the king of the Latin people at the time of *AENEAS'* arrival in Italy after the long voyage from Troy.

FLORA see *FORCES OF NATURE*

THE FURIES, from the Roman name, Furiae, were the avenging goddesses of Greek mythology and were known as the Erinyes ("the angry ones"). They were born from the blood of Ouranos that fell into the womb of *GAIA*, when *CRONOS*, his son, castrated him. The Furies

A FURY, goddess of punishment, wields a torch, scourge and spears – the tools of her vengeance. The Furies pursued without mercy in life and in death all wrong-doers. Sometimes they were winged, symbolizing the swiftness of their vengeance. (ILLUSTRATION FROM DR SMITH'S CLASSICAL DICTIONARY, 1895.)

were portrayed as ugly women with snakes entwined in their hair, and were pitiless to those mortals who had wrongly shed blood. They relentlessly pursued *ORESTES*, who avenged his father *AGAMEMNON's* murder by killing *CLYTEMNESTRA*, his mother. The Furies were only persuaded to abandon their persecution of Orestes after his acquittal by the Areopagus, an ancient Athenian council presided over by the goddess *ATHENA*. The verdict calmed the anger of the Furies, whose name was then changed to the less-threatening Eumenides, ("the soothed ones").

GAIA, in Greek mythology, was the earth, who came out of Chaos and gave birth to Ouranos the sky god, who was her son and husband. So passionate was their relationship and so overwhelming Ouranos' embrace that their offspring could not emerge from her womb. One of these buried children, *CRONOS*, the youngest son, decided to overthrow Ouranos. Gaia conceived a great sickle which Cronos used to cut off his father's penis within the earth womb. The god was emasculated and the sky separated from the earth. From Ouranos' blood, Gaia conceived the *FURIES*, the avenging goddesses who pursued murderers.

Ouranos then faded from the mythological scene and Cronos ruled the universe, taking his sister *RHEA* as a wife. The Greeks regarded this as the golden age of the *TITANS*. Cronos, however, turned out to be as tyrannical to his own family as Ouranos had been before him. He had been warned by an oracle that he would be displaced by one of his sons, so he swallowed his children as soon as they were born. Rhea, on Gaia's advice, gave him a stone wrapped in swaddling instead of the infant *ZEUS*, who was secretly taken to Crete in order to grow up there in safety. When Zeus was grown, he compelled his father to disgorge his brothers and sisters, including his future wife *HERA*, the sea god *POSEIDON*, the god of the underworld *HADES* and *DEMETER*, the goddess of vegetation.

Gaia may have saved Zeus from a fate similar to that of Ouranos and Cronos when she warned him that a child of his born by Metis

GAIA, *the great earth mother, pushes through the fruitful earth with her gifts of fertility and abundance. Not only was she the mother of all and the nourisher of children, but she was also a goddess of death who, like the earth, calls her creatures back to her.* (ILLUSTRATION BY NICK BEALE, 1995.)

("thought") would replace him as the supreme god. So Zeus swallowed Metis and later the goddess *ATHENA* sprang from his head.

The story of the separation between sky and earth is an ancient one. It is found in a variety of forms in West Asian mythology. The Hurrians, who lived on the borders of modern Turkey and Iraq, had in their myths the most violent version of the sky's emasculation. Kumarbi, the equivalent of Cronos, bit off and swallowed his father's penis. As a result of his unusual action, however, Kumarbi became pregnant with terrible deities, one of whom at last overthrew him.

GANYMEDE, in Greek mythology, was the son of Tros, the king of Phrygia, and brother of Ilus. He was such a beautiful young man that *ZEUS* abducted him and took him to Mount Olympus to be his cupbearer. It was believed that Ganymede also became Zeus' lover, and gained his immortality as the constellation Aquarius, the water-carrier.

GANYMEDE, *a handsome boy, excited the passion of Zeus who, in the guise of an eagle, bore him away to Mount Olympus.* (THE RAPE OF GANYMEDE, BY PETER PAUL RUBENS, CANVAS, 1577-1640.)

HADES (above), lord of the underworld, with his wife, Persephone, receives the souls of the dead, who are guided by Hermes. Hades appears with typically dark looks and unruly hair over which he often wore a magic helmet. (ILLUSTRATION FROM DR SMITH'S CLASSICAL DICTIONARY, 1895.)

HECTOR (below), the Trojan champion, snatches a moment of peace with his loving wife and small son. He was portrayed as both a raging warrior and a gentle family man who had taught himself to be valiant out of duty rather than any natural courage. (ILLUSTRATION BY ALAN LEE, 1994.)

THE GIANTS (above) were gigantic creatures with snake-like tails. After they were defeated by the gods, they were buried beneath volcanoes. Here we see the hound of Artemis killing a giant at the battle of the Giants and the gods. (ZEUS ALTAR OF PERGAMON, MARBLE, C. 180 BC.)

THE GIANTS, from the Roman name, Gigantes, in Greek mythology, had human shape, except for the snake-like tails that were attached to their legs. They were born at the same time as the *FURIES*, from the blood that fell into *GAIA's* womb from Ouranos' severed penis. When the Giants attacked Olympus, the gods stood their ground, but knew that they would not be able to defeat them, because the Giants could not be killed by divine hands. *ZEUS* therefore fathered the great hero *HERACLES* through a mortal woman. During the great battle between the gods and the Giants, Heracles played a decisive part, finishing off each opponent with poisoned arrows. It is important to realize that the Giants are quite different from the *TITANS*, who were the oldest generation of the gods and were led by *CRONOS*, Zeus' father.

THE GORGON MEDUSA (above) was once a beautiful woman whose locks were turned to writhing snakes by a vengeful goddess. The image of her frightful face was carved, like an evil eye, on warriors' shields, city walls, charms and amulets. (ILLUSTRATION FROM DR SMITH'S CLASSICAL DICTIONARY, 1895.)

THE GORGONS were three sisters named Stheno ("strength"), Medusa ("queen") and Euryale ("wide-leaping"), and were the children of Phorcys, son of *GAIA*. The only mortal of the three was Medusa, the victim of the Greek hero *PERSEUS*. Like her immortal sisters, she had snakes for hair and one look at her face could turn any living man or thing to stone.

THE GRACES, from the Roman name, Gratiae, were the daughters of *ZEUS* and Eurynome, and were minor goddesses to both the Greeks and the Romans. According to the most widely accepted myth, their names were Aglaia, Euphrosyne and Thalia. They were attendants to *APHRODITE* and *VENUS*, the love goddesses of Greece and Rome respectively. A favourite subject for artists, the Graces were thought to represent beauty, gentleness and friendship.

THE GRACES, or Charities, graced the world with beauty, bloom and brilliance, lifting the spirits of gods and men. In the earliest works of art, the Graces appear in flowing chitons, veiling their beauty, but later on they were depicted as nudes. (THE THREE GRACES BY RAPHAEL, WOOD, C. 1501.)

HADES (whose name means "the unseen") was the Greek god of the underworld, the realm of the dead. He was the son of CRONOS and RHEA, and the brother of ZEUS, POSEIDON, HERA, DEMETER and Hestia. He forcibly married PERSEPHONE, Demeter's daughter. At the division of the universe after the overthrow of their father, Zeus took the sky, Poseidon the sea, and Hades the underworld; the earth was to be shared among them. Another name for Hades was

Polydegmon ("receiver of many guests") on account of the multitudes who had died and come to his kingdom. The ghosts of the dead were escorted by HERMES, the messenger god, to the boatman Charon who ferried across the Styx, a subterranean river, only those ghosts who could pay the fare. CERBERUS, the three-headed dog, guarded the entrance to the underworld and prevented anyone from returning to the world of the living.

As in Egyptian mythology, the Greeks associated the underworld with the west, the place where the sun sets. Neither the Greeks nor the Romans, however, ever thought of Hades as an evil force like Satan in Christianity. He was certainly a grim and implacable deity, and worshippers always averted their

eyes when making a sacrifice. In order to avoid any reference to the nature of the underworld it was usual to call Hades by the title of Pluto ("the giver of wealth").

Hades' chief myth concerns the abduction of Persephone, who was the daughter of Demeter and his brother Zeus. Persephone was abruptly taken underground by Hades when she beheld a special narcissus planted by the earth mother GAIA to please the god of death. The conflict between Hades and Demeter over Persephone's fate was decided by Zeus, who gave the husband and the mother equal shares of her time. As a dying-and-rising goddess, Persephone sank and rose annually from the underworld, in tune with the natural cycle of sowing and harvesting.

Although usually a faithful husband, Hades at one time became enamoured of the nymph Minthe. When Persephone discovered this, however, she became so jealous that she turned the nymph into the sweet-smelling herb, mint.

HARPIES see MONSTERS AND FABULOUS BEASTS

HECATE was believed by some to be descended from the TITANS. A Greek goddess with two quite separate aspects, in the day she was supposed to have a benign influence on farming, but during the hours of darkness she was interested in witchcraft, ghosts and tombs. In many ways similar to the vegetation goddess DEMETER, Hecate uncomfortably combined fertility with death as a power of the earth. The witch MEDEA, JASON's rejected Colchian princess, used to invoke Hecate in her magic arts. Hecate is usually portrayed with three faces. The Athenians were particularly respectful towards her, and once a month they placed offerings of food at crossroads, where her influence was said to be felt.

HECTOR was the eldest son of PRIAM, the king of Troy during the Greek siege. The bravest of the Trojan warriors, he was unbeaten on the battlefield. He mistakenly killed Patroclus, the squire and lover of ACHILLES, the Greek hero. Achilles had quarrelled with AGAMEMNON and refused to fight, but Patroclus borrowed his divine armour in order to rally the Greeks, only to be slain by Hector. Roused from his lethargy, Achilles sought out Hector and compelled him to fight to the death. Such was Achilles' anger that for twelve days he dragged Hector's corpse round Patroclus' tomb. In the end ZEUS himself intervened, by sending Achilles' mother THETIS to stop this humiliation. So in exchange for a great treasure, Hector's body was returned and properly buried.

H

HELEN was the daughter of *LEDA* and *ZEUS*, the wife of the Spartan king *MENELAUS*, and the cause of the Trojan War. Her immortality as the daughter of the supreme Greek deity suggests that Helen was once a goddess and that her incorporation into myth as an unfaithful queen only occurred when her worship was largely forgotten.

Zeus mated with Leda, wife of the Spartan king Tyndareos, in the guise of a swan. Leda laid an egg, and when Helen hatched from it she brought her up as a member of the royal family. Helen's brothers were Castor and Polydeuces, the mysterious *DIOSCURI*, and her sister was King *AGAMEMNON*'s unfaithful wife *CLYTEMNESTRA*.

At the time of her marriage to Menelaus, the younger brother of Agamemnon, Helen was the most

HELEN (above) paces the walls of Troy. The most beautiful woman of the ancient world, she was also, according to Homer, a thoughtful heroine, given to self-mockery and ever aware of the misery caused by her beauty. (HELEN ON THE WALLS OF TROY BY LORD LEIGHTON, CANVAS, C. 1880.)

desirable bride in Greece. At first Menelaus and Helen were very happy, but then *PARIS*, one of the many sons of King *PRIAM* of Troy, visited Sparta and, with the help of the love goddess *APHRODITE*, gained Helen's affection. They even eloped with a part of Menelaus' treasury. When the Trojans refused to return Helen and the stolen treasure, Agamemnon assembled a great army to help his brother Menelaus. For ten years the city of Troy was besieged and then only captured through the trick of the Wooden

Horse. Throughout this long war the sympathies of Helen were mainly with the Greeks, although she was treated as the proper wife, and not merely the mistress, of Paris. After the fall of Troy, Helen and Menelaus were reconciled and they lived undisturbed at Sparta.

HELIOS was the Greek sun god and son of the *TITAN* Hyperion. To the Romans he was known as Sol. It was thought that Helios, after crossing the sky, sailed during the night around the earth in a golden bowl on the encircling waters of *OCEANOS*, and so arrived back in the east just before dawn. Both the Greeks and the Romans held that the inhabited world was a large

HELIOS, god of the sun, appears in works of art as a strong and beautiful youth with gleaming eyes, and a crown of flaming rays. Just as the sun's rays penetrate everywhere, so Helios saw everything, and was invoked as a witness of oaths. (ILLUSTRATION FROM DR SMITH'S CLASSICAL DICTIONARY, 1895.)

island surrounded by an ocean. Although Oceanos was sometimes described as a river, it stretched into the unimaginable distance and far from any shore.

One myth of Helios concerns the death of his son *PHAETHON*. Once this impetuous youth tried to steer his father's radiant chariot, but he quickly lost control. Only the timely action of *ZEUS* steadied its runaway horses and prevented the earth from catching fire. Phaethon fell from the vehicle and was drowned. However, Helios had

many other children, among them Augeas, *CIRCE* and *PASIPHAE*. A gigantic statue of the sun god was erected at the harbour of Rhodes, an island sacred to him. This so-called Colossus was one of the seven wonders of the ancient world, but was toppled by an earthquake around 226 BC.

HEPHAISTOS was the son of *ZEUS* and *HERA*, and was the Greek smith god. His Roman equivalent was *VULCAN*, whose smithy lay beneath the crater of Mount Aetna in Sicily. Hephaistos was lame as a result of having interfered in a quarrel between his parents. So angry did Zeus become that he flung his son from the top of Mount Olympus and let him fall heavily on the volcanic island of Lemnos, in the northern part of the Aegean Sea. In another version, Hera tried to drown her imperfect child, only to be thwarted by sea nymphs who took him to a beach. A sequel to this tale has the smith god gain his revenge as a fully grown man by making a golden throne for his mother which was actually a trap. None of the gods could release Hera, so Hephaistos was invited to return permanently to Mount Olympus. There, under the influence of drink, he was persuaded by his friend *DIONYSUS* to unlock the cunning device and let his mother escape.

Hephaistos seems to have come originally from Asia Minor, where iron mines date from a very early period. His cult was strong in Caria and Lycia, along its south-western shore. His marriage to the love goddess *APHRODITE* may have something to do with this eastern connection, as she also came to Greece from West Asia. Their relationship was almost as tumultuous as that of Zeus and Hera. Once Hephaistos fashioned a trap to catch his unfaithful wife in bed with the war god *ARES*. The Olympian gods merely laughed at Hephaistos' situation; the sea god *POSEIDON* only

HEPHAISTOS, god of fire, fashions exquisite golden works in his fiery forge. Lame, he leans on one leg. By him stands Apollo, who reveals that his wife, Aphrodite, loves Ares, and Hephaistos resolves to trap the guilty pair. (THE FORGE OF VULCAN BY DIEGO VELASQUEZ, CANVAS, 1630.)

promised some remedy if he agreed to release Aphrodite and Ares.

A myth about *ATHENA*'s birth recounts how Hephaistos split open Zeus' head with an axe in order to release the fully grown goddess. Apparently, Zeus had swallowed Athena's mother, Metis, once he realized she was pregnant with a powerful deity. Later, Hephaistos fell in love with Athena, but was rejected by her and his semen fell to earth where it gave birth to the serpent Erichthonius. (See also *FORCES OF NATURE*)

HERA means "lady" and was undoubtedly the title of a powerful mother goddess whom the Greeks inherited from the earlier inhabitants of Argos, which was a major city in the Peloponnese. It was claimed that she was the daughter of *CRONOS* and *RHEA*; however, her addition to the Greek pantheon was not an easy or straightforward matter, as the ceaseless conflicts between her and her husband *ZEUS* readily bear witness. Often her fits of jealousy and quarrelsomeness led to disaster for gods, heroes and men, when she relentlessly persecuted Zeus' mistresses and their children. For example, against the baby *HERACLES*, whom Zeus had fathered in order to help in the coming battle against the *GIANTS*, she sent two serpents to kill him, but the infant hero strangled them

HERA, queen of heaven, directs Helios across the sky. She is crowned with a diadem and veil, symbolizing her status as Zeus' bride. Her sceptre is tipped with a cuckoo, sacred to her as the messenger of spring, the season in which she married Zeus. (ILLUSTRATION FROM STORIES FROM LIVY, 1885.)

in his cradle. However, later in his life, Hera succeeded in driving Heracles temporarily mad.

There are a number of myths about Zeus' courtship of Hera. In one of them he disguised himself as a cuckoo and took shelter inside her clothes during a heavy downpour. Once out of the rain, Zeus resumed his normal shape and promised to marry Hera. Later she bore him the war god *ARES*, the goddess of birth Eileithyia, and Hebe, the cupbearer of the gods. Another child was the smith god *HEPHAISTOS*, who is said in some myths to have been the son of Zeus and Hera, but in others the offspring of Hera alone. Hera was worshipped with particular reverence in Crete and at Samos, where a great temple was said to have been built for her by the *ARGONAUTS*.

HERACLES, the son of ZEUS and ALCMENE, was the greatest of all the Greek heroes. To the Romans he was known as Hercules, and they added various encounters in Italy to his already large cycle of adventures. The name Heracles means "Hera's glory" – a circumstance that firmly ties the hero to Argos, the site of the goddess HERA's temple. It remains a mystery that Heracles should have been persecuted so much by Hera, even going mad at one point during his life.

Because Zeus needed a mortal champion in the forthcoming battle between the gods and the GIANTS, he fathered Heracles at the court of Thebes. The chosen mother was Alcmene, the Theban queen. Zeus intended Heracles to be ruler of Mycenae or Tiryns, strongholds close to Argos, but Hera frustrated this plan so well that the hero became the slave of Eurystheus, king of Tiryns. She struck Heracles with a fit of madness, in the course of which he killed his wife and their three sons with arrows. To atone for this terrible deed he had to become Eurystheus' dependent and undertook his famous twelve labours.

These labours began with the killing of the Nemean lion, which could not be harmed by arrows.

Heracles had to fight it with his bare hands and a wooden club. After overcoming the lion, he cured the skin and wore it as a trophy. His next opponent, the Hydra, was a nine-headed serpent sacred to Hera. It lived in a swamp at Lerna, not far from Argos. The problem that the hero encountered when fighting with the Hydra was that for every head he cut off with his sword two new ones grew in its place. But with assistance from his nephew Iolaus he was able to triumph, for Iolaus burned the stumps of the necks as soon as Heracles severed each head. When he returned to Eurystheus, the king refused to count the exploit as a labour, because Heracles had received help from his nephew.

The next labour was not quite so bloody. Heracles had to capture the Ceryneian hind, which was a beast sacred to ARTEMIS, goddess of the wild. According to different accounts, he returned to Tiryns with either its golden antlers or the hind itself. Another labour required

him to capture the Erymanthian boar, which plagued the country-side of Arcadia. He trapped it with a net, and during the hunt Heracles encountered a band of CENTAURS, beast-like men who lived in wood-lands. One of them, Nessus, was later to cause the hero's death.

The fifth labour was the cleansing of Augeas' stables. The son of the sun god, Augeas had vast herds of animals, which he pastured in the kingdom of Elis in the western Peloponnese. King Eurystheus told Heracles to remove the immense piles of dung from the stables, a feat he achieved by diverting the course of a nearby river. The last labour that the hero performed in the Peloponnese was the removal of the Stymphalian birds. Although they had steel-tipped feathers with which they killed both men and animals, these birds were frightened away by the noise of a rattle, which the goddess ATHENA had specially made for Heracles.

On the island of Crete the hero tracked down the bull that MINOS had failed to sacrifice to the sea god POSEIDON. The bull had mated with Minos' wife, PASIPHAE, who then gave birth to the MINOTAUR, the bull-headed man slain by the Athenian hero THESEUS. Heracles captured Poseidon's bull alive and brought it back to Tiryns, where he let it go free at the end of this seventh labour. The eighth labour was more gruesome. It took Heracles to Thrace in pursuit of the man-eating mares of Diomedes, which he subdued after feeding them on their master's flesh.

The last four labours were quite different in nature. First of all Eurystheus had Heracles fetch the girdle of Hippolyta, queen of the fierce AMAZONS. Then he captured the cattle of Geryon, a western king who had three heads, three bodies and six hands. After this labour Heracles brought back the golden apples of the HESPERIDES, female guardians of the fruit that the earth goddess GAIA gave to Hera on her

HERMAPHRODITOS, the beautiful son of Aphrodite and Hermes, inspired the love of the water nymph Salmacis. Here, the golden boy bathes in a shower of sunlight, unaware of his beautiful admirer on the river bank. (SALMACIS AND HERMAPHRODITOS BY BARTHOLOMEUS SPRANGER, CANVAS, C. 1581.)

wedding to Zeus. The last exploit of Heracles was the most testing, for it meant a descent into the underworld, the realm of the dead. From there the hero managed, with some help from *PERSEPHONE*, queen of the underworld, to bring briefly back to Tiryns the three-headed hound *CERBERUS*. As a result of this labour, hard-working Heracles attained immortality for himself. No other hero gained this honour.

Heracles' death on earth, an event that the Greeks expected to precede his translation to Mount Olympus as a god, was the work of the Centaur Nessus, who gave the hero's second wife a poisoned garment for him to wear. Realizing that his death was near, Heracles consulted the Delphic Oracle, which told him to build a funeral pyre in Thessaly. When the dying hero climbed on to it, there was a great flash of lightning and Zeus took his son to join the immortals.

Some of the labours of Heracles are reflected in the names of certain constellations, such as Leo, which represents the Nemean Lion, and Cancer, the crab that was allegedly sent by Hera to help the Hydra. (See also *HEROES*)

HERMAPHRODITOS

HERMAPHRODITOS was the bisexual offspring of the messenger god *HERMES* and *APHRODITE*, the goddess of love. According to one Greek myth, this handsome boy excited the passion of Salmacis, who was a nymph of a fountain near to the city of Halicarnassus in Asia Minor. When the young Hermaphroditos ignored her attentions, Salmacis prayed to the gods that she might be eternally united with him. The wish was granted when he bathed in some waters and she merged with him physically. The result was a female boy, hence the term hermaphrodite. But Hermaphroditos was not emasculated like Attis, the lover of the Phrygian mother goddess Cybele, for this West Asian god intentionally cut off his own manhood.

HERMES

HERMES was the Greek messenger god, and the son of *ZEUS* and Maia. He enjoyed playing tricks and games. During the Trojan War, it was Hermes who was always sent to steal something that was otherwise unobtainable. Before the sea nymph *THETIS* persuaded her son *ACHILLES* to stop mutilating the corpse of *HECTOR*, the gods considered that the simplest solution might be to let Hermes steal the broken body. Hermes was the god who most easily crossed the line between the living and the dead, for the Greeks believed that he guided the dead to the realm of *HADES*, the underworld. This duty helps to explain the later identification of the Germanic god Odin with the Roman equivalent of Hermes, *MERCURY*. Odin was the champion of warriors and the father of the slain.

Hermes is usually depicted as a young man with a wide-brimmed hat and winged sandals, carrying a herald's staff crowned with two snakes. In ancient Greece this staff assured the messenger safe passage even during time of war. Hermes' greatest passion was for the love goddess *APHRODITE*.

The two sons that are attributed to them were both renowned for their unusual sexuality. *HERMAPHRODITOS* was the first female boy, while the gnome-like Priapus was famous for his enormous penis. Like that of Hermaphroditus, the cult of Priapus originated in Asia Minor, though some distance farther north at Lampascus, near the Black Sea.

HERMES leads Eurydice (centre) and Orpheus (right) through the underworld. As psychopomp, Hermes conducted souls from life on earth to death in Hades. (ILLUSTRATION FROM DICTIONARY OF CLASSICAL ANTIQUITIES, 1891.)

VOYAGERS

T HE LURE OF THE UNKNOWN prompts all restless heroes to strike out on a new path in search of a fabulous treasure or shining dream, or for the sheer joy of discovery and adventure. Three intrepid explorers stand out in Classical mythology: Jason, Aeneas and Odysseus. Jason set sail with his fearless crew of Argonauts in search of the Golden Fleece; while Aeneas' seven-year voyage after the fall of Troy led him to the site of future Rome. Most famous and appealing, perhaps, was the fabled Odyssey of the shipwrecked wanderer, Odysseus. Tossed from shore to shore by the angry sea god, Poseidon, he found his way home after ten years' wandering through fabulous lands. The lure of the underworld, or a foray into a monster's den, attracts many heroes, too, such as Theseus who went into the Labyrinth to slay the Minotaur, and found his way out again. Aeneas and Odysseus both journeyed to the underworld in search of prophetic counsel.

AENEAS' (above) seven-year voyage after the fall of Troy was described in Virgil's epic tale, the Aeneid, *in part a Roman Odyssey. After fleeing with his father and son from burning Troy, Aeneas and his comrades sailed away by way of Thrace and Delos to Crete and onwards to Sicily and Carthage, before reaching Latium in Italy where he became the ancestral hero of the Romans. Here, Aeneas, arriving on Delos, is kindly welcomed by King Anius. (AENEAS IN DELOS, MAIOLICA DISH, 1497.)*

ORPHEUS (left) went down into Hades, the underworld, to bring back his wife, Eurydice. Charming the shades and even Persephone with his music, he was allowed to take Eurydice back to the upper world as long as he did not look back until clear of Hades. Just as they were about to step out into the light, Orpheus turned round only to see Eurydice slip back into the world of shades forever. Here, Orpheus bids farewell to Eurydice, while Hermes (left), waits to lead Eurydice back through the world of shades. (HERMES, EURYDICE AND ORPHEUS, MARBLE, C. 420 BC.)

ARION (right), a lyrical poet and cithara player, sailed to Sicily to take part in a magical contest which he won. On his way home in a Corinthian ship, he was robbed by the sailors, and forced to leap overboard where he was borne away to safety by song-loving dolphins. Here, Arion plays his cithara on the prow of the ship, invoking the gods of the sea, before leaping overboard. (ILLUSTRATION FROM TANGLEWOOD TALES, C.1920.)

ODYSSEUS (above), celebrated traveller, was renowned for his wits and silver tongue, for his cunning, craft and curiosity. On his way home from Troy, he beached at Sicily, home of the lawless race of one-eyed giants, the Cyclopes. Bold and inquisitive, Odysseus wandered into a Cyclops' den where he and his comrades became trapped by the hostile giant. To escape, they blinded the giant and slipped out, hidden under sheeps' bellies. Here, Odysseus and his comrades pierce the giant's single eye with a sharpened stake. (THE BLINDING OF POLYPHEMUS BY ALESSANDRO ALLORI, FRESCO, 1580.)

JASON (below) sailed across the seas on a perilous voyage in his famous ship, the Argo, accompanied by all the heroes of the age. They went in search of the Golden Fleece, guarded by a watchful dragon at Colchis. After snatching the treasure from under the dragon's eye, Jason and his Argonauts sailed away, finally arriving at Iolcus. Here, Jason steals past with his trophy, casting a furtive glance at a statue of Ares in the sacred grove of the god. (JASON AND THE GOLDEN FLEECE BY ERASMUS QUELLINUS, CANVAS, C. 1670.)

ODYSSEUS (above), fast asleep, is laid on his own coat by Phaeacian sailors. As predicted by the seer, Tiresias, Odysseus reached home alone on a foreign ship, only after many years' wandering. Once back on his island kingdom of Ithaca, he had another battle to fight – with the suitors of his wife – before he could regain his throne and settle down with Penelope. (ILLUSTRATION FROM STORIES FROM HOMER, 1885.)

HERO AND LEANDER were one of the great pairs of lovers in Greek mythology. Hero was a priestess of *APHRODITE* at Sestos in the Dardanelles, while Leander lived on the Asian side of the channel at Abydos. They met and fell in love, but because of her religious calling Hero was barred from marriage. In order to keep their affair secret, they arranged that Leander should swim across to Hero each night, guided by a light that she placed in her tower. Next morning he would swim back at dawn. One stormy night the light blew out,

Leander lost his sense of direction and he drowned in the cold waters. When his body was washed ashore at Sestos, Hero threw herself from her tower and died.

THE HESPERIDES were supposedly the daughters of Hesperus, the evening star. Their names were Hespera, Aegle and Erytheis, and they were the guardians of a tree of golden apples given by *GAIA*, mother earth, to the goddess *HERA* on her marriage to *ZEUS*, chief of the Greek gods. This tree stood in the Garden of the Hesperides on the

HERO (below) looks for her Leander, who usually swam to her across the Hellespont guided by a light in her tower. But her light blew out in a storm and Leander was drowned. (THE LAST WATCH OF HERO BY LORD LEIGHTON, CANVAS, 1880.)

THE HESPERIDES (right) guarded the golden apples in the garden of the gods. The serpent recalls the myth of the dragon Ladon who guarded the apples until he was slain by Heracles. (THE GARDEN OF THE HESPERIDES BY EDWARD BURNE-JONES, CANVAS, 1869-73.)

slopes of Mount Atlas in the far west. For one of his labours the hero *HERACLES* tricked the Titan *ATLAS* into getting him the golden apples, offering to hold up the heavens in his stead.

HORATIUS (below), a Roman hero, held the Sublician Bridge, with two of his comrades, against the Etruscan army. While other Romans hacked down the bridge, he held off the enemy until the last moment when he leapt into the stream and swam to safety. (ILLUSTRATION FROM STORIES FROM LIVY, 1885.)

HORATIUS was a Roman hero who saved the early Republic from the Etruscans, when they tried to restore *TARQUINIUS SUPERBUS* to the Roman throne by force of arms. The Etruscans mounted a surprise attack and attempted to capture Rome by crossing a poorly defended bridge over the River Tiber. With two comrades, Horatius held the enemy back until the Romans had destroyed the wooden bridge. As the final supports were sawn away, he ordered his comrades

INO rescues shipwrecked Odysseus by throwing him her veil which saves him from drowning. She was honoured along the Greek shores as a marine deity who aided sailors in distress and guided ships through storms. (ODYSSEUS AND THE GODDESS INO BY ALESSANDRO ALLORI, FRESCO, 1580.)

back to the Roman bank. They just made it, but Horatius was obliged to swim back in full armour. Only prayer saved the hero as he dodged the Etruscan arrows and struggled across the waters of the Tiber.

His full name was Horatius Cocles ("Horatius the one-eyed"). Whether he was wounded in the eye remains uncertain, though tradition says that an ancient statue of a lame, one-eyed man was erected near the bridge in his honour. He was also given as much land as he could drive a plough over in a day. (See also *HEROES*)

HYPNOS ("Sleep"), in Greek mythology, was the son of Nyx, the night goddess, and the brother of Thanatos ("Death"). Morpheus, the god of dreams, was his son. Hypnos lived in the underworld, the realm of *HADES*, and never saw the sun. On several occasions *HERA* asked Hypnos to lull her husband *ZEUS* to sleep so that she could attack his son *HERACLES*. Hypnos usually refused to anger Zeus, possibly because he had already come close to having a thunderbolt hurled at him. He was saved by taking refuge with Night, whose power Zeus always respected.

ILUS see *FOUNDERS*

INO was the daughter of *CADMUS*, the Phoenician king of Thebes, and Harmonia. In Greek mythology, she brought up *DIONYSUS*, the son of *ZEUS* and Semele, who was Ino's dead sister. Semele had been tricked by the goddess *HERA*, the jealous and vengeful wife of Zeus, who advised her to test the divinity of her lover by telling him to come to her in his true form. This Zeus was also tricked into doing, and the unfortunate result was that he appeared to Semele as lightning and thunderbolts, and she was

killed. The unborn Dionysus, however, was taken from her womb and placed in Zeus' own thigh until it was time for his birth. Then, at the suggestion of *HERMES*, the messenger god, Ino suckled the divine child and kept him safe from Hera. However, such a powerful goddess could not be thwarted without great personal cost. When she discovered the deception, Hera made Ino kill her own children. After she had done this Ino killed herself by jumping off a cliff into the sea. In another myth, she and her infant son Melicertes leapt into the sea and became marine deities.

IO was the daughter of the river god Inachus, and was one of the mortal women who bore children by *ZEUS*. Although Io was a virgin priestess of *HERA*, Zeus's wife, at her temple in Argos, this did not prevent Zeus from having her expelled from Argos so that he could make love to her without any difficulties. According to one version, he turned Io into a beautiful heifer, and would have mated with her at once had not Hera guessed his intentions and sent a gadfly to prevent the animal from standing still. It seems that Zeus eventually made love to Io on a cloud over Egypt, where she was returned to her human form. Surprisingly, she was forgiven by Hera. Because Io had been bovine in shape on her arrival, she became identified with the Egyptian cow goddess Hathor.

IO, "the wanderer", was loved by Zeus who changed her into a heifer in order to avoid his jealous wife Hera. Hera ordered all-seeing Argus to watch Io, but Zeus, in his turn, sent Hermes to lull Argus to sleep by the dreamy notes of his flute. (MERCURY AND ARGUS BY PETER PAUL RUBENS, CANVAS, C. 1635.)

J

IPHIGENIA was the eldest daughter of King *AGAMEMNON* and Queen *CLYTEMNESTRA* of Mycenae. When Agamemnon and the Greek fleet were about to sail for Troy, contrary winds caused by *ARTEMIS* kept the ships at Aulis. The goddess of the forest and wild animals had been offended, either by Agamemnon himself or by an action committed by his father *ATREUS*. In any event, Artemis demanded that Iphigenia should be sacrificed. To bring the sacrificial victim all the way from Mycenae to the port of Aulis in Boeotia, without his wife Clytemnestra's becoming suspicious, Agamemnon pretended that Iphigenia was to be married there to the Greek hero and champion *ACHILLES*. After she discovered his true intention, Clytemnestra never forgave her husband, and years later on his return from the Trojan War helped her lover Aegisthus to murder him.

IXION was a Thessalian king of Larissa and supposedly the son of Phlegyas, though some say his father was *ARES*, god of war. In order to avoid paying a bride-price to Eioneus for his beautiful daughter Dia, Ixion prepared a trap for his unsuspecting father-in-law – a pit filled with fire. Eioneus fell into it on a visit to Larissa and died, and Ixion thus became the first man to shed the blood of a kinsman.

IXION, chained to a rolling wheel, expiates his sins in Tartarus, a hell beneath Hades. Alongside him, fellow prisoners Sisyphus and Tantalus endure their own ordeals – Sisyphus condemned to endless toil and Tantalus to endless thirst. (ILLUSTRATION FROM DR SMITH'S CLASSICAL DICTIONARY, 1895.)

IPHIGENIA, the young daughter of Agamemnon and Clytemnestra, was offered as a "sacrificial lamb" to appease Artemis who was angry with Agamemnon. Here, while the high priest Calchas raises his arms in prayer, Agamemnon (right) bows his head sorrowfully. (ILLUSTRATION FROM STORIES FROM HOMER, 1885.)

Because he was polluted by this unprecedented act, the Thessalian king could not properly rule his land. Perhaps a secret passion for Dia prompted *ZEUS* himself to devise special rites of purification for Ixion. At first Ixion was grateful to the god, but it was not long before he took an interest in *HERA*, Zeus' wife. It was therefore Ixion's turn to be trapped, when Zeus made an exact copy of Hera from a cloud and enticed the unwary king to rape it. The punishment for such sacrilegious crime was to spend eternity in Tartarus, the prison beneath the underworld.

JANUS was a very old Italian god whom the Romans associated with beginnings. In Rome, his double-gated temple in the Forum was always kept open in time of war and closed in time of peace. The month of January – a time for people to look backwards and forwards – was sacred to Janus. There are few myths concerning him, although his extra eyes did on one occasion enable him to catch the nymph Carna, who liked to tease her lovers with sexual advances before suddenly running away. Their son became a king of the important city of Alba Longa.

JASON, the son of Aeson and Philyra, was a Greek hero and voyager, born in Iolcus, a town in Thessalian Magnesia. However, difficulties arose when Aeson, ruler of Iolcus, was deposed by his half-brother Pelias. Either because Philyra distrusted Pelias' intentions towards Jason, or simply because it would better for the boy if he were educated elsewhere, she placed him in the care of the wise Centaur *CHIRON*, who lived in the Thessalian woodlands. Chiron was skilled in many things, including medicine, and may have given the boy the name Jason ("healer").

The Delphic Oracle warned Pelias that he would be turned off the throne of Iolcus by a man wearing only one sandal. So the usurping king was amazed and frightened when a mature Jason arrived

JANUS, a dual-faced god, presided over all that is double-edged in life. His image was found on city gates, which look both inwards and outwards, and he was invoked at the start of each new day and year when people look both backwards and forwards in time. (ILLUSTRATION FROM DR SMITH'S CLASSICAL DICTIONARY, 1895.)

in the city with only one of his sandals. The hero had lost it while carrying what seemed to be an old lady across a swift stream; it was in fact the goddess *HERA* in disguise. Unable to harm the unwelcome guest because he had arrived at the time of a religious festival, Pelias decided to rid himself of the threat he represented by sending Jason on an impossible quest. He offered to name Jason as his successor provided he should bring home from Colchis the Golden Fleece belonging to a wonderful ram which had flown there from Iolcus.

Jason gathered together his companions, who became known as the *ARGONAUTS*, and crossed a sea of marvels, overcame difficult tasks, defeated a guardian serpent and returned with the magic fleece. Part of his success was due to the aid of the Colchian princess and witch, *MEDEA*, whom Jason made his wife with the assistance of the goddess *ATHENA*. On returning to Iolcus, the Argonauts found that Pelias had assumed that they had died in a shipwreck and murdered Jason's father Aeson. Two versions of the myth exist from this point onwards. In one of them Pelias is destroyed by means of Medea's magic. In another the Argonauts, seeing that Pelias will not honour his promise to Jason, sail off to Corinth after failing to capture Iolcus. Jason seems to have accepted exile in Corinth with Medea, where for some ten years they lived happily together and had three sons. Then the hero was offered the hand of a princess named Glauce. When he deserted Medea for her, Jason brought down on his own head the full fury and magical powers of the Colchian princess. For Medea not only killed Glauce but she also destroyed her sons by Jason. Alone and depressed, the hero lingered at Corinth until one day, as he sat in the shade of the *Argo*, his old ship, a piece of rotten timber fell and crushed his skull. (See also *HEROES; VOYAGERS*)

JUNO was the Roman equivalent
of *HERA*, the wife of *ZEUS*, the chief
god of the Greeks. Juno was the
queen of the sky and the wife of
JUPITER. She was always associated
with the Greek goddess of birth,
Eileithyia, and was called by the
Romans "the one who makes the
child see the light of day". At the
touch of a magical herb specially
grown by Flora, the goddess of
flowering and blossoming plants,
Juno became pregnant with the
war god *MARS*. Juno's own warlike
aspect is apparent in her attire. She
often appears armed and wearing a
goatskin cloak, which was the garment favoured by Roman soldiers
on campaign. In Rome she was
worshipped on the Capitol hill
along with Jupiter and *MINERVA*,
goddess of wisdom and the arts.
The festival of Matronalia was held
in her honour on 1 March.

L

JUPITER was the Roman sky god, the equivalent of ZEUS. The cult of Jupiter Optimus Maximus ("the best and greatest") began under the Etruscan kings, who were expelled from Rome around 507 BC. At first, Jupiter was associated with the elements, especially storms, thunder and lightning, but he later became the protector of the Roman people and was their powerful ally in war. The games held in the circus in Rome were dedicated to him.

LAIUS, son of Labdacus, king of Thebes, was the father of OEDIPUS and one of the most tragic figures in Greek mythology. The fate that destroyed his family was due to a curse uttered by PELOPS in revenge for Laius carrying off Pelops' young son Chrysippus, who later hanged himself for shame.

In Thebes, Laius took Jocasta as his wife, but they had no children, which the Delphic Oracle told them was fortunate, because Laius was destined to be killed by his own son. For a time Laius and Jocasta did not share the marriage bed. Then one night, full of wine, Laius slept with her and Jocasta conceived a son. So as to overcome the prophecy, the baby was left to die on a distant mountainside, his feet having been cut through with a spike. This action may have been intended to hasten death, but it is not impossible that Laius was also concerned to prevent the child's ghost from walking freely. But the effect was quite the opposite. A shepherd heard the baby's screams and took him to Corinth, where the childless King Polybus adopted him and gave him the name of Oedipus ("swell-foot").

When Oedipus reached manhood he went to Delphi to ask about his parentage. He was told that he would be reunited with his parents in a terrible manner, for he was destined to kill his father and marry his mother. Concluding incorrectly that Corinth was his place of birth, Oedipus travelled towards the north and approached Thebes. On the road he encountered Laius, who was on his way to consult the Delphic Oracle about the SPHINX, a monster with the face and breasts of a woman, the body of a lion and wings, which was causing havoc in the Theban countryside. Oedipus refused to stand aside for the king, a fight ensued and Laius was killed. Thus was Laius' destiny, and the first part of his son's, fulfilled.

LAOCOON was a Trojan, said by some to be the brother of Anchises, and a priest of the sea god POSEIDON. Both the Greeks and the Romans remembered him as the man who warned the Trojans not to accept the so-called Greek gift of the Wooden Horse. He even drove a spear into its side to show his fellow countrymen that inside the hollow belly could lurk a terrible danger to Troy. However, like the prophetess CASSANDRA, Laocoon was ignored. Worse than the fate of Cassandra was that of Laocoon and his two sons, for no Trojan lifted a hand to help when two great sea-serpents suddenly arrived and crushed them to death.

There was no agreement, however, among the Greeks or the Romans about why Laocoon and his sons were killed by the sea-serpents. One opinion was that Laocoon's punishment was not connected with the Trojan War at all. The god of prophecy, APOLLO, was simply punishing the priest for disobeying a divine command. An alternative view was that the death of Laocoon and his sons was the work of ATHENA or Poseidon for causing damage to the dedicatory horse. A Greek named Sinon had informed the Trojans that it was an offering to the goddess Athena: if they destroyed it, then Troy would fall, but if they dragged it inside the city walls, then the Wooden Horse was a guarantee of Troy's safety. In the event the cunning plot worked for the benefit of the Greeks, as those warriors hidden within the horse began a slaughter that led to the eventual overthrow and destruction of the besieged city.

As for the two serpents, once they had crushed Laocoon and his sons to death, they hid themselves in either the temple of Apollo or the temple of Athena.

LETO was the daughter of the *TITANS* Coeus and Phoebe, and she was one of the few Titanesses to be worshipped in ancient Greece. However, her cult was commonly associated with those of her more famous son and daughter *APOLLO* and *ARTEMIS*, whose father was the sky god *ZEUS*. Leto may have given birth to her divine children on the sacred island of Delos, which a helpful *POSEIDON* is said to have fastened permanently to the bottom of the sea with a huge pillar. Later, one of Apollo's most important temples was built on the island. Even the invading Persians respected this sanctuary, when in 490 BC their fleet passed by on its way to punish the Eretrians and Athenians for providing aid to the Greek rebels who were fighting Persia in Asia Minor.

LETO (below), clutching her tiny twins, children of Zeus, flees a giant serpent sent by the vengeful Hera who relentlessly plagued her husband's lovers. The boy, Apollo, plucks a cithara, his attribute as god of the arts, while Artemis clutches a tiny bow, symbol of her role as goddess of the wild. (ILLUSTRATION BY NICK BEALE, 1995.)

LEDA was the daughter of King Thestius of Aetolia, which was a state in north-western Greece. Her husband was King Tyndareos of Sparta. Two of Leda's children were *CLYTEMNESTRA*, the murderous wife of *AGAMEMNON*, and *HELEN*, who was the unfaithful wife of *MENELAUS*, Agamemnon's brother, and the cause of the Trojan War. Leda was also the mother of the *DIOSCURI*, the twin sons Castor and Polydeuces. Various accounts are given of the fathers of her children, for Leda was loved by *ZEUS* who came to her disguised as a swan. Some say that as a result of their union Leda produced two eggs, one contained Clytemnestra and Helen, and the other the Dioscuri, but that Helen's and Polydeuces' father was Zeus while Tyndareos was the father of the mortals Clytemnestra and Castor. In the case of Helen there is little doubt that the myth of the Trojan War turned a goddess into a Queen. She clearly has a connection with older Aegean goddesses who were associated with birds and eggs.

MONSTERS AND FABULOUS BEASTS

CLASSICAL MONSTERS come in all shapes and colours, sometimes hideous, but sometimes bewitchingly fair, sometimes half-human and sometimes entirely demonic. Monsters generally symbolize the dark and unresolved forces in life and in human nature. Greek mythology is full of composite creatures, such as the Chimaera, Sphinx and Scylla, symbolizing complex evil. Not all monsters were cruel, and some, such as Ladon, guarded a precious treasure, while the Sphinx guarded the pass to the city of Thebes. Other monsters ravaged the land, such as the Hydra and Chimaera. Still others were raised by a curse, as when Poseidon sent a sea monster in response to Theseus' rage. Savage beasts, such as satyrs and Centaurs, part human and part animal, represent man's unruly, instinctive nature. Although less awesome than demons, they still harassed and haunted humans.

PYTHON (above), a monstrous serpent, son of Gaia, haunted the caves of Parnassus until slain by Apollo with his first arrows. Apollo founded the Pythian games to commemorate his victory and was afterwards named Apollo Physius. The monster's defeat was celebrated every nine years at the festival of Stepteria at Delphi and involved an enactment of the whole event. (ILLUSTRATION BY GLENN STEWARD, 1995.)

SCYLLA (above), a six-headed sea monster, fished for dolphins, sea-dogs and sailors from her cavern in the Strait of Messina. According to one myth, she was originally a beautiful sea nymph, loved by Zeus and Poseidon in turn, until changed by the jealousy of Circe into a snapping, barking monster. Here, she snatches up the crew of Odysseus as his ship sails past her cavern. (ILLUSTRATION FROM STORIES FROM GREECE AND ROME, 1930.)

THE SIRENS (right) were beautiful sea nymphs who charmed sailors by their alluring songs. Although initially depicted as bird-maids, they later became fair temptresses. Here, Odysseus sails past with his crew; having advised his men to stop their ears with wax, he had himself bound to the mast so that he could hear the sirens' magic song without being lured away. (ODYSSEUS AND THE SIRENS BY FRANCESCO PRIMATICCIO, CANVAS, 1505-70.)

SATYRS (above), wild spirits of the forest, appeared as goat-like creatures with puck noses, bristling hair, budding horns and goat's ears, tails and sometimes hooves. Usually portrayed as wanton and crafty, they frolicked in the forest, chased after nymphs and played impish tricks on men. Here, Diana's forest nymphs are plagued by licentious old satyrs. (DIANA'S NYMPHS CHASED BY SATYRS BY PETER PAUL RUBENS, CANVAS, C. 1670.)

CENTAURS (below), apparently the offspring of Ixion and a cloud, were man-horse beasts who led a wild and savage life in Thessaly, and were fond of riotous revelries. They came to symbolize the dark, unruly forces of nature. The wise Centaur, Chiron, who instructed heroes, was a unique case. Here, the centaurs, writhing in a fierce battle, symbolize the blind and brute force of human nature. (BATTLE OF THE CENTAURS BY ARNOLD BOCKLIN, CANVAS, 1873.)

HARPIES (left), storm goddesses, were feared as robbers and spoilers who raged over battlefields and carried away the weak and wounded or stole children without warning. Originally they were imagined as winged goddesses with beautiful hair. Later on, they appear as awful monsters and spirits of mischief, half-birds, half-maids. (ILLUSTRATION BY GLENN STEWARD, 1995.)

M

LUCRETIA, after her suicide, returned to haunt Sextus Tarquinius, "false Sextus", the high-handed Etruscan who had raped her, incensing the whole of Rome. She appears as a pale, shrouded phantom who sings as she spins through the watches of the night.
(ILLUSTRATION FROM LAYS OF ANCIENT ROME, 1881.)

LUCRETIA was the wife of Tarquinius Collatinus and represented the ideal of Roman womanhood. When Sextus, youngest son of the Etruscan king *TARQUINIUS SUPERBUS*, raped her at dagger point around 507 BC, she made her father and her husband promise to avenge her honour before she stabbed herself to death. According to Roman legend, Lucretia's funeral roused the people and their anger was channelled by the inspiring eloquence of Lucius Junius *BRUTUS* into a desire for the overthrow of the monarchy.

MARS, the son of *JUNO* and a magical flower, was originally the Roman god of fertility and vegetation but later became associated with battle. As the god of spring, when his major festivals were held, he presided over agriculture in general. In his warlike aspect he was offered sacrifices before combat and was said to appear on the battlefield accompanied by Bellona, a warrior goddess variously identified as his wife, sister or daughter. Mars, unlike his Greek counterpart,

MARS, god of war, forces himself on gentle Pax and Abundanti, spirits of peace and plenty, while Minerva skilfully steers him away. The allegory dramatizes an age-old conflict, keenly felt in the warring Roman heart. (MINERVA DRIVING MARS BY JACOPO ROBUSTI TINTORETTO, CANVAS, C. 1576.)

ARES, was more widely worshipped than any of the other Roman gods, probably because his sons *REMUS AND ROMULUS* were said to have founded the city.

MEDEA was the daughter of Aietes, king of Colchis, a country adjoining the Black Sea, and the first wife of the voyager *JASON*. Medea means "the cunning one" – a suitable name for a princess skilled in the magic arts. In fact, to the Greeks she hovered somewhere between witch and goddess.

Medea fell in love with the Thessalian hero Jason as soon as he landed in Colchis with the *ARGO-NAUTS*, and she used magic to help him gain the Golden Fleece, the object of their expedition. On the hasty voyage back, when the Colchian fleet gave pursuit, Medea sacrificed her brother to slow the pursuers. On their return to Iolcus, Jason's birthplace, she managed to rejuvenate an old ram by boiling him in a magic pot whereupon he turned into a lamb. She also disposed of Jason's enemy, King Pelias of Iolcus, by persuading his daughters to give him a similar course of beauty treatment, but which killed him. As a result, Jason and Medea were banished to Corinth.

The relations between Jason and Medea went badly wrong. Jason put his first wife aside in order to marry Glauce, a Theban princess. Medea, feeling very insulted, took a terrible revenge on Jason. Glauce was burned alive in a poisoned wedding dress, and Medea saw to it that her own children by Jason were also killed. She then escaped to Athens in a magic chariot, which was said to belong to her grandfather *HELIOS*, the sun god.

In Athens, Medea married its king, *AEGEUS*, and bore him a son named Medus. At this time Aegeus believed he was childless, although he already had a son in the hero *THESEUS*. Through her wily skills, Medea prevailed upon Aegeus to reject Theseus when he came to Athens to claim his inheritance, and she may also have persuaded him to send Theseus to subdue the bull of Marathon. When Theseus succeeded in this dangerous task and at last Aegeus recognized him as his own successor, Medea fled with Medus to Colchis, where they avenged the recent overthrow and death of Aietes. Medus became a ruler of Colchis, but nothing else is known of Medea.

MENELAUS, king of Sparta, was the younger son of *ATREUS*. It was to recover Menelaus' wife *HELEN* that his older brother *AGAMEMNON*, king of Mycenae, led the Greek expedition against Troy. In spite of being warned, Menelaus not only entertained *PARIS*, the eldest son of King *PRIAM* of Troy, but he also

MEDEA, a ruthless sorceress, flees from Colchis with Jason and the Golden Fleece across the seas to Greece, with her father, Aietes, in pursuit. To slow him down, she cut up her brother and cast the parts into the sea, forcing Aietes to pick up the pieces for a pious burial. (THE GOLDEN FLEECE BY H J DRAPER, CANVAS, C. 1880.)

went off to Crete and left Helen alone at Sparta with the handsome visitor. Paris and Helen eloped, taking many of the treasures for which Menelaus was famous.

During the ten-year struggle against Troy, Menelaus played a secondary role to Agamemnon and the other Greek kings, although he was no coward. In single combat with Paris, Menelaus tried to settle the dispute between the Greeks and the Trojans. He won and was only prevented from killing his rival

by the intervention of the love goddess APHRODITE. She was indebted to Paris for judging her more beautiful than the goddesses HERA and ATHENA; in gratitude she had given him the love of Helen, the most beautiful woman alive.

After the fall of Troy, Menelaus could not bring himself to kill Helen because of her outstanding beauty. Once again the goddess Aphrodite cast her spell and they were reconciled and returned to Sparta, where they lived happily for many years. When Menelaus died he went to live in the Elysian Fields with his immortal Helen.

MERCURY was the Roman messenger god, and was also the deity who watched over trade and commerce, as his name suggests. He was associated with peace and

prosperity. He was apparently imported from Greece around the fifth century BC. Mercury is usually depicted in the same way as his Greek counterpart HERMES, with a winged hat and staff.

MIDAS was said to be the son of Gordius and Cybele, or to have been adopted by Gordius. He was the king of Phrygia and renowned for his wealth. According to the Greeks, his fabulous riches were the result of a kindness he showed to SILENUS, the old goat-like tutor of DIONYSUS, the god of vegetation, wine and ecstasy. So pleased was Dionysus with this behaviour that he offered Midas whatever he wished. The king asked for everything he touched to be turned into gold. At first Midas was overjoyed with the gift, but once he realized that even his food and drink were being transformed on touching his lips, he was horrified. Out of pity

Dionysus told him how to wash away his golden touch, which Midas did in the River Pactolus, thereafter famous for the gold dust to be found on its bed.

Another myth told about Midas concerns a musical competition between the gods APOLLO and PAN, the divine inventors of the lyre and pipes respectively. When the prize was awarded to Apollo, Midas incautiously expressed his surprise at the outcome and received from Apollo a set of ass's ears for his foolish presumption.

MIDAS, the fabled king of Phrygia, was fabulously rich, yet chose, when granted a wish by the gods, to become richer still, by asking for everything he touched to turn to gold. His wish was granted, but joy quickly turned to grief when he could neither eat nor drink. (ILLUSTRATION BY NICK BEALE, 1995.)

MENELAUS (left) was usually a gentle, even-tempered man, but here he fights fiercely over the fallen body of Patroclus who lies naked, for Apollo had struck off his helmet, splintered his ash spear and broken his corselet, stripping him bare so that he would be easily killed by Hector. (ILLUSTRATION FROM STORIES FROM HOMER, 1885.)

MINERVA (whose name may have originally meant "thought") was the Roman goddess of wisdom and the arts, the equivalent of the Greek goddess *ATHENA*. She was worshipped throughout Italy, though only in Rome did she take on a warlike character. Minerva is usually depicted wearing a coat of mail and a helmet, and carrying a spear. The Romans dedicated the spoils of war to her.

MINOS was the son of *ZEUS* and *EUROPA* and became the king of Crete, with his palace situated at Knossos. The Greeks regarded him both as a just lawgiver and as a cruel oppressor. To build his wonderful palace, Minos employed the Athenian craftsman *DAEDALUS*, whose creations were thought to be almost divine. So lifelike were his statues, for instance, that they had to be chained down in order to stop them running away. Minos was less pleased, however, with the hollow cow that Daedalus made for his queen, *PASIPHAE*, so that she might satisfy her desire for the white bull which *POSEIDON* had sent from the waves as a sign that Minos should ascend the Cretan throne. The *MINOTAUR*, a man with a bull's head, was the outcome of Pasiphae's unnatural union. This monstrous creature was housed in the Labyrinth, a special maze built by Daedalus at Minos' request.

Minos was known to the Greeks as an ancient ruler of the seas. His naval strength could well have owed something to Daedalus' inventiveness. Certainly he was not prepared for another ruler to enjoy the remarkable services of the craftsman. When Daedalus and his son Icarus left Crete without permission, Minos sailed to Sicily in hot pursuit. There, in the city of Kamikos, Minos met his death. Daedalus had arrived in Sicily as a refugee. He quickly went to ground and was hidden by King Cocalos of Kamikos. In order to find out where the craftsman was hiding,

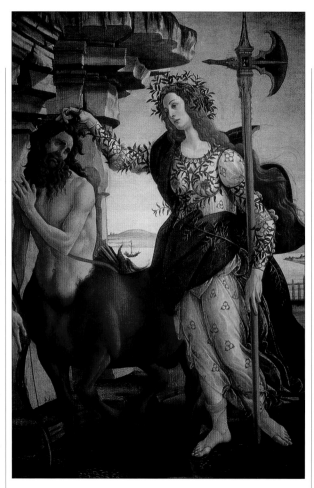

Minos carried a shell and promised to reward anyone who could pass a thread through it. Daedalus alone could solve the problem, which eventually he was unable to resist. When King Cocalos, on Daedalus' behalf, claimed the prize, Minos demanded that the craftsman be surrendered to him. But the daughters of Cocalos were unwilling to lose the inventive man who made them beautiful toys, and with his help they plotted Minos' death. When they took their royal guest to the bathroom, Daedalus led a pipe through the roof and boiling water, or oil, was poured down upon the

unsuspecting Cretan king. After his death Minos became a stern judge in the realm of *HADES*, the underworld, the land of the dead.

THE MINOTAUR was the monstrous son of a white bull, which was sent by the sea god *POSEIDON*, and *PASIPHAE*, the wife of King *MINOS* of Crete. When the child was born it had the head of a bull and the body of a man, and was given the name Minotaur ("Minos' bull").

The creature was fed on seven boys and seven girls sent annually as tribute by the Athenians. To free his countrymen of this terrible burden the hero *THESEUS* came to Knossos, entered the maze-like Labyrinth where the Minotaur lived and killed it. He was assisted by King Minos' daughter *ARIADNE*, who gave him a ball of thread, instructing him to unravel it on his way into the maze so that he could find his way out again. She also gave Theseus a sword.

In the strange story of the Minotaur the Greeks recalled in a garbled form the glories of the older inhabitants of Crete. It is now known that the bull games of the ancient Cretans involved young athletes leaping over bulls, even attempting somersaults holding the horns. Although some of them doubtless sustained serious injury, or may even have been killed, there is nothing to suggest that a man-eating creature was involved.

MOERAE see *FATES*

THE MUSES, from the Roman name, Musae, were the daughters of *ZEUS* and Mnemosyne, a *TITAN*, whose name means "memory". They used to dance and sing at parties held by the gods and heroes. For the Greeks, the Muses were the inspiration of poetry, music and dance. Later, other intellectual activities were added to their care. Although accounts of their number differ, it is generally accepted that the echo of her voice. Narcissus was then condemned by Nemesis, goddess of retribution, to spend the rest of his days admiring his own reflection in a pool. At last he died and was turned into the flower that bears his name.

NEPTUNE was an ancient Italian water god whom the Romans identified with *POSEIDON*. Compared to Poseidon, however, Neptune plays a minor role in Roman mythology.

NOTUS see *FORCES OF NATURE*

OCEANOS was a *TITAN*, the son of Ouranos and *GAIA*, but never an enemy of *ZEUS*. On the contrary, he protected Zeus' wife *HERA* and mother *RHEA* when the gods fought the Titans. As ruler of the encircling sea, which the Greeks believed surrounded the world, Oceanos married his sister Tethys and they produced three thousand rivers.

THE MUSES, guiding spirits of the arts, inspired all gifted artists, though they resented any serious competition and deprived the Sirens of their feathers for daring to be better than them in song. The nine Muses appear here amid the aspiring artists of the Renaissance. (THE REALM OF THE MUSES BY LORENZO COSTA, CANVAS, C. 1506)

OCEANUS (left), father of the river gods, is depicted here with a typically tempestuous face, unruly locks and horned brow. Above him, Selene, the crescent moon, sheds a mild light; and on either side flash the stars, Phosphorus (left) and Hesperus (right). (ILLUSTRATION FROM DICTIONARY OF CLASSICAL ANTIQUITIES, 1891.)

there were nine Muses altogether – Clio, Euterpe, Thalia, Melpomene, Terpsichore, Erato, Polyhymnia, Urania and Calliope.

NAIADS see *FORCES OF NATURE*

NARCISSUS, according to Greek mythology, was the beautiful son of the River Cephissus in Boeotia and the nymph Liriope. Among the many who loved him, including immortals and mortals, was Echo, who slowly pined away, leaving just

NARCISSUS (right), a beautiful youth, was loved by the nymph Echo who, failing to attract him, died of grief. He, in his turn, fell in love with his own reflection and pined away until changed by the gods into the flower that bears his name. (ECHO AND NARCISSUS BY J W WATERHOUSE, CANVAS, 1880.)

O

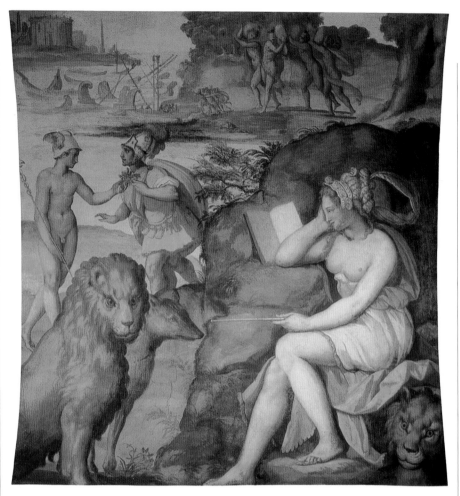

ODYSSEUS alights on the island of Aeaea where he is warned by Hermes of the horrors of Circe's enchanting wine, which turns men into swine. This fate has already befallen one comrade and so Odysseus must keep his guard. (CIRCE WITH THE COMRADES OF ODYSSEUS BY ALESSANDRO ALLORI, FRESCO, 1580.)

ODYSSEUS, king of Ithaca, was one of the Greek leaders who took part in the Trojan War. He was celebrated for both his part in this conflict and his remarkable voyage home to his island kingdom in the Ionian Sea.

A brave and clever man, Odysseus was sometimes thought to have been the son of *SISYPHUS*, the trickster of Greek mythology. But his real father was probably Laertes, whom he succeeded as king of Ithaca. His mother was named Anticleia and his faithful wife Penelope was the sister of King Tyndareos of Sparta.

From the start of the campaign against Troy it is clear that King *AGAMEMNON*, the Greek leader, placed great store upon Odysseus' cunning. He was sent with Nestor, the aged king of Pylos, to discover where the great warrior *ACHILLES*

was hidden. Again, at Aulis, where the Greek fleet was stranded by contrary winds, it was Odysseus who tricked Agamemnon's wife *CLYTEMNESTRA* into sending her daughter *IPHIGENIA* from Mycenae, supposedly to marry Achilles. Instead, however, Iphigenia was to be sacrificed to *ARTEMIS*, goddess of the wild, in order to obtain a fair wind to Troy. Throughout the ten-

year struggle against the Trojans, Odysseus was important not so much as a fighter but as a counsellor and a schemer. His eloquence was renowned, and it was probably Odysseus who thought of the Wooden Horse, which gave the Greeks victory.

Odysseus deceived the Trojans with this horse built of wood whose hollow belly was filled with

Greek warriors under his own command. The Trojans dragged the Wooden Horse inside their walls when they learned from a Greek, deliberately left behind when the rest put to sea, that the offering would bring their city a guarantee of divine protection. But in the night the Greeks emerged from it, and surprised the Trojans. Hence, the ancient saying "Never trust the Greeks bearing gifts".

Although Troy fell, the wildness of the looting and the slaughter deeply offended the gods. In particular, the goddess *ATHENA* was enraged at the rape of *CASSANDRA* within the sanctuary of her own temple. Odysseus tried to appease Athena, and he escaped drowning in the great storm which the angry goddess sent to shatter the victorious Greek fleet on its homeward journey. But he could not entirely avoid blame, and *POSEIDON* saw to it that he was the last Greek leader to reach home, after a voyage lasting some ten years.

The long period of wandering that Odysseus suffered was a favourite story of both the Greeks and the Romans, who knew the voyager by the name of Ulysses. The exact route that he followed remains a mystery, not least because his travels took him beyond known territory and into strange and dangerous lands. From Troy Odysseus sailed first to Thrace, where he lost many of his

ODYSSEUS raises his great bow and, with effortless might, stretches the bowstring which the suitors had struggled in vain to bend. He then slays the suitors who have devoured his wealth and plagued his wife during his long voyage home. (ILLUSTRATION FROM STORIES FROM HOMER, 1885.)

ODYSSEUS, *on his way through the ghostly underworld, consults the shade of Tiresias, who warns him that if he offends Helios he will return home alone on a foreign ship only after many years' wandering.* (TIRESIAS COUNSELS ODYSSEUS BY ALESSANDRO ALLORI, FRESCO, 1580.)

men in battle. After this bloody incident the places he touched upon are less easy to identify. Storms drove him to the land of the Lotophagi ("the lotus-eaters"), whose diet made visitors forget their homelands and wish to stay on forever. Then he encountered in Sicily, it was later believed, the Cyclops POLYPHEMUS, whose father was Poseidon. By putting out Polyphemus' single eye when the gigantic man was befuddled with wine, Odysseus and his companions managed to escape becoming his dinner. They then arrived on the floating island of Aeolus, who was the ruler of the winds. There Odysseus received a rare present, a sack full of winds. The idea appears in many different mythologies, but according to the Greeks, it was of little use on the voyage because the curiosity of Odysseus' men got the better of them and they opened the sack and the winds no longer blew in a helpful direction.

A tragedy overcame the squadron of ships that Odysseus led among the Laestrygones, a race of giant cannibals. Only his own ship survived the attack and reached Aeaea, the island of the enchantress CIRCE, later considered to be situated off Italy. Odysseus resisted her spells, with the aid of the messenger god HERMES, and made the enchantress restore to human shape his men who had been turned to swine. Afterwards, on Circe's advice, he sailed to the western edge of the encircling sea,

the realm of OCEANOS, where ghosts came from the underworld realm of HADES to meet him. The shade of the blind seer TIRESIAS gave Odysseus a special warning about his homeward journey to Ithaca. He told him that if the cattle of the sun god HELIOS on the isle of Thrinacia were harmed by him he would never reach his home. The ghost of Odysseus' mother also spoke of the difficulties being faced by Penelope in Ithaca at the time. The ghost of Agamemnon, his old comrade-in-arms, also warned him about his homecoming; when he returned home he had been murdered by his wife and lover in the bathroom.

Turning eastwards, Odysseus sailed back towards Greece and was the only man who dared to listen to the alluring song of the Sirens, bird-women of storm. He filled his men's ears with wax and had himself bound with strong cords to the mast. Odysseus then passed through the straits between Sicily and Italy, where six of his crew were seized by the six-headed monster Scylla. On the island of Thrinacia, as Tiresias had foretold, the voyagers were tempted by hunger to slay some of Helios' cattle. Despite his warning, the desperate men killed and cooked several cows when Odysseus was asleep. Later they deserted him, but were drowned in a storm sent by ZEUS at Helios' request.

Alone, Odysseus was almost swallowed by the great whirlpool

Charybdis. In an exhausted state he drifted to the wondrous island of the sea nymph Calypso, who cared for him and eventually proposed marriage. But not even immortality would tempt him, and after seven years the gods forced Calypso to let Odysseus set off again. Shipwrecked once more in the land of the Phaeacians, he was welcomed as an honoured guest and offered a passage back to Ithaca. So it was that he was secretly landed near his own palace, which he entered disguised with Athena's aid as a beggar.

Penelope had been patiently awaiting Odysseus' return from the war. Although pressed to marry one of her many noble suitors, she had put them off for a while by pretending that she could not marry until she had finished weaving a shroud for Laertes, her father-in-law. But Penelope unrav-

elled it each night, until one of her maids betrayed the trick. Finally, after ten years, Penelope agreed to marry the suitor who could bend and string Odysseus' great bow. This challenge was proposed on the advice of the goddess Athena. The only suitor who succeeded at the challenge was a beggar, who then threw off his disguise and revealed himself as Odysseus.

Assisted by his son Telemachus and two loyal retainers, Odysseus dispatched the suitors and hanged the treacherous maids. Reunited with his family at last, including his father Laertes, Odysseus then defeated an attack by the relations of the suitors and returned Ithaca to peace. Zeus himself threw down a thunderbolt to signal an end to the fighting. (See also VOYAGERS)

ODYSSEUS *the wanderer returns home after twenty years and embraces Penelope at last. She had refused to acknowledge her husband until he had reminded her of the secret of their bed, which was carved out of a great olive tree grown in the courtyard.* (ILLUSTRATION FROM STORIES FROM HOMER, 1885.)

OEDIPUS ("swell-foot") was the unlucky son of King LAIUS and Queen Jocasta of Thebes. Because, as a guest at the court of PELOPS, Laius had taken sexual advantage of Pelops' young son Chrysippus, a curse was laid on the ruling house of Thebes. Indeed, an oracle warned Laius that any son Jocasta bore him would kill him. For a long time the king and queen abandoned the marriage bed, but drink one night caused Laius to throw caution to the winds and a son was duly conceived. At birth, the infant was pierced in the feet and left to die on a distant mountainside, a fairly common practice for unwanted children in ancient Greece. However, a shepherd found the baby and took it to King Polybus of Corinth, who, having no children, adopted the boy and chose the name of Oedipus because of his damaged feet. When he grew up, Oedipus was taunted that he was not Polybus' son, so he went to ask

the Delphic Oracle about his parentage. He was told that he was destined to kill his father and marry his mother, and in horror he fled north. *En route* he encountered Laius, whose charioteer deliberately ran over Oedipus' foot. The result was that Oedipus killed everyone there, except one of his father's servants who ran away.

Arriving in Thebes, Oedipus discovered its people were greatly distressed at the news of Laius' death and terrified of the SPHINX, an ugly monster causing havoc in the countryside. When the regent CREON announced that whoever rid the city of the Sphinx would be offered the throne and the hand of

Jocasta, Oedipus decided to try or die in the attempt. By outwitting the Sphinx and causing its death, Oedipus unwittingly fulfilled his own destiny: he had killed his father, now he married his mother.

For a time Oedipus and Jocasta lived happily together, having a family of two sons, Polynices and Eteocles, and two daughters, ANTIGONE and Ismene. Then a dreadful plague settled on Thebes, and Creon was sent to ask the Oracle at Delphi for a remedy. The divine command he brought back to the city was to drive out the murderer of Laius. Although the famous seer TIRESIAS announced

OEDIPUS, after years of wandering since his exile from Thebes, leans on his loyal daughter Antigone; they travel to Colonus where it is destined that Oedipus will finally find peace and death in a sacred grove. (ILLUSTRATION BY NICK BEALE, 1995.)

ORESTES (right) finds some peace at the shrine of Apollo in Delphi where he has fled, pursued by the Furies, after murdering his mother. At Delphi, Orestes is partly purified by Apollo, and even the Furiae, asleep on the altar, find rest. In time, Orestes is acquitted by the Areopagus. (ORESTES, MARBLE, C. 200 BC.)

that Oedipus was the guilty one, the new king would not believe this was true until he traced those involved in his own exposure as a child. Convinced at last of his exceptional crime, Oedipus blinded himself and left Thebes. His mother and wife, Jocasta, had already committed suicide. In the company of his daughter Antigone, a broken Oedipus eventually found spiritual peace in a sacred grove at Colonus near Athens. His death there was considered to be a good omen by the Athenians, because in gratitude for the sanctuary he was given, Oedipus had foretold that his bones would save them from any future attack by the Thebans.

ORESTES was the son of King *AGAMEMNON* of Mycenae and *CLYTEMNESTRA* and is renowned for having committed matricide. In ancient Greece there were many places associated with his purification after such a terrible crime. For example, in front of the sanctuary of *APOLLO* in Troezen, there was a hut used by Orestes, which was said to have been built to avoid receiving the polluted murderer as a guest in a normal house.

When Agamemnon left to lead the Greek expedition against Troy, his wife Clytemnestra took a lover, Aegisthus. When Agamemnon returned, some ten years later, the two lovers murdered him, and it was to avenge this crime that Orestes killed his mother. The great horror felt by the Greeks over Orestes' actions runs deep in his myth. Correct though he was to seek vengeance for his father's murder, as the Delphic Oracle had advised him to, the killing of a mother by her son could not be expected to bring anything other than dire misfortune. The *FURIES* were avenging deities who tracked down all those with blood on their hands, and they now relentlessly pursued Orestes.

Wild-eyed and distraught, Orestes wandered as an outcast throughout Greece. When finally he went to Delphi for help, since Apollo had advised him to slay his father's murderers, Orestes was told to go to Athens and stand trial by the Areopagus, an ancient council presided over by *ATHENA*. The verdict in his favour calmed the Furies, so they were renamed the Eumenides ("the soothed goddesses"). It is likely, however, that the Greeks called them by this euphemism because they were afraid to use their real name, the Erinyes, "the angry ones".

ORION see *GIANTS*

ORPHEUS was a Thracian singer much revered in ancient Greece. He was said to be the son of Calliope, *MUSE* of epic poetry. His chief myth concerns the death of his wife, the nymph Eurydice. One day she died of a snake bite. Orpheus was so saddened and grief-stricken by this sudden loss that he no longer sang or played. Then he decided to risk his own life in a desperate journey to the land of the dead in the forlorn hope of bringing Eurydice home. By using his miraculous music, Orpheus was able to charm the boatman, Charon, who ferried him across the Styx, and the three-headed *CERBERUS* so that he could enter the underworld. Even the ghosts of the dead were greatly moved by his song, but the rulers of the underworld, *HADES* and his wife *PERSEPHONE*, granted Orpheus his only desire on one condition: under no circumstances was Orpheus to look back at Eurydice until both of them were completely returned to the land of the living. But so overcome was the singer by love for his departed wife that just before they reached the surface of the ground, he could not resist a quick glance in the half-light. The result was that Eurydice turned into a ghost again and sank back to Hades' kingdom forever. Orpheus' own fate was to be dismembered by Thracian maenads, the female worshippers of *DIONYSUS*, the god of vegetation, wine and ecstasy. Apparently, they tore the singer to pieces except for his head, which was then cast into a river and went floating downstream calling out "Eurydice!"

Ancient fascination with this romantic story was probably connected with religious ceremonies and rituals that were aimed at securing personal salvation after death. The worshippers of both Orpheus and Dionysus believed in some form of afterlife. Paintings of Orpheus have even been found in the catacombs, the early burial chambers of Christians in Italy. (See also *VOYAGERS*)

FORCES OF NATURE

THE WONDERS AND MYSTERIES OF NATURE are explained in mythology through the will and actions of the gods. Sunrise and sunset, storms and tidal waves, summer and winter unfold as part of a divine drama. For the ancient Greeks, the sun rose and set because Phoebus Apollo drove the glittering sun-chariot on a fiery course across the sky, preceded by Eos who sprinkled morning dew from her vase. Springtime came when Persephone, who symbolized the seed-corn, rose from the underworld to live in the light of day with her mother, Demeter, goddess of corn. The tempestuous sea god, Poseidon, could stir up sea-storms, or soothe the waves; while mighty Zeus could strike from afar with a bolt of lightning or brighten the sky with rainbows. In addition to the great gods of sky, land and sea, nature spirits or nymphs infused the forests, fields and rivers.

APOLLO (above), god of light, symbolized not only sunlight – for originally Helios (the sun) radiated daylight and was only later identified with Apollo – but also the bright, life-giving, pure, healing light of divinity. Apollo's light underlies his other roles as god of healing, god of prophecy and god of the arts. He withdrew in winter to sunny Lycius and returned in spring to dispel winter. Here, he drives the sun-chariot on its course across the heavens. (ILLUSTRATION FROM STORIES FROM LIVY, 1885.)

POSEIDON (above), the turbulent god of the seas, symbolized the might of the sea-storm. He dwelt in a golden palace in the depths of the ocean, and rode the waves in his sea-chariot, drawn by sea-horses, speeding so fast that he passed from Samothrace to Aegae in three great strides. Beside him basks his wife, the sea nymph Amphitrite, while a school of tritons (part men, part fish) frisk around his chariot blowing their conches, which they used to raise or calm the waves. (POSEIDON AND HIS CHARIOT BY MIRABELLO CAVALORI, C. 1497.)

ZEUS (left), the chief deity, governed the winds and clouds, rain, thunder and lightning. By striking his aegis he caused storms and tempests to rage, but equally, he could calm the elements and brighten the sky. As the father of the hours, he governed the changing seasons. An awesome but benign god, he is seen here resplendent in fiery light, bearing his aegis, symbol of his sovereign power over all forces of nature and all other gods. (JUPITER AND SEMELE BY GUSTAVE MOREAU, CANVAS, DETAIL, 1896.)

FLORA (right), blooming Roman goddess of spring, was honoured every year at the time of the Floralia, a theatrical festival when the people decked themselves in flowers and enjoyed a great feast lasting for six days. Flora, serene and benign, is here honoured in a lavish parade. Poussin's atmospheric scene vividly revives the pagan splendour of the early Greek pastoral festivals. (THE TRIUMPH OF FLORA BY NICOLAS POUSSIN, CANVAS, C. 1627.)

HEPHAISTOS (below), the smith god, is typically depicted as a grave, intense man wearing a workman's cap and immersed in his fiery craft. He had forges beneath volcanoes but also on Olympus where 20 bellows worked at his bidding. Famed for his artistry, he crafted works of wonder, such as Achilles' shield, embossed with a dramatic scene of life and death, joy and grief, peace and war. (APOLLO IN THE FORGE OF HEPHAISTOS BY DIEGO VELASQUEZ, CANVAS, DETAIL, 1630.)

THE NAIADS (above), or water nymphs, dwelt beside running water. Like their cousins, the Nereids and Oceanids of the oceans, the Oreads of the hills and the Dryads of forests and trees, they were usually sweet, benign spirits. Naiads, especially, were helpful and healing, nurturing fruits, flowers and mortals. Yet the youth Hylas who went to draw water from a pool was lured by the nymphs into the water and never seen again. (HYLAS AND THE WATER NYMPHS BY J W WATERHOUSE, CANVAS, C. 1890.)

NOTUS (below), the south wind, brought with it fog and rain. Here, as a winged deity, Notus pours rain from a vase, much as his mother, Eos, goddess of dawn, sprinkles dew from a vase before the sun-chariot in the early morning. (ILLUSTRATION FROM DR SMITH'S CLASSICAL DICTIONARY, 1891.)

ZEPHYRUS (below), the west wind, dwelt with his brother wind, Boreas, in a palace in Thrace. He was father of the immortal horses, Xanthus and Balius, Achilles' battle steeds who galloped with the speed of wind. (ILLUSTRATION FROM DR SMITH'S CLASSICAL DICTIONARY, 1891.)

P

PAN (above) plays his pipes at dusk. As a spirit of the dark forest, he often startled solitary travellers, arousing sudden awe and panic. He is usually depicted with shaggy head, goat's horns and hooves, dancing or playing a syrinx. (ILLUSTRATION FROM TANGLEWOOD TALES, c. 1920.)

PAN was the son of the messenger god *HERMES*. As the Greek god of the mountainside, the pastures of sheep and goats, he was himself goat-horned and goat-legged. Pan was especially associated with Arcadia, the mountainous state in central Peloponnese. He was playful and energetic, but very irritable, especially if disturbed during his afternoon nap. He liked to play on a pipe, which was known as a syrinx after a nymph of that name who turned herself into a reed-bed to avoid his advances. For Pan could also be a frightening god when he blew on his conch. Our

PANDORA (below), "all-gifts", was the first woman to appear on earth, created by the gods to work mischief for men. Irrepressibly curious, she could not resist opening a sealed jar, containing the horrors of life: strife and sickness, sorrow and grief. (ILLUSTRATION BY NICK BEALE, 1995.)

word "panic" derives from this aspect of his divinity. His worship spread from Arcadia to Athens immediately after the Athenian and Plataean victory over the Persians at Marathon in 480 BC, because he made the Persians flee in panic. He rendered a similar service for *ZEUS* during the battle against *CRONOS* and the *TITANS*. His conch deeply worried Zeus' opponents.

PANDORA was the Greek Eve, the bringer of all sorrows for mankind. She was the first woman and was created by *HEPHAISTOS*, the smith god, on *ZEUS*' orders in order to upset *PROMETHEUS*, the Greek god of fire and friend of men. When she went to live among men, she was given a gift from the gods which was a sealed jar that contained all the misfortunes of existence. But soon Pandora's great curiosity overcame a natural fear of what might be inside, and she broke the seal, releasing sorrow, disease and conflict. As a result, the men who originally comprised the human race gained a mortal, female companion, but also untold woes. Appropriately, the name Pandora means "all gifts" – the bad as well as the good.

PARIS (above), the judge of a divine beauty contest, chose Aphrodite as the winner because she offered him the world's fairest woman. Behind her, wise Athena had promised him fame, while queenly Hera had offered him power. (THE JUDGEMENT OF PARIS BY JEAN REGNAULT, CANVAS, 1820.)

PARIS was one of the fifty sons of King *PRIAM* of Troy. According to the Greeks, he was responsible for causing the Trojan War. Paris was a very handsome young man and wooed *HELEN* so well that she left her husband *MENELAUS*, king of Sparta, and fled with her lover to Troy. His unusual attractiveness was believed to have been a gift from *APHRODITE*, the goddess of love. In return for choosing her as the fairest of goddesses, Aphrodite offered Paris the most beautiful woman in the world, Helen.

During the long siege of Troy Paris cut a poor figure as a warrior. His single combat with Menelaus, Helen's husband, was supposed to have settled the outcome of the whole war. Instead it revealed Paris as a coward, who only escaped with his life through the intervention of Aphrodite. As a result, the Trojan champion *HECTOR*, his eldest brother, treated him very badly. It was an irony of fate that a poisoned arrow shot from Paris' bow should have found the one vulnerable spot on the mighty Greek champion *ACHILLES*, his heel. Paris himself was killed by an arrow, prior to the fall of Troy.

PASIPHAE, in Greek mythology, was the daughter of *HELIOS*, the sun god, and wife of *MINOS*, king of Crete. The sea god *POSEIDON* sent a white bull as a sign of Minos' right to rule the island, but the king refused to sacrifice the animal when it emerged from the waves, and Poseidon pronounced a curse in anger at the lack of respect

PASIPHAE, queen of Crete, was drawn irresistibly to a mysterious white bull which emerged from the waves. She developed a strange passion for the bull, and from her union with the creature she bore a dreadful bull-man, the Minotaur, who was kept hidden in an underground maze. (ILLUSTRATION BY NICK BEALE, 1995.)

PEGASUS, a magnificent winged horse, dips and dives through the flames of the fire-breathing monster, the Chimaera. On his back, Bellerophon urges him on. The hero had successfully tamed Pegasus with a golden bridle given to him by Athena. (ILLUSTRATION FROM TANGLEWOOD TALES, C. 1920.)

shown to himself. Pasiphae was to be stricken with a passionate desire for the bull. In order to gratify her lust, the great craftsman *DAEDALUS* made a cow, into which Pasiphae fitted and so could mate with the bull. Later, she gave birth to the *MINOTAUR* ("Minos' Bull"), which was kept in the Labyrinth.

PEGASUS, in Greek mythology, was the flying horse belonging to the Corinthian hero *BELLEROPHON*. The winged steed was born from blood which spilled from the severed head of the *GORGON* Medusa, who was already pregnant by the sea god *POSEIDON* (a deity always associated with bulls and horses). Bellerophon was given a magic bridle by *ATHENA* to help him tame Pegasus. When the hero tried to fly to Mount Olympus, Pegasus threw him on the instruction of *ZEUS*.

PELOPS was the son of King *TANTALUS*, the ruler of a kingdom in Asia Minor. Pelops' name is still recalled in the Peloponnese ("the isle of Pelops"), which is the large peninsula of southern Greece.

The sea god *POSEIDON* so loved Pelops that he seized the youth and carried him off to Mount Olympus. Possibly because of this divine favour shown to his son, Tantalus was honoured by the gods as no other mortal. He was allowed to eat nectar and ambrosia, the immortal food served to the deities on their mountain home. But Tantalus fell from divine favour and suffered eternal torment as a result.

According to one version of the myth, Tantalus cut up, boiled and served his own son Pelops to the gods in order to test their omniscience. Only *DEMETER*, the goddess of vegetation, partook of the feast, inadvertently eating a piece of Pelops' shoulder. Later, when the gods returned the youth to life, the missing piece of his body was replaced by ivory.

By favour of Poseidon the restored Pelops became famous as a champion charioteer, which was an accomplishment that the ancient Greeks regarded as one of the greatest. So when Oenomaus, king of Elis, offered his daughter Hippodameia in marriage and also his lands to anyone who could defeat him in a chariot race, Pelops accepted the challenge. But he had to agree that Oenomaus could shoot an arrow at him if he caught up with his chariot. Thirteen contestants had already perished.

It was said that Pelops bribed a certain Myrtilus, the king's charioteer, to remove the linchpins from his master's chariot, but when he won Pelops refused to acknowledge this assistance. In different versions of the story, he either threw Myrtilus into the sea, or he spurned him. As a consequence, the father of Myrtilus, who was the messenger god *HERMES*, saw that a curse afflicted the descendants of Pelops. The consequences of this curse on the house of *ATREUS*, Pelops' eldest son and the father of *AGAMEMNON*, is the basis for that family's tragic story.

PELOPS, in the winning chariot, races along the Greek track, fast outstripping his rival Oenomaus, whose chariot swerves and crashes. Pelops' white shoulder was made of ivory, fashioned by the gods after he had been partly eaten by Demeter. (ILLUSTRATION BY GLENN STEWARD, 1995.)

PENELOPE was the daughter of Icarius, king of Sparta, and a nymph Peribaea. As the faithful wife of *ODYSSEUS*, the ruler of Ithaca, she was celebrated for her patience in waiting almost twenty years for his return from Troy. Beset by suitors, Penelope kept them at bay for a long time by pretending to weave a shroud for her father-in-law Laertes. Each night she would secretly unravel the day's work. Eventually, the return of Odysseus saved her from an enforced second marriage, but she remained cold towards her saviour until she was absolutely certain of his identity. Penelope refused to be convinced that the new arrival really was Odysseus until he described their bed, carved in part from a tree trunk still rooted in the ground.

PERSEPHONE was the daughter of *ZEUS* and *DEMETER*, the earth goddess, and became queen of the underworld as the abducted wife of *HADES*. According to the Greeks, Zeus promised his beautiful daughter to Hades without consulting her mother. When Hades rose from the underworld and took his bride by force, Demeter was beside herself with grief. The goddess wandered the earth searching for her daughter, two burning torches in her hands. As a result the land was no longer fertile. Plants wilted, animals

PENELOPE (right), patient wife of Odysseus, shared her husband's cleverness. During his long absence, she kept her many suitors at bay by refusing to marry until she had completed a shroud which she secretly unravelled each night, until the suitors discovered her ploy. (ILLUSTRATION FROM STORIES FROM HOMER, 1885.)

PERSEPHONE (far right), goddess of death, spent the winter in the underworld, rising each spring to live with her mother, the goddess of corn. She symbolizes the seed-corn that is buried, rises and falls again in a cycle of constant renewal – a theme central to the Eleusian mysteries. (PERSEPHONE, MARBLE, DETAIL, C. 490 BC.)

PERSEUS and Andromeda (above) peer gingerly at the face of Medusa, reflected in the water. Burne-Jones' Medusa recalls the tranquil air and death-like beauty of the Greek Medusas carved on amulets and charms, which remind us that she was once beautiful. (THE BALEFUL HEAD BY EDMUND BURNE-JONES, CANVAS, 1887.)

bore no offspring and death stalked mankind. In the end, Zeus was obliged to intervene and ruled that Persephone should spend time each year with both her husband and her mother. Persephone could never return entirely to the living world because she had eaten in Hades' realm: a very old idea that strictly divided the food of the dead from that of the living.

The story of Persephone's abduction, disappearance and return parallels the fertility myths of West Asia. She may well have been a pre-Greek goddess, a deity worshipped by earlier settlers of the country who was later incorporated into Greek religion. Her association with the dead may have a similar origin. The Athenians, who were originally a non-Greek speaking people, referred to the dead as "Demeter's people".

PERSEUS was the son of ZEUS and DANAE, daughter of Acrisius, king of Argos. Danae had been shut up in a bronze tower in order to thwart a prophecy that if she had a son he would kill Acrisius. But Zeus visited her as a golden shower and Perseus was born. A terrified Acrisius placed mother and son in a wooden chest and cast it on the sea. The protection of Zeus, however, was enough to bring them safely to the shores of the island of Seriphos, where Perseus grew up among fishermen.

On reaching manhood Perseus was sent by the local ruler, Polydectes, to fetch the head of the GORGON Medusa, a very dangerous task. Luckily for the hero the goddess ATHENA hated Medusa and instructed him how to proceed.

PHAEDRA, seen here with her sister Ariadne and husband Theseus, was the unfortunate daughter of King Minos and Queen Pasiphae of Crete. She fell in love with her stepson Hippolytus which eventually proved to be her downfall.
(THESEUS WITH ARIADNE AND PHAEDRA BY BENEDETTO GENNARI THE YOUNGER, CANVAS, 1702.)

First he visited the Graiae, three old hags who shared a single eye. Perseus seized the eye and obliged the Graiae to tell him about the nature of the Gorgons, their three dreadful sisters.

Most important of all, they informed him how a direct glance from Medusa's eyes would turn him to stone. He also received three useful gifts from some friendly nymphs: a cap of invisibility, winged shoes and a bag for Medusa's head. Ready for the exploit at last, Perseus put on the shoes and flew to the Gorgon's cave in the far west. Careful not to look at Medusa directly, he approached by watching her reflection in his shield. Having cut off Medusa's head and stowed it in his bag, Perseus flew away unseen by her two sisters.

The chilling powers of the head were used to good purpose by Perseus on his way home. Having

saved the beautiful ANDROMEDA from a sea monster, he married her, but several people had to be turned to stone before he and his bride returned safely to Danae. Having returned his magical equipment to HERMES, the messenger god, Perseus visited Argos only to find that Acrisius had already fled to Larissa on hearing of his grandson's arrival. The prophecy was fulfilled, nevertheless, when Perseus was invited to compete in the games at Larissa and his discus hit the old man on the head.

Because of the accident the hero chose to be king of Tiryns rather than Argos. On hearing of their deaths Athena placed both Perseus and Andromeda in the sky as constellations. (See also HEROES)

PHAEDRA was the daughter of King MINOS and Queen PASIPHAE of Crete. According to the Greeks, the Athenian hero THESEUS made

her his second wife. He seems to have abandoned her sister ARIADNE not long after she helped him kill the MINOTAUR, the bull-headed creature kept in the Labyrinth at Knossos. Like her mother Pasiphae, who gave birth to the Minotaur, Phaedra was soon overcome by an illicit desire. It was not for an animal this time, but for her stepson, Hippolytus, the son of Theseus' earlier marriage to the queen of the AMAZONS, Hippolyta. When she saw how Hippolytus was horrified by her passion for him, Phaedra hanged herself and left a message to Theseus saying that his son had tried to rape her. Theseus exiled his son, who was later killed in a chariot accident. In another version, Theseus cursed his son and asked POSEIDON to destroy Hippolytus, which he did by sending a seamonster. Phaedra, filled with sorrow, then killed herself.

PHAETHON was the son of the sun god HELIOS and Clymene, daughter of OCEANOS. He drove his father's four-horse chariot so fast that he lost control and threatened the world with a terrible heat. ZEUS stopped him with a thunderbolt, which sent Phaethon crashing to the earth. The great god may have also flooded the earth in an attempt to reduce the temperature. It was believed that Phaethon's mad exploit could be traced in the shape of the Milky Way, while he was reflected in the constellation of Auriga, the charioteer.

THE PLEIADES were the seven daughters of the Titan ATLAS, and were named Maia, Electra, Taygete, Celeno, Merope, Asterope and Alcyone. They may have become stars, or doves, in order to escape from the passionate intentions of Orion, the giant hunter. Their appearance in the night sky in May coincides with the beginning of summer, and the constellation of Orion then appears to be in perpetual pursuit of them.

POLYPHEMUS, *a one-eyed giant, was in love with the nymph Galatea, but she scorned him, loving instead the handsome Acis. In a jealous rage, the giant crushed Acis with a rock; but Galatea turned her beloved into a Sicilian river bearing his name.* (POLYPHEMUS AND THE NYMPH GALATEA BY ANNIBALE CARRACCI, FRESCO, C. 1595.)

POLYPHEMUS

POLYPHEMUS was the son of POSEIDON and the sea nymph Thoosa. He was a Cyclops, a one-eyed giant, and was thought to have lived on the island of Sicily. ODYSSEUS, during his long journey home, came to the island and asked for hospitality, but called himself Nobody. Polyphemus indeed proved to be a dangerous host and treated the Greeks as part of his flock, shutting them up in his cave and eating them one by one for his evening meal. Odysseus dared not kill the Cyclops during the night because his men lacked the strength to move the boulder blocking the entrance to the cave. So Odysseus thought of a cunning plan to enable their escape. He got Polyphemus drunk on wine and then put out his single eye with a stake. The injured giant roared with

pain, but in response to the other Cyclopes' questions he cried out that he was being attacked by Nobody, so they went away, considering him drunk or mad. In the morning Polyphemus opened the entrance to the cave to let out his flock and felt the back of each animal as it passed to ensure no men escaped. But Odysseus and his men tied themselves to the undersides of the sheep and managed to leave undetected. For this crime against his son, Poseidon promised revenge on Odysseus.

POSEIDON

POSEIDON was the son of CRONOS and RHEA. He was the Greek god of the sea, and the equivalent of the Roman NEPTUNE. He was particularly associated with horses and bulls. After the overthrow of Cronos, his three sons divided the world between them:

POSEIDON, god of the oceans, rode the waves in a chariot drawn by golden seahorses. With his three-pronged trident, symbol of his power, he shattered the rocks, called forth storms and shook the earth. (NEPTUNE AND HIS HORSES BY E K BIRCE, CANVAS, C. 1880.)

ZEUS took the sky, HADES the underworld and Poseidon the sea, while the land was ruled by all three. It was agreed that Zeus was the senior deity, though Poseidon frequently asserted his independence. Once he even chained up Zeus, with the aid of HERA, Zeus' wife, and his daughter ATHENA. Possibly because his element was the tempestuous sea, Poseidon was thought of as an unruly god. Earthquakes were attributed to his anger, and Hades was often afraid that the roof of the underworld would cave in because of the shaking Poseidon gave the earth.

Poseidon was pictured riding the deep in a chariot pulled by golden seahorses. In his hands was a mighty trident, a weapon capable of stirring the waters to fury, like the sudden violence of an Aegean storm. His wife was Amphitrite, a sea nymph whose name recalls that of the sea monster Triton. This fearful pre-Greek creature was turned by the Greeks into the merman. One of Poseidon's children by Amphitrite bore this name. However, the sea god had many other offspring by other partners. He even mated with the GORGON Medusa, much to the annoyance of the goddess Athena. From the severed head of Medusa sprang the winged horse PEGASUS, surely a favourite of Poseidon. Worship of the sea god was widespread among

PRIAM, *the king of Troy, savours a moment of rare peace with Helen on the city walls, as she describes the kings and chieftains of the Greek host, who circle the city on the plains below.* (ILLUSTRATION FROM STORIES OF GREECE AND ROME, 1930.)

the Greeks, although the maritime state of Athens did not always enjoy the best relations with him.

Because the Athenians chose Athena as the deity of their city, Poseidon flooded the countryside until Zeus brought about an understanding. The temple of Athena stood on the acropolis in Athens and Poseidon's own sanctuary was conspicuously sited on Cape Sunium, which majestically juts out into the Aegean Sea.

Another naval power that offended Poseidon was Crete. When its ruler, King MINOS, asked

ZEUS, all-powerful father of the gods, enthroned on Olympus, is begged by Thetis to help her son, Achilles; she tugs his beard and clasps his knee in her affectionate way, as described in the Iliad, *and the great god nods his assent.* (ZEUS AND THETIS BY JEAN-AUGUSTE INGRES, CANVAS, 1811.)

After the overthrow of Cronos, Zeus divided up the world between himself and his two brothers, *HADES* and *POSEIDON*. Zeus chose to rule the sky, Hades the underworld, and Poseidon the sea: the earth and Mount Olympus, which was the home of the gods, were regarded as common territory. A rare visitor to either of them was Hades, who preferred to be among the dead. Zeus' influence, however, was felt everywhere, although he had no control over destiny itself. Rather he was the god who saw that fate took its proper course.

The many lovers taken by Zeus, both mortal and immortal, form the very stuff of mythology. It is highly likely that they describe the coming together of several religious traditions, as Zeus incorporated the attributes of rival deities and gained credit for all important events. The continual antagonism between Zeus and his wife *HERA*, who was definitely an ancient, pre-Greek mother-goddess in origin, often broke out into major conflict. So jealous was Hera that she spent most of her time persecuting Zeus' lovers and their children. Once Zeus became so angry about Hera's cruelty to the hero *HERACLES*, his greatest son by a mortal woman, that he suspended the goddess from a pinnacle by her wrists and hung weights on her ankles. (See also *FORCES OF NATURE*)

ZEUS was the supreme deity in Greek mythology and the son of the Titans *CRONOS* and *RHEA*. The Romans identified Zeus with their *JUPITER*, an all-powerful sky god. The tyrannical Cronos insisted on swallowing all Zeus' older brothers and sisters as soon as they were born, but Zeus escaped this fate when his mother Rhea offered Cronos a stone wrapped up in swaddling clothes to swallow instead. In secrecy, Zeus was raised on the island of Crete. He grew to manhood determined to topple his father. The wise Metis, an early love and daughter of *OCEANOS*, gave Zeus the idea of a potion that would make his father vomit up all the children he had swallowed.

XANTHUS AND BALIUS, immortal horses and children of the west wind, "tore with the speed of wind". They were Achilles' battle steeds during the Trojan War, and wept for fallen heroes on the field. Here, Zeus leads them as a gift of the gods to Peleus on his wedding day.
(ILLUSTRATION BY GLENN STEWARD, 1995.)

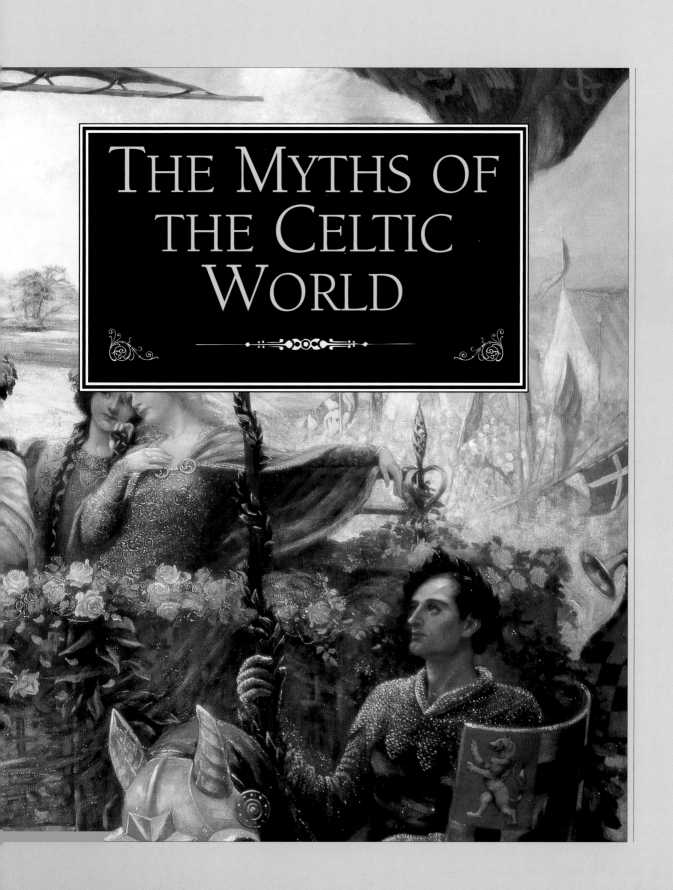

THE MYTHS OF
THE CELTIC
WORLD

INTRODUCTION

T ODAY PEOPLE OF CELTIC DESCENT IN Europe are concentrated on its western shores. They live chiefly in Brittany, Cornwall, Wales, Scotland, the Isle of Man and Ireland. At one time, however, the Celts were spread over a large part of the Continent, and in 278 BC one roving band even penetrated as far east as Asia Minor, where they gave their name to Galatia. Until the rise of Roman power, the Celts were a force to be reckoned with. Rome itself had been sacked by them in 385 BC, a historical fact not forgotten by the legionaries who gave Julius Caesar victory between 59 and 49 BC over the Celtic tribes living in Gaul, present-day France. Although largely incorporated into the Roman Empire, the Celts continued to worship their own gods and goddesses right up to the time of the official adoption by the Romans of the Christian faith. Then their religion and mythology waned in importance, except where people remembered tales about the Celtic gods and heroes of the past. Even in distant Ireland, an island that was never under Roman control, the influence of Christianity was soon felt. But here conversion did not mean the wholesale destruction of the Celtic heritage, for monks took great care from the fifth century onwards to write down the ancient sagas.

To this remarkable effort of preservation we owe almost our entire knowledge of Celtic mythology. For except in Wales, where a small group of stories was recorded, nothing else was ever committed to writing. The Celts always distrusted script and preferred to rely on speech and properly trained memories.

In Ireland the poet was held in particular esteem. Possibly because there was a clear distinction there between druid and poet in pre-Christian times. The newly-founded monasteries could therefore undertake the work of recording the ancient texts without any fear of paganism. It seems that poets went on reciting the sagas long after St Patrick converted the Irish and cleared the country of snakes, because these tales were seen as entertainment. Irish folklore insists, however, that they kept something of their magic, since the Devil could never enter a house where the exploits of the heroes were being sung.

BRANWEN was a classic Celtic heroine who remained calm and dignified under pressure. A falsely slandered wife, she was forced to suffer unjustly, until rescued by her brother, Bran the Blessed. (BRANWEN BY G SHERRINGHAM, CANVAS, C. 1920.)

Irish myths nearly always include fighting, though the combat is undertaken more often by heroes than by gods. The fearless warrior Cuchulainn, the lone defender of Ulster during the invasion of forces raised by Queen Medb of Connacht, is very much the ideal. He was chosen as the Irish champion after a beheading contest with the water giant Uath. No other man had courage enough to receive the giant's return blow. Yet Cuchalainn, "the Hound of Culann", enjoyed but a brief life; his refusal to return the affections of Morrigan, the goddess of slaughter, sealed his fate. Not even the intervention of his father Lugh, the sun god, could save him.

The apparently endless conflict appears less terrible when it is recalled how the Celts believed in reincarnation. Their otherworld, unlike the Greek or Roman underworld, was not a dismal abode of the dead. Rather it was a paradise in which souls rested prior to their rebirth in the world. The warrior-poet Oisin, son of the Fenian leader Finn MacCool, spent three hundred years there before returning to Ireland. Oisin was warned that he would never be able to go back to the underworld if he dismounted from a magic steed. When the saddle slipped and he fell to the ground, Oisin was immediately changed from a handsome youth into a blind, grey-haired, withered old man. Only St Patrick is said to have bothered to listen to his fantastic story as it was being written down.

The interest of St Patrick in the adventures of Oisin and, indeed in the exploits of many other heroes of old, is obviously a later embellishment, but it does indicate a degree of tolerance not readily found elsewhere in Christian Europe. Yet saints in Ireland could curse as well as anyone else when the occasion demanded. For instance, the troublesome King Suibhne Geilt was cursed by St Ronan for his violence towards the faith, and

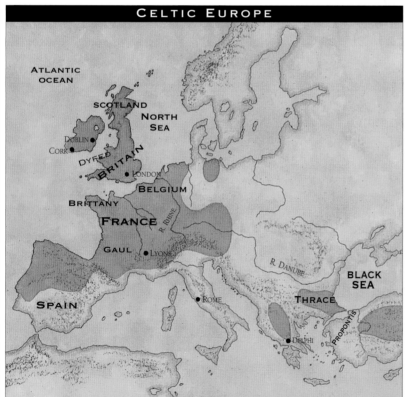

CELTIC EUROPE

ATLANTIC OCEAN

SCOTLAND

NORTH SEA

DUBLIN

CORK

DYFED

BRITAIN

LONDON

BELGIUM

BRITTANY

FRANCE

R. RHINE

GAUL

LYONS

R. DANUBE

BLACK SEA

THRACE

ROME

SPAIN

DELPHI

PROPONTIS

HEROIC combat was a feature of Celtic culture and myth. Champions, such as Cuchulainn, fought to the death, often defending their clan alone. The warriors here wear helmets with boar and raven motifs; symbols of ferocity and death. (GUNDESTRUP CAULDRON, GILDED SILVER, C. 100 BC.)

spent the rest of his life with the characteristics of a bird, leaping from tree to tree and eating at nights nothing but watercress.

In late Celtic mythology, especially the Arthurian myths, Christianity has become a central element. The quest for the Grail is the most obvious example. Although similar to a Celtic magic cauldron, this holy vessel was the cup used at the Last Supper and, at the Crucifixion, the one that received the blood which flowed from the spear thrust in Christ's side. It was brought to Britain by Joseph of Arimathea, but was later lost and its quest preoccupied King Arthur's knights. Only Sir Galahad was pure enough to be granted a full vision of the Grail, which he took as "Our Lord's body between his hands".

Whether or not Arthur was a historical

figure is still uncertain. It is quite likely that he may have been a successful warlord in the confused and violent period following the withdrawal of the Roman legions from Britain around 410 AD. That his myth blames the ultimate victory won by the Anglo-Saxon invaders on civil strife perhaps reflects a kernel of truth. The Celtic peoples were notorious for only rarely combining against an external, common foe, so deep-rooted were their own bitter quarrels. Thus British chivalry came to an end with King Arthur's disastrous battle against his nephew Modred near Salisbury. Hardly a knight survived and the King himself was badly wounded. His departure to Avalon, accompanied by three mysterious ladies, gave rise to the idea of his undeath. In an otherworld, it was believed, King Arthur lingered, awaiting reincarnation as a national saviour.

ARTHUR *and his Christian Fellowship of Knights probably derived from the earlier Welsh warlord Arthur, who journeyed to the otherworld with his warband in search of a wondrous cauldron. Here, the Knights of the Round Table experience the Grail vision for the first time, amid divine light and splendour.* (MANUSCRIPT ILLUSTRATION, C. 1470.)

CELTIC BRITAIN AND IRELAND

CALEDONIA

LINDISFARNE

TORY ISLAND

ULSTER

EMAIN MACHA

IRELAND   MEATH   ISLE OF MAN

BRIGANTES   PARISI

CONNAUGHT

KELIS

R. BOYNE

Setantii

TARA   NEW GRANGE

R. LIFFEY   DUBLIN   ANGLESEY

R. SHANNON

BRITAIN

LEINSTER

IRISH SEA

DYFED

R. SEVERN

MUNSTER

CORK

CAMULOS

LONDINIUM

STONEHENGE

GLASTONBURY   SALISBURY

TINTAGEL

A

ABARTA, which probably means "doer of deeds", was, in Irish mythology, a mischievous god. He was one of the *TUATHA DE DANANN*, who ruled Ireland until they were overcome by the Milesians, war-like invaders from Spain. Driven underground, Abarta and his kin appear in the Irish sagas more like heroic mortals than gods, although in the tale of his trick on the Fenian warriors there remains a strong trace of his original divinity.

Abarta offered himself as a servant to *FINN MACCOOL*, one of the foremost Irish heroes, and hereditary leader of the *FIANNA*. Abarta tried to serve Finn MacCool shortly after the hero had succeeded his father as leader of the band. As a gesture of goodwill, tricky Abarta presented the Fianna with a wild, grey horse. Only after great effort did the warriors manage to get a bridle on the animal, and then it refused to move even one hoof when mounted. It was not until fourteen warriors had climbed on its powerful back that it would stir at all. Once Abarta had mounted behind them, it broke immediately into a gallop, even pulling along a fifteenth warrior

who was unable to let go of the horse's tail. Abarta took them to the otherworld, for that was the reason for his appearance on earth. This wonderful land was thought by the Celts to be the home of the gods and goddesses, and the place where souls briefly rested before rebirth. The rest of the Fianna, or Fenians, acquired a magic ship to give chase to Abarta's steed. The best tracker among them was Finn MacCool's assistant Foltor. He succeeded in navigating a course to the otherworld for the rescue expedition. There Abarta was compelled to release the prisoners as well as to run back to Ireland himself holding on to the horse's tail. Honour being satisfied, the Fenians agreed to a peace with Abarta.

AILILL, who was the brother of Eochaidh, a High King of Ireland,

fell in love with his brother's wife, *ETAIN*, who was actually a goddess, one of the *TUATHA DE DANANN*. Etain had been the second wife of the proud and handsome god *MIDIR*, who lived under a mound in the middle of Ireland. She had been reborn as a human as punishment for her great jealousy of Midir's first wife, Fuamnach. When High King Eochaidh was looking for a bride himself, he heard reports that described Etain as the fairest maiden in Ireland. So he brought the beautiful former goddess back to his palace at Tara, the capital. There Eochaidh and Etain enjoyed a happy married life. Ailill, however, gradually succumbed to a terrible wasting disease because of his unrequited passion for the new queen.

Etain was steadfast in her love for Eochaidh, but she also

felt sorry for ailing Ailill and eventually promised to satisfy his desire as the only means of saving his life. It was arranged that they should meet secretly in a house outside Tara. However, Ailill never came because he fell into an enchanted sleep.

AILILL MAC MATA, according to some versions of the myth, was the king of Connacht and husband of the warrior-queen *MEDB*. He is generally portrayed as a rather weak character who was entirely under the influence of Medb. It was due to her taunting that he agreed to go to war with Ulster over the Brown Bull of Cuailgne. Ailill finally met his death at the hands of *CONALL*, who killed him in revenge for the death of *FERGUS MAC ROTH*.

AINE was the Irish goddess of love and fertility. She was the daughter of Eogabail, who was the foster son of the Manx sea god *MANANNAN MAC LIR*. Her main responsibilty was to encourage human love, although one mortal lover of hers, King Aillil Olom of Munster, paid for his passionate audacity with his life. When he

AINE, Irish goddess of love and fertility, was worshipped on Midsummer Eve by the local people who lit up her hill with torches. When some girls stayed late one night, Aine appeared among them and revealed the hill to be alive with fairies, which were only visible through her magic ring. (ILLUSTRATION BY NICK BEALE, 1995.)

AMAETHON, though the fruitful rustic god of agriculture, was not always helpful. It was Amaethon that robbed Arawn, thereby provoking the Battle of Trees, and who refused to help hard-pressed Culhwch to plough, sow and reap a hill in a day – a task in his quest to win Olwen. (ILLUSTRATION BY NICK BEALE, 1995.)

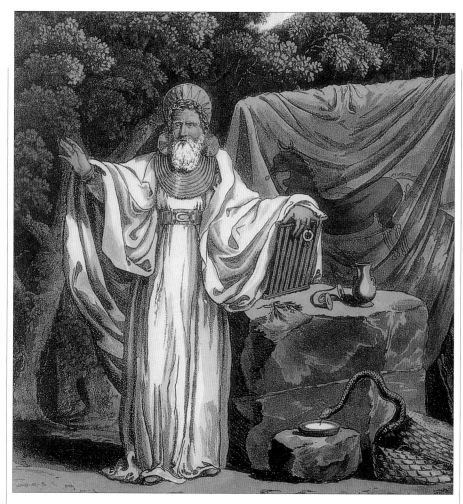

brothers plunged the country once again into dreadful strife. The fighting came to an end only with the death of Eber. Amairgen then installed Eremon as High King of Ireland at Tara. Even then conflicts still occurred because of the ceaseless rivalries between lesser rulers.

AMFORTAS see *PELLES.*

ANNWN was a Welsh otherworld that was an idyllic land of peace and plenty. In Annwn there was a fountain of sweet wine and a cauldron of rebirth, which, it would seem, was the basis of the medieval Grail myth. In one Welsh tradition, *ARTHUR* lost most of his warriors in a disastrous attempt to seize this magic cauldron.

The lord of Annwn was the grey-clad *ARAWN*, with whom the Dyfed chieftain *PWYLL* agreed to exchange shapes and responsibilities for a year. Arawn had a pack of hounds, the Celtic "hounds of hell", which were believed to fly at night in pursuit of human souls. (See also *CELTIC OTHERWORLDS; WONDROUS CAULDRONS*)

attempted to force himself upon Aine and rape her, she slew him with her magic.

Aine's worship was always associated in Ireland with agriculture, because, as a goddess of fertility, she had command over crops and animals. Even as late as the last century, celebrations were still held in her honour on Midsummer Eve at Knockainy, or "Aine's hill", in County Kerry.

AMAETHON (whose name means "labourer" or "ploughman") was the god of agriculture and the son of the Welsh goddess *DON.* Amaethon was said to have stolen from *ARAWN*, the lord of the otherworld *ANNWN*, a hound, a deer and a bird, and as a result caused the Cad Goddeu or Battle of Trees. It was in this battle that Amaethon's brother, *GWYDION,*

magically transformed trees into warriors to fight in the battle.

AMAIRGEN, sometimes known as Amergin, was one of the first Irish druids, the ancient priests in Celtic lands. He came to Ireland with the Milesians. These children of *MILESIUS*, or Mil, who was a leader of the Celts who lived in Spain, were believed to be the ancestors of the present-day Irish. Having defeated the divine rulers of Ireland, the *TUATHA DE DANANN*, the Milesians could not agree on which of their leaders should be king. Two sons of Mil, Eremon and *EBER*, contested the throne and for the sake of peace the island was divided into two kingdoms, one in the north, the other in the south. However, peace was not to survive for long, and renewed fighting between the followers of the two

AMAIRGEN (above) was one of the first druids in Ireland. He possessed both spiritual and political authority, and pronounced the first judgement in the land, deciding who would be the first king. An inspired shaman and seer, he is credited with a mystical poem in the Book of Invasions. (ILLUSTRATION ANON.)

ANNWN (below), a Welsh otherworld, was a land of fruitfulness and rest, filled with the song of birds. Annwn's magical cauldron, guarded by nine maidens, healed the sick and restored the dead to life. A recurrent motif in Celtic myth, magic cauldrons feature in the tales of Bran and Dagda. (ILLUSTRATION BY NICK BEALE, 1995.)

ANU, *a great earth goddess and mother of all the heroes, was known as the "lasting one" and also as Dana, mother of the Tuatha De Danann. In Munster there are two hills known as the Paps of Anu because they symbolized her breasts. (ILLUSTRATION BY GLENN STEWARD, 1995.)*

ANU, sometimes called Danu or Dana, was the mother goddess of Irish mythology. The *TUATHA DE DANANN* ("the people of the goddess Dana") were her divine children and the gods and goddesses who ruled Ireland prior to the arrival of the Milesians. It is quite possible that the monks who wrote down the Irish sagas from the fifth century onwards underplayed the original role of goddesses in their compilations. Certainly, the stories they recorded show us a man's world, a place where warriors seem most at home. The cult of Anu was especially associated with Munster, and two hills in County Kerry are still known as Da Chich Anann ("The Paps of Anu").

AOIFA, sometimes known as Aoife, was the daughter of Ard-Greimne and an Irish warrior-princess in the Land of Shadows, an otherworld kingdom. Her sister *SCATHACH* instructed the Ulster hero *CUCHULAINN* in the arts of war. But when the sisters went to war Scathach was frightened to take the hero with her into battle in case Aoifa killed him. Undeterred by Aoifa's reputation as a fighter, Cuchulainn challenged her to single combat. Before the fight took place, Cuchulainn asked Scathach

what Aoifa loved best and Scathach told him that above all else she treasured her chariot. At first the combat went as expected in Aoifa's favour, but Cuchulainn distracted her attention at a critical moment by calling out that her chariot horse was in trouble. Afterwards, Aoifa became Cuchulainn's lover and bore him a son named *CONLAI*. It was, however, the boy's fate to be killed by his own father.

AONGHUS was the Irish love god. His father was *DAGDA*, the father of the gods and the protector of druids, and his mother was the water goddess *BOANN*. Rather like Zeus, Dagda deceived Boann's husband and lay with her. The monks

who wrote down the Irish sagas tried to legitimize the birth by making Boann the wife of Dagda, but it is obvious that Aonghus was a divine love-child.

Aonghus was handsome and four birds always hovered above his head which were said to represent kisses. Birds also feature in his courtship of *CAER*, a girl of divine descent who came from Connacht and lived as a swan. Her father, Ethal, was one of the *TUATHA DE DANANN*. He seems to have been reluctant about the marriage until Aonghus' father, Dagda, made Ethal his prisoner. It was finally agreed that Aonghus could marry Caer provided he could identify her and she was willing to be his bride. On the feast of Samhain, Aonghus found Caer swimming on a lake with a hundred and fifty other swans. He instantly recognized her and she agreed to marry him.

An interesting tale that has attached itself to Aonghus concerns his foster-son *DIARMUID UA DUIBHNE*, or "Diarmuid of the Love Spot". This attractive young man received a magic love spot on his forehead from a mysterious girl one

ARAWN, king of Annwn, strides through his enchanted forest accompanied by his flying hounds, the Celtic "hounds of hell", one of whose duties was to escort souls on their journey to the otherworld. Like some other fairy creatures, they appear white with red ears, a token of the otherworld. (ILLUSTRATION BY JAMES ALEXANDER, 1995.)

night during a hunt. From then on, no woman could ever see Diarmuid without loving him. This included *GRAINNE*, the princess who had been promised by the High King of Ireland to his Fenian commander *FINN MACCOOL*. Aonghus saved the lovers from the great warrior's wrath, but he could not protect Diarmuid from the fate given to him at birth by the gods, that he should be killed by a magic boar. Nevertheless, Aonghus brought Diarmuid's body back to his own palace at New Grange, on the banks of the River Boyne, where he breathed a new soul into it so that he could talk to his foster-son.

ARAWN was the ruler of the Welsh otherworld *ANNWN*, which was a paradise of peace and plenty. The Dyfed chieftain *PWYLL* became friends with Arawn and was allowed to claim in his title some authority over the otherworld. The two rulers met by chance. While out hunting, Pwyll encountered a strange pack of hounds chasing a stag, so he drove them off and set

AOIFA, a warrior-princess from the Land of Shadows, spars with her young son, Conlai, instructing him in the martial arts. The tradition of warrior-women was strong in Celtic society, where women bore arms as late as AD 700, and where the fiercest gods were often women. (ILLUSTRATION BY JAMES ALEXANDER, 1995.)

AONGHUS (left), *an engaging god of love and courtesy, a Celtic equivalent of Eros, appears in this fanciful portrayal as a charming, if somewhat whimsical character, who calms the foamy sea with his fairy magic.* (AONGHUS, GOD OF LOVE AND COURTESY, PUTTING A SPELL OF SUMMER CALM ON THE SEA BY JOHN DUNCAN, CANVAS, DETAIL, 1908.)

ART (above) *confronts an army of savage and venomous giant toads on his perilous journey through the Land of Wonder, in search of Delbchaem. A taboo laid on the young hero by the jealous goddess Becuma, forced him to find and win the lovely girl imprisoned by her wicked parents.* (ILLUSTRATION BY ARTHUR RACKHAM, C. 1900.)

than she gave birth to *DYLAN* and *LLEU*. *GWYDION*, Arianrhod's brother, immediately took charge of Lleu and brought him up, but this did not prevent Arianrhod placing a series of taboos upon him, including the stricture that he was to have no wife in the human race.

ART, in Irish mythology, was the son of Conn of the Hundred Battles. In one myth, Conn's jealous mistress, the goddess Becuma Cneisgel, contrived to send Art off on a perilous journey through the Land of Wonder in search of Delbchaem ("Fair Shape"). After facing untold dangers, he managed to find and rescue Delbchaem. Art's son by another woman was *CORMAC MAC ART*. Art was killed by the rebel Lugaide Mac Con in the battle of Moy Muchruinne.

his own hounds on to the prey. Just as the stag was about to fall, a grey-clad figure appeared and rebuked Pwyll for this discourtesy in the field. It was Arawn. In order to placate Arawn and to gain his friendship, Pwyll accepted a proposal that he should exchange forms with him for a year and then slay Arawn's enemy, Havgan. It was also agreed that Pwyll would share the bed of Arawn's queen for the same period of time, but without making love to her.

Arawn warned Pwyll that he must kill Havgan by a single blow, for if struck a second time he instantly revived. When Pwyll and Havgan fought, the Welsh chieftain dealt him a fatal blow and ignored Havgan's plea to finish him off with another strike. As a result of this service, Arawn and Pwyll became close allies and Dyfed prospered.

ARIANRHOD was the daughter of the Welsh goddess *DON* and niece of *MATH*, king of Gwynedd. Math could sleep only if his feet were held in a virgin's lap, and when Goewin, the virgin who usually acted this part for him was raped by his nephew Gilvaethwy, it was suggested that Arianrhod should take her place. To test her purity Arianrhod had to step over Math's wand. No sooner had she done so

ARTHUR is undoubtedly the best known of the Celtic heroes. He was most popular during the Middle Ages, when the exploits of his followers, the Knights of the Round Table, impressed the greater part of western Europe. It was with some misgivings that the Church permitted a Christianized version of these Celtic myths to occupy such an important place in the medieval imagination. It was never quite at ease with the story of the Grail, or *SANGREAL*, which *JOSEPH OF ARIMATHEA* was believed to have brought to Britain, since its miraculous properties were clearly derived from the Celtic cauldron, a vessel of plenty as well as of rebirth. The strength of popular feeling for the Arthurian myth can be appreciated by a riot that occurred in 1113 at the town of Bodmin in Cornwall because the French servants of visiting nobility denied Arthur's undeath.

Although some of the earliest stories concerning Arthur are found in Welsh poems of the seventh century, there can be little doubt that the warlike king belongs to the heroic traditions of both Ireland and Wales. He appears in several

ARTHUR, prompted by Merlin, asks the Lady of the Lake for the sword, Excalibur. The young king marvelled at the shining sword but Merlin insisted that the scabbard was worth ten of the swords because it prevented loss of blood in battle. (ILLUSTRATION BY AUBREY BEARDSLEY, C. 1870.)

ARTHUR, a child of destiny, was guarded and guided by spiritual forces from birth. Smuggled out of Tintagel Castle by Merlin, the mage, he was fostered in safety and secrecy, unaware of his destiny until his rightful time to draw the sword from the stone, thus proving his birthright. (MERLIN AND ARTHUR BY W HATHERELL, CANVAS, C. 1910.)

Irish sagas, one of which describes how he stole the hounds of the Fenian leader *FINN MACCOOL* on one of his daring raids. Indeed, as a warrior, hunter of magic boars, killer of giants, witches and monsters, and as leader of a band of heroes whose adventures led them into untold mysteries and marvels, Arthur had much in common with Finn MacCool. But according to the ninth-century monk Nennius, Arthur was a historical leader who rallied the people of Britain against Anglo-Saxon invaders after the Roman legions had gone. Nennius credits Arthur with twelve victories, but does not mention the account of his death recorded slightly later in a history of Wales, which states that Arthur and his sworn enemy *MODRED* both fell in 537 at the battle of Camluan.

Arthur was the son of the British king *UTHER PENDRAGON* and Igraine, wife of the Cornish duke Gorlois. He was conceived out of wedlock and brought up away from his parents by the wizard *MERLIN*. The resourceful Merlin had already designed for Uther Pendragon a wonderful stronghold and placed in it the famous Round Table, at which one hundred and fifty knights could be seated. This unusual piece of furniture may

have a connection with Joseph of Arimathea, not least because it had a special place reserved for the Grail. While Joseph of Arimathea was imprisoned in Palestine, the Grail is said to have kept him alive. Later he brought it to Britain, where it disappeared due to people's sinfulness. Thus the recovery of the Grail became the great quest of Arthur's knights.

When Uther Pendragon died, the Knights of the Round Table were at a loss to know who should be the next king. They decided that Merlin should guide them. The wizard told them that they would know who Uther's successor was when he drew a magic sword from a stone, which had mysteriously appeared in London. Many knights tried to pull the sword from the stone, but none could move it.

After a number of years Arthur journeyed to London to watch his first tournament. A knight who had been appointed by Merlin to act as the boy's guardian was taking part, but finding he was without a sword, he sent Arthur to get one. Without realizing the significance of the sword in the stone, Arthur pulled it out and gave it to the amazed knight. Thus was the heir of Uther Pendragon revealed.

Even then, there were knights who would not accept Arthur as

ARTHUR, at rest in an enchanted forest, gazes in wonder at the amazing Questing Beast at the well. It was a ferlie or bewitching otherworldly wonder, which defied capture. Sir Pellinore and later Sir Palomides spent years in futile pursuit of the tantalizing chimaera. (ILLUSTRATION BY AUBREY BEARDSLEY, C. 1870.)

ARTHUR'S Round Table served many purposes: it prevented quarrels over precedence; symbolized wholeness; and commemorated the Table of the Last Supper, with the Grail at the centre. (KING ARTHUR AND THE KNIGHTS OF THE ROUND TABLE SUMMONED TO THE QUEST BY A STRANGE DAMSEL BY E BURNE-JONES, TAPESTRY, 1898–99.)

king. Only with Merlin's aid was the young ruler able to defeat his opponents and bring peace to Britain. How much he depended on magic became obvious to Arthur early in his reign. Having drawn his own sword without cause against one of his knights, Arthur was dismayed to see the blade shatter. Merlin saved him by putting the knight to sleep, for Arthur was otherwise unarmed. In despair the king wandered along the shore of a lake when, to his amazement, he saw a hand and arm rise out of the water, holding another magic sword. This was the famous Excalibur, his sure support, according to the Lady of the Lake, who handed it to him.

Rearmed and reassured, Arthur went on to be a great king. He defeated the Anglo-Saxons, aided King Leodegraunce of Scotland in his wars against the Irish and even campaigned as far away from his kingdom as Rome. In return for the aid given to Leodegraunce, Arthur was betrothed to his daughter

GUINEVERE. At first Merlin objected to the match, since he knew of Guinevere's love for Sir *LANCELOT*, the most handsome of the Knights of the Round Table. But he later blessed the married couple and, according to one version of the myth, gave Arthur the Round Table as a wedding gift. Nevertheless, the queen and Lancelot were soon lovers, and when Arthur found out about his wife's unfaithfulness Lancelot fled to Brittany.

Arthur pursued Sir Lancelot and besieged him in his Breton stronghold. The siege had to be lifted, however, because news reached the king that his nephew Sir Modred had seized Camelot and even forced Guinevere to consent to marriage, after spreading stories of the king's death on campaign. Returning to Britain, Arthur summoned his knights to do battle with the rebels. Prior to the conflict, it was agreed that the king and his nephew would meet between the two armies to discuss the possibility of peace. Because neither one trusted the other, each ordered his forces to attack if they saw anyone draw a sword. When a knight unsheathed his weapon to kill a snake, a terrible battle was fought, in which the flower of British chivalry fell.

Only two of Arthur's knights were left alive on a battlefield that

was covered by the dead and dying. Although he had won, King Arthur had to be carried away by these knights, such was the severity of his wound. Knowing his own end was near, he had Excalibur thrown into a lake, where a hand swiftly seized it. Then Arthur boarded a magic boat and disappeared. His last words were that he was going to *AVALON* to be cured of his wounds so that he might return one day to lead his people once more.

The inscription on Arthur's tomb at Glastonbury picks up this Celtic idea of reincarnation. It reads: "Here lies Arthur, king that was, king that shall be." Such an undeath was not enough to save

his weakened kingdom from the Anglo-Saxons, however. The whole of the Arthurian myth turns on the disintegration of the chivalric unity that was established by the Round Table, but which was finally destroyed by the implacable hatred between Arthur and Modred. (See also *MAGIC AND ENCHANTMENT; HEROIC QUESTS*)

ARTHUR rests in peace in Avalon, guarded by four fairy queens. Morgan le Fay, cowled in black, consults her book of magic crafts, to heal the wounds of the "undead" king. The winged apparition carrying the Grail symbolizes the hope and future promise of Arthur's reign. (LA MORT D'ARTHUR BY JAMES ARCHER, CANVAS, 1860.)

B

AVALON was another name for the Welsh otherworld, ANNWN, and its name suggests that it was an island of apples. The mortally wounded ARTHUR was ferried there by three mysterious women in a black boat, following the terrible battle against Sir MODRED's army. The undead king was expected to return from Avalon and lead the oppressed Celtic population of Britain to victory over their Anglo-Saxon and, later, Norman conquerors. According to one version of the myth, Excalibur was forged there. Traditionally, Avalon has been identified with Glastonbury, the supposed site of Arthur's tomb. (See also CELTIC OTHERWORLDS)

BADB (meaning "crow") was an Irish goddess of battle. She was one of a group of war deities who could influence the outcome of conflict by inspiring the combatants with fear or courage. The others were known as MORRIGAN, NEMAIN and MACHA. Myth connects Badb with the historical battle of Clontarf in 1014, when the High King Brian defeated the Viking invaders and Badb was said to have appeared over the warriors' heads.

BALOR, a formidable one-eyed god of death, led the misshapen Fomorii against the younger Tuatha De Danann. Here his grandson, Lugh, casts a fatal stone into Balor's deadly eye, forcing it back through his head where its lethal gaze destroys his warriors marching behind him.
(ILLUSTRATION BY MIRANDA GRAY, 1995.)

BALOR was the Irish Cyclops. This one-eyed god of death was the most formidable of the FOMORII, the violent and monstrous sea gods who ruled Ireland before the arrival of the TUATHA DE DANANN. So dreadful was his one eye that he destroyed whoever he looked upon and his eyelid had to be levered up by four servants. It was prophesied that he would be slain by his own grandson. To avoid this fate he locked his only daughter ETHLINN in a crystal tower on Tory Island, off the north-west coast of Ireland. Even so, Balor was killed in battle with a sling-shot by the sun god LUGH, Ethlinn's son and the champion of the Tuatha De Danann.

Lugh's father was Cian, a lesser member of the Tuatha De Danann. With the assistance of a female druid, Cian had entered the crystal tower and slept with Ethlinn. When Balor learned that his daughter had given birth to three sons, he ordered that they be drowned in a whirlpool near Tory Island. Balor's servants duly rolled them up in a sheet, but on the way to the whirlpool one of the boys fell out unnoticed. Either the druid then handed the fortunate baby to the smith god GOIBHNIU, or alternatively MANANNAN MAC LIR, the god of the sea, decided to foster him. In either event, Lugh was saved and set on the road to his destiny as the slayer of Balor.

The fateful meeting between Lugh and Balor occurred at the second battle of Magh Tuireadh, a fierce contest between the Fomorii and the Tuatha De Danann. Nobody could stand Balor's lethal gaze, not even the Tuatha De Danann leader NUADA, the owner of a sword which previously none could escape. The battle was just turning into a Tuatha De Danann rout, when Lugh noticed that the

BANSHEE, or bean sidhe, women of the fairies, lived underground in sparkling sidhe – fairy heavens hidden beneath grassy mounds on Irish hillsides. Legend has it that a banshee attaches itself to a family and warns of impending death with an eerie wail. (ILLUSTRATION BY H J FORD, 1902.)

AVALON, Arthur's last resting place, was an otherworldly retreat of wonder, mystery and peace. Its nine guardian queens recall an actual, historical order of nine nuns who lived off the coast of Roman Brittany, as well as the nine mythical maidens guarding Annwn's magic cauldron. (KING ARTHUR IN AVALON BY E BURNE-JONES, CANVAS, 1894.)

single eyelid of Balor was slowly closing through weariness. Lugh crept near to him with a magic sling-shot in hand. The moment the eyelid opened again, he hurled the stone so hard that it forced the eyeball backward through Balor's head, with the result that it was the Fomorii who now suffered from the destructive effect of its paralysing stare. The Tuatha De Danann were able to defeat the Fomorii, who were driven from Ireland for ever. (See also CELTIC OTHERWORLDS)

BANSHEE is the modern name for the *bean sidhe* ("woman of the fairies"), the traditional fairy of the Irish countryside. After the arrival of the Milesians from what is now Spain (the ancestors of the present-day Irish) the gods and goddesses known as the TUATHA DE DANANN disappeared underground and dwelt in mounds, and over the centuries they were slowly transformed in the popular imagination into fairies. It was believed that the wailing of a banshee foretold the approach of a human death.

figure who had long ago embarked on a great voyage to the otherworlds, so he set sail again; but not before one desperate hero forgot the warning and jumped ashore, and immediately turned into a pile of ash, as though he had been dead for centuries.

The voyage of Bran is certainly an ancient myth, although it was not written down until the eighth century by monks. Even though the monks added certain Christian elements such as references to Jesus Christ and Adam's sin, they did not obscure the tale's original magical atmosphere. (See also *FABULOUS VOYAGES*)

BRAN (below), on his epic voyage, visited the Isle of Women, where the chief woman brought his ship to shore with magic thread. Here, she holds a cup of plenty, symbolizing the idyllic delights of the island. The voyagers stayed for what they thought was a year before they left for home.
(ILLUSTRATION BY DANUTA MEYER, 1993.)

BRAN THE BLESSED, the son of the sea god Llyr, played a different role to *BRAN*, son of Febal. In Welsh mythology, he was called Bendigeidfran and seems to have been an otherworld god, although he was also active as a British king in mortal affairs. He allowed his sister *BRANWEN* to marry the Irish king *MATHOLWCH*, without the consent of her half-brother *EFNISIEN*.

Because of this slight, Efnisien cut off the lips, ears and tails of Matholwch's horses during the wedding feast in Wales. Not unnaturally, hostilities almost broke out between the Irish and the Britons as a result, but Bran managed to

BRAN THE BLESSED (right), the mighty ruler of Britain, sailed to Ireland to rescue his beautiful sister, Branwen. In the ensuing battle, Bran was mortally wounded, but his head, cut from his body, lived on. His magical cauldron of rebirth is seen here, restored, along with his head.
(ILLUSTRATION BY ALAN LEE, 1984.)

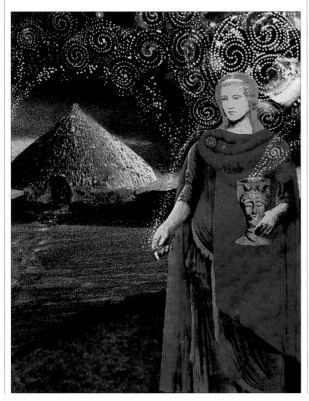

avoid a war by presenting Matholwch with a magic cauldron. This otherworld vessel could bring men back to life, but without restoring their speech.

Back in Ireland, Matholwch was unable to convince his warriors that Bran's gift was adequate compensation for the damage done to the horses. So Branwen ceased to be the Irish queen and was made to work in the palace kitchens, even though she had already given Matholwch a son and heir, *GWERN*. When Bran learned of how she was being treated, he raised a great army and sailed to Ireland. In the ensuing battle the Britons slew every Irish man there was, but only seven of their own army survived. Even Bran was killed, by a wound caused by a poisoned arrow. On his deathbed he told his followers to cut off his head, which apparently was still able to eat and talk during the voyage home. A later addition to the myth says that the head was brought to London and buried facing Europe, to ward off foreign invaders. King Arthur is said to have used the head for its power.

The Celts believed that heads were the seat of the soul, which may partly explain their practice of head-hunting. Even more curious, was the medieval Christian claim that Bran was the first British man. (See also *WONDROUS CAULDRONS*)

*BRANGAINE (above) and Iseult peer
quizzically at the shy young stranger in the
palace garden, puzzling over his identity.
But as soon as the dog leapt fondly onto his
lap, they recognized the stranger as Tristan,
who had been assumed dead. They were
confused at first because he was much
changed after his wanderings in the
wildwood. (ILLUSTRATION BY EVELYN PAUL, C. 1920.)*

BRANGAINE was the maid of
ISEULT, princess of Ireland and
lover of TRISTAN. Iseult had been
promised in marriage to King MARK
of Cornwall. Tristan, his nephew,
came to Ireland to escort her across
the sea. Before the ship sailed,
Iseult's mother gave Brangaine a
love potion for Iseult and Mark on
their wedding night, as it caused
those who drank it to love only
each other for the rest of their lives.
However, during the voyage, Tristan
became thirsty and unwittingly
drank the potion, and then offered
some to Iseult.

Through all the ensuing difficulties Brangaine was always loyal,
sharing their secrets, such as when
Tristan was brought to Mark's
castle mistaken for a wild man,
even taking Iseult's place in Mark's
bed on the wedding night.

*BRANWEN (right) releases a starling,
bearing a plea for help, across the sea to
her giant brother, Bran. When he reads
of her plight in Ireland, he sets sail
immediately with a fleet to rescue her.
(ILLUSTRATION BY ALAN LEE, 1984.)*

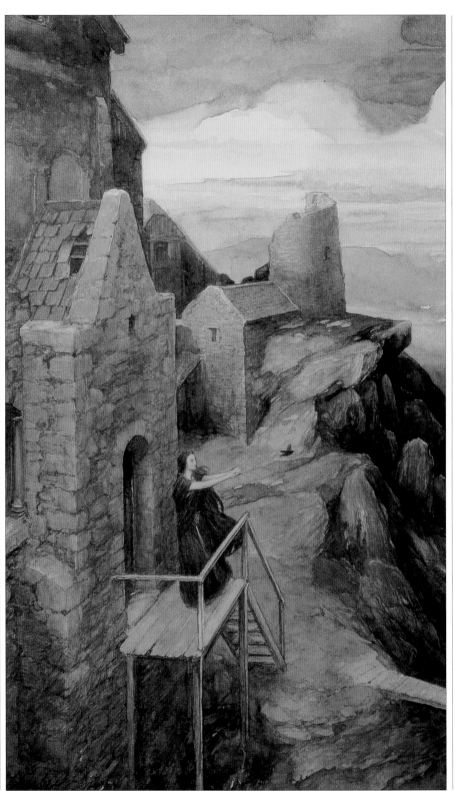

BRANWEN was the daughter of Llyr, the Welsh equivalent of the Irish sea god LIR, and sister to BRAN THE BLESSED, and MANAWYDAN. When High King MATHOLWCH of Ireland came to Bran's court at Harlech it was agreed that Branwen should be given to him in marriage. But her half-brother EFNISIEN was not consulted and, feeling insulted, he cut off the lips, ears and tails of Matholwch's horses. To restore peace Bran offered the Irish king replacement horses and a magic cauldron. Matholwch returned to Ireland with Branwen, who was at first received with great rejoicing for she was generous with gifts, and before long she gave birth to a son, GWERN. But after a few years Matholwch's friends and family began to complain that the compensation he had received from Bran was not enough. To satisfy them, Matholwch insisted that Branwen relinquish her position as queen and become a cook for the court.

During the next three years, as Branwen worked in the palace kitchens, she reared a starling and taught it to recognize her brother Bran. Then she sent it across the sea with a letter tied to its leg, telling of her treatment. When Bran and the Britons learned of her fate they brought an army to Ireland.

BRENDAN the Navigator was the title given to a sixth-century Irish saint. Indeed, the account of the two voyages undertaken by St Brendan was just as popular in the Middle Ages as the stories told about the Knights of the Round Table. This wonder tale is in the same tradition as that of BRAN, son of Febal, although its direct inspiration was the voyage of the Aran hero MAELDUN. Having taken holy orders, Brendan prayed to go on a pilgrimage into unknown lands. An angel then showed him an island in a vision. In search of this beautiful land, St Brendan set sail twice, first in a craft made from skins, and

BRENDAN, the Irish saint and navigator, returns to Ireland after his wondrous voyage in search of the Land of Promise. His tour of twelve mysterious islands included a land of birdlike spirits, which was possibly the Land of Promise. His amazing tale seems to be a blend of earlier voyages. (ILLUSTRATION BY JAMES STEPHENS, C. 1920.)

second in a boat made of wood. Miraculous events took place due to the saint's faith. One Easter a whale appeared so that St Brendan and his followers could hold a service on its broad back. After the service, the whale plunged under the waves and swam away. This great animal was made docile by St Brendan, as were numerous whirlpools. Even the Devil was unable to disturb the saint's serenity when he showed him the pain of Hell. St Brendan also restored to life one of the monks who were his companions after he had insisted on seeing this forbidden sight for himself.

On the voyages he also encountered a heathen giant, whom he baptized, terrifying mice and an enormous sea cat. Finally, they reached the island in St Brendan's vision. Inhabited by a hermit clothed in feathers, it was probably the Land of Promise, a place of Christian resurrection similar to the Celtic otherworlds. On his return to Ireland, St Brendan refused to stay in his old monastery but moved instead to a retreat near Limerick, where he died. (See also *FABULOUS VOYAGES*)

BRES, in Irish mythology, was briefly the leader of the TUATHA DE DANANN, the implacable enemies of the FOMORII, the sea gods who ruled Ireland long before them. Bres was an unusual leader of the Tuatha De Danann because his father was ELATHA, who was a Fomorii king of a land that lay under the sea. Elatha had met a Tuatha De Danann goddess named Eri on the sea-shore and made love to her on the sand. Bres was born as a result, although Eri was careful to say nothing to her husband about the boy's real father.

When Bres grew up, he fought against the existing inhabitants of Ireland, the FIRBOLG, at the first battle of Magh Tuireadh. In this engagement NUADA, the leader of the invading Tuatha De Danann, lost a hand and in consequence he retired for a time. Nuada tried to use a silver replacement without success, until Miach, son of the healing god DIAN CECHT, made him a hand of flesh and blood. However, until Nuada was fully recovered and able to resume his

BRIAN and his brothers set out on a perilous voyage across the world to fulfil eight tasks, set by the sun god Lugh. With daring and resource they sought and found wondrous treasures, such as an invincible sword and healing pigskin, which helped the De Danann in their battle with the Fomorii. (ILLUSTRATION BY STEPHEN REID, 1912.)

leadership, the De Danann were under the command of Bres. But Bres had no gift for leadership and became something of a tyrant. On the restoration of Nuada, Bres and his mother Eri fled to Elatha in order to seek Fomorii assistance. This caused the second battle of Magh Tuireadh, in which Nuada was killed. Through the bravery of the sun god LUGH, however, the Fomorii were routed and Bres was taken prisoner. One version of the myth explains how, in return for his life, Bres promised to instruct the Tuatha De Danann in the arts of planting and sowing crops. It is possible that Bres, like his wife, the fertility goddess BRIGID, was a deity connected with agriculture.

BRIAN was one of the three sons of TUIREANN, whose family were engaged in a feud with the family of Cian, father of the god LUGH. When Lugh sent Cian to summon the warriors of the TUATHA DE DANANN to battle, Brian and his brothers, Iuchar and Iucharba, killed him during his journey. To atone for this act of murder they were given by Lugh eight tasks to perform. Among the objects they had to retrieve were three apples from the Gardens of the Sun, a healing pigskin from the king of Greece, a poisoned spear from the king of Persia, a cooking-spit belonging to the nymphs of an undersea kingdom and the seven pigs of King Asal of the Golden Pillars, which could be cooked and eaten one day and found alive the next. Finally, they were to shout three times on the Hill of Mochaen. Having successfully brought back to Lugh all the magical objects he required, they then set out to perform their last duty. However, they were mortally wounded by Mochaen and his sons. Tuireann therefore asked Lugh if he might borrow the magical pigskin and so heal his sons, but the god refused and Brian and his brothers died. (See also *FABULOUS VOYAGES*)

BRICIU was one of the trouble-makers of Irish myth. An Ulster lord, he arranged a great feast to which he invited all the Ulster heroes, and ordered that the hero's portion be given to the greatest among them. At which point the three great warriors, CUCHULAINN, CONALL and Laoghaire, sprang up at once and began fighting each other for the honour. In order to settle the argument it was agreed that a monster should be summoned to test the courage of the three heroes. Briciu did this by challenging each one to cut off the demon's head, on the understanding that the following day that man should then lay his own head on the block. Cuchulainn stepped up

first and beheaded the monster, whereupon the creature rose, took up its head and departed. The next day Cuchulainn offered his own head and the monster pronounced him the bravest man in Ireland.

BRIDE see BRIGID

BRIGANTIA ("High One" or "Queen") was the chief goddess of the Brigantes, the dominant tribe in the north of England before the invasion of the Romans. She was associated with water, war and healing, and also with prosperity. A widely revered goddess, she was worshipped throughout the Celtic world. In Ireland she was known as BRIGID and in France as Brigindo.

BRIGID, sometimes known as Brigit, was a goddess of healing and fertility who was believed to assist women in labour. She seems to have been widely worshipped in Ireland and Britain, where she was most likely known as BRIGANTIA. In Irish mythology, she was the wife of BRES, the half-FOMORII god who briefly led the TUATHA DE DANANN after the first battle of Magh Tuireadh against the FIRBOLG. Bres was handsome but also oppressive, like all Fomorii, so his reign was short. Brigid, however, bore him three sons. She often appears as an alternative for her mother ANU, which suggests that they were probably different aspects of the same mother goddess.

ST BRIDE is ferried by angels from Iona to Bethlehem on the eve of Christ's birth to foster the infant Christ. Celtic and Christian motifs merge in this scene, while the angels' soaring flight beyond the frame enhances the powerfully spiritual effect.
(ST BRIDE BY JOHN DUNCAN, CANVAS, C. 1913.)

St Brigit, or St Bride, one of Ireland's patron saints, may have been a priestess of the goddess Brigid prior to her conversion to Christianity. It was said that she was able to feed animals without reducing the available food for the people, and this also links her with Brigid, who was celebrated at the Celtic festival of Imbolc on the first of February, at the same time as the ewes came into milk.

CAER was a fairy maiden who was loved by Aonghus. She chose to live as a swan for part of her life. When the swans gathered on the Lake of the Dragon's Mouth, Aonghus went to find Caer and win her love. As he reached out to her he was also turned into a swan, and they flew away together. (ILLUSTRATION BY GLENN STEWARD, 1995.)

BRIGIT see BRIGID

CAER was a fairy maiden loved by AONGHUS, the Irish love god. Her father Ethal was one of the TUATHA DE DANANN. Aonghus became aware of Caer in a dream and so attracted was he to her beauty that he fell into a deep sickness. When the identity of Caer was discovered, Aonghus immediately asked her father for her hand, but Ethal said it was not in his power to grant this because his daughter had taken the form of a swan. It was agreed, however, that Aonghus could ask Caer to marry him but only if he was able to recognize her from among the large flock of swans with whom she lived.

When the swans arrived at the Lake of the Dragon's Mouth, Aonghus went to the shore and, recognizing Caer, called out her name. Afterwards Aonghus and Caer were married.

CAMELOT, a mythical castle-city named after Camulos, was the heart of Arthur's kingdom, the seat of his power, symbol of his golden age and his most beloved home. Its shining towers drew knights from all over the world. Part of the mystique of Camelot is its elusive location which has yet to be found. (ILLUSTRATION BY ALAN LEE, 1984.)

CAILTE, son of RONAN, was a Fenian warrior and poet, and a cousin of FINN MACCOOL, leader of the FIANNA, the warrior bodyguard of the High King of Ireland. Cailte, though exceptionally thin, was a formidable fighter and is credited with killing LIR, the sea god who was the father of MANANNAN MAC LIR. But it was as a poet that he was most admired, and his most famous audience was St Patrick. Possibly after returning from an otherworld, Cailte was said to have travelled through Ireland recounting to the saint the legends of the hills, woods and lakes that they encountered, and also the great exploits and battles of the Fianna.

CALATIN, in Irish mythology, was a misshapen druid of FOMORII origin who was said to have studied sorcery for seventeen years. Queen MEDB of Connacht dispatched Calatin along with his numerous sons to fight the Ulster hero CUCHULAINN. All of them had their left hands and right feet missing, but they never missed with their poisoned spears, and Cuchulainn only succeeded in beating them with the assistance of a Connacht warrior who disapproved of such a one-sided contest. The destruction of the male Calatins did not spell the end of Cuchulainn's troubles, however, for not long afterwards Calatin's wife gave birth to three daughters, who were blinded in one eye, like the Germanic god Odin, so as to learn the magic arts. Soon the three Calatin sisters became powerful witches, and they deceived Cuchulainn with their spells, and so assisted Queen Medb's invasion of Ulster. When Cuchulainn rode out in his chariot against the invaders, he came across these hideous women cooking a dog next to the road. Either

CAILTE, a Fenian warrior and bard, was renowned for his songs and legends. Bards or lyric poets played a central role in Celtic society, perpetuating the mysteries, praising their leaders and satirizing their enemies. Bardic schools flourished in Ireland right up to the seventeenth century. (AQUATINT BY R. HAVELL. C 1890.)

because the dog was his namesake, or because it would have been discourteous to refuse a piece of the cooked meat, Cuchulainn stopped and took hold of the dog's shoulder. As a result, his own hand and shoulder withered. Gravely weakened, he still advanced with his faithful charioteer LAEG.

CAMELOT see HEROIC QUESTS

CAMULOS was the god of the Remi, a Celtic tribe living in what is now Belgium, although there is evidence that he was also worshipped as a divinity of war in northern Britain and at the town of Camulodunum ("The Fort of Camulos"), modern Colchester, in Essex. The name of the town formed the basis for the mythical city of Camelot. The Romans associated Camulos with their god Mars. He was said to wield an invincible sword.

CARADAWC, in Welsh mythology, was the son of BRAN (son of the sea god, Llyr). When Bran sailed with his army to Ireland to avenge the ill-treatment of his sister BRANWEN by the High King MATHOLWCH, he left Caradawc as chief steward. When news of Bran's death arrived, Caradawc was overthrown by Caswallon, son of the death god Beli.

CARBONEK see CELTIC OTHERWORLDS

CATHBAD (above), the inspired druid and seer, predicted Deirdre's tragic destiny at her birth. Druids, both male and female, held high rank in Celtic society. They were counsellors, judges, teachers and ambassadors. Even a high king could not speak at an assembly before his druid. (ILLUSTRATION BY NICK BEALE, 1995.)

CATHBAD, in Irish mythology, was a seer and druid, and advisor to *CONCHOBHAR MAC NESSA*, the king of Ulster. Cathbad prophesied that though *DEIRDRE* would have great beauty she would bring destruction to Ulster. He also foretold that the hero *CUCHULAINN* would have a glorious but short life. When King Conchobhar Mac Nessa became cruel towards the end of his reign, Cathbad cursed the king and his stronghold at Emain Macha. Cathbad had three children, *DECHTIRE*, the mother of Cuchulainn, Elbha, the mother of *NAOISE*, and Findchaem, mother of *CONALL* Cearnach.

CERIDWEN was a Welsh goddess of fertility and the mother of Afagddu, reputedly the ugliest man in the world. To compensate for his looks Ceridwen boiled a cauldron of knowledge for a year and a day so that Afagddu could become wise and respected, and she set Gwion Bach, the second son, to watch over the pot. But Afagddu was denied the prophetic gift when a drop fell on Gwion Bach's finger and he unthinkingly sucked it. In fury, Ceridwen chased and ate Gwion Bach, only later to reincarnate him as *TALIESIN*, who was the greatest of all the Welsh bards. Ceridwen had another equally ugly son, Morfan, who was also a fearsome warrior. He fought with King

CERIDWEN boils a magical brew hoping to endow her ill-favoured son with wisdom. At the end of a year, the broth would yield just three precious drops of inspiration; but these splashed on to the hand of Gwion Bach, who became all-knowing. (ILLUSTRATION BY JAMES ALEXANDER, 1995.)

ARTHUR in his last battle, at Camlan. At first none of Sir *MODRED*'s men would fight Morfan because they thought he was ugly enough to be a devil.

CERNUNNOS was a Celtic god worshipped in both France and Britain. He is usually depicted sitting cross-legged and wearing a sleeveless tunic and bead necklace. He has an impressive pair of antlers, and the name Cernunnos means "the Horned One", which suggests that he was a god of wild animals and the forest, although he has also been seen as a god of plenty. The Romans identified him with their god Mercury, the messenger god and the guide of the dead to the underworld. In medieval Ireland the antlers of Cernunnos were transferred to the Devil.

CESAIR was the daughter of Bith, son of Noah and one of the earliest arrivals in Ireland. In her myth, Celtic and Hebrew traditions were brought somewhat uncomfortably together by the monks who wrote down the sagas and who suggested that the first settlers had reached Ireland before the Flood. Although Bith was denied a place in the Ark, he was fortunate to be advised by a god to build his own boat. Cesair appears to have guided him to this decision as well. They sailed for seven years and eventually reached

CESAIR, granddaughter of Noah, set sail with her father, Bith, to escape the Flood. After a seven-year voyage, they reached the shores of Ireland. Yet neither Cesair nor her father survived the Flood when it engulfed the land, although her husband, Fintan, escaped by changing into a salmon. (ILLUSTRATION BY JAMES ALEXANDER, 1995.)

CERNUNNOS, a Celtic hunter god of beasts, is typically depicted in a lotus position. The "horned one" was a lord of animals and is here surrounded by wild creatures such as the stag, boar and lion. In one hand he clasps a warrior's torc, in the other a serpent, demonstrating his power. (GUNDESTRUP CAULDRON, GILDED SILVER, C. 100 BC.)

Ireland, where Cesair was married to FINTAN. When the rising waters of the Flood engulfed the land, Fintan saved himself by changing into a salmon, but the rest of Bith's family drowned. This myth is known as the first invasion of Ireland. Subsequent invasions were by the PARTHOLON and Nemed, the FOMORII and TUATHA DE DANANN, who were all more or less supernatural in nature. The final invasion of Ireland was by the sons of MILESIUS, who came from Spain and brought human rule to the island.

CLIODHNA, in Irish mythology, was an otherworld goddess of beauty. It was said that her three magical birds could sing the sick to sleep and cure them. Cliodhna was passionately in love with a mortal named Ciabhan, a youth with wonderful curling locks. One day on the shore near Cork, while Ciabhan went hunting inland, Cliodhna was put into a magic sleep by the sea god MANANNAN MAC LIR, who then sent a wave to pull her back to the Land of Promise.

CONAIRE MOR was a High King of Ireland. He was the son of a cowherd's foster-daughter named Mess Buachalla and the bird god NEMGLAN. His mother was actually

the daughter of Etain Oig and CORMAC king of Ulster. However, Cormac was so disappointed not to have a son that he ordered Mess Buachalla to be thrown into a pit. According to the myth, the baby girl was saved by two kind-hearted servants, who could not bring themselves to carry out the king's order. Instead they gave Mess Buachalla to a cowherd. When she grew up, her beauty was so remarkable that Eterscel, the High King of Ireland, decided to marry her. He was also persuaded by a prophecy which said that an obscure woman would bear him a famous son. But on the night before the wedding, Mess Buachalla slept with the god Nemglan, who had magnificent plumage. From this union was born Conaire Mor, whom Mess Buachalla passed off as the son of Eterscel. The one instruction that Nemglan told Mess Buachalla to give to their child was that he was never to kill a bird.

When Conaire Mor was a young man, Eterscel died and the right of succession was raised in Tara, the Irish capital. It was agreed to follow the ancient custom of the dream. After a feast, one of the court would have a spell of truth sung over him as he slept. The man the courtier dreamed about would then be the next High King. In the succession dream a naked man was revealed, walking along the road to Tara with a sling in his hand.

At this time Conaire Mor was some distance from Tara. As he headed back to the palace in his chariot, a flock of birds descended upon him. They had such wonderful plumage that Conaire Mor forgot the taboo about killing birds and got out his sling. The birds shed their feathers and attacked the charioteer as warriors. But one of the birdlike fighters, who was more handsome than the rest, protected Conaire Mor. He introduced himself as his father Nemglan and reminded the young man that he must never cast stones at birds for they were his own kin. As a penance, Nemglan told his son to walk naked along the road to Tara, carrying only his sling. If he did this, and promised to rule Ireland in peace, Conaire Mor would be made High King.

So it was that Conaire Mor was received at Tara as the High King. Peace and prosperity at first marked his reign, although the lure of plunder gradually drew the Irish back to their old habit of cattle-raiding. Since Conaire Mor was reluctant to punish severely those who took

CLIODHNA fled to Glandore to live with her mortal lover, Ciabhan, but the sea god, Manannan Mac Lir, sent a great wave to scoop her up and bring her home. Here, lulled to sleep by fairy music, she drifts back to fairyland. The Wave of Cliodhna is still one of the three great waves of Ireland. (ILLUSTRATION BY JAMES ALEXANDER, 1995.)

CONAIRE MOR was burdened by more geis (taboos) than any other Irish warlord. Violation of geis led to misfortune or death and marked a tragic turning-point in the hero's life. Despite his wisdom, Conaire Mor was lured by his enemies into breaking his geis one by one. (ILLUSTRATION BY STEPHEN REID, 1910.)

part in the growing disorder, the country soon slid back into clan warfare. Eventually, the High King had to forgo the ways of peace and break his promise to his father. Conaire Mor soon realized that this would bring about his own downfall. While on campaign, he came to a roadside hostel where he was greeted by three strange horsemen, whose clothes, weapons, bodies and horses were all red. A hideous old woman told Conaire Mor that during his stay in the hostel "neither skin nor flesh of you will escape from the place to which you have come, save what the birds will take in their claws." The same night a rebel force surrounded the hostel and attacked. Three times the building caught fire and three times the flames were brought under control, but all the water had now been used. When a druid accompanying the rebels laid a spell of thirst on the High King, he sent one of his companions to fetch some water. On returning, the warrior saw that the fight was over and Conaire Mor's severed head lay on the floor. So he poured the water into the king's head, at which Conaire Mor's decapitated head praised him for his sense of duty.

115

SAGES AND SEERS

THE SPIRITUAL SEERS and shamans of Celtic myth were endowed with extraordinary gifts of prophecy, wisdom and healing. They enjoyed a profound rapport with natural and supernatural forces, and acted as intermediaries between the realms of the living and the dead, between the visible world of men and the invisible otherworld, a realm of wondrous spirits. Most famous of all was Arthur's wise counsellor, Merlin; but other inspired druids – Amairgen, Taliesin and Cathbad – feature in Celtic myths as prophetic bards and counsellors to clan chiefs and kings. Some lived as hermits in the wilderness, while remaining powerful in Celtic society. Although on the whole helpful to mortals, some dark sorceresses, such as Morgan, Nimue or the Calatins, used their supernatural gifts to bewitch and manipulate mortals for their own ends.

MORGAN LE FAY (above right), Queen of Avalon, the otherworldly Isle of Apples, bears an apple bough, the Celtic symbol of peace and plenty. A gifted sorceress, she is often portrayed as a dark soul, thwarting Arthur and manipulating heroes. At a deeper level, she is a winter goddess of darkness and death, opposing Arthur, the Lord of Summer. She reveals the redeeming aspect of her character in her role as sovereign healer of Avalon and guardian of Arthur's body in death. (ILLUSTRATION BY STUART LITTLEJOHN, 1994.)

MERLIN (right) is best remembered as the fatherly and spiritual guardian of Arthur. A wise seer, Merlin counselled the young king, sometimes sternly and sometimes gently, but always with wisdom. Merlin was also a peerless sage, credited with the design of the Round Table, the plan for Camelot and the stone ring at Stonehenge. He learnt his craft from a master, Bleise, portrayed here as an historian recording the deeds of Arthur's reign, as reported by Merlin. (MANUSCRIPT ILLUSTRATION, C. 1300.)

HELLAWES (below) was a sorceress in the Arthurian myths who had set her heart on the noble knight Sir Lancelot, whom she had loved from afar for some seven years. Eventually, she managed to lure him into her Chapel Perilous and there she tried all the methods she knew to inspire his love for her. But it was to no avail because the steadfast and loyal knight loved one woman only, Arthur's queen, the fair Guinevere, and he had come to the chapel with but one mission in mind, which was to collect healing talismans for the wounded knight Sir Meliot. When Lancelot left with the talismans, he was completely untouched by Hellawes' love and even her magical craft. The sorceress finally realized that he would never love her and she died of a broken heart. (ILLUSTRATION BY AUBREY BEARDSLEY, C. 1870.)

DRUIDS (above) held both political and spiritual power in Celtic society and were gifted not only as shamans and seers but also as legal and moral advisors. Druids underwent a long apprenticeship of at least twenty years, learning the mysteries and laws by heart. Here, druids on a snowy hill celebrate the winter solstice by gathering a bough of mistletoe, cut with the sacred golden sickle borne by the foremost druid. (THE DRUIDS BRINGING IN THE MISTLETOE BY G HENRY AND E A HORNED, CANVAS, 1890.)

TALIESIN (left), a prophetic poet and shamanistic seer, was gifted with all-seeing wisdom after consuming a "greal" of inspiration from Ceridwen's cauldron. Wales's greatest bard, he foretold the coming of the Saxons and the oppression of the Cymry as well as his own death. He appears here as an eagle, the bird often chosen by shamans on their spirit-flights or trance journeys to the otherworld. The eagle's gold nimbus symbolizes Taliesin's radiant brow. (ILLUSTRATION BY STUART LITTLEJOHN, 1994.)

CONALL, in Irish mythology, was the foster-brother of the Ulster hero *CUCHULAINN*. As children, they swore that if either was killed first the other would avenge him. When Queen *MEDB* of Connacht invaded Ulster, Cuchulainn faced her army single-handed, but he was doomed because he had offended the war goddess *MORRIGAN*. After Cuchulainn had been killed, and his head and sword-hand cut off by the enemy, the warriors of Ulster were stirred by Conall to wreak bloody revenge. They caught up with Queen Medb's army and Conall slew those who had killed his foster-brother. Later, Conall went on to ravage the whole of Ireland as he punished Queen Medb's allies one by one. In doing so he earned his title, Caernach ("of the Victories").

CONALL of the Victories, a veteran warlord, avenged Cuchulainn's death by slaying his killers one by one. From the brain of one of his victims, Mac Da Tho, he made a magic brain ball, a lethal weapon. Conall here is welcomed by his Ulstermen at a feast in Mac Da Tho's dun.
(ILLUSTRATION BY STEPHEN REID, 1910.)

CONCHOBHAR MAC NESSA, in Irish mythology, was an Ulster king. He was the son of Fachtna Fathach and *NESSA*, a local beauty who, according to one tradition, conceived Conchobar on the eve

CONCHOBHAR MAC NESSA, a high king of Ireland, granted arms to the young Cuchulainn, but when the boy grasped his spears, they splintered in his hand; next, a chariot shattered beneath his stamp. No weapons withstood the hero's mighty grasp until he was given the king's own arms.
(ILLUSTRATION BY STEPHEN REID, 1910.)

of her royal marriage through a secret affair with a druid. When her husband died shortly after the wedding, Nessa was courted by his half-brother and successor, *FERGUS MAC ROTH*. But she would only agree to become his wife on the condition that he would first let her son Conchobhar rule as king of Ulster for a year. An ambitious and determined woman, Nessa instructed her son how to be a great ruler so that when the time arrived for Fergus Mac Roth to return to the throne, the people of Ulster simply refused to let Conchobhar step down.

Although he was married, King Conchobhar fell deeply in love with *DEIRDRE*, who was sometimes called Derdriu ("of the Sorrows"). She was the daughter of an Ulster chieftain, and at her birth the druid *CATHBAD* had warned that, though Deirdre would be the most beautiful woman in Ireland and would marry a king, she would be the cause of death and destruction throughout the land. By the time Deirdre grew up, Conchobhar was an old man, and she in disgust

refused his advances and eloped with a handsome young warrior named *NAOISE*. But the king never gave up his passion, and so eventually he had Naoise killed and was married to Deirdre. She found her situation so intolerable that she committed suicide by throwing herself from a speeding chariot. Fergus Mac Roth, appalled by Conchobhar's behaviour, offered his services to Ulster's enemies and a long war ensued. Conchobhar was himself killed by a magic slingshot. It was the famous "brain ball" made by Conall out of the brains of a slain Leinster king. The ball lodged in the king's skull, and his doctors advised him to avoid any strenuous exercise and excitement. Some years later Conchobhar Mac Nessa got into a rage and the "brain ball" caused his death.

CONLAI, sometimes known as Connla, was the doomed son of the great Ulster hero *CUCHULAINN*. According to one Irish tradition, Cuchulainn had visited the Land of Shadows in order to challenge the warrior woman *AOIFA* to single combat. After the fight, which the

hero just managed to win by the use of cunning, they became lovers and Conlai was conceived. When he left, Cuchulainn gave Aoifa a gold ring. Years later Conlai wore this ring on a visit to Ulster, where he challenged the local heroes to combat. Just like his father, Conlai was quick to anger and soon overcame *CONALL*, Cuchulainn's foster-brother. Despite the misgivings of his wife *EMER*, Cuchulainn could not resist fighting the young stranger himself. Too proud to announce his own identity when challenged by Cuchulainn, Conlai accepted the possibility of death and drew his sword. Although Cuchulainn was impressed by sword-play that matched his own, he lost his temper the moment Conlai cut off one of his locks of hair. The terrible combat only

CONLAI, the ill-starred son of Aoifa and Cuchulainn, grew up in Skye, a stranger to his father. When he went to Ulster to challenge the local heroes, he met Cuchulainn in single combat and was killed. Recognizing his son too late, Cuchulainn was overwhelmed with grief.
(ILLUSTRATION BY JAMES ALEXANDER, 1995.)

D

contenders for the championship – Laoghaire, Cuchulainn's foster-brother *CONALL*, and *CUCHULAINN* himself – were invited by Cu Roi to a beheading contest, which only Cuchulainn had enough courage to go through with. Later, Cu Roi and Cuchulainn carried off *BLATHNAT*, a beautiful woman. Although she expressed her love for Cuchulainn, Cu Roi took her to his castle in Munster. When Cuchulainn laid siege to the stronghold, Blathnat betrayed Cu Roi by showing how the place could be entered.

CYNON, according to a late Arthurian myth, was a knight who encountered a black man with one foot and one eye, and bearing a large wooden club. This Fomorii-like fighter, doubtless a cousin of the violent and misshapen Irish sea gods, ordered Cynon to go to a fountain and fill with water a silver bowl that he would find there , and then to throw the water against a marble slab. Sir Cynon did as he was instructed and a Black Knight appeared to the sound of thunder and the singing of magic birds. Sir

CYNON, an Arthurian hero, battles with the Black Knight, a mysterious warrior who appeared by magic. Although defeated, Cynon returned home on foot to tell the tale, and thus inspired Owain to set out on his memorable quest. Years later Cynon retraced his steps in search of Owain. (ILLUSTRATION BY H THEAKER, 1920.)

Cynon then fought his mysterious opponent but was defeated.

DAGDA means "the good god". He was in fact the great god of Irish mythology, and was usually depicted as a man in rustic clothes dragging an enormous club on wheels. With one end of this weapon he could slay his enemies and with the other he could restore the dead to life. Dagda was believed to be wise, full of knowledge and well versed in the magic arts. He was a chief of the *TUATHA DE DANANN*.

Dagda was a great fighter and the lover of *MORRIGAN*, the war goddess. The bones of his enemies were described as "hailstones under horses' hooves" when he wielded his mighty club. Like an all-powerful chieftain, Dagda led the Tuatha De Danann on the bat-tlefield, slaying all those who dared to confront him. Yet he was also associated with abundance, being able to satisfy the hunger of every-body by means of an inexhaustible cauldron. That Dagda took great pleasure in eating was apparent, when just before the second battle of Magh Tuireadh he visited the camp of the *FOMORII*, his bitter enemies, during a truce at the time of the New Year festival. There they made for him a porridge of milk, flour, fat, pigs and goats, enough for fifty men.

On pain of death Dagda was

ordered by the Fomorii to consume this massive meal, which he readily did with a huge wooden ladle "so big that a man and a woman could have slept together in it". This test turned Dagda tem-porarily into a gross old man, but it did not prevent him from making love to a Fomorii girl, who promised to use her magic on behalf of the Tuatha De Danann. The story may recall, in a distorted form, a holy marriage between a chieftain and a maiden at the beginning of each year; similar to

DANA, the great mother goddess, gave her name to the Tuatha De Danann, a race of wonderful, beautiful but often vulnerable gods who lived in the sparkling otherworld. Here, they gather to hear the poignant song of Lir's children, ill-starred gods who were turned into swans. (ILLUSTRATION BY STEPHEN REID, 1912.)

DAGDA, father of the gods, owned a wondrous cauldron of plenty and a double-edged magic club, carried on wheels. This bronze relief of a powerful Celtic deity, with a wheel, is regarded by some to be Dagda, with the wheel symbolizing his treasures. (GUNDESTRUP CAULDRON, GILDED SILVER, C. 100 BC.)

the sacred rite that was performed by a Sumerian ruler and a priestess in Mesopotamia. This union was meant to ensure prosperity, strength and peace.

Although the eventual defeat of the Fomorii at the second battle of Magh Tuireadh was really due to the sun god *LUGH*, it was Dagda who was held in the greatest respect, even after the Tuatha De Danann were in their turn overthrown by the sons of *MILESIUS*, the ancestors of the present-day Irish.

To Dagda fell the important task of settling the defeated Tuatha De Danann underground. Just as the Fomorii had retreated beneath the waves, so the vanquished De Danann disappeared underground. Over the centuries these powerful deities were gradually transformed into fairies – the *bean sidhe* or *BANSHEES* of Irish folklore. (See also *WONDROUS CAULDRONS*)

DANA, another name for *ANU*, was the goddess after whom the *TUATHA DE DANANN* were named – "the people of the goddess Dana".

DECHTIRE, in Irish mythology, was the mother of *CUCHULAINN*. She was a daughter of Maga, the child of the love god *AONGHUS* and of the druid *CATHBAD*, advisor to King *CONCHOBHAR MAC NESSA* of Ulster. When Dechtire married *SUALTAM MAC ROTH*, a fly flew into her cup during the wedding feast and she swallowed it. She fell into a deep sleep and dreamed that the sun god *LUGH* insisted that she and fifty of her kinswomen follow him to the otherworld as a flock of birds. Three years later a flock of brightly coloured birds reappeared at Emain Macha, the capital of Ulster. The Ulstermen went after them with slings, but were unable to hit any of them. It was decided, therefore, to surprise the birds at night as they rested. So it was that the warriors came upon Dechtire, her women and Lugh sleeping in a hut on a site renowned for its magical properties. When Conchobhar was told of of this he sent for Dechtire at once, but she told her captors that she was too ill to be able to travel for another day. The next morning she showed them her new-born son, a gift to Ulster.

DECHTIRE, who had disappeared mysteriously on her wedding day, returned three years later with the shining sun god, Lugh. Dechtire brought with her a gift from the otherworld – her child, Setanta, who became Ulster's greatest hero, Cuchulainn. (ILLUSTRATION BY G DENHAM, C. 1900.)

DEIRDRE was the cause of Ulster's sorrows, according to Irish mythology. The druid *CATHBAD* foretold this before she was born, as well as telling of how beautiful she would become. When she grew up, King *CONCHOBHAR MAC NESSA* wished to marry her, even though he was already advanced in years, but Deirdre would have none of this. She persuaded *NAOISE* and his brothers to run away with her to Alba. After living for many years in their voluntary exile, they were tricked into returning to Ulster on the understanding that they would come to no harm. But Conchobhar arranged to have Naoise killed and then forced Deirdre to agree to marry him. Once married, however, Deirdre remained sad and kept her distance from the king, with the result that he handed her over to the killer of Naoise. Rather than sleep with this man, she threw herself from his speeding chariot and smashed her brains out on a rock. From each of the graves of Naoise and Deirdre grew a pine, which eventually intertwined and grew as a single tree.

DERBFORGAILLE was the daughter of a ruler of Lochlann. When her father left her on the shore as a tribute for the *FOMORII*, she was rescued by the Ulster hero *CUCHULAINN* and fell in love with him. In order to follow him, she turned herself into a swan. However, unaware of the bird's true identity, Cuchulainn brought her down with a sling-shot. She returned to human form and he sucked the stone out of the wound, but now they were linked by blood and so he could not marry her.

DIAN CECHT was the Irish god of healing. It was said that with his daughter Airmid, he had charge of a spring whose waters restored the dying gods to life. After *NUADA*, the leader of the *TUATHA DE DANANN*, lost his hand fighting the *FIRBOLG* at the first battle of Magh Tuireadh, Dian Cecht gave him a silver hand, thus earning him the title Nuada "of the Silver Hand". Impressed though the Tuatha De Danann were by Dian Cecht's handiwork, Nuada was felt to be no longer fit to be a war leader and *BRES*, who was

DEIRDRE grieves for the death of her beloved Naoise and his brothers, slain by the jealous King Conchobhar. Over the brothers' grave, she sang her pitiable lament, "May my heart not break today for the sea-tides of our everyday sorrows are strong, but I am sorrow itself..." (DEIRDRE OF THE SORROWS BY JOHN DUNCAN, C. 1912.)

half *FOMORII*, took his place. But Bres was a tyrant and became very unpopular, so Nuada was restored to the leadership, once Dian Cecht's son Miach had made him a new hand of flesh and blood. Apparently the god of healing grew jealous of his son's medical skills and so killed him.

DIARMUID UA DUIBHNE, or Diarmuid "of the Love Spot", was the foster-son of the Irish love god *AONGHUS*. His mortal father gave him to the god as a child, a gift that was returned when Diarmuid received the famous love spot as a young Fenian warrior. One night, when out hunting, Diarmuid and three companions took shelter in a small hut in a wood. There a beautiful young woman received them but chose to sleep only with Diarmuid. She told him that she was Youth, and that the love spot she put on his forehead would make him irresistible to women. As a consequence, Diarmuid's life was almost continuously troubled by desperate women, the worst being *GRAINNE*, the passionate daughter of High King *CORMAC MAC ART*. Grainne was betrothed to *FINN MACCOOL*, the Fenian commander, but she wanted Diarmuid and forced him to elope with her. For sixteen years the Fenians pursued them until, at the request of the king and the love god, a peace was grudgingly made.

It seemed that Diarmuid and Grainne would settle down to a contented family life and they had several children. But Diarmuid's own destiny was about to catch up with him. His mortal father had killed his brother at birth because

DIAN CECHT (above), god of healing, guards the sacred spring of health with his daughter, Airmid. Its miracle waters cured the sick and restored the dead to life. Known as the father of medicine, Dian Cecht is credited with a remarkable sixth-century Brehon Law tract on the practice of medicine. (*ILLUSTRATION BY NICK BEALE, 1995.*)

DIARMUID (below), a gifted Fenian warrior, was lured underground by the De Danann who often recruited champions to fight in their otherworldly battles. To test his skill, they sent a mysterious warrior to challenge him as he drank from their forest well. (*ILLUSTRATION BY STEPHEN REID, 1912.*)

DON (below), the Welsh mother goddess, was as popular as her Irish counterpart, Dana. This female figure, surrounded by birds and children, is widely assumed to be a Celtic mother goddess. She is one of several Celtic deities embossed on the gilded panels of the Gundestrup Cauldron. (*GILDED SILVER, C. 100 BC.*)

he believed that Aonghus' steward, Roc, was responsible for the pregnancy. However, Roc revived the infant as a magic boar and told it to bring Diarmuid to his death. When hunting one day with Cormac Mac Art and Finn MacCool, Diarmuid came face to face with this creature. His hounds fled in terror, his sling-shot had no impact on the charging boar's head and his sword broke in two, so the irresistible Diarmuid was left bleeding to death on the ground. Finn MacCool refused to fetch the dying Diarmuid a drink of water, and by the time the other hunters arrived on the scene, he was too near to death to be saved. Grainne was devastated by the loss, although she was moved by the way that Aonghus took care of Diarmuid's corpse. He took the body to his own palace by the River Boyne, where he breathed a new soul into Diarmuid so that they could converse each day. This was how the young man came to live with the *TUATHA DE DANANN*, who had by this time left the upper world and lived beneath the soil of Ireland.

DIARMUID, gored by a wild boar, was denied healing water by Finn, still smarting over Diarmuid's love affair with Grainne. A Celtic Adonis, the hero was loved by women often against his will, and, like Adonis, was killed by a boar, but enjoyed some form of immortality. (*ILLUSTRATION BY H J FORD, 1912.*)

DON was the Welsh equivalent of the Irish mother goddess *DANA* and was the daughter of Mathonwy, sister of *MATH*, and the wife of Beli, the god of death. She had many children, including *AMAETHON*, *ARIANRHOD*, Govannon, *GWYDION*, Gilvaethwy and *NUDD*.

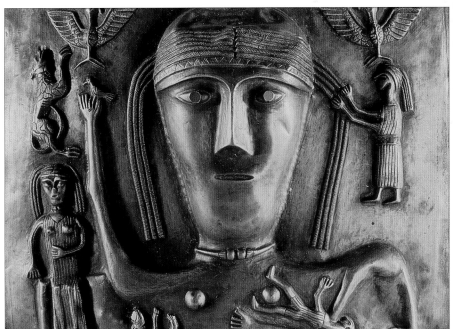

MAGIC AND ENCHANTMENT

ENCHANTMENT PERMEATES Celtic myth, shrouding the tales in a haunting, dreamlike quality. The all-pervasive otherworld lies behind much of the mystery and magic, penetrating the forests and lakes, and crafting charmed rings and weapons. Yet spells and magic also arose in the visible world where bards, druids and some privileged heroes, such as Finn MacCool, possessed magical powers. Bards could weaken the enemy with satire or enchanted sleep, while druids bewitched the host with magical illusions. Off the battlefield, love and romance were also subject to spells, love philtres or magical

trickery, as in the romances of Sadb, Rhiannon and Iseult. On the brighter side, many heroes enjoyed the gifts of the otherworld, such as Arthur's sword, Excalibur, or Fergus Mac Roth's *sidhe* sword; while Fergus Mac Leda's water-shoes afforded underwater adventures; and countless heroes were nourished or reborn from magical cauldrons.

FERGUS MAC LEDA, (above), a high king of Ulster, owned a pair of water-shoes with which he enjoyed underwater travel. He never tired of exploring the depths of the lakes and rivers of Ireland until he encountered a fierce river-horse in Loch Rury. The incident so terrified Fergus that his face became permanently distorted with fear. As only an unblemished king could rule Ireland, Fergus returned to the loch to slay the monster before going down himself, but with a face at last restored and serene. (ILLUSTRATION BY STEPHEN REID, 1912.)

THE ENCHANTED FOREST (left) of Arthurian legend, was alive with beguiling fairy maidens, who often taunted errant knights. One such, La Belle Dame Sans Merci, described by the poet Keats, was a banshee who attracted mortal lovers for her own amusement, inspiring them with a hopeless infatuation and then leaving them bereft of will or purpose until they withered on the lake, "alone and palely loitering". As the languishing knight here sleeps, he dreams of the pale kings and warriors whom La Belle Dame holds in thrall. (LA BELLE DAME SANS MERCI BY H M RHEAM, CANVAS. 1897.)

EXCALIBUR *(above), Arthur's enchanted sword, shone with the light of thirty torches and dazzled his enemies. The precious scabbard prevented the loss of blood in battle, but Arthur rather rashly handed this talisman over to his half-sister Morgan Le Fay for safekeeping; she instantly made a duplicate for Arthur, passing the original on to her lover, Accolon. Here, Arthur marvels at the sword rising from a white-clad arm in the enchanted lake. (ILLUSTRATION BY AUBREY BEARDSLEY, C. 1870.)*

PWYLL'S *(above) family wander in an enchanted wilderness after their country, Dyfed, had been spirited away in a peal of thunder. The baffling enchantment was part of a lingering curse placed on Pwyll to avenge Gwawl, a rival suitor for the hand of Rhiannon. Even after Pwyll's death, the spell blighted his family, until Rhiannon's new husband, Manawydan, struck a deal with the enchanter, who at last restored Dyfed to its former beauty. (ILLUSTRATION BY ALAN LEE, 1984)*

MERLIN *(right), wise and thoughtful though he was, was enchanted by the ravishing Lady of the Lake, Nimue, and despite his foresight, he allowed himself to be lured deep beneath a stone and bound there by his own magic spells. In another legend, Nimue put Merlin into a trance beneath a thorn tree and then trailed her veil around him, creating an invisible tower of air in which he was trapped forever. It is said that his voice can still be heard in the plaintive rustling of leaves. (ILLUSTRATION BY ALAN LEE, 1984.)*

E

DONN ("the Dark One") was the Irish god of the dead. He is sometimes confused with *EBER* Donn, one of the leaders of the sons of *MILESIUS*, who insulted *ERIU*, one of the *TUATHA DE DANANN*, and was drowned off the south-west coast of Ireland. Donn's home, the House of Donn, was thought to be an assembly point on the journey to the otherworld.

DRUIDS see *SAGES AND SEERS*

DUBH was a druidess. According to one Irish tradition, her anger at her husband Enna's passion for another woman ultimately led to the name of Dublin. Dubh used magic to drown her rival, but her husband in turn drowned her in what became known as Dubhlinn ("Dubh's pool").

DYLAN ("Son of the Wave") was a Welsh sea god whose parents were *ARIANRHOD* and her brother *GWYDION*. As soon as he was born

DONN, god of the dead, gathers souls around him as they assemble on his stormy island before setting out on their journey to the otherworld. Inevitably, he became associated in popular folklore with shipwrecks and sea storms, and was often confused with Eber Donn, who died at sea. (ILLUSTRATION BY JAMES ALEXANDER, 1995.)

DYLAN, a Welsh sea deity, leapt from his mother's arms at birth and plunged straight into the sea and swam as well as any fish. Beloved by the sea, all the waves wept when he was killed, and his death-groan can still be heard in the roar of the incoming tide. (THE BAPTISM OF DYLAN, SON OF THE WAVE BY GEORGE SHERRINGHAM, CANVAS, C. 1900.)

he headed straight to the sea, where he immediately swam as well as a fish. When his uncle, the smith god Govannon, killed him, all the waves of Britain and Ireland lamented his death.

EBER was the name of two of the three leaders who led the Milesians in their conquest of Ireland. They were Eber Donn, or Eber "the Brown", and Eber Finn, or Eber "the Fair". The third was named Eremon. Eber Donn failed to reach the Irish coast because his ship foundered in a storm caused by, it was said, his bloody war cry. The

druid *AMAIRGEN* had only just succeeded in casting a spell over the turbulent waves, when Eber Donn was seized by a battle-frenzy and the charm was broken by his wild cries. After the defeat of the *TUATHA DE DANANN*, the advice of Amairgen was ignored by Eber Finn, who refused to acknowledge the right of his older brother Eremon to be king of the whole island. So it was that Ireland was partitioned into two kingdoms, with Eremon ruling the north and Eber Finn the south. But Eber Finn invaded Eremon's territory and laid waste to his lands until he fell in battle. Eremon then became the first High King of all Ireland.

EFNISIEN, in Welsh mythology, was the troublesome half-brother of *BRAN THE BLESSED* who caused the rift between Bran and King *MATHOLWCH*. Because Efnisien had not been consulted by Bran over the marriage of his half-sister *BRANWEN* to the Irish king, he proceeded to cut off the lips, ears and tails of Matholwch's horses during the wedding feast. To compensate for this act, Bran gave Matholwch a magic cauldron that was capable of restoring dead warriors to life, but with one small imperfection – they came back to life without the power of speech. However, the

Irish did not consider this gift a sufficient redress for Efnisien's act of mutilation, and some time after her arrival in Ireland Branwen was demoted from being queen to just a lowly cook in the palace kitchens. Efnisien accompanied the army that was sent against Matholwch to avenge this insult. It was fortunate for Bran that his half-brother did come, because Efnisien foiled a cunning trap that had been laid for the Britons by Matholwch in his hall. He had placed behind each of Bran's strongest warriors a sack hung from the wall containing an armed Irishman, and at a signal they were to fall upon the Britons during what was supposed to be a feast of welcome. When Efnisien inspected the hall beforehand, he asked what was in one of the bags. On being told it was corn, Efnisien laid hold of the sack and felt about till his fingers closed on the head of the warrior within it, then he squeezed and cracked his skull. One by one Efnisien asked about the contents of the sacks and each time repeated his squeezing.

The feast took place therefore not as Matholwch had planned. An even more unexpected turn of events occurred when Efnisien threw Matholwch's three-year-old son by Branwen on to the fire. Branwen would have leapt after her

ELATHA (above), a Fomorii king, lived beneath the waves with his violent and misshapen people. Unlike the other Fomorii, Elatha was a godlike being with long golden hair. Emerging from the sea one day in his silver ship, he met the lovely goddess, Eri, who fell immediately in love with him. Soon after, they had a handsome but troublesome son, Bres. (ILLUSTRATION BY NICK BEALE, 1995.)

EBER DONN (above) and the Milesian chiefs drift in the fairy sea mists off the Irish coast. On board Eber's ship, the druid Amairgen charmed the sea with magic of his own, but Eber let out his great war cry which broke the druid's spell and stirred up a storm in which he was drowned.
(ILLUSTRATION BY JAMES ALEXANDER, 1995.)

EFNISIEN (below) inspects sacks in Matholwch's hall. In each sack he felt a warrior's head, which he crushed between his fingers. The moody trickster went on to provoke a deadly contest, but then, in remorse, sacrificed himself to save his comrades. (ILLUSTRATION BY STEPHEN REID, 1910.)

son, but Bran held her back. In the fight that took place afterwards the Britons were almost defeated by the magic cauldron that Bran had given Matholwch, because at night it restored to life the Irish warriors who had been slain during the day. The Britons were in a desperate predicament and so Efnisien, at the cost of his life, destroyed the magic cauldron. He hid among the Irish dead and was thrown into the boiling cauldron, where he stretched and burst its sides, but the great effort involved killed him.

ELATHA, in Irish mythology, was the son of Delbaeth, the leader of the *FOMORII* and father of *BRES*, who was briefly the leader of the *TUATHA DE DANANN*. Unlike the other Fomorii, who were described as being hideous and deformed, Elatha was fair and had golden hair. He met the goddess Eri on the sea shore and there they conceived their child Bres. When Bres was removed from the leadership of the De Danann, he and his mother went to Elatha to ask for help, but the Fomorii were defeated at the second battle of Magh Tuireadh and driven from Ireland.

EMER, in Irish mythology, was the daughter of Fogall and the wife of *CUCHULAINN*, who first saw her when he was at the court of the High King of Ireland at Tara. She appeared "dark-haired almost as himself, and her skin white as mare's milk, and her eyes wide and proud and brilliant like the eyes of Fedelma, his favourite falcon". Emer's father was a chieftain from Meath and was against the match. He told Cuchulainn to travel to improve his fighting skills and only then would he consider him as a son-in-law. Cuchulainn survived and returned to claim his bride. Indeed, Cuchulainn was forced to attack the reluctant Fogall's fortress before the wedding could take place. Although Emer was totally enraptured by her handsome husband, their marriage was not without its troubles, not least because many other women also found the Ulster hero attractive. Just before his final battle, when he fought the army of Queen *MEDB* alone, Emer tried to persuade him to remain in the fortress of Emain Macha, the seat of King *CONCHOBHAR MAC NESSA*. However, he got on his chariot when it was brought

around to the front of his house. Even then, he thought of Emer's request, but his enemies the witches of *CALATIN* cast a spell to harden his resolve to fight single-handed.

ENID see *CELTIC ROMANCE*

EMER, a peerless Irish maiden, inspired the love of Ulster's great hero, Cuchulainn. She was blessed with the six gifts of womanhood: beauty, chastity, wisdom, sweet speech, song and needlecraft. When the hero courted her, she smiled at his youth, and said that he had "deeds to do".
(ILLUSTRATION BY STEPHEN REID, 1912.)

F

*ETAIN (right), one of the High Queens of Ireland, appears with her peers in power and beauty: from left to right, Etain, Greek Helen, Medb and Fand, the fairy queen. The jewelled cup of plenty recalls Etain's links with the otherworld. (*ETAIN, HELEN, MEDB AND FAND *BY* HARRY CLARKE, *GLASS, C. 1900.)*

EPONA, the Celtic horse goddess, won the favour of the Roman army and was depicted in monuments set up at its cavalry barracks as a woman riding a fast steed, her cloak billowing with air behind her. She was even given her own festival in Rome on December 18. Originally, Epona was almost certainly seen by the Celts as a mare, possibly like the great white horse carved in the chalk downs near Wantage, in southern England. The fact that she is often depicted riding a horse with a foal suggests that she was also a goddess of fertility. In the Welsh myth of *PWYLL* there is a connection between Epona and his wife *RHIANNON*, who is made to carry visitors into her husband's palace.

ERIU, or Erinn, was the wife of Ma Greine, son of *OGMA*, and herself one of the *TUATHA DE DANANN*. When the Milesians invaded, she and her two sisters, Banba and

*EPONA (below), the Celtic horse goddess, was adopted by the Roman cavalry who spread her cult across Europe. Her effigy, often placed in stables, portrayed her riding side-saddle, sometimes with a foal, which reflected her role as a fertility goddess, symbolized here by the wheat and birds. (*ILLUSTRATION BY MIRANDA GRAY, 1995.)*

GAWAIN, in Welsh Gwalchmai, was the most courteous knight at *ARTHUR*'s court. He was a strict upholder of chivalry and the enemy of Sir *LANCELOT*. Sir Gawain's most extraordinary adventure concerned the Green Knight. Rather like the hazard faced by the Ulster hero *CUCHULAINN*, when a water giant came to test the courage of Irish warriors, the gigantic Green Knight strode into King Arthur's hall at Camelot one New Year's Eve and challenged the Knights of the Round Table to a beheading contest. Sir Gawain accepted and cut off the stranger's head in a single blow. As the severed head rolled around the hall, the royal court relaxed and thought the challenge over. But to the amazement of all

present, the giant behaved as if nothing had happened. Calmly stooping, he picked up his head and mounted his green charger. Then, from the saddle, the Green Knight pointed his severed head in Sir Gawain's direction and told him to be at a lonely chapel a year from that day in order to take a turn at receiving a blow from an axe. On the journey to this dangerous appointment Sir Gawain stayed with Sir Bercilak de Hautdesert who had a beautiful wife. He was sorely tempted by Sir Bercilak's wife but managed to resist her advances for two days. However, on the third day Sir Gawain accepted from her a green sash, which was the usual token worn by a knight to show his love for a lady.

At the meeting between Sir Gawain and his fearful opponent, the Green Knight turned out to be none other than Sir Bercilak himself. Three times the axe was swung at Sir Gawain's neck. Twice it was deflected because he had not abused his host's hospitality by making love to his wife. The third time it made a slight cut, at which Sir Gawain flinched. It did not cut off his head because Sir Gawain had only accepted the green sash out of good manners. Yet Sir Gawain realized that courtesy was no equal to moral purity, and thereafter he always wore the green sash as a reminder of his lapse.

This late British version of the Celtic beheading contest was quite clearly influenced by Christianity.

GAWAIN, an active and restless knight, lost interest in the Grail Quest quite early on. Although one of the first to set forth, inspiring the rest of the Knights, he lost heart, lacking the necessary discipline, patience and humility. (THE FAILURE OF SIR GAWAIN BY W MORRIS, TAPESTRY, 1895–96.)

Unlike Sir Gawain, Cuchulainn had no hesitation in slipping away from the battlefield in order to keep a secret meeting with a lover, even during Queen *MEDB*'s invasion of Ulster. The magical transformation of Sir Bercilak de Hautdesert into the Green Knight was explained as the work of the witch *MORGAN LE FAY*, King Arthur's half-sister.

GERAINT see *CELTIC ROMANCE; SINGLE COMBAT*

GOIBHNIU was the Irish smith god and one of the *TUATHA DE DANANN*. He could make a perfect sword or spear with three blows of his magic hammer. Just before the second battle of Magh Tuireadh, a *FOMORII* spy came to see how Goibhniu made such impressive weapons, and even wounded the god. Goibhniu was said to preside over an otherworld feast called *Fled Goibnenn*, for which he brewed the ale. His Welsh counterpart was named Govannon.

THE GRAIL see *SANGREAL*; see also *WONDROUS CAULDRONS*; *HEROIC QUESTS*.

GRAINNE, in Irish mythology, was the daughter of *CORMAC MAC ART*, the High King of Ireland. She was promised to *FINN MACCOOL*, leader of the *FIANNA*, the body-guard of the High King. Although still powerful, Finn MacCool was quite old and Grainne preferred *DIARMUID UA DUIBHNE*, who was

GOIBHNIU, the Irish smith god, was an outstanding craftsman and armourer. Along with his gifted brothers, Creidhne the goldsmith, and Luchtar, the carpenter, he repaired the Tuatha De Danann armour with miraculous speed on the battlefield. (ILLUSTRATION ANON.)

the foster-son of the love god *AONGHUS*. By using magic, Grainne managed to escape from Tara, the Irish capital, with a rather reluctant Diarmuid. Gradually, however, he came to love Grainne, although for sixteen years they had to keep moving in order to avoid capture

by the Fenians. But Diarmuid was killed by a magic boar in a hunting accident after Cormac Mac Art and Finn MacCool had finally accepted his marriage to Grainne. Although Grainne blamed Finn MacCool for Diarmuid's death and swore to obtain vengeance through her four sons, the wily Finn wooed her until she agreed to marry him.

GUINEVERE, whose Welsh name, Gwenhwyfar, probably means "white spirit", was the wife of *ARTHUR* and the secret lover of Sir *LANCELOT*. In the stories about the Knights of the Round Table, Guinevere is always compared with Helen of Troy, the famous beauty of Greek mythology. Such a comparison is not unjustified, for both these women brought disaster to those who loved them. In Guinevere's case the love affair with Sir Lancelot weakened the unity of the Round Table. It was her beauty that also attracted Arthur's nephew Sir *MODRED*, who seized Camelot

GRAINNE (above), a passionate and wilful maiden, fell for the irresistible Diarmuid. As she was betrothed to Finn MacCool, Diarmuid politely refused her advances. But she persisted until he agreed to elope, with the Fianna in hot pursuit. Here, the guilty pair hide in a magic tree. (ILLUSTRATION ANON.)

GUINEVERE (below), in her original role as Flower Bride, is crowned May Queen in a bower of petals. On May Morning, Arthur and his knights celebrated with sports and contests. Lancelot, her champion, always excelled. (LANCELOT AND GUINEVERE BY HERBERT DRAPER, CANVAS, 1900.)

I

GUINEVERE (above), condemned to death for her affair with Lancelot, was rescued by him. In the bloody contest that ensued, Lancelot slew many knights. Arthur wept at the loss of "the fairest fellowship of noble knights". (LANCELOT RESCUES GUINEVERE BY W HATHERELL, CANVAS, C. 1910.)

and forced Guinevere to consent to marry him during the king's absence abroad. The confrontation between Arthur and Modred at the battle of Camlan brought to a bloody end the golden age of British chivalry, as hardly a knight was left alive. Arthur, mortally wounded, was taken to AVALON, while Guinevere became a nun at Amesbury, where she later died. It is believed by some that her body was buried at Glastonbury, not far from Arthur's tomb. (See also CELTIC ROMANCE)

GWERN, according to Welsh mythology, was the son of the Irish king MATHOLWCH and the Welsh princess BRANWEN. A dispute between the two royal families led to Branwen becoming a cook, which caused her brother, BRAN THE BLESSED, to sail to Ireland to avenge the insult. Matholwch suggested a compromise to settle the

quarrel. He proposed that Gwern, though only three, should be placed on the Irish throne. But Branwen's half-brother EFNISIEN would not agree and threw the child on to a fire.

GWYDION was the nephew of MATH, lord of the Welsh kingdom of Gwynedd. In order to help his brother, Gilvaethwy, sleep with Gowein, the young woman who was Math's footholder, Gwydion stirred up a quarrel between Math and PRYDERI, which meant that the king went away to war. When Math returned and discovered the deception, he turned his nephews into a stag and a hind for one year, into a boar and a sow for the next, and into a pair of wolves for the third. Later, Gwydion took charge of his sister ARIANRHOD's son LLEU.

GWION BACH see TALIESIN.

GWYN AP NUDD, in Welsh mythology, was an otherworld king who crossed swords with King ARTHUR. Gwyn abducted Griddylad, the daughter of Lludd Llaw Ereint, on her wedding day. According to one late myth, Lludd Llaw Ereint was the son of the death god Beli

and the builder of London. King Arthur set out after Griddylad and demanded that Gwyn ap Nudd return her to her rightful husband, his loyal follower Gwythyr. The siege of the otherworld king's castle proved to be long and difficult, so a strange compromise was agreed by both sides. Gwyn ap Nudd and Gwythyr agreed to meet in combat each May Day until the end of time; whoever was the winner on doomsday could have Griddylad.

HELLAWES see SAGES AND SEERS.

IRNAN, in Irish mythology, was a witch who once spun a magic web to catch some members of the FIANNA, or Fenians, the bodyguard of the High King of Ireland. When this plan failed, Irnan changed herself into a monster and challenged any one of the Fenians to single combat. FINN MACCOOL, the leader of the Fenians, stepped forward but was persuaded that it would not be heroic enough for a warrior of his stature to fight a hag, even if she was in the form of a monster. So another Fenian, Goll, slew Irnan and as a reward Finn allowed him to marry his daughter.

GWYDION (above) and Gilvaethwy flee from Pryderi's castle with his precious swine. The daring theft was part of an ingenious plan to help Gilvaethwy win Gowein. A resourceful magician, Gwydion had tricked Pryderi into exchanging his swine for some illusory horses. (ILLUSTRATION BY ALAN LEE, 1984.)

IRNAN (below) was one of three sister witches. She spun a magic web to snare the Fenian warriors. The warriors were rescued by Goll who slew two of the sisters, but spared Irnan when she begged for mercy. However, Irnan instantly changed into a monster and Goll killed her. (ILLUSTRATION BY STEPHEN REID, 1910.)

ISEULT, sometimes Isolde, was an Irish princess, and the story of her love for *TRISTAN* was extremely popular in medieval times. The Celtic myth of Tristan and Iseult originated in Brittany and was retold in almost every European country. It became attached to the Arthurian stories by the later addition of *ARTHUR* to the myth.

Iseult, a beautiful woman with wonderful golden hair, cured the orphan Tristan of a wound in the side; a lingering ailment similar to the one afflicting the "Maimed King" in the story of the Grail. On Tristan's arrival in Cornwall, his uncle King *MARK* wanted to name the young man his successor, but the nobles objected to this arrangement, so the king said that he would marry only the girl to whom belonged the golden hair a swallow had just dropped. Sir Tristan, recognizing the hair as belonging to Iseult, suggested to his uncle that he should go on his behalf to ask for her hand.

Disguised as a Cornish trader, Sir Tristan arrived in Ireland to find the country terrorized by a dragon,

ISEULT (below), an Irish beauty, was also a gifted healer, and cured the Cornish knight Tristan of a lingering wound. While nursing him to health, they fell in love, but their bliss was shortlived as Tristan was forced to leave the Irish court for political reasons. (ILLUSTRATION BY EVELYN PAUL, C. 1900.)

an enormous "crested serpent". Realizing that the best way to advance King Mark's suit would be to slay this monster, Sir Tristan sought out its lair and fought it. Although he just managed to overcome the dragon, its poisonous breath weakened him temporarily and an imposter claimed to have won the contest. Iseult and her mother, however, suspected trickery and discovered the injured young knight. While they were nursing Sir Tristan back to health, Iseult noticed that his sword had a piece missing exactly like the fragment of metal found in the head of *MORHOLT*, the Irish champion. Sir Tristan had mortally wounded him on the last occasion the Irish tried to collect tribute from Cornwall.

Iseult wanted to kill Sir Tristan in revenge, but she found that her heart would not let her wield the sword against him. It came as a

shock then, on his recovery, that Sir Tristan asked for Iseult on behalf of King Mark. When her own father readily agreed to the marriage as a means of restoring good relations between Ireland and Cornwall, Iseult was deeply upset. But her mother gave Iseult's maid *BRANGAINE* a love potion which, if drunk on their wedding night, would make the couple love each other forever. All would have been well had not Tristan accidentally drunk the potion and given some to Iseult on the journey to King Mark's court. Although Iseult did marry the Cornish king, on the wedding night, under the cover of darkness, Brangaine took her place in the royal bed so that he would suspect nothing. For a time the lovers managed to meet in secret, but, like the love of *GUINEVERE* and *LANCELOT*, they were eventually discovered. It happened one day

ISEULT and Tristan unwittingly drank a love philtre which heightened their already awakened passion, forging an unbreakable and finally tragic bond. Duncan's strongly Celtic portrayal captures the intense and undying nature of their love. (TRISTAN AND ISOLDE BY JOHN DUNCAN, CANVAS, 1912.)

that King Mark found them asleep with Sir Tristan's sword between them, but he decided not to slay them there and then. Instead he exchanged Sir Tristan's sword for his own and left them sleeping. Overcome by the mercy shown by his uncle, Tristan persuaded Iseult to return to her husband and he left for voluntary exile in Brittany.

In Brittany Sir Tristan married but without happiness. On several occasions he returned to Cornwall in disguise and secretly met Iseult again, but war took up most of his energies. A serious wound forced Sir Tristan to send for Iseult. It was

K

agreed that Iseult should indicate her imminent arrival with a white sail. Jealous of the reunion of the lovers, Sir Tristan's Breton wife said a ship with a black sail had been sighted. Tristan lost the will to live and threw himself on his sword before Iseult could land and reach his bedside. Iseult followed him into death shortly afterwards.

Stories about elopements, courtships and ill-fated lovers were always popular with the Celts, for whom this story of frustrated passion held great appeal. (See also CELTIC ROMANCE)

ITH was said to have dwelt in a great tower in Spain, from which he was able to see Ireland and so decided to go there. He landed with ninety followers just after the TUATHA DE DANANN had defeated the FOMORII at the second battle of Magh Tuireadh. The Tuatha De Danann suspected Ith of harbouring invasion plans and so killed him. When his body was returned to Spain, his sons swore to conquer the island. The leader of this

IUBDAN (below), one of the Wee Folk, was inclined to brag of his greatness, inciting his bard to cut him down to size by insisting that far greater men lived in Ulster, a veritable race of giants. To prove his valour, Iubdan ventured off to the dun of the "giant", Fergus Mac Leda. (ILLUSTRATION BY STEPHEN REID, 1910.)

invasion of Ireland, the last to be recorded in Irish mythology, was Ith's uncle Mil, or MILESIUS.

IUBDAN was a ruler of tiny people. According to Irish mythology, King Iubdan liked to boast a lot; to put a stop to this annoying habit his court poet told him that Ulster was a land of giants. He even made King Iubdan and his wife, Queen Bebo, travel there in secret and try the porridge of the king of Ulster, Fergus Mac Leda. Unfortunately, Iubdan fell into the porridge and, along with his wife, was taken prisoner by Fergus. No ransom offer proved acceptable to the king of Ulster, although the tiny people offered him an abundant crop of corn. So they went on to the offensive: milk became scarce, rivers and wells were made foul and polluted, mills burned and during the nights the

JOSEPH OF ARIMATHEA (above), the man who interred Christ's body in his own tomb, is believed to have brought the Grail to Glastonbury. After building a church for it where Glastonbury Abbey now stands, he founded a family of Grail Guardians. (MANUSCRIPT ILLUSTRATION C. 1450.)

hair of men and women was entirely cut off. After a year and a day of this harassment Fergus Mac Leda eventually agreed to release Iubdan and Bebo, but only on the condition that in return he was given the king's most valuable and treasured possession, a pair of magic shoes. Whoever wore these shoes was able to travel underwater or across the surface as if walking on dry land; when Fergus Mac Leda put them on they grew to fit his feet exactly. Echoes of the tiny people in this Irish myth can be found in Jonathan Swift's novel, *Gulliver's Travels*.

KAI (above), Arthur's steward, was a knight of legendary might and prowess. Endowed with unusual skills, he could go for nine days underwater and could grow as tall as a forest tree at will. He was very gruff, thwarting both Peredur and Culhwch at the gate. (MANUSCRIPT ILLUSTRATION C. 1450.)

JOSEPH OF ARIMATHEA was a biblical figure who was included in Arthurian mythology because of the Grail story. Joseph allowed Christ's body to be placed in his own tomb. His own long life was said to have been due to the Grail. Either Joseph, or his brother-in-law Bron with his son Alan, brought the Grail to Glastonbury. Later, it disappeared and its recovery was the greatest quest for the Knights of the Round Table. Only GALAHAD was granted a complete vision of the Grail. It was handed to him by Joseph of Arimathea, a "bishop already dead for more than three hundred years"; this "good man took Our Lord's body between his hands, and offered it to Sir Galahad, who received it with humble joy".

KAI, in Welsh mythology, was one of the senior warriors of ARTHUR's court. In medieval romance, he became the steward Sir Kay. In one tradition, he is a Cornishman and Arthur's foster-brother. He was said to have magical powers: he could go nine days and nine nights without sleep and breathe for nine days and nine nights under water.

KAY see KAI

CELTIC ROMANCE

THE LIVELY AND COMPELLING character of Celtic romance stems from the heated rivalries and passions of the lovers. Most, if not all, tales involve a love triangle with two men contesting one desirable woman. Sometimes one of the rivals is young and handsome, while the other is an oppressive guardian, as in the tale of Naoise and Conchobhar; elsewhere, the two suitors are simply rival admirers, one loved and the other despised, as in the case of Pwyll and Gwawl. This recurrent rivalry probably symbolizes a seasonal battle between a Lord of Summer and a Lord of Winter for the Spring Maiden. Celtic love triangles create tension, drama and colourful characters of timeless appeal. The attractive young heroes, such as raven-haired Naoise, or Diarmuid of the Love-Spot, are quite as irresistible as the ravishing Celtic beauties, Deirdre and Fand. While all the characters are portrayed with touching flaws, the heroines emerge as strong and independent women, expressing warmth and wisdom.

LANCELOT (above) and Guinevere's abiding love for each other wounded Arthur, shook his court and split the Fellowship of Knights. Yet both lovers are portrayed by Malory as essentially good but tragic characters. Even Arthur realized that Guinevere had been true to him in her way as a generous and faithful consort, and he was never lessened by their love. Here, the couple kiss at their first meeting, contrived by Galleot in an embroidered medieval setting. Although their love grew out of the courtly tradition, it went far beyond what the courtly code would have allowed. (MANUSCRIPT ILLUSTRATION C. 1400.)

TRISTAN (above) and Iseult snatch a tense moment together in their clandestine romance. They had grown obsessively attached to one another after accidentally drinking a love philtre intended for Iseult and her betrothed, King Mark of Cornwall. The doomed lovers embarked on a desperate and tragic romance, fraught with guilt and unrequited longings. (TRISTAN AND ISOLDE BY A W TURNBALL, CANVAS, 1904.)

THE LADY OF THE FOUNTAIN (right), *a shining vision in gold, appeared to young Owain as the fairest, wisest, noblest, most chaste, most generous woman in the world. But, as Owain had just slain her husband, the Black Knight, he had to press his suit with care. The Lady's faithful handmaiden, Luned, helped Owain woo her mistress by reminding her that the realm required a strong guardian. Luned here escorts Owain to her Lady's chamber.* (ILLUSTRATION BY ALAN LEE, 1984.)

FAND (above), *a breathtaking beauty from the otherworld, set her heart on the Ulster hero, Cuchulainn, and lured him to her realm to fight a Fomorii giant. After a month in her delightful company, the two arranged a tryst where the hero's wife, Emer, joined them, lamenting, "What's new is sweet, what's well-known is sour…" Her heartfelt plea inspired the generous Fand to give up her beloved Cuchulainn, realizing that he had a worthy mate in Emer.* (ETAIN, HELEN, MAEV AND FAND BY HARRY CLARKE, GLASS, DETAIL, C. 1900.)

GERAINT (right), *suspecting his wife of infidelity, forced her to accompany him on a gruelling journey of errands, and so tested her love and obedience every step of the way. Like other strong-minded Celtic heroines, Enid endured her ordeal calmly, remaining loyal and loving throughout. Geraint, for his part, finally felt "two sorrows" of remorse for having mistrusted and mistreated her so. At one stage in their journey, the pair passed through a wonderful walled tower, as seen here.* (ILLUSTRATION BY ALAN LEE, 1984.)

L

LAEG, *charioteer of Cuchulainn, drove the hero on all his adventures, acted as scout and comrade and finally cast himself in front of a spear meant for his master. War chariots played a key role in Celtic battle, with driver and warrior acting as a single unit. (ILLUSTRATION BY J LEYENDECKER, 1916.)*

LANCELOT, *most handsome and gifted of Arthur's knights, attracted both mortal and immortal queens. Four fairy queens here kidnap the sleeping knight and hold him in their castle, demanding that he choose one of them to be his mistress. (HOW FOUR FAIRY QUEENS FOUND LANCELOT SLEEPING BY W F CALDERON, CANVAS, C. 1900.)*

LAEG was CUCHULAINN's charioteer. The Celts were renowned in the ancient world for their skill in handling chariots on the battlefield, and Laeg's skill was crucial to many of Cuchulainn's victories. He was also a great friend and companion. When FAND invited Cuchulainn to the Land of Promise, he sent Laeg before him to survey the place. During Cuchulainn's final and mortal combat, Laeg threw himself in front of a spear aimed at his master. Id, Laeg's brother, was charioteer to CONALL Caernach.

LANCELOT was one of the greatest and noblest knights in the Arthurian tales. He was known as Lancelot of the Lake because the Lady of the Lake had plunged him into a magic pool when he was a child. Sir Lancelot, described as "the flower of knights", was very attractive to women, not unlike the handsome Irish warrior DIARMUID UA DUIBHNE. Once King ARTHUR's half-sister and enemy MORGAN LE FAY cast a spell over the sleeping knight and shut him in a dungeon. There she demanded that he must choose among four enchantresses who would be his "paramour", or

mistress. When he turned them all down, including Morgan Le Fay, the knight admitted his love for GUINEVERE. All of Sir Lancelot's great adventures and exploits were indeed informed by this secret love. For a time Queen Guinevere would not allow Sir Lancelot to come to her, but they eventually became lovers. Sir Meliagaunt, however, was suspicious and confronted Sir Lancelot in the presence of King Arthur and Queen Guinevere. A tournament was held to discover the truth. "With such great force Sir Lancelot smote Sir Meliagaunt on the helmet that the stroke carved the head into two parts."

LANCELOT, *after much fasting and praying, came at last to Carbonek, the Grail Castle. Being tainted with sin, he could not enter but was granted a vision. When he stepped too close he was struck by fire and left dazed for 24 days. (LANCELOT REFUSED THE GRAIL BY E BURNE-JONES, CANVAS, 1870.)*

Honour seemed satisfied and the reputation of Arthur's queen also appeared unblemished, but there were other Knights of the Round Table who could not accept this judgement by arms. So Sir Agravain and Sir MODRED led twelve knights to Guinevere's chamber and surprised the lovers. Although Sir Lancelot managed to make a fighting exit and several days later saved Queen Guinevere from being burnt to death, his actions effectively split the Round Table and weakened the strength of King Arthur's realm. First, Arthur conducted an unsuccessful siege of Sir Lancelot's castle in Brittany. Then a second and more deadly challenge to the king's authority came from Sir Modred, his nephew. In the subsequent battle at Camlan, near Salisbury, most of the Knights of the Round Table were slain. King Arthur was mortally wounded and taken by a magic boat to AVALON. Queen Guinevere retreated from the world and became a nun at Amesbury, where she died. Sir Lancelot and Guinevere met only once more before the knight renounced the ways of war to lead the life of a hermit. (See also CELTIC ROMANCE)

MATHOLWCH'S (left) convoy of ships glides up to the ragged Welsh shore in the prelude to a doomed marriage between himself and Branwen, the beautiful sister of Bran the Blessed. The ships had ensigns of brocaded silk and an uptilted shield as a sign of peace. (ILLUSTRATION BY ALAN LEE, 1984.)

MEDB (above), the magnificent but malevolent queen of Connacht, was a warrior who fought as fiercely as Morrigan. A wild and wilful woman, she precipitated and perpetuated the bloody war with Ulster in which Cuchulainn and other heroes lost their lives. (ILLUSTRATION BY J LEYENDECKER, 1916.)

MATH was the brother of the Welsh mother goddess *DON* and a great magician. At the time that *PRYDERI* ruled over Dyfed in the southern part of Wales, Math was the lord of Gwynedd in the north. Except during war, Math could only live if his feet were held in the lap of a virgin. When Gilvaethwy, one of his nephews, fell in love with the young woman who held Math's feet in her lap, his brother, *GWYDION*, tricked Math into going to war with Pryderi so that the girl might be left behind. On discovering that he had been deceived, however, the furious Math turned his nephews into animals.

MATHOLWCH, in Welsh mythology, was the Irish king married to *BRANWEN*, the sister of *BRAN THE BLESSED* and half-sister of *EFNISIEN*. Efnisien, because he claimed that he had not been consulted over Branwen's wedding, "cut off the lips of Matholwch's horses at their teeth, their ears to their heads, and their tails to their bodies". Later, when Bran took his army to Ireland to avenge the insult of Branwen being made a cook, Efnisien tossed Matholwch's three-year-old son *GWERN* into a fire. In the battle that followed, nearly all the Britons were killed and all of the Irish except for five pregnant women.

MAXEN see *FABULOUS VOYAGES*

MEDB, also known as Maeve, was the warrior-queen of Connacht. According to Irish mythology, no king could reign in Connacht unless he was married to Medb, who was believed to hold the kingdom's sovereignty in her person. It was also said that she "never was without one man in the shadow of another". Medb's most famous action was the invasion of Ulster, when her forces captured the great brown bull of Cuailgne and killed the Ulster hero *CUCHULAINN*. She was herself slain by Forbai, the son of King *CONCHOBHAR MAC NESSA*, while she was bathing in a pool. Forbai had discovered that Queen Medb was in the habit of regularly taking her bath in a Galway pool. He very carefully measured the exact distance between the spot where she bathed and the shore, then he returned to the Ulster stronghold of Emain Macha and practised with a sling-shot until he was able to knock an apple from the top of a pole over the same distance. Satisfied at last that his aim was perfect, he stealthily made his way back to the pool and hit Queen Medb in the centre of her forehead using his sling-shot. Thus was Ulster revenged.

149

SINGLE COMBAT

I N WAR, THE ANCIENT CELTS relied on heroic single combat, rather than all-out warfare, as a means of settling disputes. Shortage of manpower forbade multiple pitched battles. Instead, chosen champions, such as Cuchulainn or Morholt, duelled to the death. Even in a large-scale epic war, like the campaign of Cuailgne, the Ulster champion fought in single combat every day with a different warrior. In the Arthurian legends, single combat continued in the form of knightly jousts. While the Celtic heroes wore scant armour, Arthur's mounted knights encased themselves in glittering iron. In addition to the basic weapons of spear, sword, sling and shield, the hero of legend had recourse to magical skills and a range of enchanted weapons, such as Arthur's Excalibur or Fergus Mac Roth's Caladcholg, the original Excalibur.

CUCHULAINN (left), the Irish champion, enjoys a short respite between battles. Exhausted by continual combat, he suffered from chronic lack of sleep, snatching cat-naps between duels. Once, his father Lugh, pitying him, cast the hero into a magical sleep for three days and nights, during which he healed all his wounds. When Cuchulainn defended Ulster alone against the forces of Medb, he confronted chosen champions one by one. Between duels, the restless hero harassed the army with his sling. (*ILLUSTRATION BY YVONNE GILBERT, 1994.*)

CELTIC CAVALRY (right) ride their battle horses to war, armed with spears and crested helmets. Their comrades on foot wear breeches and caps, and bear spears and long bossed shields, while trumpeters bring up the rear. The Celts were heavily reliant on their long shields, which were usually made of wood and sometimes covered with decorative bronze work. Other sharp-rimmed shields could also be used as missile weapons. (*GUNDESTRUP CAULDRON, GILDED SILVER, C. 100 BC.*)

GERAINT (left) and the Knight of the Kestrel engage in single combat with such ferocity that they shatter each other's armour. Ostensibly, the duel was over the kestrel, but really Geraint was intent on avenging an insult to Guinevere's handmaiden, made by the knight's dwarf. Goaded on by their seconds, both champions fought tirelessly, until Geraint's rage gave him the edge and he overcame, but spared, the knight. (ILLUSTRATION BY ALAN LEE, 1984.)

OWAIN'S (below) kindness to a lion earned him a faithful friend who proved to be a valiant comrade-in-arms. In this unequal match, the giant was winning until Owain's lion leapt to Owain's defence. When the giant complained that he could handle Owain well enough if it were not for his lion, Owain pushed his pet back into the fortress, but the irrepressible creature leapt over the fortress walls and mauled the giant to death. (ILLUSTRATION BY ALAN LEE, 1984.)

HOW MORGAN LE FAY GAVE A SHIELD TO SIR TRISTRAM

MORGAN LE FAY (above) charmed the unsuspecting Tristram into accepting a beautiful gold shield decorated with a strange motif. The shield's design portrayed a knight, Lancelot, enslaving a royal couple, Arthur and his wife. Innocent of the shield's true motif or motive, Tristram rode to Arthur's court and jousted in the royal tournament. When he duelled with Arthur, the king's spear shattered on the enchanted shield. Such enchanted weapons could help or hinder the best of heroes. (ILLUSTRATION BY AUBREY BEARDSLEY, C. 1870.)

MERLIN, sometimes Myrddin, was the famous wizard of Arthurian mythology. So powerful was his magic that one medieval tradition credits him with the magical construction of Stonehenge, the outstanding British monument that has survived from ancient times. Another of his works was supposed to be King ARTHUR's famous Round Table, a late copy of which can still be seen at Winchester today.

Merlin's birth was the subject of a strange story. Apparently, the Britons were told that a great fortress they had built on Salisbury plain, possibly near Stonehenge, would never be safe until the ground there had been soaked by the blood of a child who had no

MERLIN (below), for all his wisdom, was bewitched by the Lady of the Lake who turned his love to her own ends. She sapped his power and plundered his store of secret knowledge, and when done, she bound him in stone by his own spells. (MERLIN AND NIMUE BY E BURNE-JONES, CANVAS, C. 1870.)

MERLIN (left), sage from another world, was an inspired seer and mystic mage, a wise counsellor and faithful friend to three able kings. This powerful portrayal captures the mystical and visionary nature of Celtic bards, rooted in a deep affinity with nature. (MERLIN BY ALAN LEE, CANVAS, 1984.)

MIDIR (right), one of the Tuatha De Danann, appeared at the palace of Tara to carry off Etain, the Ulster woman he loved, long since lost to him by enchantment. The pair drifted upwards and disappeared through a palace window, and flew to an otherworld. (ILLUSTRATION BY STEPHEN REID, 1910.)

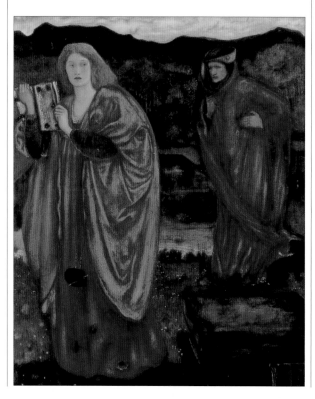

mortal father. Such a half-human sacrifice seemed impossible to achieve, until it was learned that a beautiful girl was with child by a demon. The child turned out to be Merlin, who, though baptized as a Christian, still possessed fabulous powers inherited from his demon father. Somehow the boy did not need to be sacrificed for the sake of the fortress because it is likely that Merlin was able to deal with the problem by means of magic. Two dragons were, in fact, responsible for the problem.

This mixture of pre-Christian and Christian ideas sits strangely with Merlin's later assistance to King Arthur, whose father UTHER PENDRAGON was said to have successfully invaded Britain about this time. Merlin sided with Uther and employed his powers to enable him to sleep with Igraine, the wife of a Cornish nobleman, by disguising him as her husband. Due to this deception Arthur was conceived. Once he ascended the throne, King Arthur had Merlin as his trusted advisor and often used the wizard as a messenger because, as with many of the Celtic gods and goddesses, he could assume any shape he pleased.

There are various accounts of Merlin's death. One tells how the wizard forgot about the seat at the Round Table that only GALAHAD could use, being the only knight worthy enough to see the GRAIL. Merlin sat down and was at once swallowed up by the earth, like other sinful men who had tried it before him. Another story blames the wizard's death on his passion for women. Either Viviane, possibly the Lady of the Lake, or Nimue, the daughter of a Sicilian siren, imprisoned him in an enchanted wood after Merlin had explained all about the secrets of his own magic. As Merlin told Sir GAWAIN, who once

passed by: "I am also the greatest fool. I love another more than I love myself, and I taught my beloved how to bind me to herself, and now no one can set me free." (See also SAGES AND SEERS; MAGIC AND ENCHANTMENT)

MIDIR, in Irish mythology, was the proud son of DAGDA, father of the gods. Unlike his father, who is usually portrayed as a rough, coarse figure, Midir always appeared as a splendidly dressed young man. Midir's first wife was Fuamnach, the daughter of Beothach. She became furious with jealousy when Midir married a second wife, ETAIN, from Ulster. With a druid's aid, Fuamnach turned Etain first into a pool, then into a worm and finally into a fly in order to keep her away from Midir. As a fly Etain was swallowed by the wife of Etar, an Ulster warrior, and reborn as the wife of the High King of Ireland. Although Midir recovered Etain, he had to accept in the end that she was the High King's consort and leave her alone. Midir also had some difficulty in accepting his father's successors as leaders of the TUATHA DE DANANN. The conflict that he started seems to have had a dangerously weakening effect on this generation of gods just before the invasion of the Milesians, who then went on to defeat the gods.

MIL OR MILE see MILESIUS

MILESIUS sails for Ireland to avenge the death of his nephew, Ith, who was slain by the Tuatha De Danann, rulers of Ireland. Although Milesius did not reach shore himself, his family succeeded, defeating the De Danann who retreated into an invisible otherworld. (ILLUSTRATION BY STEPHEN REID, 1910.)

MILESIUS, sometimes Mil or Mile, was the name given to a Spanish soldier whose sons were said to have organized the final invasion of Ireland. The murder there of their kinsman *ITH* caused the Milesians to take revenge by conquering the island. This they achieved by defeating the *TUATHA DE DANANN*, "the people of the goddess Dana", the existing rulers. Following the final decisive battle between the two forces, which the Milesians won, the Tuatha De Danann retired to an otherworld beneath the soil of Ireland.

MODRED was the treacherous nephew of King *ARTHUR*. While he was away waging war in Brittany, Arthur had appointed Modred his regent, but his scheming nephew tried instead to take the throne and force *GUINEVERE* to marry him. On the king's return, a terrible battle was fought near Salisbury and most of the Knights of the Round Table were killed, including Modred. Arthur, who had been mortally wounded during the battle, was then taken to *AVALON* in a black boat by three mysterious women.

MONGAN was the son of the Manx sea god *MANANNAN MAC LIR*. According to Irish mythology, his conception had been made possible by the use of a deception akin to the one used by *MERLIN* so that *UTHER* could sleep with Igraine and so conceive *ARTHUR*. Manannan Mac Lir had assumed the shape of an Ulster king in order to sleep with his beautiful queen. When Mongan was three days old, his father took him to one of his other-world realms, the Land of Promise, where the boy remained until he had grown to manhood. It is claimed by some traditions that Mongan then returned to Ireland reincarnated as *FINN MACCOOL*, the famous leader of the *FIANNA*, but in other accounts he retained his own identity. The stories about Mongan describe how he used his shape-changing ability to get his own way, and mention in particular the recovery of his wife Dubh Lacha. He had inherited the divine ability of metamorphosis from his father.

MORGAN LE FAY was King *ARTHUR*'s half-sister and in some versions of the story she is said to have been the mistress of Sir Accolon of Gaul. Throughout all the British myths that tell of Arthur's incredible reign Morgan Le Fay is always depicted as the king's implacable enemy, often plotting his downfall. According to one story she is supposed to have stolen the magic sword Excalibur and sent it to Accolon, who then challenged Arthur to single combat. When Accolon dropped the sword Arthur recognized it and the other knight admitted his guilt and surrendered. However, after the bloody battle against Arthur's rebellious nephew Sir *MODRED*, Morgan le Fay was one of the three women who took the grievously wounded king in a black boat to *AVALON*. The other two were "the Queen of Northgales and the Queen of Wastelands". (See also *SAGES AND SEERS; SINGLE COMBAT*)

MORGAN LE FAY'S (below) paradoxical nature is reflected in her dual role as both healer and dark magician, as Arthur's thorn in life, yet also his guardian in death. Although educated at a convent, she managed to emerge as a gifted magician. (MORGAN LE FAY BY A SANDYS, WOOD, 1864.)

MODRED (above), Arthur's treacherous nephew, abused his role of regent and usurped the throne, forcing Arthur to quash the rebel forces. Both perished in the final battle that ended the war and so came to an end the Arthurian golden age. (ARTHUR AND MODRED BY W HATHERELL, CANVAS, C.1910.)

N

MORHOLT was the gigantic brother of the king of Ireland, to whom King Mark and Cornwall were expected to pay an annual tribute. Mark's nephew *TRISTAN* was determined to put an end to this practice. He therefore sailed to Ireland and succeeded in killing Morholt, but not before he had been wounded by the giant's great poisoned sword. Before he died, Morholt told Tristan that only his sister *ISEULT* would be able to cure his poisoned wound.

MORRIGAN, sometimes known as Morrigu, was an Irish goddess of death on the battlefield who helped the *TUATHA DE DANANN* at both battles of Magh Tuireadh. She was associated with the other war deities *MACHA*, *BADB* and *NEMAIN*. Her favourite form was the crow, and as such she settled in triumph on the shoulder of the Ulster hero *CUCHULAINN* when he was finally killed in the war against Queen *MEDB*'s forces. Cuchulainn had not only refused Morrigan's love, but in anger he had even wounded her. For such a deed his fate was sealed.

MORRIGAN, the terrible goddess of war, appeared sometimes as a warrior in a battle, siding with her favourites. Most often she soared overhead as a raven or crow, shrieking and flapping her wings to scare the host, or to signify imminent death, as here. (ILLUSTRATION BY STEPHEN REID, 1910.)

MORHOLT, the Irish champion, confronts Tristan, the Cornish newcomer, in a duel over Irish taxes. Despite Morholt's greater power and skill, the young Tristan fought like a mighty lion and dealt the older knight a mortal blow to his helm, lodging a piece of sword in his brain. (ILLUSTRATION BY EVELYN PAUL, C. 1900.)

NAOISE was the eldest son of Usna and his wife Elbha, daughter of *CATHBAD*. When *DEIRDRE* persuaded him to run away with her so that she could avoid marriage to the Ulster king *CONCHOBHAR MAC NESSA*, Naoise and his two brothers fled with her to Alba. Conchobhar sent *FERGUS MAC ROTH* to bring them all home. Suspicious of Conchobhar, but trusting Fergus' promise that no harm would come to them, Naoise agreed. In the event, Conchobhar had Naoise killed, and so enraged was Fergus Mac Roth that he joined the forces of Conchobhar's great enemy, Queen *MEDB* of Connacht.

NECHTAN was an Irish water god and, according to some versions, the husband of *BOANN*. On Nechtan's hill there was a holy well that was the source of all knowledge, to which only Nechtan and his three cup-bearers had access. When Boann found her way to the well, the waters rose from the ground and chased after her, becoming the River Boyne.

NEMAIN (whose name means "dreadful" or "venomous"), in Irish mythology, was a goddess of war. Along with *BABD*, *MORRIGAN* and *MACHA*, she formed one of a group of war deities who sometimes appeared as beautiful young women and sometimes as crows, screeching over the battlefield. Nemain was said to have been the wife of *NUADA*, the leader of the *TUATHA DE DANANN*.

NEMGLAN, an Irish bird god, fell in love with Mess Buachalla, the betrothed of Eterscel, High King of Ireland. On the eve of the wedding, Nemglan came to her in a bird skin and seduced her, and this was how she conceived *CONAIRE MOR*. The child was passed off as High King Eterscel's son, but Mess Buachalla was careful to warn the boy that he must never, whatever the circumstances might be, kill a bird. When Conaire Mor was a young man, Eterscel died and the question of the succession was raised in Tara, the Irish capital. Unknown to Conaire, there was a prophecy to the effect that Eterscel's successor would be a naked man walking along the road to Tara with a sling in his hand. It happened one day that Conaire was driving his

NAOISE elopes with the great Irish beauty, Deirdre. They fled across the sea to Scotland, pursued by Fergus Mac Roth. By Loch Ness, they found refuge and hunted deer and salmon, living in pastoral bliss until they were lured back to a deadly trap in Ireland by an unsuspecting Fergus Mac Roth. (ILLUSTRATION ANON.)

NEMAIN, one of the dreadful goddesses of war, appeared sometimes as a washer at the ford, presaging doom. Before his last combat, Cuchulainn saw a washer weeping and wailing as she rinsed a heap of bloody raiment belonging to the great hero. (ILLUSTRATION BY STEPHEN REID, 1910.)

chariot down this very road when a flock of birds with beautiful plumage descended upon him. Forgetting his mother's instruction never to harm any bird, he loaded his sling, at which point the birds immediately turned into armed warriors. The leader of these incredible warriors, however, introduced himself to Conaire as his real father Nemglan. To make up for his misconduct towards the birds, Conaire was told to undress and return home to Tara on foot, carrying only his sling. He thus became the next High King of Ireland.

NESSA, in Irish mythology, was the mother of *CONCHOBHAR MAC NESSA*, the Ulster ruler during the lifetime of the hero *CUCHULAINN*. Nessa's husband was King Fachtna of Ulster and when the king died his half-brother, *FERGUS MAC ROTH*, succeeded to the throne and proposed marriage to Nessa.

However, she would agree to the match only on the condition that her son should be allowed to rule Ulster for one year. Fergus Mac Roth was so in love with her that he readily agreed, but at the end of the year the people of Ulster refused to let Conchobhar step down from the throne, so excellent was his rule.

NEMGLAN, a bird god from an other-world, came to Mess Buachalla before her wedding to the High King. As he flew in, his plumage moulted to reveal a beautiful youth. Like Leda and Danae before her, she loved the god and bore him a son, Conaire Mor. (ILLUSTRATION BY NICK BEALE, 1995.)

NIAMH was the wife of *CONALL* Caernach. While *CUCHULAINN* was recovering from wounds sustained during the war against the men of Connacht, Niamh nursed him and became his mistress. She then tried to prevent him returning to battle. But the witch *BADB*, one of the daughters of *CALATIN*, cast a spell on Niamh so that she wandered away into the countryside. Badb then assumed the form of Niamh and told Cuchulainn that he must return to the war and fight.

NIAM OF THE GOLDEN HAIR was a daughter of the sea god *MANANNAN MAC LIR*. She fell in love with the poet *OISIN* and they lived happily together in the Land of Promise, which was one of the otherworld realms. Niam bore the poet a daughter, Plur nam Ban ("Flower of Woman").

NODENS was a British god of healing, whose magic hounds were also believed to be able to cure the sick. Nodens was worshipped during the Roman occupation; the ruins of a great temple have been found on the banks of the River Severn. In Ireland, he became *NUADA* of the Silver Hand and in Wales *NUDD* of the Silver Hand, also known as Llud to the Britons.

NUADA, also known as Nuada Airgetlamh ("Nuada of the Silver Hand"), because of a temporary replacement for a hand he lost at the first battle of Magh Tuireadh, was an important Irish god and leader of the *TUATHA DE DANANN*. He was married to *NEMAIN*. The De Danann were a younger generation of gods than the *FOMORII*, the sea gods who were soon to challenge them at the second battle of Magh Tuireadh. For a while between the two battles, Nuada appointed *BRES* as leader because of the loss of his hand. The silver replacement was made by *DIAN CECHT*. But Nuada was dissatisfied with it and turned to Dian Cecht's son Miach, who made him a new hand of flesh and blood. Dian Cecht slew Miach out of jealousy. Nuada's restoration as leader caused the second battle of Magh Tuireadh, because the half-Fomorii Bres complained to his kinsmen about his treatment.

At the second battle the lethal eye of *BALOR* killed both Nuada and Nemain before the sun god *LUGH* destroyed it with a sling-shot. Their victory saved the Tuatha De Danann, but later they in turn were defeated by the sons of *MILESIUS*. That Nuada was the great De Danann leader, there is no doubt. He is described as sitting on his throne "with a white light about him as it had been a fleece of silver, and round his head a wheel of light pulsed and beat with changing colours". Nuada is cognate with the Welsh *NUDD*.

NUDD, known as Llud to the British, is the Welsh equivalent of *NUADA*. He also had a silver hand, and in one tale was known as Llud Llawereint ("silver-handed").

NUDD, or Llud, ruled Britain at a time when it was plagued by a strange May Eve scream. It transpired that two subterranean dragons caused the scream during an annual battle. They were soothed by sinking mead into a pit dug through the centre of the earth. (ILLUSTRATION BY ALAN LEE, 1984.)

O

OGMA was the Irish god of eloquence and the inventor of Ogham, the earliest system of writing used in Ireland. Ogham is made up of a series of vertical or sloping lines inscribed on a base line. The sagas tell of vast libraries of Ogham writing, though only inscriptions in stone carvings have survived, and the sagas themselves were later recorded by monks using the Roman alphabet.

Ogma was a son of *DAGDA*, who was a god described as the "Lord of Knowledge". Besides having a truly remarkable skill as a poet, Ogma was a fighter like other Irish gods and also, like the the Greek god Hermes or the Roman Mercury, he was responsible for conveying souls to the otherworld. Whereas for the Greek and Roman messenger gods this was a sad duty, not least because the kingdom of Hades was not an inviting place, Ogma's task was a happier one since the Celtic otherworld was a delightful and peaceful resting-place for the soul prior to its next rebirth in the world. It is thought that Greek colonists in the western end of the

OISIN and the fairy maiden, Niamh, flew away on a snow-white steed through golden mist to the Land of Promise, which was a delightful otherworld beyond all dreams, filled with birdsong and scented flowers, with overflowing mead and wondrous creatures. (ILLUSTRATION BY STEPHEN REID, 1910.)

OGMA, god of eloquence, invented the Ogham script, consisting of vertical lines crossing a lateral baseline. Ogham messages were carved on stone and inscribed on barks and wands of hazel or aspen. Over 400 ancient messages have survived. (ILLUSTRATION BY NICK BEALE, 1995.)

Mediterranean first encountered the idea of the transmigration of souls from their Celtic neighbours. In the sixth century BC the famous and unusual Greek philosopher Pythagoras left the Aegean island of Samos and went to live in the city of Croton in southern Italy. He became extremely interested in the theory of reincarnation. His followers, who believed that the soul was immortal, accepted transmigration through animals and plants as well, and as a result proposed the kinship of all living things.

In some Irish myths Ogma is said to have married *ETAIN*, who was the daughter of the god of healing *DIAN CECHT*. At the second and final battle of Magh Tuireadh Ogma slew Indech, son of the *FOMORII* goddess Domnu. Indech was one of the leaders of the Fomorii, who were the older sea gods who had challenged the *TUATHA DE DANANN*, the younger generation of gods of which Ogma was one. After the terrible battle was over and the De Danann were victorious, Ogma claimed as his prize a magic Fomorii sword that was capable of recounting all the deeds it had performed.

OISIN, sometimes Ossian, was the son of the Fenian, or *FIANNA*, leader *FINN MACCOOL*. According to Irish mythology, Oisin was the greatest poet in Ireland, perhaps not a surprising achievement considering how as a young man his father had eaten the Salmon of Knowledge. Oisin's mother was none other than the goddess *SADB*, the granddaughter of *DAGDA*. This made *OGMA*, the god of eloquence, Oisin's uncle.

One day, as Finn MacCool with his companions and dogs was returning homewards, a beautiful deer started up on their path and the ensuing chase took them towards Tara, the Irish capital and the base of the Fenians. At last the exhausted animal stopped and crouched down on the ground, but instead of attacking their quarry the hounds began to play round her, and even to lick her head and limbs. So Finn MacCool ordered that no harm should be done to the deer, which followed them on the way home until sunset.

That same night Finn MacCool awoke to find the most beautiful woman he had ever seen standing next to his bed. It was Sadb. She explained how a spell had been placed upon her, but that she had learned that if Finn MacCool came to love her, then all the enchantments would cease to have power and she could resume her normal shape. So it came to pass that Sadb lived with Finn MacCool as his mistress, and for months neither of them stirred from their dwelling. Then news arrived of invaders in ships off Dublin, most likely a Viking raid, and the Fenians were called to arms. For only one week Finn MacCool was absent dealing with the Vikings. On his return, however, he discovered that Sadb had been lured away by someone disguised as himself (a common trick among shape-changers in Irish mythology). Realizing that it must be the enchanter whom Sadb had rejected, Finn MacCool organized a search of every remote hill, valley and forest in the country, but without success. Eventually he gave up all hope of finding his mistress and returned to his pleasure of hunting. It happened, by chance, that his dogs tracked down a very strange quarry and Finn MacCool came upon them surrounding a naked boy with long hair. His two best hounds were, in fact, keeping the pack from seizing the child.

Having driven off the dogs, Finn MacCool and the other huntsmen regarded the boy with curiosity. He told them that he did not know the identity of his father, but that his mother was a gentle hind, with whom he lived in a quiet valley safely shut in by steep cliffs. To their home a tall, dark stranger came every now and again to see his mother, but she always shrank away in fear and the man left in anger. When the stranger finally

His famous adventure concerns *NIAMH*, the daughter of the sea god *MANANNAN MAC LIR*. Oisin met her while on a hunt by the shores of a lake. She suddenly appeared riding a horse with silver hooves and a golden mane. When Niamh told Oisin how she had travelled a great distance to invite him to her father's otherworld realm, the Land of Promise, he readily mounted the magic steed and was never seen by his father again. In the otherworld kingdom he fought against a *FOMORII* giant in an undersea combat worthy of his father. But after a number of other exploits Oisin began to miss his own land of Ireland. Niamh gave him her magic horse so that he could visit his home, but told him not to dismount otherwise he would never be allowed to return. Ireland appeared to Oisin almost a strange land, for everyone he knew had died long before. The people seemed far sadder and more careworn than the heroes he had grown up with. By chance he came upon a ragged group of men attempting to move a boulder, which he easily lifted for them while still seated on his mount. However, his saddle slipped and he fell to the ground. In an instant the magic horse vanished and the valiant young warrior was turned into a blind and frail old man.

A Christian addition to the end of this myth includes St Patrick. Because everyone took Oisin to be mad he cried out: "If your god has slain Finn MacCool, then I would say that he is a strong man." So he was taken to the saint, who recorded his strange tale and explained the changes to Ireland since the arrival of Christianity.

struck her with a magic hazel wand, the hind was forced to follow him, although she tried to comfort her son as she left.

As soon as the boy finished this account, Finn MacCool embraced him as his own son by Sadb, and immediately named him Oisin ("Little Fawn"). He was trained as a Fenian warrior, which involved one of the most difficult courses of training imaginable, and became a skilled fighter like his father, but he also inherited the gentler ability of eloquence from his mother, and his songs and poetry were admired throughout Ireland.

HEROIC QUESTS

THE THRILLING PURSUIT of a real or visionary goal forms the plot of many compelling tales of adventure. The goal is not always the most tantalizing part of the venture and might seem like a tedious or even trivial task, but serves to spur the traveller on his way. Other goals, such as the Grail, seem barely attainable, but serve as shining symbols of aspiration. The impetus is sometimes romantic, as when Culhwch set out to find fair Olwen; or retributory, as when Geraint went forth to avenge a wrong; while Peredur, Owain and the Grail Knights were inspired by otherworldly visions and ideals. Whatever the goal, the quest usually takes on a magic of its own, leading the hero down unexpected bypaths of adventure and discovery. *En route* he meets new friends and travelling companions, learns much-needed lessons and catches sight of even more tantalizing quests ahead.

OWAIN (above), inspired by the tale of Cynon, set off in search of the Castle of the Fountain, which was guarded by the Black Knight. He passed through the fairest vale until he saw a shining castle on the hill. After entering its otherworldly domain Culhwch defeated the Black Knight, and went on to woo his widow. After a rather difficult beginning, he overcame her resentment, and guarded her realm until his yen for adventure lured him off again. (ILLUSTRATION BY ALAN LEE, 1984.)

CAMELOT (left), Arthur's shining city-castle, drew knights from far and wide to join the Fellowship of the Round Table, inspired by ideals of courage, honour and vision. From Camelot, the questing knight set forth on journeys of adventure and discovery, to seek honour, to avenge wrongs and to win ladies and renown. The figure of the questing knight became a symbol of aspiration. (ILLUSTRATION BY ALAN LEE, 1984.)

THE GRAIL QUEST (right) proved to be the hardest, highest and greatest of all quests. Many knights set forth but few returned. When Arthur's warriors resolved to undertake the Grail Quest, Arthur wept, lamenting that the fairest fellowship of noble knights would never meet again around the table at Camelot. He was right, for few of his company were fitted for the quest and many perished. (THE ARMING AND DEPARTURE OF THE KNIGHTS BY E BURNE-JONES AND W MORRIS, TAPESTRY, 1895–96.)

CULHWCH'S (left) quest for the fair Olwen involved thirty-nine impossible tasks, the longest series of tasks in Celtic mythology. En route *the hero enlisted the help of Arthur's war-band who assisted Culhwch in one of his hardest tasks, which was the retrieval of a comb, razor and scissors from between the ears of the terrible, enchanted boar, Twrch Trwyth.* (ILLUSTRATION BY ALAN LEE, 1984.)

PEREDUR'S (above) quest for adventure led him through many wondrous lands. At one point he passed through a lovely river valley, filled with colourful pavilions and a wondrous multitude of windmills and water-mills. He lodged with the head miller and jousted in the tournament, defeating countless warriors with such skill and might that he impressed the local empress. After fighting her battles, he ruled with her for fourteen years before continuing his search for new adventures. (ILLUSTRATION BY ALAN LEE, 1984.)

159

OLWEN, in Welsh mythology, was the daughter of the giant Yspaddaden and her suitor was *CULHWCH*, one of King *ARTHUR*'s warriors. Culhwch's stepmother hated him so much that she cursed him to marry only Olwen, a girl whom the warrior came to love dearly. Yspaddaden was so upset by the obvious affection between Olwen and Culhwch that he set his daughter's lover a series of tasks in order to prevent the marriage. Among other things, Culhwch had to uproot a forest, burn the wood for fertilizer and plough the cleared land in one day; force *AMAETHON*, the god of agriculture, to nourish its crops; make the smith god Govannon forge tools for the work; bring four strong oxen to help; obtain magic seed; provide honey nine times sweeter than that of a virgin swarm; get a magic cup and a hamper of delicious meat; borrow the drinking-horn of the underwater king Gwyddbwyll and the magic harp belonging to Teirtu (an instrument that played itself); capture the birds of *RHIANNON*, whose song could wake the dead and lull the living to sleep; provide a magic cauldron; a boar's tusk for the giant to shave with and shaving cream made from a witch's blood;

OWAIN and Arthur (below) appear in a warrior's dream, playing gwyddbwyll. During the game, Arthur's knights battle with Owain's ravens, but the players simply play on, until Arthur smashes the pieces. The game symbolizes a battle, possibly for sovereignty. (ILLUSTRATION BY ALAN LEE, 1984.)

steal a magic dog, leash and collar; hire as a huntsman *MABON*, son of Modron, who had first to be released from prison; find a wonderful steed and swift hounds; steal a comb, scissors and a razor from between the ears of a fierce boar; and persuade a number of unlikely guests to come to Yspaddaden's stronghold. Undaunted by the

OLWEN (left), in flaming red, wanders through the otherworld, depicted here as a vibrant, brooding wooded idyll. Olwen was loved by Culhwch, a warrior of King Arthur's court, who had to go to great lengths to secure his bride.
(ILLUSTRATION BY ALAN LEE, 1984.)

sheer size and complexity of the challenges, Culhwch said that "King Arthur will provide horses and men to help him win Olwen". He also informed the giant that he would return to slay him. Culhwch succeeded and married Olwen "and she was his only wife as long as he lived". The giant was killed by one of Culhwch's fellow knights.

OWAIN (below) peers through the tangled branches of the wildwood, like a shy, wild creature. Overcome with shame after wronging his wife, he fled into the wilderness and lived as a wild man, wasting away until rescued by a noblewoman.
(ILLUSTRATION BY ALAN LEE, 1984.)

PARTHOLON (above) *found a lush, primal country when he first landed in Ireland. The forests and plains were alive with strange, shy and beautiful creatures. Partholon cleared the land for cultivation and in his time three new lakes appeared, one of which was named after his son.* (ILLUSTRATION BY ARTHUR RACKHAM, C. 1910.)

OSCAR, in Irish mythology, was the son of *OISIN* and the grandson of *FINN MACCOOL*. His name means "deer lover" and recalls his grandmother, the goddess *SADB*, whom Finn MacCool first encountered while he was hunting. Sadb had been changed into a hind by a spell, which Finn MacCool briefly lifted. Oscar's mother was Eibhir, who was said to be "a yellow-haired maiden from a warm country".

Oscar was a mighty fighter, one of the best of all the *FIANNA*, or Fenians, the warriors who acted as a bodyguard to the High King of Ireland. But he lived during a time when the ruler, Cairbe, felt that the Fenians had too much power, and

a bloody struggle ensued. High King Cairbe refused to pay the Fenians for their services and raised another band of fighters to replace them. In a battle fought at Gabhra, near present-day Dublin, Oscar killed Cairbe in single combat but was himself mortally wounded. According to one version of the myth, Finn MacCool returned briefly from the otherworld to mourn Oscar's death.

OWAIN, in Welsh mythology, was the son of *URIEN* and one of King *ARTHUR*'s warriors. When a fellow warrior named *CYNON* was defeated by a mysterious Black Knight, Owain set out to find this stranger. He severely wounded the Black Knight but did not unseat him, and when the knight galloped off to a nearby castle, he gave chase only to find himself almost a prisoner once he entered its walls. Owain was saved by a lady named Luned, who gave him a ring of invisibility. Soon the lord of the

castle, the Black Knight, died of the wound Owain had inflicted on him. Not deterred by her grief, Owain persuaded Luned to plead his cause with such success that his widow consented to marry him. Thus he became master of the Castle of the Fountain, as the Black Knight's stronghold was called. But the long absence of Owain worried King Arthur a great deal, so he sent out a party of knights to find him. Owain returned with them to King Arthur's court, and he gradually forgot about his wife.

When a very angry lady arrived at court to accuse Owain of deceit, treachery and unfaithfulness, he was overcome with shame. A remorseful Owain fled to the forest and pursued the solitary life of a hermit. There he would have died but for a well-born lady who used a magic potion to restore his health. Sir Owain took up his arms, slew a dragon and befriended a lion. The knight and the lion had numerous adventures, which included saving Luned from death by burning and slaying a giant. Owain returned to the Castle of the Fountain, where he was reconciled with his wife. They seem to have spent the rest of their lives together in King Arthur's court. (See also *CELTIC ROMANCE; SINGLE COMBAT; HEROIC QUESTS*)

PARSIFAL see *PERCIVAL*

PARTHOLON, son of Sera, was believed to have led one of the early invasions of Ireland. Together with twenty-four men and their wives, he is said to have come out of the west after the waters of the Flood had receded and cleared the island of trees ready for cultivation. According to the myth, after living in Ireland for some five thousand years, the race of Partholon were stricken by disease and they all died within the space of a week.

PELLES was one of the names given to the "Maimed King" of the *GRAIL* story in whose castle of Carbonek the holy vessel was kept. In other versions of the tale he is known as Amfortas. Pelles was said to have been the father of Elaine, who fell in love with Sir *LANCELOT* and bore him the pure knight Sir *GALAHAD*, who was the only one of *ARTHUR*'s knights granted a vision of the Grail and allowed to hold it.

PELLES, *the Grail King, guarded the Grail in Carbonek, the Grail Castle. Maimed by an incurable wound, symbolizing some spiritual imperfection, he lived in a twilight state, while his country wasted, awaiting the coming of Galahad, the redeeming knight.* (ILLUSTRATION BY ALAN LEE, 1984.)

PERCIVAL, who was also sometimes called Perceval or Parsifal in
different traditions, was in later
Arthurian mythology something of
an outsider. He was brought up in
a forest far from the court of
Camelot and was completely ignor-
ant of courtly manners. However,
he travelled to King *ARTHUR*'s court
and was duly made a knight, and
then set off in quest of the Grail,
the holy vessel that was used at the
Last Supper and which received the
blood that flowed from the spear
thrust in Christ's side at the time of
the Crucifixion. The Grail had been
brought to Britain by *JOSEPH OF
ARIMATHEA*, the rich man who had
allowed Christ's body to be placed
in his tomb. However, the Grail
was later lost and its recovery
became the great quest for the
Knights of the Round Table.

The purity of Sir Percival may
have meant that he was permitted
a brief glimpse of the Grail, but he
was denied the complete vision
and heavenly release that was eventually granted to Sir *GALAHAD*, Sir
LANCELOT's son. Only Galahad was
allowed to touch the Grail, "Our
Lord's body between his hands",
and then to die in the company of
angels. The mysterious Queen of
the Wastelands, one of the three
ladies who took the dying King
Arthur to *AVALON* after he had been
wounded in the battle against
MODRED, was Sir Percival's aunt.
On his personal quest for the Grail,
Sir Percival unfortunately fell somewhat short of the high standard of
conduct required for recovering the
Grail. One day on his journey he
encountered a wondrous and
mysterious ship and at once fell in
love with its beautiful owner.
Indeed, he was on the point of

entering her bed when, "by chance
and grace, Sir Percival saw his
unsheathed sword lying on the
ground, and on its pommel was a
red cross, the sign of the
Crucifixion, which reminded him
of his knightly duty to behave as a
good man. So he made the sign of
the cross on his forehead, at which
the boat was upended, then
changed into a cloud of black

smoke." So annoyed and filled with
remorse was Percival by this moral
lapse that he felt obliged to inflict a
punishment on the weakness of his
own flesh by wounding himself in
the thigh. Meanwhile, the enchantress who had attempted to waylay
him and divert him from his quest
"set off with the wind roaring and
yelling, that it seemed all the water
was burned after her".

PEREDUR, in Welsh mythology,
was the seventh son of Evrawg and
the only surviving male. His father
and brothers were killed before his
own coming of age. This did not
prevent Peredur from becoming
one of *ARTHUR*'s warriors and his
many adventures formed the basis
for the later stories about *PERCIVAL*.
Possibly because of his position as
a seventh son, always a significant

SANGREAL (above) was attained by three very different knights. Galahad, the purest, beheld its contents; Bors, the most worldly, returned to tell the tale; Percival, the simplest, became its guardian. (THE ATTAINMENT BY WILLIAM MORRIS, TAPESTRY, C. 1870.)

SCOTA was said to be the earliest known ancestor of the Scots. According to one version of the myth, she was the daughter of an Egyptian pharaoh. A wise teacher named Niul, who had settled in Egypt, became her husband and they had a child, Goidel, who gave his name to the Gaels. In another tradition, she was the wife of MILESIUS and was killed fighting the TUATHA DE DANANN.

SEARBHAN, in Irish mythology, was a FOMORII warrior, one of the ancient sea gods. This one-eyed, one-armed and one-legged fighter

guarded a magic tree, which no one dared approach. However, during the sixteen-year flight of GRAINNE and DIARMUID UA DUIBHNE from the FIANNA, the hard-pressed lovers managed to become friends with Searbhan and he allowed them to shelter in the branches of the magic tree, which made it difficult for FINN MACCOOL to find them. However, Searbhan and Diarmuid came to blows when Grainne attempted to eat some of the magic berries that grew on the tree, and the Fomorii warrior was slain.

SETANTA see CUCHULLAIN.

SUALTAM MAC ROTH, in Irish mythology, was the brother of FERGUS MAC ROTH. An Ulsterman, he accepted CUCHULAINN as his own son, although the hero's real father was the sun god LUGH. On

SEARBHAN (left), the surly one-eyed Fomorii giant, guarded a magic tree, squatting at its foot all day. The eloping lovers, Diarmuid Ua Duibhne and Grainne sheltered in its branches, but Grainne developed a craving for the tree's magic berries. This so enraged the giant that he and Diarmuid fought and the mighty Searbhan was slain with his own club. (ILLUSTRATION ANON.)

SUALTAM MAC ROTH'S (right) head rallied the Ulstermen to battle, even after his death. He had exhorted them in life without success, as they were weakened by Macha's curse. The cries of the severed head at last broke the spell and roused the men to fight. (ILLUSTRATION BY STEPHEN REID, 1910.)

the night of her wedding to Sualtam Mac Roth, DECHTIRE had swallowed a fly and fallen into a deep sleep. In this state she went to the otherworld with Lugh and there conceived Cuchulainn. While Cuchulainn was single-handedly defending Ulster against the invading forces of Queen MEDB of

Connacht, Sualtam Mac Roth attempted to gather the men of Ulster who had been weakened by MACHA's curse. So desperately did he turn his horse that Sualtam cut off his own head with the sharp edge of his shield. But the severed head continued the call to arms long enough to rouse the warriors.

169

T

SUIBHNE GEILT, "the mad one", in late Irish mythology was a king cursed by St Ronan. One day King Suibhne was outraged to learn that, without his permission, Ronan was founding a church on his land. Although his wife, Eorann, tried to restrain him, the king rushed to the new foundation, seized the saint's psalter and threw it in a nearby lake. He then laid hands on St Ronan, when a messenger arrived to summon him to an ally's aid on the battlefield. Next day an otter returned the psalter unharmed. St Ronan thanked heaven for this and cursed Suibhne, who assumed the characteristics of a bird, leaping from trees for seven years before his reason returned.

When St Ronan heard about this recovery, he prayed that the king would not return to persecute Christians. So Suibhne was once again on the brink of madness as headless bodies and severed heads harried him. Another priest took pity on the tormented man and wrote down his sad tale, after which Suibhne "died a Christian and his soul ascended to heaven".

TARANIS, "the thunderer", was a Celtic sky god whom the Romans equated with their supreme deity Jupiter. The wheel, which is sometimes used as a symbol of the sun in Celtic art, here represents the electric light of a thunderbolt, symbolized by the trident, a three-pronged spear. (ILLUSTRATION BY MIRANDA GRAY, 1994.)

TAILTU was the daughter of a ruler of the *FIRBOLG* and wife of Eochaidh Mac Erc, another Firbolg king. She was said to have cleared the forest of Breg so that it became a plain, a task which killed her. Because she was the foster-mother of the sun god *LUGH*, he declared that the festival of Lughnasadh be held in her honour, which took place on the first day of August. It was originally the occasion of a national sporting competition, not unlike the Olympic Games.

TALIESIN ("Shining Brow") was a Welsh wizard and bard and according to Welsh mythology he was the first person to acquire the skill of prophecy. In one version of his story he was the servant of the witch *CERIDWEN* and was named Gwion Bach. Ceridwen prepared a magic brew that, after a year of boiling, was to yield three drops of knowledge. Whoever swallowed these precious drops would know all the secrets of the past, the present and the future. As Gwion Bach was tending the fire beneath the cauldron, some of the hot liquid fell on his finger and he sucked it to relieve the pain (much like *FINN MACCOOL* when he was cooking the Salmon of Knowledge). The furious Ceridwen employed all her magic powers to pursue the boy. During the chase he transformed himself into a hare, a fish and a bird before being eaten by the witch in the form of a grain of wheat. Later Gwion Bach was thrown into the sea and was caught in a fish-trap and renamed Taliesin because of his radiant forehead. "I am old, I am new," he said. "I have been dead, I have been alive." (See also *SAGES AND SEERS*)

TALIESIN was a prophetic bard who was gifted with all-knowing vision, which was symbolized by his shining brow. At the young age of thirteen, he already surpassed all of Arthur's bards in spiritual insight. He is portrayed here as a visionary spirit who was at one with the forces of nature. (ILLUSTRATION BY STUART LITTLEJOHN, 1994.)

TARANIS (whose name means "Thunderer") was one of the few Celtic gods with whom the Romans identified and he was often equated with Jupiter. Monuments to Taranis have been found all over the Celtic world, from the Adriatic coast to the northern regions of Britain. Taranis is usually depicted with his symbol, the wheel. The word "taran" is still used in modern Welsh and Breton to mean thunder.

TEIRNON was lord of Gwent Is Coed and foster-father of *PRYDERI*. Teirnon owned a beautiful mare, and every year on the eve of the first of May the animal gave birth to a foal, which mysteriously disappeared. One year Teirnon decided to keep watch to see what would happen. A giant clawed hand came through the stable window and took the new-born foal. He hacked off the hand but heard a crying coming from outside and found a three-day-old baby boy lying on the doorstep.

Teirnon and his wife took the child in and raised him as one of their own, but as he grew, the resemblance to *PWYLL* became increasingly marked until they knew that he was the missing son of Pwyll and *RHIANNON*.

TEUTATES, also called Toutatis, was one of the Celtic gods mentioned by the Roman historian Lucan and is often equated with the god Mars. His name means "a people" or "a tribe" and so it may well be that the many inscriptions to him are actually dedicated to local deities of a region rather than to a single pan-Celtic figure.

to Cornwall, where King Mark waited to marry her. The ensuing tale relates the sad course of their love, separation and their deaths. The lovers' end was particularly touching. Having agreed to part, Tristan went to Brittany, but later was gravely wounded and sent for help from Iseult, who had once before cured him of a serious wound. So she sailed to Brittany with a magic cure. It had been agreed that the ship carrying Iseult would hoist a white sail to indicate that she was aboard. However, an incorrect report of a black sail caused Tristan to lose the will to live and he died of his wound. When Iseult was told of her lover's death she too quickly died, but of a broken heart. (See also *CELTIC ROMANCE; SINGLE COMBAT*)

THOMAS THE RHYMER see
CELTIC OTHERWORLDS

TRISTAN, the nephew of King MARK of Cornwall, was one of the great lovers of medieval mythology. His name is said to have been given to him after his mother's death in childbirth. Of Breton origin, the story of Tristan and *ISEULT* was popular in Cornwall, Ireland and Brittany. A love potion prepared by Iseult's mother, the Irish queen, was the cause of their great love. Tristan and Iseult drank it accidentally when Tristan was escorting her

TRISTAN humbly sought the Grail, even though he doubted his chances because of his illicit love for Iseult. At one stage in his quest, he found a splendid castle all alight and alive with song. Sadly, however, he was struck back by a burning beam of light, for only the purest could attain the Grail. (ILLUSTRATION BY EVELYN PAUL, C. 1900.)

TRISTAN and Iseult (left), enchanted by a love potion, gaze at each other in rapture. In one legend, the two had fallen in love before sipping the potion, which only served to quash their scruples. The Victorian design captures the extreme nature of courtly love. (ILLUSTRATION BY EVELYN PAUL, 1900.)

TUATHA DE DANANN were "the people of the goddess Dana" in Irish mythology. They were the last generation of gods to rule Ireland before the invasion of the sons of MILESIUS, the ancestors of the present-day Irish. The Tuatha De Danann overcame the FOMORII, violent and monstrous sea gods, at the second battle of Magh Tuireadh largely because of their superior magic. They were said to have learned magic, crafts and knowledge in four marvellous cities of the north, Falias, Gorias, Finias and Murias. From these cities the Tuatha De Danann brought to Ireland four talismans: the Stone of Fal, which screamed aloud when the rightful king of Ireland placed his foot upon it; the magic sword of NUADA, their great war-leader, which was a weapon that could only inflict fatal blows; the spear or

TWRCH TRWYTH (below) was a boar that guarded three treasures between his ears which Culhwch sought to retrieve. Arthur's war-band hunted the boar, and here Mabon, the renowned hunter, skilfully snatches one treasure from between the boar's ears. (ILLUSTRATION BY ALAN LEE, 1984.)

TUATHA DE DANANN (above), an ancient race of Irish gods, went to live underground after their defeat by the Milesians. Beneath grassy mounds, each had his own sparkling sidhe, a subterranean court which glittered with wonders within. (ILLUSTRATION BY ALAN LEE, 1984.)

sling-shot of the sun god LUGH, who, as the slayer of BALOR, was the bringer of victory over the Fomorii; and the cauldron belonging to DAGDA, father of the gods, which was an inexhaustible pot that was capable of satisfying every appetite.

It is clear that the gods known in Ireland as the Tuatha De Danann were common to all Celtic peoples. Their names can be found in Welsh myths and in inscriptions on the continent of Europe. In Ireland they were not entirely lost with the advent of Christianity. Apart from having their exploits recorded by the monks who wrote down the Irish sagas, the Tuatha De Danann took up residence underground as the fairies. On the ancient Celtic feast of Samhain, celebrated on the last day of October to mark the new year, the De Danann were believed to allow mortals to enter their realm.

TUIREANN was the Irish father of three sons who killed Cian, father of the son god LUGH. To atone for this crime, Lugh demanded that the sons of Tuireann should perform a series of near impossible tasks, bringing back to Ireland such magical objects as a healing pigskin belonging to a king of Greece and a cooking spit from an undersea kingdom. When fulfilling their final labour they were badly wounded and Tuireann begged Lugh for the pigskin to cure his sons, but the god refused and they died.

TWRCH TRWYTH, in Welsh mythology, was a king who was turned into a gigantic boar for his sins. Between his ears he kept a comb, a pair of scissors and a razor. The retrieval of these objects was one of the hardest of the tasks that the giant Yspaddaden set CULHWCH who wanted to marry his daughter OLWEN. The boar was an important animal to the Celts and appears in many myths, as well as in statues and carvings. It represented both war and feasting.

UAITHNE was the god Dagda's inspired harpist. He had three equally gifted sons who played such sad music that on one occasion twelve men died weeping from sorrow. The Celtic bards accompanied their music with lyrics which perpetuated the legends down the generations. (ILLUSTRATION ANON.)

UATH submitted three Irish heroes to a beheading contest to test their courage and find the champion of Ireland. The rules allowed a hero to behead the giant but only if he could return the favour on the next day. Only Cuchulainn had the courage to behead the giant and place his head on the block. (ILLUSTRATION BY JAMES ALEXANDER, 1995.)

UAITHNE, in Irish mythology, was the magic harp of the *TUATHA DE DANANN* god *DAGDA*. It was stolen by the *FOMORII*, the enemies of the De Danann. When Dagda discovered where it was, he called out to the harp to free itself. The harp responded by killing nine Fomorii and then singing Dagda's praises. Uaithne was also the name of Dagda's harpist.

UATH ("Horror") was the name of the water giant who challenged the three Irish heroes *CUCHULAINN*, Laoghaire and *CONALL* to a beheading contest. Each was invited to take an axe and chop off the giant's head, provided that he would then lay his own head on the block for the giant to decapitate. Only Cuchulainn rose to the challenge, and was proclaimed by the giant as the Irish champion. After the announcement Uath revealed himself to be *CU ROI*, the Munster king.

UATHACH was one of the lovers of the great Ulster hero and champion *CUCHULAINN*, and, according to Irish mythology, the daughter of the female warrior *SCATHACH*, who had been Cuchulainn's tutor in the martial arts. When Uathach served

UTHER PENDRAGON, Arthur's father, hit upon the incredible idea of having a round table at which 150 knights could see each other and sit without quarrelling. Turning to Merlin, he asked him to design a table "round in the likeness of the world". (ILLUSTRATION ANON.)

the hero food, he forgot his own strength and accidently broke her finger while taking a dish from her hand. Her scream brought her previous lover to Uathach's immediate aid, but Cuchulainn easily slew him in the fight that followed and afterwards Uathach transferred her affection to the victor.

VORTIGERN, a fifth-century ruler of Britain, tried to build a grand castle, but the walls kept crumbling. The boy Merlin, a precocious seer, was consulted and revealed that two dragons battled beneath the site every night, destroying the castle walls. (ILLUSTRATION BY ALAN LEE, 1984.)

URIEN, father of *OWAIN*, ruled Rheghed in north-west Britain. His courage and skill as a warrior were celebrated in many songs, including the work of *TALIESIN*. When the Angles invaded, Urien is said to have fought a successful campaign against them and besieged them on the island of Lindisfarne.

UTHER PENDRAGON (whose name means "dragon head") was *ARTHUR*'s father. According to late-British mythology, Uther was able to sleep with Igraine because he was disguised as her husband, Gorlois, Duke of Cornwall, and the result of their union was Arthur. The wizard *MERLIN* helped in this deception and later Uther killed Gorlois and married Igraine, while Arthur was taken by Merlin.

VORTIGERN was a British ruler who hired Jutish mercenaries, but as increasing numbers of Saxons came into Britain he fled to Wales. Here he tried to build a stronghold, but it kept collapsing. When *MERLIN* was consulted he said that a red dragon (the Saxons) battled with a white dragon (the Britons) beneath the fort and that the red dragon would eventually win.

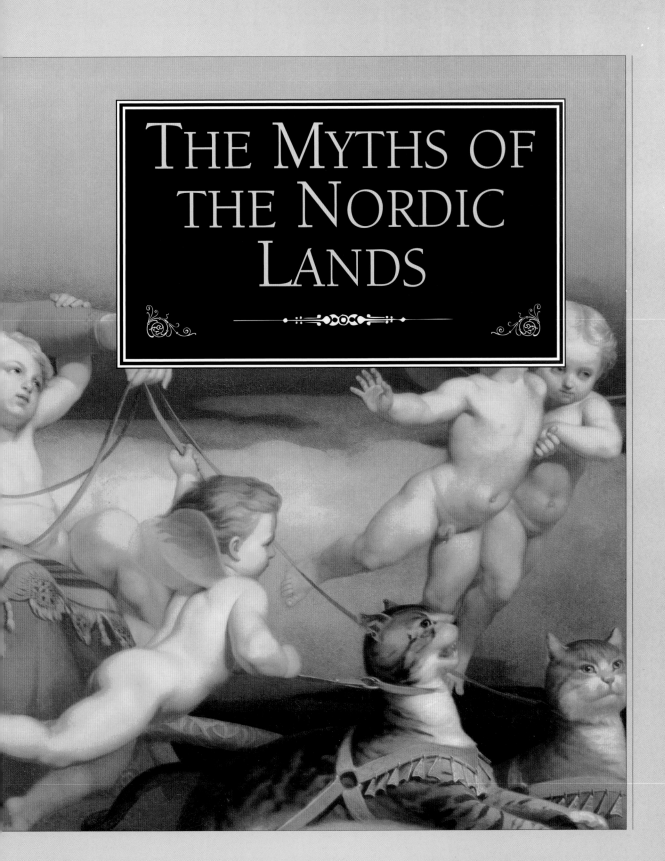

THE MYTHS OF
THE NORDIC
LANDS

INTRODUCTION

THE MYTHOLOGY OF NORTHERN AND eastern Europe is essentially that of two main groups, peoples of Germanic and of Slavic descent. Today the former group includes Germans, Dutch, Danes, Swedes, Norwegians, Icelanders, English, and any of their extraction, while the Slavs are made up of Russians, Serbs, Croats, Bulgarians, Rumanians, Slovacs and Poles. Other peoples have also contributed to the mythological tradition of the region, such as the inhabitants of the Baltic shore: the Prussians, Lithuanians and Letts. Further north there are contributions from the Finns and the Lapps of Sweden and Norway. The northernmost people of all, the Lapps of Finland and their cousins, the Samoyeds of Russia, are actually the scattered remnants of the Uralians, an ancient group once spread right across the tundra of Europe and Asia. Their beliefs remained similar to those held by the tribespeople of Siberia until quite recent times. For the purpose of this book these traditions have been grouped together under the generic term, Norse.

It is a fact that the overwhelming bulk of mythology surviving from northern and eastern Europe is Scandinavian and Icelandic in origin. Most Slavic gods are not much more than names, and the little we know about their worship is usually as a consequence of its Christian termination. In Russia the conversion of Vladimir in 989 to the Orthodox faith involved the ransacking of pagan temples at Kiev. Fortunately, chroniclers of this event noted the strange worship accorded to the thunder god Perunu or Veles, the god of flocks. Without such passing testimony our scant knowledge would be almost nonexistent. Even so, there are difficulties with Vladimir's own pagan beliefs prior to his conversion to Christianity. He was of Swedish descent and the "Rus" state he ruled on the River Dnieper was a by-product of Viking exploration. It is therefore likely that the Slavic thunder god Perunu had already absorbed much of Thor's mythology. Although a native hammer-god undoubtedly existed before the Vikings arrived in the 860s, the importance of northern warriors in Novgorod and Kiev made it inevitable that the Russian god would be identified with his Germanic counterpart. The strength of the Viking presence can be judged from the Arab traveller Ibn-Fadlan's account of the ship cremation of a "Rus" leader on the Volga river in 922.

In the Balkans the Slavs not only encountered Orthodox Christianity, but were later for a time under Islamic rule also. This long isolation from such Slavonic influences did not bode well for Balkan mythology. As the myths were never written down, the influence of Christianity and Islamic rule replaced the native story-telling. Of Baltic mythology next to nothing now exists, although some idea can be formed of the pantheon. The brutal truth is that European mythology has escaped the Baltic fate only where by historical accident it was written down. In the case of Celtic

ODIN, the leading warrior god of the Vikings, at left, bears the weapons of his warcraft, an axe and spear. The stylized tree depicted beside him symbolizes Yggdrasil, the World Tree. At centre is the thunder god Thor, wielding his fiery thunderbolt, Mjollnir; while at right, Freyr bears an ear of corn to represent his fertility. (TAPESTRY, 12TH CENTURY.)

mythology we are fortunate in the care taken by Christian monks in Ireland to record the ancient sagas. The classical heritage of Greece and Rome was preserved like that of the Celts in monastic libraries, after the Germanic peoples overran the western provinces of the Roman empire. And much of Germanic mythology would have been lost in its turn without the efforts of the Icelandic scholar and statesman Snorri Sturluson.

At the turn of the thirteenth century Snorri Sturluson wrote a handbook for poets on the world of the Germanic gods, providing detailed explanations of the old myths. He was recalling the sagas of the Viking era, approximately 750–1050, when a vigorous tradition formed around the heroic deeds of Odin, Thor and Freyr. Still untouched by Christianity, the restless and adventurous Northmen – the Danes, Norwegians and Swedes – put to sea in search of plunder and land. Viking warriors were largely organized in small bands or ships' crews, only joining together in temporary alliances for military expeditions, trading voyages or piracy. They might serve under a famous leader for a while, and then break up again, although on occasion they built up armies or large fleets of warships, like the forces that attacked France in 842 or invaded England in 866. Their magnificent ships and expert seamanship gave them mastery of rivers and seas, and enabled them to travel far and wide.

The Irish lamented the Viking onslaught most. "The sea spewed forth floods of foreigners over Ireland," noted the *Annals of Ulster*, "so that no harbour, no beach, no stronghold, no fort, no castle, might be found, but it was sunk beneath waves of northmen and pirates." In 836 the Vikings had decided to set up a permanent raiding base on the site of present-day Dublin.

It is hardly surprising that aggressive Viking

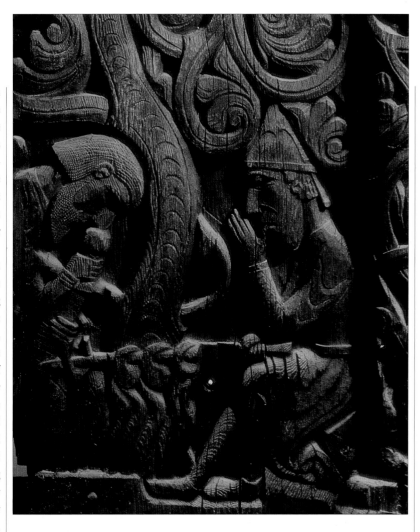

SIGURD *roasts the heart of the terrible dragon, Fafnir, and sucks his thumb which was splashed with the dragon's blood. On tasting the otherworldly blood, Sigurd gained the power to understand birdsong and learnt from the birds that Regin, his tutor sleeping by the fire, planned treachery.* (WOOD CARVING, 12TH CENTURY.)

warriors loved hearing about the exploits of one-eyed Odin. This chief of the Germanic gods exerted a special fascination as "father of the slain". He shared those who fell on the battlefield with Freyja, the goddess of fertility. He also inspired the frightful berserkers, the shield-biting fighters who rushed unheeding and naked into the fray. When the Danish king Harald Wartooth complained about Odin's fickleness, the way he gave luck in battle and then suddenly withdrew it again,

the war god said "the grey wolf watches the halls of the gods". Gathering to Valhalla the heroic warriors slain in battle was the only policy Odin felt he could sensibly follow under the constant threat of Ragnarok, the doom of the gods. These dead warriors, the *Einherjar*, were desperately needed for the final battle on the Vigrid Plain, where nearly all would fall in an encounter between the gods and the frost giants. Odin himself was destined to be killed by the wolf Fenrir, the monstrous offspring of the fire god Loki and the frost giantess Angrboda. Whether Harald Wartooth accepted this as an adequate answer is uncertain, since Odin, who was acting as his charioteer, flung the old king down and slew him with his sword as he fell.

177

VALHALLA (below), the splendid, many-spired Hall of the Slain, housed Odin's phantom army of heroic warriors, gathered to fight at Ragnarok – the preordained doom of the gods. On the right, the massive World Serpent, Jormungand, was destined to overwhelm the world at Ragnarok. (ILLUSTRATION FROM THE PROSE EDDA, 1760.)

The "axe-age, sword-age", which was the age that would lead up to the catastrophe of Ragnarok, must have seemed like a description of contemporary times to the footloose Vikings. But for those who settled down as colonists, either as farmers or traders, an alternative god to worship was Thor, Odin's son. Although "allergic" to frost giants, Thor is represented in the sagas as an honest and straightforward person. He was very popular with Icelandic colonists, who had fled southern Norway to avoid the Odin-like activities of leaders like Erik Bloodaxe. Thousands of them revealed their allegiance in the choice of family name: Thorsten or Thorolf were most common. Thor was indeed a reassuring supernatural presence in both divine and human crises, be they encroachments by frost giants on gods, or local tyrants on farmers, or even overzealous Christian missionaries on pagan temples. Ever handy was his thunder-hammer Mjollnir, a magic instrument with powers of destruction, fertility and resurrection. It was hardly surprising then that Thor became a greater god than Odin at the close of the Viking era, just a century or so before Scandinavia was converted to Christianity.

LOKI (below), the fiery trickster god, was to begin with a mischievous and playful prankster, but he became so dark and twisted that his malice threatened the stability of the world and precipitated Ragnarok. Here, the troublesome god taunts the Rhine Maidens, who are grieving the loss of their Rhinegold. (ILLUSTRATION BY ARTHUR RACKHAM, C. 1900.)

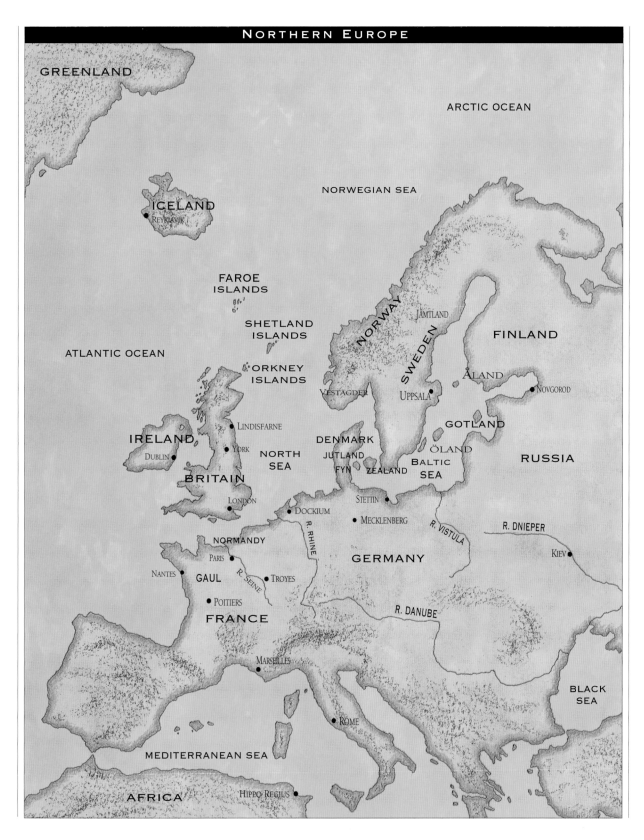

NORTHERN EUROPE

GREENLAND

ARCTIC OCEAN

NORWEGIAN SEA

ICELAND
Reykjavik

FAROE
ISLANDS

SHETLAND
ISLANDS

ATLANTIC OCEAN

ORKNEY
ISLANDS

NORWAY

SWEDEN

JÄMTLAND

FINLAND

ÅLAND

VESTAGDER

UPPSALA

NOVGOROD

LINDISFARNE

IRELAND

YORK

DUBLIN

GOTLAND

DENMARK

JUTLAND

NORTH
SEA

ÖLAND

RUSSIA

FYN

ZEALAND

BALTIC
SEA

BRITAIN

LONDON

STETTIN

DOCKIUM

MECKLENBERG

R. VISTULA

R. DNIEPER

R. RHINE

NORMANDY

PARIS

GERMANY

KIEV

NANTES

GAUL

R. SEINE

TROYES

POITIERS

R. DANUBE

FRANCE

BLACK
SEA

MARSEILLES

ROME

MEDITERRANEAN SEA

AFRICA

HIPPO REGIUS

A

AEGIR, or Eagor, was a Germanic sea god, the husband of *RAN* and father of nine daughters, the waves. He seems to have belonged to an older generation of the gods than either the *AESIR* or the *VANIR*, although no details of his descent survive. Aegir was sometimes depicted as a very old man with white hair and claw-like fingers. Whenever he rose from his underwater hall, he broke the surface of the sea for a single purpose, the destruction of ships and their crews. To ensure a calm voyage, prisoners would usually be sacrificed to Aegir before a Viking raiding party set sail for home.

One myth tells how the proud sea god was outwitted by *THOR*. Aegir had been ordered by Thor to brew some ale for the gods, but he pretended that he had no cauldron large enough for the task. In fact he disliked being told what to do. But undaunted, Thor acquired a vast cauldron from the frost giant *HYMIR*. It was so big that when he hoisted it onto his shoulders, the

AEGIR (above), a tempestuous and powerful god of the sea, resided in a glistening underwater palace from where he directed the swirling waves through his nine daughters, who were known as the billow maidens. The hissing, seething Nordic sea was called "Aegir's Brewing Kettle". (ILLUSTRATION BY JAMES ALEXANDER, 1995.)

AEGIR'S sister-wife, Ran, was famous for her drowning net, which she used to snatch unsuspecting sailors from the decks of ships and drag them down to the seabed. She entertained them in her coral caves, which were lit by gleaming gold and where mead flowed as freely as in Valhalla. (ILLUSTRATION BY PETER HURD, 1882.)

handles reached his ankles. Hymir tried to stop Thor leaving with the cauldron, but the god's hammer saw off Hymir and his gigantic friends. As a result, a humiliated Aegir had to accept the cauldron and supply *ASGARD*, the home of the gods, with ale.

It was at a subsequent feast for the gods held by Aegir that *LOKI* showed how evil he had become when he insulted the assembled company and stabbed Aegir's servant Fimafeng.

THE AESIR, in Germanic mythology, were one branch of the family of the gods; the other branch were the *VANIR*. At one time there was a war between the younger Aesir and the older Vanir, which ended in a peace that left the Aesir dominant. Both branches had in fact grown weary of fighting, and were pleased to come to terms. In order to cement the peace, several of the leading Aesir went to live among the Vanir, while a number of important Vanir went to *ASGARD*, the Aesir's home.

The Aesir, under the leadership of *ODIN*, included his sons *BALDER* ("the bleeding god") and *BRAGI*, the god of eloquence; the justice god *FORSETI*, who resolved quarrels in a splendid hall supported by pillars of red gold and covered with a roof inlaid with silver; the fertility god *FREYR*, once a leading Vanir; the vigilant *HEIMDALL*, whose duty it would be to summon every living creature to *RAGNAROK*, the day of doom, with his horn; blind *HODR*, the unwitting killer of Balder; the trickster *LOKI*, god of fire and ally of the frost giants; the sea god *NJORD*, one of the gods exchanged with the Vanir; another of Odin's sons, *THOR*, whose mighty magic hammer was the only weapon the frost giants feared; the god of war *TYR*, a son of Hymir; *VILI* and *VE*, the brothers of Odin; and *VIDAR*, a son of Odin who was destined to avenge his father's death at Ragnarok.

The goddesses of the Aesir were *FREYJA*, the fertility goddess and twin sister of Freyr; *FRIGG*, Odin's wife; *SIF*, the wife of Thor; and *IDUN*, who was the keeper of the apples of youth.

Almost all the Aesir were to be killed at Ragnarok (the doom of the gods), when a terrible battle was destined to take place between the forces led by Odin, and the forces led by Loki.

ALBERICH see *ANDVARI*

ALVIS ("All Wise"), in Germanic mythology, was a dwarf who was outwitted by *ODIN*'s son *THOR*, the possessor of a magic hammer of irresistible force. In payment for the weapons Alvis had forged for them, the gods promised that he could marry Thor's daughter *THRUD*. However, Thor was displeased with the arrangement and so devised a test of knowledge to stop the dwarf from marrying his daughter. When Alvis came to *ASGARD*, Thor questioned him all night long because sunlight turned dwarfs to stone.

ALVIS, a dwarf famed for his wisdom, hoped to marry Thor's giant daughter, Thrud, but first he had to prove that his great wisdom made up for his small stature. Thor quizzed him and prolonged the test until sunrise when the first ray petrified Alvis who, like all dwarfs, turned to stone in daylight. (ILLUSTRATION BY JAMES ALEXANDER, 1995.)

In the netherworld the brave Hermod found his brother Balder seated in a high position. When he asked for his release, Hel said Balder could leave only on condition that "everything in the nine worlds, dead and alive, wept for him". Messengers were sent out and soon even the stones were weeping. But THOKK, an old frost giantess, refused, saying, "Let Hel hold what she has." So upset were the gods at this refusal to mourn that it took some time for them to realize that Thokk was none other than Loki in disguise. Nevertheless, Balder remained with Hel.

Balder's good looks and early death recall the myths of the Egyptian Osiris and the Sumerian Tammuz, as well as that of Adonis, who was the dying-and-rising god the ancient Greeks adopted from the Phoenicians. For the Germanic peoples believed that the return of the wounded, dying Balder would occur in a new world, a green land risen from the sea, after RAGNAROK, the doom of the gods. Like the undead Celtic King Arthur, Balder was expected to return and rule over a world cleansed by catastrophe. It would seem that some of the initial appeal of Christianity in northern Europe was connected with the triumphant return of the risen Christ on Judgement Day. (See also RAGNAROK)

BALDR see BALDER

BALDUR see BALDER

BEOWULF was the Germanic hero who slew two water monsters. He was said to be the nephew of the king of Geats, whom some interpret as the Jutes. His story is set in Denmark. One night a dreadful creature known as GRENDEL came to the hall of King Hrothgar and ate one of the warriors sleeping there. Although invulnerable to weapons, Grendel was seized by Beowulf and held in a powerful grip, from which it could only

BEOWULF, seen here with raised drinking horn, gazes up at the gory trophy hanging from the splendid vault of Denmark's Victory Hall. The giant hairy hand belonged to the fearsome sea monster, Grendel, who had continually terrorized and devoured the Danes, until Beowulf tore the creature's arm right out of its socket. (ILLUSTRATION BY ALAN LEE, 1984.)

BEOWULF wrestles with a monstrous merwoman in the crystal cavern of her underwater den. Grieving for the death of her son, Grendel, slain by Beowulf, the merwoman fought with frenzy, but Beowulf battled calmly and took her by surprise. (ILLUSTRATION BY JAMES ALEXANDER, 1995.)

break away by losing an arm. Mortally wounded, the water monster fled to its home, deep in a nearby lake, and bled to death.

Delighted by this feat of courage and strength, King Hrothgar loaded Beowulf with gifts, since his kingdom had been rid of a menace. But neither the king nor the warrior reckoned on Grendel's mother, an even more dreadful creature. She returned to the attack and ate another sleeping warrior. In pursuit, Beowulf followed her into a lake and dived down to her cavern-like lair. A desperate struggle then took place and Beowulf lost his

trusty sword. Like Arthur, he was fortunate to find another magic weapon in the water and he used this to finish off Grendel's mother.

Having once again saved King Hrothgar's kingdom from danger, Beowulf returned home to southern Sweden, where his father ruled. Towards the end of his popular reign a dragon attacked his land. Going out with twelve followers to slay the fiery beast, Beowulf soon found himself almost on his own, for all his companions but one ran away in terror. Although he managed to kill the dragon, it was at the cost of his own life.

In contrast to the Celtic myths that describe combat with water-giants, the Germanic stories tell of heroes who face actual monsters rather than magical opponents. This is quite unlike the great Ulster hero and champion Cuchulainn's beheading contest with Uath, or Sir Gawain's with the Green Knight, for in these traditions their monstrous opponents were able to restore themselves to life after they had been decapitated.

BEOWULF, even in his old age, tackled fire-breathing dragons. Yet neither his might nor his fabled armour, crafted by Wayland, could withstand the dragon's crushing teeth. Beowulf was mortally wounded in the combat, but he did not die before seeing the dragon's treasure released for his people. (ILLUSTRATION BY JAMES ALEXANDER, 1995.)

BERGELMIR, according to Germanic mythology, was the son of Thrudgelmir and the grandson of YMIR. When ODIN, VILI and VE killed Ymir and threw his body into the middle of GINNUNGAGAP, all the frost giants drowned in the giant's blood except Bergelmir and his wife. By using a hollowed tree trunk as a boat, they escaped to

BIFROST (above) was a gigantic rainbow causeway, reaching from the shining citadel of Asgard to the earthly realm of Midgard. Composed of fire, water and air, it shimmered with rainbow-coloured light in hues of red, blue and green. Over the ethereal arch, the gods moved to and fro.
(ILLUSTRATION BY ALAN LEE, 1984.)

continue the race of giants, who never lost their hatred for the gods. At RAGNAROK the frost giants and the dead of HEL were destined to settle the final account for Ymir's dismemberment.

BIFROST, in Germanic mythology, was the flaming three-strand rainbow bridge between ASGARD and Midgard (heaven and earth respectively). It was said to have been built by the gods out of red fire, green water and blue air, and was guarded by the watchman god HEIMDALL. Every day the gods rode across the bridge to hold meetings at the well of URD.

BILLING, in Germanic mythology, was the father of RIND. According to some traditions, he was king of the Ruthenians, or Russians. So strong-willed was Rind that ODIN could not woo her, even though Billing approved of the god's suit. On the contrary, she treated the chief of the Germanic gods with undisguised contempt. Eventually, however, she gave way to his advances and she bore a son, VALI, who killed HODR with his bow and arrow.

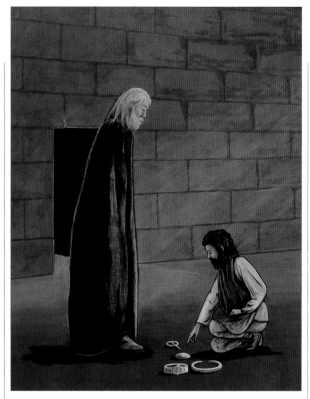

BERGELMIR (below) and his wife were the only frost giants to escape drowning in the torrent of Ymir's blood that flowed from his mortal wounds. They journeyed in a hollowed-out tree trunk to the edge of the world where they founded the realm of Jotunheim and bred a new race of giants.
(ILLUSTRATION BY NICK BEALE, 1995.)

BILLING (above) gazes in wonder at the glittering trinkets fashioned by the dwarf goldsmith Rosterus. Unknown to King Billing, the dwarf is Odin in disguise, who was intent on wooing the king's daughter, Rind. She was destined to bear Odin a son, Vali, who would avenge Balder's death.
(ILLUSTRATION BY NICK BEALE, 1995.)

BOR was the son of BURI, husband of the giant Bestla and father of ODIN, VILI and VE. An ancient god, Bor lived in the time before the world had been made, when there was no earth, sky or sea, only mist, ice, fire and the gaping pit of GINNUNGAGAP. Bor's father-in-law, the giant Bolthur, also had a son who imparted his wisdom to his nephew Odin.

BRAGI was the son of ODIN and Gunnlod, a female giant, and was the Germanic god of poetry and eloquence. He was married to IDUN, the goddess who kept the magic apples of youth. When LOKI returned to ASGARD, after being instrumental in causing BALDER's death, Bragi, who was never at a loss for words, told him that he was

BRAGI (above) was born in a glittering stalactite cave, where his mother, Gunnlod, guarded the Mead of Poetry, until seduced by Odin. The dwarfs gave the fair child a magical harp and set him afloat on one of their fine-crafted vessels from which he sang his poignant Song of Life which rose to the heavens. (ILLUSTRATION BY PETER HURD, 1882.)

unwelcome company at their feast. Enraged, Loki called Bragi "the bragger", whereupon Bragi threatened to twist off Loki's head as the only sure method of stopping his lies. Although Odin tried to calm the gathering, the effect of Bragi's words on Loki was to make him

THE BRISINGAMEN (below) was an exquisite necklace crafted by dwarfs so finely that it shone like liquid flame. The goddess Freyja, beside herself with longing, paid dearly for possessing the treasure. An emblem of the stars, it so enhanced her beauty that she wore it continually, night and day. (ILLUSTRATION BY J PENROSE, C. 1890.)

even more threatening. He finally prophesied the destruction of the gods and then fled from Asgard.

Possibly Bragi was a late addition to the Germanic pantheon. It is not unlikely that Bragi was added through the divine elevation of a poet, since in Germanic courts poets were venerated second only to kings. Bragi was portrayed as an old, bearded man carrying a harp, and when oaths were sworn they were solemnized by speaking over a vessel called the Cup of Bragi.

BRISINGAMEN see *RINGS OF POWER*

THE BRISINGS, also known as the Bristlings, were the mysterious owners of a golden necklace, called the Brisingamen, that the fertility goddess *FREYJA* craved. To *ODIN*'s disgust she slept on four successive nights with the dwarfs Alfrigg, Dvalin, Berling and Grer in order to acquire it. When she returned to *ASGARD*, Odin accused her of debasing her divinity by paying such a price. As a penance he made her stir up war in Midgard, the world of men. Freyja and Odin shared those slain on the battlefield.

No agreement exists about the meaning of this strange myth, not least because the identity of the Brisings is unknown. It has been suggested that necklaces were the special adornment of mother goddesses, but this hardly does more than explain Freyja's attraction to this particular one. What seems more likely is that the sexual price Freyja paid for it represents the other side of love, namely, blind passion and lust. Nothing could stop her, not even Odin's great disapproval, when she desired something badly enough. The Brisingamen came to be identified so closely with Freyja that when *THOR* wished to disguise himself as the goddess to retrieve his hammer from *THRYM*, she lent it to him to make his costume convincing. (See also *TREASURES AND TALISMANS*)

THE BRISTLINGS see *BRISINGS*

BRUNHILD see *BRYNHILD*

BRYNHILD was a *VALKYRIE* who defied *ODIN* and so was banished to earth and imprisoned within a ring of fire. When *SIGURD* braved the fire and broke her charmed sleep, they fell in love. He gave her his ring, Andvarinaut, unaware of its curse. On his travels he was bewitched by Grimhild into betraying Brynhild, first by marrying Gudrun and then by helping Gunner win Brynhild. On discovering Sigurd's betrayal, Brynhild planned his death, but then killed herself in despair. (See also *THE VALKYRIES*; *TRAGIC LOVERS*)

BURI, in Germanic mythology, was the ancestor of the gods. He was released from the ice by *AUDHUMLA*, the primeval cow. One day Buri's hair appeared where she licked; on the second day, his head was free of ice; and, on the third, his entire body. He had a son, *BOR*, who married a frost giantess, and their sons were *ODIN*, *VILI* and *VE*.

BRYNHILD, one of the leading Valkyries, was punished by Odin for meddling with his will in warfare. The god put her to sleep and imprisoned her in a ring of fire, where she would remain until a peerless hero freed her. Only Sigurd braved the scorching fire, waking her from her enchanted sleep. (ILLUSTRATION BY ARTHUR RACKHAM, C.1900.)

NATURE SPIRITS

T
HE DRAMATIC LANDSCAPE of Scandinavia, with its electric skies, icy wastes
and seething springs, was easily peopled with nature spirits. Such spirits
roamed the mountains and snow slopes as fearsome frost, storm and fire
giants, personifying the mysterious and menacing forces of nature. So great
were the terrors of crushing ice and searing fire that the giants loomed large in the
Norse myths as evil and ominous forces. Yet other less dramatic but no less important
spirits were the invisible *landvaettir*, or land spirits, who imbued the land and guarded
its welfare. Helpful and timid, the *landvaettir* easily took fright, shying away from
Viking dragon ships. In the underground caverns, dark dwarfs unearthed glittering
gems and metals, while light elves inspired the forests and lakes. In Slavonic myth, a
host of vital forces filled
the world and imbued
the forests, fields and
rivers with whirling
spirits of nature.

*THE FROST GIANTS (below) personified the icy
terrors of the Nordic landscape. Mighty, menacing
and numbing, the ice masses of the North were a
constant threat to the Norsemen, much like the frost
giants, whose undying enmity would overwhelm the
gods at Ragnarok. In the interim, the frost giants
sent freezing blasts to nip the buds of spring, or
shook avalanches from their icy shoulders and brows.
(RONDANE AT NIGHT BY H SOHLBERG, CANVAS, C. 1890.)*

*THE SUN (above), in one myth,
was fashioned by the gods from a
bright spark of fire. Its glowing orb
was placed in a chariot, drawn by
two white steeds and driven by the
sun-maid, Sol. Fearing that the
sun's heat might be harmful, the
gods placed a shield, Svalin, or
Cooler, in front of the golden car.
In another myth, the gods gave a
giant, Day, a chariot and horses to
drive round the earth once every 24
hours. Day's horse, Shining Mane,
lit up the earth and sky with the
radiance of his shining hair. (SUN
DISC, GILDED BRONZE, C. 1000 BC.)*

RAN (left), a stormy spirit of the sea, reflected the shifting moods of the ocean, sometimes helpful, sometimes harmful. She gathered sailors in her drowning net and dragged them down to the depths of the sea. There, with her husband, Aegir, she entertained her victims in her gleaming coral caves, which were lit by the shining gold of the sea. Ran loved gold, named the Flame of the Sea, after the fluorescent quality of Nordic waves. Sailors seeking Ran's favour wisely pocketed some gold for the trip. (ILLUSTRATION BY ARTHUR RACKHAM, C. 1900.)

DARK DWARFS (below) were formed from maggots in the rotting flesh of the slain giant, Ymir. The gods thought them too ugly to be seen, however, and condemned them to a life underground. Like giants, they turned to stone in daylight, thus explaining the many smaller stones and rocks scattered across the Nordic landscape. The twin peaks of Trold Tindterne, for example, are two bands of warring dwarfs who forgot to retreat before sunrise. As dwarfs had a habit of whispering behind rocks, the mountain echoes were known as "dwarfs' talk". (ILLUSTRATION BY ALAN LEE, 1984.)

THE RHINE MAIDENS (above) were ethereal sprites who dwelt in lakes and rivers during the winter, emerging from the water to flit through the forests in summer. The river's colours reflected the nymphs' moods, turning black with grief when the Rhine Maidens lost their gold. Here, the Rhine Maidens bemoan their loss to the gods crossing the rainbow bridge above. (ILLUSTRATION BY ARTHUR RACKHAM, C.1900.)

ROCK AND STORM GIANTS personified the vast craggy mountains and storm clouds. Rocky chasms and outcrops were created by giants treading too heavily at the dawn of time. Best suited to mist and fog, the mountain giants, like dwarfs, were petrified by the light of day, which explains some fantastic rock formations, such as the Riesengebirge (right), formed by foolish giants who were caught outside at sunrise. Similarly, in Iceland the highest peaks are named Jokul which derives from Jotun or Giant. (ILLUSTRATION BY NICK BEALE, 1995.)

F

DAZHBOG was the Slavic sun god, known as Dabog to the Serbs and Dazbog to the Poles. Son of Svarog, the god of the sky, and brother of *SVARAZIC*, god of fire, he was born again every morning and rode through the sky on his diamond chariot until he became an old man in the evening. In some versions he is married to *MYESYATS*, the moon, and quarrels between them are said to cause earthquakes.

DRAUPNIR see *RINGS OF POWER*

DIETRICH see *RINGS OF POWER*

EAGOR see *AEGIR*

THE EINHERJAR were the "heroic dead" of Germanic mythology. They were gathered from the battlefields by the *VALKYRIES*. In *VALHALLA*, the Einherjar formed *ODIN*'s private army, which he raised to fight at *RAGNAROK*, the doom of the gods. This was the final battle between the gods and the frost giants on the *VIGRID* Plain. Until then, these dead warriors would fight every day and feast every night, and any wounds they sustained were magically healed. (See also *THE VALKYRIES*)

FAFNIR slays his father, Hreidmar, because he is bewitched by the treasure trove stolen from the dwarf Andvari. The dwarf's cursed ring can be seen glittering on Hreidmar's forefinger as he writhes in the dust. Behind the warring pair, the gods gaze on in numb dismay. (ILLUSTRATION BY F VON STASSEN, 1914.)

FAFNIR, son of the magician *HREIDMAR*, was corrupted by the cursed ring Andvarinaut. Lusting after the fabulous ring-hoard, he slew his father, helped by his brother *REGIN*. Greed made him monstrous in nature and form, as he turned into a dragon to guard his hoard. The legend of his treasure drew many aspiring heroes to his lair in search of fame and fortune. Most met their deaths on the blasted heath outside his lair, but the youthful *SIGURD*, armed with his father's sword and guided by Regin, outwitted the dragon and won his ill-fated treasure.

FARBAUTI ("Cruel striker") was a giant and father of the fire god *LOKI*. According to one tradition, his wife was another giant, Laufey ("Tree island") who gave birth to Loki when hit by a lightning bolt unleashed by Farbauti. Little else is known of Loki's parents.

FENRIR, or Fenris, according to Germanic mythology, was the son of the mischief-making god *LOKI* and the frost giantess *ANGRBODA*. He was the devouring wolf, the

beast of *RAGNAROK*, the doom of the gods. His was "an axe-age, a sword-age, a wind-age, a wolf-age, before the wrecking of the world". *ODIN*, the chief of the gods, was destined to become his victim.

Kidnapped by the gods and brought to *ASGARD* where they could keep an eye on him, Fenrir was so savage that only the war god *TYR* dared to feed him. At first Odin was uncertain about the wolf, but when the *NORNS*, the goddesses of destiny, warned him about his own fate, he decided that Fenrir should be restrained. No chain, however, was strong enough to hold the animal. Finally, the dwarfs made a magic fetter called Gleipnir from strange materials such as the roots of a mountain and bird's spittle. Although it seemed to be a silken ribbon, Fenrir would not have it round his neck unless one of the gods put his hand between his jaws as a pledge that it was as harmless as it seemed. Tyr was the only one prepared to risk his hand, and the other gods laughed when the wolf bit it off on finding that the chain could not be broken. Fenrir was then secured to a rock and his

THE EINHERJAR, or "heroic dead", were gathered up from the battlefield by the Valkyries who galloped over the fray, choosing the bravest heroes for Odin's ghostly army. A chosen hero saw a soaring Valkyrie just before the fatal blow. (THE RIDE OF THE VALKYRIES BY W T MAUD, CANVAS, C. 1890.)

mouth was kept open by a sword so he could not bite.

When freed from captivity at Ragnarok, Fenrir was a fearsome spectacle. His vast mouth gaped so wide that the lower jaw touched the ground and the upper one reached the sky, and Odin was swallowed by him.

FENRIS see *FENRIR*

FJALAR and his brother Galar, in Germanic mythology, were the wicked dwarfs who killed the wise man *KVASIR* in order to gain his magic powers. They mixed his blood with honey in a cauldron and made a mead that bestowed wisdom. But Fjalar and Galar lost the wonderful drink to Suttung, a frost giant whose parents they had also killed. Unlike the dwarfs, Suttung was boastful about his

FORSETI, *the fair god of justice, was a Solomon-like force for peace. He sat in judgement in his golden hall, Glitnir, and settled the disputes of gods and men, allaying strife and resolving feuds. He never failed to reconcile even the bitterest foes.* (ILLUSTRATION BY NICK BEALE, 1995.)

FENRIR *(above), the wolf fathered by Loki, was so savage that the gods chained him to an underground rock. Only a magical cord was strong enough to bind him. Here, the brave god Tyr fetters Fenrir at the cost of his own hand, which he placed in the wolf's mouth as a sign of trust.* (DIE, 8TH CENTURY.)

FJALAR *(below) and his brother Galar slew the wise Kvasir and drained his blood to extract his wisdom. Two glistening bowls and the Kettle of Inspiration contained the magical fluid, which the brothers mixed with honey to produce the golden Mead of Poetry.* (ILLUSTRATION BY JAMES ALEXANDER, 1995.)

acquisition and it was not long before the gods heard about the mead. ODIN himself decided that he would go to JOTUNHEIM, the land of the frost giants, and lay hold of the magic drink. Disguised as evil Bolverk, he journeyed to Jotunheim and persuaded the frost giant Baugi to tunnel through a mountain to where Suttung kept the mead under the care of his daughter Gunnlod. Once the hole was drilled, Odin changed his shape from Bolverk's to a snake, and slithered downwards to the hidden treasure as quickly as he could. Reaching the secret cave, he changed himself into a handsome one-eyed giant and for three days and nights he was Gunnlod's lover. The passionate giantess let Odin drink up every drop of the mead, before he turned himself into an eagle and flew back to ASGARD, the home of the gods. There he spat the mead into jars left empty for his return. Suttung gave chase as another eagle, but just failed to catch Odin.

In the account of Kvasir's death, it is clear that this is a myth about

fermentation. To put the seal on their peace agreement the two branches of the gods, the AESIR and the VANIR, had spat into a jar, and it was from the spittle that Kvasir had been formed. Spittle, like yeast, causes fermentation, and so when Fjalar and Galar mixed Kvasir's blood with honey in a cauldron they created a magical mead. The connection between inspiration, poetry and wisdom and some form of potent drink occurs in several mythological traditions.

FORSETI was the Germanic god of justice, and was known to the Frisians as Forsite. He was the son of BALDER and Nanna. Both of his parents were killed, his father stabbed by a piece of mistletoe, thrown unwittingly by the blind god HODR, and his mother with a broken heart shortly after this tragic event. Although Forseti plays only a relatively small role in Germanic mythology, we are told in detail that his hall of Glitnir "had pillars of red gold and a roof inlaid with silver." There he sat in judgement and resolved strife.

FREA see FREYJA

FREY see FREYR

FREYA see FREYJA

FREYJA, the voluptuous, blue-eyed goddess of love, rode in a chariot drawn by cats, which were symbols of her warm affections. Accompanied by a flock of airborne love spirits, she toured heaven and earth in search of her roving husband, Odur, shedding tears of gold all the while.
(FREYJA BY N J O BLOMMER, CANVAS, 1852.)

FREYJA ("Lady"), sometimes known as Freya or Frea, was the daughter of the sea god *NJORD* in Germanic mythology and sister of *FREYR*. She was an important fertility goddess and a member of the *VANIR*, one of the two branches into which the Germanic gods were divided. After a war the Vanir seem to have been supplanted by the younger *AESIR*, who were led by *ODIN*. When peace was agreed between the two sides, Njord went with Freyr and Freyja to *ASGARD*, where they lived with the Aesir as a token of friendship.

Freyja's greatest treasure was the *BRISINGS*' necklace, which she obtained by sleeping with its four dwarf makers. Her beauty won her many admirers, including *OTTAR*, whom she changed into a boar. She was said to be a sorceress who could fly in a falcon's skin. Some traditions state that, on her arrival in Asgard, she taught the gods the spells and charms of the Vanir.

Both Odin and Freyja took an interest in the heroic dead, dividing the slain between them at the end of every battle. Odin's share went to live in *VALHALLA*, while Freyja's lived in her hall, Sessrumnir. It is possible that Freyja's lost husband Odur, or Od, of whom nothing is known but his name, was Odin. For she was the goddess of lust as well as love, a suitable partner for Odin who was the father of battles and the lover of destruction. (See also *SORCERY AND SPELLS*)

FREYR ("Lord"), sometimes Frey, was the twin brother of the Germanic fertility goddess *FREYJA*. Their father was *NJORD*, the god associated with the wind and the sea. Freyr, with *ODIN* and *THOR*, was one of the principal gods. He was mainly concerned with fertility, having control of sunlight, rain, fruitfulness and peace. His title of Skirr means "shining", and the name of the frost giantess he married, *GERDA*, derives from "field". As late as 1200, Freyr's statue in his temple at Uppsala, Sweden was noted for the size of its penis. Possibly for this reason the Romans had always identified him with Priapus, the virile son of Dionysus and Aphrodite. Although a member of the *VANIR* by descent, Freyr moved to *ASGARD* to live with the *AESIR*, the younger branch of the gods under the leadership of Odin, along with his father Njord and his

FREYJA (below) flew over the earth, sprinkling morning dew and summer sunlight behind her. She shook spring flowers from her golden hair and wept tears which turned to gold, or to amber at sea. She was so beautiful that she was wooed and pursued by all living creatures.
(ILLUSTRATION BY F VON STASSEN, 1914.)

FREYR (right), a gentle god of summer sun and showers, was lord of the fairy realm of Alfheim, home of the Light Elves. Here, he is sailing his ship, Skidbladnir, personifying the clouds. His flashing sword, symbolizing a sunbeam, fought of its own accord. (ILLUSTRATION BY JAMES ALEXANDER, 1995.)

sister Freyja, as a gesture of good-will that had been agreed at the end of the war between the Vanir and the Aesir.

Freyr's myth is about his woo-ing of Gerda, the daughter of the frost giant Gymir. When Freyr first saw Gerda he immediately fell in love with her, and because he did not know how to gain her affection he became ill. Njord became so worried about him that he asked his faithful servant Skirnir to find out what was amiss. Having learned of this love, Skirnir went to *JOTUNHEIM*, the land of the giants, taking two of Freyr's greatest treasures, his magic horse and his magic sword. The servant was instructed to bring Gerda back to Asgard, whether her father liked it or not. On reaching Gymir's hall, Skirnir tried to persuade Gerda to

FRIGG (below), a deity of the atmosphere, spun long pearly webs of cloud from her jewelled distaff which shone in the night sky as the constellation of Frigg's Spinning Wheel. Her heron plumes symbolize her discretion, while her keys signify her divine housewifery. (ILLUSTRATION BY NICK BEALE, 1995.)

declare her love for Freyr in return for "eleven of the apples of youth". She refused both this gift and Skirnir's second offer of one of Odin's arm-rings. Gerda's resolve was only strengthened further when Skirnir then threatened to decapitate her with Freyr's sword. Finally, Skirnir said that he would impose on her an unbreakable spell that would make her a permanent outcast and it was this that per-suaded Gerda to pledge herself to

the fertility god with an agreement to meet Freyr in a forest in nine days' time. In this way the passion of Freyr was fulfilled, though it cost him his horse and sword which he gave to Skirnir. At *RAGNAROK*, the doom of the gods, he sorely missed his mighty magic weapon, since it could fight giants on its own. (See also *TREASURES AND TALISMANS*; *TRAGIC LOVERS*)

FRICKA see *FRIGG*

FRIGG, also known as Frigga, Frija and Fricka, in Germanic mythology, was the daughter of Fjorgyn, goddess of the earth and atmosphere, wife of *ODIN*, the chief of the gods, and mother of *BALDER*. She has given her name to Friday. Frigg was a fertility goddess who "will tell no fortunes, yet well she knows the fates". When Balder dreamed of impending danger, Frigg extracted a promise from each and every thing, except the mistletoe, that no harm should happen to him. Apparently, the mistletoe appeared such a harmless

plant that she did not bother about it. This proved to be a mistake because the fire god *LOKI* got the blind god *HODR* to throw a branch of mistletoe at Balder which killed him. Frigg's subsequent effort to have her son released from the land of the dead also failed, because Loki refused to mourn on behalf of Balder. Thus it would seem that Frigg was a fertility goddess not unlike the Sumerian deity Inanna, though she lacked that goddess's ability to enter the netherworld.

Frigg has much in common with *FREYJA*. Although her role as consort of Odin shows her to be a devoted wife and mother, she too possesses a falcon skin and has a great passion for gold. It is quite possible that the two goddesses had their origins in a single earth-mother deity.

FRIGGA see *FRIGG*

FRIJA see *FRIGG*

FRITHIOF see *TRAGIC LOVERS*

GEFFINN see *GEFION*

FRIGG enjoyed the privilege of sitting beside her husband, Odin, on his fabulous throne, Hlidskialf, from where the divine pair could view the nine worlds, witnessing events present and future. A paragon of silence, she never revealed her foreknowledge. (ILLUSTRATION BY H THEAKER, C. 1920.)

GEFION, also known as Gefinn and Gefjon, was a Germanic goddess of fertility akin to FREYJA, the sister of the fertility god FREYR, and FRIGG, the wife of ODIN. Appropriately for a goddess of agriculture, Gefion's name is connected with "giving". She was usually imagined as a virgin and as the protector of virgins after their deaths. However, LOKI accused Gefion of selling herself, like Freyja, for a necklace.

Her myth concerns ploughing and doubtless recalls the ancient ritual of ploughing a token strip of land each spring. Gefion, disguised as an old beggar, managed to trick King Gylfi of Sweden out of a great tract of land. In return for her hospitality, the king offered Gefion as much of his kingdom as she could plough with four oxen during one day and one night. With the aid of her four giant sons, transformed into oxen, she cut from the mainland the whole island of Zealand, part of present-day Denmark.

GEIRROD was a frost giant, the father of two daughters, GJALP and Greip, and was one of THOR's most formidable enemies. It happened that LOKI, a constant companion of Thor, had taken the form of a hawk and was captured by Geirrod. The only way Loki could avoid death was to promise to bring Thor to Geirrod's hall without his magic belt and magic hammer which protected the god against frost giants.

Because Thor trusted Loki he went with him to Geirrod's hall. Fortunately, they rested on the way at the home of a friendly giantess named GRID, and she warned Thor about the plan while Loki was asleep. She also lent the god her own magic belt of strength, magic iron gloves and magic staff. Thus equipped, Thor arrived at their destination, with Loki hanging as usual on his belt. Geirrod was not at home, but the giant's servants received the visitors. It was not long, though, before Geirrod's two

GEIRROD's (left) immense body, slain by Thor, lay in the City of the Not-Dead, shrouded in cobwebs. Beyond the sleeping giant sparkled the Chamber of Treasures full of jewels and weapons. Here came the Danish hero, Thorkill, years later, on a raid for his king. (ILLUSTRATION BY NICK BEALE, 1995.)

GEFION (above), disguised as a beggar, ploughed a vast field in Sweden with four giant oxen, her supernatural sons. They dragged the tilled field to the coast and floated it across the sea to Denmark, where it formed the island of Zealand. (ILLUSTRATION BY JAMES ALEXANDER, 1995.)

daughters tried to kill the slumbering Thor by lifting up his chair and dashing out his brains on the ceiling. But with the aid of Grid's staff, Thor succeeded in driving the chair downwards and crushed the frost giantesses instead. However, Geirrod himself then appeared in the hall and using a pair of tongs he picked up a red-hot iron ball and threw it at Thor, who caught it in Grid's iron gloves. Angered beyond measure by this extremely discourteous action, Thor threw the still hot and smoking ball back down the hall, straight through an iron pillar and deep into Geirrod's stomach. After this, the thunder god laid about the frost giant's servants with the magic staff.

GERDA, in Germanic mythology, was a beautiful frost giantess and daughter of the giant Gymir, who reluctantly became the wife of FREYR, the fertility god. Although initially resistant to the idea, she was persuaded to marry by Freyr's faithful servant SKIRNIR, when he threatened to recite a terrible spell. This spell would have made Gerda so ugly than no man would ever come near her again. She would be transformed into "a sight to make the blood run cold". So it was that Gerda met Freyr in a forest after nine nights, representing the nine months of the northern winter. The Aurora Borealis was believed by some to be the radiance of Gerda. (See also TRAGIC LOVERS)

GINNUNGAGAP, in Germanic mythology, was a "yawning emptiness" at the time of creation, which lay between the realms of fire and cold. As the warm air from the south met the chill of the north, the ice of Ginnungagap melted and from the drops was formed YMIR, the frost giant, and AUDHUMLA, the primeval cow. By licking the ice, Audhumla uncovered BURI, ancestor of the gods. Buri's three grandsons, ODIN, VILI and VE, killed Ymir and took his body to the centre of Ginnungagap. There they made Midgard, the world of men, from his body. Ymir's flesh became the earth, his bones the mountains, his teeth rocks and stones, his hair the trees and his blood turned into the lakes and seas. The brothers used his skull to form the sky, with four dwarfs named Nordi, Sudri, Austri and Westri holding up the corners.

GJALP ("Howler") was a frost giantess, daughter of GEIRROD, who, along with her sister Greip, tried to kill THOR, the Germanic thunder god. When Thor, accompanied by the fire god LOKI, came to the hall of Geirrod, Gjalp did what she could to harm the visitors. Even before their arrival she added a torrent of her menstrual blood to a river in order to drown Thor and Loki. A well-aimed stone stopped Gjalp and sent her howling home. However, she and Greip then tried to ram the head of sleeping Thor against the rafters by suddenly raising his chair. The thunder god woke just in time to force the chair downwards by using a magic staff. Its massive weight broke the backs of the two giantesses and they died in agony on the floor.

GINNUNGAGAP (right), the primal abyss at the dawn of creation, lay between the icy north and fiery south. Twelve swirling streams gushed into its vacuum and froze into massive ice blocks. In the south, fiery sparks slowly melted the ice, and from the icy droplets slowly emerged a frost giant. (ILLUSTRATION BY NICK BEALE, 1995.)

GERDA (above), a frosty beauty, inspired the love of Freyr who sent Skirnir to win her hand. Although he offered her the apples of youth, and revealed his master's glowing portrait reflected in water, she remained unmoved until forced by threat of magic to consent. (ILLUSTRATION BY H THEAKER, C. 1920.)

GJALP (right) stirs up a river into a great flood, engulfing Thor as he wades across. Thor managed to stem the torrent by striking Gjalp with a boulder. He then heaved himself ashore by grasping a mountain ash named "Thor's Salvation". (ILLUSTRATION BY JAMES ALEXANDER, 1995.)

H

GRENDEL, *a man-devouring monster, met his match in the fearless warrior Beowulf, who seized the creature's hairy limb in a vice-like grip and wrenched it from its socket. Howling with pain and rage, Grendel fled back to his watery lair and bled to death. (ILLUSTRATION BY ALAN LEE, 1984.)*

GRENDEL was the name of a water monster which was invulnerable to weapons and troubled the kingdom of King Hrothgar of Denmark. One night Grendel, "grim and greedy, brutally cruel", came to the royal hall and ate a sleeping warrior, but a visiting warrior, BEOWULF, held one of the monster's arms in a vice-like grip. In the fierce struggle that ensued, Grendel's arm was torn off and he ran away and bled to death in his watery lair. It was in this lair that, later, Beowulf killed the monster's mother. Grendel's head was so large that when Beowulf brought it back as a trophy to King Hrothgar, he needed the assistance of four men to carry it.

GRID was a kindly frost giantess who helped the Germanic thunder god THOR in his struggle against GEIRROD. Thor had been lured by LOKI, the fire god, into danger without the protection of his magic belt of strength and his magic hammer. Grid loaned Thor her own belt, iron gloves and unbreakable staff to face Geirrod. In some traditions she is said to have borne ODIN a son, the silent god VIDAR, and to have made for him a special shoe which enabled him to stand in the mouth of the wolf FENRIR.

GRIMHILD see SORCERY AND SPELLS

GROA, according to Germanic mythology, was a seeress and the wife of Aurvandil, whose frozen toe THOR turned into a star by throwing it up into the sky. Exactly who this Aurvandil, or Aurvandill, was remains uncertain, though it has been suggested that he may have

been a fertility god of the wetlands. Groa herself tried by magic to remove whetstone fragments from Thor's head after his fight with the frost giant HRUNGNIR. They had come from Hrungnir's sharp-edged, three-cornered stone when it had collided with Thor's hammer in mid-air. So excited was Groa, however, by Thor's news about the

star and the return of her lost husband that she unfortunately failed to finish the spell, and this was why a few fragments of whetstone remained in Thor's head. Some time after her death, Groa was roused from the grave by her son, Svipdrag, who needed her advice on how he could win the love of the beautiful Menglad.

GUNGNIR was the magic spear belonging to ODIN, the leader of the Germanic gods. It was forged by dwarfs, the sons of Ivaldi, at the same time as a wig of spun gold, which the fire god LOKI ordered as a replacement for the golden hair of THOR's wife SIF. Mischievous Loki had cut off her beautiful locks as a joke. Having made the wig, the dwarfs decided to please the gods by using the furnace to make a ship for FREYR and, for Odin, a spear that managed to be both strong and slender, and never missed its mark. It was required in Viking custom that a spear should be thrown over the heads of an enemy before battle commenced, as an entreaty for Odin's aid. When the god hung himself on the cosmic tree YGGDRASIL for nine nights in order to obtain wisdom, he was, just like Christ, stabbed with a spear. (See also TREASURES AND TALISMANS)

GUDRUN see THE VALKYRIES

GUNNER see NORSE HEROES

HARBARD ("grey-beard"), in Germanic mythology, was a surly boatman. Wishing to cross a deep river, the god THOR summoned Harbard to ferry him over, only to be met by insults. Thor could think of no response to Harbard's abuse other than anger, but the boatman remained away from the bank. In his fury, Thor failed to notice that Harbard was his father ODIN. The meeting between the two gods reveals their different characters: Odin, the deceitful troublemaker and braggart; while Thor is hot-tempered but honest.

GROA, *a gifted healer, chants charms over Thor in order to loosen the stone splinters lodged in the god's forehead. Feeling relief and gratitude, Thor rashly revealed that her long-lost husband was alive. The happy news so excited Groa that she forgot her spells and so left a splinter in Thor's head.* (ILLUSTRATION BY NICK BEALE, 1995.)

HEIMDALL (right), bright guardian of the Bifrost Bridge, was ever alert, sleeping less than a bird. Gifted with special sight and hearing, he could see for 100 miles by night or day, and hear grass growing on the hillside. With his curved herald's horn, he would summon the gods to Ragnarok. (ILLUSTRATION BY NICK BEALE, 1995.)

GUNGNIR'S (below) spear shaft was carved from the sacred wood of Yggdrasil. After gaining wisdom at the World Tree, Odin broke off a bough, and fashioned a perfect staff from its holy wood. Here, the one-eyed, all-seeing god peers through the boughs of the sacred ash. (ILLUSTRATION BY ALAN LEE, 1984.)

GUNGNIR (above) was the name of Odin's spear; both slender and strong, it was unswerving in its flight. The weapon was so sacred that oaths were sworn on its point. Dvalin, the dwarf, forged its head, and Odin made the staff, carving it with magic runes. (ODIN BY R FOGELBERG, MARBLE, C. 1890.)

HEIMDALL, or Heimdalr, was the son of nine mothers and the watchman for the Germanic gods. Originally, he may have been an omniscient sky god. He could hear the sound of grass and wool grow-ing, and see for over a hundred miles. He stood upon *BIFROST*, the three-strand bridge that linked *ASGARD* and Midgard (heaven and earth respectively). There he stood ready to blow his horn Gjall at the onset of *RAGNAROK*, during which he was to be the last to fall in single combat with *LOKI*. Heimdall's name may be related to the con-cept of a "world tree", as he was thought to be the supreme watch-man perched at its top, above the highest rainbow. He disguised him-self as *RIG*, the mortal who estab-lished the three social groups: the nobles, the peasants, and the enslaved. Disguised as Rig, the god visited in turn three houses in Midgard and fathered handsome children for the nobility, sturdy children for the peasants and ill-favoured children for the slaves.

HEIMDALR see *HEIMDALL*

TREASURES AND TALISMANS

THE MOST CELEBRATED CRAFTSMEN of the Norse world were wise and gifted dwarfs who laboured underground in caverns studded with gems. With superhuman artistry and secret wisdom, they fashioned fabulous treasures and talismans for gods and heroes. Some of their creations were exquisitely beautiful, such as the Brisingamen necklace; others were supernaturally powerful, such as the silken thread which fettered the fierce wolf, Fenrir. Most indispensable were the gods' wondrous weapons – Thor's boomerang hammer, Mjollnir, and Odin's infallible spear, Gungnir. The tireless dwarfs were also innovative engineers who crafted a collapsible, flying ship for Freyr and a sword that fought of its own accord once drawn. Most amazing of all, perhaps, were their living treasures, the gold-bristled boar, Gullinbursti, and Sif's golden hair which grew naturally. Some precious marvels were created by nature, such as the golden apples of youth. Among mortals, only Volund the smith could match the dwarfs in artistry and craft while, among sorcerers, the Finnish Ilmarinen excelled in magical craft and produced a peerless talisman, the Sampo.

IDUN'S (left) golden apples kept the gods eternally young. The fabulous fruit tree was tended and guarded by the three wise Norns who allowed only Idun, the deity of Spring, to pick the magic fruit. Yet such precious gifts were coveted by the giants who sought to strip the gods of their vigour and youth. Here, the giant Thiassi, disguised as a bird, carries Idun and her apples off in an ill-fated attempt to steal the gods' elixir of life. (ILLUSTRATION BY H THEAKER, C. 1920.)

THE BRISINGAMEN (above) necklace was crafted by four dwarfs with such artistry that it glittered like a constellation of stars in the night sky. Around Freyja's lovely neck it became an emblem of the fruits of the heavens and earth. She, in her turn, produced treasures for the earth whenever she cried, and Freyja wept profusely, especially during her search for her husband, Odur. When her tears fell on rock, they turned to gold, but tears shed at sea turned to amber. (FREYJA BY N J O BLOMMER, DETAIL, CANVAS, 1852.)

MJOLLNIR (left), Thor's wondrous hammer, was never far from his grasp, as seen here in this characteristic pose of the god with his hammer clutched close to his heart. The Mjollnir was used as a fiery thunderbolt, launching shafts of lightning, and as a weapon for smashing giants' skulls. It was a talisman of both creativity and destruction, and was used to hallow both birth and death ceremonies. (BRONZE, 10TH CENTURY.)

GUNGNIR (right), Odin's great spear, never missed its mark. The spear shaft was fashioned by Odin from the sacred ash of Yggdrasil and carved with the god's magic runes. Just as valuable was Odin's fabulous ring, Draupnir, which produced eight similar gold rings every nine days, an everlasting source of wealth and power. (ILLUSTRATION BY H HENDRICH, C. 1906.)

THE SAMPO (below) was forged by Ilmarinen, the Eternal Hammerer of Finnish myth, who hammered out the sky at the dawn of time. Over three days, the talisman was fashioned mysteriously from one swift quill, milk of the fertile cow, a grain of barley and the fleece of a summer lamb. So out of the magical flames of the forge the Sampo was created; it consisted of a flour mill, salt mill and money mill, ensuring lasting prosperity and power. Here, the master smith looks intently into the furnace to see what the fire has produced. (THE FORGING OF THE SAMPO BY A GALLEN-KALLELA, CANVAS, C. 1852.)

WONDROUS LONGSHIPS (above) belonged to both Freyr and Thorstein. The god's ship, Skidbladnir, was crafted by the dwarfs. A personification of the clouds, it glided across land, sea and air. Although massive enough to convey all the gods and an entire host, it could be folded up and pocketed like a handkerchief. Thorstein's fabulous dragon boat, Ellida, was a gift from the sea god, Aegir. Shaped by swelling planks which grew together in the form of a winged dragon, Ellida raced with the whistling wind and outstripped the eagle. The floating fortress was famed far and wide. (ILLUSTRATION BY I J BILIBIN, C. 1900.)

HEL was the daughter of trickster *LOKI*, the fire god, and the frost giantess *ANGRBODA*. She was ruler of the Germanic netherworld (also called Hel), to which she had been banished by *ODIN*, the chief god. Once there, however, her powers were stronger than Odin's, for when Odin's son *BALDER* was killed Hel refused to return him to his parents. Her brothers, *FENRIR* the wolf and *JORMUNGAND* the serpent, were as terrifying as she, though it was Hel and her ghastly home which were adopted by the Christians as the name for their realm of eternal damnation.

The unpleasantness of Hel's realm stands in marked contrast to the pleasurable and enviable afterlife that was enjoyed by the heroic dead who dwelt in Odin's wondrous hall *VALHALLA*. However, Hel's subjects were little more than silent attendants of the semi-decomposed queen. She was only partly decomposed because she had the face and body of a living woman, but her thighs and legs were those of a corpse. Hel's throne was known as the Sick Bed and her subjects were "all who died through sickness and old age".

HERMOD leaps bravely into misty Hel on his vain mission to seek Balder's release from death. The great noise made by the hero and his eight-hoofed horse Sleipnir when they crossed the crystal Gioll Bridge, provoked the grim guardian, Modgud, to complain irritably that Hermod must be alive. (ILLUSTRATION BY PETER HURD, 1882.)

HEL, the grim goddess of the dead, listens unimpressed to Hermod's plea to release the much-loved god Balder from her dismal realm. Behind her, kneeling, there are rows of her sad subjects – souls of the old, sick or criminal who suffered ceaseless cold, pain and hunger in their cheerless, dreary home. (ILLUSTRATION BY JAMES ALEXANDER, 1995.)

HERMOD, in Germanic mythology, was the son of *ODIN* and *FRIGG*, and brother of *BALDER*. Rather like the Greek god Hermes and the Roman Mercury, he acted as a divine messenger. Hermod also shared these gods' interest in the dead, for it was he who was sent to *HEL* after Balder's death to ask for his brother's release. He rode there on Odin's famous horse, the eight-legged *SLEIPNIR*. When Hel refused to let Balder go until everything wept for him, Hermod was allowed to take back to *ASGARD* the arm-ring which Odin had fastened to Balder's body as a memento.

Hermod nearly met his own death on a journey to Midgard, the land of men. He was sent there by Odin to consult a Finn named Rossthiof about his worries concerning the future. He was saved by magic, however, and returned to reassure his father as best he could.

HIMINBRIOTER see *HIMINRJOT*

HIMINRJOT, or Himinbrioter, ("Sky Bellower") was the head of a gigantic black ox. The ox belonged to *HYMIR* with whom *THOR* went fishing for *JORMUNGAND*, the sea serpent. Thor had no trouble in breaking Himinrjot's neck, despite the animal's vast size, and used its head to bait his hook. Jormungand rose for this delicacy, but the head stuck in his throat. Thor would have landed the prize had not the sight of the serpent rising from the depths of the sea terrified Hymir. In the confusion that ensued Hymir was able to cut the great sea serpent free.

HOD see *HODR*

HODR, sometimes Hodur or Hod, the son of *ODIN* and *FRIGG*, was the blind god of Germanic mythology. In the Icelandic tradition, Hodr unintentionally killed his brother *BALDER*. When Balder was troubled by dreams of his coming death, his mother Frigg exacted a promise from each and every thing not to do her son any harm. A sole exception was the mistletoe, a plant the goddess considered to be too insignificant. The trickster god *LOKI* learned about the mistletoe, however, and guided Hodr's hand when he threw it at his brother. The branch of mistletoe went straight through Balder, who fell down dead. Once it became clear that Balder would have to stay in the land of the dead, Hodr was sent to join him as a punishment. In a very different version of the story, Hodr and Balder are rivals for the hand of Nanna, and Balder is portrayed as a hateful figure. Their conflict is finally resolved when Hodr kills Balder with a magic sword. This Danish version shows the brothers in a very different light.

HERMOD (below) spurs his fabulous steed to assail the barred gate of Hel. Within, Balder can be seen waiting stoically beside an alarming creature, who is possibly one of the starved inmates of Hel. Balder, who knew the future well, knew that he was destined to remain in cheerless Hel for ever. (ILLUSTRATION FROM THE PROSE EDDA, 1760.)

LEMINKAINEN (above) was slain and dismembered during one of his exploits. But his magician mother gathered him up and restored him to life. Here she calls upon a bee to bring life-giving honey from beyond the highest heaven. (LEMINKAINEN'S MOTHER BY A GALLEN-KALLELA, CANVAS, C.1890.)

KULLERVO see *SORCERY AND SPELLS*

KVASIR was a wise man in Germanic mythology. His name means "spittle" and recalls his creation when the gods spat into a jar to mark the end of conflict between two branches of the divine family, the *VANIR* and the *AESIR*. The Aesir then took the jar and Kvasir was made from the spittle. Renowned for his great wisdom, he travelled the world and wherever he went people stopped what they were

doing to listen to him. He was killed by two dwarfs, *FJALAR* and Galar, who wanted his wisdom. They mixed his blood with honey in order to make a wonderful mead which gave the gift of poetry to everyone who drank it.

LEIB-OLMAI ("Alder man") was a Lapp bear god. At bear festivals hunters used to sprinkle their faces with an extract of alder bark. As the protector of bears, Leib-Olmai required certain prayers before he would allow any man to kill a bear.

LEMINKAINEN ("Lover") was one of the heroes in Finnish epics. As a child, he was bathed by his mother three times in one summer night and nine times in one autumn night to ensure that he would become a wise adult, gifted

KVASIR (right), a character endowed with wondrous wisdom, was created from the spittle of the gods. He travelled the world inspiring gods and mortals with his sense and wisdom. After his death his blood was used to make a mead of inspiration. (ILLUSTRATION FROM THE PROSE EDDA, 1760.)

with a talent for song. A carefree young man, many of his adventures involve the pursuit of women and he accompanied *VAINAMOINEN* on a journey to the land of Pohja in search of wives. His most dangerous exploit was an attempt to kill the swan of *TUONI*, the god of the dead. Failing to protect himself with magic, he was torn apart by Tuoni's son and his remains were scattered in the river. But his magician mother put his body back together again and restored him to life. (See also *NORSE HEROES*)

NORSE HEROES

T HE VIKINGS were famed for their fighting spirit, facing death and doom with vigour and courage. Their hardy heroism was doubtless shaped by the crushing Nordic climate, but also by a stoic fatalism. While accepting the inevitability of death on the field and doom at the end of the world, the Norsemen fought with undiminished spirit. For the Vikings, word-fame was everything, redeeming and surviving a hero's death. After death, the bravest heroes went to Valhalla where they awaited the fated and fatal showdown at Ragnarok. No less than the heroes, the Norse gods were heroic, facing doom at Ragnarok with fighting spirit. Finnish heroes were quite as determined and brave in their way, though perhaps less grand and stoic. Armed with magical forces, they battled with incantations rather than force of arms. For the Finns, death was not always final: Leminkainen had more than one life, while aged Vainamoinen could always slip out of a tight corner by shifting shape.

GUNNER AND HOGNI (left), the Nibelung brothers, died gallantly though neither lived a flawless life. Drawn into the web of tragedy woven by a cursed ring, they slew the peerless hero Sigurd, and hoarded his gold. When seized by Atli, who coveted their gold, they refused to surrender under threat of death. Hogni died laughing as his heart was cut out; and Gunner, here, cast into a serpent's pit with bound hands, played his harp with his feet, defying death to the last. (WOOD CARVING, 12TH CENT.)

THOR (right), supernaturally strong and armed with the magical Mjollnir, was a formidable foe. Being neither immortal nor invulnerable, he fought with a fearless spirit, slaying giants with effortless ease and reckless rage. Along with some of the other gods, Thor was destined to die heroically at Ragnarok, after putting up a fierce fight and slaying his arch-foe, the World Serpent. (THOR AND THE GIANTS BY M E WINGE, CANVAS, DETAIL, C. 1890.)

SIGURD (above), the most famous of Iceland's heroes, slew the terrible dragon, Fafnir. Armed with his father's invincible sword, Sigurd hid in a hole in the dragon's slime track and, as Fafnir slithered across on his daily trip to the foul forest pool, thrust his sword into its belly. The bloated creature had grown increasingly monstrous in shape and character; all the better to guard his cursed treasure. Although Sigurd's heroic deed won him fame and fortune, his life from then on was blighted by the curse that came with the ill-fated treasure. (ILLUSTRATION BY ALAN LEE, 1984.)

SIGMUND THE VOLSUNG (right) proved his heroic status by drawing forth a magical sword thrust into the Branstock oak by Odin. With this sword he won fame throughout Scandinavia, but also provoked the envy of his brother-in-law, Siggeir, who resolved to slay all the Volsungs. All ten sons were tied to forest trees, prey to the beasts of the forest. Only Sigmund escaped, by biting off a wolf's tongue, and sought vengeance for his kinsmen. (ILLUSTRATION BY P WILSON, C. 1900.)

THE LESHY, also known as Lesovik and Lesiye, was the Slavonic spirit of the forest who led travellers and hunters astray in the woods. Although human in form, he had a long green beard and cast no shadow. His chief attribute, however, was his ability to change size: he could become as small as a mouse or as tall as the highest tree. Every October the Leshy went into a kind of hibernation, disappearing from his woodland home until the following spring, when he would return wilder and noisier than ever.

LESIYE see THE LESHY

LESOVIK see THE LESHY

LIF and Lifthrasir ("Life" and "Eager for Life") were the man and woman who were to hide in the cosmic ash tree *YGGDRASIL* at *RAGNAROK*, the doom of the gods. They were destined to survive this catastrophe and then repopulate a new world, which would rise from the sea like a volcanic island. "The bellowing fire will not scorch them; it will not even touch them, and their food will be the morning dew. Through the branches they will see a new sun burn as the world ends and starts again."

LIFTHRASIR see LIF

LODDFAFNIR, in Germanic mythology, was a man who learned the wisdom of the gods. He visited the Well of *URD*, where the gods held their daily assembly, and stayed in *VALHALLA*, *ODIN*'s hall. His myth comprises a retelling of the knowledge he gathered there. It is an interesting mixture of commonsensical advice about good conduct and superstitions concerning the avoidance of witchcraft.

LOKI, sometimes Lopt, was the Germanic fire god and son of the giants *FARBAUTI* and Laufey. He was a mischief-maker, trickster and shape-changer, and grew progressively more evil until eventually the gods bound him in a cave until the coming of *RAGNAROK*, the end of the world. Boredom was a problem for Loki, who "was tired of the string of days that unwound without a knot or a twist in them".

The fact that his parents were giants may help to explain his tendency towards evil deeds. He

SAULE (above), the Baltic sun goddess, poured golden light from her heavenly height through the summery clouds down to the earth below. The snake on her crown symbolizes her fertility and abundance. The Morning Star, her child, flashes above her. (ILLUSTRATION BY JAMES ALEXANDER, 1995.)

SIF (above right) was famous for her gold, flowing hair, symbolizing ripe harvest corn. When Loki cut off her locks her misery represented the winter season when the cornfields are reduced to stubble. Here, Loki lurks menacingly behind the dreaming beauty. (ILLUSTRATION BY NICK BEALE, 1995.)

SIGNY (right) Queen of Gotaland, rushes down the glacial fjord to greet her kinsmen. She warns them of an ambush planned by her vengeful husband, Siggeir, a sore loser, who bitterly resented her brother Sigmund's victory in a magical sword contest. (ILLUSTRATION BY JAMES ALEXANDER, 1995.)

caverns where the dwarfs lived, Loki also met the dwarf brothers Brokk and Eiti. They were so jealous of the workmanship that had gone into the wig, the boat and the spear that Loki persuaded them to make something better; he even staked his own head on their inability to do so. As a result, the dwarf brothers fashioned the magic hammer known as MJOLLNIR, the scourge of the frost giants.

The gods were delighted with the treasures Loki and Brokk had brought back. However, Brokk demanded Loki's head. The gods would not agree, but they had no objection to Brokk sewing up Loki's lips with a thong when Thor dragged the god back home after

he tried to flee, which caused Loki to plan a revenge against Thor. (See also TREASURES AND TALISMANS)

SIGMUND see NORSE HEROES

SIGNY, in Germanic mythology, was the unfortunate daughter of VOLSUNG, supposedly a descendant of ODIN. Married against her will to the Gothic king Siggeir, she tried to warn her father and her ten

brothers about Siggeir's plot against them, but they were ambushed in a forest and bound to a fallen tree. Each night a wolf devoured one of them in turn, until only her youngest brother Sigmund was left alive. Signy got a slave to smear Sigmund's face with honey so that the wolf would lick him instead of biting him. Sigmund was thus able to catch the wolf's tongue in his teeth and overcome the beast.

Signy helped Sigmund to plot revenge. She even slept with him in disguise and bore a son named Sinfiotli. When Sinfiotli grew up she placed him in Sigmund's care, but they were both captured by Siggeir. A magic sword freed them and killed Siggeir and his sons. Signy chose to die herself in the burning Gothic palace, but not before she had told Sigmund the truth about Sinfiotli's parentage.

SIGRYN see SIGYN

SIGUNN see SIGYN

SIGURD, or Siegfried as he was known in German, was a northern Germanic hero similar to the Celtic King Arthur. He was the foster-son of REGIN, the smith at the court of King Hjalprek in Jutland, who sent him to recover a fabulous hoard of gold. Regin's father HREIDMAR had first acquired this treasure, which once belonged to the dwarf ANDVARI. To get their hands on the gold Regin and his brother FAFNIR had then killed Hreidmar, but Fafnir wanted the treasure for himself and turned into a dragon to guard it. By cunningly stabbing the monster from underneath, Sigurd succeeded in slaying Fafnir, thus apparently gaining both dwarfish wealth and wisdom, since Fafnir was said to have understood the language of birds. When he realized that Regin intended to kill him for the gold, Sigurd slew him before carrying it away himself. (See also NORSE HEROES; TRAGIC LOVERS; RINGS OF POWER)

SIGYN, also known as Sigunn or Sigryn, in Germanic mythology, was the faithful wife of the fire god LOKI and mother of his sons Narvi and VALI. Once the gods realized that in Loki they had allowed the growth of evil in their midst, they

SIGURD (above) watches with fascination as Regin forges the broken shards of his father's wondrous sword, a gift from Odin. The conquering sword would help Sigurd in his destined mission to slay the dragon, Fafnir, guardian of a fabulous but ill-fated treasure. (SIEGFRIED IN THE FORGE OF REGIN BY W VON HANSCHILD, FRESCO, 1880.)

SIGURD (right) confronts the fire-breathing dragon, Fafnir, and slays him, winning fame and a fateful fortune. On the advice of his mentor, Regin, he roasted the creature's heart, licking some spilt blood from which he learnt the speech of birds. (SIEGFRIED AND FAFNIR BY H. HENRICH, CANVAS, 1906.)

ocean, lift the massive sea serpent Jormungand and wrestle with old age. As soon as this message was delivered, Utgard vanished. Only then did it dawn on Thor that Skrymir and Utgard were illusions, vast creations sent out by frightened frost giants. But it gave Loki some satisfaction to learn that brain had indeed triumphed over brawn.

Even Thor had to admit that on certain occasions Loki's cleverness was necessary to hold the frost giants in check. Such a moment in time was when Mjollnir, Thor's magic hammer, fell into their hands after it was stolen by the dwarfs. Its new owner, the frost giant *THRYM*, demanded as the price of the hammer's return the hand of *FREYJA*, the fertility goddess. Loki got Thor to dress in Freyja's clothes and go to Thrym's hall instead. Despite his god-like appetite, Thor was passed

THOR (above) impulsive as ever, confronted mighty Skrymir with his tiny hammer, bashing him over the head to silence his snores, but to no avail. Each time the giant woke he scratched his brow and nodded off again. Later, Thor learnt that Skrymir had been an illusion. (ILLUSTRATION BY J HUARD, 1930.)

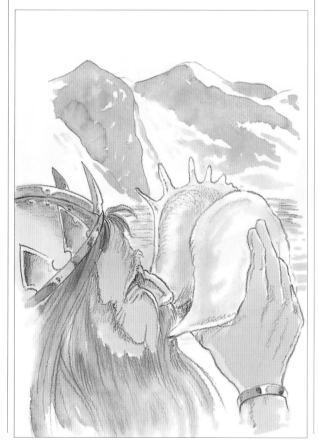

THOR (left) and his party visited the icy citadel of Utgard, the stronghold of the frost giants, where they underwent a series of allegorical tests. Thialfi was outstripped by the speed of Thought, Loki out-eaten by Wildfire, and Thor overcome by Age. Here, Thor fails to drain a horn brimful of the ocean. (ILLUSTRATION BY JAMES ALEXANDER, 1995.)

THOR (above) wrestles with Jormungand in their final combat at Ragnarok. Trapped within the serpent's crushing coils, Thor smashed its ugly head with a fatal blow of his hammer; he then staggered back nine paces and drowned in the flood of venom flowing from the beast's gaping jaws. (ILLUSTRATION BY JAMES ALEXANDER, 1995.)

off by his "bridesmaid" Loki as a blushing bride, and an excited Thrym handed over Mjollnir. The ensuing massacre did a great deal to restore Thor's fierce reputation, which had been tarnished by the god having to dress like a woman.

Mjollnir was the sole protection of the gods against the frost giants. It was the thunderbolt which terrorized them prior to the catastrophe of Ragnarok. Apart from its destructive side, the hammer had other magic powers over fertility and death. It seems to have had the ability to restore animal life. It also hallowed marriage, for otherwise Thrym would not have been so ready to place Mjollnir between

Thor's knees when the thunder god was disguised as Freyja. But throughout the myths relating to Thor we are never unconscious of its unlimited destructive powers. For it was the thunder god's purpose to quell the enemies of the gods – "to smash their legs, break their skulls, and crush their backs". Like his Hindu equivalent Indra, Thor was the scourge of evil and in Germanic mythology this could only mean frost giants. Loki's eventual siding with these grim opponents is therefore one of the saddest events to befall Thor, for the two gods "both enjoyed each other's company". (See also *NORSE HEROES; RAGNAROK*)

RINGS OF POWER

AMONG THE VIKINGS, the ring was a potent symbol of power, fortune and fame. A gift of honour and form of currency, it was also sometimes a royal heirloom, such as the Swedish Sviagriss. The magical rings of Norse myth were also symbols of destiny and, in their bleakest form, symbols of doom. One famous example was the cursed ring, Andvarinaut, which blighted many lives. Another ring of doom was Thor's Domhring, formed by a circle of stone statues surrounding a punishment pillar in front of his temple. The Domhring possibly symbolized the inevitability of retribution. Much more joyous and fabulous rings were Odin's astounding Draupnir which literally dripped eight similar gold rings every nine days; or Thor's Oath Ring, a symbol of fair play and good faith. The rings of heroes inevitably brought wealth and power, but not always happiness and sometimes tragedy, if corrupted by greed. Yet the pure rings of Orthnit, Wolfdietrich and Dietrich were symbols of a ring-lord's circle of power and everlasting fame.

DRAUPNIR,
Odin's fabulous ring,
was an emblem of abundance
and power. Precious beyond compare, it
dripped eight similar gold rings every ninth night, consolidating
his vast wealth and dominion over the nine worlds. Draupnir
was crafted by the dwarf, Sindri, while his brother, Brokk,
pumped the bellows. In an extravagant gesture of grief, Odin
cast the ring upon Balder's funeral pyre, but later retrieved it
when Hermod ventured to Hel. The return of the ring symbolized
the promise of fertility after winter bleakness. Here, the dwarf
Sindri fashions the magnificent ring with fire and arcane magic
in his underground forge. (ILLUSTRATION BY ALAN LEE, 1984.)

THE GOLD RING *among the Vikings was*
a precious token of power, fame and
fortune. Sometimes bequeathed as an
heirloom, it was also often buried with the
ring-lord for the journey to the otherworld,
such as this burial treasure. Exquisitely
wrought, the ring's clear, bold lines express
the vigour and strength of Viking craft.
(GILT SILVER, 10TH CENTURY.)

ALBERICH (above), a dwarf in the Niebelungenlied, forged a ring of power from the Rhinegold stolen from the Rhine Maidens. News of the gold robbery and ring of power incited gods and giants alike to action. The giants Fafner and Fasolt demanded the ring in payment for building Valhalla, and carried off Freyja as a hostage. In the border, the gods, Odin, Frigg, Loki, Freyr and Thor all search despairingly for the hidden treasure. (ILLUSTRATION BY F VON STASSEN, 1914.)

DIETRICH (above), a Gothic hero, won a wondrous ring from the dwarf, Laurin, who ruled a fabulous underground kingdom lit by gems. After various battles and intrigues, Dietrich overcame the wily dwarf, and claimed his magical gold ring as well as a girdle of strength, a cape of invisibility, a magical sword and a vast ring-hoard. Laurin's ring was the very one owned by Dietrich's great-grandfather, the Emperor Wolfdietrich. Here, Dietrich breaks into Laurin's enchanted, ever-flowering rose garden, before winning the ring treasures. (ILLUSTRATION BY ALAN LEE, 1984.)

THE RING ANDVARINAUT wove a fortune of gold much like Draupnir, but was tainted by the bitter curse of Andvari. Heidmar, who had demanded the ring as wiergold from Loki, was the first to suffer from the curse by falling at the hands of his son, Fafnir, who lusted after the gold. Next, Fafnir turned himself into a monstrous dragon to guard the ring-hoard. When the youthful hero Sigurd (above) slew the dragon, he inherited the fabulous ring-hoard, but with it a terrible curse. (WOOD CARVING, 12TH CENTURY.)

SIGURD (right) won the cursed ring, Andvarinaut, after slaying its dragon guardian, Fafnir. Although innocent himself, he suffered from the ring's web of doom. After falling in love with the splendid Valkyrie, Brynhild, he was bewitched by Grimhild into betraying Brynhild by marrying Gudrun. When his memory returned, he suffered from guilt and grief. Sigurd's gold in turn evoked the envy of the Nibelung brothers who slew him, urged on by a vengeful Brynhild, seeking to assuage her honour. As the hero breathed his last, he died calling to Brynhild. (ILLUSTRATION BY ARTHUR RACKHAM, C. 1900.)

239

THRUD, in Germanic mythology, was the daughter of the thunder god *THOR* and his wife *SIF*. She was promised to the dwarf *ALVIS* as a payment for his handicraft. But Thor prevented the dwarf from claiming Thrud by keeping him talking until morning, when the sunlight turned Alvis into stone.

THRYM, in Germanic mythology, was the frost giant who came to acquire *THOR*'s magic hammer. The gods were at a loss because only this weapon could protect them against the frost giants. When Thrym said he would exchange the hammer for the fertility goddess *FREYJA*, the fire god *LOKI* persuaded Thor to go to the frost giant's stronghold disguised as the bride in order to recover the hammer. Loki also went along in the form of a maidservant. Thus the unusual pair arrived at Thrym's hall. Even though the frost giant was quite suspicious about his bride-to-be, Loki cleverly managed to talk him into producing the hammer, which Thor then used to lay low all the frost giants in sight.

THRYM (left), a daring storm giant, stole Thor's sacred hammer, causing panic at Asgard. Here, the giant broods on his rocky hilltop overlooked by Loki, disguised as a falcon, and scouting the icy wastes in search of the hammer, buried eight fathoms down. (ILLUSTRATION BY JAMES ALEXANDER, 1995.)

TIR see *TYR*

TIWAZ see *TYR*

TRIGLAV was a three-headed god of the Slavs living in central Europe. At Stettin in present-day Poland, Triglav once boasted four separate temples. These were maintained by war booty, one tenth being the amount due to the god at the end of a campaign. The best temple at Stettin housed a black horse for Triglav's use. In the twelfth century Christianity arrived and Triglav's statues were broken and their multiple heads sent to the Pope in Rome as curiosities.

TUONI was the Finnish god of the dead, who lived in the dark land of Tuonela, from which few travellers return. With his wife Tuonetar he had several children who were deities of suffering, including Kipu-Tytto, goddess of illness. One of the few heroes who managed to escape from Tuonela was *VAINAMOINEN*. After successfully crossing the river that marked the border of Tuonela, he was received there by Tuonetar, who gave him beer to drink. But while her visitor slept, her son created a vast iron mesh across the river so that Vainamoinen could not return that way and would be trapped forever. But when he woke, the hero changed into an otter and swam easily through the net.

TUONI guarded the dark realm of Tuonela on the banks of a black river. When Vainamoinen visited Tuoni in search of magic charms, he was trapped by a vast iron net, flung across the river; but the hero changed into an otter and slipped through. (ILLUSTRATION BY NICK BEALE, 1995.)

U

TYR (left), famed for his bravery and might, was assigned the task of feeding Fenrir, the fierce wolf-son of Loki. Yet Fenrir kept on growing, stronger and fiercer every day, until all-seeing Odin realized the danger and the gods decided to bind the beast underground. (ILLUSTRATION BY J HUARD, 1930.)

TYR (above left), a popular sword god, was invoked before battle, honoured with sword dances, and had his rune engraved on blades. He lost his right hand in a fight with Fenrir, but was just as skilful with his left, and at Ragnarok slew the hell-hound Garm. (ILLUSTRATION BY JAMES ALEXANDER, 1995.)

URD (above), a wise Norn, personified the past, while her sisters represented present and future fate. The Norns warned the gods of future evil and drew lessons from the past. Urd fed two swans on the Urdar pool who gave birth to the swans of the world. (ILLUSTRATION BY JAMES ALEXANDER, 1995.)

TYR, also known as Tiv and Tiwaz, was the Germanic war god, and the son of *ODIN* and his wife *FRIGG*. The Anglo-Saxons usually called him Tiw and gave his name to Tuesday (Tiwesdaeg in Old English). He was closely associated with Odin and, like that god, received sacrifices of hanged men. It is not unlikely that Tyr was an early sky god whose powers were later passed to Odin and Thor. *GUNGNIR*, Odin's magic spear, may once have belonged to Tyr, since it was customary for the Vikings to cast a spear over the heads of an enemy as a sacrifice before fighting commenced in earnest, and over recent years archaeologists have found numerous splendidly ornamented spears dedicated to Tyr.

The myth of Tyr relates to the binding of the wolf *FENRIR*. This monstrous creature had grown so powerful that the gods decided to restrain it. No ordinary chain was strong enough, and before Fenrir would consent to a magic one being placed round his neck, Tyr had to put his hand in the wolf's mouth as a sign of goodwill. When the wolf discovered the chain could not be broken, he bit off Tyr's hand. Although Tyr was in agony, the other gods just laughed. The downgrading of Tyr may not be unconnected with the loss of a hand. A Celtic god by the name of Nuada was forced to give up the leadership of the Irish Tuatha De Danann ("the people of the goddess Dana") after he lost a hand at the first battle of Magh Tuireadh. But Tyr was still able to fight at *RAGNAROK*, during which it was destined that the hound Garm, which stood at the gates of *HEL*, acting as watchdog to the land of the dead, was to leap at Tyr's throat and they would kill each other.

URD, or Wyrd (meaning "Fate" or "Past"), was one of three sisters who were the Germanic fates and were known as the *NORNS*. The two other sisters were Verdandi ("Being" or "Present") and Skuld ("Necessity" or "Future"). Urd gave her name to the well that was situated beneath one of the roots of *YGGDRASIL*, the cosmic tree, and that was where the gods would hold their daily meeting. As was also the case in Greek mythology, the gods were not superior or beyond the influence of the fates. Indeed, Urd warned the chief of the Germanic gods, *ODIN*, that he was destined to be killed by the terrible wolf *FENRIR* at *RAGNAROK*, the doom of the gods.

V

UTGARD ("Outer Place"), in Germanic mythology, was the huge giants' stronghold in *JOTUNHEIM*, where *LOKI*, *THOR* and Thor's servant *THIALFI* found themselves in contests against unequal opponents. Loki failed to consume more food than wildfire; Thialfi could not keep pace as a runner with thought; and Thor was unable to drink the sea dry, pick up the sea serpent *JORMUNGAND* or wrestle old age. When they left, the gods realized that Utgard was an illusion made by the frightened frost giants to deter Thor, their greatest enemy.

VAFTHRUDNIR, in Germanic mythology, was a wise frost giant. He was believed to have gained his impressive store of wisdom by consulting the dead. Possibly like *ODIN*, the chief of the gods, who voluntarily hanged himself for nine nights on *YGGDRASIL*, the cosmic tree, in order to become wise, Vafthrudnir had also temporarily died. Seeking to test his knowledge against the giant's, Odin decided to journey to Vafthrudnir's land in disguise. There he challenged the gigantic "riddle-master" to match their knowledge of the past, the present and the future. After an impressive display on the part of both Odin and Vafthrudnir, the giant was eventually defeated by a quite unanswerable question, when the god asked the giant what he had whispered to his dead son *BALDER* before he lit the pyre on which he lay. It is implied in the story that Odin's foreknowledge allowed him to assure Balder of future resurrection and worship on the new earth, "risen out of the water, fresh and green", after *RAGNAROK*, the doom of the gods and the end of the world.

UTGARD, the icy citadel of the frost giants, was carved out of snow blocks and glittering icicles. The Norse poets, who knew all about the terrors of the ice of their northern homes, inevitably portrayed the evil giants in just such a harsh realm, where numbing cold froze the muscles and paralysed the will. (ILLUSTRATION BY ALAN LEE, 1984.)

Now Vafthrudnir recognized Odin and admitted that no one could tell what the god had whispered into the ear of the dead Balder. The frost giant's last words were: "So I have pitted myself against Odin, always the wisest."

242

VAFTHRUDNIR spars with Odin in a friendly contest of wits. Ever thirsty for knowledge, Odin had resolved to test the wise frost giant and learn any new snippets of wisdom. Yet, after quizzing each other on every aspect of life and death, Odin emerged as the wisest of the wise.
(ILLUSTRATION BY JAMES ALEXANDER, 1995.)

VAINAMOINEN, the chief hero of Finnish epic, was the son of a primal goddess, *LUONNOTAR*. He was always depicted as a vigorous and sensitive old man, who from birth possessed the wisdom of the ages, for he was in his mother's womb for at least thirty years. As

the champion of the Kalevala (which means "the fatherland of heroes"), Vainamoinen was gifted with extraordinary magical powers. He was less lucky in love, however. When he sought a bride from among the women of Pohja, he was promised one of Louhi's daughters if he made the magic talisman, the Sampo. He gave the task to his comrade Ilmarinen and so Louhi's daughter was married to Ilmarinen instead. But the bride was killed and the magic talisman stolen, so Vainamoinen and Ilmarinen, joined by *LEMINKAINEN*, set off to find the Sampo. After several great adventures, they succeeded in recovering it. However, Louhi raised a great storm and, in the form of a griffin, descended onto their ship. Only the swift action of Vainamoinen saved them, but during the storm the Sampo was lost to the winds. When the storm had passed, Vainamoinen collected all the scattered pieces together and was able to restore some of the talisman's former power. With his mission completed, Vainamoinen built a ship and embarked on an endless voyage. (See also *TREASURES AND TALISMANS; SORCERY AND SPELLS*)

VAINAMOINEN (above), a peerless mage, was also a gentle, humane hero. A tireless explorer, he journeyed across the known world and, alone among heroes, returned from the underworld. At the end of his life, he set sail in a copper boat and embarked on a voyage without end. (VAINOMOINEN BY A GALLEN-KALLELA, CANVAS, C. 1890.)

VAINAMOINEN (below) courts reluctant Aino in her father's grove. Promised to the old man against her will by her brother, she drowned herself rather than marry, only to wind up as a salmon on his fishing line, before leaping back into the river and returning to her human form. (THE AINO TRIPTYCH BY A GALLEN-KALLELA, CANVAS, C. 1890.)

The newly fallen joining the residents in Valhalla had to enter by a door called Valgrind ("the sacred barred-gate of the slain"). Even before they reached this entrance, they must pass several obstacles, including a fast-running river of air. Once in Valhalla "the men killed in war" were miraculously cured of their wounds and were able to indulge endlessly in the pleasures of feasting and fighting. The meat of a magic boar was prepared as wonderful stew in an inexhaustible cauldron. The same boar was eaten day after day through a process of resurrection. Mead was provided from the teats of a goat. It was said that every day the Einherjar put on their armour, went to the practice ground and fought each other. If killed, they were restored to life. At midday they returned to Valhalla and started drinking. Such an existence for a Viking helps to explain Odin's popularity in Denmark, southern Norway and Sweden, the regions where most of the raiding expeditions came from.

VALHALLA'S Valkyries – beautiful battle-maidens – welcomed the chosen slain with open arms. At other times, Odin's sons, Hermod or Bragi, received the heroes, conducting them to the foot of Odin's throne; while Odin himself rose to greet the bravest Vikings at the gate. (ILLUSTRATION BY E WALLCOUSINS, C. 1920.)

VALHALLA was a Viking's paradise where chosen heroes fought and feasted from dawn to dusk. Wounds healed overnight, and mead and meat flowed freely. The hectic round of combat ensured that heroes stayed in fighting form, fit for the final battle at Ragnarok. (ILLUSTRATION BY W B DRACK, 1900.)

VALHALLA (above), the Hall of the Slain, was built in the shimmering grove of Glesir. Encircled by strong outer walls, the magnificent hall glittered with precious metals, its walls were built of spears and its roof of shining shields. This starlit scene evokes a sense of the untold wonders that lie within. (ILLUSTRATION BY F VON STASSEN, 1914.)

VALHALLA, or Valholl, in Germanic mythology, was the hall of the *EINHERJAR* ("heroic dead"), those warriors slain on the battle-field and chosen by *ODIN* himself as his followers. Built in *ASGARD* by Odin, Valhalla was enormous. It had over five hundred doors, each wide enough to allow up to eight hundred men to march through abreast. These wide doors were designed to allow the chosen warriors to pour forth at the first sign of *RAGNAROK*, the doom of the gods. Then they were destined to fall again, alongside the gods, in a great battle on the *VIGRID* Plain.

Odin was known as the father of the slain and he was the host who presided over Valhalla, and daily sent out the VALKYRIES to add to the number of the dead. In Valhalla the Valkyries would carry food and drinks for the Einherjar.

Ragnarok was always given as the reason for creating Valhalla. When asked about his habit of giving luck to a warrior in a battle and then suddenly taking it away, Odin said that "the grey wolf watches the halls of the gods": that is to say, the gods were constantly threatened by Ragnarok, the catastrophe in which they would die in mutual destruction with the frost giants and the forces of evil. The gathering of the "heroic dead" in Valhalla was the only way the gods could prepare to face their own fate, no matter how vain the attempt would prove to be. At least Odin's men, caught up in a berserk fury, could be guaranteed to tear into the enemy ranks in one last battle. (See also THE VALKYRIES)

VALHOLL see VALHALLA

VALI was one of the few bright young gods to survive Ragnarok. Destined from birth to avenge Balder's death, he grew at an amazing rate, reaching manhood in a single day and rushing off with uncombed hair to slay Hodr. Here, he is portrayed striding across the new earth after Ragnarok. (ILLUSTRATION BY NICK BEALE, 1995.)

VALI was the son of *ODIN* and *RIND* and was destined to kill blind *HODR* in revenge for his unwitting murder of *BALDER*. Fulfilling a prophecy, he grew from a baby to manhood in a single day and rushed off to kill Hodr. Along with his half-brother *VIDAR*, he survived *RAGNAROK*. Another Vali was one of the unlucky sons of *LOKI*.

THE VALKYRIES ("female choosers of the slain") were *ODIN*'s battle- or shield-maidens. They rode over battlefields and selected the *EINHERJAR* ("heroic dead") who would go to *VALHALLA*. They probably derived from something more dreadful than the attendants of Valhalla, and must have originally been the goddesses of slaughter itself, wild Amazon-like creatures who took great delight in the severed limbs and bloody wounds of battle. Something of this early terror can be imagined in an account of the battle of Stamford Bridge, King Harold's victory over the Norwegians shortly before his defeat by the Normans at Battle in 1066. A soldier in the Norwegian army dreamt of a Valkyrie before the battle. He thought he was on the king of Norway's ship, when he beheld a great witch on an island, with a fork in one hand to rake up the dead and a trough in the other to catch the blood. (See also *THE VALKYRIES*; *RAGNAROK*)

VALKYRIES (above), Odin's martial maidens, alighted on the battlefield to select the bravest warriors for Valhalla, the idyllic abode of Odin's ghostly army. Although quite charming in Valhalla, on the battlefield the Valkyries became sinister spirits of slaughter, goading heroes to their death. (THE VALKYRIES BY G VON LEEKE, 1870.)

VALKYRIES (below) rode through the stormy sky on magnificent pearly steeds, personifying clouds, and whose soaking manes sprayed the earth with fertile frost and dew. They also scoured the seas, snatching sailors from ships, or sometimes beckoning from the strand. (THE RIDE OF THE VALKYRIE BY H HERMAN, CANVAS, C. 1890.)

RAGNAROK

RAGNAROK WAS THE preordained doom of the gods, and the climax of the cosmic drama. The seeds of doom were sown at the dawn of time when the world and its first creatures emerged from the violent extremes of ice and fire. Inherently fragile, the universe was beset by forces of destruction and flawed from the outset. The inevitable climax was precipitated by a series of disasters. Loki, a catalyst of evil, spawned three fearsome monsters against whom the gods were ultimately powerless. Consumed with hate, Loki went on to slay Balder, symbol of goodness and beauty. Beyond Asgard, the enmity of the hostile giants gathered momentum until, at Ragnarok, all the world's destructive forces burst forth in cataclysmic disaster. Apocalypse is a common mythical theme, but the Norse vision is starker than most and unique in the loss of its gods. In one hopeful version, some gods survive and the earth emerges fresh and green, purged by flood and fire. Ragnarok casts a dark shadow over the Norse myths, yet also highlights the heroism of gods and heroes.

LOKI (left), ever envious of anyone who was good and beautiful, guided blind Hodr to slay his brother, Balder, with a dart of mistletoe. The wanton destruction of the best of the gods marked a turning-point in Loki's downward spiral of evil. Yet even after the crime, the gods allowed Loki to roam unrestrained, growing ever more bitter and twisted. (LOKI AND HODR BY C QVARNSTROM, MARBLE, C. 1890.)

THE MIGHT OF THOR (above) and his hammer, Mjollnir, symbolized the foremost defence of the gods against the threat of the giants and the doom of Ragnarok. Yet Thor's sustained might proved ultimately inadequate to withstand the combined onslaught of giants and monsters. At the end, however, Thor rid the world of the giant monster, Jormungand, before dying himself from its venom. (THOR BY B FOGELBERG, MARBLE, C. 1890.)

JORMUNGAND *(above) was one of the evils threatening the survival of the Norse world. Along with his monster siblings, Fenrir and Hel, Jormungand epitomized darkness and destruction. The massive serpent lurked in the ocean depths, circling the world in a stranglehold. Coiled in upon itself, this striking snake motif recalls the World Serpent curled around Midgard with its tail in its mouth, until it burst forth at Ragnarok. (*BROOCH, 7TH CENTURY.*)*

LOKI *(above) gate-crashes Aegir's feast and ridicules the gods with his sardonic wit, undermining and humiliating each in turn. None can either match or silence him, until Thor enters and threatens Loki with his hammer. Odin, at the right, looks on in speechless sorrow, recognizing the signs of Ragnarok. (*AEGIR'S FEAST BY C HANSEN, CANVAS, C. 1861.*)*

ODIN *(left), despite all his wisdom and power, was powerless to prevent the imminent doom of the gods. Yet he tried everything to fend off the fateful moment. Here, he carves magic runes on his spear, setting out rules of conduct for giants and dwarfs, gods and mortals. Odin learnt the wisdom of the runes from the dead when hanging from the sacred Yggdrasil in voluntary self-sacrifice. He also paid for wisdom with one eye at Mimir's well. Yet all his spies and sources only reinforce his own foreknowledge of doom. (*ILLUSTRATION BY F VON STASSEN, 1914.*)*

AT RAGNAROK *(above) the mighty walls of Asgard, home of the Aesir gods, were destroyed and the heavenly Bifrost Bridge was set alight by Surt, the fearsome flame giant. Jormungand, the gigantic World Serpent, burst from the seething ocean and engulfed the Vigrid Plain, spewing venom in all directions. Fenrir broke his bonds and roamed the earth with his savage brood, spreading death and destruction. The wolves swallowed the sun and moon, and even Yggdrasil itself shuddered. Over the whirling seas, Loki sailed with his giant host, while his daughter Hel rose from misty Niflheim with her pale army of the dead, and the assembled host issued forth over the Vigrid Plain. At the very end, Surt set all the nine worlds ablaze and the earth sank beneath the boiling ocean. (*ILLUSTRATION BY ALAN LEE, 1984.*)*

THE VALKYRIES *(left), Odin's formidable martial shield-maidens, gathered up the heroic slain from the battlefield and ferried them to Valhalla where they kept in fighting form until Ragnarok. By raising a heroic army, Odin determined to put up a fighting stand against the enemy host at Ragnarok. (*THE RIDE OF THE VALKYRIES ANON.*)*

247

THE VANIR were the older of the two branches of the Germanic family of gods and were fertility deities. They lived at Vanaheim, far from ASGARD, the fortified residence of the AESIR, the younger branch, who were primarily war gods. Myth relates how the Vanir and the Aesir fought for supremacy not long after creation. After the Aesir had won, peace was sealed by an exchange of gods and goddesses. The Vanir sent to Asgard the sea god NJORD and his twin son and daughter FREYR and FREYJA, and also KVASIR, who was believed to be second to none in his wisdom. The Aesir despatched to Vanaheim long-legged HONIR and wise MIMIR.

At first Honir and Mimir were welcomed and accepted by the Vanir, but the gods gradually came to the conclusion that they had got the worst of the exchange with the Aesir. The problem was the terrible indecisiveness of Honir, which reached embarrassing proportions whenever Mimir was absent. To the Vanir it seemed that Mimir was not only Honir's voice but also his brain, so in anger they cut off Mimir's head and sent it back to Asgard. Although this did not rekindle the conflict, it effectively caused a rift between the Aesir and the Vanir which greatly reduced the mythological significance of the Vanir, so they slowly faded into the background.

The distinction between the older Vanir and the younger Aesir was uncertain even in Viking times. When the sagas were collected in the late twelfth century, there was speculation about the origins of the two groups. The Icelander Snorri Sturluson thought that the name of the Aesir recalled their homeland in Asia, and that THOR was the grandson of King Priam of Troy and ODIN his descendant in the twentieth generation, while the Vanir were originally inhabitants of the land by the River Don, formerly called Vanaquisl. Today, however, these theories have been discounted.

THE VANIR, deities of fertility, wealth and health, were worshipped by farmers. The three main Vanir gods, Njord (centre) and his lovely twins, Freyja and Freyr, were all gentle, benign spirits of nature, who nourished the earth and seas, and granted fair weather and good harvests. (ILLUSTRATION BY JAMES ALEXANDER, 1995.)

VE, in Germanic mythology, was one of the sons of BOR and the brother of ODIN and VILI. At the beginning of creation the primeval cow AUDHUMLA sustained herself by licking the ice and from her ample teats flowed enough milk to feed the frost giant YMIR, the first living creature. He is described as being utterly evil. However, Audhumla's licking also uncovered BURI, the grand-father of Ve. All the gods were descended from Buri, because his son Bor married the frost giantess Bestla and had three sons – Odin, Vili and Ve.

Although the blood of the frost giants and the gods intermingled, the implacable enmity between them could not be denied or resolved, for it went right back to the killing of Ymir. Odin, Vili and Ve disliked Ymir and his growing band of frost giants. Eventually, their dislike turned to hatred and they slew Ymir, making the world in GINNUNGAGAP (the "yawning emptiness") from the giant's body.

Afterwards the three brothers found on the seashore two fallen trees, an ash and an elm. From the wood they made first man and then woman. Odin breathed into them the spirit of life; Vili gave them intelligence and emotion; and Ve added the ability to see and hear. In some versions of the creation myth, Ve is known as Lodur or Lothur.

THE VANIR were famed for magic and foresight of which the macho Aesir were a little suspicious, except for Odin who, ever eager to increase his knowledge, rapidly absorbed the Vanir arts. Here, the fruitful Vanir twins follow Odin and Frigg over the Bifrost Bridge, with Thor and Loki in the rear. (ILLUSTRATION BY F VON STASSEN, 1914.)

VIDAR (above), a strong, silent and solitary god, lived alone in a leafy palace deep in his primal forest. He personified the imperishable forces of nature, and was one of the few gods destined to survive Ragnarok. He slew the wolf Fenrir with his iron-shod foot.
(ILLUSTRATION BY NICK BEALE, 1995.)

VE (above) and his brothers, Vili and Odin, fashioned human forms from two pieces of driftwood lying on the cosmic beach at the dawn of time. Odin created a man from the ash, while his younger brothers formed a woman from the elm, and then Odin breathed life into them.
(ILLUSTRATION BY JAMES ALEXANDER, 1995.)

VELES guarded cattle and flocks for the Slavs. Especially popular with farmers, he survived into the nineteenth century, when Russian farmers still honoured him in the harvest fields by curling the ears of one sheaf of corn (see right), symbolizing the god's curly hair and beard.
(ILLUSTRATION BY NICK BEALE, 1995.)

VELES, or Volos, was the Russian god who had authority over flocks and herds. It was customary to swear oaths in the names of Veles and *PERUNU*, who was the thunder god. When Vladimir, ruler of Kiev, was baptized into the Orthodox faith in 988, he had a statue of Veles thrown into the River Dniepner. In Russian folklore, however, the god of flocks survives. For instance, at harvest time the ears of the last sheaf of corn are still woven into a plait known as "Veles' beard". Also in Russian Orthodox tradition, Veles was incorporated into the Christian faith by identifying him with St Blasius, who was a shepherd and martyr from Cappadocia. Prayers offered to this saint are expected to protect and increase flocks of sheep and goats.

VIDAR was the silent and solitary god of Germanic mythology. He was the son of *ODIN* and the frost giantess *GRID*, and lived in a place called Vidi, where all was quiet and peaceful. It was Vidar's destiny to avenge his father's death at *RAGNAROK*, the doom of the gods and the end of the world. When the terrible wolf *FENRIR* had overcome Odin in a fierce and bloody struggle and swallowed him, Vidar stepped forward, smashed one of his well-shod feet against the wolf's lower jaw, and then with both hands he forced the upper jaw open till the ravenous beast's throat was torn asunder. It is more than likely that the meaning of Vidar's own name refers in some way to this ripping in half of evil.

249

VIGRID, in Germanic mythology, was the name of a plain that was destined to be the scene of the final conflict between the gods and the frost giants. There at *RAGNAROK* the two sides and their allies would engage in mutual destruction. A huge expanse of land, Vigrid was said to stretch 120 leagues in every direction. Even so, it was predicted that the assembled hosts would cover it completely.

VILI, in Germanic mythology, was the son of *BOR* and Bestla and the brother of *ODIN* and *VE*. At the beginning of creation he helped his brothers to slay the frost giant *YMIR* and form the world from his carcass. When they later created the first man and woman from wood, Vili's contribution was sharp wits and feeling hearts. Odin gave them the breath of life, while Ve added the powers of sight and hearing. In one Icelandic poem Vili is given the name *HONIR*.

VLKODLAK was the Slavic wolfman. More a figure of folklore than mythology, he exists because of the ancient respect accorded to the ravenous wolf, which in the forests of northern and eastern Europe was the animal most feared. According to Germanic mythology, the chief god *ODIN* was destined to be killed by the wolf *FENRIR* at *RAGNAROK*, the doom of the gods.

VOLOS see *VELES*

VOLSUNG was the subject of a late Germanic myth. He was said to be a descendant of *ODIN*. When Signy, Volsung's only daughter, was married against her will to the Gothic king Siggeir, a one-eyed stranger appeared among the wedding guests. It was Odin, chief of the Germanic gods. He stuck a sword deep into an oak and told the company that the weapon would belong to the man who pulled it out. Whoever wielded the sword could never be defeated.

THE VIGRID PLAIN (above) was mapped out as the battlefield of Ragnarok. When Heimdall sounded the call to battle, the warring hosts converged from all corners of the earth; gods and heroes poured over the Bifrost Bridge, while Loki and the fiery host swarmed in from the swirling seas. (ILLUSTRATION BY JAMES ALEXANDER, 1995.)

Out of courtesy Volsung invited his son-in-law Siggeir to try his luck first. But Siggeir did not succeed. Nor was anyone else able to pull out the sword, except the youngest of Volsung's sons, Sigmund. When Siggeir offered to buy the magic weapon, Sigmund refused to part with it at any price.

This refusal made the Gothic king really angry. Despite Signy's

VOLSUNG's (below) great hall, built around a sacred oak, was the scene of a magical event when Odin appeared one night and thrust a sword, hilt-deep, into the great oak. He challenged the heroes to pull it out, offering the divine gift to the winner. Sigmund was the much-envied champion. (ILLUSTRATION BY ALAN LEE, 1984.)

warning, Volsung and his ten sons walked into Siggeir's trap when they accepted an invitation to visit his court. They were ambushed on the way and left in the forest, bound to a fallen tree. Each night a wolf came and ate one of them, until only Sigmund was left alive. Signy succeeded in rescuing him.

As a result, Siggeir wrongly believed that no one had escaped the attentions of the wolf. He relaxed his guard and Signy was able to bury her family and help Sigmund. It took a long time to prepare a revenge, however. First of all Signy tried to have her own sons trained by Sigmund, but they lacked courage. A second attempt to reinforce her brother involved incest. Without his knowledge, Signy slept with him and bore Sinfiotli, a warrior with double Volsung blood. When Sinfiotli grew up, Signy sent him to her brother to be trained as a warrior.

Although Sigmund and Sinfiotli were captured by Siggeir, the magic sword secured their release and allowed them to take revenge on the king and his sons. Afterwards Sigmund returned home, and had another son, *SIGURD*, known in German legend as Siegfried.

VOLUND see *WAYLAND*

WAYLAND was the smith god of the Anglo-Saxons. The son of a sailor and a mermaid, he was renowned for making coats of mail and swords. In Scandinavia he was known as Volund, or Volundr, and in Germany as Wielund.

Wayland's myth is a story of revenge. King Nidud of Sweden cut Wayland's leg sinews and placed him and his forge on a remote island. The smith god avenged this mutilation by killing Nidud's two sons, who came to see his treasures, and sending their heads studded with precious jewels and mounted on silver to King Nidud. He may also have raped Nidud's daughter, but this is not certain.

WAYLAND's (above) smithy was visited not just by warriors seeking arms, but by noblewomen wanting dainty trinkets of purest gold. Wayland was also a craftsman on the grand scale, designing a fabulous Icelandic maze, known as Volund's House. (WHALEBONE CARVING, 8TH CENTURY.)

WAYLAND (below), captive on a desolate island, laboured in his underground forge, fashioning wondrous ornaments and weapons for his oppressive master, Nidud of Sweden. Like Daedalus, Wayland fashioned wings and flew away to freedom. (WIELAND BY MAX KOCH, WATERCOLOUR, 1904.)

WAYLAND (above right) and his brothers chanced upon three Valkyries bathing in a lake. They took their plumage left on the bank and kept them on earth for nine years, until they escaped. Fashioning wings for himself, Wayland flew after his wife, Alvit, to Alfheim. (ILLUSTRATION BY H THEAKER, 1900.)

Afterwards Wayland is said to have flown to *VALHALLA*, like the Greek inventor Daedalus, on wings he had made for himself. Near Uffington in Wiltshire, a long barrow has ancient associations with Wayland, and is locally known as his smithy. His lameness parallels that of Hephaistos, the Greek smith god whose injury had two different explanations. In one version it was claimed that his limp was the result of his having interfered in a violent quarrel between his parents, Zeus and Hera. So annoyed did Zeus become that he flung his son out of Olympus and let him fall heavily on the island of Lemnos. A second explanation tells how Hephaistos was born a dwarfish figure with a limp. Hera even tried to drown him, but he was saved by sea nymphs. The latter version of the myth is most relevant to Wayland. In Germanic mythology the master craftsmen were mainly dwarfs, and Wayland's own mother was a mermaid. It is interesting to note that Lemnos was an island with volcanic activity, like the remote island to which Wayland had been banished.

WIELAND see *WAYLAND*

WODEN see *ODIN*

WOTAN see *ODIN*

Y

YGGDRASIL, or Yggdrasill, (which means something like "dreadful mount") was the cosmic ash tree in Germanic mythology. Its name is a reference either to the gallows or *ODIN*'s horse. Not only did Odin hang himself on Yggdrasil for nine nights in order to learn wisdom, but sacrificial hangings from gallows trees were also a favourite Viking way of worshipping the god. An archaeological find that reveals the extent of this ghastly ritual is the Tollund Man, found in a Jutland peat bog in 1950. The corpse was so well preserved that it was possible to deduce that he was a prisoner of war who had been sacrificed as a thank-offering after a battle.

The parallel between Odin's voluntary death on Yggdrasil and

YGGDRASIL (right) the World Tree, lay at the heart of the universe. Here, the whirling patterns of Viking art strikingly capture the swirling vitality at the centre of life. A stag browses on its evergreen foliage while a serpent nips the stag's neck, reflecting the life and death struggle at the root of life. (WOOD CARVING, 8TH CENTURY.)

YMIR (below) was the first creature to emerge from the primal wastes of ice in the yawning abyss of Ginnungagap at the dawn of creation. As fire from the south melted ice from the north, the icy droplets fused to form a massive frost giant. As he slept, his sweat formed other frost giants. (ILLUSTRATION BY NICK BEALE, 1995.)

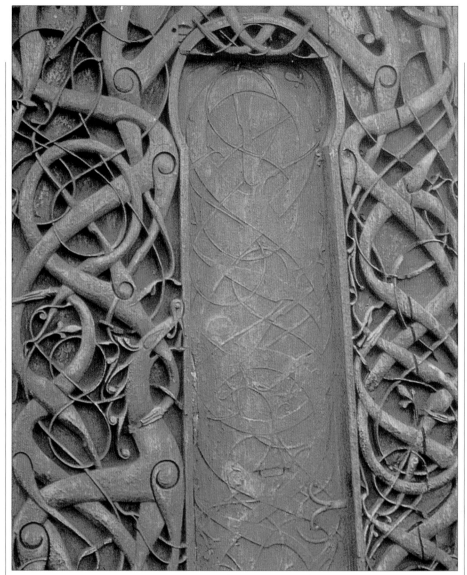

the Crucifixion remains striking. Odin was also pierced with a spear and, like Christ, cried out before he died. Although it is possible that the Crucifixion was known at the time that the Odin myth was recorded, there is little doubt that his hanging on the cosmic tree had pre-Christian origins and derived from ancient pagan worship. Odin had long been the god of the spear, the god of the hanged.

Yggdrasil is described as the largest and most stately tree ever to have grown. Its branches overhung the nine worlds and spread out above the heavens. It was supported by three great roots: one descended to *JOTUNHEIM*, the land of the giants, where *MIMIR*'s well stood; the second ended in foggy Niflheim, close by the spring of Hvergelmir, where the dragon *NIDHOGG* gnawed the root from below whenever it tired of chewing corpses; the last root was embedded near *ASGARD*, the stronghold of the gods, beneath *URD*'s well, where the gods held their daily assembly. Water was taken from the well each day by the *NORNS*, the three fates, Urd, Skuld and Verdandi, and mixed with earth as a means of preventing Yggdrasil's bark from rotting. An eagle perched on the very top of the cosmic tree was daily harassed by a squirrel named Ratatosk, who brought unpleasant comments and insults up from the dragon Nidhogg. Another bird in its branches was a cock, sometimes referred to as "Vidofnir the tree snake".

The idea of a cosmic tree is common in the myths of the northern parts of both Europe and Asia. It was thought of as the backbone of the universe, the structural support of the nine worlds. In Ireland, however, the sacred tree acquired a different role. Although always associated with otherworld splendour, the musical branches of Irish mythology acted as cures for

YGGDRASIL's mighty limbs held up the nine worlds of the Norsemen. Seen here (above) are the three highest realms of gods and light elves, lying under the rainbow bridge; next, the worlds of mortals, dwarfs and dark elves rise from the ocean, with the frost giants' land at the icy edge.

(ILLUSTRATION FROM NORTHERN ANTIQUITIES, 1847.)

YGGDRASIL (right) filled the known world, taking root not only in the dark depths of Niflheim (bottom), but also in Midgard and Asgard. Its topmost boughs reached heaven, while its lowest root touched hell. It was generally thought of as the structural support of the universe.

(ILLUSTRATION BY ALAN LEE, 1984.)

sickness and despair. In a number of tales these magic branches of silver or gold were brought by messengers from otherworld lands. Thus the fabulous voyage of Bran began with the sound of music that caused him to fall asleep. It came from a branch of silver with white blossoms, which a beautiful lady took away after telling of the delights of her world beyond the sea. Hints of such magic are also present in Germanic mythology. The obvious example must be the apples belonging to the goddess IDUN. Only this magic fruit prevented the gods from growing old. They were clearly the gift from

another sacred tree. How much trees were once revered can be seen from the reactions to early Christian missionaries like St Boniface. In the eighth century he cut down sacrificial trees, to the terror of the Frisians, until he himself was felled at Dockum by an outraged pagan.

YGGDRASILL see YGGDRASIL

YMIR, in Germanic mythology, was the first living creature. He was a frost giant who emerged from the ice in GINNUNGAGAP ("the yawning emptiness"). He was evil and the father and mother of all frost giants, who first came from the sweat of

his armpit. Ymir fed on the milk of the primeval cow AUDHUMLA. He was slain by the brothers ODIN, VILI and VE, who were the grandsons of BURI, whom Audhumla had licked free of the ice.

Growing tired of the brutality of Ymir and his ever-increasing band of frost giants, Odin, Vili and Ve took up arms. They slew Ymir and then drowned all the frost giants in his blood, with the exception of BERGELMIR and his wife, who managed to escape by sailing on a hollowed tree trunk.

Odin, Vili and Ve then threw Ymir's carcass into Ginnungagap. His flesh became the earth, his

unbroken bones mountains, his teeth and jaw rocks and boulders, his blood rivers, lakes and the sea, and his skull the sky, which was held up at its four corners by dwarfs. Sparks were used to make the sun, the moon and the stars.

Such an extremely violent creation myth is by no means unique. The Babylonian champion of the gods, Marduk, slew the chaos-dragon Tiamat with raging winds and an arrow, before splitting her carcass into two parts. One he pushed upwards to form the heavens, the other he used to make a floor above the deep, the emptiness at the bottom of the universe.

253

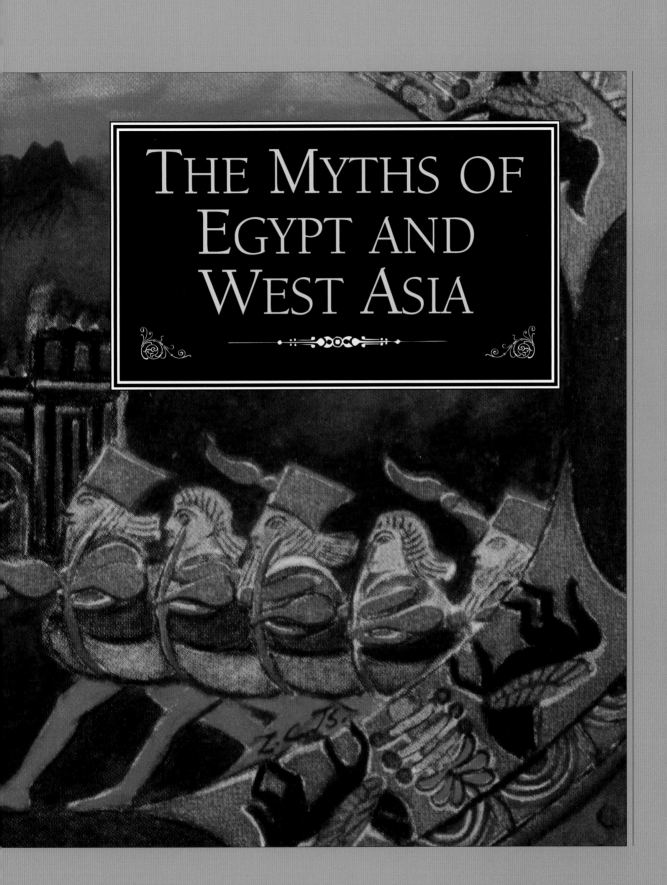

THE MYTHS OF
EGYPT AND
WEST ASIA

INTRODUCTION

THE ANCIENT MIDDLE EAST, the so-called "cradle of civilization", was the birthplace of Judaism, Islam and Christianity, the three faiths that came to have such an immense impact on human culture and, by tradition, originated amongst the descendants of Shem, one of the sons of Noah. Zoroastrianism, probably the most powerful religion of its time, also arose in the Middle East, whereas the wider area of West Asia witnessed the rise of the powerful Egyptian and Hittite empires.

What was it about this region that enabled it to bear witness to such remarkable achievements? One answer at least lies in the geography of the area: it was here that crop farming first began, and with it the beginnings of a settled, civilized way of life, which proceeded to bear rich cultural fruits.

The annual flooding of the Nile inspired many of the myths of ancient Egypt. The people there depended on the revival of the parched land for their livelihood, a concern that was reflected in the myth of Osiris, their dying-and-rising vegetation god, who finally retired from life to rule over the underworld. A preoccupation with death haunts Egyptian mythology, prompted by this sense of man's vulnerability in the face of forces beyond his control. Even the great sun god, Ra, was believed to die each evening and be born again at dawn.

It was on the fertile land produced by the Nile's annual floodings that Egypt's first city states grew up, each with its own gods. Eventually, around 3100BC, these separate states were unified under a succession of pharaohs. Many of the local gods were admitted into the national pantheon, giving

SYMBOLIZING the divine relationship between pharaohs and the gods, Horemheb, the last Egyptian pharaoh of the 18th dynasty, sits beside the god Horus, son of Isis and Osiris. (c. 1320BC.)

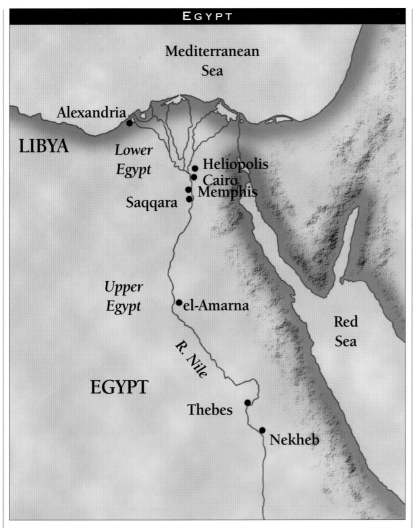

EGYPT

Mediterranean
Sea

Alexandria

LIBYA

Lower
Egypt

Heliopolis
Cairo
Memphis
Saqqara

Upper
Egypt

el-Amarna

R. Nile

Red
Sea

EGYPT

Thebes

Nekheb

featured dying and rising gods. The Mesopotamians' existence was, however, much more precarious than that of the Egyptians. Not only could the flooding of their rivers be sudden and unpredictable, but the people were also under constant threat from marauding tribes and foreign invaders. Their myths, therefore, tended to portray life as a constant battle against the forces of chaos.

Despite its political instability, ancient Mesopotamia produced an extensive written literature. As a result, the Mesopotamian deities and myths were transmitted to other West Asian peoples, including the Assyrians and Hittites. The Hittites, who originally hailed from Anatolia, came to be known in the Old Testament as one of the peoples occupying Canaan, the promised land of the Israelites. Many of the ancestors of the Israelites had themselves migrated from Mesopotamia to Canaan soon after 2000BC; some of them continued into Egypt where, at a date which is uncertain, they were taken into slavery by a pharaoh. However, in the

BAAL, an ancient fertility god, is a dying and rising god whose actions symbolized the growth and decay of vegetation. (BRONZE AGE, 1400–1300BC.)

rise to a vast and splendid array of deities who flourished virtually unopposed by alien beliefs. Seen as divinely appointed mediators between the world of men and the gods, the pharaohs gave a political and religious focus to Egyptian civilization and culture. Their power was such that it came to extend into Canaan and Syria. However, in about 1387BC the pharaoh Akhenaten instigated vast religious reforms, which, though eventually overturned when he died, began to weaken Egyptian power.

Like the Egyptians, the Mesopotamian settlers were attracted to the rich land left by the flooding of rivers. The Sumerians, a non-Semitic people (not descended from Shem), had settled in Mesopotamia, the area lying between the rivers Tigris and Euphrates, around 4000BC. Some 2,000 years later, Babylon was made the region's capital and Sumer was gradually absorbed into Babylonia. The livelihood of these Mesopotamians, like that of the Egyptians, depended on the agricultural cycle, and their pantheon likewise

MOSES delivered the tribes of Israel from slavery in Egypt and led them through the desert to freedom. Here he strikes the rock to produce water. (19TH CENTURY ENGRAVING.)

13th century BC, Moses led the Israelites out of slavery in Egypt and back towards Canaan. On this journey, they made a solemn promise to worship only one god – Yahweh.

The Canaanite pantheon, which the Israelites encountered at the end of their journey, was dominated by the god of rain, fertility and storms, Baal. Many other gods also went under this name, which translates as "Lord", but the chief Baal was a warlike dying and rising god. His attributes reflected the Canaanite way of life which, like that of all the other peoples of the region, was closely bound up with the agricultural cycle.

As the tribes settled in Canaan, they united in their worship of Yahweh, who became the supreme god, although rites associated with

MOSES delivered the tribes of Israel from slavery in Egypt and led them through the desert to freedom. Here he strikes the rock to produce water. (19TH CENTURY ENGRAVING.)

ZOROASTER, the great religious reformer of ancient Iran, receives fire and the law of reform, which is brought to him by Ahura Mazda, the principle of good. At the age of 30, Zoroaster received numerous revelations from the Amesa Spentas, or holy immortals. (19TH CENTURY ILLUSTRATION.)

other gods persisted for some time. The followers of the new faith were based around Jerusalem. In 587BC, the city was conquered by the Babylonians, and the leading Israelites were taken into exile in Babylon. Nearly 50 years later, the Achaemenids of Iran, whom the Greeks called Persians, conquered Babylon in turn.

The Persian conquerors introduced the Babylonians to their Zoroastrian faith, which, though often loosely adhered to, saw the world as in the grip of the forces of good and evil. Zoroaster, who founded the religion and who is now believed to have lived around 1200BC, had preached of his vision of a single, supreme god. Faced with encroaching monotheism, and sometimes directly overthrown, the Mesopotamian gods finally began to lose their power. In 525BC the Persians also occupied Egypt. Since the pharaoh Akhenaten had tried to bring about religious reform back in 1367BC, the country had never quite recovered its harmony or strength, and its glorious pantheon of gods was becoming increasingly threatened by outside beliefs.

Monotheism, as preached by both the Israelites and the Zoroastrians, was thus beginning to threaten the vast and dramatic array of gods and goddesses until then prevalent across West Asia, and the region was to see yet more turmoil. Over the following centuries it was overrun by the Greeks and Romans. However, Cybele, the great mother goddess of Asia Minor, Isis, the great mother goddess of Egypt, and Mithra, originally an ancient Iranian sun god, all arrived in Rome. There they became the focus of mystery cults, which flourished in the early centuries of the Christian era. When many of the old gods of West Asia were losing their power, these ancient deities were believed to renew the spirit and put their devotees in touch with the divine.

Monotheism eventually triumphed in West Asia. By the time the prophet Muhammad was born, around AD 570, Judaism and later Christianity had already spread throughout the region, and had also encroached on the Arabian peninsula. With the arrival of the strictly monotheistic Islam, the days of the old gods were numbered.

RA-HERARHTY (below), god of the rising sun, symbolized by his falcon wings and sun-disc headdress, is carved on the polished granite capstone of the pyramid of Amenemhet III. Coiled around the sun disc is the symbol of the cobra goddess Wadjet, representing the pharaoh's royal authority and power over the life and death of his people. The carvings below include a bee and an ibis, representing Thoth, the wise counsellor of the gods and the judge of the dead. (PYRAMIDION, C. 1818–1772BC.)

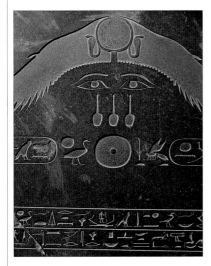

APIS (above), the sacred bull, was worshipped as a living animal believed to be the reincarnation of the god Ptah at his temple at Memphis. Mythical bulls, symbols of strength and potency, occurred in many belief systems from the earliest times. Hathor, the Egyptian goddess of maternal and sexual love, took the form of a cow (above right) who nourished humankind with her milk. She was the protector of women, helping them to conceive and give birth, and was regarded as the mother of the pharaohs. (EGYPTIAN BRONZE, 7TH–6TH CENTURY BC.)

DRAGONS (right) symbolized Marduk, the tutelary god of the fabled city of Babylon. These composite creatures had the head and tail of a serpent, the body and forelegs of a lion and the hind legs of a falcon, and were emblazoned on the monumental Ishtar Gate at the climax of the ceremonial route through the city. The processional way was lined with rows of lions sacred to Ishtar, the goddess of love and fertility. (GLAZED BRICK RELIEF, 6TH CENTURY BC.)

KHNUM (above), the ram-headed god, took mud from the life-giving Nile and used it to create humanity on his potter's wheel. He was also responsible for supervising the annual flooding of the river. At his sanctuary near its mythical source, offerings of mummified rams decorated with gold leaf were buried in stone tombs. His consort was Satis, who was depicted pouring water on to the dry earth.

SEBEK (left), the crocodile god, represented the skill and strength of the pharaoh in battle. The qualities he needed to display could be seen in the crocodiles of the Nile, which inspired awe with their speed and agility in catching their prey and the fearsome strength of their jaws. The mortuary goddess Serket took the form of a scorpion, though she was sometimes depicted in human form with a scorpion headdress. Her role was to guard the canopic jars containing the vital organs of the dead, and to protect the throne of the pharaoh. (EGYPTIAN BRONZES, 6TH CENTURY BC.)

APIS, or Hapi, was the most renowned of Egypt's sacred animals. He was worshipped at Memphis, where his temple lay opposite that of the great creator god *PTAH*. Apis, in the form of a real black bull, was believed to be the reincarnation or "glorious soul" of Ptah, who was said to have inseminated a virgin cow in the form of fire, and to have been born again as a black bull.

Each day, Apis was let loose in the courtyard attached to his temple, and the priests would use his movements as a means for divining the future. Usually, the Apis bull was allowed to die of old age, but he was drowned in a fountain if he reached the age of 25. The bull was twice assassinated by the Persians.

Ptah's priests were said to be able to recognize the next holy bull by discovering certain markings on the creature's body, including a white triangle on his forehead and a crescent moon on his right side. The extent of the reverence with which the sacred bulls were regarded can be gauged by the fact that their mummified bodies were buried with great ceremony in huge underground burial chambers. (See also *SACRED ANIMALS*)

APSU, in Mesopotamian mythology, was the watery abyss or primordial, fresh-water ocean, which existed at the beginning of time and which circled and supported the earth. Apsu spread happiness and abundance over the earth and was the source of knowledge and wisdom. Eventually, the waters of Apsu merged with those of *TIAMAT*, the primordial, salt-water ocean, and gave rise to Mummu, the waves, and the primal couple, Lahmu and Lahamu. *ANSHAR* and Kishar, the next divine couple to arise from the waves, were the male and female principles who bore the great gods *ANU* and *EA* as well as the other divinities who peopled the sky, the earth and the underworld.

In time, Apsu became troubled by the gods and plotted with Tiamat to destroy them. Tiamat was at first unwilling to take part in the battle, but, when Apsu was slain by the god Ea, she was prompted to seek revenge. Ea's son, the great god *MARDUK*, who had been born in the waters of Apsu, was chosen to challenge Tiamat. The bloody battle that ensued gave rise to the creation of the world and the sky. According to one tradition in Sumerian mythology, the goddess Nammu formed the first men from clay dug out of the waters of Apsu. In the epic of *GILGAMESH*, the hero descended into the waters of Apsu to find the plant of eternal life.

AQHAT see *AHAT*.

ARINNA was the name of a Hittite town. Its chief goddess was known as the "Sun of Arinna", or Ariniddu. The "Queen of Heaven and Earth", the goddess Arinna became the supreme patroness of the Hittite kingdom, protecting it from enemies and helping out in time of war. Her symbol was the sun disc. Arinna was identified with the Hurrian goddess *HEPAT*; both deities were said to be married to the weather god *TESHUB*.

The sun goddess Arinna was sometimes addressed as a masculine deity, the "Inspired Lord of Justice". The sun god was also an important figure in Hittite mythology, although his actual name has been lost. He was regarded as the king of the gods and a dispenser of truth and justice. In one prayer he was addressed as "Sun god of heaven, my lord, shepherd of mankind! Thou risest, O sun-god of heaven, from the sea and goest up to heaven. O sun-god of heaven, my lord, daily thou sittest in judgment upon man, dog, pig, and the wild beasts of the field." There was also a sun god of the water and a sun god of the underworld, through which the sun was believed to travel during the night.

ARSU see *RUDA*.

ASHERAT; ASHTORETH see *ASTARTE*.

ASHUR see *ANSHAR*.

ASTARTE was the principal goddess of the Phoenicians and Canaanites. She was incorporated into Egyptian mythology as a daughter either of the sun god *RA*, or of *PTAH*, and she was often depicted naked, bearing weapons and riding a horse.

According to one story from Egyptian mythology, Ptah and the other great gods were forced to pay tributes to the sea. Gifts of silver, gold and precious stones were brought to the seashore, but the sea wanted more. The gods then

ASTARTE was the principal goddess of the Phoenicians and the Canaanites. This figurine shows her, perhaps, as a fertility deity. She was associated with love and procreation. (CERAMIC FIGURINE, GATH, 8TH–7TH CENTURIES BC.)

told Astarte to take more offerings to the sea. When she arrived at the shore, Astarte mocked the sea, who responded by insisting that he have Astarte herself as a gift. The great gods covered Astarte with jewels and sent her back to the shore, but this time *SETH* accompanied her in order to fight the sea. Although the end of the story is missing, it is usually presumed that Seth fought the sea, and saved Astarte.

The name Astarte is sometimes translated as "Womb", or "That Which Issues from the Womb", and Astarte the light, heavenly aspect. In one text, they are both described as the daughters of NEITH, an Egyptian mother goddess. Moreover, they were both known as "Lady of Heaven". Aphrodite is widely believed to have developed from Astarte.

ATAR, or "Fire", was said to be the son of the Iranian deity AHURA MAZDA, although fire worship probably existed long before the naming of the supreme being. According to the teachings of Zoroastrianism, fire was one of Ahura Mazda's seven creations. Atar was said to bring men comfort and wisdom, and to defend the world from evil. It represented the light of truth and the divine spark in humankind, which signified the presence of the supreme god.

The monstrous dragon AZHI DAHAKA sought to extinguish the divine fire in a bloody battle, which took place across land, sea and air. Eventually, Atar caught the dragon and chained it to a mountain.

ATEN was a sun god who came to pre-eminence in the 14th century BC under Amenhotep IV, a PHARAOH of the 18th dynasty. He was regarded as none other than the sun god RA himself.

Amenhotep IV built temples to Aten close to those of the supreme god AMON and, to the disgust of Amon's priests, piled Aten's temples high with gifts. Four years into his reign, the pharaoh pronounced that the religion of Aten was the only official faith and that the god was to be worshipped as the exclusive creator of humankind. Worship of all other gods – especially Amon – was forbidden.

In an attempt to spread the religion of Aten throughout the empire, Amon's temples were closed and his images defaced. The pharaoh changed his name from Amenhotep, meaning "Amon is Satisfied", to Akhenaten, "Glory of Aten" or "He Who is Devoted to Aten", and relocated his capital from Thebes to a city known today as el-Amarna, which he had built specifically to glorify Aten.

Aten is always depicted as an enormous red disc, from which rays of light emanate. The rays, ending in hands, were believed to extend the beauty of Aten to the ruler. When Akhenaten died, Amon and the other gods were reinstated, and Aten's rays were sliced through to prevent his beauty reaching Akhenaten.

suggesting that the goddess was primarily a fertility deity. Astarte was also associated with love and procreation, and her cult included the practice of temple prostitution among her devotees.

In the Old Testament of the Bible, she appears as Ashtoreth, and SOLOMON had a temple built in her honour near Jerusalem. Indeed, the Israelites sometimes revered the goddess as the queen of heaven and wife of YAHWEH.

The goddess Asherat, or Ashera-of-the-Sea, tends to be viewed as identical with Astarte. She was called "Mother of the Gods" and was said to have had 70 children. According to texts dating from the 14th century BC, the supreme god EL took two women, generally believed to be Asherat and ANAT, as

his consorts, and by them fathered SHACHAR and Shalim, "Dawn" and "Dusk", and many other deities.

It is still not certain whether Anat and Astarte were two separate goddesses or different aspects of the same goddess. Anat may have been the dark aspect of the goddess

ATTAR was worshipped in southern Arabia in pre-Islamic times. A god of war, he was often referred to as "He who is Bold in Battle". One of his symbols was the spear-point, and the antelope was his sacred animal. He had power over Venus, the morning star, and was believed to provide humankind with water.

ATTIS was the consort of *CYBELE*, the great mother goddess of Phrygia in Asia Minor. A vegetation god, he was sometimes known as Papas, or "Father". One of the oldest stories concerning the birth of Attis tells how the hermaphrodite *AGDISTIS* fell asleep, whereupon the gods tied its genitals to a tree. Agdistis awoke with a start, and the severed genitals fell to the ground. An almond tree grew up on the spot, and in due course Nana, the daughter of the river god, became pregnant by one of its fruits. The girl eventually gave birth to Attis. Other legends say that the god was a foundling or the son of a king.

The best-known story of Attis is that in which his desperate love for Cybele drove him insane, leading him to castrate himself under a pine tree. Flowers and trees grew up from his blood. Although he died, the god was reborn and united with Cybele.

The cult of Cybele spread to Greece and Rome, and with it, that of Attis. Cybele was said to have fallen in love with Attis, who was regarded as a handsome young shepherd. She chose him as her priest and imposed a vow of chastity upon him. However, Attis fell in love with a river nymph, so Cybele caused him to suffer a fit of madness, during which he mutilated himself. When the god recovered, he was about to kill himself when Cybele changed him into a fir tree. In another version of the story, Attis was gored to death by a boar sent by Zeus.

Each spring, at the end of March, a five-day festival was held in honour of Attis. The first day was

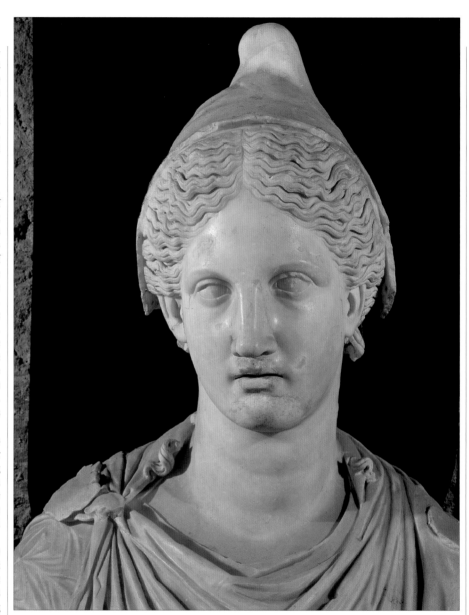

ATTIS was a vegetation god in Phrygia in Asia Minor. His death and rebirth symbolized the natural cycle. In a Roman legend, Attis was gored to death by a boar sent by Zeus. (MARBLE BUST, IMPERIAL ROME.)

one of mourning. The god, represented by a sacred fir tree taken from the grove near Cybele's temple, was bound with bandages, decorated with ribbons and flowers, and carried through the streets. On the second day, Cybele's priests performed frenzied dances, and on the third day they castrated themselves, sprinkling the altar and effigy of Attis with their blood. The fourth day was that on which the resurrection of Attis was celebrated. The fifth day was one of rest. A ritual marriage between Cybele and Attis formed part of the ceremony, with Cybele's high priest taking the role of the god.

The Romans generally represented Attis as a shepherd, usually holding a shepherd's crook and sometimes carrying a sheep on his shoulders. He plays a pipe and wears a pointed cap on his head. The rays of the sun, or ears of corn, protrude from the cap, symbolizing his function as a god of regeneration and rebirth. (See also *DYING AND RISING GODS*)

AZHI DAHAKA, the monstrous dragon of ancient Iranian mythology, was said to have had three heads, six eyes and three pairs of fangs. He was sometimes regarded as a mythical king of Babylon, Iran's

B

enemy, or as the enemy of YIMA, the great king. Originally, Azhi Dahaka was believed to kill cattle and men. One story tells how the hero FERIDUN cut the creature open with his sword and was horrified to find lizards and toads pouring out of its insides.

In time, Azhi Dahaka came to be seen as the embodiment of falsehood and the servant of ANGRA MAINYU, the principle of darkness. ATAR, the fire god, went into battle against the monster and harried him through land, sea and air before finally catching him and chaining him to a mountain.

It was believed that at the end of time Azhi Dahaka would succeed in breaking free from his chains and ravage the earth again. Eventually, the hero KERESASPA would kill the monster. (See also SERPENTS AND DRAGONS)

THE BA AND KA were believed by the ancient Egyptians to be the soul and spirit, or vital essence, of a dead person. The Ba hovered over the deceased and was usually depicted as a bird with a human head. The Ka was said to appear to the deceased in the form of a blue phoenix and was believed to return to the tomb, where it ate food left by relatives and priests. So deeply entrenched was this belief that menus were sometimes inscribed on the walls of tombs.

BAAL, meaning "Lord" or "Owner", was the name given by many Canaanite tribes to their chief god. When the Israelites entered the land of Canaan, they took up the word and used it to describe any alien god – it is as a general term for a "false god" that the name Baal is used in the Bible. The most renowned Baal of Canaanite mythology was the rain and fertility god associated with the storm god, Hadad. He lived on a mountain in the north of the region and was sometimes referred to as "Lord of the North".

One story tells how this Baal defeated YAM, the sea deity. Yam asked the supreme god EL to crown him king. El agreed but warned him that first of all he would have to defeat Baal. Learning of the forthcoming battle, Baal equipped himself with magic weapons made by the gods, and as a result, he succeeded in killing Yam and scattering his remains. Baal then proclaimed himself king, built a sumptuous dwelling place on Mount Saphon and took control of several cities.

After this victory, Baal became so proud that he decided to challenge MOT, the god of death. He forced Mot to live in the barren wastelands and barred him from all fertile regions. In response, Mot challenged Baal to come to his underground dwelling and eat mud, the food of the dead. Baal took up the challenge and died.

BAAL was said to have a voice like thunder, and that he watered the earth through a hole in the floor of his palace. In the Greco-Roman period, Baal became assimilated in the Palestine region with Zeus and Jupiter. (GILDED BRONZE, SYRIA, C. 14–15TH CENTURY)

All the gods mourned Baal's death. His wife, the ferocious ANAT, descended to the underworld to retrieve his corpse. However, she was unable to revive Baal and so appealed to Mot for help. When Mot refused to come to her aid, Anat burst into a frenzy and slaughtered him, whereupon Baal returned to life. Baal is thus seen as a dying and rising god. He is often depicted wielding a thunderbolt, or a flash of lightning. (See also DYING AND RISING GODS)

C

BASAMUM was worshipped in southern Arabia in pre-Islamic times. His name may come from the Arabic word for a balsam bush, suggesting that he was a god of healing. One ancient text tells how the god cured two wild goats.

BASTET was the local goddess of Bubastis, or "House of Bastet", the capital of a province of Lower Egypt. She was usually regarded as the daughter of the sun god *RA*, although she was sometimes said to be his sister and consort. Later, she became the wife of the creator god *PTAH*. According to some accounts, it was Bastet, rather

Can any under I thun the spread wings of the Churile the mane of his Tabernacle.

Behold now Behemoth which I made with thee

than *NEPHTHYS*, who was the mother of the jackal-headed god *ANUBIS*.

Originally a lioness goddess symbolizing both the warmth of the sun and the rage of the sun god's eye, from about 1000BC Bastet came to be represented as a cat, or a cat-headed woman. However, in some stories she continued to possess the qualities of Sekhmet (see *HATHOR*), the lion-headed goddess. Usually a benevolent goddess, Bastet protected humanity from diseases and evil spirits. Most importantly, she was a goddess of fertility, sex and love, and enjoyed music and dancing. In the fourth century BC fertility festivals were held in her honour at her temple at Bubastis. Cats were venerated as Bastet's sacred animals, and their mummified bodies were buried at her sanctuaries. (See also *SACRED ANIMALS*)

BEHEMOTH was a terrifying monster of Hebrew mythology, the dry-land equivalent of the monstrous sea serpent *LEVIATHAN*. According to the Old Testament

BASTET (left) was usually portrayed as either a cat or a cat-headed woman. Originally a local goddess of Bubastis, her cult reached its height in the Late and Ptolemaic periods (c 660–30BC) when animal cults became a major feature of popular religion. Bronze figurines and mummified cats were given as offerings. (BRONZE, C. 5TH CENTURY BC.)

BEHEMOTH (left) and the sea monster Leviathan were used in the Book of Job as examples of the largest and strongest animals imaginable. (HAND-TINTED ENGRAVING BY WILLIAM BLAKE, C. 1793.)

Book of Job, Behemoth was associated with the hippopotamus. The monster is sometimes said to have developed from *TIAMAT*, the fearsome Babylonian goddess.

BEL see *ENLIL*.

BELILI see *TAMMUZ*.

BORAK (below) with a human head, the body of a winged horse and a peacock's tail, carries the prophet Muhammad to heaven, surrounded by winged peris. (QAJAR LACQUERWORK, C. 1870.)

BORAK was a fabulous beast of Islamic mythology. Part human, part animal, the prophet Muhammad was said to have ridden on its back on the night of his ascension to heaven. The creature's name means "Lightning".

CORYBANTES see *KORYBANTES*.

CYBELE was the great mother and fertility goddess of Phrygian mythology. She probably originated as a mountain goddess and was sometimes referred to as the "Lady of Ida", a mountain in western Anatolia. She inhabited the wild and dangerous regions of the earth and ruled over the fiercest of wild animals. Cybele's origins have

NOAH (above) released his dove a third time, seven days after her return carrying the olive branch. This time, she left the ark for good. Noah, looking out, saw dry land once more and was able to disembark. God promised him and his family that they were safe, and as a token of his covenant, he set a rainbow in the sky, which would appear when rainclouds threatened as reassurance that the flood would not return. (THE DOVE SENT FORTH FROM THE ARK BY GUSTAVE DORÉ, 19TH CENTURY.)

NOAH (above right) was given a precise specification for the ark by God, detailing the dimensions of the boat, its roof and door, the number of decks, the type of wood to use and how it should be waterproofed. Noah was already an extremely old man at the time of the flood and lived on for many more years after it – his longevity recalls the eternal life granted to the survivors in the Mesopotamian versions of the myth. (DETAIL OF THE VERDUN ALTAR, 1181.)

UTNAPISHTIM'S (right) boat eventually came to rest on Mount Nisir and, as the water began to subside, he sent out a dove and a swallow. Both returned to the boat unable to find food or a place to perch. However, when a raven was released, it did not come back, and Utnapishtim concluded that it had found dry land. He offered a sacrifice on the summit of the mountain, which placated the gods. (ILLUSTRATION FROM GILGAMESH BY ZABELLE C. BOYAJIAN, 1924.)

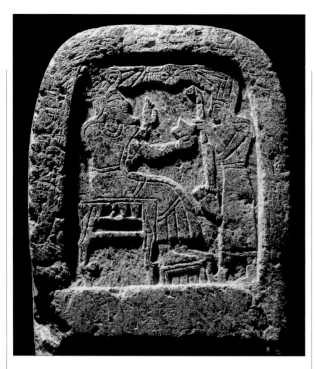

EL, the creator god, sits on his throne and listens to the prayer of a supplicant. (RELIEF ON A STELE, SYRIA, 13TH CENTURY BC.)

EL, a Canaanite deity, was referred to as the "Father of the Gods". He caused the rivers to flow, thus making the land fertile, and made his home near the seashore. Sometimes referred to as "Creator of the Earth", he was also known as "Bull", or "Bull-El", to signify his strength and powers of fertility. His name is usually translated as "Mighty One" or "First One". In 1929, stories about El were found on clay tablets at Ras Shamra in Syria, the site of the ancient city of Ugarit. The tablets dated from the 14th century BC.

Although El was usually regarded as the consort of Asherat (see *ASTARTE*), one myth found at Ras Shamra tells how he had intercourse with two women, probably representing Asherat and *ANAT*. The women subsequently gave birth to the deities *SHACHAR*, "Dawn", and *SHALIM*, "Dusk". According to the story recorded on the clay tablets, El walked along the shore, then plunged into the waves. His hands reached out like the waves, and he made his wives fruitful. He kissed their lips, which tasted as sweet as grapes, and in the kiss, and the conception and the embrace, Dawn and Dusk were born. El went on to father many more deities. He was depicted as an old man, sitting on a throne and wearing bull's horns.

EL-'OZZA see *AL-UZZA*.

ENKI see *EA*.

ENLIL was originally worshipped in Sumer as "Lord of the Wind", the god of hurricanes who represented the power of nature. He was believed to have absolute power over humans and was represented among men by the earthly kings.

Long before humankind was created, Enlil was said to have supervised the gods in their task of digging out the beds of the Tigris and Euphrates rivers. In time, the gods became exhausted by their ceaseless toil and decided to rebel. Enlil was devastated, but the god Enki (see *EA*) came to his aid, suggesting that the goddess Nintur create humankind in order to take over the work from the gods. For hundreds of years, all went smoothly, but then the cities became so overpopulated that the clamour made by the men and women kept Enlil awake. Enlil decided to solve the problem by sending a plague down to earth. However, Enki warned the people of the impending disaster, and they made huge efforts to keep quiet.

In time, the men and women forgot Enlil's threat and reverted to their noisy ways. This time, Enlil threatened to send a drought down to earth. Once again, Enki warned the people and they became quiet. The next time that Enlil was disturbed by the people's clamour, the god threatened to instigate a famine, but again Enki warned humankind and they were quiet.

Finally, when the men and women again began to create a huge clamour, Enlil lost all patience and sent down a massive flood. However, Enki had advised a wise man to build a ship and to save himself and his family from the flood. In some versions of the myth, the wise man was called Atrahasis, in others, Ziusadra. For seven days and seven nights, the rains lashed down, and the world was submerged by a massive flood. When the waters finally subsided, only Atrahasis (or Ziusadra), his

ENLIL, Sumerian "Lord of the Wind", receives worshippers at his throne. Son of the sky god, Anu, he represented the power of nature and threatened to destroy humankind because the clamour they made kept him awake. (CYLINDER SEAL, MESOPOTAMIAN, 3RD MILLENNIUM BC.)

family and the animals on the boat remained alive. In another version of the flood myth, which forms part of the epic of *GILGAMESH*, the hero *UTNAPISHTIM* survives the flood with his family.

In earliest times, Enlil's consort was believed to be *NINHURSAGA*, the "Lady of the Great Mountain". Later, however, he was associated with the grain goddess, *NINLIL*.

The Babylonians often equated Enlil with the great god *MARDUK*, calling him Bel, or "Lord". He was also assimilated into the Hittite pantheon, by way of the Hurrians. There, he features in the myth of the monstrous being *ULLIKUMMI*. (See also *MYTHS OF THE FLOOD*)

ENNUGI see *UTNAPISHTIM*.

ERESHKIGAL was the queen of the underworld in both Akkadian and Babylonian mythology. The underworld lay beneath the waters of *APSU*, the primordial ocean. It was a dry and dark realm, sometimes referred to as a mountain, sometimes as enemy territory. According to the epic of *GILGAMESH*, Ereshkigal, rather than having chosen her kingdom, was "given the underworld for her domain." Enthroned therein, she ate only clay and drank dirty water.

The goddess had an insatiable sexual appetite and never let compassion for others stand in the way of her desires. According to one story, when the war god Nergal entered the underworld, Ereshkigal

EVE was created by God, who placed her in paradise as a companion for Adam.
(NUREMBERG BIBLE, 1483.)

copulated with him for six days and nights. None the less, when he left, she remained unsatisfied.

In order that no one should return to the land of the living, the underworld was guarded by seven walls. At each of its seven gates, people had to take off an item of clothing, each representing one of their earthly attributes. When they finally reached the centre, they found themselves naked and imprisoned forever in eternal darkness. According to one tradition, Ereshkigal was the sole ruler of the underworld until Nergal invaded her territory, posting two demons at each gate. In order to achieve peace, Ereshkigal agreed to marry Nergal and to give him authority over the underworld. Ereshkigal was the sister of the fertility goddess *ISHTAR*, the counterpart of the Sumerian goddess *INANA*.

ETANA was the 12th king of the city state of Kish after the flood. King Etana grew miserable because he had no children and appealed to the sun god *SHAMASH* for help. Shamash told Etana to go to a particular mountain. There, on the mountain, an eagle and a serpent had recently had a terrible quarrel. Each of the creatures had children but the eagle had eaten all the serpent's offspring. The serpent

complained to Shamash, who told him to trap the eagle and leave him to die. Etana found the dying eagle and asked him for a special herb that would enable him to have a son. The eagle promised Etana that he would bring him the herb if he would cure him. For several months, Etana brought the eagle food and drink until finally the bird was fully recovered. Then, the eagle told Etana to sit on his back so that he could carry him up to the sky of *ANU*, the supreme god. The eagle flew up to the gods and continued flying upwards towards the dwelling place of *ISHTAR*, the fertility goddess. In some versions of the tale, Etana seems to succeed in his quest and is given the herb by Ishtar. In another version, Etana grows dizzy and begs the eagle to return to earth. However, the eagle's strength suddenly runs out, and the two of them fall to the ground with a mighty crash.

EVE was the first woman, according to the Hebrew creation story. She was said to have been formed from her husband *ADAM*'s rib. A serpent tempted Eve to eat the one fruit which God had forbidden the couple, and she persuaded Adam to join her. As a result, both Adam and Eve were expelled from paradise. Eve was seen as responsible for the Fall and for bringing death, sin and sorrow into the world.

Christians have often viewed Eve's sin as a sexual failing. However, the Fall also opened the way for growth and learning. Adam refers to Eve as Hawwah, which is usually translated as "Mother of All Living", or "She who gives Life". According to one tradition, Adam was buried in paradise and was promised resurrection, whereas Eve was buried with her son, Abel. (See also *SERPENTS AND DRAGONS*)

EVE bears the apple, traditionally the forbidden fruit that led to the Fall and expulsion from paradise. (EVE BY LUCAS CRANACH THE ELDER, OIL ON WOOD, C. 1528.)

G

EYE see *HATHOR*.

FATIMA, the prophet Muhammad's daughter, is regarded by Isma'ilis as the "Mother of the Holy Imams". The Imams are the semi-divine leaders of Shi'ism, one of the two great forms of Islam of which the Isma'ilis form a subsect. Fatima is revered within esoteric Islam and is seen as symbolizing the "supra-celestial earth". She is considered to be the source of the Imams' wisdom because she is the "hidden tablet; upon which God has written."

FERIDUN, according to ancient Iranian mythology, was the hero destined to overthrow *ZOHAK*, the evil king sometimes regarded as the embodiment of the terrifying monster *AZHI DAHAKA*.

Zohak was warned in a dream that he would be deposed by someone called Feridun, and consequently ordered the massacre of all children. However, Feridun's mother, Firanak, saved her baby by hiding him in a garden, where he was suckled by a miraculous cow called Purmajeh. Firanak then hid the baby in Hindustan.

Throughout Feridun's childhood years, Zohak was obsessed with the thought that his destroyer was alive somewhere. Sure enough, Feridun grew up determined to overthrow the evil king.

One day, a man whose children had been killed by Zohak led a group of rebels to Feridun's palace. Feridun decided that the time was ripe for action. As he marched towards the king, an angel taught him magic and comforted him with tales of his future happiness. Zohak, learning of Feridun's approach, clad himself in armour. He attacked Feridun with his sword, whereupon Feridun smashed it with a club. However, an angel told Feridun not to kill the king but to chain him in a cave under a mountain. Feridun did as he was told and then succeeded to

FATIMA, daughter of the prophet Muhammad, on her way to a Jewish wedding party with Muhammad, A'isha, Umm Salma and Umm al-Ayman, receives a gift of a green cloak brought by Gabriel from paradise.

the throne. His reign lasted for several hundred years. (See also *SERPENTS AND DRAGONS*)

THE FRAVASHIS, according to the mythology of ancient Iran, were benevolent spirits or guardian angels. They helped *AHURA MAZDA* to create the world, and defended heaven from its enemies with their sharp spears while riding their fleet-

GEB, the Egyptian god of the earth, was the brother and consort of the sky goddess, Nut. (PAPYRUS.)

footed steeds. They were believed to be the ancestral spirits of believers, a part of the human soul that Ahura Mazda had created before each individual's birth, and thus might be regarded as prototypes for living beings. Fravashi is usually translated as "She who is Chosen".

GABRIEL, or Jibril, is known as the spirit of truth or "Angel of Revelations" in Islamic tradition. He stands at the apex of the angelic host and is said to have dictated the Qur'an to Muhammad. Gabriel is also believed to stand at the north-east corner of the *KA'ABA*, Islam's most sacred shrine.

In the Bible, Gabriel appears as the messenger of *YAHWEH*. He visited the Old Testament patriarch *DANIEL* twice, to announce the return of the Hebrews from captivity in Babylon and to explain the diversity of nations. In the New Testament, it is the archangel Gabriel who brings Mary the tidings that she is to conceive Jesus. Gabriel is also the trumpeter who will sound the Last Judgment. According to Hebrew apocalyptic literature, Gabriel is an angel of retribution and death. (See also *ANGELS AND DJINN*)

GADD was the name given to a variety of beneficent deities in pre-Islamic northern Arabia. It is sometimes believed to refer merely to a personification of good luck.

GAYOMART was the primeval being of ancient Iranian mythology. His corpse, together with that of the primeval bull *GEUSH URVAN*, was said to have given rise to all life. According to tradition, Gayomart existed for 3,000 years as a spirit until, in the second great epoch, he was made into a physical being by *AHURA MAZDA*, the principle of goodness. He was killed by *ANGRA MAINYU*, the principle of darkness. According to one myth, all the parts of the universe were created from his body; another tale tells how the seed of Gayomart was buried in the ground for 40 years, until it gave rise to the first human couple, *MASHYA AND MASHYOI*, as well as the seven metals. Gayomart's name is translated as "Mortal Life", or "Dying Life".

GEB, the Egyptian god of the earth, was the brother and consort of *NUT*, and the eldest son of *SHU* and Tefnut, the deities of air and moisture. Shu, or in some stories *RA*, was said to have separated Geb and Nut from a passionate embrace by violently pushing them apart so that Nut formed the sky and Geb the earth. Until then, there had not been sufficient space between the two bodies for Nut to give birth. Geb was said to grieve continuously for having been parted from his beloved Nut, and his distress was said to cause earthquakes.

He was usually regarded as a beneficent deity who provided humanity with crops for their fields, and who healed the sick. However, it was also feared that he might trap the dead within his body and thereby prevent them from entering the underworld. The god was usually depicted as a bearded man, often lying under the feet of Shu. He was sometimes coloured green, to indicate that vegetation was believed to grow from his body. Occasionally he was accompanied by a goose or portrayed as a bull.

Geb, the "Father of the Gods", and Nut were said to have begat *OSIRIS*, *ISIS*, *NEPHTHYS* and *SETH*. The kings of Egypt called themselves the "Heirs of Geb".

GEUSH URVAN, the primeval bull of ancient Iranian mythology, was created, along with the primeval man *GAYOMART*, by *AHURA MAZDA*, the essence of good. According to one tradition, Geush Urvan died, like Gayomart, at the hands of *ANGRA MAINYU*, the essence of darkness. Another tradition teaches that Geush Urvan was slain by *MITHRA*. All kinds of plants and animals were said to emerge from his corpse.

Widely believed to be the guardian of cattle, Geush Urvan's name means "Soul of the Cow". The sacrifice of a bull was an important part of Mithraic rituals.

GILGAMESH, the famous Mesopotamian hero, is believed to be based on a real person, who was most probably a Sumerian king. *The Epic of Gilgamesh*, a poem recording the hero's exploits, was transcribed on to tablets in the second millennium BC.

Gilgamesh was two-thirds god, one-third man. He was so active and such a womanizer that the inhabitants of Uruk, or Erech, the city where he lived, appealed to the gods for help. The deities responded by creating another man called Enkidu, or Eabani, who turned out to be a wild and savage being, even more troublesome than Gilgamesh. Eventually, it was Gilgamesh who helped the people of Uruk to hatch a plot whereby they succeeded in taming the wild being. Enkidu subsequently became Gilgamesh's friend and constant companion, and the two men lived a life of luxury together.

In time, however, Gilgamesh was instructed by the gods to leave his home in order to fight Khumbaba, or Huwawa, the horrible monster who lived some 20,000 marching hours away from Uruk at Cedar Mountain. Enkidu and Gilgamesh set off on their quest and, after entering the cedar forest, eventually found Khumbaba's home. Gilgamesh

GILGAMESH with a lion. Gilgamesh is the Mesopotamian hero of an epic poem, which describes his legendary adventures, taking him to death and back. (RELIEF FROM PALACE OF SARGON, KHORSABAD, 8TH CENTURY BC.)

challenged the monster to battle and, after a fearsome struggle, the two men overcame him, although it was Enkidu's spear that struck the fatal blow.

Soon afterwards, the goddess *INANA* tried to seduce Gilgamesh. When the hero turned her down, she complained to the god An (see *ANU*) who was eventually persuaded to give Inana the bull of heaven to send against Gilgamesh. However, Enkidu caught the bull and Gilgamesh stabbed it to death. The gods, outraged that the bull had been killed, took their revenge by striking Enkidu down with illness. After a few days, he died.

Gilgamesh was devastated at the death of his friend, and became terrified at the thought of death. He decided to try and discover the secret of immortality and set out on a quest to find *UTNAPISHTIM*, the hero who, after surviving the flood, had been granted immortality by the gods. When he reached Mount Mashu, Gilgamesh was confronted by the scorpion men who guarded its gates. However, they recognized that he was in part divine and let him pass by them to proceed into the mountain.

At length, Gilgamesh came to a beautiful garden beside a sea and saw before him the tree of the gods, laden with amazing fruits, the ground covered with jewels. There, he met the goddess Siduri Sabitu, who tried to deter the hero from his quest. At Gilgamesh's insistence, the goddess eventually advised him to seek the help of Ushanabi, Utnapishtim's boatman. Ushanabi took Gilgamesh through the waters of death into the underworld, and at last, the hero reached Utnapishtim. Gilgamesh told him: "Because of my brother I am afraid of death; because of my brother I stray through the wilderness. His fate lies heavy upon me. How can I be silent, how can I rest? He is dust, and I shall die also and be laid in the earth for ever." The hero of the flood told Gilgamesh that death, like sleep, was necessary for humankind. To prove his point, he told Gilgamesh to try staying awake for six days and seven nights. Gilgamesh agreed, but fell fast asleep almost as soon as he had sat down.

Before Gilgamesh returned home, Utnapishtim showed him the plant of youth, which lay at the bottom of the ocean. Gilgamesh found the plant, but as he bent to pick it, it was stolen by a snake. The tale ends on a sad note, with the ghost of Enkidu telling Gilgamesh of the misery of life in the underworld. (See also *UNDERWORLDS; HEROES AND QUESTS*)

GUBABA see *KUBABA*.

GULA see *NINURTA*.

GULASES see *GULSES*.

THE GULSES, or Gulases, were Hittite goddesses whose name means either "Scribes", or "Female Determiners of Fate". The Gulses allotted the destinies of individual men and women, dispensing good and evil as well as life and death. The Hurrians called them Hutena.

HADAD see *BAAL*.

THE HAFAZA, according to Islamic mythology, are a type of guardian spirit. They look after people, protecting them from *DJINN*, or demons. Everybody is said to be protected by four hafaza: two to watch over them during the day and two during the night. The hafaza record each individual's good and bad deeds. People are said to be most at risk from the djinn at sunset and at dawn since, at those times, the hafaza are changing guard.

HAHHIMAS, the disappearing god, according to one version of the Hittite myth of *TELEPINU*, was responsible for having caused the great devastation that afflicted the earth. The myth tells how "Hahhimas has paralysed the whole earth, he has dried up the waters, Hahhimas is mighty!" In response to this desperate state of affairs, the weather god *TARU* called on his brother, the wind, to breathe on the earth, thereby reinvigorating it. However, on his return, the wind simply reported that the whole earth was paralysed and that people were doing nothing but eating and drinking. Hahhimas then began to seize and paralyse the gods, including Telepinu. Hahhimas's name is sometimes translated as "Torpor".

HAN-UZZAI see *AL-UZZA*.

HANNAHANNA was the Hittite mother goddess and goddess of birth. Her name is usually translated as "Grandmother". She was served by the bee who eventually found the fertility god *TELEPINU* after he had disappeared from the world, leaving decay and death behind him. *TESHUB* protested at the bee being sent on the mission, saying, "The gods great and small have sought him but have not found him. Shall this bee now search and find him?" However, Hannahanna ignored Teshub's objections and told the bee to bring Telepinu home.

The bee searched the earth, and eventually found Telepinu asleep in a field. As directed by Hannahanna, the insect stung the god. Enraged, Telepinu embarked on a bout of destruction, killing humans and animals. The story may be influenced by the belief that honey has the power to expel evil spirits.

HAOMA, according to ancient Iranian mythology, was the lord of all medicinal plants. He was able to confer immortality on his followers and was sometimes said to be the son of *AHURA MAZDA*, the supreme god and principle of good. Equivalent to the Indian Soma, haoma was also a real herb from which an intoxicating drink could be made. The drink was believed to heighten spiritual awareness and also to confer immortality. It was used in sacrificial rituals, which

GILGAMESH and his friend Enkidu fought bulls during their quest together, which culminated in the death of the monster Khumbaba. (AKKADIAN CYLINDER SEAL IMPRESSION, 3RD MILLENNIUM BC.)

were said to drive away evil spirits. The spirit of the great religious reformer *ZOROASTER* was said to be strengthened by drinking haoma.

HAOSHYANGHA, or Hoshang or Husheng, the son of Siyamek, was the first king, according to ancient Iranian mythology. Siyamek, the son of *MASHYA AND MASHYOI*, the first human couple, was killed by a demon. After killing the demon, Haoshyangha spread peace throughout his kingdom and then proceeded to spread justice throughout the world. He introduced all the arts of civilization to human beings. After extracting iron from a stone, he taught humankind how to make axes, saws and hoes. He then organized a system of irrigation, leading water from the rivers to the fields, and tamed wild animals so that they could be used to cultivate the land. He also taught people to make clothing from the skins of wild animals.

HAPI see *APIS*.

HARSIESIS see *HORUS*.

HAOMA was both a god of medicine and the name of a magical herb. Zoroaster was said to have drunk a fortifying potion made from haoma. (LIEBIG "CHROMO" CARD, 19TH CENTURY.)

HATHOR (above), was depicted as a cow, or as a woman wearing a horned headdress with a solar disc. (TEMPLE OF HUREMHEB, EGYPT.)

HATHOR (left), daughter of the god Ra, in her usual form of a cow. She nourished the living with her milk and carried the dead to the underworld. (TEMPLE OF HATSHEPSUT, EGYPT.)

HATHOR, the Egyptian sky goddess and daughter of the sun god, *RA*, was usually represented as a cow. The goddess of joy and love, dance and song, she looked after mothers and children. She nurtured the living and carried the dead to the underworld. There, she refreshed them with food and drink from the sycamore tree, in which it was believed she was incarnated. Royal coffins were made from sycamore trees, in the belief or hope that death was no more than a return to the womb.

HATHOR, as the goddess Sekhmet, is depicted in human form, with the head of a lioness surmounted by a sun disc, identifying her as the daughter of Ra.

The Eye of Ra was identified with Hathor. When Ra grew old, humankind began to plot against him. Hearing of this, the enraged god decided to send the divine Eye, the terrifying, burning power of the sun, to slaughter them. The Eye took the form of Hathor who, as the lioness Sekhmet, or the "Powerful One", threw herself at all the wicked men and women and killed them in a massive bloodbath. Eventually, Ra decided that enough carnage had been inflicted, and he called an end to the slaughter. Only by Ra's intervention was Sekhmet prevented from destroying humanity.

In order to put an end to Sekhmet's relentless slaughter, Ra drenched the battleground in thousands of jugs of beer mixed with pomegranate juice. The bloodthirsty Sekhmet drank the bright red potion, believing it was blood, and became so inebriated that she ceased her attack and was transformed back into the beautiful Hathor. In remembrance of the event, great jugs of beer and pomegranate juice were drunk annually on Hathor's feast day. (See also *SACRED ANIMALS*)

HAZZI was a mountain god worshipped by both the Hurrians and the Hittites. He formed part of the retinue of the weather god, *TARU*, and was invoked at Hittite state occasions as a god of oaths. Hazzi was also the home of the gods; it is thought to have been situated on Mount Sapon, near Ugarit.

HEBAT see *HEPAT*.

HEPAT, or Hebat or Hepit, the chief goddess of the Hurrians, was sometimes referred to as the "Queen of Heaven". The wife of the tempest god *TESHUB*, she was often granted almost equal status with her husband, and occasionally took precedence over him. She and Teshub produced a son, Sharruma, who was represented as a pair of human legs. When Hepat heard that *ULLIKUMMI* had forced Teshub to abdicate, she nearly fell off the roof of a tower in horror: "If she had made a single step she would have fallen from the roof, but her women held her and did not let her fall." Hepat was assimilated into the Hittite pantheon, where she was often equated with *ARINNA*, the sun goddess. She was depicted either sitting on a throne or standing on a lion, her sacred animal.

HEPIT see *HEPAT*.

HERARHTY see *HORUS*.

HORUS, in the story of *ISIS* and *OSIRIS*, is sometimes known as Harsiesis to distinguish him from the twenty or so other Horuses in the Egyptian pantheon. He was depicted as a falcon or with a falcon's head. He was born, after Osiris had retired to the underworld, on the island of Chemmis near Bhutto and was raised there in secret by Isis. Harsiesis eventually avenged Osiris's death at the hands of *SETH*, and reclaimed the throne. He ruled peacefully, and was worshipped throughout Egypt.

Horus was worshipped as the god of the sky. His eyes were said to be the sun and moon.

Herakhty, or "Horus of the Horizon", was a sun god who rose each morning on the eastern horizon. He was often identified with the sun god, *RA*, and was eventually absorbed by him, forming Ra-Herakhty.

HOSHANG see *HAOSHYANGHA*.

monstrous dragon or snake *ILLUYANKAS* with a rope after Inaras had trapped the creature at a feast. The weather god *TARU* then killed Illuyankas. Inaras rewarded Hupasiyas for his help by building him a house. She warned him that he must never look out of the windows of his new home in case he saw his mortal wife and children. When Hupasiyas disobeyed the goddess, she killed him.

HUSHEDAR, according to ancient Iranian mythology, is a saviour and a son of the prophet *ZOROASTER*. Hushedar would be succeeded every thousand years by other saviours, culminating in *SAOSHYANT*, who is expected to introduce the universal judgment of humankind.

Eventually, after a final conflict between good and evil, the universe will be made pure again, and humanity will dwell in perfection with *AHURA MAZDA*.

HUSHENG see *HAOSHYANGHA*.

HUTENA see *GULSES*.

IBLIS is the name for the devil in Islamic belief. He is a rebel against God and tempts humankind to evil. Originally, he was the angel Arazil. When *ALLAH* created the first man, *ADAM*, out of clay, Arazil refused to worship him. When Allah summoned the angels to praise his creation, Arazil refused to attend. As a result, Arazil was thrown out of paradise, and from then onwards he encouraged the *DJINN* to make war against Allah. Eventually, he brought about Adam and Eve's fall from grace by tempting them into sin.

On the Day of Judgment, Iblis and his hosts of evil spirits will be consigned to the fires of hell. It is disputed whether Iblis was an angel or a djinn since, though he behaved like a fallen angel, he was said to have been made from smokeless fire like a djinn.

HORUS (above) was the son of Osiris and Isis, and a cosmic deity. He was depicted as a falcon or with a falcon's head. As the first ruler of all Egypt, he wore the double crown of the united kingdom. (RELIEF OF THE TEMPLE OF SETI I IN HYPOSTYLE, 1303–1290BC.)

HORUS (left) in battle. Raised in secret by his mother, Isis, he eventually avenged his father Osiris's death at the hands of Seth and reclaimed the throne.

HOURIS, in Islamic mythology, were black-eyed women who provided dead men in paradise with sexual pleasure. Each man was said to be given 72 houris, whose virginity was eternally renewed.

HUBAL was a god worshipped in Arabia in pre-Islamic times. His image, made from red carnelian, still stands in the sacred *KA'ABA* in Mecca, Islam's holiest city. It is believed that the Black Stone of the Ka'aba might be connected with the god in some way. Hubal was particularly famed for his oracle.

HUPASIYAS was the lover of *INARAS*, the Hittite goddess whose duties seem to have been those of protecting gods and tradesmen. A mortal being, Hupasiyas bound the

SERPENTS AND DRAGONS

HUMAN FEARS OF POWERFUL, ungovernable forces were crystallized in visions of huge and terrifying monsters. Serpents and dragons were composite images of everything that was inhuman: scales, claws and wings, of fantastic, fearful strength and size. They might also exhibit the characteristics of other animals, such as the head of a lion and the talons of an eagle. Their hybrid appearance added to their monstrous nature. Many were sea creatures, embodying the malign power of unpredictable nature and the threat of chaos. The most dramatic myths concern human or immortal heroes who killed dragons that threatened the world. By destroying the monsters, heroes were able to restore order and preserve the safety of civilization. As emblems of chaos, serpents featured in creation stories such as the myth of the snake Apep, coiled in the primeval water, who fertilized the cosmic egg of the Egyptians. In time, snakes came to represent not just disorder, but evil.

THE SERPENT (above) in the Garden of Eden is frequently portrayed with the face of Lilith, who in Hebrew legend was Adam's first wife. She considered herself his equal and left him – and Eden – rather than submit to him. She was often depicted as winged, with the body of a snake, and was said to be the temptress of Eve. She acquired the character of a wicked demon who killed new-born babies and was the enemy of men. (ANONYMOUS ENGRAVING.)

EVE (left), with her partner Adam, was free to eat the fruit of every tree in the Garden of Eden except one, the tree of the knowledge of good and evil. The serpent, more subtle than any other beast, persuaded Eve that this was the one fruit she desired and, having tasted it, Eve gave it to Adam to eat. According to the Old Testament of the Bible, their disobedience condemned humans to lives of toil, hardship and death. The serpent's punishment was to crawl on its belly and eat dust, and to be the enemy of humankind thereafter. (ILLUSTRATION BY RICHARD RIEMERSCHMID.)

LEVIATHAN (left), the great sea monster, was said to have existed from the fifth day of creation, and to represent the forces of chaos subordinated by Yahweh. According to later Hebrew traditions, Leviathan will be vanquished in a great final battle with the archangel Gabriel, and the banquet celebrating the eventual arrival of the Messiah will take place in a tent made from the monster's skin. (LEVIATHAN BY ARTHUR RACKHAM, 1908.)

AARON'S ROD (above), was turned into a serpent by Yahweh to help Moses and Aaron persuade the pharoah to allow the Israelites to leave Egypt. The pharaoh sent for all the sorcerers and magicians of Egypt, who responded by miraculously turning their own staffs into serpents as well, but they were all eaten by Aaron's. (AND HE THREW DOWN HIS ROD..., BY QAJAR, MINIATURE, C. 1860–70.)

APEP (left) the great serpent, lay in wait in the Egyptian underworld to ambush the sun god, who had to voyage through it each night ready to rise again. Night was a time of uncertainty and danger for the god, as it was for humans on earth. The return of the sun in the morning represented the triumph of life over death, symbolized by Ra-Herakhty, the falcon, vanquishing the serpent. (SMALL LIMESTONE PYRAMID.)

MARDUK's (above) battle with Tiamat is part of the Babylonian creation myth. Tiamat was the primeval salt-water ocean, which had to be tamed to allow the universe to come into existence. Marduk subdued her and eventually split her in two to create the earth and sky. Her eyes became the sources of the rivers Tigris and Euphrates. Marduk went on to kill her son, Kingu, and mixed his blood with earth to create humankind. (ILLUSTRATION FROM GILGAMESH BY ZABELLE C BOYAJIAN, 1924.)

DRAGONS (right) were appropriate emblems for the stars mapped by Arabic astronomers. These cosmic creatures engaged in battles far beyond human realms, such as the encounter between the Persian hero Feridun and the mighty dragon Azhi Dahaka. When Feridun stabbed the monster, snakes, toads and scorpions began to pour out, so instead of cutting him up, the hero imprisoned him in Mount Demavend. (ILLUSTRATION FROM A DESCRIPTION OF THE FIXED STARS, 1629.)

IBRAHIM see *ABRAHAM*.

ILLUYANKAS was the monstrous snake or dragon of Hittite mythology. He waged war against the gods, particularly against the weather god, *TARU*. However, the monster was eventually slain by Taru, who was assisted in his assault by the goddess *INARAS* and her mortal lover, *HUPASIYAS*. In another version of the tale, Illuyankas seized the heart and eyes of the weather god. Taru responded by fathering a son whom he married to the daughter of Illuyankas, demanding the missing organs as a dowry payment. Taru then succeeded in slaying the monster.

The story of Illuyankas and Taru was assimilated into Canaanite mythology as the struggle of the gods against the *LEVIATHAN*. The Hittite monster was also the prototype for Typhon, the hundred-headed beast of Greek mythology. The tale of Taru's battle against Illuyankas was recited at an annual feast either of the New Year or of spring. The destruction of the monster was believed to signal the beginning of a new era.

IMHOTEP was a sage and scholar attached to the court of the ancient King Zoser, who ruled Egypt in the third millennium BC. A great architect, as well as an astronomer and scientist, Imhotep designed and oversaw the construction of the first pyramids. Until then, rulers had been buried in underground chambers. Imhotep's Step Pyramid at Saqqara was the first monumental stone building ever constructed. The sage was also credited with ending a seven-year famine by advising the king to make offerings to *KHNUM*, the god who controlled the flood waters of the Nile.

Admired during his lifetime, Imhotep gradually came to be celebrated as a god. According to some tales, he was the son of the great god *PTAH* and provided the high priest of Ptah with a son. The patron of scribes, he is usually depicted as a priest with a shaven head. He was also the patron of doctors. His name means "He Who Comes in Peace." (See also *GATEWAYS TO THE GODS*)

INANA, the goddess of love, fertility and war, queen of heaven and earth, was the most important goddess in the Sumerian pantheon. Her symbol was the reed bundle, and she was often portrayed with bright sunbeams radiating from her image. Inana's Babylonian equivalent was the goddess *ISHTAR*.

Like Ishtar, Inana descended to the underworld kingdom of *ERESHKIGAL*. At the gate, Inana explained why she had come: "Because of my sister Ereshkigal". Then, however, she claimed that she wanted to see the funeral of Gugalanna, the "Bull of Heaven".

At each of the gates of the underworld, Inana divested herself of one of her items of clothing, or earthly attributes, including her priestly office, her sexual powers and her royal powers. Finally, she was condemned to death and killed, becoming part of the underworld kingdom.

The goddess Ninshubur, Inana's handmaiden, mourned grievously for her queen and eventually appealed to the gods for help. Neither *ENLIL* nor Nanna (see *SIN*) would become involved. However, the god *EA* came to Inana's aid. From the dirt of his fingernails, he created two beings who, because they were sexless, were able to enter the land of infertility. These beings were mourners who eased the ceaseless pain of Ereshkigal, whose existence had been one of continuous rejection. In reward for thus soothing the ruler of the underworld, the beings asked that they be allowed to revive Inana. Ereshkigal agreed and the goddess was reborn.

Before leaving, Inana had to agree to find someone to take her place in the underworld. The goddess was escorted on her homeward journey by a group of horrific demons.

When she reached the world of the living, Inana found her handmaiden, Ninshubur, waiting for her by the gates of the underworld and

INANA with Ea and Gilgamesh. She was the most important goddess in the Sumerian pantheon. (AKKADIAN CYLINDER SEAL, 3RD MILLENNIUM BC.)

her two sons waiting for her in their temples. All three were in mourning. However, she was aghast to discover that her husband *DUMUZI*, far from mourning her death, was thoroughly enjoying himself. Not only was he seated on his throne but he was also dressed in the splendid garments which she herself had given him. Furious with rage, Inana immediately appointed Dumuzi as her substitute in the underworld.

Although Dumuzi attempted to hide, he was eventually dragged off by the demons who had accompanied Inana on her homeward journey. Geshtinanna, Dumuzi's sister, was so distraught that she offered to share Dumuzi's sentence with him. On the way to the underworld, Inana granted eternal life and death to both Dumuzi and Geshtinanna. For half of each year Inana and Dumuzi were together, while Geshtinanna took Dumuzi's place. When Dumuzi joined Inana, the milk flowed, the crops ripened and the fruit trees blossomed. During the barren months, however, Dumuzi had to return to the realm of Ereshkigal.

In ancient Sumer, a ceremony took place each year in which the king of each city would impersonate Dumuzi and the chief priestess would assume the role of Inana. The couple would take part in a marriage ritual, which was believed to ensure fertility and prosperity.

IMHOTEP, studying a papyrus. Probable architect of the famous Step Pyramid at Saqqara, and greatly admired during his lifetime, Imhotep gradually came to be celebrated as one of the gods.

INANA (left), often identified with Ishtar, the goddess of love and war, is shown here with Anubanini, king of the Lullubians.

ISHTAR (right), the Babylonian goddess of love and war, had countless lovers, both men and gods, but was fickle and cruel. (ILLUSTRATION FROM LEWIS SPENCE'S MYTHS OF BABYLONIA AND ASSYRIA.)

INARAS features in Hittite mythology as the goddess who helped bring about the death of the monstrous dragon or serpent *ILLUYANKAS*. She is sometimes said to be the daughter of the weather god *TARU*. When Taru failed to overcome Illuyankas, Inaras devised a plot to bring about the monster's downfall. She prepared a marvellous feast, then asked a mortal, *HUPASIYAS*, to help her in her task. Hupasiyas agreed, on condition that she sleep with him.

Once she had carried out his request, Inaras invited the dragon, together with his offspring, to attend the banquet. When the monsters had eaten and drunk their fill, they found they were unable to squeeze back into their underground home. Hupasiyas then bound Illuyankas with a rope, and Taru killed him. Inaras built Hupasiyas a house in gratitude for his help. Then she said, "Farewell! I am now going out. Do not look out of the window; for if you look out, you will see your wife and children." When 20 days had passed, Hupasiyas threw open the window and saw his family. As soon as Inaras returned from her journey, Hupasiyas begged her to let him go home, whereupon the goddess killed him.

ISHTAR, the goddess of love and fertility, was a fearsome, often violent, deity, sometimes known as the "Lady of Battles". The Babylonian form of the Sumerian goddess *INANA*, she was the guardian spirit of life and the creator of wisdom. Her symbol was the eight-pointed star. Although she had countless lovers, she usually treated them cruelly.

On one momentous occasion, Ishtar descended to the underworld realm of her sister *ERESHKIGAL*. However, Ereshkigal cursed her sister, who subsequently died. As a result of Ishtar's death, the earth became infertile and neither birds nor beasts nor human beings mated. *EA*, the water god, eventually managed to save Ishtar by using his magic incantations, but Ereshkigal demanded she be given someone in her sister's stead. It was finally decided that *TAMMUZ*, her husband, should replace her for six months of each year.

Uruk or Erech, Ishtar's holy city, was called the town of the sacred courtesans, for prostitution formed part of her cult and she protected harlots, as well as alehouses. The personification of the planet Venus, Ishtar was sometimes believed to be the daughter of the moon god, *SIN*, sometimes of the sky god *ANU*. (See also *DYING AND RISING GODS*; *SACRED ANIMALS*)

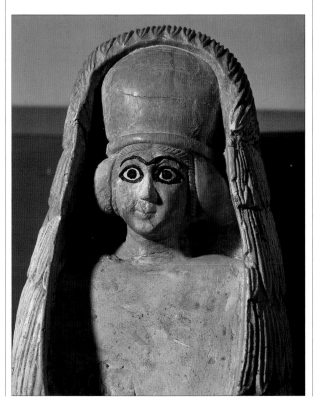

ISHTAR (left) became the principal goddess of the Babylonians and Assyrians. Like Inana, she was identified with Venus, the evening star. (ALABASTER, 2800–2300BC, SYRIA.)

ISHTAR (right), in her violent form as "Lady of Battles", is shown heavily armed and mounted on a lion.

ISIS, the Egyptian mother goddess, was the daughter of *GEB* and *NUT*, and the sister and consort of *OSIRIS*. She is usually depicted with huge, sheltering wings, and she is sometimes regarded as a personification of the throne. The hieroglyph for her name is the image of a throne, and her lap came to be seen as the throne of Egypt.

Isis helped Osiris to civilize Egypt by teaching women to grind corn as well as how to spin and weave. She also taught people how to cure illness and instituted the rite of marriage. When Osiris left Egypt on his world travels, Isis ruled the country wisely and well in his stead. Aspects of the myth of Isis occur in various Egyptian texts, and were assembled into a single narrative by Plutarch in the first century AD.

On hearing of Osiris's death at the hands of the evil god *SETH*, Isis was distraught. She cut off her hair, put on mourning clothes and set off in search of his body. A group of children told Isis they had seen the chest that enclosed Osiris's body floating down the Nile and out into the sea. It was eventually washed up underneath a beautiful tree on the shores of Byblos in the Lebanon. The tree immediately began to grow, so quickly that it had soon enclosed the coffin in its trunk. Hearing of the astonishing tree, the king of Byblos ordered it to be cut down and brought to his palace, where it was used to support the roof.

News of the remarkable tree rapidly spread. Isis immediately guessed what had happened and rushed to Byblos where, after disguising herself, she sat by a well in the city centre. When some of the queen's servants came to fetch water from the well, Isis braided their hair for them, breathing on it such beautiful perfume that a short

ISIS (above) is usually depicted as a woman seated on a throne. She wears a headdress and huge wings which are outspread, protecting Egypt and its people. (SARCOPHAGUS OF RAMESES III, GRANITE.)

ISIS (left) was the sister and consort of Osiris, the murdered god. She sought his body throughout the land of Egypt when he was slain by the evil god Seth.

while later the queen sent for the stranger and made her the nurse of her child.

Each night, Isis placed the queen's child in the fire of immortality while she transformed herself into a swallow and flew around the pillar that enclosed Osiris's corpse. One evening, the queen came into the room and saw her son lying in the flames. She was so horrified that she let out a piercing scream, thereby causing her child to lose his chance of immortality. Isis then revealed her true identity and asked to be given the pillar.

Her wish was granted, and so at last she recovered Osiris's corpse. The goddess carried the body of Osiris back to Egypt where she hid it in a swamp. However, Seth discovered the body and cut it into 14 pieces, which he then scattered up and down the country. With the help of several other gods, Isis located all the pieces, except for the penis, which had been swallowed by a fish. According to one version of the story, Isis then reassembled the body and, using her healing and magical powers, restored Osiris to life. Before departing to the underworld, Osiris and Isis conceived a child, *HORUS*.

Isis became so famous throughout Egypt, and beyond, that in time she absorbed the qualities of almost all the other goddesses. She was a great mother goddess, a bird goddess, a goddess of the underworld who brought life to the dead and a goddess of the primeval waters. Her following spread beyond Egypt to Greece and throughout the Roman Empire. She was worshipped for more than 3,000 years, from before 3000BC until well into Christian times. Her cult, and many of her images, passed directly on to the figure of the Virgin Mary.

ANUBIS (above) presided over mummification and funeral rites. Since the Egyptians regarded the afterlife as a continuation of their earthly existence, the correct preservation of the corpse was vital. Detailed incantations, designed as a guide to the underworld, accompanied the body, at first carved inside tombs, and later written on an illustrated papyrus scroll known as the Book of the Dead. (THE BOOK OF THE DEAD OF KHENSUMOSE, 11TH–10TH CENTURY BC.)

THE PYRAMIDS' (below) vast size attested to the Egyptians' overriding concern with the continuation of life after death. Tens of thousands of men laboured for decades to construct them, under the direction of a single architect, who was given the title of "Overseer of All the King's Works". Most of the stone was quarried locally, and the huge blocks were hauled on sleds up ramps that rose higher and more steeply as the pyramid grew.

THE TOWER OF BABEL (above) was said to have been built on the plain of Shinar in Babylonia, according to the Bible, by the descendants of Noah, with the intention of reaching up to heaven. Yahweh, the god of the Israelites, disapproved of this product of human pride. He thwarted their plan by confusing their speech so that they no longer understood one another's instructions. The tower, and the planned city, were abandoned, and the people scattered. (MEDIEVAL MANUSCRIPT REPRODUCED IN STRUTT'S ANTIQUITIES, 1773.)

THE PYRAMIDS (above) of Giza were regarded by the Greeks as one of the Seven Wonders of the World, and are the only one of the seven to have survived virtually intact. Their awesome size and mysterious nature made it difficult to believe that they were the work of human hands. Imhotep, the architect of the first pyramid – and the first stone building in Egypt – achieved great renown by his feat: by the Late Period, 2,000 years after his death, he had become a god. (ENGRAVING BY JACQUES PICART FROM THE SEVEN WONDERS OF THE WORLD, 17TH CENTURY.)

M

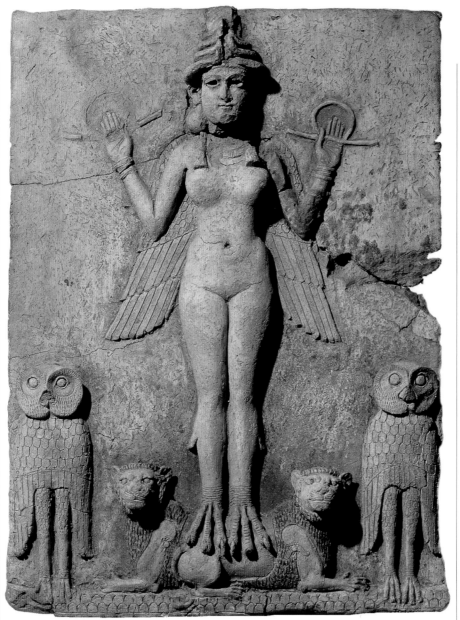

LILITH is flanked by owls, her sacred animals. Created with Adam, she rejected his authority and consorted with demons. She wears a crown of lunar horns and a rainbow necklace. (TERRACOTTA.)

LILITH, according to Hebrew legend, was the first woman to be created. She was portrayed as part snake, part woman and wearing wings. YAHWEH blamed her for having tempted EVE to reveal the mysteries of the Garden of Eden to ADAM. In the Old Testament, she is the demon who disturbs the night. Her name means "Storm Goddess", or "She of the Night". The owl was her sacred creature.

According to Talmudic legend, Lilith was created at the same time as Adam. She refused to lie down beneath him, believing herself to be his equal, and flew away to the desert. There, she consorted with demons and became the mother of numerous other demons, at the rate of more than a hundred each day. God sent three angels to bring Lilith back from the desert, but she refused. The angels threatened to drown her, but she warned them that she had the power to kill children. Eventually she agreed not to harm children: "Whenever I shall see you or your names or your images on an amulet . . ." Lilith then wandered the world, looking for unprotected children who deserved to be punished because of the sins of their fathers. She killed them by smiling at them.

According to another tradition, Lilith desired to join the ranks of the cherubim, but God forced her to descend to the earth. When Lilith saw that Adam already had a partner, Eve, she attempted to return to the cherubim but instead found herself cast out into the desert. One Hebrew myth tells how Yahweh made Lilith, like Adam, from earth. However, instead of using clean earth, Yahweh made her from filth and sediments.

Lilith originated in Sumerian mythology as a goddess of desolation. She is also associated with the Babylonian demon Lilitu, who preyed upon men. (See also SERPENTS AND DRAGONS)

LILITU see LILITH.

LUCIFER see SATAN.

MAAT was the Egyptian goddess of truth, justice and harmony. A daughter of the sun god, RA, she ruled over the judgment of the dead in the throne room of OSIRIS. Each person, when they died, had to appear before the 42 judges of the dead and declare whether they were innocent or guilty of numerous crimes. The soul of the dead person would be weighed on a pair of scales against the goddess, represented by a single ostrich feather. The scales were held by the jackal-headed god, ANUBIS, and their verdict was recorded by Maat's consort, the moon god, THOTH. If the heart was weighed down by crimes, the terrifying female monster Ammut, part crocodile, part hippopotamus, part lion, would devour the dead person. If, however, the deceased had lived "with Maat in his heart", and was thus pure and virtuous, he became a spirit, and could live with the gods to fight against the serpent APEP.

Maat was depicted wearing on her head the feather that was said to be put in the scales of judgment. As the "Breath of Life", she was often pictured ministering to the PHARAOHS by holding the ankh, a symbol of life, to their noses. All human beings were intended to live "by Maat, in Maat and for Maat."

MAAT, goddess of truth and justice, is depicted wearing a single ostrich feather, which is an ideogram of her name. (TOMB OF HUREMHEB, EGYPT.)

THE MALA'IKA, according to Islamic belief, are angels. They are sometimes said to be made from light and are believed to be superior to ordinary humankind but inferior to the prophets. The four chief angels are Jibril or *GABRIEL*, the holy spirit; Mikha'il, the guardian of the Jews; Israfil, the angel who will sound the trumpet at the resurrection; and Arazil, the "Angel of Death". *IBLIS* is either regarded as the fallen arazil or as one of the *DJINN*.

MANAT, or Menat, was a goddess of pre-Islamic Arabia who was worshipped in the region between the holy cities Mecca and Medina. She was believed to be one of the three daughters of *ALLAH*, the supreme god, the others being *AL-UZZA* and *AL-LAT*. As a goddess of fate, Manat had control over human destiny.

MANDAH was the name given to a pre-Islamic group of Arabian gods who were concerned with irrigation as well as being protective deities.

MARDUK, the chief god of Babylon, was the oldest son of *EA*, the water god. Born in the waters of *APSU*, the primordial, fresh-water ocean, Marduk was originally regarded as a fertility or agricultural deity whose attribute was an agricultural implement with a triangular blade, called a "mar". However, he gained a reputation as a fearless warrior and was usually depicted armed for battle. His name means "Calf of the Sun God", and he was associated with the planet Jupiter. This most splendid of gods apparently had four eyes and four ears, and fire blazed forth when his lips moved.

In time, Marduk's reputation for bravery grew to such an extent that he was chosen by the gods to attack the terrifying monster *TIAMAT*. He was given a thunderbolt as a weapon and also equipped himself with his bow, spear and mace. After a ferocious battle, Marduk slaughtered Tiamat: "When Tiamat opened her mouth to consume him, he drove in the evil wind that she close not her lips. As the fierce winds charged her belly, Her body was distended and her mouth was wide open. He released the arrow, it tore her belly, It cut through her insides, splitting the heart. Having thus subdued her, he extinguished her life."

MARDUK (right), the supreme god, with Shamash (left), the Babylonian god of the sun. (AKKADIAN CYLINDER SEAL, 3RD MILLENNIUM BC.)

The great god cast down Tiamat's carcass, stood upon it and, after slicing her body in two, thrust one half upwards to form the vault of the heavens and pushed the other half down to form the floor of the deep. Thus, the earth and sky were created. Marduk then divided the year up into 12 months, made the constellations and appointed the sun and moon to their places in the sky. He then addressed his father saying "Blood I will mass and cause bones to be. I will establish a savage, 'man' shall be his name."

The gods tied up *KINGU*, who had sided with his mother, Tiamat, in the battle, and severed his blood vessels. Out of his blood, which they mixed with clay, they fashioned human beings.

Before agreeing to attack Tiamat, Marduk had successfully persuaded the gods that, if he rose to the challenge, he should be granted additional powers, including the ability to determine fates and the right to pardon or kill captives taken in battle. After killing the monster, he was awarded 50 titles, each of which corresponded to a powerful divine attribute. In this manner, Marduk came to absorb all the other gods and to symbolize total divinity. He even threatened *ANU*'s status as supreme god, taking from him the power of his dignity.

According to one tale, the evil genies were annoyed by the moon god, *SIN*, whose light revealed their wrongdoings for all to see. The genies, together with *SHAMASH*, *ISHTAR* and *ADAD*, devised a plot whereby they eventually succeeded in eclipsing Sin's light. However, Marduk, displaying no fear whatsoever, simply overcame the conspirators and put them to flight. (See also *SACRED ANIMALS; SERPENTS AND DRAGONS*)

MARDUK became the chief god of Babylon and took over many of the functions of Enlil. His symbol is a tool, like a hoe or spade, called a "mar", before which his priest prays. (BABYLONIAN SEAL, 7TH CENTURY BC.)

MASHYA AND MASHYOI

were the first human couple of ancient Iranian mythology. In some traditions, they were said to have been born from the seed of GAYOMART, the primeval man, after it had lain in the soil for 40 years. Their first act was to walk, their second to eat. Then, however, they were sent a thought by a demon and, as a result, they became victims of ANGRA MAINYU, the principle of darkness. However, the good spirits continued to protect them. In time, Mashya and Mashyoi begat seven couples. One of these couples, Siyamek and Siyameki, became the parents of HAOSHYANGHA and of Fravak and Fravakain, who were said to be the ancestors of the 15 different peoples into which humankind was divided.

MEHUERET see NEITH.

MEN, a Phrygian moon god, was said to rule over both the underworld and the heavens. He was attributed with the good health of plants and animals and was referred to as Tyrannos or "Master".

MENAT see MANAT.

MIN, an ancient and popular Egyptian god, was always depicted with an erect phallus and with a flail raised in his right hand. On his

MIN (left), the god of roads and travellers, wore upon his head a crown decorated with two upright plumes. (RELIEF, KARNAK.)

head he wore a crown decorated with two tall, straight plumes. It is thought that Min may originally have been worshipped as a creator deity, but in classical times he was venerated as the god of roads and protector of those who travelled through the desert. His main cult centre was at Koptos, a centre for commercial travellers, and prayers were offered to the god before the travellers embarked on their expeditions. Min was also a god of fertility and growth, and a protector of crops. His main feast was known as the Feast of the Steps. Seated on his step, the god received the first sheaf of the harvest, which had been cut by the king.

MINUCHER, according to ancient Iranian mythology, was a descendant of FERIDUN, the great hero. When Feridun grew old he gave each of his three sons, Selm, Tur and Irej, a share of his kingdom. However, Selm and Tur plotted to take Irej's share from him. Irej was willing simply to give his brothers his part of the kingdom, and so he came before them unarmed. Without hearing what he had to say, Tur struck him over the head with a golden chair and then slashed him with his sword from head to foot until Irej's body

was streaming with blood. Tur tore Irej's head from his body, filled his skull with musk and amber, and sent it to Feridun. The king, who was waiting for his youngest son to return home, was stricken with grief when he heard what had happened and sought revenge.

Eventually Irej's grandson MINUCHER attacked and killed Selm and Tur in a bloody and ferocious battle. Feridun then died, leaving the throne to Minucher.

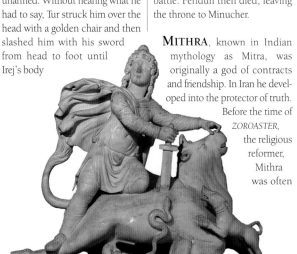

MITHRA, known in Indian mythology as Mitra, was originally a god of contracts and friendship. In Iran he developed into the protector of truth. Before the time of ZOROASTER, the religious reformer, Mithra was often associated with AHURA MAZDA, the principle of good. Mithra was the light: he was believed to ride his golden chariot, the sun, across the sky, drawn by four white horses. He had 10,000 ears and eyes, possessed both strength and knowledge, and was renowned for his bravery in battle. The god was able to bless those who worshipped him with victory over their enemies as well as wisdom, but he showed no mercy to his foes. As a god of fertility, he caused the rain to fall and the plants to grow.

According to one tradition, Mithra, as the sun, formed a link between Ahura Mazda and ANGRA MAINYU, the principle of darkness. This supposition was built on the understanding that the sun marked the continual revolutions of light and dark. Under Zoroaster's reforms to Iranian religion, Mithra was ousted from power, and Ahura

MITHRA was a forerunner of the Graeco-Roman god Mithras, shown here. Mithra was worshipped in underground shrines, many of them decorated with a relief showing him slaying the bull Geush Urvan. (MITHRAEUM OF SIDON, 4TH CENTURY AD.)

the entire earth was submerged. After some time had passed, Noah sent out a dove to see if the flood had abated but it returned to the ark. Eventually, another dove returned with an olive leaf in its mouth. God promised never again

to flood the earth and offered the rainbow as a sign of good faith: "This is the token of the covenant which I make between me and you and every living creature that is with you, for perpetual generations: I do set my bow in the cloud."

Flood myths are found throughout the ancient world, from Greece to India. The story of a flood destroying earth appears in the epic of *GILGAMESH* as well as in the myth of the Sumerian water god Enki (see *EA*) and the hero

NOAH was instructed by God to build an ark and take into it two of every living thing, to preserve them from the destruction of the flood. (FRENCH BOOK ILLUSTRATION, C. 1260.)

Atrahasis, or Ziusadra. (See also *MYTHS OF THE FLOOD*)

303

UNDERWORLDS

T HE MYTHOLOGY OF EVERY CULTURE included the idea that life in some way continued after death. The spirit might inhabit another physical body and live on earth again, or lead a perpetual existence in a murky netherworld. The concept of judgment invariably accompanied death and determined the future of the soul. A tribunal of gods or angels awaited the deceased to weigh up their conduct. The religion of the Egyptians was dominated by their funerary cult, but far from being obsessed with death itself, they saw it simply as a brief interruption. They aspired to an afterlife that was a continuation of their existence on earth in every

respect, preserving their social status, family connections and even their physical possessions. Only for those who had failed to please the gods during their mortal lives, or who had not prepared themselves for their journey through the underworld with the proper rituals and incantations, was death really a termination.

OSIRIS (right) was originally a deity of vegetation and agriculture, but the myth of his death became central to his cult and raised his status to that of a great god. The pharaoh, who was considered to be an incarnation of Ra the sun god while he was alive, became identified with Osiris on his death. Osiris was depicted wearing the crown of Egypt, and carrying the royal insignia of the crook and flail, but was tightly wrapped in mummy cloths. As lord of the underworld, he presided over the judgment of the dead on their arrival in his realm. (WALL PAINTING FROM THE GRAVE OF SENNUTEM, 14TH CENTURY BC.)

an old man with a blue beard, and he was called the "Shining Boat of Heaven". Every evening, he would climb into his crescent-shaped boat and sail across the skies. Sometimes, the crescent moon was regarded as the god's weapon and the full moon as his crown.

Sin was the enemy of the wicked, for his light revealed their evil ways. On one occasion, the utukku, or evil genies, hatched a plot against Sin and, with the help of Shamash, Ishtar, the goddess of love and fertility, and ADAD, the god of thunder, they eclipsed his light. However, the great god MARDUK waged war against the conspirators and gave Sin back his radiance.

Sin was also held to be wise and was believed to measure time with his waxing and waning. Moreover, by raising the marsh waters around

the city of Ur, where his temple stood, he ensured the well-being of cattle by enabling them to enjoy an abundant supply of food. (See also *GATEWAYS TO THE GODS*)

SIYAMEK see *HAOSHYANGHA*.

SOBEK see *SEBEK*.

SIN (right) was the Babylonian moon god, whose symbol, the crescent moon, is depicted on this carved stone. The god was held in supreme regard in Mesopotamia. His chief cult centres were at Ur and Harran. (KUDURRU, C. 1120BC.)

SHU (below), supports a head-rest found in the tomb of Tutankhamen. The god of air, Shu was the father of the sky goddess, Nut, and was often depicted in this position, supporting the sky above his head. (CARVED IVORY, 14TH CENTURY BC.)

T

SOLOMON

SOLOMON was the Old Testament king who ruled over Israel in the tenth century BC. He was noted for his great wisdom and for building YAHWEH's marvellous temple at Jerusalem. Under the influence of his many foreign wives, Solomon also built shrines for other gods, thereby incurring Yahweh's wrath. Solomon's seal, a six-sided star, became an important symbol used as an amulet or talisman. According to Arabic mythology, the star and the real name of God were etched on King Solomon's magic ring, thereby enabling him to command armies of demons. (See also *ANGELS AND DJINN*)

SPENTA ARMAITI is one of the *AMESA SPENTAS*, or the "Holy Immortals", of ancient Iranian mythology. Like the other Amesa Spentas, she is believed to have originated before the religious reforms of *ZOROASTER* and to have been assimilated into the purified religion as an aspect of *AHURA MAZDA*, the supreme being. Spenta Armaiti was patroness of the earth, and symbolized submission and devotion. She was widely believed to be the spiritual mother of all human beings, and people were taught to say, "My mother is Spendarmat, Archangel of the Earth, and my father is Ohrmazd, the Lord Wisdom."

According to one tradition, she was the mother of *GAYOMART*, the primordial being. As Gayomart lay dying, his body separated into seven metals. Spenta Armaiti gathered together the gold and grew a plant from it. From this plant came the first human couple.

The name Spenta Armaiti is sometimes translated as "Wisdom" or "Devotion".

SRAOSHA was known as the "Ear" of *AHURA MAZDA*, the principle of good in ancient Iranian mythology. He was one of the *YAZATAS*, Zoroastrianism's "Beings Worthy of Worship". As the "Ear" of Ahura Mazda, he was the means by which those who worshipped the supreme being could gain access to him. During the night, Sraosha guarded the whole of creation from evil demons.

SUEN see *SIN*.

TAHMURAS, according to ancient Iranian mythology, was the son of *HAOSHYANGHA*, the first king. He taught people how to spin and weave, and how to train birds of prey. On one occasion, he succeeded in capturing *ANGRA MAINYU* and, after leaping on to his back, forced the evil being to carry him on a tour of the world. However, while Tahmuras was away on his travels, the *DAEVAS* began to create havoc, so Tahmuras had to return and take up arms against them.

The daevas gathered together a noisy army, which hid itself in thick black smoke. Undeterred by this, Tahmuras captured two-thirds of the aggressors with the help of his magic arts and struck down the remainder with his massive club. The daevas pleaded for mercy and promised Tahmuras that if he spared their lives, they would teach him a marvellous secret. Tahmuras relented and, in return, the daevas taught him how to write and made him extremely wise and learned.

TAMMUZ, the Babylonian god of vegetation and the harvest, was a dying and rising god. Relatively low in standing among the gods, he was nevertheless extremely popular with the people and had a widespread following. His marriage to *ISHTAR*, the lustful goddess of love and fertility, led to his death: just as corn is cut down suddenly at the height of its splendour, so Tammuz was forced to retire to the underworld. Ishtar was devastated at his loss and underwent a period of wailing and lamentation. Each year after the harvest, those who worshipped Ishtar and Tammuz took part in a mourning ritual.

Ishtar eventually sought out Tammuz in the underworld and managed to secure his release, on condition that he return to the underworld for half of each year. Tammuz returned to the land of the living and took up his position at the gate of the sky god, *ANU*. It was there that the wise man *ADAPA* encountered him, when Adapa was summoned before Anu for demonstrating too much power. Adapa flattered Tammuz, who rewarded him by interceding on his behalf.

Tammuz's sister was Belili. In Sumerian myth, he was known as *DUMUZI*, the consort of *INANA*. (See also *DYING AND RISING GODS*)

HEROES AND QUESTS

MYTHS ABOUT MORTAL HEROES HAVE AN immediacy that comes from their recognizable human characteristics. Though the great heroes performed astonishing acts of bravery and achieved feats that were far beyond the capability of any real man, their adventures took place on earth and, in some ways, they behaved as other men did – falling in love, falling asleep, making friends, making mistakes – so that those who listened to their stories could identify with them as they could not with remote gods and goddesses. These men feared death and could not avoid it, hard as they tried. A perilous journey was usually central to the hero's story. There were many thrilling adventures on the way, with twists and turns that diverted him from his path, and selfless deeds such as killing monsters that frustrated him in his quest but saved the day for ordinary folk.

GILGAMESH (above), king of Uruk, or Erech, was the hero of a number of Sumerian stories that were combined and written down by Babylonian scribes in about 2000BC. Gilgamesh was said to be two-thirds god and one-third man because his mother was the goddess Ninsun. From her he derived his great strength. Despite his heroic stature, he began his reign as a tyrannical king, whose people were eventually driven to call on the gods for help in subduing him. (ASSYRIAN CYLINDER SEAL IMPRESSION, 1350–1000BC.)

ENKIDU (above left) was a wild man sent by the gods to deal with Gilgamesh, in answer to his people's prayers. He was, however, even more unruly than the king. Gilgamesh conceived a plan to civilize Enkidu. As a test of strength, they fought in a great wrestling match, but neither could outdo the other, and the two became friends. Their adventures together included the killing of fierce bulls and the fire-breathing demon Humbaba. (AKKADIAN CYLINDER SEAL IMPRESSION, C. 2300BC.)

GILGAMESH (left) resisted the seductive advances of the goddess Ishtar. Incensed, she sent the bull of heaven to avenge her honour, but with Enkidu's help, Gilgamesh managed to stab the bull. The gods were outraged and decided that Enkidu must pay for his part in the exploit. Within a few days, he had fallen ill and died. The loss of his friend instilled the fear of death in Gilgamesh and he embarked on a quest to find eternal life. (ILLUSTRATION BY E. WALLCOUSINS FROM MYTHS OF BABYLONIA AND ASSYRIA BY DONALD MACKENZIE.)

USHANABI (above), the ferryman, was the only man who knew how to cross the treacherous waters of death safely. He guided Gilgamesh over them on his way to reach the old man Utnapishtim, the sole survivor of the great flood, who had been granted immortality by the gods. Gilgamesh hoped that Utnapishtim would be able to tell him the secret of eternal life. (ILLUSTRATION FROM GILGAMESH BY ZABELLE C. BOYAJIAN, 1924.)

UTNAPISHTIM (above) reluctantly told Gilgamesh of a plant growing at the bottom of the sea which had the power to give him eternal youth. Gilgamesh found the plant, but as he bent to pick it, a serpent smelt it and stole it. In this way, snakes acquired the ability to stay young forever by simply shedding their ageing skin. Gilgamesh was forced to understand that his death was inevitable and returned to his kingdom. (ILLUSTRATION FROM GILGAMESH BY ZABELLE C. BOYAJIAN, 1924.)

RUSTEM (left), alone of all men, dared to fight the great White Demon in order to free the king, who had been inspired by the evil Angra Mainyu to try to usurp the throne of the ruler of Mazinderan. Rustem found the demon sleeping in his mountain lair, woke him and wrestled with him until "blood and sweat ran down in rivers from their bodies." Rustem was victorious and cut off the demon's head. (ILLUSTRATION FROM SHAH-NAMEH, LITHOGRAPH.)

RUSTEM (above), the Iranian hero, was born in a mysterious fashion, as a result of the incantations of a wizard and with the help of the magical feathers of the Simurgh bird. He was as tall as eight normal men and was famed for his strength and prowess in battle. One of his exploits in his youth was the killing of a rogue white elephant with a blow from an ox-headed mace.

(ILLUSTRATION FROM SHAH-NAMEH BY SHIRAZ, C. 1545.)

RUSTEM (left) searched the country for a horse and eventually caught one that had in fact been set aside for him from birth. Rakhsh was as magnificent and brave as the hero himself, with the strength of an elephant and the speed of a racing camel. On one occasion, when Rustem was sleeping and unarmed, his horse saved his life by killing a lion before it could attack him.

(ILLUSTRATION FROM SHAH-NAMEH BY INJU SHIRAZ, 1341.)

TARU, the Hittite weather god, was the father of *TELEPINU*. Like many other myths originating in West Asia, those featuring Taru are concerned with the annual cycle of vegetation. The tales relate his battles against a terrible monster, the giant serpent or dragon *ILLUYANKAS*. When Taru overcame the monster, vegetation flourished, but when he was vanquished all plant life withered and died.

According to one tale, Illuyankas managed to defeat the weather god. However, the goddess *INARAS* then hatched a plot whereby she managed to trap the terrible monster. The goddess prepared an enormous banquet and invited Illuyankas and his numerous offspring to come and join her in feasting.

When they had eaten their fill, the monsters discovered that they were too fat to fit through the tunnel that led to their underground home. The hero *HUPASIYAS*, Inaras's human consort, then tied the monsters up with a rope, whereupon Taru, assisted by the other gods, overcame them.

According to another version of the myth, the serpent overcame Taru, and seized his heart and eyes. Taru then fathered a son whom he married to the daughter of Illuyankas. The son asked for his father's missing organs as a dowry

payment and returned them to Taru. The weather god then slew Illuyankas in a terrifying sea battle. He also killed his son, probably in revenge for his having sided with the monster during the battle.

TEFNUT see *SHU*.

TELEPINU was a Hittite god of agriculture who controlled the fertility of plants and animals. His father, *TARU*, the weather god, said of him: "This son of mine is mighty; he harrows and ploughs, he irrigates the fields and makes the crops grow."

On one famous occasion, which has become known as the "myth of the disappearing god", Telepinu suddenly vanished; his haste was such that he put his boots on the wrong feet. Immediately, all life on earth began to wither and die. Even the gods began to starve. Fire was extinguished, animals perished, the trees lost their leaves, and the fields became dry and parched. "Barley and emmer wheat throve no more, oxen, sheep and humans ceased to conceive, and those who were pregnant could not bear." The sun threw an enormous feast for the gods, but his guests were unable to eat their fill or quench their thirst. Finally Taru explained that his son was angry and had disappeared, taking all good things with him.

TESHUB (above) god of the tempest and head of the Hittite pantheon, bears an axe and a three-pronged lightning fork. He was also a god of battle and overcame Kumarbi, the father of the gods. Kumarbi's son Ullikummi fought to take control of Teshub's city, but without success.

THOTH (below), the Egyptian moon god and vizier of Osiris, records the result of the weighing of a heart. As Osiris' sacred scribe, he was associated with secret knowledge and helped at the burial of Osiris. (FROM THE BOOK OF THE DEAD OF HUNEFER, C. 1310BC.)

All the gods, both great and small, proceeded to search for Telepinu. The sun sent out the eagle saying, "Go, search the high mountains, search the hollow valleys, search the dark-blue waters." However, although the eagle explored the entire country, he failed to find the missing god. Then, the weather god asked the mother goddess, HANNAHANNA, for advice. Hannahanna told the weather god to go himself and look for Telepinu, but Taru soon gave up and sat down to rest. Then Hannahanna suggested sending a bee to look for the god. Although the weather god objected, the goddess ignored him and told the bee to find the Telepinu, sting him on his hands and feet to wake him up, and then bring him back home.

At length, the bee found Telepinu asleep in a field. When the bee stung him, the god fell into such a frenzy that he proceeded to cause yet more devastation, killing human beings, oxen and sheep in his wake.

Eventually, the goddess Kamrusepas managed to calm him down using her magic spells: "She stilled his anger, she stilled his wrath, she stilled his rage, she stilled his fury." Telepinu flew home on the back of an eagle, and life returned to normal: "He released the embers of the hearth, he released the sheep in the fold, he released the oxen in the stall. The mother attended to her child, the ewe attended to her lamb, the cow attended to her calf."

TESHUB was a god of the tempest who was worshipped throughout western Asia. He is believed to have originated among the Hurrians, although the chief myth concerning his activities has been passed down by the Hittites. In the Hittite mythological texts, it is recorded how the fearsome god Teshub overcame KUMARBI, the father of the gods. Kumarbi fathered a son, ULLIKUMMI, who was made of diorite stone and grew to a huge size on the back of the giant, Upelluri. In order to view the vast creature, Teshub climbed to the summit of a high mountain. On seeing the monster, the terrified weather god persuaded the other deities to join him in launching an attack. However, their assault proved unsuccessful. Ullikummi succeeded in advancing as far as the gates of Teshub's city, whereupon he forced the god to abdicate his throne.

Teshub sought advice from the wise god EA who, after pondering a while, unearthed the ancient saw with which heaven and earth had been divided, and used the tool to sever the diorite stone at its feet. As a result, Ullikummi's power quickly faded, whereupon the gods decided to renew their attack on him. Although the end of the myth is missing, it is generally believed that Teshub eventually regained his kingdom and throne.

Teshub was the husband of HEPAT, who was often given almost equal standing with her husband, and sometimes took precedence over him. Teshub's attributes were an axe and lightning flashes, and he was sometimes depicted as a bearded figure, holding a club, with his feet resting on mountain deities. His chariot was drawn by two bulls.

THOTH, the Egyptian moon god, presided over scribes and knowledge, and was "Lord of the Sacred Words". He was sometimes said to be the sun god RA's eldest son, although, according to one tradition, he sprang from the head of the evil god, SETH.

Thoth is usually regarded as the vizier of OSIRIS, god of vegetation and the dead, as well as his sacred scribe. Because he was associated with secret knowledge, Thoth was able to help at the burial of Osiris. He also helped to look after HORUS when ISIS was bringing him up.

Eventually, Thoth succeeded Horus to the throne of Egypt and reigned peacefully over the land for more than 3,000 years. Afterwards, he took his place in the sky as the moon.

According to one story, he was ordered by Ra to light up the sky at night. There, he was slowly devoured by monsters who were, however, repeatedly forced to disgorge him bit by bit. Thoth was usually depicted as an ibis or as a baboon. It was said that Thoth wrote a book of magic, known as the *Book of Thoth*, which lies buried in a tomb near Memphis. The spells within the book were said to give the user power over the gods. Thoth was also said to record the verdict of the judgment of the dead in the underworld. (See also *SACRED ANIMALS*)

THOTH, god of the moon, writing and knowledge, with a scribe. Thoth was often depicted as a baboon, one of his sacred animals. (BRONZE, ARMARNA, C. 1340BC.)

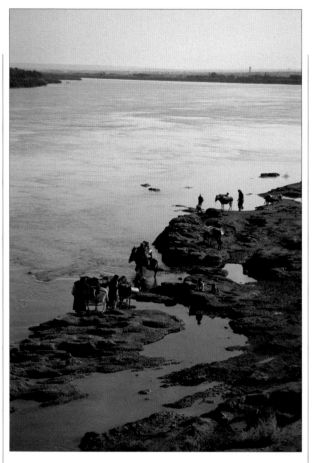

TIAMAT *embodied the raw energy of the ocean. In the Babylonian creation story, she was split in two by Marduk to form the sky and the ocean floor. Her eyes became the sources of the great rivers Tigris (left) and Euphrates, on which the lives of the Mesopotamians depended.*

useful plants. It was said that he helped AHURA MAZDA, the principle of goodness, in his struggle against every evil.

TISTRIYN see *TISHTRYA*.

ULLIKUMMI was the son of KUMARBI, originally an ancient Anatolian deity who was later introduced into Hittite mythology. The myth of Ullikummi concerns Kumarbi's attempt to wreak vengeance on his first son, *TESHUB*, who had overthrown him.

Kumarbi nursed the thought of creating an evil being and eventually slept with a vast stone, which subsequently gave birth to a son, Ullikummi. The boy was made of diorite stone, and in order that he might grow up in safety the deities placed him on the shoulders of the giant Upelluri in the middle of the sea. The child rapidly grew bigger and bigger until the water reached no higher than his middle, at which point the sun god noticed him and immediately told Teshub of the impending threat. Teshub wept

TIAMAT *was the personification of the primeval ocean who, with Apsu, initiated the creation of the gods. Depicted as a mighty dragon, she eventually marched against Ea and the other gods. Only Marduk, Ea's son, stood against her and overcame her.* (ILLUSTRATION BY EVELYN PAUL.)

TIAMAT, according to Mesopotamian mythology, was the turbulent, salt-water ocean that existed at the beginning of time. The universal primeval mother, she was depicted as a monstrous female dragon and was believed to embody the forces of chaos. The waters of Tiamat mingled with the fresh-water primordial ocean, APSU, and, in doing so, initiated the creation of the gods.

In time, Apsu grew tired of the clamour of the gods and began to plot their destruction. Tiamat at first refused to take part in Apsu's plan, but when the water god EA captured both Apsu and Mummu, the waves, Tiamat was spurred into action. After giving birth to an army of monsters, "sharp of tooth and merciless of fang", she marched against Ea and the other gods.

For some time, all attempts to subdue Tiamat failed until finally MARDUK, Ea's son, was chosen to confront her. Tiamat opened her jaws to swallow Marduk, but the god threw a raging storm into her mouth so that she was unable to close it. Marduk then caught Tiamat in a net and, after piercing her with an arrow, tore her innards apart. After slaughtering Tiamat's army of monsters, Marduk split Tiamat's skull and slashed her body in two. From one half of her body, he made the vault of the heavens, from the other half, the floor of the ocean. Then Marduk pierced Tiamat's eyes to form the sources of the rivers Tigris and Euphrates and bent her tail up into the sky to make the Milky Way. (See also *SERPENTS AND DRAGONS*)

TISHTRYA, or Tistriyn, was the name given by the ancient Iranians to the dog star. He was regarded as the god of water, whether that of the clouds, lakes, rivers or seas. Tishtrya also provided the seeds of with fear but, after being comforted by his sister, resolved to attack the monstrous being. However, though Teshub summoned the thunder and rain to help him, he was unable to defeat the creature.

Before long, Ullikummi had reached the gates of Teshub's city and forced the weather god to abdicate. Distraught, Teshub sought help from the wise god EA, who retrieved a saw that had originally been used to separate heaven from earth. Ea sliced through Ullikummi's ankles, and the monster's power

UTNAPISHTIM was told by Ea to build a boat and take every kind of living thing aboard. The gods were about to punish the wicked city of Shurripak with a deluge, but Ea wished Utnapishtim to survive. (ILLUSTRATION FROM GILGAMESH BY ZABELLE C. BOYAJIAN, 1924.)

faded. The gods then renewed their attack on Ullikummi, and Teshub regained the throne.

UTNAPISHTIM, according to one version of the Mesopotamian flood myth, was the wise man who alone survived the flood. The gods ANU, ENLIL, NINURTA and Ennugi decided to destroy humankind, having grown tired of their ways. However, EA, the water god, warned Utnapishtim of the conspiracy, and told him to build a boat and in it store the seeds of all life. Utnapishtim built a huge vessel 120 cubits high and loaded it with his family, his cattle and numerous other animals and birds.

On the evening that he finished his work, a filthy rain began to fall, and everyone on earth was stricken with terror. For six days and six

nights, the deluge continued until, at daybreak on the seventh day, it suddenly ceased and all that was left of humanity was a vast heap of thick mud.

Utnapishtim, whose marvellous boat had come to rest on the summit of Mount Nisir, cried out in grief. He let loose one bird after another from his boat, but they all returned, having found nowhere they could alight. However, when at last Utnapishtim released a raven, it failed to return, signifying that it must have found dry land.

In gratitude to the gods, Utnapishtim placed offerings to them on the summit of the mountain. Enlil, however, was furious to see that a human being had escaped the wrath of the gods. Ea eventually managed to calm Enlil down, whereupon Enlil took

Utnapishtim and his wife by the hand and said that from now on they would be immortal, like the gods themselves.

Some time after these events, the hero GILGAMESH, a descendent of Utnapishtim, sought out the immortal in the hope of learning the secret of eternal life from him. Utnapishtim refused to disclose the secret, but nonetheless directed Gilgamesh to the bottom of the sea to find the plant of rejuvenation. Unfortunately, on Gilgamesh's journey home, it was stolen from him by a serpent when the hero stopped to bathe and rest. (See also MYTHS OF THE FLOOD; HEROES AND QUESTS)

UTTUKU see SIN.

UTU see SHAMASH.

W

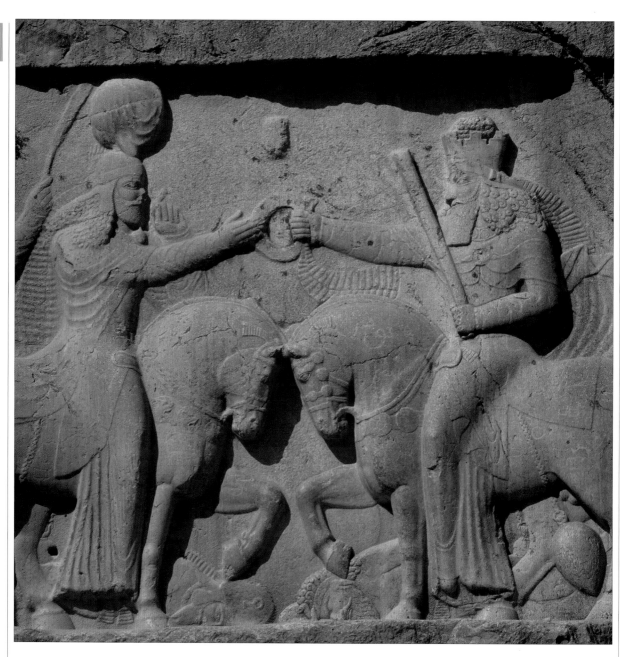

VOHU MANO was one of the *AMESA SPENTAS*, or "Holy Immortals", of ancient Iranian mythology. These divine beings were believed to people the universe and to look after humanity. They are thought to have been worshipped before the time of the religious reformer *ZOROASTER*. Although Zoroaster denounced the old gods, he continued to venerate the Amesa Spentas as aspects of *AHURA MAZDA*, the one true spirit set in opposition to *ANGRA MAINYU*, the spirit of darkness. It was said that when Zoroaster was about 30 years old, Vohu Mano transported his spirit to Ahura Mazda, thereby bringing about his spiritual enlightenment. Vohu Mano ("Good Thought" or "Spirit of Good") reigned over useful animals and was often represented by the cow.

WADD was a moon god worshipped in certain parts of southern Arabia from the fifth to second centuries BC. His name means "Love" or "Friendship", and his sacred animal was the snake. Wadd is referred to in the Qur'an as a pagan divinity, one of five idols erected by the descendants of Cain.

VOHU MANU, the "Good Thought", was one of the Amesa Spentas of Iranian mythology. He personified the wisdom of Ahura Mazda, portrayed here presenting the crown of the kingdom of Persia to Ardechir I. (ROCK CARVING, EARLY 3RD CENTURY BC.)

was "Ruler River". According to one myth, Yam asked the supreme god, EL, to grant him power over the other gods. El agreed but warned him that he must first conquer BAAL.

The fertility god equipped himself with magical weapons made by the smith gods and went into battle. He succeeded in killing Yam, proceeded to scatter his remains and then crowned himself king. The myth symbolizes the chaotic forces of nature being overcome by its civilizing aspect, which ensures the fertility of the crops.

Another tale tells how Yam was compensated for his defeat by being given the goddess ASTARTE as his bride. Yam was sometimes referred to as a dragon or serpent, or as the sea monster, LEVIATHAN.

YAMM see YAM.

THE YAZATAS, or "Beings Worthy of Worship", were the protective spirits of Zoroastrianism. Most of them were ancient Iranian gods who were incorporated into ZOROASTER's reformed religion as helpers of the supreme being, AHURA MAZDA. Some of the Yazatas corresponded to the stars and planets, others to the elements, while many embodied abstract concepts. Sometimes, the celestial Yazatas were said to be led by Ahura Mazda and the terrestrial Yazatas by Zoroaster. They included in their number RASHNU and SRAOSHA.

YAM, the Phoenician sea god, represented the turbulence of nature. He was defeated by the fertility god, Baal. In some versions of his myth he married the goddess Astarte, though she is more often described as the consort of Baal himself. (GILDED BRONZE, 19TH–18TH CENTURY BC.)

WADJET was the cobra goddess of Lower Egypt. She was usually represented as a cobra about to strike, although she sometimes appeared as a lioness. In the myth that relates how ISIS brought up her child HORUS in secret, Wadjet appears as the young god's nurse. Both Wadjet and NEKHBET were believed to protect the PHARAOH. (See also SACRED ANIMALS)

YAHWEH, or Jahweh, was regarded by the tribes of Israel as the creator of all things and the judge of all nations. He probably originated as a mountain god and was identified with EL, the supreme deity of the Canaanite pantheon. Yahweh intervened in earthly affairs, often through his prophets. He demanded that his followers should worship no other deity and was a jealous god. Though he dealt severely with anyone who strayed from his teachings, he was a god of

YAHWEH's followers avoided pronouncing the four Hebrew letters that made up his name, considering it too sacred to be pronounced aloud.

righteousness and ultimately merciful. No physical likeness was ever attributed to him.

The Third Commandment decrees, "Thou shalt not take the name of the Lord thy God in vain", so his followers avoided pronouncing the four Hebrew letters, YHWH or JHWH, which made up his name. The letters are supposed to represent the identity of God and are usually interpreted as meaning "I am that I am". From the 13th century, Yahweh was sometimes known in English as Jehovah. (See also SERPENTS AND DRAGONS; ANGELS AND DJINN)

YAM, or Yamm, or Jamm, was the Phoenician god of the sea and water in general. One of his titles

329

ANGELS AND DJINN

NGELS ARE INTERMEDIARIES BETWEEN heaven and earth, sent to bring messages to humankind – their name comes from the Greek word for "messenger". The Hebrew patriarch Jacob had a vision of angels on foot, ascending and descending a ladder which stood on the earth and reached up to heaven. Later concepts of heaven were of a more remote realm, from which winged angels flew down to earth. Angels are mentioned frequently in the Bible, praising Yahweh or appearing to humans bearing announcements or instructions from him. Islamic angels are also winged messengers; another of their tasks is to record the good and bad deeds of men, and they examine the faith of the dead on their first night in the grave. Djinn are less predictable. Originally nature spirits, they are a disruptive influence on humankind, capable of causing madness. A sinful man risks being turned into a djinnee (a lesser djinn) after his death.

THE PROTECTIVE SPIRITS (above) of ancient Iranian mythology were portrayed as winged creatures, and it was perhaps this imagery that influenced the development of the idea of angels' wings. Protective, sheltering wings were an important symbol of the beneficence of Ahura Mazda, the supreme god of the Iranians, and are used to represent him. (PERSIAN MINIATURE, C. 1370–80.)

LUCIFER (above left), arriving in hell with Beelzebub, entered a new and dreadful domain, where he plotted his revenge as the adversary of humankind. Early Christian tradition, based on a passage of Isaiah and the words of Jesus – "I beheld Satan falling as lightning from heaven" – held that Satan had originated as an angel who had been thrown out of heaven because he was too proud to acknowledge the supremacy of Yahweh. (ILLUSTRATION TO MILTON'S PARADISE LOST BY JOHN MARTIN, 1827.)

THE DJINN (above) were ugly and evil supernatural beings in pre-Islamic times, the fiery spirits of wild, desolate places who exercised their malign powers under a cloak of invisibility or by changing their shape at will. Their name means "furious" or "possessed". Though they were capable of redemption under Islam, those who refused to acknowledge Allah became demons. (SYRIAN RELIEF SCULPTURE, 9TH CENTURY BC.)

THE ANGELS (left), who were created before human beings, objected to Allah's plan to populate the earth, on the grounds that humanity would rebel against him. However, when Allah created Adam as the first prophet and taught him the names of all things, all the angels agreed to bow down before him. The single exception was Iblis, the devil, who considered that as he was born of fire he was superior to a being made of earth. (OTTOMAN MINIATURE, 1558.)

THE ARCHANGEL GABRIEL (below) sits on the left hand of Yahweh and, in Hebrew literature, guards the left side of humans while they sleep. As a warrior, he will fight the last great battle with Leviathan, the symbol of chaos, at the end of time. According to Christian tradition it was Gabriel who was sent to announce the births of John the Baptist and Jesus. In Islam, he is Jibril, the angel of revelations. (ARCHANGEL GABRIEL, BYZANTINE SERBIAN ICON, 14TH CENTURY.)

SOLOMON (left), the son of David, was king of Israel for 40 years in the tenth century BC. His wisdom was legendary, and his reign prodigiously successful: his wealth and knowledge, together with his interest in the various religious practices of his many wives, led to his being credited with supernatural powers. He was said to converse with spirits such as peri and djinn, and the six-pointed star called Solomon's Seal was a powerful talisman. (KING SOLOMON AND A PERI BY QAZWIN, C. 1570.)

THE TEMPLE (above) in Jerusalem was the outstanding achievement of Solomon's long reign. It was built using a labour force of 180,000 men, but its scale and splendour prompted the legend that Solomon's magic powers gave him command over an army of djinn who had carried out the work. When the temple was completed, it was dedicated in a ceremony lasting 14 days, during which 22,000 oxen and 120,000 sheep were sacrificed. (ILLUSTRATION FROM CALMET'S DICTIONARY OF THE HOLY BIBLE, 1732.)

MUHAMMAD (above) travelled as a young man to Syria, where he met Christians, Jews and others who believed in a single god. He became convinced that they were right. When he was about 40 he retreated to a cave on Mount Hira to wrestle with his beliefs alone. There, he was visited by the angel Jibril, who insisted that Muhammad should "recite" his beliefs, in other words, that he should preach the truth about Allah. (ILLUSTRATION FROM AN UNDATED MINIATURE.)

Z

YIMA, or Jam, or Jemshid, according to ancient Iranian mythology, was a great king. He was usually regarded as the son of *TAHMURAS*, one of the civilizing heroes, although according to some traditions the boy was born in a pillar of fire when a bolt of lightning struck the earth.

Yima governed the land wisely and justly, earning the title of the "Good Shepherd". As a priest, he was pious; as a warrior, he was strong; and as a herdsman, he was rich in cattle. He lived in a time known as the Golden Age, when death did not exist.

Because nobody died, Yima had to enlarge the earth three times, with the aid of his magic instruments. However, it came to pass that Mahrkusha, an evil demon, sent terrible floods followed by scorching summers down to earth, with the intention of annihilating all living creatures, both human beings and animals. Seeing what was about to happen, *AHURA MAZDA*, the principle of good, decided that the noble and upright Yima should be saved. He told him to build an underground dwelling place and to take into it every variety of man and beast. The fabulous chamber should also contain running water and trees, flowers and fruits. No diseased, wicked, ill-natured or deformed creature should be allowed entrance. Yima asked how he was to make this chamber, and Ahura Mazda replied that he should mould the earth with his hands and feet, as potters do. After the disaster, Yima emerged unscathed.

A later tradition claims that Yima eventually fell victim to the evil monster *AZHI DAHAKA*, who sawed him in two. It seems that he deserved this fate because he had committed the sin of pride.

ZAL, a hero of ancient Iranian mythology, was the son of Sam, a descendant of *FERIDUN*. Zal was born with white hair. Horrified by his strange appearance, his father ordered him to be left to die on the slope of a mountain. However, Simurgh, a noble vulture, rescued the baby and carried him to her nest on the peak of Mount Elburz. Simurgh was a mythical bird, said to be so old that she had seen the world destroyed three times, and had thus acquired great wisdom.

Zal grew up to become an extraordinarily beautiful young man. Sam, by now consumed with guilt for having abandoned his son, went in search of the child. He reached the home of Simurgh and entreated the vulture to return the young man to him. The bird agreed, and Sam blessed his son and called him Zal.

Zal had many adventures. On one occasion, he visited Kabul, which lay in his father's land of Hindustan. While staying with Mihrab, one of his father's servants, he learnt that his host had a beautiful daughter, Rudabeh. Without even having seen the young woman, Zal fell in love with her and she, hearing of Zal, fell in love with him. They arranged to meet in secret in a palace, which Rudabeh had filled with beautiful flowers and strewn with jewels. Rudabeh stood on a high terrace and looked down on Zal. Then, let-

ZAL was rejected as a baby by his father Sam, and exposed on a mountain. He was rescued by a fabulous bird called Simurgh, who raised him in her nest. (MINIATURE, MID 15TH CENTURY.)

ting down her beautiful hair, she told Zal to climb up it to her. Zal refused to do anything that might harm Rudabeh and instead climbed up a rope, which he managed to throw on to the terrace.

Although the young couple were deeply in love, they had to overcome the fact that Rudabeh's family were old enemies of Sam's employer, King MINUCHER. At length, Sam agreed to let Zal marry Rudabeh, particularly since astrologers had said that the couple would give birth to a great hero. That hero proved to be RUSTEM.

ZARATHUSTRA see ZOROASTER.

ZOHAK, according to ancient Iranian mythology, was the son of a desert king. He was persuaded by ANGRA MAINYU, the principle of darkness, to kill his father and seize the throne. Angra Mainyu then took up residence in Zohak's castle as his cook and persuaded the new king to introduce meat to his diet. Zohak was so pleased with his new cuisine that he promised Angra Mainyu a gift of his choosing. Angra Mainyu asked that he might kiss Zohak's shoulders, and rest his

face and eyes there. After kissing the king, Angra Mainyu disappeared. Suddenly, a snake appeared from each of Zohak's shoulders. His courtiers tried to destroy them, but each time the snakes were sliced off, they grew again.

Disguised as a doctor, Angra Mainyu returned and told Zohak that he should feed the snakes each day with human brains. In this way, Zohak himself became a demon and ruled over the world for a thousand years, during which time evil reigned supreme. Finally, one night Zohak had a terrifying dream; when

ZAL was carried by Simurgh to the highest peaks of Mount Elburz, where he grew up without his father's knowledge. Eventually, Sam was prompted by a dream to seek his son in the mountains, and the two were reconciled.

his advisers interpreted it for him, they said that it signified that he would be overthrown by a man called FERIDUN. Zohak ordered all children to be put to death, but the baby Feridun survived. When Feridun grew up he succeeded in killing Zohak and taking over the reins of power.

ZOROASTER, or Zarathustra, was a great religious reformer of ancient Iran. He was thought to have lived in the north-east of the country, some time in the sixth or fifth centuries BC, but scholars now believe that he lived much earlier, around 1200BC. The compelling figure of Zoroaster gave rise to many myths. It was said that his birth was foretold from the beginning of time. The moment he was born, he burst out laughing and the whole universe rejoiced with him.

Although the evil demons, the *DRUJS*, tried to destroy the child, he was protected by *AHURA MAZDA*, the principle of good. When he reached the age of 30, Zoroaster was given numerous revelations from the *AMESA SPENTAS*, or "Holy Immortals". Once armed with these spiritual insights, Zoroaster was able to resist the temptations of *ANGRA MAINYU*, or Ahriman, the principle of darkness.

Zoroaster denounced the worship of numerous gods, which until then had been prevalent in Iran, and instead preached a purified faith, focused on the struggle between good and evil, or Ahura Mazda and Angra Mainyu. His faith was a type of monotheism, although it inclined to dualism.

It was said that on one occasion, Zoroaster visited the court of a king and performed numerous miracles, including curing the king's favourite horse, before finally winning him over to his religion. The king then waged war against numerous neighbouring kings in an attempt to convert them. According to tradition, Zoroaster was murdered at the age of 77 while at his prayers.

ZOROASTER was traditionally said to have had a miraculous birth. According to legend, his mother, Dughdova, who was a virgin, conceived after she had been visited by a shaft of light. Though evil forces repeatedly tried to destroy the baby, he was protected by Ahura Mazda. (LIEBIG "CHROMO" CARD, 19TH CENTURY.)

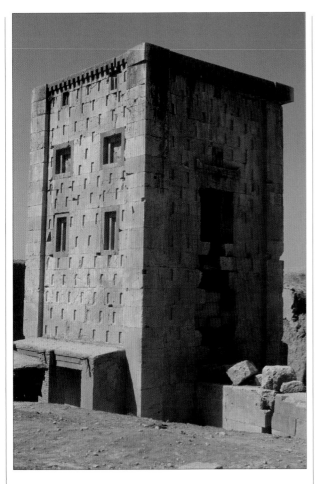

ZOROASTER's teaching was embraced by the Achamenian rulers of Iran, who built this square tower facing the royal rock tombs at Naqsh-i-Rustam near their capital, Persepolis. Known as the Ka'bah-i-Zardusht, it may have been used as a fire temple; fire was a Zoroastrian symbol of purity and wisdom.

It is probable that Zurvan Akarana originated as an important god of early Iranian mythology. However, in the centuries following ZOROASTER, devotees of the religious movement known as Zurvanism came to regard him as the primal and eternal being, beyond good and evil, who formed Ahura Mazda and Angra Mainyu in order that they should both struggle to dominate creation.

According to one tradition, Zurvan Akarana promised authority to the firstborn, leading Angra Mainyu to tear his way out of the womb. As a result, evil reigned for several thousand years. It was also said that Zurvan Akarana conceived his two offspring at the very moment when he began to doubt that he would ever give birth. In consequence, Ahura Mazda embodied his wisdom and Angra Mainyu his doubt.

ZU was the demonic tempest bird of Mesopotamian mythology who lived in the underworld and stole the tablets of fate from ENLIL, "Lord of the Wind". The tablets gave whoever possessed them control of the universe. The supreme god ANU promised sovereignty over the gods to whoever recovered the tablets. Although the fragmentary nature of the surviving text makes the outcome difficult to establish for certain, it seems that the god MARDUK succeeded in regaining the tablets, although in some versions of the tale Zu is overcome by NINURTA, Enlil's son.

ZURVAN AKARANA came to prominence in Iranian mythology as the transcendent being who gave rise to AHURA MAZDA, the principle of good or light, and ANGRA MAINYU, or Ahriman, the principle of evil or darkness.

The religious reformer ZOROASTER had taught that Ahura Mazda was the one true god, who was set in eternal opposition to Angra Mainyu. This dualism, which became sharper as time passed, presented a problem: if Ahura Mazda was all-powerful, then he must have created evil. The concept of Zurvan Akarana, or "Infinite Time", managed to circumvent this intellectual dilemma.

ZOROASTER was a priest, prophet and thinker who made huge innovations in religious thought. He preached a purified faith that focused on the struggle between light and darkness, or Ahura Mazda and Angra Mainyu. (SYRIAN MURAL.)

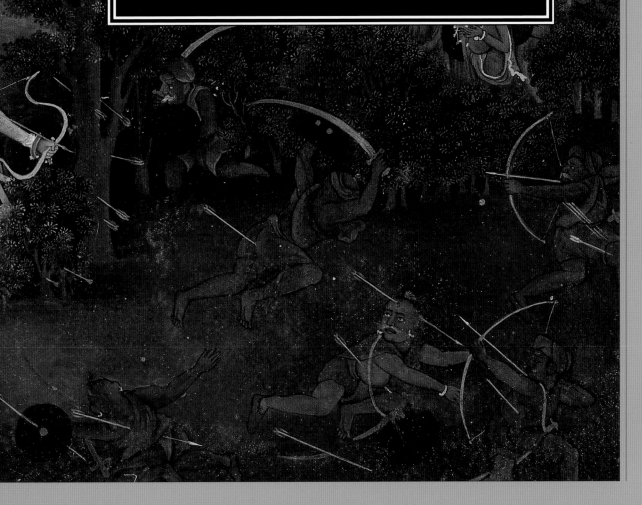

THE MYTHS OF
SOUTH AND
CENTRAL ASIA

INTRODUCTION

THE IMMENSE INDIAN subcontinent encompasses an astonishing diversity of geographical regions. In the north lie the rugged Himalayan mountains, further south the vast agricultural plains of the river Ganges; there are high plateaux and low-lying coastal regions, vast rainforests and deserts. The climate is extreme, with scorching heat followed by drenching monsoons. This tremendously varied and unpredictable land has given rise to a rich mythology, many of whose deities have spread elsewhere, for example to Tibet and Sri Lanka, the other countries that are under consideration here.

A significant feature of Indian belief is the desire to transcend the chaos and unpredictability of the world in order to find the truth, nirvana (spiritual ecstasy) or enlightenment. From the earliest times, evidence suggests that people believed that they might achieve this goal through the practice of meditation. For example, modern excavations have uncovered evidence that the people of the Indus Valley civilization, which flourished around the middle of the third millennium BC in the region of modern Pakistan, worshipped a deity associated with meditation.

In the second millennium BC, the remarkable Indus Valley civilization collapsed under the constant incursions of the Aryan invaders, a group of Bronze Age tribes. The Aryans, or

GAUTAMA BUDDHA, the founder of Buddhism, attained enlightenment after many incarnations as a bodhisattva, or "buddha-to-be", setting an example for all Buddhists to follow. (GANDHARA-STYLE RELIEF, 3RD CENTURY BC.)

ARJUNA, having broken a vow he had made to his brothers, had to endure 14 years' exile. During this time, he journeyed to the river Ganges, where he became the lover of the river goddess Ganga. She gave him the power to become invisible in water. (PAINTING BY WARWICK GOBLE.)

devas forged a huge and dazzling disc, so bright that no-one could look at it.

Meanwhile, Jalamdhara tried to seduce Shiva's wife, PARVATI, although the goddess managed to escape him. Vishnu then disguised himself as Jalamdhara and succeeded in seducing Vrinda. When Vrinda realized what had happened, she died of grief.

Jalamdhara was furious. He resurrected his dead asuras and summoned them to battle once more. Shiva threw the marvellous disc at Jalamdhara, cutting off his head. However, the asura simply grew a new head in the old one's place each time Shiva beheaded him. Eventually, Shiva summoned the wives of the gods. Taking the form of monstrous ogres, the goddesses drank all the asuras' blood, whereupon the gods won the battle and regained their kingdom.

The Hindu epic the *Mahabharata* tells how Brahma granted three DAITYAS – asuras descended from Diti – permission to establish three cities: one of gold in heaven, one of silver in the air and one of iron on earth. The three brothers ruled over them for many years. Countless asuras flocked to the cities where they were provided with their every desire. Eventually,

Shiva burned the three cities to the ground, together with all the asuras, and threw them into the depths of the ocean.

THE ASVINS, or "Horse

Drivers", according to Hindu mythology, are golden-coloured twins who drive a three-wheeled golden chariot drawn by horses or birds. Known individually as Nasatya and Dasra, they bring divine bliss to humankind, and symbolize strength and energy. The offspring of the sun and the cloud goddess Saranyu, the Asvins are both married to daughters of the light. Each morning, they make a path through the clouds for the dawn goddess USHAS and scatter the dew with their whips.

In the *Rig Veda*, the ancient Hindu hymns, the Asvins often intervene with the gods on behalf of humankind. They also guard the *RISHIS*, or seers, from drowning in the sea of ignorance. The doctors of the gods, they are friends of the sick and unfortunate. They heal the blind and the lame, and rejuvenate the aged. They are chiefly associated with the war god INDRA and prepare the equipment of the warrior gods.

THE ASURAS, outwitted by Vishnu, chose to hold the head end of the serpent Vasuki during the churning of the ocean, and were nearly suffocated by the creature's hot breath. (KANGRA MINIATURE, 18TH CENTURY.)

Although they are kind and beautiful, the gods originally forbade the Asvins entry to heaven. However, the rishi Syavana eventually came to their aid. Despite being well advanced in years, Syavana had a beautiful young wife, Sukanya. One day, the twins saw her bathing in a river and, after flattering her, tried to persuade her to leave her husband for one of them. Sukanya refused, whereupon the twins said that they would make Syavana young and beautiful again and that Sukanya should then choose from among the three of them. Syavana agreed and, after bathing in the river, the three men emerged, all looking young and handsome. Sukanya took a long time to come to a decision, but finally chose to stay with her husband. Syavana was delighted: not only had he kept his wife, but he had regained his youth and beauty. In gratitude, he persuaded Indra to allow the Asvins into heaven.

MYTHICAL MOUNTAINS

THE VAST MOUNTAIN RANGE OF THE Himalayas inspired awe in all those who beheld it. Its peaks appeared to reach up out of the human world to touch the realms of the gods, and the range was regarded as sacred by both Tibetans and Hindus as a transitional domain between the human and the heavenly worlds. Mount Meru, the mythical axis of the cosmos, lay at its centre. One legend credited the mighty god Indra with the formation of the mountains: it was said that they had been a herd of flying elephants who had displeased him. He punished them by cutting off their wings. All the gods were thought to make sacrifices on the mountains, but Shiva was particularly associated with them. Mount Kailasa was his mythological paradise and, as an ascetic, his deep meditation on this mountain ensured the continued existence of the world.

PARVATI (above right) was the daughter of the god Himavat, king of the Himalayas, who was a deified personification of the mountains. Parvati's name means "Daughter of the Mountain" and she was an aspect of the mother goddess, Devi. She became the consort of the great god Shiva, who had his home on Mount Kailasa. Another daughter of Himavat was Ganga, the deity of the sacred river whose source is in the Himalayas and was said to flow through Shiva's hair. (SHIVA AND PARVATI WITH SKANDA, BRONZE, 10–11TH CENTURY.)

MERU was supported on the hood of the coiled primeval cobra, Vasuki, who created earthquakes when he yawned and will consume the whole world with his fiery breath at the end of the present age. Both Hindus and Buddhists acknowledge the mountain's sacred status, and its shape is symbolized in conical objects of worship and meditation called yantras, on which the material world is depicted at the outer edge, and the absolute and eternal at the centre. (NEPALESE YANTRA.)

MERU (left) *was the mythical mountain at the centre of the cosmos, the navel of the world, and was sacred to both Hindus and Buddhists. All the spheres of existence, from Brahma's heavenly city of gold at its summit, to the seven nether worlds at its foot, centred on the mountain, and the sacred river Ganges sprang from it. Its slopes glittered with precious stones and were clothed with trees laden with delectable fruits. It was surrounded by a vast lake and ringed with golden peaks.* (MURAL PAINTING, WAT KO KEO SUTTHARAM, THAILAND.)

THE GODS (below) *assembled on Mount Meru in search of the elixir of immortality, Amrita, which had been lost with other precious treasures in a catastrophic flood. Vishnu's solution was to churn the cosmic ocean until the treasures emerged. The gods uprooted Mount Mandara and set it on the back of the tortoise Kurma. The gods, with the help of the asuras, coiled the world serpent Vasuki around the mountain like a rope and each took an end.* (THE CHURNING OF THE MILKY OCEAN, BASOHLI, C. 1700.)

MOUNT MANDARA (right), *as it was spun, churned the cosmic ocean until it turned to milk, and then to butter. Eventually, the precious things it contained began to emerge: the sacred cow, Surabhi; the sun; the moon; Lakshmi, the goddess of good fortune; and, finally, the physician of the gods, Dhanvantari, holding the precious Amrita. The demon Rahu got hold of the elixir, but Vishnu rescued it by chopping off Rahu's head. The gods drank the Amrita to regain their power, and restored Mount Mandara to its proper place.* (KANGRA MINIATURE, 18TH CENTURY.)

351

AVALOKITESHVARA is the most popular *BODHISATTVA* or "buddha-to-be" of Mahayana or "Great Vehicle" Buddhism. His name is translated as "Lord of Compassionate Sight" or "Lord Who Looks From On High". The Bodhisattva of the present age, Avalokiteshvara is said to have emanated from the great buddha *AMITABHA*. Although his residence is in Amitabha's paradise, he remains in this world in order to attend to the salvation of humans and animals. He is usually represented as a handsome man, with several heads and arms.

According to one myth, when Avalokiteshvara was looking down on the suffering in the world, his head burst open in pain. Amitabha put the pieces back together as nine new heads. Then, because Avalokiteshvara wanted to help all creatures, he grew 1,000 arms, and in the palm of each hand was an eye: "From his eyes were derived the sun and the moon, from his forehead, Mahesvara, from his shoulders, *BRAHMA* and other gods, from his heart, Narayana, from his thighs, *SARASVATI*, from his mouth, the winds, from his feet, the earth, from his belly, *VARUNA*."

Avalokiteshvara helps everyone who asks for his assistance. He visits hell to take cooling drinks to those suffering the heat of the damned, and he preaches the Buddhist law to beings incarnated as insects or worms. He is also said to protect people from natural disasters and to bless children. Moreover, the bodhisattva is said to have converted the female ogres of Sri Lanka and to have been given the task of converting Tibet to Buddhism.

In Tibet, his name is sPyan-ras-gzigs or *CHENREZIG*. In China, Avalokiteshvara developed into the goddess Kuan Yin, or Guanyin, and in Japan into the god, or sometimes goddess, Kwannon. (See also *BODHISATTVAS*)

AVALOKITESHVARA (left) is also known as Padmapani, or "Lotus-bearer", and holds a pink lotus blossom in his hand. In eastern religions, the lotus signifies non-attachment, freedom from ignorance, and the path to enlightenment.

AVALOKITESHVARA (above) the bodhisattva of universal compassion, is an emanation of the meditation of the Dhyanibuddha Anitabha, and therefore wears an effigy of the great buddha in his headdress. (BRONZE, 14TH CENTURY.)

THE AVATARS of *VISHNU* are his incarnations on earth in order to help humankind in moments of great crisis. It is generally accepted that Vishnu has ten avatars, although their number varies, and their identities are also flexible. Usually, the incarnations are said to consist of Matsya, *KURMA*, Varaha, *NARASIMHA*, Vamana, Parashurama, *RAMA*, *KRISHNA*, *GAUTAMA BUDDHA* and Kalkin.

Matsya, the first avatar, appeared as a fish who protected *MANU*, the first man, during the great deluge. The second avatar, Kurma the tortoise, supported Mount Mandara on his back during the churning of the ocean. Varaha, the boar, rescued the earth. The story tells how the earth, lost beneath floods, had been captured by a demon, whereupon Vishnu, as the boar Varaha, plunged into the waters and traced the earth by its smell. He killed the demon who had captured the earth and raised it out of the ocean on his tusks. Vishnu as Varaha is depicted as a giant with a boar's head, carrying the goddess of the earth.

The fourth avatar was Narasimha, who killed the powerful demon Hiranyakashipu, an incarnation of *RAVANA*. The demon had persuaded *BRAHMA* to give him the power to dethrone the storm god, *INDRA*, and to send the sky gods into exile. The demon then proclaimed himself king of the universe. Hiranyakashipu's son, Prahlada, was, however, a devotee of Vishnu. This so enraged Hiranyakashipu that he tortured the young man in an effort to dissuade him from his worship. Prahlada remained unswayed. Hiranyakashipu then ordered Prahlada to be put to death, but nothing could harm the young man. Eventually, Hiranyakashipu flew into such a rage that he struck a pillar, saying that if Vishnu was so important and omnipresent, why was he not right there, within the pillar? Immediately, the pillar collapsed, and Vishnu emerged

in the form of Narasimha, a man with a lion's head. Narasimha immediately seized Hiranyakashipu and tore him to pieces, whereupon Prahlada succeeded his father to the throne.

Vamana, a dwarf, was the fifth avatar who came to save the world from the demon Bali. The sixth avatar was Parashurama. When his mother had impure thoughts, Parashurama decapitated her at his father's command. However, when his father granted him a wish, Parashurama asked that his mother be brought back to life. Later, when

King Kartavirya insulted his father, Parashurama destroyed the whole kshatriya, or warrior, caste to which the king belonged. He then ordered the brahmans to sleep with the widows of the kshatriya men, in order to produce a new and purer warrior caste.

Rama, the warrior, is the seventh avatar of Vishnu, and the god, Krishna, is the eighth. Vishnu was said to assume his ninth avatar, the Buddha, in order to mislead the sinful so that they would receive their just deserts. Kalkin, the final avatar, has yet to come. He will

THE AVATARS surround this picture of the god Vishnu. Taking the form of various animals, the avatars appeared on earth to help humankind during times of crisis.

(JAIPUR, RAJASTHAN, 18TH CENTURY.)

appear at the end of the present age, or Kali *YUGA*, to establish a new era. It is thought that he will take the form of a warrior on a white horse, or a man with a horse's head. Kalkin will put an end to the wicked, and everything will be reabsorbed into the "Absolute" until creation begins again. (See also *THE AVATARS OF VISHNU*)

B

BALARAMA was the elder brother of *KRISHNA*, the eighth *AVATAR* of *VISHNU*, and was himself regarded as a partial avatar of the great Hindu "Preserver of the Universe". When the evil King Kamsa heard of Krishna's amazing exploits, he determined to kill him. He announced a wrestling match, challenging all the local young men to try their strength against the champions of his court. Krishna and Balarama, eager to take up the challenge, immediately made their

BALARAMA holding a horn, with his younger brother Krishna, playing the flute. The brothers overcame the champions of the court of the evil King Kamsa. (PAINTING BY BECHERAM DAS PANDEC, 1865.)

way to the city where the contest was to take place. However, when it was their turn to fight, King Kamsa released a wild elephant into the ring. The elephant charged towards the two young men, but Krishna simply leapt on to its back, put his arms round its neck and squeezed it to death. King Kamsa then sent his two strongest champions into the ring, but Krishna broke the neck of the first and Balarama crushed the other so hard that his heart burst.

Krishna later killed King Kamsa, but Balarama was killed in a drunken brawl involving Krishna's kinsmen, the Yadavas.

BALI see *VISHNU*.

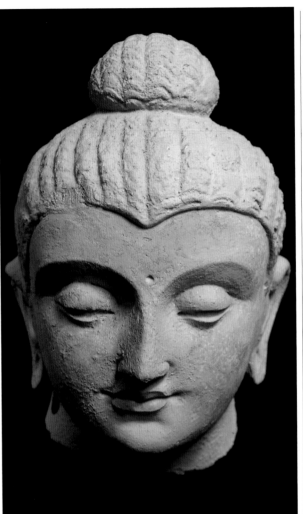

BANA see *ANIRUDDHA*.

BANDARA was the title that was originally given to important officials within the Singhalese kingdom of Sri Lanka. In time, however, the term came to be used for a group of gods who were considered superior to the lesser deities, or *YAKSHAS*. For example, the god *DADIMUNDA*, treasurer to the supreme god *UPULVAN* and protector of Buddhism, is held to be a Bandara. Very often, a principal local god will be known simply as Bandara.

BCAN see *BTSAN*.

BODHISATTVAS are living symbols of compassion. They choose to delay the moment of entering nirvana in order to help others along the path to enlightenment. (STONE, 2ND–4TH CENTURY AD.)

THE BDUD were the heavenly spirits of the indigenous Bon religion of Tibet. However, within Tibetan Buddhism, the bDud came to be seen as devils. They were said to be black and to live in a castle.

BEG-TSE, a *DHARMAPALA*, or "Protector of the Teaching", is a mythical warrior who is regarded as a symbol of the conversion of the Mongols to Tibetan Buddhism. He

A MANDALA (left) has Avalokiteshvara at its centre. He is shown with many heads because he was so distraught by his vision of the sufferings on earth that his head split open with pain. In the mandala, a symbolic representation of the universe, the four walls and four open gateways are taken to include within them the whole external world, at the centre of which sits the bodhisattva in the position of lord of the world. (TIBETAN PAINTING.)

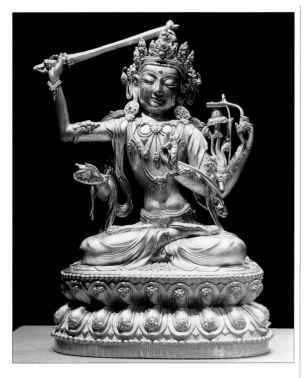

MANJUSHRI (above), the great bodhisattva, personifies wisdom and learning. The sword he wields in his right hand is used to cut through the veil of ignorance. In his left hand he carries a lotus blossom, holding a scroll which contains the "Perfection of Wisdom": these writings describe the ideal of the bodhisattva as the highest aspiration of religious life, and the emptiness of phenomena which characterizes Mahayana Buddhism. (CHINESE, 15TH CENTURY.)

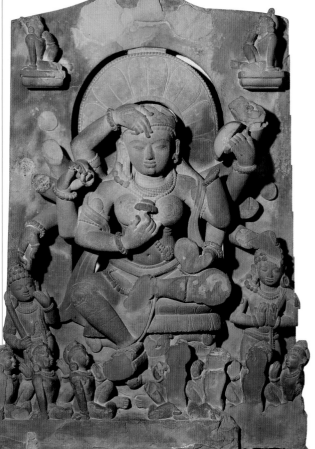

CUNDA (left) is a female bodhisattva, sometimes called the "Mother of the Buddhas". She is said to be kindly to the good but terrifying to the wicked: she is portrayed with as many as 16 arms, each of which holds a threatening weapon, but for a worshipper who knows how to regard her, her hands are in the positions of teaching and charity. (RELIEF FROM CENTRAL INDIA, 10TH CENTURY.)

VAJRAPANI (left), the indigo bodhisattva, is one of the most important wrathful deities. Vajrapani is the destroyer of evil. His fierce demeanour represents the attitude needed to turn hatred against itself and transcend it. He is armed with a Vajra, or thunderbolt, which is the weapon of the Hindu gods Indra and Karttikeya. Vajrapani is also said to be the embodiment of skilful actions. (TIBETAN PAINTING.)

361

THE DAKINI, according to traditional Buddhist belief, are supernatural beings, or low-ranking goddesses. They fly through the air and are said to eat human beings. The dakini have magical powers and are able to initiate novices into the secret wisdom of the Tantra, a series of ritual texts dealing with the attainment of enlightenment. They can also help Yogis who wish to further their spiritual progress since they are able to concentrate the powers that the Yogi releases.

The dakini are usually shown dancing and appear as young naked women, as horrible monsters, or with the heads of lions or birds and the faces of horses or dogs. They also feature in Hindu mythology, as witch attendants on the goddess KALI.

In Tibetan Buddhism, dakinis are known as khadromas, female beings who move in celestial space. Their nakedness symbolizes their knowledge of perfect truth. The khadromas are said to live in Urgyen, a mythical realm that is also regarded as the birthplace of PADMASAMBHAVA, one of the founders of Tibetan Buddhism. In Tibet, eight goddesses, represented as beautiful young women, are sometimes included within the group of dakinis. They are known as the "Eight Mothers" and are thought to have developed from Tibetan shamanism.

DAKSHA, according to Hindu mythology, is the lord of cattle and the son of the mother goddess ADITI. He chose Sati, one of his 60 beautiful daughters, to be the wife of the great god, SHIVA. One tale tells how Daksha prepared an important sacrifice to which he invited all the gods, including INDRA. However, he failed to invite Shiva. Sati was outraged at this slight to her husband but decided that, even if her husband were not invited, she herself would attend the ceremony. Shiva was highly impressed by his wife's loyalty. However, he told her that Daksha was sure to insult him and that she must be strong and not respond to his insults.

When Sati arrived at her father's house, Daksha immediately began to insult Shiva, scorning his wild dancing and his appearance. Sati, finally overwhelmed with fury, denounced her father in front of all the gods. Then, since she had broken her promise to Shiva, she threw herself on to the sacrificial fire and was burnt to death.

Shiva was so angry and distraught at this turn of events that he sent one of his emanations, a terrifying demon, to kill everyone who had attended the ceremony. At length, the great god VISHNU, the preserver of the universe, persuaded Shiva to bring the guests back to life. Daksha finally acknowledged that Shiva was indeed a great god, and as a sign that he recognized his own stupidity he adopted the head of a goat. Shiva entered into a deep and prolonged meditation and awaited the time when Sati would be reincarnated as PARVATI.

In another version of the myth, Daksha's head was torn off, and Sati was brought back to life after the massacre. The goddess begged Shiva to restore her father to life. The great god agreed but, because nobody could find Daksha's head, he was given that of a ram.

THE DANAVAS are half-divine, half-demonic beings of Hindu mythology who were banished by the war god, INDRA, to live in the ocean. The monster Bali, whom it is said that VISHNU overcame in his incarnation as Vamana the dwarf, was a danava. The danavas were ASURAS, and although they are often described as "demons", they were not totally evil.

Vishnu, for example, recognized that Bali had shown himself to be capable of honourable behaviour and so rewarded him by making him king of the underworld.

DASRA see ASVINS.

DEVADATTA was a cousin of GAUTAMA BUDDHA. He became a member of the Buddhist community but grew jealous of Gautama and planned to murder him. First of all, he sent a group of assassins to murder the great teacher. However, the men were so impressed by the Buddha that they repented their evil intentions and became his followers. Then, Devadatta tried to crush Gautama by rolling an enormous boulder on

DHANVANTARI features in the ancient Indian myth of the churning of the ocean. It was he who appeared bearing *AMRITA*, the elixir of immortality, from the milk ocean. Dhanvantari was also known as Sudapani, or "One Who Bears Nectar in His Hands". The master of universal knowledge, he came to be regarded as the physician of the gods. He is the guardian deity of hospitals which are usually in the vicinity of a sanctuary of *VISHNU*.

top of him. However, the boulder stopped before it reached its target. Finally, he sent a wild elephant to gore the Buddha to death. The elephant was, however, tamed by the Buddha's kindness. When he died, Devadatta was condemned to lengthy sufferings in hell.

DEVAKI see *KRISHNA*.

DEVI (above), the great Hindu goddess, is the subject of an attempted seduction by her husband Shiva. On the right, he praises her for having resisted temptation. (SANDSTONE, CAMBODIA, 13TH CENTURY.)

DEVI (left) is honoured by the Hindu gods, Shiva, Vishnu, Brahma, Ganesha and Indra. (ILLUSTRATION BY J. HIGGINBOTHAM, 1864.)

THE DEVAS are the divine beings of the Veda, the ancient sacred teachings of India. The devas were regarded as immortal, and their chief attribute was their power, which enabled them to help human beings.

They later came to be regarded as those gods who are less important than great gods such as *ISHNU* and *SHIVA*. Although they inhabit a realm higher than that of human beings, they are still mortal. Among these Hindu devas are groups such as the *ADITYAS*, the rudras and the vasus.

In Buddhism, the devas are divine beings who live in the celestial heavens but are none the less subject to the ongoing cycle of death and rebirth. Most of the Buddhist devas originated in the Indian pantheon. They have long, pleasurable lives, and promote and protect Buddhism.

DEVATA BANDARA see *DADIMUNDA*.

DEVI is an aspect of the "Great Goddess" in Hindu mythology. It is the name by which the god *SHIVA*'s wife is sometimes known and is also the name given to female Hindu deities in general. Devi, as Shiva's *SHAKTI*, or consort, is both a benevolent and a fearsome deity, and is regarded as a major goddess within Hinduism.

She is a complex figure, taking many different forms, including those of *DURGA*, *KALI*, *PARVATI* and Sati. Sometimes, she also takes the form of goddesses who are independent of Shiva. Her main attributes are the conch, hook, prayer wheel and trident. (See also *THE MOTHER GODDESS*)

DEVADATTA, the Buddha's cousin and his rival from childhood, hatched a plot to murder him, but his hired assassins were all stricken with remorse as soon as the Buddha touched the wall behind which they were hidden.

THE DAKINI include eight Tibetan goddesses, of which images such as this one were used in rites of exorcism which drew on shamanistic practices. (CARVED HUMAN BONE, TIBET, 18TH CENTURY.)

DHARMAPALAS are "Protectors of the Dharma", or teaching. In Buddhism, particularly in Tibetan belief, they are regarded as ferocious divine beings who protect the faithful from the evil demons and bad influences which might thwart their spiritual progress. As such, the Dharmapalas are similar to the GUARDIAN KINGS. In Tibet, the Dharmapalas are worshipped either individually or in groups of eight, when they are known as the "Eight Terrible Ones" or Drag-shed. The eight are usually said to be KALADEVI (Lha-mo), BRAHMA (Tsangs-pa), BEG-TSE, YAMA, Kuvera (Vaishravana), HAYAGRIVA, MAHAKALA or Mahalka ("Great Black One") and YAMANTAKA. Vaishravana is also one of the Guardian or Celestial Kings.

In Tibet, the Dharmapalas are usually shown frowning, with tangled hair surmounted by a crown of five skulls. Most of them are in Yab-Yum, the posture of embrace, with their SHAKTI.

Some of the Dharmapalas were also Lokapalas (Guardian Kings) who existed in pre-Buddhist times as members of the Bon pantheon. PADMASAMBHAVA, one of the founders of Tibetan Buddhism, assimilated some of these ancient deities and transformed them into deities who protected the Buddhist law. However, some of the Lokapalas were adopted from the Hindu religion.

THE DHYANIBUDDHAS, or
five "Great Buddhas of Wisdom", are the five meditating buddhas who, according to some traditions, are said to have arisen from the primeval buddha, ADIBUDDHA. They are sometimes referred to as Tathagatas ("Perfected Ones"), Transcendent Buddhas, or Jinas.

***DHARMAPALAS** with ferocious frowns decorate these ritual implements. They wear jewellery of writhing snakes and each have a third eye in its forehead. (NEPALESE RITUAL FLAYING KNIVES, 18–19TH CENTURY.)*

DURGA, mounted on a lion, in combat with Mahisha, the terrible buffalo demon who threatened the power of the gods. (PAINTING BY BIKANER, RAJPUT SCHOOL, 1750.)

The term Jina means "Conqueror", and refers to someone who has succeeded in overcoming the cycle of rebirth and suffering.

The Dhyanibuddhas are *VAIROCANA* or Mahavairocana, *AKSOBHYA*, *RATNASAMBHAVA*, *AMITABHA* and *AMOGHASIDDHI*. They are sometimes regarded as symbols of the various aspects of enlightened consciousness. On the other hand, they are sometimes believed to represent the body of the Dharma or teaching. Whereas followers of the non-Mahayana schools of Buddhism tend to venerate *GAUTAMA BUDDHA*, Mahayana Buddhists make any one of the five Dhyanibuddhas their chief object of worship. Occasionally, Gautama Buddha replaces Amoghasiddhi as one of the Dhyanibuddhas and sometimes *KSHITIGARBHA* is considered one of their number. (See also *DHYANIBUDDHAS*)

DIPANKARA, or the "Lighter of Lamps", was a Buddha of a past age whom Shakyamuni, or *GAUTAMA BUDDHA*, met in a previ-ous life when he was the sage Sumedha. After having honoured Dipankara, Sumedha determined that he would become a Buddha himself. He became a *BODHISATTVA*, or "buddha-to-be", and passed through countless lives before entering the *TUSHITA* heaven prior to his final birth, to Queen *MAYA*. Dipankara recognized that Sumedha would become Gautama Buddha, and proclaimed his glorious future.

DITI see *ADITI*.

THE DMU were supernatural beings of the indigenous Bon religion of Tibet. They are said to have lived in heaven.

DRAG-SHED see *DHARMAPALAS*.

DURGA is the great Hindu mother goddess whose name means "She Who is Difficult to Approach", or "Inaccessible". She is an aspect of the *SHAKTI* of *SHIVA*, and can be terrifying and ferociously protective. She is usually depicted with a beautiful face and with eight or ten arms, in which she carries various weapons given to her by the gods.

Other goddesses are often identified with her, including Candi, who protects against wild animals, and Shitala, who protects against smallpox. She also manifests herself as the bloodthirsty *KALI*.

Durga is said to have been born fully formed, ready to do battle against demons. When the terrible buffalo demon Mahisha threatened the power of the gods, not even *VISHNU* nor Shiva dared stand against him. However, Durga rose to the occasion. The demon changed first into a buffalo, then into a lion, whereupon Durga sliced off his head. Mahisha then turned into an elephant, but the goddess cut off his trunk. Although he hurled mountains at her, Durga overcame the monster, crushing him and killing him with her spear (See also *THE MOTHER GODDESS*)

DUSHYANTA see *APSARAS*.

THE GANDHARVAS are a class of Hindu demigods who are said to inhabit the heaven of the war god *INDRA* along with the *APSARAS*. They are part human, part horse and, as nature spirits, are associated with the fertility of the earth. The gandharvas guard the *SOMA*, the sacred drink that conveys divine powers. Some of them appear at Indra's court as divine musicians and singers. According to the *Rig Veda*, the ancient hymns composed by Vedic Aryans who came to India from central Asia, at the beginning of existence a gandharva united with an apsara to produce the first pair of human beings, *YAMA* and Yami.

DURGA is a slayer of demons who threaten the order of creation. She killed Mahisha, who was invulnerable to man and beast. (ILLUSTRATION BY J. HIGGINBOTHAM, 1864.)

GANESHA is the Hindu god of wisdom and literature, and the son of *PARVATI*, the wife of the great god *SHIVA*. He is portrayed with the head of an elephant and a pot belly, a symbol both of his greed and his ability to dispense success. He has four arms but only one tusk. An extremely popular deity, he is invoked at the outset of new undertakings. He is regarded as the patron of business, and businesspeople hold ceremonies in his honour. He was traditionally the first scribe of the great Hindu epic, the *Mahabharata*. He was said to have been so keen to write it down that he tore off one of his tusks to use as a pen.

One myth tells how, when Shiva was away from home, Parvati grew bored and lonely. She decided to make herself a baby and created Ganesha, either from the rubbings of her own body, from dew and dust, or from clay. She later ordered the child to stand guard outside the entrance to her rooms. When Shiva returned home and tried to see his wife, Ganesha, not realizing who he was, barred his entrance, whereupon Shiva knocked his head off. Parvati was distraught and demanded that her son be brought back to life. The first head Shiva

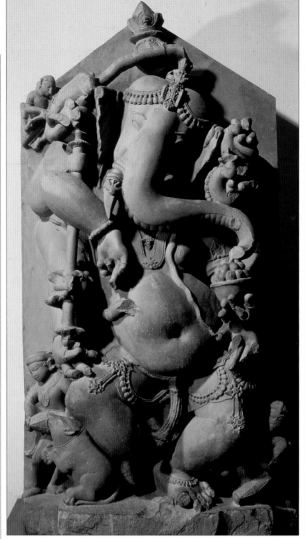

GANESHA (below), patron of literature, with Sarasvati, goddess of learning and the arts, mounted on a peacock and holding a lute. (ILLUSTRATION BY J. HIGGINBOTHAM, 1864.)

GANESHA's (above) mount, the rat, was originally a demon, who was vanquished and transformed by the elephant-headed god. (STONE, 11TH CENTURY.)

could find was that of an elephant. Parvati was delighted. Ganesha subsequently looked after the ganas, Shiva's attendants.

According to another myth, Parvati invited the god Sani, the planet Saturn, to visit her son. However, she had forgotten how dangerous the god could be and when he looked at Ganesha, the child's head burst into flames. *BRAHMA* told Parvati to repair her child with whatever she could find, which turned out to be the head of the elephant, *AIRAVATA*.

GANGA (right) the personification of the sacred river Ganges, is usually depicted holding a waterpot and a lotus in her hands. (STONE, BENGAL, 12TH CENTURY.)

GANGA, according to Hindu mythology, is the goddess of the sacred river Ganges. Ganga is the holiest of the three great river goddesses, the others being Yamuna and *SARASVATI*. The confluence of the three rivers, known as the Tirtha, is regarded as particularly sacred and is situated at the town of Allahabad, where a great mass pilgrimage takes place each year.

Ganga is said to have emerged from one of *VISHNU*'s toes. Until her descent, she was believed to live in the sky, but when the earth became filled with the ashes of the dead, the sage *BHAGIRATHA* prayed that the gods might allow her purifying waters to come down to earth. The gods agreed. However, the descent of the great river threatened to engulf and destroy the entire earth, so *SHIVA* allowed it to land on his head as he sat meditating on Mount Kailasa. After spending several years in Shiva's hair, the river separated into seven different streams and flowed down over the earth.

According to one myth, Ganga nourished the semen of Shiva in her waters, eventually producing the warrior god Skanda, also known as KARTTIKEYA. The tale tells how Shiva offered up six of his seeds to the fire god AGNI, who gave them to Ganga for safekeeping. Swaha, the daughter of a sage, visited the river on six successive nights and was impregnated by the seeds, eventually giving birth to Karttikeya. The child had six heads, and six or 12 arms and legs.

Another myth tells how INDRA's power was beginning to threaten that of Shiva, whereupon a form of anger manifested itself before Shiva and asked that it might serve him. Shiva told the form to submerge itself in the Ganges and to marry the goddess to the ocean. A son called Jalamdhara, an ASURA, resulted from the union, and BRAHMA gave the asura the power to conquer the gods. (See also SACRED RIVERS)

GARUDA, according to Hindu mythology, was the prince of birds and the son of the sage KASYAPA. According to one account of Garuda's birth, Kasyapa had two beautiful wives, Kadru and Vinata. The sage promised to provide both wives with heirs. Kadru chose to give birth to 1,000 splendid serpents, whereas Vinata asked for only two sons. However, Vinata requested that her sons' strength and prowess should surpass that of Kadru's offspring.

Eventually, Kadru laid 1,000 eggs and Vinata laid two. After 500 years, 1,000 serpents emerged from Kadru's eggs. However, Vinata's two sons failed to appear. Impatient, Vinata broke open one of her eggs to find an embryo with only the upper half developed. The embryo became Aruna, the red glow of dawn. Aruna cursed his mother and ascended into the sky, where he remains to this day. Another 500 years passed and Vinata's remaining egg finally broke open to reveal Garuda.

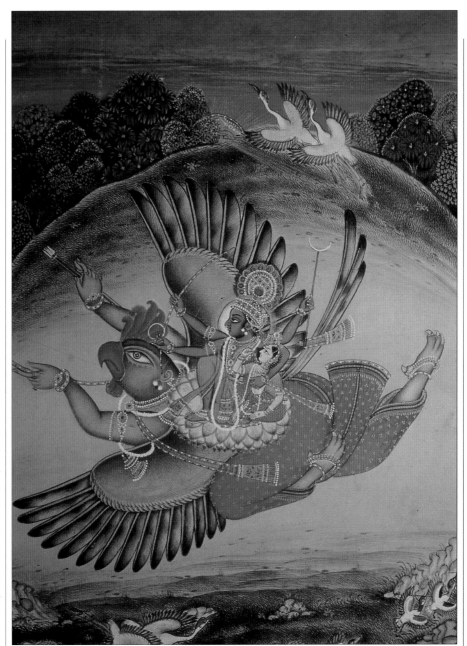

Another tale tells how, in order to free herself from a curse, Vinata was forced to acquire AMRITA, the elixir of immortality and to give it to her nephews, the 1,000 serpents. Vinata asked Garuda to seize the drink from the gods and, after a mighty struggle, he succeeded in doing so. He put the drink down in front of the serpents, but said that they must purify themselves before drinking it. While they were busy performing their ablutions, INDRA retrieved the Amrita, as had been previously arranged with Garuda.

Garuda was a devotee of VISHNU, the preserver of the universe, and he was chosen by the god to be his mount. He appeared whenever summoned by Vishnu's thought, and fought with him against demons and demonic ser-

GARUDA, half human, half eagle, was the chosen mount of Vishnu, who rides him with his consort, Lakshmi, seated on a lotus flower. (PAINTING, BUNDI, C. 1770.)

pents. Garuda is depicted with the head, wings and claws of an eagle. In Buddhism, garudas are divine bird-like creatures.

GAURI see PARVATI.

367

GAUTAMA BUDDHA was the founding master of Buddhism and is regarded as the most perfect of holy men, rather than as a deity. By most accounts, he was born in the sixth century BC into the kshatriya, or warrior, caste at Kapilavastu, just inside the border of what is now Nepal. Gautama was the Buddha's family name; his given name was Siddhartha. In later legend he was known as Shakyamuni, or the sage of the Shakya clan. Gautama is venerated by all Buddhists, although for the "Pure Land" sect of Japanese and Chinese Buddhism, the Buddha *AMITABHA*, or Amida, has supreme importance.

The story of Gautama's life has become a legend. According to tradition, while in one of the Buddhist heavens, Gautama realized that the time had come for him to descend to earth. The spirit of the Buddha appeared in a dream to Queen *MAYA*: a small, snow-white elephant floating on a raincloud, a symbol of fertility, seemed to circle around the queen three times and then enter her womb. At that moment, all around the world, musical instruments played, trees and flowers bloomed and lakes were suddenly covered with lotus blossoms. Astrologers forecast that Queen Maya and the Buddha's father, the local ruler King Suddhodana, would have a son who would become either a universal emperor or a buddha.

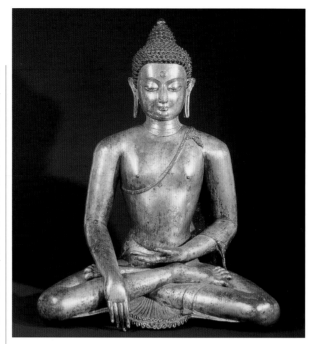

When the boy was born, he immediately began to walk, and a lotus sprang from the place where his foot first touched the ground. The child took seven steps in the directions of the seven cardinal points, and thus symbolically took possession of the world. Soon after his birth, his mother died of joy.

When Gautama was 12 years old, a wise man predicted that, if he were to witness old age, sickness or death, or to see a recluse, he would leave the palace in order to become an ascetic, one who shuns physical pleasures. In fear of the prophesy, the king surrounded his son with luxury and had high walls built around his palaces.

When Gautama reached the age of 16, he was married to Princess Yasodhara and 12 years later, their son *RAHULA* was born. At about this time, Gautama's curiosity about the outside world was aroused and he decided to set out to explore the land outside the palace grounds. The king immediately ordered that every sign of suffering and sadness should be removed from his son's path. However, on the first day of his excursion, Gautama saw a wrinkled old man; on the second day, he saw someone suffering from an incurable disease, as well as a funeral procession; and on another day, he came across a wandering ascetic. Gautama finally decided to leave home and become an ascetic. His father was devastated and provided even more amusements for the prince. However, nothing would deter the young man.

After six years of asceticism, Gautama realized that he was no nearer enlightenment than he had

GAUTAMA BUDDHA (left), seated in the witness attitude, is assailed by the powers of evil, led by the demon Mara. Demons in threatening human and animal shapes seek to terrify him, and Mara's daughters try to seduce him. (MURAL, AJANTA, BERAR.)

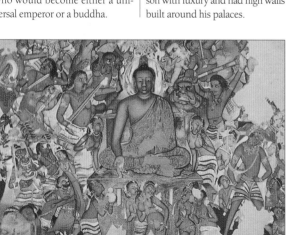

GAUTAMA BUDDHA (left) has an urna, or symbolic circle of hair, between his eyebrows, derived from Indian images of Shiva's third eye: it indicates spiritual vision. (GILT-COPPER, NEPAL.)

GAUTAMA BUDDHA (right), having decided to renounce the world, cuts off his hair. (TIBET, 18TH CENTURY.)

been while living his former life of luxury. Deciding that he must free himself from desire, he set off for the town of Bodh Gaya; as he journeyed, light radiated from his body, attracting peacocks and kingfishers. When Gautama reached Bodh Gaya, he sat down beneath the branches of a sacred tree, whereupon the earth shook six times.

While Gautama was meditating, he was tested by the demon *MARA*, the Buddhist equivalent of Satan. First, he was subjected to fear, then enticed with pleasure. However, Gautama remained unmoved. Eventually he became aware of the "Four Noble Truths" that became the basis of his teaching: that life is full of suffering, that suffering depends on certain conditions such as craving, that these conditions can be removed, and that the way to make suffering cease is to practise the eightfold path: right view, right thought, right speech, right action, right livelihood, right effort, right mindfulness and right concentration or contemplation.

Gautama had reached a state of perfection and at that moment attained complete spiritual insight. The earth swayed, breezes blew, flowers rained down from heaven, the gods rejoiced and all living things were happy. Seven weeks later, he preached his first sermon at Sarnath, on the outskirts of the holy city of Benares.

Gautama preached for more than 40 years, during which time he performed many miracles and converted all who heard him, including his father, his son, his first cousin Ananda, his wife and his adoptive mother,

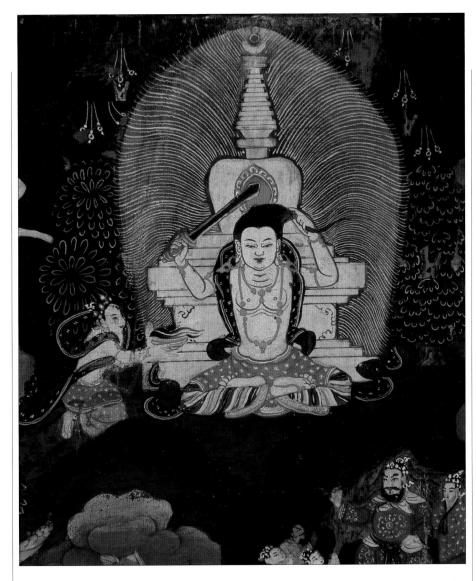

MAHAPRAJ-APATI GAUTAMI. He even ascended into heaven, where he converted his mother, Queen Maya, before climbing back down to earth on a ladder, accompanied by the gods. At the age of 80, Gautama entered nirvana, the ultimate state of spiritual bliss, near his birthplace. (See also *THE AVATARS OF VISHNU; THE LIFE OF THE BUDDHA*)

GESAR was a mythical king who inspired the greatest epic of Tibetan Buddhism. Tales of his exploits began to arise in the 11th century, at the time when Buddhism was beginning to infiltrate Tibet and threaten the indigenous Bon religion. The legends describe King Gesar's battle against the ancient beliefs and are said to be several times the length of the Bible.

Gesar, whose name means "Lotus Temple", was said to have been born in the kingdom of Ling in eastern Tibet. He is regarded as the embodiment of the *BOD-HISATTVA AVALOKITESHVARA*, as well as of *PADMASAMBHAVA*, one of the founders of Tibetan Buddhism. His warriors are said to be incarnations of the Mahasiddhas, great ascetics.

Although the stories about Gesar are influenced above all by Buddhism, traces of the Bon religion can also be found in the tales that tell of mountain deities and spirits of places. Travelling singers transmitted the early versions of the epic, whereas the later tales were said to arise from Tibetan monks.

The story of Gesar tells how an old woman died cursing all religions. Her final wish was that in a future life she and her three sons might rule over all Buddhist lands and wreak their revenge on the Buddhist teaching. The gods, hearing that the woman and her sons were threatening to return to the world as horrifying monsters, decided to send one of their number, Gesar, down to earth in order to do battle against them.

Gesar was reluctant to assume human form and so, before agreeing to descend to earth, he drew up several conditions that he set before the gods, believing that they would be impossible to fulfil. He demanded that his father should be a god and his mother a snake; that he should be given an immortal horse, which could fly through the sky and speak all languages; that he should be supplied with a magical bow and arrow and strong companions; that he should be given a beautiful wife, for whom everybody would be willing to fight; and a clever uncle, who would be able to assist him with battle plans. He also insisted that the gods should protect and help him at all times. To Gesar's distress, the gods agreed to all his demands, so he was forced to descend to earth.

The earthly Gesar was conceived when a god descended in the form of a rainbow and gave Gongmo – a *NAGA* who had transformed herself into a beautiful young girl – a drink of water from a holy vase. Gongmo became pregnant, and in due course, Gesar emerged from his mother as a globe of golden light, which eventually broke open to reveal a baby. According to some versions of the tale, the baby had three eyes, whereupon his horrified mother immediately plucked one out.

Having been warned that he would be overthrown by Gesar, the ruling king tried to kill the child almost as soon as he was born, but, despite his every effort, the boy remained unharmed. However, Gesar and his mother were forced into exile. At the age of 15, Gesar entered a horse race, and on winning it, was made King of Ling and given the former king's daughter as his wife. King Gesar then fought and conquered several demons and converted several countries to Buddhism.

He finally returned to heaven, although in the knowledge that he would have to return to earth one day. Gesar came to be regarded as a warrior god and god of wealth; his consort was a *DAKINI*.

369

TIRTHANKARAS

JAINISM IS AN INDIAN RELIGION and philosophy which offers an austere path to enlightenment. Much of its mythology was inherited from Hinduism, including huge numbers of gods, and ideas on the structure of the universe, but Jains differ from Hindus in that they do not believe in the idea of creation, considering that time is cyclic. Jain ascetics attempt to conduct their lives following five vows: to injure no living thing (because everything has a soul); to speak the truth; to take only what is given; to be chaste; and to achieve detachment from places, people and things. Their examples in following this discipline are 24 tirthankaras, or "spiritual

teachers", who have appeared in the present cycle of time. A *tirtha* is a ford or crossing-place, or a sacred place, person or path which enables believers to cross over into liberation from an endless round of rebirth: for Jains, the tirthankaras were the builders of the ford.

RISHABHA (left) also called Adinatha, was the first tirthankara of the present cycle. He lived for an extremely long time, and was credited by Jains with the establishment of the caste system, the monarchy and the rule of law. He also organized the cultivation of the land, the pursuit of the arts, and taught humankind the 72 sciences, including arithmetic and writing. In Hindu mythology, he was a minor avatar of Vishnu. He is represented by the bull motif and is usually shown naked in a standing yoga posture. (TIRTHANKARA, SRI ADINATH TEMPLE, KHAJURAHO, INDIA.)

MAHAVIRA (above), the twenty-fourth tirthankara, was a contemporary of Gautama Buddha. At the age of 30, he renounced family life and embarked on life as a wandering ascetic. He endured 12 years of fasting, silence and meditation to achieve enlightenment, then spent the next 30 years preaching throughout northern India. He and his followers went about naked to indicate their conquest of passion, and he and other tirthankaras are traditionally portrayed with downcast eyes, dead to the world. (HEAD OF A TIRTHANKARA, STONE, 10TH CENTURY.)

THE TIRTHANKARAS (above) were all considered to have come from the kshatriya, or warrior caste, and were not deities but human teachers who had achieved enlightenment. Worship of their images focuses on their teaching and achievements rather than on themselves. They are all depicted as identical, except for an animal or other symbol which identifies each one, such as the boar that is associated with Vimala (top) and the goat that distinguishes Kunthu (bottom). (DETAIL FROM THE TWENTY-FOUR JAIN TIRTHANKARAS, BUNDI, C. 1720.)

PARSHVA (left) was the twenty-third tirthankara, born to Vama, queen of Benares, in the ninth century BC. He spent 70 years as a wandering ascetic before attaining nirvana when he died at the age of 100 on Mount Sammeda. His symbol was the snake, and he was often depicted under a canopy of cobras. He systematized the Jain religion, dividing its adherents into monks, nuns, and male and female laity, and giving his chief disciples responsibility for the Jain community. (TIRTHANKARA PARSHVANATHA, ORISSA, 11TH CENTURY.)

GNOD-SBYIN see *YAKSHAS*.

THE GNYAN are Tibetan spirits who live in trees and stones. They send plagues, diseases and death down on humankind.

GREAT BUDDHAS OF WISDOM see *DHYANIBUDDHAS*.

GRI-GUM, according to Tibetan belief, was a king who, unlike the rulers who preceded him, cut the magic rope that connected him to heaven. The first human ruler was said to have come down from the sky, landing on top of a mountain. At the end of his reign, he returned to heaven by means of a magic rope. The six kings who followed him did the same. However, Gri-gum, the eighth king, failed to return to heaven. During a duel, the air became so filled with soot that, unable to see while waving his sword around, he severed the magic rope. He was then killed by his opponent.

GSHEN-LHA-OD-DKAR, in the Tibetan Bon religion, was the "God of White Light" from whom all other gods emanated. When nothing else existed, two lights emerged; one was black and the other was white. A rainbow then appeared and gave rise to hardness, fluidity, heat, motion and space.

THE GUARDIAN KINGS (below) who guard the four quarters of the world. Acolytes of the bodhisattva Avalokiteshvara, they are said to have assisted at the birth of Gautama Buddha.

These phenomena merged with one another and formed a gigantic egg. From that egg, the black light produced sickness, disease, pain and countless demons, whereas the white light produced joy, prosperity and numerous gods. The gods and demons together gave rise to all kinds of creatures. These beings inhabit the mountains, trees and lakes of the land.

GSHEN-RAB, or Shenrab Miwo, is traditionally said to have been the founder of the later or purified form of the Bon religion of Tibet, which came into being after the introduction of Buddhism to the country. He is said to have come from a mystic land known as Zhang Zhung, and he came to be regarded as identical to *GAUTAMA BUDDHA*. Some scholars have also identified him with Laozi, the founder of Daoism. He is represented seated on a lotus.

THE GUARDIAN KINGS, according to Buddhist belief, guard the four quarters of the world and protect the Buddhist law. They are said to live on the mythical Mount *MERU*, at the gates of the paradise of *INDRA*, the protector of Buddhism. The Guardian Kings are acolytes of the *BODHISATTVA AVALOKITESHVARA*.

Originally, they were regarded as benevolent, but they developed into menacing warriors. They are usually shown wearing armour and helmets or crowns. The kings are said to have assisted at the birth of *GAUTAMA BUDDHA* and to have held

up the hooves of his horse when he left the palace of his father for the outside world. In Indian art, they are usually shown riding elephants, whereas in Tantrism they are often shown trampling demons.

The chief Guardian King is Vaishravana, the guardian of the north and of winter. His name means "He Who is Knowing", and he is lord of the *YAKSHAS*, divine beings who protect and serve their ruler.

The guardian of the south, Virudhaka or the "Powerful One", fights ignorance and protects the root of goodness in human beings. He rules over the summer, and, in

Tibet, he is often shown with a helmet made from an elephant's head. The guardian of the east, Dhritarashtra, or "He Who Maintains the Kingdom of the Law", presides over the spring and maintains the state. The guardian of the west, Virupaksha, or "He Who Sees All" presides over the autumn. Virupaksha is usually represented standing on a rock or on demons, and wearing armour.

In Hinduism, the guardians are known as Lokapalas. Vaishravana is worshipped as Kuvera, a god of wealth who guards his buried treasure. Kuvera became the king of

HANUMAN (above) wrestles with the demons of Ravana as he strives to find Rama's wife, Sita. (TERRACOTTA, 5TH CENTURY.)

HANUMAN (left), the Hindu monkey god, was well known for his extraordinary agility, which enabled him to escape from the demon Ravana. (JAIPUR, 17TH CENTURY.)

LANKA and drove a magnificent chariot, which the demon king *RAVANA* used in battle in the Hindu epic, the *Ramayana*.

HANUMAN

is the monkey god of Hindu mythology. He is regarded as the patron of learning and is the son of *VAYU*, god of the winds. According to one myth, Hanuman once tried to snatch the sun from the sky, thinking it was something to eat. To prevent the catastrophe, the war god *INDRA* threw his thunderbolt at the monkey, smashing his jaw.

In the great Hindu epic the *Ramayana*, Hanuman is the minister of the monkey king Sugriva and the loyal companion of *RAMA*, the famous *AVATAR* or incarnation of *VISHNU*, the preserver of the universe. Hanuman assisted Rama when the hero was locked in battle with the demon king *RAVANA*, who had run off with Rama's wife, *SITA*. It was Hanuman who discovered Sita's whereabouts, on the island of *LANKA*, Ravana's kingdom.

Hanuman's extraordinary agility enabled him to leap across the waters to the island like an arrow.

However, in mid-flight, a sister of the demon king caught Hanuman's shadow and managed to pull the monkey beneath the waters, where another demon tried to swallow him. Hanuman succeeded in escaping by stretching out so that the demon had to open her jaws, then contracting, so that he was able to leap from her mouth.

Hanuman finally found Sita in a grove of trees. Each day, Ravana threatened the goddess with torture and death if she refused to marry him, but Sita insisted on remaining faithful to Rama. Although Hanuman offered to carry her away, Sita refused to touch any man but her husband. As Hanuman left to tell Rama that he had found Sita, Ravana and his demons set his tail on fire. However, the fire failed to hurt the monkey god, who instead caused vast destruction on the island by swishing his tail from side to side, setting light to countless buildings.

Back in India, Hanuman encouraged an army of monkeys to build a bridge across the sea from India to Lanka, thereby enabling Rama and his troops to approach and attack the demon king. Rama rewarded Hanuman for his help by giving him the gift of eternal life.

Hanuman was said to be as large as a mountain, with yellow skin, a red face and a tremendously long tail. His roar was like thunder, and he flew through the clouds with a great rushing sound.

HAYAGRIVA

is one of Tibetan Buddhism's *DHARMAPALAS*, or "Protectors of the Teaching". He is the lord of wrath, the leader of the terrifying gods known as Dragshed. His name means "Horse's Neck", and he is small, with a pot belly and a horse's head. In Buddhism, Hayagriva is regarded as an emanation of either the buddha *AMITABHA* or the buddha *AKSOBHYA* and as the terrifying aspect of the *BODHISATTVA AVALOKITESHVARA*.

In a Hindu myth, Hayagriva was one of the *DAITYAS*, giant *ASURAS* who opposed the gods. He stole the Veda, the sacred knowledge of Hinduism, when it fell from *BRAHMA*'s mouth. *VISHNU*, reincarnated as the *AVATAR* Matsya the fish, managed to kill Hayagriva and retrieve the sacred texts.

Hayagriva is also regarded as an avatar of the god Vishnu, who is said to have taken on this form in order to retrieve the Veda, after it had been stolen from the gods by two daityas.

HERUKA

is a Buddhist deity, an emanation of the buddha *AKSOBHYA*. In Tibet he is regarded as one of the protective deities, or *ISHTADEVATAS*. Heruka is usually depicted with three eyes, wild hair and bared teeth. His body is smeared with ashes, and he holds a severed human head in his hand. The deity sits or dances on a corpse and is sometimes shown with his female partner, Prajna, with whom he creates nirvana (spiritual bliss). Heruka confers buddhahood and protects the world from evil.

The herukas as a group are terrifying energies who are usually portrayed with haloes of flame. They dance with their huge and terrifying consorts. The herukas exist in the head region, and meditators who achieve their level are believed to be capable of reaching a realm of the ultimate reality.

HAYAGRIVA, the leader of the terrifying gods known as Drag-shed, wreathed with his enemies' heads. (BRONZE, TIBET.)

HEVAJRA is a *YIDAM*, or tutelary god, worshipped in Mongolia, Cambodia, Thailand and Tibet. He is usually represented with four legs and eight heads; his body is blue, and his heads are different colours. He is sometimes shown alone, but often in Yab-Yum, the posture of embrace, with his *SHAKTI* or corresponding female energy.

HIMAVAT see *PARVATI*.

HIRANYAKASHIPU see *AVATARS* and *RAVANA*.

INDRA, one of the chief deities of Indian mythology, is a god of storms and war. He appears in the *Rig Veda* – the ancient hymns forming part of the Veda, the sacred knowledge of Hinduism – as the king of the gods. Indra is red or gold in colour, and is large, fierce and warlike. In his right hand he carries a thunderbolt, which he uses either to slay his enemies or to revive those killed in battle. He is said to ride through the heavens in a chariot, often said to be the sun. In later times, he was frequently depicted on the elephant, *AIRAVATA*.

Indra was born from heaven and earth, which he separated for ever. He challenged the old order and became the leading deity, a less remote figure than the Vedic god, *VARUNA*. Indra was best known as a destroyer of demons, who led the gods against the *ASURAS*. He fought and destroyed the serpent *VRITRA* with a pillar of foam and, in doing so, gave form to chaos, liberating the waters, generating life and causing the sun to rise.

On another occasion, Indra set free some cows which had been stolen from the gods. This myth is interpreted as symbolizing how Indra released the sacred force, or light of the world. Indra was also worshipped as the god who provided rain. As the bringer of light and water, he absorbed many of Varuna's functions, becoming a fertility god and a god of creation.

A vast drinker with a huge belly, Indra was also associated with *SOMA*, an intoxicating drink used in religious rituals. It was from Soma that the god was said to derive his special powers. After drinking it, he became so large that he filled both heaven and earth.

Indra's importance gradually declined. Although he remained a terrifying god of thunder, he came to be regarded as a divine earthly monarch who reigned in Swarga, a luxurious heaven situated on the sacred Mount *MERU*.

According to one myth, it was Indra, rather than *VISHNU's AVATAR* Vamana, who fought the demon Bali. While Indra was attacking a host of demons led by Jalamdhara, Bali fell, and a stream of jewels poured from his mouth. Indra was

HEVAJRA is the Buddhist equivalent of the Hindu god Shiva Nataraja. He is shown in Yab-Yum with his shakti, Nairamata, who stands on two corpses. (TANTRIC BRONZE.)

so amazed that he struck open the demon's body with one of his thunderbolts. The different parts of Bali's body then gave rise to the seeds of precious stones. Diamonds were produced from his

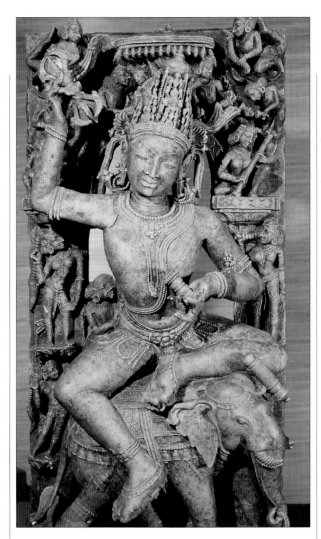

the guru will be able to discern which aspect of the divine will be most useful to the disciple.

JALAMDHARA see *THE ASURAS* and *GANGA*.

JINAS see *DHYANIBUDDHAS*.

KADAVUL see *KATAVUL*.

KADRU see *GARUDA*.

KALADEVI, known in Tibet as Lha-mo, is the only female *DHARMAPALA*, or protector of the Buddhist law. She is said to have been created by the other deities and provided with weapons, in order that she might defend Tantrism, a tradition of gaining enlightenment through ritual practices. Kaladevi rides a mule whose reins are made from poisonous snakes and whose back is covered with the skin of a *YAKSHA*. According to one myth, the skin is that of Kaladevi's son, whom she is said to have devoured. Kaladevi has three protruding eyes, ten arms and, like all Dharmapalas, wears a crown and garland of skulls. She is sometimes said to be the wife of a yaksha king of Sri Lanka and is occasionally depicted walking on a lake of blood along with two other female beings. A terrifying and bloodthirsty goddess, she is often regarded as a consort of *YAMA*, god of the dead. She helps those who earnestly seek her protection.

KALADEVI, a bloodthirsty goddess who is the only female Dharmapala, or protector of the Buddhist teaching. (BRONZE AND ENAMEL, TIBET, 18TH CENTURY.)

INDRA (above) is a weather and fertility god, and a leading Hindu deity. He is shown wielding a vajra, or thunderbolt, and is seated on his mount, the elephant Airavata. (11TH CENTURY.)

bones, sapphires from his eyes, rubies from his blood, emeralds from his marrow, crystal from his flesh, coral from his tongue and pearls from his teeth.

In a story from the Hindu epic, the *Ramayana*, Indra seduced Ahalya, the wife of the great sage Gautama. One day, when he knew that the sage was away from his home, Indra disguised himself, visited Gautama's wife and pressed her to become his lover. Despite his disguise, Ahalya immediately recognized Indra and, because she was curious about the chief god, she agreed. Afterwards, as Indra was leaving, he met Gautama returning. Realizing what had happened, the sage caused the god's testicles to fall off. Gautama then cursed Ahalya, condemning her to lie on ashes and eat only air until *RAMA* visited her. The gods later replaced Indra's testicles with those of a ram. (See also *MYTHICAL MOUNTAINS*)

ISHTADEVATAS are protective Buddhist deities or sacred beings who are especially common in Tibet. Ishtadevata means "Beloved (or Desired) Divinity".

Each individual who decides to enter the path of Bhakti yoga – that of loving submission to a deity – chooses their own ishtadevata. Alternatively, the individual's guru may choose the ishtadevata, since

KALI, *dancing on the god Shiva in a frenzy of blood lust. Eventually she realized what she was doing, and the world became safe once more.* (INDIAN PAINTING, 18TH CENTURY.)

KALI, the "Black One", is the terrifying aspect of the great mother goddess and SHAKTI of SHIVA. The personification of death and destruction, she is said to spring from the forehead of DURGA, another aspect of the goddess, when she becomes angry. Kali is usually depicted with blood-red eyes, four arms and with her tongue lolling out of her mouth in search of blood. She is naked, but for a girdle of severed heads or hands, a necklace of skulls and a tiger skin.

Like Shiva, Kali has a third eye in her forehead. In one hand she holds a weapon, in another the severed head of a giant, while her remaining two hands, in contrast, are raised in blessing. Her devotees regard her as a loving mother goddess who can destroy death as well as demons.

One myth tells how a monster, Raktabija, was destroying the world. Each time he was wounded, 1,000 demons sprang from each drop of his blood. The gods asked Kali to destroy the monster and, as she set about killing the demons, she drank their blood before it reached the ground, so that they were unable to multiply. When only the original monster remained, Kali gulped him down in one mouthful.

In celebration of her victory, she began to dance. As her movements became more and more frenzied, all creation began to shake, and the whole of existence was threatened with destruction. The gods begged Shiva to stop the goddess from dancing, but even the great god was unable to calm her. Eventually, Shiva threw himself on the ground in front of the goddess, whereupon she began to dance on his body. Finally, Kali realized what she was doing and stopped dancing.

The city of Calcutta is called after the goddess: its name means "Kali Ghat" or "Kali's Steps". Each day, animals are sacrificed to her, and it is believed that human sacrifices were made to her in the past. (See also THE MOTHER GODDESS)

KAMA, *in the form of Kamadeva, is the god of love. Often depicted as a young man riding on a parrot, he bears a bow and arrows made of sugar cane and decorated with flowers.* (ILLUSTRATION BY J. HIGGINBOTHAM.)

KALKIN see AVATARS.

KAMA, according to the ancient sacred teachings of India, is either sexual desire or the impulse towards good. However, Kama is sometimes regarded as a deity. Described as the first being to be born, he is superior to gods and humanity and, as a symbol of original desire, he is said to have brought about the created world.

In the form of Kamadeva, he is the god of love. He is sometimes regarded as the son of Dharma, god of justice and Shraddha, goddess of faith. Elsewhere he is described as the son of LAKSHMI, or as having arisen from the heart of BRAHMA. His consort is Rati, or "Voluptuousness", the goddess of sexual passion. Kama is said to rule over the APSARAS, the heavenly nymphs.

According to one myth, the goddess PARVATI grew bored because her consort, the great god SHIVA, was deep in meditation on Mount Kailasa. Parvati persuaded Kama to come to her aid. Kama was loathe to intervene, but Parvati insisted, whereupon Kama prepared to fire his arrow at Shiva's heart in order to remind him of his duties to his wife. The god Mahesvara saw what was about to happen; since it was

KARTTIKEYA, the Hindu warrior god, is named after the Kirttikah, or Pleiades.
(SANDSTONE, PUNJAB, 6TH CENTURY.)

self-born, emerged from Time". One of his wives, Kadru, gave birth to 1,000 serpents, while the other, Vinata, gave birth to *GARUDA*, the bird chosen by the great god Vishnu to be his mount. Kasyapa is sometimes said to have fathered the *ADITYAS* by *ADITI* and the demonic *DAITYAS* by her sister, Diti. He is described in the Hindu epics, the *Mahabharata* and the *Ramayana*, as the son of *BRAHMA* and the father of Vivasvat, or the sun, who in turn was the father of *MANU*, the first man, from whom all human beings are descended.

In Buddhism, Kasyapa is one of the six Manushi, or "human", buddhas. He is the immediate predecessor to *GAUTAMA BUDDHA*. He is often shown seated on a lion, and is coloured yellow or gold because he represents the light of the sun and the moon.

KATARAGAMA DEVIYO is one of the four great gods of Sri Lanka. He is the equivalent of the Indian god *KARTTIKEYA* and the southern Indian Tamil god, *MURUKAN*. Originally, Kataragama Deviyo was called Ceyon, or "God with the Red-coloured Body".

KATAVUL, or Kadavul, is the name for the supreme personal being of the Tamils of southern India and Sri Lanka. The source of all existence, his name means "He Who Is". He is the judge of humankind, rewarding or punishing people according to their deeds during life.

KATUKILAL see *KORRAWI*.

KHADROMAS see *DAKINI*.

KHYUNG-GAI MGO-CAN was an ancient Tibetan god who may have been connected with the sun. He was said to have had the head of a bird.

KORRAWI is the Tamil goddess of battle and victory. She also takes the form of Katukilal, a goddess of the woods. The mother of *MURUKAN*, her temples are guarded by demons and spirits.

necessary for Shiva to finish his meditation in order for the cycles of creation to run their course, he struck Kama with a thunderbolt. Later, however, he brought Kama back to life. In another version of the myth, Shiva struck Kama with a flash of his third eye and burned him to ashes. As a result, Kama was sometimes called Ananga, or "Bodiless".

KAMSA see *KRISHNA*.

KARTTIKEYA, also known as Skanda, is a warrior god who campaigns against demons. The deity is sometimes said to have been raised by the stars of the Pleiades, or Kirttikah. He is sometimes also regarded as a god of fertility.

In the great Hindu epics the *Mahabharata* and the *Ramayana*, Karttikeya is described as the son of *SHIVA*. He is said to have been

conceived when Shiva offered his seeds to the fire god *AGNI*, who gave them for safekeeping to the river goddess *GANGA*. Eventually, a child with six heads, and six or 12 arms, was born.

Alternatively, Shiva is said to have directed the fire of his third eye at a lake. Six children emerged and were brought up by the wives of the *RISHIS*, or seers. One day, *PARVATI* hugged the children so tightly that they were squeezed together into one child, although the six heads remained.

KASYAPA was an ancient Indian sage whose name means "Tortoise". According to the sacred Hindu *Atharva Veda*, "Kasyapa, the

KARTTIKEYA is sometimes shown riding a peacock, holding a bow in one hand and an arrow in the other.

THE AVATARS OF VISHNU

THE GREAT GOD VISHNU WAS SEEN as the protector of the world, having measured out the universe in three giant strides and established it as the home of both gods and humanity. He was a benevolent deity, and his consort Shri, or Lakshmi, was the beautiful goddess of good fortune. In token of his willing involvement with the human race, he descended to earth and became incarnate at times when the world of mortals was threatened by evil. His incarnations, or avatars, follow an evolutionary pattern, from fish and reptile, through animals and the dwarf Vamana, to men and finally to the future creator, Kalkin. The number was traditionally fixed at ten, although the individual avatars varied slightly in different texts. The Buddha was assimilated into the series much later than the others, while the seventh and eighth avatars, Rama and Krishna, are important heroes of Hindu mythology.

MATSYA (above), the fish, was Vishnu's first incarnation. It was rescued by Manu from being eaten by a larger fish. Manu looked after it while it grew, then released it to the ocean. In return, the fish warned Manu of a catastrophic flood. It helped him build a boat on which he could save seeds and animals to repopulate the world, and towed the boat to safety. (ILLUSTRATION FROM DEVOTIONAL TEXT, 17TH CENTURY.)

KURMA (left), the tortoise, supported Mount Mandara on his back during the churning of the cosmic ocean. As the gods had uprooted the mountain and turned it upside down for this task, the peak drilled into the earth when the churning began. Vishnu, in his second incarnation as Kurma, dived underneath it and twisted with the mountain, acting as a paddle to speed up the operation. The milk ocean turned to butter and tossed up Amrita, the elixir of immortality. (ILLUSTRATION BY J. HIGGINBOTHAM, 1864.)

VARAHA (right) was the rescuer of the earth. The demon Hiranyaksha tossed the earth into the cosmic ocean, but in his third avatar, as Varaha the boar, Vishnu plunged into the ocean and killed the demon. He then found the earth in the form of a beautiful woman, whom he carried back up to the surface on his tusks. (BRONZE, GURJARA PRATIHARA, 10TH CENTURY.)

NARASIMHA (above) was the fourth avatar. Hiranyakashipu the demon, the twin brother of Hiranyaksha, dethroned the god Indra and proclaimed himself king of the universe. He was enraged by his son's veneration of Vishnu and condemned him to death, but failed to kill him. In his anger, the demon struck a pillar demanding to know why Vishnu did not show himself. The pillar split open, and Vishnu was incarnated as the man-lion Narasimha, who disembowelled Hiranyakashipu. (ILLUSTRATION BY J. HIGGINBOTHAM, 1864.)

VAMANA (above), the dwarf, rescued the universe from the demon Bali, who had assumed power over it. To release it from his grasp, Vishnu assumed the form of a dwarf for his fifth incarnation. He requested from Bali as much territory as he could cover in three strides. Bali easily granted this apparently trivial request, and Vishnu, transformed into the giant, Trivikrama, covered the underworld, the earth and the heavens in three vast strides. (ILLUSTRATION BY J. HIGGINBOTHAM, 1864.)

PARASHURAMA (above), although he was born a brahman, was destined to lead the life of a warrior. He was armed with a celebrated axe that had been given to him by Shiva. In revenge for insulting his father, he wiped out all the male members of the warrior caste and ordered their widows to sleep with brahmans to produce a new and purer caste of warriors. He was Vishnu's sixth avatar. (PARASHURAMA KILLING ARJUNA KARTAVIRYA BY CHAMBA OR BILASPUR, C. 1750–60.)

RAMA (left) was Vishnu's seventh avatar, assumed at the gods' request to destroy Ravana, the evil ruler of Lanka (the island of Sri Lanka). Rama, son of the king of Ayodhya, won his wife, Sita, by bending and breaking Shiva's unbendable bow. He was banished by his stepmother for 14 years to the forest, where Sita was abducted by Ravana. After many adventures, Rama killed Ravana, won Sita back, returned to his kingdom and reigned for 1,000 years. (ILLUSTRATION TO THE RAMAYANA BY MIR KALAN, C. 1750–60.)

GAUTAMA BUDDHA (left), Vishnu's ninth incarnation, was not identified until the third or fourth century AD. In the earliest accounts of it, Vishnu was said to have assumed this avatar in order to convert demons to Buddhist beliefs, with the intention of weakening them in their war against the gods, or to mislead sinful mortals so that they would receive their just punishment. Later, a more positive reason was suggested: Vishnu was said to want to abolish animal sacrifices.

KRISHNA (above), the god and the eighth avatar, was hidden at birth because of a prophecy that his mother's eighth child would kill the evil King Kamsa. Krishna was brought up in obscurity among a community of cowherds. After killing a succession of demons, including Vatsasura, who came in the guise of a calf, Krishna killed Kamsa. He assisted the hero Arjuna in the great battle of Kurukshetra, disguised as his charioteer. (ILLUSTRATION TO THE BHAGAVATA PURANA BY MANKOT, C. 1730–40.)

KALKIN (above right) is Vishnu's tenth and final avatar, and is still to come: he will appear at the end of the present age, the Kali Yuga, which began in 3102BC and will last 432,000 years. In its final years, humanity will face a breakdown of civilization and a loss of spiritual and moral values. The divine incarnation of Kalkin, riding a white horse, will be needed to wipe out the wickedness of the world and establish a new era. (STONE CARVING ON PRASANNA CHENNAKESHAVA TEMPLE, SOMNATHPUR.)

KRISHNA, according to Hindu mythology, is an *AVATAR* of *VISHNU*, the preserver of the universe. He is traditionally referred to as the only complete avatar. A divine hero, Krishna is said to have been miraculously born in the town of Mathura in northern India. The gods wanted to destroy the evil oppressor King Kamsa, and so Vishnu decided to be born as the eighth son of the king's sister Devaki. According to one story, Vishnu plucked out two of his hairs, one black, one white. The black hair became Krishna and the white hair *BALARAMA*, Krishna's older brother. Krishna's name means the "Dark One".

King Kamsa learned that he was to be assassinated by one of his nephews, so he imprisoned Devaki and her husband Vasudev and killed each of their sons as they were born. When Devaki gave birth to Krishna, Vishnu told the couple to exchange their baby for the daughter of some cowherds who lived on the other side of the river Yamuna. The doors of the prison miraculously opened, and Vasudev carried the baby to the river. As soon as the child's toe touched the waters, they parted, allowing the father and son to pass through safely. Vasudev left the baby with the cowherds Yashoda and Nanda. However, King Kamsa discovered what had happened and sent a demon disguised as a nurse to look after the infant. Krishna sucked at the demon's breast until he drained her life away.

Krishna was a playful child, teasing

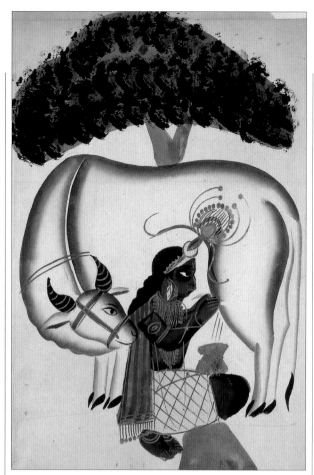

KRISHNA (above), an avatar of Vishnu, spent his childhood as the adopted son of cowherds. (KALIGHAT PAINTING, C. 1860.)

KRISHNA (left) is said to have taught the science of Bhakti yoga to the sun god, Surga, who instructed Manu, father of humankind.

the cows, laughing at his elders and stealing butter and sweets. He also displayed signs of his divine origins by, among other pranks, uprooting two trees at once; on another occasion, his adopted mother, Yashoda, was amazed to see the whole universe when she looked down his throat. Once, when the cowherds were about to worship the great god INDRA, Krishna told them that instead they should worship Mount Govardhana and their herds. The mountain, he explained, provided their herds with food and the cows themselves gave them milk to drink. Krishna then declared that he himself was the mountain. Indra was furious and sent down torrents of rain. However, Krishna lifted Mount Govardhana and held it above the storms for seven days and seven nights. Indra was so amazed that he came down from the heavens and asked Krishna to befriend his son, the hero ARJUNA.

One of the most popular myths concerning Krishna is that of his youthful dalliances with the gopis, the female cowgirls, and in particular with a girl called *RADHA* with whom the young hero fell passionately in love. Once, when the cowgirls were bathing in the river Yamuna, Krishna stole their clothes, then hid in a tree. He refused to return their garments to them until they came out, one by one, their hands clasped in prayer. Because all the cowgirls wanted to hold Krishna's hands when they danced, he multiplied his hands countless times. The sound of

Krishna's flute, calling the cowgirls out to dance in the moonlight, is believed to symbolize the voice of the supreme lord calling all who hear him to divine pleasures.

As Krishna grew older, he began to rid the neighbourhood of monsters and demons. Eventually, King Kamsa heard of his exploits and determined to kill him. However, Krishna not only succeeded in killing Kamsa but also went on to destroy numerous other oppressive kings as well as demons.

The most important battle he participated in was that of Kurukshetra. On the eve of the

KRISHNA visiting Radha, a young gopi, or cowgirl, with whom he fell passionately in love. His name means "Dark One" and he is often depicted as dark-skinned.
(ILLUSTRATION TO RASAMANJARI BY BHANUDETTA, BASOHLI, C. 1865.)

battle, Krishna, disguised as a charioteer, is said to have preached to the hero Arjuna the *Bhagavad Gita,* or "Song of the Lord", which forms part of the great Hindu epic, the *Mahabharata.* The war ended in the destruction of both armies, with only the merest handful of survivors on each side. Krishna died shortly afterwards. He was sitting in the forest, meditating, when a huntsman mistook him for a deer and shot an arrow, which struck him on his left heel, his only vulnerable spot. Krishna told the huntsman not to grieve or be afraid, and then ascended into the sky in a beacon of light.

Krishna is believed to embody divine beauty, joy and love, using his charm, playfulness and compassion to draw his devotees into the embrace of the supreme lord. (See also *THE AVATARS OF VISHNU*)

KSHITIGARBHA, who is a *BOD-HISATTVA*, or "buddha-to-be", is said to look after the six paths taken by souls after they have been judged. These paths are the destinies of humankind, *ASURAS*, demons, gods, animals and the damned. Patient and persevering, he consoles those who live in hell, seeking to lighten the burdens that they have brought upon themselves by evil actions when alive.

Kshitigarbha came to be regarded as the protector of all travellers. In India, he had only a small following, but he attracted many devotees both in China and Japan. According to one Chinese myth, he was a young Indian boy of the brahman caste who was so upset by how his late mother was suffering in hell that he determined to save all the other inhabitants of hell from such a terrible fate.

Kshitigarbha's name means "He Who Encompasses the Earth". In China, he is known as Dizang Wang, and in Japan as Jizo-Bosatsu.

KUNTI see *ARJUNA*.

KUN-TU-BZAN-PO, according to the Bon religion of Tibet, created the world from a lump of mud, and living beings from an egg.

KURMA, the tortoise, was the second incarnation, or *AVATAR*, of the Hindu god *VISHNU*, the preserver of the universe. During the churning of the ocean, Kurma supported Mount Mandara on his back in order to prevent the mountain from boring a hole in the earth. The gods were thus able to obtain *AMRITA*, the elixir of immortality, to restore their power. (See also *THE AVATARS OF VISHNU*)

L

KURUKULLA is a Buddhist goddess who emanates from *AMITABHA*. She is said to be able to cast spells on men and women in order to ensure that they serve her. In Tibet, she became a goddess of riches. Her main attributes are a red lotus, a bow and an arrow. She is often represented as reddish in colour, seated in a cave and with four arms. Her two upper arms are held in a threatening posture, while the two lower arms offer comfort.

KUVERA see *GUARDIAN KINGS*.

LAKSHMANA, according to Hindu myth, was the son of King Dasaratha and Sumitra and the half-brother of *RAMA*, an incarnation of the great god *VISHNU*. When Rama was exiled from his late father's kingdom, Lakshmana accompanied him on his travels. While the two brothers were living in the wilderness, Surpanaka, one of the demon king *RAVANA*'s sisters fell in love with Rama. He sent the woman to Lakshmana who in turn sent her back to Rama. The demoness, seeking revenge for being thus insulted, attacked Rama's wife *SITA*, but to no avail. Rama then asked Lakshmana to disfigure the seductress, which he did by cutting off her nose and ears. The demoness demanded that Ravana avenge her, and it was during this great battle that the demon king succeeded in abducting Sita.

LAKSHMI, or Shri, according to the Veda, the sacred knowledge of the Hindus, was alleged to have been many deities, including the consort of *VARUNA* or *SURYA*. However, she is best known as the beautiful consort or *SHAKTI* (female power) of the great Hindu god *VISHNU*. The goddess of wealth and good fortune, Lakshmi is usually depicted as a beautiful golden woman sitting on a lotus flower, the symbol of the womb, immortality and spiritual purity. During the Hindu celebration of Diwali, the

LAKSHMANA and Rama wandering in search of Rama's abducted wife, Sita. (ILLUSTRATION TO THE RAMAYANA, KANGRA, 1780.)

festival of lights, thousands of lanterns are lit and fireworks exploded in order to please the goddess. People gamble and feast, while the goddess is said to wander from house to house looking for somewhere to rest, and blessing with prosperity all houses that are well lit.

Lakshmi was said to have been born several times. For example, when Vishnu was incarnated as *RAMA*, Lakshmi was born as *SITA*.

Everyone wants to possess Lakshmi, but she insists that no one can keep her for long. She immediately leaves anyone who puts her on their head, which is what the demons do whenever they manage to catch hold of her. In early myths, Lakshmi was sometimes associated with *INDRA*, the war god. However, even Indra had to divide her into four parts in order to keep hold of her for any length of time. Lakshmi's presence is believed to bring fertility. According to one tale, when the goddess sat down next to Indra, he

began to pour down rain so that the crops flourished. Another myth tells how Lakshmi was born by her own will in a beautiful field, which had been cut open by a plough.

Lakshmi appears in the famous myth of the churning of the ocean. Using the snake Vasuki as a rope to turn Mount Mandara, the gods churned the cosmic ocean for 100 years. Eventually the ocean turned to milk and gave rise not only to *AMRITA*, the elixir of immortality, but also to the "Fourteen Precious Things", including the beautiful goddess Lakshmi, who rose seated on a lotus flower. The heavenly musicians and great sages began to sing Lakshmi's praises; the sacred rivers asked her to bathe in their

LAKSHMI (far left), laden with flowers, is a beautiful golden woman. Her presence is believed to bring fertility, and ancient Indian rulers would perform a marriage ritual in which they took Lakshmi as their bride to secure wealth and fertility.

LAKSHMI (left) sat on Vishnu's lap and refused to look at the demons who wanted to own her as goddess of prosperity when she emerged from the cosmic ocean. (ILLUSTRATION BY J. HIGGINBOTHAM, 1864.)

LANKA was the site of the battle between Rama and Ravana, the demon king. Ravana's horde of demons was eventually defeated by Rama's army of monkeys, assembled by Hanuman. (ILLUSTRATION TO THE RAMAYANA, RAJASTHAN, EARLY 19TH CENTURY.)

MAHALKA see *MAHAKALA*.

MAHAMAYA see *MAYA*.

MAHAPRAJAPATI GAUTAMI was the stepmother and aunt of *GAUTAMA BUDDHA*. She raised him after his mother, Queen *MAYA*, died of joy a few days after his miraculous birth. The devotion of Mahaprajapati became legendary. After the death of her husband, Mahaprajapati persuaded the Buddha to allow her to found a Buddhist order of nuns.

MAHAKALA is a destructive aspect of the god Shiva. Threatening and armed with a sword, he is known as the "Great Black One". (TIBETAN, 19TH CENTURY.)

waters; the sea of milk offered her a crown of immortal flowers; and the sacred elephants who hold up the world poured the holy water of the Ganges over her.

LANKA was the old name given to Ceylon, now Sri Lanka. It was also the name of its capital. The walls of Lanka are said to have been made from gold by Vishvakarma, a creator deity and the architect of the gods. Originally, Lanka was intended as a home for Kuvera, god of riches, but the demon king *RAVANA* later captured it and took it as his own.

According to one tale, *VAYU*, a god of the winds, was responsible for creating the island. Narada, a sage, or *RISHI*, challenged Vayu to break off the summit of Mount *MERU*, the world mountain. *GARUDA*, the mythical bird, normally protected the mountain,

but one day, in the bird's absence, Vayu succeeded in breaking off the summit. He immediately threw the summit into the depths of the ocean, where it remained as the island of Lanka.

THE LHA-DRE are gods, or supernatural beings, of the indigenous Bon religion of Tibet. When Buddhism entered Tibet, the Buddhist teachers assigned to the Lha-Dre the role of protectors of the new faith, thereby assimilating them into the Buddhist pantheon, where they are regarded as "Deities of the World" rather than the symbolic deities of Buddhism.

LHA-MO see *KALADEVI*.

LOKAPALAS see *DHARMAPALAS* and *GUARDIAN KINGS*.

THE LU are supernatural beings of the indigenous Bon religion of Tibet, who were assimilated into Buddhism as protectors of the faith. They live in lakes and rivers, and require regular placation.

MAHAKALA, or Mahalka, is known in Tibet as Mgon-po. The destructive form of the god *SHIVA*, he is one of the *DHARMAPALAS* of Tibetan Buddhism, and a *YIDAM*, a tutelary god of Tibet. He is known

as the "Great Black One", and has three eyes. He is covered with a tiger or elephant skin and holds a noose made from snakes.

His function, like that of all Dharmapalas, is to destroy all known enemies of the Buddhist teaching. Mahakala's most important duties are to pacify, enrich, magnetize and destroy. In the 17th century, he was accepted as the tutelary god of Mongolia, then under Tibetan influence.

LANKA (left) burns as Hanuman, the monkey god of Hindu mythology, leaps across the water to safety.

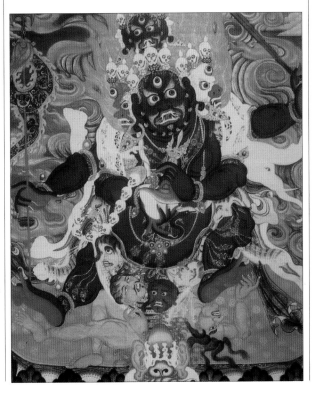

MAITREYA is the buddha of the future and the last earthly buddha. Regarded as the embodiment of love, his name means the "Benevolent" or "Friendly One". Maitreya is currently a *BODHISATTVA* dwelling in the *TUSHITA* or "Joyful" Heaven. In due course, *GAUTAMA BUDDHA* will enthrone him as his successor. Maitreya is expected to appear at the end of the present Buddhist age, in around 30,000 years' time.

Maitreya is often depicted as one of a triad with Gautama and the bodhisattva *AVALOKITESHVARA*. In non-Mahayana, or "Great Vehicle" Buddhism, the term *bodhisattva* usually refers either to Maitreya or to the historical Gautama Buddha, prior to his spiritual enlightenment.

The cult of Maitreya is very widespread in Tibetan Buddhism. According to one Tibetan tale, Asanga, a learned sage who founded the Yogachara school of Mahayana Buddhism, received his teaching directly from Maitreya. The Yogachara school teaches that everything consists of "mind only" and puts particular emphasis on the practice of yoga.

Asanga spent many years meditating on the future buddha. He eventually began to feel that his efforts to attain wisdom were fruitless and started to feel frustrated. One day, Asanga noticed that the wings of birds had worn a groove in a rock against which they always brushed when landing. The sage then heard the drip of water on a stone and saw that the drip had cut a deep passage through the rock. These two observations caused him to renew his determination to attain wisdom. However, though he continued to meditate, and though he continued to invoke Maitreya, he still got nowhere.

Some time later, while he was searching for food, Asanga met a man who was rubbing an iron bar with a piece of cotton. When Asanga asked the man what he was doing, the man replied that he was making a needle. Once again, Asanga determined to continue his pursuit of wisdom.

Many years passed, and still Asanga had failed to achieve his goal. Finally, he decided to leave his cave for good. As he was making his return to the outside world, Asanga met a dog who was suffering excruciating pain from a wound infested with worms. Although Asanga felt great compassion for the animal, he knew that if he removed the worms, they would die for want of food. Eventually, he decided that he would pick off the worms and allow them to eat his own flesh. However, he then worried that he might crush the worms, and so he decided to lick them off the dog instead.

Just as his tongue brushed against the worms, the dog disappeared and in its place stood Maitreya. Asanga asked Maitreya why he had failed to appear to him during his many years of meditation, whereupon the future buddha replied that only in this act of pure

MAITREYA (above) will appear far in the future, when India becomes an earthly paradise. (TIBETAN BRONZE, 11TH CENTURY.)

MAITREYA (right), the buddha of the future, and the last earthly buddha.

compassion had Asanga's vision been cleansed, although he had been with the sage throughout his many years of meditation.

Maitreya then told Asanga to carry him on his back into the city so that everyone might see him. Asanga did as instructed, but nobody saw Maitreya because their vision was so clouded. Maitreya then took Asanga to the Tushita heaven, where he was able to gain the spiritual insight which he had sought for so many years.

MANJUSHRI

MANJUSHRI is the *BOD-HISATTVA* of wisdom and one of the most important members of the Buddhist pantheon. His name means "He Who is Noble and Gentle", and his *SHAKTI*, or female energy, is *SARASVATI*. Manjushri is usually depicted with two lotus

blossoms, on which rest his attributes, a sword of wisdom and a sacred text. He dispels ignorance, bestows eloquence and is a symbol of the enlightenment that can be reached through learning. He is said to be the father and mother of the bodhisattvas, as well as their spiritual friend.

In Tibetan Buddhism, certain great saints and scholars are regarded as incarnations of Manjushri. The Tibetans often depict Manjushri with several heads and arms. In Nepal, he is believed to have introduced civilized life, and his festival is celebrated on the first day of the year. According to legend, Manjushri originally came from China. In Japan he is known as Monju-Bosatzu. (See also *BOD-HISATTVAS*)

MANU

MANU, according to Hindu mythology, was the first man and the precursor of humankind. One myth tells how Manu was the son of *BRAHMA* and a young woman whom the god had produced from his own body. According to

MANJUSHRI, enthroned and surrounded by deities, is flanked by two lotus blossoms, on which rest a sword of wisdom and the Prajnaparamita-sutra, a holy text that advocates the ideal of the bodhisattva. (TIBETAN PAINTING.)

another tradition, Manu was the son of the sun god *SURYA*. Manu was saved from a cataclysmic flood by Matsya, an *AVATAR* or incarnation of the great god *VISHNU*, the preserver of the universe.

One day, Manu was washing in the river when he found a tiny fish, Matsya, which begged the sage to protect it. Manu took the fish home, where it grew bigger and bigger until eventually it asked to be taken to the sea. Before the fish swam away, it warned Manu that there would be a huge flood, which would engulf the earth, and it advised the sage to save himself by building a huge boat. Manu did as the fish advised, taking on board the boat all kinds of creatures and seeds of plants.

Almost before he had finished his task, the rains began to fall heavily and soon the whole world was flooded. The waters grew rough and threatened to capsize Manu's craft. However, Matsya appeared again, this time as a gigantic fish, and towed the boat safely through the waters. The fish then told Manu to fasten the boat to the summit of a mountain, which still remained above the water, and to wait for the floods to subside. Before leaving, the fish confessed to Manu that he was in fact Vishnu.

In gratitude to the god, Manu made a sacrifice of milk and melted butter. After a year, the offering turned into a beautiful woman who revealed that she was his daughter, Ida. The couple proceeded to engender the human race.

MANJUSHRI, seated on a lotus-moon throne, wields his sword of wisdom, poised to strike down ignorance.

MARA is the evil demon of Buddhist belief who tempted *GAUTAMA BUDDHA* as he sat meditating under the sacred tree at Bodh Gaya. Mara's name means "Death". He realized that if Gautama achieved enlightenment, his own power would be destroyed, and he therefore sent his three beautiful daughters to tempt the sage. Although Mara's daughters sang and danced and tried every trick they knew to beguile him, Gautama remained unmoved. Eventually, they admitted defeat.

Mara then sent an army of terrifying devils to threaten Gautama. Some of the creatures had 1,000 eyes, others were horrifically deformed; they drank blood and ate snakes. However, as soon as they came near to the sacred tree, they found that their arms were bound to their sides. Finally, Mara himself attacked Gautama with his fearsome weapon, a disc which could slice mountains in two. None the less, when the disc

MARA (below) sent his three beautiful daughters to tempt Gautama and tried in every way to threaten the sage as he sat meditating under the sacred tree at Bodh Gaya. (TIBETAN PAINTING, 18TH CENTURY.)

MAYA (above) gave birth to Gautama Buddha while holding on to the branch of a tree. He is also shown taking seven symbolic steps. (TIBETAN PAINTING, 18TH CENTURY.)

reached Gautama, it was transformed into a garland of flowers. At last, the demon realized that he was beaten.

THE MARUTS are a group of either 27 or 60 storm gods, usually said to be the sons of the goddess Prisni and *RUDRA*, an ancient Vedic deity who later came to be identified with *SHIVA*. The Maruts accompanied the war god *INDRA* and were armed with lightning arrows and thunderbolts. According to the *Rig Veda*, the ancient collection of sacred hymns, they wore golden helmets and breastplates, and used their axes to split the clouds so that rain could fall. They were widely regarded as clouds, capable of shaking mountains and destroying forests.

According to a later tradition, the Maruts were born from the broken womb of the goddess Diti, after Indra hurled a thunderbolt at her to prevent her from giving birth to too powerful a son. The goddess

had intended to remain pregnant for a century before giving birth to a son who would threaten Indra.

MATSYA see *MANU*.

MAYA, or Queen Mahamaya, was the mother of *GAUTAMA BUDDHA*. According to Buddhist tradition, she possessed all the qualities required of a woman destined to bear a buddha. She was not passionate, she drank no alcohol and she observed the precepts of a lay Buddhist. On the day she conceived Gautama, she is said to have had a dream in which a small white elephant, carrying a white lotus in its trunk, entered her right side. In due course, Maya gave birth to Gautama from her side as she stood holding on to a tree. She suffered no pain. Seven days later, she died of joy and joined the gods.

Maya, or "Miraculous Power", was a term used in Hinduism to describe the power of the Vedic gods. Later, Maya was regarded as the illusion of reality which we perceive, which will be dispelled when the universal reality of Brahman or the "Absolute" is understood. (See also *THE LIFE OF THE BUDDHA*)

MAYA (above) dreams of a small white elephant and conceives Gautama Buddha, who is seen arriving for reincarnation, riding on the elephant.

MERU is a mythical world mountain, also known as Sumeru. According to ancient Indian beliefs, both Buddhist and Hindu, it is situated at the centre of the universe and is the dwelling place of the gods. In Hindu tradition, the sacred Ganges flows from the summit of Mount Meru, and *BRAHMA*'s magnificent golden city is situated at its peak. Beneath the mountain lie seven lower worlds, in the lowest of which lives the snake Vasuki, who bears Mount Meru and all the worlds on his coils and destroys them at the end of each *YUGA*.

In Buddhist belief, Meru is surrounded by seas and worlds, beneath which lie the hells. The realms of the gods and the Buddha-fields are situated above the mountain. According to one Tibetan myth, in the very beginning, there was nothing but emptiness. Eventually, a wind began to stir, caused by the karma of the inhabitants of a previous universe. After many ages, the winds

grew stronger, and rain began to fall. Many years later, the primeval or cosmic ocean arose, and the winds began to move the waters of the ocean, churning them until they gave rise to the cosmic mountain Meru, or Rirap Lhunpo. In due course, Meru became the abode of the gods and semi-divine beings.

Meru is made of precious stones; its slopes are covered with trees and fruits. Around the mountain lies a vast lake, and around the lake lies a ring of golden mountains. Altogether, there are seven rings of mountains and seven lakes. The final lake is Chi Gyatso, within which lie the four worlds. Each world is like an island and has its own unique inhabitants. Our own world is called Czambu Ling. At first, Czambu Ling was inhabited by gods from Mount Meru. Everyone was happy, there was no illness or pain.

However, it so happened that one day, one of the gods noticed a creamy substance lying on the sur-

MERU (right), the golden mountain, is the centre of the world in both Hindu and Buddhist mythology. (MURAL PAINTING, WAT KO KEO SUTTHARAM, THAILAND.)

face of the earth. The cream tasted delicious, and soon all the other gods began to eat it. The more the gods ate, the less powerful they became. Eventually, the light the gods had radiated was extinguished, the world became dark and the gods became human beings. When the creamy food ran out, the people began to eat fruit. Each individual had his own plant, and each day the plant would produce just one piece of fruit, which was just enough to satisfy one person's hunger.

One day, a man noticed that his plant had produced two pieces of fruit. He ate both pieces and, when the next day his plant produced no fruit, he stole some from his neighbour's plant. In this way, theft and greed were introduced to the world. (See also *MYTHICAL MOUNTAINS*)

MGON-PO see *MAHAKALA*.

MITRA, according to Vedic mythology, was a god of light. He was one of the *ADITYAS*, and was

closely associated with *VARUNA*, the supreme Vedic deity. Sometimes regarded as twins, Mitra and Varuna maintained universal order and justice and were said to embody the power that formed the essence of the kshatriya, or warrior caste. A good-natured deity, Mitra has particular responsibility for friendships and contracts. He is believed to direct human beings towards the light and to enable them to live happily with one another. In Iran, his parallel is the god Mithra.

MURUKAN, or the "Youthful One", was a deity of the Dravidians of southern India. He is sometimes known as Ceyon, or the "Red One". He is an important figure in present-day Tamil religion. Murukan is usually represented riding an elephant or a peacock, and he carries a spear and a garland of flowers. He is sometimes identified with *KARTTIKEYA*, the Hindu warrior god. His equivalent in Sri Lanka is *KATARAGAMA DEVIYO*.

SACRED RIVERS

THE GREAT RIVER GANGES, which rises in the Himalayas and flows across north-east India, is sacred to Hindus, who believe that bathing in her water will enable them to reach Indra's heaven, Svarga, on Mount Meru. They also revere the holy city of Prayaga (now Allahabad), where the Ganges is joined by her two tributaries, the Yamuna and the subterranean Sarasvati. This is a place of pilgrimage so sacred that a tiny piece of its soil is believed to be capable of wiping away sin. Each of these great rivers was deified as a goddess, of which the most holy was Ganga, daughter of the mountain god Himavat and an aspect of the great mother goddess, Devi. She was said to have emerged from the toe of Vishnu, and to have descended from heaven to cleanse the earth of the accumulated ashes of the dead. The ashes of the faithful are still committed to her care.

SARASVATI (above), the goddess, was originally identified with the sacred river which flows into the Ganges at Prayaga. As the deity of a natural force, she had the power to smash mountains and spoke with the roar of the waterfall. Later, she was said to be the creation and consort of Brahma. She became the goddess of music and wisdom, was credited with the invention of Sanskrit, and was known as the "Mother of the Veda". (MARBLE STATUE, 12TH CENTURY.)

VARANASI (left), the city on the west bank of the Ganges, is a holy place for Hindus. They believe that to die here, or to have their ashes committed to the river, will release their souls from the cycle of rebirth and death. The dead are cremated on the "burning" ghats (the stone steps that run down to the water), and their ashes are given to the Ganges to be carried down to the sea.

YAMUNA (left), the river goddess, was the daughter of the sun god Surya and his wife Sanjna, and was also sometimes said to be the sister of Yama, the Vedic god of death. As a river goddess, she was thought to bring fertility and good harvests, and was therefore identified with prosperity. The river Yamuna, a tributary of the Ganges, parted miraculously to allow Krishna's father, Vasudev, to carry him to safety as a baby. (STONE CARVING, 9TH CENTURY.)

GANGA'S (above) fall from heaven was cushioned by the matted hair of Shiva, sitting on Mount Kailasa. It separated the river into seven different streams so that it would not engulf the earth. Ganga was believed to flow through the underworld too, linking all three worlds. She was seen as a symbol of purity and was portrayed as a beautiful woman, the consort of Vishnu and Shiva, and also of a mortal king, Shantanu. (ILLUSTRATION BY WARWICK GOBLE.)

THE YAMUNA (left) is one of the seven great rivers of India – the others are the Ganges, Sarasvati, Godavari, Narmada, Sindhu and Kaveri – that are particularly revered, though Hindus hold all water to be sacred. On the bank of the Yamuna lies the ancient city of Mathura, the mythical birthplace of Krishna, which is also a place of pilgrimage for Buddhists and Jains.

389

P

NAGAS, according to Hindu belief, are semi-divine but powerful serpents who guard the treasures of the earth. They are often associated with fertility but can occasionally prove dangerous. Whereas some nagas are depicted with several heads, others are represented as human beings. The naga Vasuki was used as a rope in the myth of the churning of the ocean and was afterwards worn by *SHIVA* as a girdle that had the power to dispel demons. When the great god *VISHNU* is resting, he sleeps on the naga known as Sesha, or Ananta. Seshas's hoods shade the god, but his yawns cause earthquakes.

In Buddhist belief, the nagas are often regarded as water deities who guard Buddhist texts. One story tells how the nagas took the Buddhist philosopher Nagarjuna to their realm, where he rediscovered the *Prajnaparamita-sutra* of Mahayana Buddhism. The *GAUTAMA BUDDHA* is said to have given the text to the nagas for safekeeping until a time when humans were ready to receive it. Another story tells how the naga king Elapatra disguised himself as a man to listen to the Buddha preach.

Naga kings are depicted in representations of Gautama Buddha's birth. One such king, Mucilinda, is said to have sheltered the meditating Buddha during a great storm by surrounding him with the coils of his body and forming an awning

NAGAS are semi-divine but powerful serpents who guard the treasures of the earth. (ALAMPUR, 7TH–8TH CENTURY.)

with his hood. The naga kings are said to control rainfall and to look after rivers, lakes and seas. They protect against fires caused by lightning. In spring, the nagas climb to the heavens, whereas in winter they live deep in the earth.

NANDA see *KRISHNA*.

NANDI, or Nandin, is the milk-white bull who is an animal form of *SHIVA*, the great Hindu god. As well as being Shiva's chosen mount, Nandi is a member of his retinue and represents the great god's virility and fertility.

When Shiva took the form of Nataraja, Nandi provided the music for his wild dancing. In the *Puranas*, Hindu scriptures dating from the fifth century AD, Nandi is invoked as a divinity. He is the son of Surabhi, the divine cow who arose from the churning of the ocean, and *KASYAPA*, the sage.

Nandi looks after all four-legged creatures and stands guard at the four corners of the world. A sculpture of the bull is usually situated at the entrance of temples dedicated to Shiva.

NANDIN see *NANDI*.

NANG-LHA is one of the supernatural beings of the indigenous Bon religion of Tibet. He was assimilated into the Buddhist pantheon as a protector of the religion.

NANDI's statue stands at the entrance of many temples dedicated to Shiva, and devotees customarily touch the bull's testicles as they enter the shrine. Nandi is Shiva's principal attendant.

Nang-Lha looks after the house and is usually shown with the head of a pig and the body of a human being.

NARASIMHA was the fourth incarnation, or *AVATAR*, of the great Hindu god *VISHNU*, preserver of the universe. A man-lion, he overcame the king Hiranyakashipu, an incarnation of *RAVANA*. See also *THE AVATARS OF VISHNU*)

NARAYANA see *BRAHMA*.

NASATYA see *ASVINS*.

NATARAJA see *SHIVA*.

NATHA is one of the four principal gods of Sri Lanka. His name means "Master". He was identified with the *BODHISATTVA*, or "buddha-to-be", *AVALOKITESHVARA*, and was also sometimes regarded as *MAITREYA*, the future Buddha. The Buddhist goddess *TARA* is said to be his consort.

NILARANTHA see *SHIVA*.

PADMASAMBHAVA was one of the founders of Tibetan Buddhism. His followers worship him as the

NARASIMHA was a man-lion, the fourth avatar of the Hindu god Vishnu. He overcame the demon king Hiranyakashipu. (CARVING, HALEBIDU, KARNATAKA.)

"second Buddha". A contemporary of the Tibetan king Trisong Detsen (AD755–97), Padmasambhava was allegedly born in the mythical land of Urgyen, believed to be situated in north-west Kashmir. He is said to have been created by the buddha *AMITABHA* and to have appeared, aged eight years old, in a lotus blossom, thereby earning his name, which means "He Who is Born from the Lotus".

After murdering a king's minister, Padmasambhava was condemned to live in the charnel grounds. However, while there, he mastered all the learned disciplines of his time, in particular the teachings of the Tantras, and achieved great spiritual power through conversing with the *DAKINI*, the female "Sky-goers". At that time, the ancient Bon religion still flourished in Tibet. King Trisong Detsen decided that he wanted to intro-

duce Buddhism to the country, and so sent messengers to India, instructing them to find the most learned men in order that they might teach his people. The messengers advised the king to send for Padmasambhava.

Padmasambhava arrived in Tibet and imparted the Buddhist teachings to 25 main students, as well as to the king. Some accounts say that he stayed for a few months, others that he was in Tibet for 50 years. He transformed many demons into *DHARMAPALAS*, or "Protectors of the Teaching", founded the "Inconceivable" temple with the help of local spirits, and composed the "Hidden Treasures". The treasures, known as Gter-ma, are religious instructions, which are said to have been hidden away in order to be revealed sometime in the future when the world needs a fresh revelation.

PADMASAMBHAVA was worshipped as the "second Buddha" and instrumental in introducing Buddhism to Tibet. (PAINTING, TANKA LAMA SCHOOL, 19TH CENTURY.)

One story tells how the king eventually grew worried that his people showed greater reverence for Padmasambhava than for himself. In order to demonstrate his supreme authority, he summoned all his courtiers to watch Padmasambhava bow down before him. However, as Padmasambhava raised his arms as if to prostrate himself before the king, flames sprang from his fingertips, setting the ruler's clothes on fire. Immediately, the king tore off his ceremonial scarf, already smouldering, and threw himself at Padmasambhava's feet in submission. He later gave Padmasambhava the scarf as a token of his humility, establishing the tradition of giving scarves as a sign of respect.

Before leaving Tibet, the sage promised to return every month on the tenth day of the waxing moon in order to bless anyone who called out his name. According to legend, he travelled to Bhutan, where he

PADMASAMBHAVA in his eight forms. He built the first Tibetan Buddhist monastery, at Samyé, where previous attempts had been foiled by demons, who tore down the buildings as soon as they were erected.

continued his religious teaching. Padmasambhava is said to have lived for more than 1,000 years.

THE PANDAVAS

THE PANDAVAS were the descendants of King Pandu. The five Pandava princes fought the Kauravas in the famous battle of Kurukshetra, which is described in the Hindu epic, the *Mahabharata*.

On the eve of the battle, *ARJUNA*, one of the five brothers, received spiritual instruction from *KRISHNA*, an *AVATAR* of the great god *VISHNU*, who disguised himself as Arjuna's charioteer. Krishna's teaching forms the *Bhagavad Gita* or "Song of the Lord".

PARASHURAMA see *AVATARS*.

PARVATI

PARVATI is an aspect of the divine mother of Hindu mythology, the consort of the great god *SHIVA*. She is the graceful aspect of the *SHAKTI* of Shiva. Parvati's name means "Daughter of the Mountains"; her father was Himavat, king of the mountains, and she was the mother of the elephant god *GANESHA*, whom she is sometimes said to have created from the rubbings of her own body. According to one myth, Shiva produced six

PARVATI (right), mother of the elephant-headed god Ganesha, with Shiva, who is shown with the goddess Ganga in his hair.
(ILLUSTRATION BY J. HIGGINBOTHAM, 1864.)

children without Parvati's assistance. The goddess became extremely fond of her husband's offspring and one day hugged them so tightly that they merged into one child, although the six heads remained. The boy grew up to become the warrior god *KARTTIKEYA*, or Skanda. According to another story, when Parvati first saw Karttikeya, she felt such maternal love for him that milk flowed from her breasts.

Another tale tells how Shiva criticized Parvati's dark skin, whereupon the goddess retired to the forest in shame and became an

ascetic. However, *BRAHMA* was so impressed by Parvati's austerities that he transformed her into Gauri, the golden-skinned goddess. In some versions of the story, Parvati's dark skin became the goddess *KALI*.

Shiva once turned Parvati into a fisherwoman to punish her disobedience. On another occasion, Parvati crept up behind Shiva and put her fingers over his eyes. Darkness enveloped the world, and so Shiva made a third eye appear in the middle of his forehead. (See also *MYTHICAL MOUNTAINS*; *THE MOTHER GODDESS*)

PATTINI

PATTINI is the most important Singhalese goddess. She is said to look after marriages and to keep epidemics at bay. According to one myth, she was born from a mango, which had been struck by a divine arrow. Another myth tells how she introduced the cultivation of rice into Sri Lanka.

THE PEY

THE PEY, according to the Tamils of southern India and Sri Lanka, are demons who drink the blood of the dead and of wounded warriors, and bring misery and bad luck to the living. They are wild creatures with tangled hair.

PRADYUMNA

PRADYUMNA, according to Hindu mythology, was the son of *KRISHNA*, the eighth *AVATAR* of *VISHNU*, and his wife Rukmuni. He is sometimes said to have been a reincarnation of *KAMA*, god of desire. When he was six days old, Pradyumna was kidnapped by a demon, Shambhara, who threw him into the sea. The infant was swallowed by a fish, which was later caught and brought to Shambhara's home. Pradyumna

PARVATI with her husband, Shiva, and children Karttikeya and Ganesha, in their home on Mount Kailasa, attended by Nandi, the bull. (MINIATURE, 18TH CENTURY.)

Prajapati then created night and day, the seasons, death, and people to relieve his loneliness.

The name Prajapati sometimes refers to a variety of gods, including INDRA, SOMA, SHIVA, GARUDA, KRISHNA and MANU. It is also the name given to ten sages from whom humanity is said to be descended, and to seven RISHIS, or seers. BRAHMA is sometimes attributed with myths that later became associated with Prajapati.

PRAJNA see HERUKA.

PRAJNAPARAMITA, according to Buddhist belief, is the deification of the *Prajnaparamita-sutra*, a sacred text in which GAUTAMA BUDDHA is said to have set out his teachings. According to tradition, the Buddha gave the text to the NAGAS until the time was ripe for it to be revealed to the faithful. The sutra is said to have been "restored" by the Buddhist philosopher Nagarjuna.

Prajnaparamita is thus regarded as an incarnation of the divine word. Her name means "Perfection of Insight" or "Wisdom that Reaches the Other Shore". In Tibet, the goddess is usually depicted coloured white or yellow, holding a lotus flower in one hand and the sacred text in the other.

PRITHIVI, a Vedic earth goddess, is sometimes said to be the mother of USHAS, the dawn, AGNI, the god of fire, and INDRA, the great war god. She is also the consort of Dyaus, the sky father of the Vedic religion. When giving birth to Indra, numerous portents warned the goddess that this particular son was destined to supplant the old order. As a result, she hid the child away. Prithivi is usually depicted in the form of a cow.

emerged from the fish, and Mayadevi, the mistress of the house, looked after him. The sage Narada, lord of the GANDHARVAS, told her who the child was. When Pradyumna became a young man, Mayadevi fell in love with him and told him the truth about his origins. Pradyumna then killed Shambhara and fled with Mayadevi to Krishna's palace.

PRAHLADA see AVATARS.

PRAJAPATI, according to Hindu mythology, is the lord or master of created beings. In the Hindu epic, the *Mahabharata*, he is the protector of the sexual organ. By his own powers, he produced numerous children including a daughter, USHAS, or "Dawn".

On one occasion, Prajapati attempted to commit incest with Ushas, whereupon she transformed herself into a gazelle or deer. Prajapati then took the form of a stag, whose seed gave rise to the first humans. In other versions of the myth, Prajapati succeeded in mating with Ushas when she appeared in numerous different animal forms. The couple thereby gave rise to all living creatures. Another myth tells how Prajapati rose weeping from the primordial waters. The tears that fell into the water became the earth, whereas those that the god wiped away became the sky and the air.

R

PURURAVAS see *APSARAS*.

PURUSHA was the primordial man or cosmic giant of Indian mythology. According to the ancient sacred hymns known as the *Rig Veda*, Purusha was three-quarters immortal and one-quarter mortal. From his mortal quarter, he released his wife, Viraj, and he was then born from her as a universal spirit. Purusha assumed the form of a giant with 1,000 thighs, 1,000 feet, 1,000 arms, 1,000 eyes, 1,000 faces and 1,000 heads.

In order that the world might be created, he offered himself up to be sacrificed. His head became the heavens, his navel, the atmosphere and his feet, the earth. The seasons came from his armpits, the earth from his feet, the sun from his eyes, and the moon from his mind. The gods and people of the brahman caste came from his mouth, and the wind was born from his breath. His arms became the kshatriyas, or warrior caste; his thighs became the vaishyas, or the traders and farmers; and his feet became the shudras, or servant class.

In the *Brahmanas* and the *Upanishads*, religious texts composed after the *Rig Veda*, Purusha was regarded as *PRAJAPATI*, the lord of created beings. His name is also used to denote the spiritual core of a person; in Buddhist texts, it is sometimes applied to the Buddha.

RADHA (above) and Krishna walking by the Yamuna river in the moonlight, having exchanged clothes. (ILLUSTRATION TO THE BHAGAVATA PURANA, KANGRA, C. 1820.)

PURUSHA (left) was the primal being of Indian mythology. He was sacrificed to create all living things.

RADHA, according to Hindu mythology, was the favourite gopi, or cowgirl, of *KRISHNA*, the eighth *AVATAR* of the great god *VISHNU*. She lived in Vrindavan, the village in northern India where Krishna was brought up. Radha is sometimes regarded as Krishna's wife, sometimes as his lover. According to one tale, she was married to Ayanagosha, a cowherd. When Ayanagosha heard of Radha's adultery, he went in search of the couple. However, Krishna assumed the form of a goddess, and they thereby escaped Ayanagosha's asleep with Rahula in her arms, feared he might wake them and so left them sleeping.

Rahula entered a Buddhist community at the age of seven and is regarded as the guardian of novices. He is one of the ten great disciples of the Buddha and was said to be "first in esoteric practices and in desire for instruction in the Law". He died before the Buddha. He is sometimes represented holding a fly whisk (swatter) and a scroll of scriptures, and is often accompanied by a deer or a disciple.

RAKSHASAS, according to Hindu belief, are semi-divine, usually evil-natured, spirits. They are able to assume any shape they choose. Whereas they tend to be good-natured and faithful towards one another, with outsiders they can be gluttonous, lustful and violent. They live in a magnificent city, designed by Vishvakarma, the architect of the gods. Harmless beings, such as the *YAKSHAS*, are rakshasas, as are numerous enemies of the gods, including demons who live in cemeteries and harass human beings.

According to one tradition, the rakshasas emerged from *BRAHMA*'s foot, whereas another tradition tells how they are descendants of *KASYAPA*, the great *RISHI*, or sage. In some texts, the rakshasas are described as the original inhabitants of India who were subjugated by the Aryans.

wrath. According to another tradition, Radha is an incarnation of *LAKSHMI*, the goddess of good fortune and wife of Vishnu. The goddess took the form of Radha in order that she might not be separated from her husband.

Radha's love for Krishna is seen as a symbol of the interplay between the individual soul and the divine. When Radha is apart from Krishna, she longs for his return, and Krishna likewise pines for Radha. Devotees of Krishna regard the human feeling of love and surrender as a means of achieving knowledge of and union with the divine.

RAHU see *AMRITA*.

RAHULA, whose name means "Fetter", was the son of *GAUTAMA BUDDHA* and the princess Yasodhara. He is usually said to have been born shortly before Gautama left his family to seek enlightenment, although he is sometimes said to have been born on the day of his father's enlightenment. According to the former version of the myth, Gautama crept into his wife's rooms to kiss her goodbye but, seeing her

RADHA (right) listens to her lover, Krishna, (left), entertaining her with his flute as she attends to her toilette. (MINIATURE, 18TH CENTURY.)

THE MOTHER GODDESS

DEVI, OR MAHADEVI ("THE GREAT GODDESS"), is a composite figure who includes various aspects of the female deity in a series of contrasting incarnations. In the earliest Indian cultures, the mother goddess was Shakti, the source of all energy in the universe, the creative force who brought fertility to the earth. Some of her manifestations were associated with natural forces, such as Ushas, the dawn, and Ganga, the river. Later she was subsumed in the patriarchal Hindu creation myth as the consort of Shiva. In this role she continued to appear in a variety of incarnations. Some were benign, such as Sati and Parvati, both of whom were loving and caring, but others were terrifying, such as the warrior goddesses Durga and Kali. Although she lost her autonomy in her new role as consort, she was still the creative force. While Shiva embodied potency, Shakti was the energy needed to release his power.

KALI (above), the "Black One", was the most terrifying aspect of the goddess Devi. She was portrayed as a black-skinned hag with pendulous breasts and a necklace of skulls or severed heads. Like Shiva, she had an all-seeing third eye in her forehead. Her male victims, made impotent without the goddess's activating energy, had no way of resisting her attack. (THE GODDESS BEHEADING A MAN, BUNDI, C. 1650.)

UMA (right) was an early form of the goddess Parvati, the shakti of Shiva. Uma was the consort of Chandrashekhara, an aspect of Shiva who was also called Umapati ("Uma's spouse"). She was the daughter of Himavat, the king of the Himalayas. In her fierce aspect as Uma Maheshvara, she fought with demons. (KHMER STATUE, 11TH CENTURY.)

PARVATI (above right), the wife of Shiva (above left), was a reincarnation of his first wife, Sati, who had immolated herself in shame when Shiva was not invited to her father Daksha's sacrifice. Shiva showed no interest in Parvati at first, objecting to her dark skin, but she won his love by enduring austerities. She became the personification of the loving wife and mother, domesticating Shiva, and they led an idyllic family life with their children Karttikeya (above centre) and Ganesha. (BRONZE SOMASKANDA GROUP, 16TH CENTURY.)

DURGA (left) the invincible warrior goddess, fought demons that threatened the world. She was the embodiment of the anger of the gods, whether of Shiva and Vishnu, or of Parvati. When Durga herself was angry, Kali emerged from her forehead. Durga fought the demon Mahisha in an epic battle, in which he transformed himself into a buffalo, a lion, an armed man and an elephant. Finally, Durga cut off Mahisha's head. (DURGA SLAYS MAHISHASURA, MANDI, C. 1750–60.)

KALI (right) set out to kill demons but could become so intoxicated with blood that she threatened the world as well. She vanquished the demon Raktabija, who was reproduced with every drop of his blood that touched the ground, by catching the drops in her huge mouth before they fell, and then sucking the demon dry. Inflamed by her feast, she began to dance wildly, and when Shiva tried to stop her, she danced on his body, nearly destroying the cosmos. (ILLUSTRATION BY J. HIGGINBOTHAM, 1864.)

RAMA (above) and his brothers getting married. Rama was married to Sita, regarded by devotees of Vishnu as the ideal woman. (KULU-MANDI, PAHARI SCHOOL, 1760–5.)

RAMA (left) and his half-brother, Lakshmana left Sita alone to hunt a golden deer planted in the forest by Ravana. Meanwhile, the demon captured Sita. (MUGHAL PAINTING, EARLY 17TH CENTURY.)

RAMA was an *AVATAR*, or incarnation, of *VISHNU*, the great Hindu deity known as the preserver of the universe. He is said to have been sent down to earth in order to overcome the powers of darkness as embodied by the evil demon *RAVANA*, king of *LANKA*. His life and exploits are immortalized in the Hindu epic, the *Ramayana*.

Rama probably originated as a folk hero and only gradually came to be regarded as an avatar of Vishnu. He was courageous and peace-loving, dutiful and virtuous. Devotees of Vishnu regard him as the ideal man and they regard his wife, *SITA*, as the ideal woman: chaste, faithful and devout.

Rama was said to be the son of King Dasaratha of Ayodhya. On his father's death, his stepmother Sumitra cheated him out of his inheritance and banished him into exile in the forest for 14 years. Although Rama advised his wife to stay in the palace, away from the hardships of forest life, Sita insisted on accompanying her husband: "With you it is heaven, away from you hell," she said. Once in the forest, Rama protected the sages who had their hermitages there. When Rama failed to respond to the advances of a horrible female demon, Surpanaka, she persuaded her brother, Ravana, to kidnap Sita. Ravana succeeded in abducting Sita and carried her off to the island of Lanka. Rama, mad with grief, went in search of his wife and succeeded in overcoming numerous demons, often with the help of the monkey god *HANUMAN*.

In order to reach Sita, Rama had to take his army across the sea. He asked the ocean for help and, when none was forthcoming, became so enraged that he shot his arrows at the waters in an attempt to dry them up. Nothing happened. Rama then fired an arrow tipped with a charm given to him by *BRAHMA*. Immediately, the sky grew dark, and all living creatures trembled with fear. Finally, the ocean spoke and explained that, though he was unable to halt the movements of his waters, he would support a bridge over which Rama's soldiers could cross. Soon, Hanuman's army of monkeys had built a bridge and the troops began to cross over to Lanka. Immediately, Rama and Ravana entered into a fearsome battle. Rama's army appeared to be winning when Ravana approached to attack Rama in person. Rama destroyed the demon's ten heads one after another, but new ones kept growing in their place. Finally, Rama fired an arrow which the sage *AGASTYA* had given to him. The arrow killed Ravana, then returned to Rama. The battle was won.

Despite Sita's innocence, she repulsed Rama, since her reputation had been stained by her long stay with Ravana. Sita despaired and threw herself on to a funeral pyre. *AGNI*, the fire god, rescued her from the flames. In another version of the story, Sita remained unharmed by the flames, thus publicly proving her innocence.

Rama regained his kingdom and ruled over it with wisdom, fairness and tenderness for 1,000 years. He finally returned to heaven where he was reunited with Vishnu. The

RAMA (far left) spurned the advances of the sister of the demon Ravana. In revenge, she persuaded Ravana to kidnap Rama's wife Sita. (ILLUSTRATION BY WARWICK GOBLE.)

RAMA (left) gives his ring to Hanuman for the monkey god to send to Sita. Hanuman is the courageous and ever-loyal supporter of Rama. (ILLUSTRATION BY WARWICK GOBLE.)

victory of Rama over Ravana continues to be celebrated annually in India at the festival of Dussehra. In northern India, his name refers to the supreme god. His attributes are a bow and arrows. (See also *THE AVATARS OF VISHNU*)

RATI see *KAMA*.

RATNASAMBHAVA is one of the *DHYANIBUDDHAS*, "Great Buddhas of Wisdom". He is the "Source of Secret Things" and "He Who is Born of the Jewel". In Tibet he is often shown embracing Mamaki, his *SHAKTI*. His element is fire, his heavenly quarter the south, and he is yellow in colour. His carriage is drawn by a pair of lions or a horse.

RAVANA was the demon king of *LANKA* whom *RAMA*, an *AVATAR* of the great god *VISHNU*, was sent down to earth to vanquish. He had ten heads and was said to be indestructible. In the Hindu epic, the *Ramayana*, he is portrayed as the embodiment of evil. According to one tradition, a high-ranking member of Vishnu's heaven committed a sin and was given the choice of two means to clear his name: he could either descend to earth and live out seven incarnations as a friend of Vishnu or three incarnations as the enemy of the god. The offender chose the latter option, believing that he would thereby return to heaven more quickly.

Ravana's first incarnation was as the demon king Hiranyakashipu. Such was his power that he

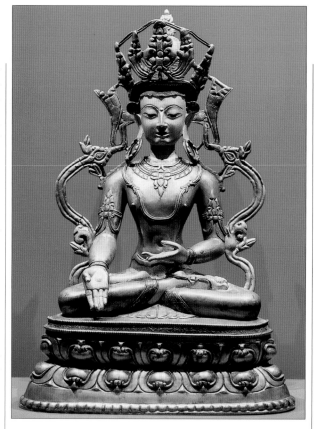

dethroned the mighty god *INDRA* and shut the gods out of heaven. He proclaimed himself king of the universe and ordered everyone to worship him. However, his son Prahlada persisted in worshipping Vishnu; try as he might, the demon king was unable to sway him from his vocation. Hiranyakashipu determined to kill Prahlada, but Vishnu protected him. Eventually, Vishnu destroyed the demon and Prahlada became king.

Ravana's second incarnation was as the enemy of Rama, another avatar of Vishnu. Ravana abducted

Vishnu's wife, *SITA*, and took her away to the island of Lanka. Helped by the monkey god *HANUMAN*, Rama found her there and made war against the demon, eventually killing him. On the eve of the great battle in which he was slain, the demon admitted that he had only kidnapped Sita in order that he might be killed and so go on to live out his third incarnation as a demon, after which he would be able to return to heaven.

In his third incarnation, Ravana appeared as the demon Sisupala. The son of a king, he had three eyes

and four arms. Although his parents were horrified at the sight of him, they were reassured by a voice which told them that, until the time of his death, Sisupala would be both famous and fortunate. The voice also announced that his mother would be able to recognize whoever it was that would eventually kill the boy: when the child sat on his knee, his third eye and extra arms would disappear.

The king and queen travelled from kingdom to kingdom, placing their son on the knee of each ruler, but nothing happened. When they returned home the young prince *KRISHNA*, the eighth avatar of Vishnu, visited the palace. As soon as Sisupala sat on Krishna's knee, his third eye vanished, and his extra two arms fell off. The queen then begged Krishna to forgive her child should he ever offend him. Krishna agreed that he would.

Years later, Sisupala attended a great sacrifice along with numerous important kings. Krishna was also present. The celebration was hosted by King Yudhishthira, who decided that the first homage should be paid to Krishna. Sisupala was outraged, saying that many of the guests present were more important than Krishna. Sisupala appealed to *BRAHMA* for advice, who simply said that Krishna himself should settle the dispute. Sisupala was furious and insulted Brahma, who proceeded to tell the guests the story of Sisupala and the predictions made about him at his birth. Sisupala became increasingly angry and, drawing his sword, continued to insult Brahma. Krishna's flaming disc then rose into the air, shot towards Sisupala and cut him in two. Sisupala's soul appeared as leaping fire and, moving towards Krishna, was absorbed into the hero's feet.

RAVANA (above left), the demon king of Lanka, is conquered by Rama, who rides away in triumph with his wife Sita.

RAVANA (above right) with Hanuman, the monkey god. When Ravana abducted Rama's wife Sita, Hanuman leapt across

the waters to the island of Lanka to discover where Ravana had hidden her. (ILLUSTRATIONS BY J. HIGGINBOTHAM, 1864.)

S

RIRAP LHUNPO see *MERU*.

RISHIS are usually regarded as the seers and great sages of Hinduism, but the term is also applied to saints and inspired poets. The Veda, the sacred knowledge of the Hindus, was said to have been revealed to the seven great rishis who preserved and transmitted it. The identity of these seven great rishis varies. According to the *Shatapatha Brahmana*, a commentary on the Veda, they were *GAUTAMA*, Bharadvaja, Vishvamitra, Janmadagni, Vasishtha, *KASYAPA* and Atri. The seven great rishis were sometimes regarded as holy beings who were identified with the seven stars of the Great Bear.

RUDRA appears in the *Rig Veda*, the great collection of ancient Indian hymns. His name means "Howler" or the "Red One". A god of storms and the dead, he was sometimes associated with the destructive aspect of the fire god *AGNI*. According to one myth, he emerged from the forehead of *BRAHMA* when the god became angry. Rudra fired his arrows of disease at gods, men and animals, but he also brought health and performed good deeds.

When *PRAJAPATI* committed incest with *USHAS*, the dawn, Rudra was about to shoot him when Prajapati promised to make

him lord of animals. In this role, Rudra was represented in the form of a bull. He gradually came to be seen as an increasingly dark god who developed into the destructive aspect of *SHIVA*. He is often regarded as the father of the *MARUTS*, companions of *INDRA*.

THE SA-DAG are the supernatural "Lords of the Soil" of the indigenous Bon religion of Tibet. They were assimilated into the Buddhist pantheon as protectors of the religion and are propitiated before any building work or farming is carried out.

SAMANTABHADRA is an emanation of the *DHYANIBUDDHA VAIROCANA*, and represents the Buddhist law and compassion. He is one of the most important *BODHISATTVAS* of Mahayana, or "Great Vehicle" Buddhism, and is worshipped as the protector of all those

SAMANTABHADRA, enthroned on a lotus, is mounted on his six-tusked white elephant, which also stands on lotus flowers. (EMEI, SICHUAN, CHINA.)

who teach the dharma, or law. Samantabhadra is often depicted together with *GAUTAMA BUDDHA* and *MANJUSHRI*, bodhisattva of wisdom. He is shown riding on a white elephant with six tusks, a symbol of the ability of wisdom to overcome all obstructions to enlightenment, including the six senses.

SAMVARA, or Chakra Samvara, is a god of initiation in Tantrism, a tradition that uses ritual practices as a path to enlightenment. One of the *YIDAMS* or tutelary gods of Tibet, he is depicted with 12 arms and four or five heads. He is associated with the buddha *AKSOBHYA*. In China, he is believed to be incarnated in the chief Tibetan Buddhist priest in Beijing. His *SHAKTI*, or corresponding female energy, is *VAJRAVARAHI*.

SANI see *AIRAVATA*.

SANJNA see *SURYA*.

SARASVATI is one of the three sacred rivers mentioned in the *Rig Veda*, a collection of ancient Hindu hymns. The Sarasvati is believed to

SAMVARA (above) in the posture of Yab-Yum with his shakti, wears a garland of heads and a crown of skulls. (BRASS AND COPPER, KASHMIR, 9TH CENTURY.)

flow underground to join the other two sacred rivers, the Ganges and the Yamuna, at Allahabad, a town in northern India where mass pilgrimages occur each year.

Sarasvati means "Watery"; as the river, she gives fertility and wisdom to the earth. In later times, Sarasvati became the wife and the creation of *BRAHMA*, the creator of the universe.

Sometimes identified with Vak, the goddess of eloquence, Sarasvati was herself the goddess of language, art and learning. She was sometimes called the "Mother of the Veda", the sacred texts of Hinduism, and was also credited with having invented the Sanskrit alphabet. Offerings are made to her by schoolchildren before classes.

Beautiful but temperamental, she was sometimes depicted with four arms and was represented riding on a swan or peacock, or sitting on a lotus. In some branches of

SARASVATI (right) with Brahma. Sarasvati was the creation and the wife of Brahma, the creator of the universe. (CHAPRA ILLUSTRATION, BIHAR, 1802.)

Buddhism, Sarasvati is the goddess of instruction and a companion of the *BODHISATTVA MANJUSHRI*. (See also *SACRED RIVERS*)

SATI see *DAKSHA*.

SESHA see *NAGAS*.

SHAKTI means "Force", "Power" or "Energy". In Buddhism, shaktis, who are female, embody the active energy of the male deities with whom they are often shown in a sexual embrace known as Yab-Yum. The five main shaktis correspond to the five male *DHYANIBUDDHAS*, or the "Great Buddhas of Wisdom": Vajradharisvari corresponds to *VAIROCANA*, Locana corresponds to *AKSOBHYA*, Mamaki corresponds to *RATNASAMBHAVA*, Pandara corresponds to *AMITABHA* and Tara to *AMOGHASIDDHI*. When in Yab-Yum, these shaktis may hold a cup made from a skull.

In Hinduism, Shakti is regarded as the creative force of *SHIVA* and is worshipped under many names, including *PARVATI*, Uma, *DURGA* and *KALI*. Shaktism is an aspect of Tantrism. Shaktas worship Shakti

and revere her as the life-force and the energy that maintains the universe. As a means towards experiencing the supreme reality, Shaktas use sexual practices, including those shown in the *Kamasutra*, the manual of erotic art. However, in some sects, these practices are meditated upon rather than actually performed.

SARASVATI, one of the three sacred rivers mentioned in the Rig Veda, *was also a beautiful but temperamental goddess, sometimes depicted with four arms and sitting on a lotus.*

SHAKUNTALA see *APSARAS*.

SHAMBHALA, according to Tibetan Buddhist mythology, is a mythical kingdom generally said to lie to the north-east of India, although it is also believed to be located in China and at the North Pole. It is claimed that the saviour of the world will appear from Shambhala when war and destruction threaten civilization. The Kalachakra teachings, a complex system of meditation, are also said to have arisen in Shambhala. According to tradition, a mythical

king Suchandra ruled over Shambhala and received the Kalachakra teachings from the Buddha in his 80th year. The king wrote the teachings down and passed them on through six further kings and 25 "Proclaimers". At the time of the 25th teacher, Rigden Pema Karpo, a golden age will dawn and Shambhala will become a universal kingdom.

SHENRAB MIWO see *GSHEN-RAB*.

SHITALA see *DURGA*.

SHIVA is one of the principal Hindu deities who, together with *VISHNU* and *BRAHMA*, forms the Trimurti, or triad of great gods. He is believed to have developed from *RUDRA*, a minor deity who appears in the *Rig Veda*, the collection of ancient Hindu hymns dating from between 1500 and 900BC. It seems that the god grew in stature after absorbing some of the characteristics of an ancient fertility god sometimes referred to as "proto-Shiva". Representations of this god, sitting in the position of a yogi and associated with animals and plants, have been ascribed to the Indus Valley culture, which dates from before 1500BC.

Shiva can be kind and protective, but he is also terrifying and is found in such places as battlefields and cremation grounds. He is often shown decorated with a string of skulls. Although he is a god of creation, he is also the god of time and thus the great destroyer. He is a fertility god, but he is also an ascetic who has conquered his desires and lives on Mount Kailasa in the high Himalayas, deep in the meditation which keeps the world in existence.

Although Shiva brings death, he also conquers death as well as disease and is invoked to cure sickness. He is sometimes depicted as half-male, half-female. The conflicting qualities and attributes found within the god are intended to symbolize a deity within whom all opposites are reconciled. Even Shiva's name, which means "Auspicious", is intended to reconcile and propitiate the dark aspect of his character, which caused him to be known as the "Destroyer".

As Nataraja, Shiva is the "Lord of the Dance", and is often depicted as such. He dances out the creation of the world, but when he grows tired he relapses into inactivity and the universe becomes chaotic. Destruction thus follows the period of creation. One myth about Shiva as Nataraja concerns the 10,000 *RISHIS*, or sages. Shiva visited the rishis in order to persuade them to become his devotees. The rishis responded by cursing Shiva and, when this had no effect, they sent a fearsome tiger to devour him. The great god simply removed the skin of the tiger with his fingernail and draped it around his neck like a shawl. The rishis then sent a snake to attack Shiva, who merely hung it around his neck as a garland. Finally, the rishis sent an evil dwarf armed with a club to attack the god, but Shiva responded by placing his foot on the dwarf's back and beginning to dance. The rishis watched the performance in wonder. Even the heavens opened so that the gods were able to look down at the astounding dance. Eventually, the rishis were no longer able to resist the dancing Shiva and threw themselves at his feet.

Shiva's principal symbolic representation is the lingam, a phallic shaped stone. One myth tells how the god visited a pine forest where some sages were meditating. The sages, not recognizing Shiva, suspected him of trying to seduce their wives and caused him to lose his phallus. Immediately, the world grew dark, and the sages lost their virility. Eventually, they made offerings to Shiva, and the world returned to normal.

Shiva is often shown with four arms and with a third eye, the eye of inner vision, in the middle of his forehead. He frequently has a serpent as a necklace, one around his waist and others wrapped around his arms. He may also be depicted smeared with ashes as a symbol of his asceticism. His throat is often coloured blue, and he is sometimes known as Nilakantha, or "Blue Throat", due to the important part he played in the myth of the churning of the ocean.

According to this popular tale, the great snake Vasuki was used as a rope with which to turn Mount Mandara and so churn the seas in order to produce AMRITA, the elixir of immortality. However, the snake became so exhausted that he eventually spewed out venom, which threatened to destroy all existence. Shiva came to the rescue by swallowing the poison, which stained his throat.

Shiva is the father of the elephant god GANESHA and the warrior god KARTTIKEYA. His mount is the bull NANDI. His consort or SHAKTI (female power) is called PARVATI in her gentle aspect.

SHIVA with the wives of the rishis, whose husbands feared he was trying to seduce them: an episode from the Puranas. *(PAHARI SCHOOL, 1710–25.)*

Her other aspects are called Uma, the gracious; Bhairavi, the terrible; Ambika, the generatrix; Sati, the good wife; Gauri, the brilliant; KALI, the black; and DURGA, the inaccessible.

One myth tells how Shiva gained his third eye as a result of a prank played by Parvati. While Shiva was meditating on Mount Kailasa, Parvati crept up behind him and covered his eyes with her hands. Immediately, the sun grew pale, and every living being trembled with fear. Suddenly, a burning eye appeared on Shiva's forehead, banishing the darkness. Flames shot out from the eye and set light to the whole of the Himalayas. Parvati was devastated and, in due course, Shiva was moved by her distress to restore the mountains to their former glory.

According to another myth, when Shiva was deep in meditation on Mount Kailasa, Parvati grew bored. She persuaded KAMA, god of

desire, to come to her aid. Kama was loathe to intervene, but Parvati insisted, whereupon Kama prepared to fire his arrow at Shiva's heart in order to remind him of his duties to his wife. The god Mahesvara saw what was about to happen; since it was necessary for Shiva to finish his meditation in order for the cycles of creation to

SHIVA, as Nataraja, dances holding a drum, symbolizing the rhythm of creation, and a flame, symbolizing destruction.

run their course, he struck Kama down with a thunderbolt. Later, however, Mahesvara brought Kama back to life.

In another version of the myth, Shiva destroyed Kama with a flash of his third eye. Parvati retired from life, having become tired of Shiva's lack of interest in her. One day she was visited by a young man who, while praising her for her asceticism, tried to persuade her to give it up. Parvati grew angry, and eventually the man revealed himself to be none other than Shiva.

The god promised his wife that he would demonstrate his love to her, but Parvati demanded that he should first return Kama to his wife. Shiva did as she requested, and the couple then retired into the mountains. The intensity of their love-making shook the whole world.

DHYANIBUDDHAS

IVE GREAT MYSTIC BUDDHAS appear together in the "Mandala of the Five Jinas", and are therefore known collectively as Dhyanibuddhas, or "Meditation Buddhas". They are said to have arisen from the Adibuddha, or "Primeval Buddha". Jinas, or spiritual conquerors, are those who have overcome the perpetual cycle of rebirth and human suffering. As subjects for meditation, they each represent a different aspect of the enlightened consciousness.

Mandala is the Sanskrit word for a circle: a mandala is both a symbolic picture of the universe and an aid to meditation, helping the onlooker to achieve different states of mind. For ritual purposes, the mandala is traced on the ground using coloured powders which are brushed away afterwards. It may also be a picture or a three-dimensional object, such as a sculpture or even a building. Mandalas can also be visualized during meditation – they do not have to exist physically.

AMITABHA reigns in the western paradise of Sukhavati, or "Pure Land". Once a king, the buddha renounced his throne and vowed to create a realm which combined all the perfections of existing lands. As its ruler, he devoted himself to good deeds and eventually became a buddha. Sitting on his lotus, his aura is bigger than a billion worlds and he has 84,000 marks of his virtues. Rebirth in Pure Land leads to the attainment of nirvana without difficulty. (TIBETAN PAINTING.)

AMOGHASIDDHI (right) rules the paradise of the north, seated on a throne flanked by a pair of garudas, or mythical birds with human heads, on which he travels. He is coloured green, and his hand is traditionally raised in a posture meaning "Fear not". His emblem is the Vajra, the thunderbolt, an indestructible weapon, as hard as a diamond. (TIBETAN PAINTING, 15TH CENTURY.)

AKSOBHYA (above), the "Immovable", was a monk who took an oath that he would never again feel anger or revulsion. His adherence to his vow eventually resulted in his attainment of enlightenment. He is the buddha of the eastern paradise, Abhirati, where the virtuous are reborn into a land without evil or suffering and where they can quickly achieve nirvana. He touches the earth with his hand to symbolize his enlightenment. (LOTUS MANDALA WITH AKSOBHYA, 12TH CENTURY.)

VAIROCANA (left) is the oldest of the Dhyanibuddhas. His name means "Coming from the Sun", and he was at one time identified with the Adibuddha. He is often depicted clasping his hands in the gesture of supreme wisdom. The great monument of Borobodur, in Java, is itself a mandala, designed in concentric circles and squares with four open entrances. A long series of stone reliefs depicting the Buddha's life story is designed to aid meditation. (RELIEF OF BUDDHA MAHAVAIROCANA AT BOROBODUR, JAVA, 9TH CENTURY.)

THE MANDALA (left) has a fixed, symbolic format. It has an outer ring of flames, protecting the area within, and burning away the impurities of the onlooker. A ring of Vajras indicates the indestructability of enlightenment, and lotus petals show the nature of the Pure Land. Within the circles is a palace, with four walls and four open gates, symbolizing the whole world. At the centre sits a presiding deity, with whom the meditator attempts to identify. (SAMVARA MANDALA, TIBET.)

405

SITA (left) and Lakshmana, Rama's half-brother, watch the monkey god Hanuman worshipping Rama.

SITA (right) finds Rama among the lotus blooms. (PAINTING BY WARWICK GOBLE.)

throwing herself on to a funeral pyre, which left her unscathed. The goddess is believed to embody all the virtues of an ideal wife: chaste and devout.

SKANDA see *KARTTIKEYA.*

SOMA, according to Hindu mythology, is the vital life force in all living beings. A plant, as well as the state of ecstasy induced by the sacred drink extracted from the plant, it played a central role in Vedic sacrificial rituals.

Soma was regarded as a deity, and one entire book of the ten that comprise the *Rig Veda*, the sacred Hindu hymns, is devoted to his glory. After swallowing the juice, the war god *INDRA* grew so vast that he filled heaven and earth. It was said to be the power of Soma that enabled Indra to overcome the monstrous snake *VRITRA* and to make the sun rise. In due course, Soma developed into the moon god. The source of water, he was associated with fertility and the powers of creation.

Sometimes regarded as the father of the gods, Soma was married to the daughters of *DAKSHA*, a lord of creation. One myth tells how Daksha believed that Soma was showing one of his daughters preference over the others, and so sentenced the moon to death by consumption. However, Daksha's other daughters intervened, causing Soma's punishment to be only periodic rather than eternal. According to another traditional myth, the waxing and waning of the moon is due to the gods'

SITA before Rama – her husband and an incarnation of Vishnu. Lakshmana waves a fan. (ILLUSTRATION BY J. HIGGINBOTHAM, 1864.)

gradual consumption of the Soma it contains. Soma is the equivalent of the ancient Iranian Haoma. Soma can appear as either a bull or a bird.

SUDAPANI see *DHANVANTARI.*

SUMERU see *MERU.*

SURABHI see *AMRITA.*

SURYA, the sun god, was one of the most important deities in the Veda, the sacred knowledge of the Hindus. His father was either the sky god Dyaus or the warrior god *INDRA*.

Sometimes, however, Surya is said to form a trinity with Indra and the fire god *AGNI*, who are regarded as his brothers. His mother is *ADITI*, the mother goddess. According to the *Rig Veda*, the sacred Hindu hymns, Aditi had eight sons known as the *ADITYAS*. She threw one of her offspring, the sun, away from her, possibly because she did not want to be associated with its burning heat. Another myth tells how Surya arose from the eye of a great giant, *PURUSHA*.

Surya has golden hair and golden arms, although sometimes he is represented as dark red in colour. His chariot is drawn by a team of horses and he holds a lotus flower in his hands. His symbol is

---

SHRI see *LAKSHMI.*

SISUPALA see *RAVANA.*

SITA appears in the Veda, the sacred knowledge of the Hindus, as a goddess who rules over agriculture and vegetation and is the wife of the war god *INDRA*. However, according to the Hindu epic, the *Ramayana*, she is the wife of *RAMA*, an *AVATAR* of the great god *VISHNU*, and the daughter of King Janaka.

Rama won Sita as his wife after proving his worth by stringing a miraculous bow, which the god *SHIVA* had given to the king. *RAVANA*, the demon king of *LANKA*, later abducted Sita and took her to his kingdom.

According to one version of the myth, when Rama finally reclaimed his wife, he suspected her of having committed adultery with the demon. Sita proved her innocence and was immediately swallowed by the earth, her mother. Shortly afterwards, Rama drowned. In another version of the traditional tale, Sita demonstrated her innocence by the swastika, which was widely used throughout the ancient world as a symbol of the sun.

Surya's scorching heat was so intense that his wife Sanjna became exhausted and left him. Before abandoning the god, she persuaded her handmaid to take her place. Surya went in search of Sanjna and found her in the forest in the form of a mare. The god transformed himself into a horse, and the couple produced the warrior Revanta and the two ASVINS. The Asvins are golden youths who act as messengers of the dawn.

Eventually, Sanjna's father cut off some of Surya's brightness so that Sanjna was able to bear his heat. Surya's shavings fell to earth, where they were made into weapons for the gods.

In the *Brahmapuranas*, sacred writings dating from the fourth century AD, Surya is attributed with 12 "splendours" and given 12 names of distinct deities including INDRA, VISHNU, VARUNA and MITRA. Surya himself is said to be "the supreme spirit who, by means of these splendours, permeates the universe and radiates as far as the secret soul of men."

SURYA (left), the sun god in Hindu mythology. (LIMESTONE VOTIVE IMAGE FROM THE SUN TEMPLE AT KONARAK, ORISSA, 11TH CENTURY.)

SURYA (below), the Hindu sun god, drives his chariot across the sky. (ILLUSTRATION BY J. HIGGINBOTHAM, 1864.)

T

TAKSHAKA, according to Hindu mythology, was king of the *NAGAS*, the semi-divine serpents. He ruled over a glorious city in the underworld. One myth tells how King Parikchit, when out hunting, mistakenly insulted a hermit who had taken a vow of silence. The hermit's son cursed the king, saying that within a week the snake Takshaka would burn and kill him with his poison. The king decided to protect himself by building a palace on top of a column in the middle of a lake. Takshaka transformed an army of serpents into monks and sent them to the king with gifts. Among the gifts, the king found a strange insect. He was so relieved that Takshaka had spared him that he boasted to his courtiers that, having no fear of death, he dared to put the insect on his neck. Immediately, the insect turned into Takshaka. The serpent bound the king in his massive coils and uttered a tremendous roar, whereupon the king's courtiers burst into tears and fled. Meanwhile,

Takshaka rose high into the air, king Parikchit fell down dead, and his palace burst into flames.

According to another tale, Takshaka coveted some beautiful jewels, which belonged to the queen, wife of King Parikchit's son. The queen decided to give the jewels to the wife of a tutor and asked Utanka, one of the tutor's students, to take them to her. On the journey, Utanka stopped to wash. Immediately, a beggar stole the jewels and ran off with them. Utanka pursued the beggar, but when he finally caught hold of him, the man turned into the serpent Takshaka, slid into a hole in the ground, and hid in his palace.

The god *INDRA* saw Utanka's distress and sent a thunderbolt down to earth. The bolt split the ground open, allowing Utanka to continue pursuing the thief. Beneath the earth, Utanka discovered a glorious kingdom filled with beautiful palaces and temples. He chanted a hymn of praise to the nagas, but the snakes remained

TARA (above) as the Green Tara, is regarded as the saviour of Tibet, and holds the blue lotus of compassion in each hand. (MONGOLIA, 19TH CENTURY.)

unmoved. Utanka then began to praise Indra. Flattered, Indra again offered to help the student, whose horse burst into flames and engulfed the nagas' kingdom in smoke. Terrified, Takshaka returned the jewels to Utanka. At long last, riding Indra's horse, Utanka arrived at the appointed place to deliver the jewels to his tutor's wife.

TARA is one of Tibetan Buddhism's most popular deities. Her name means both "She Who Delivers" and "Star". She is regarded as an emanation of the *BODHISATTVA AVALOKITESHVARA* and is said to have been born from a lotus floating in one of his tears in order to help him in his work. According to another account, Tara was born in a beam of blue light

TARA (left), in her white form, is the symbol of transcendent knowledge.

TARA (right), the patron goddess of Tibet, has 21 forms, including that of the Green Tara, who embodies the feminine aspect of compassion.

which shone from one of Avalokiteshvara's eyes. She embodies the feminine aspect of compassion and incorporates the essence of the goddess. As a result, her name is sometimes applied to other female deities.

The earliest representations of the goddess date from the sixth century AD, when Tara came to be regarded as the *SHAKTI*, or sometimes the wife, of Avalokiteshvara. In Tibet, where her cult spread widely in the 11th century, it was said that the goddess was reincarnated in every virtuous woman. Since then she has been worshipped widely as a personal deity. There are 21 different forms of Tara, each of which has its own colour, posture and attributes, and they all can appear to be either peaceful or wrathful.

The most common forms are Green Tara and White Tara. In Tibet, the White Tara is often said to be a form of the Green Tara. She is believed to be a form of *SARASVATI*, the wife of *BRAHMA*. The Green Tara, said to be the original Tara, holds a blue lotus in each hand to signify her compassion. The consorts of the seventh-century Tibetan king Songtsen Gampo are said to have been embodiments of these two Taras. When red, yellow or blue, Tara is said to be in a menacing mood, whereas when green or white she is said to be gentle and loving. Tibetan Buddhists believe that their ancestors are

Avalokiteshvara in the form of a monkey and Tara (sGrol-ma) in the form of a rock ogress.

TATHAGATAS see *THE DHYANI-BUDDHAS*.

THE TIRTHANKARAS are the ancient "Ford-makers" of Jainism, who taught the Jain doctrine. These leaders, through their own ascetic observances, succeeded in finding a way of escaping the continual round of death and rebirth, and were thus able to show others the path to enlightenment.

According to Jain belief, there are ten regions of the universe, in each of which 24 tirthankaras appear in each of the three ages – past, present and future. Since Jains do not believe in a creator god, their mythology concentrates on the figures of these tirthankaras, who have become objects of worship. Tirthankaras are usually depicted naked, each with his own characteristic colour and posture, but otherwise identical.

In the current age, the first tirthankara was Rishabha, who is usually said to be the founder of Jainism. At his birth, the great warrior god *INDRA* appeared in order to welcome the child into the world. Rishabha taught human beings how to cultivate the land, how to ply different trades and how to execute the arts. He also organized people into three castes. He then left worldly affairs and became a monk. After meditating for six months, Rishabha achieved enlightenment and finally entered nirvana. 21 tirthankaras followed Rishabha, ending with Neminatha, a cousin of *KRISHNA*.

The twenty-third tirthankara, Parshva, appeared 84,000 years after Neminatha's death. Before being born, Parshva lived in heaven as the god Indra. In order to descend to earth, he entered the womb of Queen Vama. As a child, Parshva disdained worldly life and finally withdrew to live in the forest

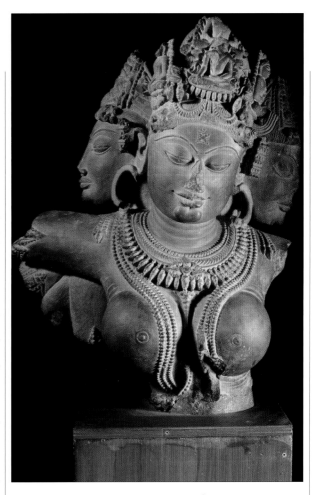

as a recluse. Eventually, he learned how to achieve liberation from the world and from then onwards he passed on his knowledge to his followers. When he died, at the age of 100, his soul entered nirvana. His death occurred 246 years before the birth of Mahavira, the twenty-fourth Tirthankara.

Mahavira, or the "Great Hero" was also known as Vardhamana. One night, he entered the womb of Devananda, the wife of a brahman. That same night, Devananda saw 14 apparitions, all of favourable omen – an elephant, a bull, a lion, the goddess Shri, or *LAKSHMI*, a garland, the moon, the sun, a standard, a vase, a lake of lotuses, the ocean, a heavenly dwelling, a heap of jewels and a flame.

Devananda's husband was delighted by this omen, as he felt sure it meant that he would father a wise and learned son. However, the

THE TIRTHANKARA Malli, the nineteenth, was a woman according to one Jain tradition. Tirthankaras are portrayed with downcast eyes, to indicate their detachment. (CHAUHAN SCULPTURE, 11TH CENTURY.)

king of the gods decided that he would prefer Trisala, the wife of Siddhartha, a kshatriya (member of the warrior caste) to bear the child, and so the embryo was transferred. Trisala also witnessed 14 splendid apparitions before the birth.

When Mahavira was born, the gods rejoiced and the demons threw gifts. As a youth, Mahavira married Yasoda, but at the age of 30, he gave away his wealth and withdrew from the world. After 12 years of austerity, he achieved enlightenment. When Mahavira died, his soul ascended to nirvana. Jainism still requires its followers to practise austerity for at least 12 years.

V

TRANSCENDENT BUDDHAS
see *DHYANIBUDDHAS*.

TUSHITA is the Buddhist heaven inhabited by contented or joyful gods. It is home to all the buddhas who need to be born on earth only once more, and is thus the abode of *MAITREYA*, the future buddha. Before his final incarnation, *GAUTAMA BUDDHA* lived in the Tushita heaven as a *BODHISATTVA*. From there, he descended to earth to enter the right side of Queen *MAYA*, his mother. In the Tushita heaven, one day corresponds to 400 years of human life.

UPULVAN is the highest of the four great gods in the Singhalese pantheon. His name means the "Water-lily Coloured One". He is said to have been the only god who remained faithful to *GAUTAMA BUDDHA* during his battle with the demon *MARA*.

URVASI see *APSARAS*.

USHA see *ANIRUDDHA*.

USHAS, the dawn, is the daughter of *PRITHIVI*, the earth goddess of Hindu mythology. Her father is usually said to be the sky god Dyaus and her lover *SURYA*, the sun god. Sometimes, however, the fire god *AGNI* is regarded as her lover, and she herself is said to be the mother of the sun. According to another tradition, Ushas was the daughter of *PRAJAPATI*, the lord or master of created beings. When the god attempted to commit incest with her, Ushas turned into a deer in order to escape his advances.

Ushas is the bringer of life in all its richness. She drives away the dark but is the source of aging. She herself is born each morning, yet because she exists for ever, she is regarded as old. It is said that through the light provided by Ushas, human beings can find their way towards the truth. Each morning, like a good housewife, she

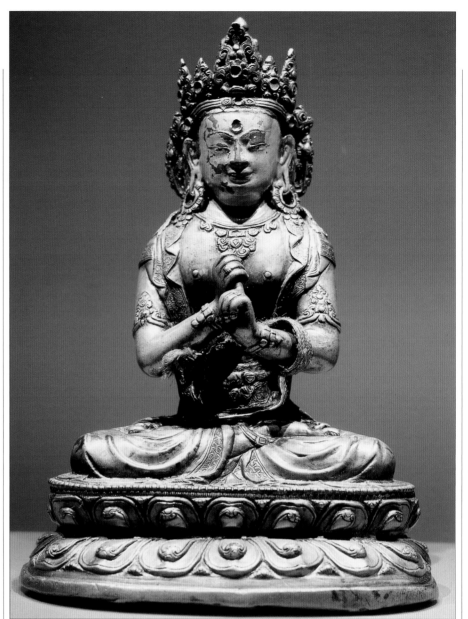

wakes all living beings and directs them towards their work. The gods implore her to leave the wicked asleep and wake only the good. In the *Rig Veda*, the ancient sacred hymns, Ushas is depicted as a bride dressed in rose-coloured garments and a golden veil. She is sometimes described as a dancing girl, covered with jewels, or as a beautiful young woman who is stepping out of her bath. The goddess drives a carriage pulled by rosy-hued cows or horses, who represent the morning clouds.

VAIROCANA, according to Hindu mythology, was an *ASURA*, the son of Prahlada, who became king of the *DAITYAS*. He was the father of Bali, who was overcome by *VISHNU* in his incarnation as a dwarf.

One account tells how, together with *INDRA*, Vairocana attempted to discover Atman, or the "Self". The gods sent Indra and Vairocana to ask *PRAJAPATI* to help them in their quest, whereupon Prajapati told them, "That which is reflected in the eye, that is the Self." Vairocana

VAIROCANA is the principal of the five Dhyanibuddhas, or "Great Buddhas of Wisdom". (TIBET, 15TH CENTURY.)

and Indra then asked whether that which was reflected in the water was the Self. Prajapati confirmed their suspicion and told them to look at themselves in the water. He added that they should let him know if there was anything they failed to understand. Vairocana decided that he now knew the Self, and returned to the asuras. Indra looked at himself in the water but was troubled by numerous questions which he put to Prajapati. Eventually, Indra achieved absolute certainty about the Self and became fully enlightened.

Vairocana appears in Buddhist teaching as the principal of the five DHYANIBUDDHAS, or the "Great Buddhas of Wisdom". He is said to be the personification of the "Absolute" and is sometimes regarded as a type of ADIBUDDHA, or primordial Buddha. In Tibet, the snow lion is regarded as Vairocana's mount. His colour is white, and he is often shown holding a disc. Vairocana is sometimes said to have introduced humankind to the Yogacara school of Mahayana, or "Great Vehicle" Buddhism, which teaches that everything is "mind only" and that the disciple's aim is to achieve mystical union with the divine. (See also DHYANIBUDDHAS)

VAISHRAVANA see GUARDIAN KINGS.

THE VAJRA, or Vajrakila, is a deified spike, sometimes known as a "Thunderbolt Sceptre", which is believed to embody a powerful god and is said to be capable of dispelling evil forces. It is mainly employed by Tantric Buddhists in Tibet. The Vajra originated in India, where the thunderbolt sceptre is the favourite weapon of INDRA.

VAJRAVARAHI is regarded as an important Buddhist deity in both Tibet and Nepal. Her name means "Diamond Sow", and she is represented with the head of a pig. Her attributes are a thunderbolt, a skull and a club.

VAMANA see AVATARS.

VARAHA see AVATARS.

VARUNA appears in the *Rig Veda*, an ancient collection of sacred Hindu hymns, as a sky god. He symbolized the heavens and lived in his palace high above the realm in which INDRA operated. In one sense, then, he was more important than Indra, but because he was more remote, the part he played was of less consequence. He could see everything going on in the world and surveyed the affairs of human beings, reading their secret thoughts and sending his messengers out to oversee their activities. Varuna was omnipresent and knew both the past and the future. Above all, he was concerned with the moral order. He presided over oaths and he initiated and sustained the *rta* or order, which was believed to govern both nature and society, and which human beings had to obey. Those who failed to follow the *rta* would be bound with Varuna's noose. However, the god had a reputation for gentleness and could undo sin easily. Varuna was sometimes said to have created the sun; at other times, the sun was said to be his eye. Later, he came to be seen as lord of the night and as the god of water, ruler of the rivers and seas. The wind was his breath,

VARUNA (left) was represented riding a sea monster and holding the noose he used to bind the disobedient. (STONE, 8TH CENTURY.)

THE VAJRA, or "Thunderbolt Sceptre", is carried by the god Indra, the Hindu god of weather, mounted on Airavata.

and the stars his eyes. He was linked with the moon, and presided over the care of SOMA, the sacred drink. He also shared with YAMA, the first person who died, the title of "King of the Dead". Sometimes regarded as one of the ADITYAS and the twin brother of MITRA, Varuna is also known as "King of the Snakes".

VASUDEV see KRISHNA.

VASUKI see NAGAS.

VAYU appears in the *Veda*. He is god of the winds and sometimes shares a chariot with INDRA. He is said to have been born from the breath of PURUSHA, the original being or world giant.

According to one myth, Vayu was responsible for creating the island of LANKA, now known as Sri Lanka. Narada, a sage or RISHI, challenged Vayu, who was known for his unstable temper, to break off the summit of Mount MERU. GARUDA, the mythical bird, protected the mountain, but one day, in the bird's absence, Vayu succeeded in his efforts. He immediately threw the mountain peak into the sea where it became the island of Lanka.

THE LIFE OF THE BUDDHA

BEFORE HE ACHIEVED enlightenment, the Buddha had lived through a long series of existences as a bodhisattva, striving to be generous and moral, to shun possessions and to gain insight. He was eventually reborn in the Tushita heaven, the domain of those who need be born only once more, where he prepared

for his final miraculous birth as Siddharta Gautama. King Snddhodana, his father, had been told in a prophecy that if his son were to be king, he must be prevented from seeing the miseries of life. So, Siddharta enjoyed a splendid and carefree life in three

palaces, surrounded by guards to stop him from looking out. He married Yasodhara and had a son, Rahula. But at about the age of 30, he ventured out of his palaces and encountered the "Four Sights": old age, disease, death and an ascetic looking for a way to transcend suffering. Siddharta resolved to do the same and left his royal existence behind.

QUEEN MAYA *(above), the Buddha's mother, dreamed on the night of his conception that an elephant laid a lotus blossom in her womb while the whole of nature shook with joy. At his birth, the Buddha emerged from his mother's side while she rested by a tree in a garden. He began to walk immediately, and lotus flowers sprang up each time his feet touched the ground. With seven symbolic steps, one in each of the cardinal directions, he took possession of the world and declared that there would be no more rebirth for him. (SCENES FROM BUDDHA'S LIFE BY MULGANDHA VIGARA.)*

GAUTAMA BUDDHA *(left), having left behind his early life of absolute luxury, endured six years of strict austerities which reduced him to little more than a skeleton. Eventually, however, he realized that this way of life would do nothing to end human suffering and that he needed to achieve a middle way. On the bank of the river Nairanjana, a woman called Sujata mistook him for a god and made him an offering of rice milk, which he accepted. Knowing now that his enlightenment was near, he divided the milk into 49 mouthfuls, one for each day he would spend in contemplation, striving to see things as they really are. (FROM A PAINTING BY ABANINDRO NATH TAGORE.)*

YAMA with his shakti, Yami, goddess of death. They stand in the posture of Yab-Yum on Yama's attendant animal, a black buffalo. Yama is a guardian of the south, the direction associated with the dead.

YAMANTAKA, or "He Who Puts an End to Yama", is one of Buddhism's *VIDYARAJAS*, or kings of mystical knowledge. He conquers *YAMA*, god of the dead, and is sometimes shown trampling him. A wrathful manifestation of the buddha *AKSOBHYA*, he is one of the *BODHISATTVAS* who welcome the faithful into Aksobhya's paradise. He is also regarded as a *DHARMAPALA*, or "Protector of the Teaching", and is said to fight pain.

Yamantaka is often shown with six arms and legs as well as six horribly contorted faces, each with three eyes. He is usually represented seated on a white cow, although he sometimes rests on a rock. His body is coloured black, dark blue or green, and he is surrounded by flames. In Tibet, he is sometimes shown holding an axe and a skull, and he may wear a tiara of skulls, a belt of skulls and carry a human corpse.

YAMI; YAMUNA see *YAMA*.

YASHODA see *KRISHNA*.

THE YIDAMS are the tutelary deities of Tibet. There are numerous yidams since each deity in the Tibetan pantheon can be adopted

YAMANTAKA is a wrathful guardian deity of Tibetan Buddhism, depicted in the posture of embrace, or Yab-Yum, with his shakti, Vidyadhara.

as a tutelary god. Their name means "Firm Mind". The yidams are invoked by people for protection, but they are more usually regarded as deities who can help in an individual's transformation. They are nearly always depicted with their *SHAKTI*, their corresponding female energies, and are usually coloured blue. The male yidams are divided into bhagavats, dakas and herukas, whereas the female yidams are divided into bhagavatis and *DAKINIS*.

THE YUGAS are Hinduism's cycles, or ages of the world. Each yuga lasts for thousands, even millions, of years.

The yugas decline in length through the cycle, reflecting the decline in righteousness. The Krita Yuga, lasting 1,728,000 human years, was the golden age, when there were no gods, demons or diseases and when human beings were saints. The Treta Yuga lasted 1,296,000 years and was the age when sacrifices began and people became less virtuous. The Dwapara Yuga was a decadent age, lasting 864,000 years, when virtue lessened even more and desire, disease and disasters entered the world. The Kali Yuga, 432,000 years long, is the degenerate age, when only a quarter of virtue remains and people have sunk into wickedness. The Kali Yuga is the age in which we are currently living.

More than four million human years make up a Maha Yuga, or great age, and one Maha Yuga equals a day and a night in the life of Brahma. Each Maha Yuga is preceded and followed by periods of twilight, which last a tenth of the length of a Maha Yuga. During this time, *BRAHMA* sleeps.

ZHANG ZHUNG see *GSHEN-RAB*.

417

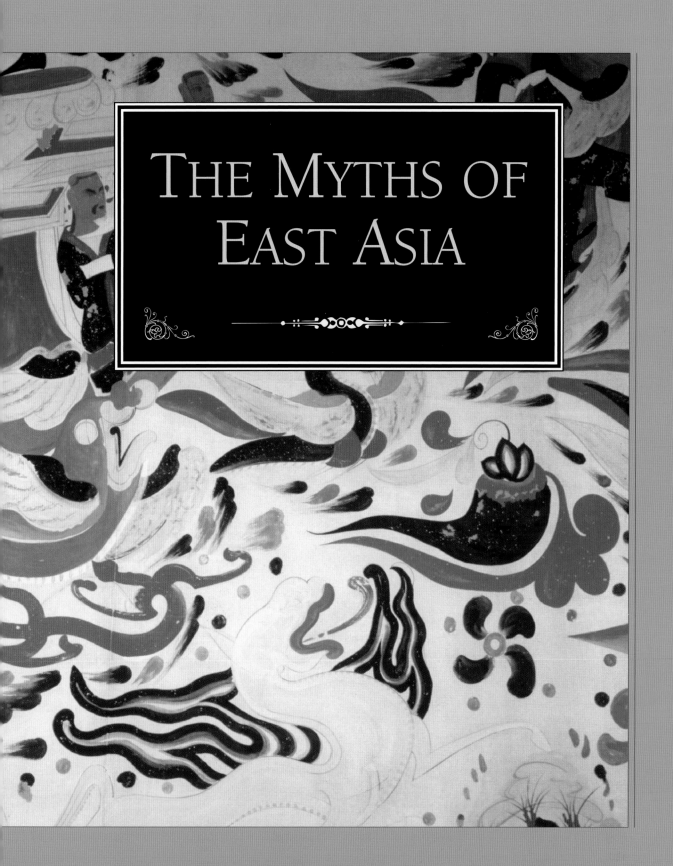

THE MYTHS OF EAST ASIA

INTRODUCTION

THE GREAT WORLD religions founded in West and Central Asia gradually spread eastwards until they encountered the gods and goddesses of the Far East. To a greater or lesser extent, Hinduism, Buddhism and Islam all influenced the indigenous beliefs of East and South-east Asia. However, the host countries tended to make the encroaching deities their own, embracing them within their own mythologies by a process of adaptation and assimilation.

China, the so-called "Mother Civilization of East Asia", did not view the incoming gods and goddesses as a threat. The immensely stable structure of Chinese society meant that, rather than feeling threatened by outside beliefs, the Chinese were able to modify and absorb outside influences while maintaining their own culture.

China has its origins in the second millennium BC, when the Shang kings founded a state which formed the basis for all subsequent development. During the ancient Shang dynasty, ancestor worship was already in evidence, and numerous gods were also venerated, including the great Shang Di. Worshipped as the ancestor of the dynasty, Shang Di came to have an important role in Chinese religious thought. The Zhou invaders, who overthrew the Shang dynasty in about 1050BC, worshipped a deity known as Tian, or "Heaven".

In the sixth century BC, Confucianism emerged, although it was not until the Han dynasty (206BC–AD220) that it became the philosophy of the state. Founded by Master Kong (551–479BC), Confucianism propounded a belief in a highly structured society and stressed the importance of the bonds of family life. Master Kong remained, however, noncommittal about the existence of supernatural beings.

Whereas Confucianism drew its adherents from all social classes, Daoism, which emerged at about the same time, tended to appeal to the underprivileged. Daoists seek out the Dao, or "Way", a type of divine

BUDDHA was widely venerated in China, especially during the Tang dynasty between the seventh and ninth centuries AD. Buddhism offered a consoling message about the transience of suffering and the possibility of eventual salvation. (BUDDHA PREACHING, BANNER FROM DUNUANG CAVES, CHINA, 8TH CENTURY AD.)

EAST ASIA

SIBERIA

Oikhon Is.

Lake Baikal

MONGOLIA

Mt. Kunlun

R. Yellow

CHINA

R. Yangtze

KOREA

Sea of Japan

JAPAN

Yellow Sea

East China Sea

Pacific Ocean

INDIA

BURMA

LAOS

VIETNAM

South China Sea

Luzon

THAILAND

CAMBODIA

PHILIPPINES

Mindanao

MALAYSIA

Celebes Sea

Indian Ocean

Sumatra

Borneo

INDONESIA

Java

Bali

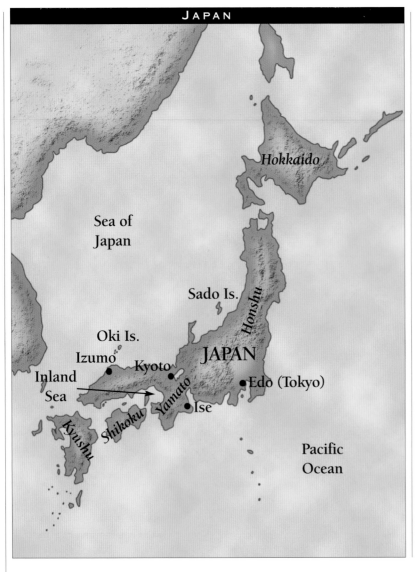

JAPAN

Hokkaido

Sea of Japan

Sado Is.

Honshu

Oki Is.

Izumo

JAPAN

Inland Sea

Kyoto

Yamato

Edo (Tokyo)

Shikoku

Ise

Kyushu

Pacific Ocean

principle underlying nature. Its followers aim to achieve harmony with the principle by stilling and emptying the mind. During the first millennium AD, Daoism developed an elaborate pantheon of gods and goddesses. Its principal deity was the "Jade Emperor", whose heaven, modelled on that of the earthly emperor, contained numerous ministries and officials.

Around the beginning of the Christian era, Buddhism entered China, introduced by Buddhist monks travelling along the ancient trade route, known as the Silk Road, from India and Central Asia. It was a peaceful invasion, since Buddhism did not feel it necessary to reject the gods and spirits of popular religion, provided that people realized that only the Buddha could offer true salvation. What made the incursion of Buddhism even smoother was the fact that the incoming religion had similarities with Daoism: both Buddhism and Daoism aimed to control mental processes. As a result, there came to be an interplay between the two faiths after Buddhism's arrival in China.

China had a widespread cultural influence on its neighbouring countries, including Japan. Shinto, the early religion of Japan, took

YU HUANG (below), the "Jade Emperor", was the chief deity of the Daoist pantheon. His supremacy in heaven mirrored that of the emperor on earth, with whom he was said to correspond directly. (CHINESE WALL PAINTING, C. 1325.)

CONFUCIUS is known in the West by the Latin rendering of his name, Kong Fuzi. Benevolence was central to his doctrine, which was adopted by the state during the Han dynasty. (CHINESE DRAWING.)

much of its cosmology, including that of an egg-shaped cosmos, from Chinese sources. However, whereas the Chinese regarded their "Jade Emperor" as a reflection of the earthly emperor, the Japanese claimed that the members of the imperial family were descended from their chief deity, the sun goddess Amaterasu, giving them a divine right to govern. In the sixth century AD, Buddhism entered Japan, spreading from China and Korea. Japan adopted Buddhism and used it to complement Shintoism, so that it still remains unclear whether some deities are Shinto or Buddhist. The overlap of Shinto and Buddhist ideas gave Japanese Buddhism its own distinctive flavour.

Chinese civilization also influenced South-east Asia, in particular Vietnam. However, Burma, Thailand, Cambodia, Laos, peninsular Malaysia and the Indonesian islands of Sumatra, Java and Bali were all affected by the advance of Indian culture, and especially by the cults of the great Hindu gods Vishnu and Shiva. On the island of Bali, Shiva and Buddha were sometimes worshipped as a joint deity.

From the beginning of the 17th century, Islam became the dominant religion of insular South-east Asia, carried there by Muslim traders. However, despite the impact of these major religions, indigenous beliefs persisted. For example, on Bali, where Hinduism is the official religion, mediums still communicate with deities and spirits; among the peoples of Borneo, the indigenous animistic beliefs continue to produce a mythology peopled by ghosts and spirits connected with natural phenomena.

In other areas of East Asia, traditional beliefs have been lost under the force of incoming religions. Many of the shamanic myths of Mongolia were lost after the introduction of Buddhism to the country in the 13th century. In Siberia, shamanism came under threat from Muslim missionaries from the tenth century onwards. However, while Islam won many converts, a reverse process also took place, with certain Central Asian Sufi orders being influenced by shamanism. Later, shamanism declined in the face of the missionary activity of the Russian orthodox church in the 19th century and, after the Russian revolution of 1917, Siberian shamans were persecuted by the Communists. Today, however, there are movements to revive shamanism to the level of influence it held in times gone by.

In general, the countries of East Asia have contributed to the already rich mythologies of the religions to which they have become hosts. In China, the goddess of mercy,

SHAMANS of Mongolia perform ritual dances with the use of drums to induce a trance state. These charismatic figures have the power to control spirits and to make journeys out of their bodies to the upper and lower spirit worlds. They are central figures in many communities, combining the functions of priest and doctor. (ILLUSTRATION FROM LE TOUR DU MONDE. C. 1850.)

Guanyin, evolved out of the Indian bodhisattva Avalokiteshvara and became a powerful mother goddess. Amitabha, the buddha of boundless light, became an important deity in both China and Japan. As Omito Fu in China and as Amida in Japan, he came to have an immense impact, in particular on the Japanese mind.

Initially identified with the great Shinto goddess Amaterasu, Amida became the focus of a school of Buddhism that teaches that all of those who call on the Buddha in faith will gain entry to his wondrous paradise. By confidently looking forward to a glorious hereafter, Chinese and Japanese devotees came to view earthly life as simply transitory. The figure of Omito Fu/Amida thus demonstrates the manner in which an incoming deity can both be transformed by and, in turn, come to transform the society in which it makes its home.

THE ABAASY, according to the Yakut people of Siberia, are evil supernatural beings who live in the lower world and are ruled over by the malevolent spirit *ULU TOYO'N*. The son of the chief Abaasy is said to have only one eye and iron teeth.

AIZEN-MYOO is regarded as the god of love in popular Japanese belief. He is a deity of both physical and intellectual desire and represents love transformed through the desire for enlightenment. His body is red and he has six arms holding various weapons, three eyes and the head of a lion in his hair. Despite his frightening appearance, he shows great compassion for humankind.

AJYSYT see *ITCHITA*.

AMATERASU is the sun goddess of Japanese mythology and one of the most important deities within the Shinto pantheon. Her full name, Amaterasu-O-Mi-Kami, means "August Person who Makes the Heavens Shine". Amaterasu was brought into being when *IZANAGI*, the male half of the primal couple, washed his face after returning from *YOMI*, the land of the dead. The sun goddess emerged from Izanagi's left eye and the moon god *TSUKIYOMI* from his right. Izanagi told Amaterasu that she should rule the high plains of heaven and gave her his sacred bead necklace.

The storm god *SUSANO-WO*, who had been born from Izanagi's nose, angered his father by saying that, rather than rule over the waters as Izanagi had decreed, he wanted to join his mother *IZANAMI* in Yomi. As a result, Izanagi banished Susano-Wo. Before leaving, Susano-Wo said that he wanted to say goodbye to Amaterasu, his sister. However, Amaterasu suspected that her brother wanted to take her kingdom from her, so she prepared for battle. Arming herself with a bow and two quivers of arrows, she

shook her bow in challenge and stamped the earth beneath her feet. Susano-Wo claimed that he had no wish to usurp Amaterasu's power. Instead, he said that they could prove which of them was the most powerful by seeing who could produce male deities.

Amaterasu began the contest by breaking her brother's sword into three, chewing the pieces, then spitting them out. A mist appeared from her mouth, soon taking the form of three goddesses. Susano-Wo then took the fertility beads with which Amaterasu bound her hair and arms. He cracked the beads with his teeth, and from them produced five male gods. He then announced that he had won the contest. However, Amaterasu said that because the gods had

AIZEN-MYOO sits on a blossoming lotus, a symbol of enlightenment. He is popularly seen as the god of romantic and erotic love.
(*JAPANESE SCULPTURE, C. 12TH CENTURY.*)

come from her own jewels, she had won the contest. Susano-Wo ignored her protest and celebrated his victory by wreaking havoc on earth. He destroyed the rice fields, filled in the irrigation ditches and

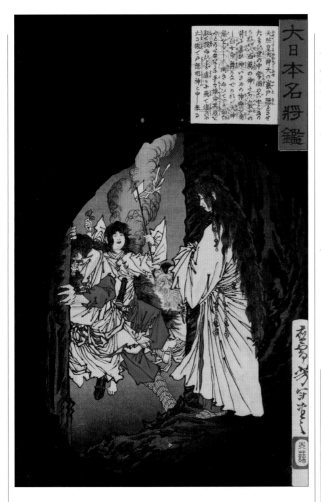

AMATERASU (above), hearing the commotion outside her cave, looked out in curiosity and light returned to the world. (WOODBLOCK PRINT BY TAISO YOSHITOSHI, 1882.)

finished his rampage by skinning a young pony and hurling it through the roof of the sacred weaving hall, where Amaterasu and her attendants sat weaving. One of the maidens died of fright, and Amaterasu fled in terror and fury.

The goddess hid in a cave, thereby casting the world into darkness. The evil gods were delighted, as the darkness enabled them to perform their wicked deeds undetected. However, the good deities beseeched Amaterasu to return to the world. The goddess refused, and so the deities hatched a plot. They found the cock whose crow precedes the dawn and made a mirror strung with jewels. Then, after setting the cock and the mirror outside Amaterasu's hiding place, they asked the goddess *AME-NO-UZUME* to dance on an upturned tub. The cock began to crow and the goddess began to dance, her feet creating a frenzied drumming noise. Eventually, the goddess was carried away by the ecstasy of her dance and removed her clothes, whereupon all the gods began to laugh. Unable to contain her curiosity, Amaterasu emerged from the cave and caught sight of her reflection in the mirror. As she was lured out to gaze at her own beauty, the world was again lit by the sun.

Amaterasu and her attendants are said to have been weaving the garments of the gods, or those of the priestesses who officiate at ceremonies associated with the sun goddess's cult. Another theory argues that the women were weaving the fabric of the universe, which remained incomplete.

Until 1945, Amaterasu was worshipped as a sacred ancestor of the Japanese imperial family, and a mirror forms part of the imperial regalia. A major shrine to the goddess at Ise is visited by millions of pilgrims each year. (See also *CREATION MYTHS*)

AME-NO-UZUME, or simply Uzume, is the dawn goddess and the goddess of laughter, according to the Shinto mythology of Japan. She helped to tempt *AMATERASU* out of a cave after the sun deity, enraged by the behaviour of the storm god *SUSANO-WO*, had taken shelter there. Ame-No-Uzume danced at the entrance to the cave, eventually becoming so carried away by her antics that she flung off all her clothes. The assembled gods burst out laughing, and the disturbance caused Amaterasu to look out of her hiding-place to see what was happening. As a result, her light returned to the world.

Another myth tells how Ame-No-Uzume distracted a local solar deity, the "Monkey Prince", who had attempted to block the descent from heaven of *NINIGI* or Honinigi, Amaterasu's grandson. In due course, Ame-No-Uzume and the Monkey Prince were married.

AME-NO-UZUME (below) helped to lure Amaterasu out of a cave by arousing her curiosity with an erotic dance. (ILLUSTRATION FROM MYTHS AND LEGENDS OF JAPAN.)

B

AMIDA is a Japanese deity who derives from the buddha Amitabha, or "Boundless Light", who postponed his own entry into nirvana in order that he might save humankind. In China, Amida is known as Omito Fu. He is the central figure in the "Pure Land" sects of Buddhism. The devotees believe that, by invoking the buddha at the hour of their death, they may be reborn in the Pure Land, Amida's western paradise. Once in the Pure Land, the faithful remain free from pain and desire until the time for their final enlightenment arrives.

Amida was originally identified with *AMATERASU*, the sun goddess and the most important Shinto deity. He is often represented welcoming the faithful to his Pure Land, surrounded by numerous bodhisattvas and celestial beings.

ANTABOGA is the world serpent of Balinese mythology. At the beginning of time, only Antaboga existed. By means of meditation, the great serpent created the world turtle, *BEDAWANG*. Two snakes lie on top of the world turtle, as well as the Black Stone, which forms the lid of the underworld.

The underworld is ruled by the goddess *SETESUYARA* and the god *BATARA KALA*, who created the light and the earth. Above the earth lies a layer of water and, above the water, a series of skies. *SEMARA*, the god of love, lives in the floating sky, and above that lies the dark blue sky, home to the sun and moon. Next is the perfumed sky, which is full of beautiful flowers and is inhabited by Tjak, a bird with a human face; the serpent Taksaka; and a group of snakes known as the Awan, who appear as falling stars. The ancestors live in a flame-filled heaven above the perfumed heaven, and beyond that is the abode of the gods.

ARA is a spirit who features in a creation myth of the Iban, one of the Dayak peoples of Borneo. The

story tells how, at the beginning of time, Ara floated in the form of a bird above a boundless ocean together with another spirit, *IRIK*. The birds eventually plucked two enormous eggs from the water. From one of the eggs, Ara formed the sky, and from the other, Irik formed the earth. However, because the earth was too large for the sky, the two spirits had to squash it until it became the right size. During the process, mountains and valleys, rivers and streams were created. Plants began to appear, and then the two spirits decided to create human beings. At first they tried to make them from the sap of trees but, when this proved unsuccessful, they used the soil. After fashioning the first humans, they gave them life with their bird-song.

AS-IGA, according to the Ostyak people of Siberia, is a benevolent spirit. His name means "Old Man of the Ob", the great river that runs through Siberia.

THE BA XIAN, or Pa Hsien, or "Eight Immortals", are symbols of good luck and important figures within the Daoist mythology of China. They are not, however, gods, although they are often viewed as such. The Ba Xian are said to have achieved immortality through the practice of the Dao, or "Way". Although accounts of how

they became immortal did not appear until the 15th century, some of the Ba Xian featured in earlier myths.

The first figure to achieve immortality was Li Tieguai ("Li with the Iron Crutch"). An ascetic, Li Tieguai was taught by Laozi, said to be the founding father of Daoism, who descended from heaven in order to help him. One day, soon after gaining immortality, Li decided to visit a sacred mountain. He left his body behind, asking his disciple to look after it for seven days and telling him that, if by then he had not returned, the disciple was to burn it.

On the sixth day, the disciple's mother fell ill. Anxious to visit her, the disciple burned Li's body. When Li's soul returned, it found only a heap of ashes, and so entered the body of an ugly beggar with a crippled leg who had died of hunger. Although Li did not want to live in such a horrible body, Laozi persuaded him to do so and gave him a crutch to help him to walk. According to another tale, Li was given the crutch by *XI WANG MU*, the "Queen Mother of the West", who healed a wound on Li's leg and taught him how to become immortal. Li is usually depicted as a beggar leaning on an iron crutch.

Li Tieguai is said to have instructed Zhong-li Quan in the Daoist doctrine. According to one tradition, Zhong-li Quan found instructions for gaining immortality behind the wall of his dwelling when it collapsed one day. Zhong-li Quan followed the guidelines, whereupon he disappeared to the heavens on a cloud. Another tale tells how, during a famine, Zhong-li Quan miraculously produced silver coins and gave them to the poor, thereby saving them from starvation. Zhong-li Quan was fat, bald and sported a long beard. He was

THE BA XIAN included Zhang Guolao, who is represented here, riding his mule back-to-front, in a paper model outside a temple during a festival in Taiwan.

often represented with a fan made from feathers or palm leaves. After gaining immortality, he became a messenger of heaven.

Lu Dongbin was born in the tenth century AD. While still a student, he met a fire dragon who gave him a magic sword with which he could conceal himself in heaven. Later, Lu Dongbin visited an inn where he met a man called Han Zhongli. While Han Zhongli warmed up a pot of wine, Lu fell asleep and saw the whole of his future life in a dream. He dreamt that he would enjoy good fortune for 50 years but then his luck would run out, his family ruined and he himself killed by bandits.

When Lu Dongbin woke up, he became convinced of the worthlessness of earthly ambition and decided to renounce the world. He followed Han Zhongli into the mountains in order to seek the Dao and achieve immortality. Lu Dongbin is said to mingle with ordinary mortals, rewarding the good and punishing the wicked. He uses his sword to conquer ignorance, passion and aggression. He is the patriarch of many Chinese sects and the most popular immortal in Chinese culture.

Han Xiang is usually said to be a nephew of a Tang dynasty philosopher. He became a disciple of Lu Dongbin, who took Han to heaven and showed him the tree that bears the peaches of eternal life. Han began to climb the tree but slipped and crashed to earth. Just before landing, he achieved immortality. Han Xiang is said to have a wild temper and supernatural powers. On one occasion, he caused peonies to blossom in the middle of winter. A prophecy was written on their petals and, though at the time the words appeared to mean nothing, they later came true. Han is traditionally portrayed carrying a peach, a flute or a bouquet of flowers.

Cao Guojiu was a brother of Empress Cao of the Song dynasty. He lived in the 11th century AD and is said either to have become disillusioned by the corrupt life of the court or to have been overwhelmed with shame when his brother was found to be a murderer. Whatever the reason, he disappeared into the mountains in pursuit of the Dao.

On coming to a river, Cao tried to persuade the boatman to carry him across by showing him the golden tablet that had allowed him entrance to court. The boatman was unimpressed and Cao, ashamed, threw the tablet into the river. The boatman turned out to be Lu Dongbin in disguise. Lu Dongbin adopted Cao as his disciple and instructed him in the Dao.

Another version of the story tells how the emperor gave Cao a golden medal, which had the ability to allow its owner to overcome all obstacles. When Cao showed the medal to the boatman, a priest asked him why he found it necessary to use such methods of persuasion. Ashamed, Cao threw the medal into the river, whereupon the priest revealed himself as Lu Dongbin and promised to help Cao gain immortality.

Zhang Guolao was an old man who lived at the time of the Empress Wu of the Tang dynasty, in the eighth century AD. He is often shown riding back-to-front on a white mule. The mule was said to be capable of travelling thousands of miles each day and, when not being ridden, could be folded up and put in a bag. To bring the mule back to life, Zhang just sprinkled it with water.

The emperor grew intrigued by Zhang and asked a Daoist master to tell him his true identity. The master replied that he was afraid to answer the emperor's question because he had been told that if he did so, he would immediately die. He finally agreed to reveal who Zhang was, on condition that the emperor promised afterwards to go barefoot and bareheaded to Zhang and ask him to forgive the master for his betrayal. The emperor agreed, whereupon the master said that Zhang was an incarnation of the chaos that existed at the beginning of time. The master died, but when the emperor went to ask Zhang for forgiveness, he was brought back to life.

Zhang could endow the childless and the newly married with children. He is sometimes shown holding the peaches of eternal life or the bag that contains his mule.

Lan Caihe was either a girl or a man who looked like a woman. In summer she wore a thick overcoat and in winter only light clothing. She wore a belt made of black wood and a boot on only one foot. Her family dealt in medicinal herbs. One day, when she was collecting herbs, Lan Caihe met a beggar dressed in filthy rags, his body covered in boils. The girl looked after the beggar, who turned out to be Li Tieguai in disguise. For her kindness, Li Tieguai rewarded the girl with immortality. Lan Caihe then toured the country singing songs and urging people to seek the Dao. One day, she took off her coat, boot and belt, and rose into the sky riding on a crane. She is sometimes represented carrying a basket of fruit or flowers.

He Xiangu became immortal after grinding and eating a mother-of-pearl stone. After swallowing the stone, He Xiangu became as light as a feather and found that she was able to fly over the mountains gathering fruits and berries. One day the emperor summoned her to his court, but she became immortal and disappeared. She is usually depicted holding either a peach or a lotus blossom. (See also *THE EIGHT IMMORTALS*)

THE BAJANG is an evil spirit who, in the folk-tales of the Malay-speaking people of South-east Asia, appears when a disaster or illness is about to occur. He usually takes the form of a giant polecat (ferret) and is particularly harmful to children.

The master of the household is said to be able to catch the Bajang and keep him in a container. If the master feeds the Bajang milk and eggs, the spirit becomes friendly and will cause the master's enemies to fall ill. However, if the master fails to feed the spirit, he will attack him.

BARONG, according to Balinese mythology, is the leader of the forces of good and the enemy of *RANGDA*, the demon queen. He is regarded as the king of the spirits and traditionally takes the form of a lion. Ritual battles, usually ending in Rangda's defeat or a compromise, are staged between the two beings. (See also *DEMONS*)

BASUKI is a giant serpent of Balinese mythology. He lives in the underworld cave that is ruled over by the god *BATARA KALA* and the goddess *SETESUYARA*.

BATARA GURU is the name by which the Hindu god Shiva was known in South-east Asia before the arrival of Islam. He was the omnipotent sky god and was also viewed as a god of the ocean. Shiva was introduced to Java, Sumatra, Bali and the Malay peninsula sometime before the fifth century AD.

The Malay people added their own stories to the Indian tales of the great god's exploits. In Sumatra, for example, Batara Guru was said to have created the earth by sending a handful of soil to his daughter, *BORU DEAK PARUDJAR*, who had jumped from heaven into a vast ocean in order to avoid the unwelcome advances of the god Mangalabulan. A swallow told Batara Guru what had happened, and the god sent the bird down to earth with the soil. When the girl

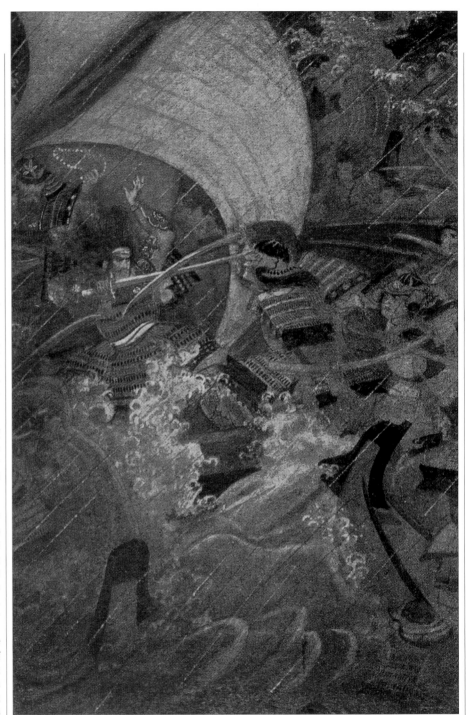

BENKEI was the companion of the hero Yoshitsune. They were once attacked by a ghostly company of the Taira clan.
(ILLUSTRATION FROM MYTHS AND LEGENDS OF JAPAN.)

threw the soil into the water, it immediately formed an island. This so annoyed the sea serpent *NAGA PADOHA* that he arched his back, causing the island to float away. Batara Guru then sent down more soil, as well as an incarnation of himself in the form of a hero. The hero managed to keep the serpent still by placing an iron weight on his back so that he sank to the lower depths. Try as he might, Naga Padoha was unable to move the huge weight, but his writhings caused the formation of mountains and valleys.

After he had created the islands of the South-east Asian archipelago, Batara Guru sprinkled them with seeds, from which arose all animals and plants. Boru Deak Parudjar and the hero then produced the first human beings.

BATARA KALA, according to the creation myth of the Balinese, is the god who rules over the underworld cave together with the goddess *SETESUYARA*. Batara Kala created the light and the earth.

BEDAWANG is the Balinese world turtle whom the world serpent *ANTABOGA* created through meditation. Two snakes lie on top of the world turtle as well as the Black Stone, which forms the lid of the underworld. The god *BATARA KALA* and the goddess *SETESUYARA* rule over the underworld.

BENKEI, according to Japanese mythology, is the companion of the hero *YOSHITSUNE*. He is said to have been conceived by a *TENGU*, or demon. He soon grew to a great height and became very strong. None the less, Yoshitsune succeeded in overpowering Benkei in a duel, whereupon the giant became the hero's servant.

BENTEN, or Benzai, was one of the *SHICHI FUKUJIN*, or seven deities of good fortune or happiness, an assembly of immortals grouped together in the 17th century by a monk who intended them to symbolize the virtues of a man of his time. Benten was said to be the sister of the king of the Buddhist hells. Later, due to a mistake, she was attributed with the virtues of good luck and was included in the group of seven deities of happiness. Benten helps human beings acquire material gains. She is said to have married a dragon in order to render him harmless, and is sometimes represented riding a dragon or sea serpent. She is associated with the sea. The goddess is

BENTEN holding a zither and riding on a dragon, is visited in her cave at Enoshima by a nobleman asking her to grant prosperity to his house. The goddess is associated with material wealth. (GOLD LACQUER SCREEN, 19TH CENTURY.)

also believed to be an exemplar of the feminine accomplishments, and she is often shown playing a musical instrument. Venerated by gamblers and jealous women, as well as by speculators and tradesmen, Benten is believed to bring good luck in marriage and is the patron saint of the geishas. (See also *THE SHICHI FUKUJIN*)

BENZAI see *BENTEN*.

BISHAMON is a Japanese god who was derived from Vaishravana, one of the Guardian Kings of Buddhism. Bishamon, like Vaishravana, was originally the heavenly guardian of the north, but he later became the protector of the law who guarded people from illness and demons. He was also a god of war. Bishamon is believed to possess enormous wealth and to dispense ten sorts of treasure or good luck. As a result, he was included in the list of *SHICHI FUKUJIN*, the seven deities of happiness or good luck, an assembly of immortals grouped together in the 17th century by a monk who intended them to symbolize the virtues of a man of his time.

Bishamon is normally represented as a blue-faced warrior clad in full armour, and his attributes include a spear and a pagoda, a symbol of religious devotion. He is sometimes known by the name Bishamon-tenno or Bishamonten, and is often shown trampling two demons. In the sixth century, Prince Shotoku called upon the god to help him in his crusade against anti-Buddhist factions. (See also *THE SHICHI FUKUJIN*)

BORU DEAK PARUDJAR, according to the mythology of Sumatra, is the daughter of the god *BATARA GURU*, the name by which the Hindu god Shiva was known in South-east Asia before the arrival of Islam. Batara Guru is said to have created the earth by sending a handful of soil to his daughter, Boru Deak Parudjar, who had jumped from heaven into a vast ocean in order to avoid the unwelcome advances of the god Mangalabulan. A swallow told Batara Guru what had happened, and the god sent the bird down to earth with the soil. When Boru Deak Parudjar threw the soil into the water, it immediately formed an island. This so annoyed the sea serpent *NAGA PADOHA* that he arched his back, making it float away.

Batara Guru then sent down more soil, as well as an incarnation of himself in the form of a hero. The hero managed to keep the serpent still by placing an iron weight on his back so that he sank to the depths. Try as he might, Naga Padoha was unable to move the weight, but his writhings caused the formation of mountains and valleys.

After he had created the islands of the South-east Asian archipelago, Batara Guru sprinkled them with seeds from which arose all the animals and plants. Boru Deak Parudjar and the hero then produced the first human beings.

BOTA ILI, according to the Kedang people of eastern Indonesia, was a wild woman who lived at the top of a mountain. Her

BISHAMON is a Japanese god of war whose attributes include a spear and a pagoda, a symbol of religious devotion. He is shown here with a ministering demon.
(WOODBLOCK PRINT BY ISAI, 19TH CENTURY.)

body was covered with hair, and she had long, pointed fingernails and toenails. She ate lizards and snakes and would cook them over a fire, which she lit by striking her bottom against a stone.

One day, a man called *WATA RIAN* noticed the smoke of Bota Ili's fire and set off to find its source. He took with him a fish to eat and some wine. When he reached the top of the mountain, Wata Rian climbed a tree and waited for Bota Ili to return with her catch of reptiles. The wild woman struck her bottom against a rock to start a fire, but to no effect. Looking up, she saw Wata Rian and shrieked at him to come down from the tree so that she could bite him to death. Wata

THE CITY GOD stands resplendent on his altar in the City God Temple in Xi Gang in Taiwan.

the god of wind. With their help he smothered Huang Di's soldiers in a thick, black fog, whereupon the latter invented the compass in order to find his whereabouts. Chiyou then called down the wind and rain, whereupon Huang Di summoned the goddess of drought, Ba, to clear the skies. Eventually, Chiyou was defeated and decapitated, although his headless body continued to run across the battlefield before finally falling down dead.

Chiyou was said to have invented warfare and weapons and was also a renowned dancer. Although his body was that of a human being, he had the feet of an ox. He was said to have four eyes and six arms, pointed horns, a head made from iron and hair as sharp as spears. He lived on a diet of sand and stones.

CH'IYU see *CHIYOU*.

CHORMUSTA see *QORMUSTA*.

CHU JONG see *ZHU RONG*.

THE CITY GOD was the impersonal tutelary deity of walled cities and towns, responsible to *YU HUANG*, the "Jade Emperor", in heaven. In each town, his temple was regarded as the "yamen", or celestial court, the counterpart to the terrestrial state yamen with its human mandarin responsible to the emperor in Beijing. The City God performed the same duties "on the other side", controlling harmful ghosts and spirits with his retinue of tamed demons within the city bounds. Prayers were addressed to him on behalf of a deceased, asking him to intercede with the ten judges of the purgatorial courts in the underworld, reflecting the widespread Buddhist concept of reincarnation.

Rian, unafraid, told her to calm herself or he would set his dog on her. The two of them lit a fire and cooked their food together.

Bota Ili drank so much wine that she fell asleep, whereupon Wata Rian shaved the hair from her body and discovered that she was really a woman. The two were eventually married.

BUJAEGN YED is a culture hero of the Chewong, a Malayan people. One day, Bujaegn Yed, a hunter, was eating the food he had caught when *YINLUGEN BUD*, an ancient spirit, appeared to him. The spirit warned the hero that he was committing a terrible sin in failing to share his food. Bujaegn Yed took heed of the warning and took some of the food home to give to his wife, who was pregnant.

When Bujaegn Yed's wife was about to give birth, the hero was on the point of cutting open her stomach to allow the baby out, as was customary at that time, when Yinlugen Bud again appeared. The spirit showed Bujaegn Yed how to deliver a baby in the correct manner, and also taught him the rules and rituals of childbirth. Then, after teaching Bujaegn Yed's wife how to breastfeed a baby, the spirit disappeared. From that time on, women did not have to die when their children were born.

CAO GUOJIU see *BA XIAN*.

CHANG E see *ZHANG E*.

CHIYOU or Ch'iyu, is variously described as a son, descendant or minister of *SHEN NONG*, the ancient Chinese god, or culture hero, associated with medicine and agriculture. Chiyou rebelled against *HUANG DI*, the "Yellow Emperor", in a struggle for the succession. After Chiyou had driven Huang Di's forces on to an immense plain, the enemies engaged in a tremendous battle.

Huang Di's army was composed of bears, tigers and other ferocious animals, whereas Chiyou's army was composed of demons. Chiyou was also supported by Chi Song Zi, the "Master of Rain", and Fei Lian,

D

been led from a country near Mecca to their present home. Demong married the daughter of a local ruler in order to ensure good relations with the existing inhabitants of Borneo. The woman, Rinda, had several children. When Demong was about to die, he ordered that a boundary stone be erected in order to mark the Ibans' territory. The stone stands to this day, and it is said that whoever attempts to move it risks incurring the wrath of Demong.

DIDIS MAHENDERA was a fabulous creature who, according to the Dayak people of Borneo, appeared together with *ROWANG RIWO* during the first epoch of creation, when a part of the universe was brought into being with each successive clash of the two cosmic mountains. The creature had eyes made from jewels.

DIMU see *DIYA*.

DIYA and Tian-Long were attendants of *WEN CHANG*, the Chinese god of literature. Diya, whose name means "Earthly Dumb", and Tian-Long, meaning "Heavenly Deaf", helped Wen Chang with the setting and marking of his examination papers, since, being deaf and dumb, they could be relied on not to leak the questions in advance. Another myth mentions these two as the primal couple, who gave rise to human beings and all other creatures. Diya was sometimes known as Dimu, meaning "Earth Mother".

DIZANG WANG, or *TI-TS'ANG WANG*, is one of the four great bodhisattvas ("buddhas-to-be") of Chinese buddhism. Long ago, Dizang Wang vowed that he would become a buddha, but only when he had liberated all creatures on earth from the relentless cycle of death and rebirth.

In one of his existences, he was a girl whose mother killed animals for food. Through meditating, the girl succeeded in saving her mother from hell. Dizang Wang is believed to succour all those who are detained in the courts of hell. He is depicted as a monk holding a metal staff which opens the gates of hell, and is often surrounded by the ten judges. He is the equivalent of the Indian bodhisattva Kshitigarbha and the Japanese *JIZO-BOSATZU*.

DONGYUE DADI, or Tung-yüeh Ta-ti, is the "Great Emperor of the Eastern Peak" according to Chinese mythology. He assists the "Jade Emperor" *YU HUANG* and supervises all areas of earthly life.

There are 75 departments within Dongyue Dadi's offices. One lays down the time for the births and deaths of all creatures, another determines people's social

DAIKOKU was one of the *SHICHI FUKUJIN,* or seven gods of good fortune, a group of deities assembled in the 17th century by a monk who intended them to symbolize the virtues of a man of his time.

Daikoku was regarded as the god of wealth and a patron of farmers. He is often depicted standing or sitting on bales of rice, which are sometimes being eaten away by rats. Daikoku remains untroubled by the rats' greed because he is so wealthy. He usually carries a mallet, with which he is able to grant wishes. His picture was sometimes placed in kitchens, and he is sometimes said to have provided for the nourishment of priests. (See also *THE SHICHI FUKUJIN*)

DAINICHI-NYORAI is the Japanese form of the buddha Mahavairocana, or the "Great Illuminator". He was introduced to Japan at the beginning of the ninth century, together with numerous other Buddhist figures. He became the supreme deity of some esoteric sects and is sometimes regarded as the "Primordial Buddha". *YAKUSHI-NYORAI,* the divine healer, is sometimes seen as an aspect of Dainichi-Nyorai.

DAISHO-KANGITEN see *SHOTEN*.

DEMONG, according to the Iban of Borneo, governed the ancestors of the Iban people after they had

E

standing, another their wealth and another the number of children they will have. Dongyue Dadi's offices are staffed by the souls of the dead. His daughter, Sheng Mu, looks after women and children. Dongyue Dadi is usually represented sitting down and wearing the garments of an emperor.

THE EARTH GOD

THE EARTH GOD, the ubiquitous local territorial deity, is the closest to the lives of villagers and is amongst those most frequently seen on the altars of the common people. The Earth God is not looked upon as powerful or fearsome. He is a celestial deity, the lowest ranking official in the bureaucracy of the celestial pantheon, and is the tutelary god of each sector of a large village or suburb; the protector of the well-being of both town and country dwellers. He has control over the wealth and fortune of the people.

The Earth God is almost universally thought to be an impersonal spirit. People appeal to him for anything that affects their lives and livelihoods. In times of peril, images of the Earth God have sometimes been taken from their shrines to be shown the cause of a problem, such as drought, flood, frost, caterpillars, locusts or mildew, to enable the deity to understand fully what his devotees are suffering.

EBISU, in Japanese mythology, was one of the *SHICHI FUKUJIN,* or seven gods of good fortune or happiness, an assembly of deities grouped together in the 17th century by a monk who intended them to symbolize the virtues of a man of his time. Ebisu himself is credited with the virtue of candour.

THE EARTH GOD (right) sits on the altar of a local temple, clutching his staff and tael of gold, symbolizing wealth.

DAINICHI-NYORAI (below), the "Great Sun Buddha", was the supreme deity of the Shingon sect. Its members held that the esoteric teachings of the Buddha were too obscure to be expressed in writing, but could be presented in painting. (PAINTING ON SILK, 13TH CENTURY.)

He is said to be the patron of labourers, wealth and prosperity, and to promote hard work. Ebisu is believed to have originated in Shinto belief as the son of *OKUNINUSHI*, the mythical hero. He is also sometimes identified with the third son of *IZANAGI AND IZANAMI*, the primal couple, and as such is regarded as one of the ancestors of the first people of Japan.

In some areas of Japan, the god of farms is called Ebisu; fishermen also invoke the god before going to sea. Ebisu is symbolized by a large stone, which a boy must retrieve from the bottom of the water. He is usually represented dressed as a peasant and smiling. He holds a fishing rod in one hand and a sea bream (sunfish), a symbol of good luck, in the other hand. (See also *THE SHICHI FUKUJIN*)

EC, according to the Yenisei people of Siberia, is the supreme god. He regularly descends to earth in order to ensure the well-being of creation. Ec drove his wife, *KHOSADAM*, out of the sky in punishment for being unfaithful to him with the moon.

THE EIGHT IMMORTALS see *BA XIAN.*

YIN AND YANG

DAOIST PHILOSOPHY CENTRED ON the principle of unity in the cosmos and the belief that a natural order, based on balance and harmony, determined the behaviour of everything in existence. Two interacting forces held the Chinese universe in delicate balance: yin, the female element, was associated with coldness, darkness, softness and the earth. It originally referred to the shady side of the mountain. Yang, the sunny side, was the male principle, associated with light, warmth, hardness and the heavens. The two forces were opposites but mutually dependent, and needed to be in equilibrium for harmony to exist. They were present in every aspect of the world, in contrasting pairs such as life and death, or good and evil, as well as in everyday activities, objects, animals and human characters. In the ancient Chinese creation myth, yin and yang were held inside the cosmic egg until the struggle of the opposing forces cracked the shell.

THE YIN/YANG SYMBOL (above) expresses the interaction between opposites that gives rise to the universe and everything in it. The dark section (yin) and the light section (yang) are directly opposed, yet interlocking and mutually dependent. Together they form a perfect circle. The two small spots show that each opposing force contains a small seed of the other within it. (CARVED CHINESE JOSS BOARD.)

THE BAGUA (left) were discovered by Fu Xi, the legendary emperor, who saw them inscribed on the back of a tortoise he found on the banks of the Yellow River in about 3000BC. The constantly changing interactions of yin and yang gave rise to the infinite variety of patterns of life, symbolized in the three-line symbols of the eight trigrams. The top line of each trigram represents heaven, the bottom is earth and the middle line is humankind. (ILLUSTRATION FROM SUPERSTITIONS EN CHINE, 1915.)

THE YIN/YANG SYMBOL (below), surrounded by the trigrams of the bagua, was hung on the house door as a protective amulet to prevent the entry of devils. With it might hang a picture of the immortal Liu Hai with his three-legged bowl, who brought good luck to those involved in commercial ventures. He carried a string of gold pieces to remind him of a visiting philosopher who suggested he tried to pile eggs to demonstrate the precariousness of high office. (ILLUSTRATION FROM SUPERSTITIONS EN CHINE, 1915.)

THE PEI TOU IMMORTALS (above) were star spirits of which the most important were the "Three Stars of Happiness": Shou Lao, the god of longevity; Fu Shen, the god of luck; and Cai Shen, the god of wealth. They are shown here contemplating the yin/yang symbol on a scroll, and surrounded by symbolic figures of long life and immortality: the pine tree with Shou Lao's white crane, the stag and a child presenting a peach. (CHINESE SILK EMBROIDERY, 17TH CENTURY.)

THE DRAGON (right) and the phoenix were often used together decoratively. For the Chinese, dragons represented the male, yang element and were a beneficent force of nature, even though they had fiery tempers. The mythical phoenix represented the female, yin element. The dragon was the emblem of the Chinese emperor, and the phoenix of the empress, and together the two creatures were used to symbolize marital harmony. (JADE RITUAL DISC WITH DRAGON AND PHOENIX, C. 481–221BC.)

F

EMMA-O (left), the king of hell, was no match for the strong man Asahina Saburo, and was humiliated by having to crawl between his legs. (KINJI INRO, 19TH CENTURY.)

EMMA-O (right) wears a magistrate's hat to indicate his office as judge of the dead. (NASHIJI INRO, 18TH CENTURY.)

EMMA-O, according to Japanese Buddhism, is the ruler of hell and the judge of the dead. He is identified with the Chinese deity YANLUO WANG and derives from the Hindu god of death, Yama.

Emma-O rules over the underground hell Jigoku, where he is surrounded by 18 generals and thousands of soldiers as well as demons and guards with horses' heads. The underworld is divided into eight hells of fire and eight of ice. According to one tradition, death begins as a journey across a vast, empty plain. In other versions of the tale, infernal beings guard the dead during their journey. At the entrance to hell lies a steep mountain, which the deceased have to climb before encountering, on the other side of the mountain, a river with three crossings. One of the crossings is a shallow ford, which those who have committed only minor sins may cross. Another is a bridge over which good people may pass. The third is a horrific torrent filled with monsters, through which evil sinners must struggle. At the other side of this third crossing waits a horrible old woman who strips her victims naked. They are then taken before Emma-O by the guards of hell. Emma-O judges only men; his sister decides the fate of women. The god sits between two severed heads, and a magic mirror reflects all the sinner's past wrongdoings. Emma-O then judges the individual's sins and allocates them to the appropriate hell. The souls of the dead can, however, be saved with the help of a bosatsu, the Japanese form of the bodhisattva.

ERLIK, according to the Altaic people of southern Siberia, is the king of the dead, an adversary of the supreme god, ULGAN. He incurred Ulgan's wrath by leading the first men to commit sin. The great sky god sent the saviour MAIDERE down to earth in order to teach men to respect and fear him, but Erlik succeeded in killing him. Flames shot forth from the saviour's blood, eventually reaching up to heaven and destroying Erlik and his followers. Erlik was then banished to the underworld. Erlik is regarded both as the first man and as the elder brother of the creator. He is depicted as a terrifying being, having taken on some of the characteristics of Yama, the Buddhist god of the underworld. He sometimes appears as a bear.

ES is the sky god of the Ket people of Siberia. Although he is invisible, he is depicted as an old man with a long black beard.

Es created the world and made the first human beings from clay. When he threw clay with his left hand towards the right, it became a woman; when he threw clay with his right hand towards the left, it became a man.

ESEGE MALAN TENGRI, or "Father Bald-head Tengri", is the sky god of the Buriat people of Siberia.

FANGCHANG see PENGLAI.

FU HSI see FU XI

FU XI, or Fu Hsi, according to Chinese mythology, is the brother and husband of NU GUA. Whereas Nu Gua rules over the earth, Fu Xi rules over the sky. They are both represented with the tails of dragons.

One popular myth tells how, long ago, a man was labouring in his fields when he heard a rumble of thunder. He ordered his son and daughter into his house, hung an iron cage under its eaves and stood in wait, holding a large iron fork. All at once, there was an enormous clap of thunder and a flash of lightning, and the monstrous thunder god, LEI GONG, appeared wielding a huge axe. The man attacked Lei Gong with his fork, pushed him into the iron cage and slammed the door shut. Immediately, the rain and wind ceased.

they knew that they would first have to be granted permission from the gods because, being brother and sister, the marriage would be incestuous. The couple climbed a sacred mountain, and each built a bonfire on its summit. The smoke from the two fires mingled, and Nu Gua and Fu Xi took this to mean that they had been granted permission to marry. Time passed and eventually Nu Gua gave birth to a ball of flesh. Fu Xi chopped the ball into numerous pieces with an axe and carried the fragments up a ladder to heaven. A gust of wind scattered the pieces of flesh all over the earth; when they landed, they became human beings. In this way, the earth was repopulated. (See also *CREATION MYTHS; YIN AND YANG*)

FU XI (below centre) became the first of the legendary emperors of China, followed by Shen Nong and Huang Di.

The following morning, the man prepared to journey to the local market in order to buy spices with which to pickle the thunder god. Before leaving home, he warned his children not to give Lei Gong anything to eat or drink. As soon as the man had left, Lei Gong began to beg the children for just the merest drop of water. At first the children heeded their father's instructions, but eventually they relented. As soon as the water touched his lips, Lei Gong became strong again and burst out of his cage. Before leaving, he thanked the children for helping him and gave them one of his teeth, which he told them to plant in the ground. The children planted the tooth and, within a few hours, it grew into a plant bearing a gourd.

It began to rain, and by the time the man returned from market, the rain had covered the whole earth. The man told his children to climb inside the gourd for safety, then he built a boat and rose up to heaven on the swelling water. There, he knocked on the door and begged

FU XI's (above) legacy to Chinese civilization included the invention of the calendar, the fishing net and the bagua, or eight trigrams. (19TH CENTURY ILLUSTRATION.)

the lord of heaven to end the flood. The lord of heaven commanded the water god to put an end to the flood, but the god was so diligent that the water immediately subsided, and the man's boat crashed down to earth, killing him. However, the children were unharmed because the gourd cushioned their fall.

The children proved to be the only survivors of the flood. They became known as Fu Xi. When they grew up, the young man suggested that they have children. The young woman was reluctant, since they were brother and sister, but agreed on condition that her brother was able to catch her in a chase. Fu Xi caught his sister, and so began the custom of marriage. The woman then changed her name to Nu Gua.

According to another version of the tale, although the two beings wanted to marry and have children,

FUDO-MYOO (left), a terrifying deity who protects Buddhism and its adherents, holds a sword in one hand and a rope in the other. (SCULPTURE, 12TH–14TH CENTURY.)

Fugen is often depicted sitting on a white elephant with six tusks, or sometimes riding four elephants. He may be shown with 20 arms.

FUKUROKUJU is one of the *SHICHI FUKUJIN*, the seven gods of good fortune or happiness, a group of deities assembled in the 17th century by a monk who intended them to symbolize the virtues of a man of his time.

Fukurokuju himself symbolizes the virtue of popularity as well as wisdom, longevity, virility and fertility. He is usually depicted with a very long, thin head to indicate his intelligence and a short, fat body. He is sometimes accompanied by a crane, a stag or tortoise, all creatures which symbolize longevity. Fukurokuju is of Chinese origin

FUDO-MYOO (above) is surrounded by a halo of flames, the symbol of his virtues. (PAINTING, C. 13TH CENTURY.)

FUGEN-BOSATSU (below) sits on a lotus blossom carried by a white elephant. (JAPANESE SILK PAINTING, 14TH CENTURY.)

FUDO-MYOO is the most important of the five great Japanese myoos, the equivalent of Indian Buddhism's vidyarajas, terrifying emanations of the five "Great Buddhas of Wisdom". Fudo-Myoo corresponds to the Buddha *DAINICHI-NYORAI*. He is usually portrayed with a terrifying face half-concealed by long hair and surrounded by a halo of flames. The flames are believed to consume the passions. In one hand, he holds a sword, which is used to conquer greed, anger and ignorance, and in the other hand he holds a rope with which he catches those who oppose the Buddha.

FUGEN-BOSATSU is the Japanese form of the bodhisattva or "buddha-to-be", Samantabhadra. He represents innate reason and is believed to be able to prolong people's lives. One tale tells how Fugen-Bosatsu appeared before a monk disguised as a courtesan with the intention of demonstrating that the nature of Buddha was latent in even the most sinful of women.

and may have been a Daoist sage. He is the godfather of *JUROJIN*, the god of longevity and happy old age. (See also *THE SHICHI FUKUJIN*)

FUXING see *SAN XING*

GAO YAO, or Ting-jian, was an ancient Chinese god of judgement. His accompanying animal, a mythical one-horned goat, helped him to detect injustice.

GIMOKODAN is the name that the Bagobo people of the Philippines give to the underworld. The Bagobo are a hill tribe living on the island of Mindanao. According to tradition, Gimokodan, the land of the dead, lies below the earth and is divided into two parts. One part is reserved for brave warriors who die in battle, the other part houses everyone else. A giantess lives in the second section and feeds the spirits of dead children with milk from her many breasts. Most of the spirits, however, turn to dew as soon as it is daylight and only become spirits again at night. A river lies at the entrance of Gimokodan, and all those who bathe in it forget their former lives.

GONG-GONG appears in Chinese mythology as a terrible monster who brings about a disastrous flood. He takes the form of a black dragon and is attended by a nine-headed snake. As the sworn enemy of the legendary benevolent emperor *YAO*, Gong-Gong decided to impale Mount Buzhou with his horn, thereby disturbing the balance of the earth and causing the rivers to overflow. He then tore a hole in the sky, disturbing the course of the sun. The monster is thus held responsible for all irregularities of weather and light.

According to another version of the tale, Gong-Gong and *ZHU RONG*, the divine lord of fire, decided to fight each other in order to determine which of them was the most powerful. The battle

GAO YAO'S (above) assistant in his pursuit of justice was a mythical one-horned animal, sometimes described as a qilin, or unicorn, who butted the guilty but spared the innocent. (SINO-TIBETAN ENAMEL QILIN.)

continued for several days. Eventually, the two creatures fell out of heaven, and Gong-Gong was defeated. Gong-Gong was so humiliated by having lost the battle that he determined to kill himself by running head first at Mount Buzhou, one of the mountains which supported the sky. When Gong-Gong struck the mountain, a great chunk fell off, a huge hole was torn in the sky and enormous cracks appeared in the earth. Fire and water gushed out, and a massive flood covered almost the entire surface of the world. The few areas that escaped the flood were destroyed by fire.

The goddess *NU GUA* selected some coloured stones from the bed of a river and melted them down. She then patched the sky with the melted stones and propped up the four points of the compass with the legs of a tortoise. However, when Gong-Gong collided with the mountain, he caused the heavens to tilt towards the northwest, which is why all the great rivers of China flow eastwards.

FUKUROKUJU (left), the god of long life and wisdom, is portrayed as a benevolent old man with an enormous brain. (JAPANESE LACQUERED VASE, 19TH CENTURY.)

GUAN DI was worshipped as the protector of state officials in thousands of temples throughout China, in which the swords of public executioners were housed.
(CHINESE PORCELAIN, 16–17TH CENTURY.)

Guanyin is believed to live on a mountain or an island in the Eastern Sea. She is said to have introduced humankind to the cultivation of rice, which she makes wholesome by filling each kernel with her own milk. The goddess comes to the aid of all those who need her help, especially when they are threatened by water, demons, fire or the sword. She is sometimes said to stand on a cliff in the middle of flaming waves and rescue shipwrecked people from the sea, the symbol of samsara, the ceaseless round of earthly existence.

The 14th-century novel *Journey to the West*, which is said to provide a popular record of Chinese mythology, tells how the "Monkey King" went up to heaven where he stole the peaches of immortality from the garden of *XI WANG MU*, the "Queen Mother of the West". The monkey incurred the wrath of all the gods and was finally taken captive by Buddha. However, Guanyin interceded on the monkey's behalf and he was allowed to accompany a Buddhist pilgrim during his journey to India.

Another myth tells how Guanyin was the third daughter of King Miao Zhong. She entered a religious order against the wishes of her father, who did all he could to persuade her to remain in the outside world. Eventually, the king decided that he would have to kill her. However, *YANLUO WANG*, lord of death, appeared and led Guanyin away to his underworld kingdom. There, Guanyin soothed the damned and transformed hell

GUAN DI is sometimes portrayed as a mandarin, sitting unarmed, stroking his beard. (SOAPSTONE FIGURE, 17–18TH CENTURY.)

GUAN DI, or Kuan-ti, is the Daoist patron deity of soldiers and policemen. He protects the realm and looks after state officials. During the Chinese Qing dynasty (1644–1912), Guan Di was venerated for his warlike functions. In other periods he was regarded as the guardian of righteousness who protects men from strife and evil. In popular belief, Guan Di was famed for casting out demons. He was also called upon to provide information about people who had died and to predict the future.

Guan Di was originally a general called Guan Gong, who lived in the third century AD, during a time of turmoil at the close of the Han dynasty. He was renowned for his military skill, but he also came to be admired for his great courage and loyalty, since he was eventually executed by his enemy as a prisoner of war because he refused to change his allegiance. Because of his many virtues he was later deified, being officially recognized as a god at the end of the 16th century. Guan Di is represented as a giant dressed in green with a long beard and a red face. He is often depicted standing next to his horse and clad in full armour.

GUANYIN, or Kuan Yin, is Chinese Buddhism's goddess of mercy or compassion. She developed from the male bodhisattva, or "buddha-to-be", Avalokiteshvara, known in Japan as *KWANNON*, and helps all beings on earth to attain enlightenment. Guanyin was herself originally regarded as male but increasingly gained female characteristics. Believed to bless women with children, she is sometimes depicted holding a child in her arms. However, she may also be represented as a bodhisattva with a thousand arms and a thousand eyes. She sometimes appears in the guise of a young woman holding a fish basket, standing on clouds or riding on the back of a dragon in front of a waterfall.

GUANYIN (above), Chinese Buddhism's
goddess of mercy and compassion, is often
depicted holding a willow branch and a
vase filled with the dew of compassion.

GUANYIN (right) helps all beings attain
enlightenment. Originally a male deity, she
increasingly gained female characteristics.
(CHINESE PORCELAIN, 13–14TH CENTURY.)

into a paradise. Yanluo Wang then
released Guanyin, and she was
reborn on an island where she protected seafarers from storms. Her
father then fell ill, and Guanyin
healed him by cooking a piece of
her own flesh for him to eat. In
gratitude, the king ordered a statue
of his daughter to be made.
However, the sculptor misunder-
stood the king's instructions and
made a statue with a thousand
arms and a thousand eyes.

Guanyin is also credited with
the ability to release prisoners from
their chains, remove poison from
snakes and deprive lightning of its
power. She is believed to be capable of curing almost every sickness.
A very popular goddess, her image
is often found in people's homes
and the festivals of her birth and
enlightenment are endowed with
great significance by Buddhists.

GUEI, or Kuei, according to
Chinese mythology, are spirits
formed from the YIN, or negative
essence, of people's souls. These
spirits or emanations are always
feared because they are said to take
their revenge on those people who
ill-treated them when they were
alive. They can be identified
because they wear clothes which
have no hems and their bodies cast
no shadows.

H

HACHIMAN is the Japanese god of war. However, he is also a god of peace, and sometimes serves as a god of agriculture and protector of children. A historical figure, he is the deified form of the Emperor Ojin, who died at the end of the fourth century AD and was famed for his military deeds and bravery. Within the Shinto religion, Hachiman became a very popular deity, although his name does not appear in the sacred texts of Shintoism. He came to be regarded as a protector of Buddhism and is viewed by Buddhists as a bosatsu, the Japanese form of a bodhisattva, or "buddha-to-be". His sacred creature is the dove.

HAN XIANG see BA XIAN.

HE XIANGU see BA XIAN.

HIKOHOHODEMI is the great-grandson of the Japanese sun goddess AMATERASU and the son of NINIGI, or Honinigi, and his wife, Kono-Hana-Sakuyu-Hime.

Hikohohodemi's name means "Fireshade". His brother is called HONOSUSERI, or "Fireshine". Hikohohodemi hunted land animals, whereas his brother was a fisherman. One day the brothers tried to swap their means of livelihood but discovered that neither was able to perform the other's tasks. Honosuseri returned the bow, but Hikohohodemi had lost Honosuseri's fish hook and so offered him another in its stead. Honosuseri, however, refused to accept the replacement.

Upset, Hikohohodemi visited the sea god Watatsumi-No-Kami at the bottom of the ocean. Having previously found the fish hook in the mouth of a fish, the sea god returned it to Hikohohodemi. Meanwhile, Watatsumi-No-Kami's daughter had fallen in love with the young god. The couple were married and lived together for many years. Eventually, Hikohohodemi decided to return home. Before

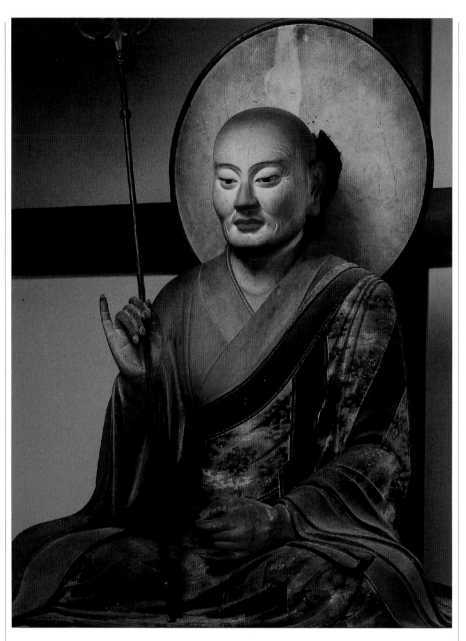

leaving, Hikohohodemi's father-in-law gave him two jewels, which made the tide rise and fall; he also gave him a friendly crocodile to transport him on his journey.

Back on land, the god returned the fish hook to Honosuseri, who, despite this gesture, continued to pester his brother. Eventually, Hikohohodemi lost all patience and made the tide rise. When

Honosuseri was almost covered by the sea, he begged forgiveness and promised to serve Hikohohodemi, whereupon the latter caused the tide to go out.

The daughter of the sea god joined Hikohohodemi on land and announced that she was about to have his child. She made Hikohohodemi promise not to look at her while she gave birth,

HACHIMAN is the Japanese god of war, the deified form of the Emperor Ojin. Centuries after his death, a vision of a child appeared at his birthplace, identifying itself with an ideogram representing the name Hachiman. (STATUE BY KAIKEI, 13TH CENTURY.)

but the god was unable to resist the temptation and peeped through a crack in the wall of his wife's hut. There, he saw his wife transformed

HIKOHOHODEMI was the grandfather of Jimmu-Tenno, the first emperor of Japan.

HONOSUSERI, according to the Shinto mythology of Japan, was the elder brother of *HIKOHOHODEMI*. Honosuseri was a great fisherman, while his brother hunted animals on land. Honosuseri's name means "Fireshine", and his brother's name means "Fireshade". The brothers are the great-grandsons of the sun goddess *AMATERASU* and the sons of *NINIGI*, or Honinigi, and his wife Kono-Hana-Sakuyu-Hime.

HOTEI is one of the *SHICHI FUKUJIN*, or seven Japanese gods of good fortune or happiness. He is represented as a Buddhist monk and is recognizable by his bald head and vast belly, a symbol both of his wealth and friendly nature and of a soul that has achieved serenity through Buddhism. Hotei is often shown leaning on a large sack, which is said to contain endless gifts for his followers. He is regarded as a friend of the weak and of children. He may have originated as a Chinese hermit called Budaishi who lived in the 10th century AD and was believed to be an incarnation of Maitreya. (See also *THE SHICHI FUKUJIN*)

HSI HO see *XI-HE.*

HSI WANG MU see *XI WANG MU.*

HSIEN see *XIAN.*

HSÜAN TSANG see *XUAN ZONG.*

HOTEI is depicted as a smiling monk with a large belly, which signifies contentment, not greed. He carries a fan and a sack. (IVORY NETSUKE, LATE 19TH CENTURY.)

into an enormous dragon. Afterwards, Hikohohodemi's wife returned to the sea and sent her sister to look after the child.

When the boy grew up, he married his aunt, the sea-god's daughter Tamayori-Hime, who had brought him up. They produced a son with two names, Toyo-Mike-Nu and Kamu-Yamato-Iware-Hiko. After his death, the boy was known as *JIMMU-TENNO*. He was the first emperor of Japan.

HINKON, according to the Tungu people of Siberia, is the god of hunting and lord of animals.

HKUN AI is a hero of Burmese mythology. He married a dragon who had taken the form of a beautiful woman. During each water festival, the woman became a dragon again, and Hkun Ai eventually became upset by his wife's metamorphoses. He decided to leave her, but before he did so, she gave him an egg. In due course the egg cracked open to reveal a son whom Hkun Ai called Tung Hkam.

When the boy grew up, he fell in love with a princess who lived on an island. Tung Hkam could not find a way to cross over the water to reach his beloved, until one day his mother appeared and formed a bridge with her back. Tung Hkam eventually became a great king.

HOMOSUBI see *KAGUTSUCHI.*

HONINIGI see *NINIGI.*

CREATION MYTHS

MYTHS OF THE CREATION OF THE WORLD begin with emptiness, darkness, a floating, drifting lack of form or a fathomless expanse of water. Out of this dim swirl comes a more tangible object which holds the promise of both solid land and human life. The egg is a potent symbol of creation, and features in mythologies all over the world, including those of China and Southeast Asia. According to the folklore of the Iban in Borneo, the world began with two spirits floating like birds on the ocean, who created the earth and sky from two eggs. In Sumatra, a primordial blue chicken, Manuk Manuk, laid three eggs, from which hatched the gods who created the world. A Chinese creation myth, which may have originated in Thailand, begins with the duality governing the universe – yin and yang – struggling within the cosmic egg until it splits, and the deity Pangu emerges.

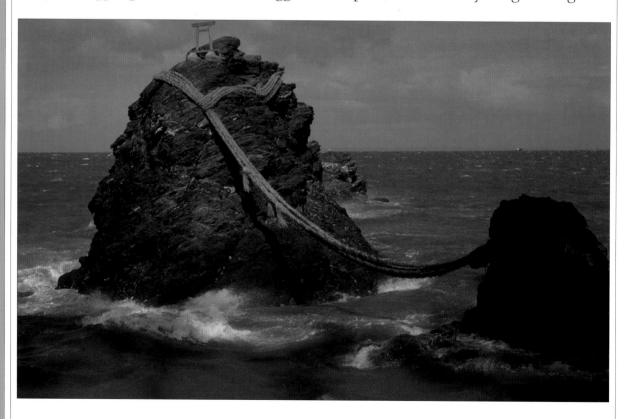

IZANAGI AND IZANAMI were the primal couple in the Japanese creation myth. The gods arose in a remote heaven far above the floating world, and generations of gods and goddesses were born before these two were instructed to complete and solidify the world below. As a result of their union Izanami gave birth to all the islands of Japan and numerous gods and goddesses, including the fire god Kagutsuchi who burnt her so badly that she died. These rocks off the Japanese coast, near Ise, are known as the Myoto-Iwa, or wedded rocks, and symbolize Izanagi and Izanami. They are bound together by a rice-straw rope.

which to rule his kingdom, he was bewitched by a god who took the form of a bear and caused the invaders to fall asleep. One of Jimmu-Tenno's followers dreamt of a magic sword sent by Amaterasu to help Jimmu-Tenno pacify the land now known as Yamato. When he awoke, the soldier found the sword and gave it to his leader. The forces continued on their journey, led by a crow. When they reached Yamato, Jimmu-Tenno built a magnificent palace and married a local princess.

JIZO-BOSATSU

JIZO-BOSATSU is the Japanese form of Kshitigarbha, the bodhisattva or "buddha-to-be" who protects children. He is also said to help pregnant women and travellers. His cult is extremely popular in Japan, where he tends to be regarded as a venerable person rather than as a deity. Each year, his devotees confess their faults to him in the ceremony known as the "Confession of Jizo".

According to one tale, dead children whose parents simply lament their deaths, rather than offering up prayers to help them to be reborn, are sent to a sandy beach or river bank in hell. There, they spend their time building shrines, which are destroyed each night by demons. However, Jizo eventually appears to console the children. He wraps them in the folds of his robe and tells them that he is their father and mother.

JIMMU-TENNO (below) was the legendary first emperor of Japan, from whom the Japanese Imperial family claims direct descent. (DRAWING, ANON. 20TH CENTURY.)

combination of earth and water. Jar-Sub can refer either to the universe as a whole, or to the native land.

JATA

JATA, according to a creation myth of the Dayak people of Borneo, was a divine maiden who made the land and the hills during the second epoch of creation. In the first epoch of creation, the clouds, the sky, the mountains, the cliffs, the sun and moon all came into being. Afterwards, the "Hawk of Heaven" and the great fish *ILA-ILAI LANGIT* were created, followed by two fabulous creatures, *DIDIS MAHENDERA* with the jewel eyes and *ROWANG RIWO* with the golden saliva. Finally, the golden headdress of the god *MAHATALA* appeared. In the third epoch of creation, the tree of life arose, thereby uniting the upper and lower worlds.

JIZO-BOSATSU (above) is sometimes represented as a monk. He carries a staff with rings whose jingling warns small creatures of his approach so he will not step on them. (CARVED WOOD, 11TH CENTURY.)

JIMMU-TENNO

JIMMU-TENNO, according to Japanese mythology, was the first Emperor of Japan and thus the founder of the Imperial line. He was said to be the descendant of the sun goddess *AMATERASU* and the grandson of *HIKOHOHODEMI*. During his life, Jimmu-Tenno was known by two names, Toyo-Mike-Nu and Kamu-Yamato-Iware-Hiko; it was only after his death that he became known as Jimmu-Tenno. Jimmu-Tenno was said to have acceded to the throne in 660BC.

One story tells how, while moving east with his troops in search of new territories and a place from

K

JUROJIN is one of the *SHICHI FUKUJIN* or seven gods of good fortune or happiness, an assembly of deities gathered together in the 17th century by a monk who intended them to symbolize the virtues of a man of his time.

Jurojin was the god of longevity and happy old age. He is depicted as a small old man with a long white beard and is shown in the company of a crane, tortoise or deer, all symbols of longevity. The god also carries a staff to which is attached a scroll or book, which is said to contain the wisdom of the world. He is said to be extremely fond of rice wine. (See also *THE SHICHI FUKUJIN*)

KADAKLAN, according to the mythology of the Tinguian people of Luzon in the Philippines, is the god of thunder. He lives in the sky and beats his drum to create thunder. His dog Kimat is the lightning; he bites whatever Kadaklan chooses.

KAGUTSUCHI, or Homosubi, is the fire god of Japanese Shinto mythology. He is the son of *IZANAMI*, the female half of the primal couple. When she gave birth to him, the goddess was so badly burned that she died. In revenge, *IZANAGI*, Kagutsuchi's father,

attacked the fire god, slicing off his head. In doing so, Izanagi created several more deities. Kagutsuchi was greatly feared by the Japanese.

KAMI was the word used in ancient Japan to refer to anything mysterious or sacred. Its range of application covered everything from objects of folk cults to important deities. The kami came to be regarded as supernatural beings with human qualities. Sometimes, they are nature deities such as mountains, trees and rivers; sometimes they embody values or ideals. They may be protective deities or important men. The Buddha was thought of as the kami of China, and, later on, local kami came to be regarded as protectors of Buddhism. Some became identified with Buddhist deities.

KAMI-MUSUBI see *OKUNINUSHI*.

KANNON see *KWANNON*.

THE KAPPA, according to Japanese mythology, are a race of monkey-like demons. They live in ponds and rivers, and lure human beings, as well as other creatures, down into the depths of the water where they then feed on them. As well as being particularly fond of blood, the kappa like cucumbers.

They are malicious creatures who can, however, sometimes be appeased or bargained with. For example, if a cucumber is inscribed with the names and ages of a particular family and thrown into the water where a kappa lives, the creature will not harm that family. The kappa also display a certain vulnerability. They always return a low bow, and in doing so they spill the water, which empowers them,

from the saucer-shaped depressions in the tops of their heads.

Because they are very knowing, they can sometimes prove helpful to human beings. According to one tale, a kappa persuaded a man on a horse to play tug-of-war with him. As soon as they had grasped hold of one another, the man spurred on his horse, and the water began to spill from the top of the kappa's head. The kappa begged the man to stop, promising that if he did so, he would teach him how to mend bones. The rider agreed, and his family became renowned for their knowledge of bone-setting.

The kappa have monkey-like faces, webbed hands and feet and yellow-green skin. They wear shells like tortoises.

KARITEI-MO see *KISHIMO-JIN*.

KHADAU see *MAMALDI*.

KHORI TUMED is a hero of Mongolian shamanism. One day, he saw nine swans fly on to the island of Oikhon on Lake Baikal. The swans removed their feathered garments and revealed themselves to be beautiful women. Believing that they were alone, they bathed naked in the lake. However, while the women were bathing, Khori Tumed stole one of their dresses and so, when they left the water, one of them was unable to fly away.

Khori Tumed married the swan woman and they lived happily together, eventually producing 11 sons. However, the time came when the swan woman asked Khori Tumed to give her back her feathers. The hero refused, but his wife continued to ask him for her dress, assuring him that she would not fly away. Eventually, Khori Tumed relented and allowed her to try the dress on. Immediately, she flew up and out of a window in their tent.

Before she finally escaped, Khori Tumed persuaded her to name their sons. The swan woman did so and then flew around the tent, bestowing blessings on the tribes.

KHOSADAM, according to the Yenisei people of Siberia, is the wife of *EC*, the supreme god. Ec drove her out of the sky after discovering

KUNLUN, where Gautama Buddha sits enthroned, is regarded as a kind of earthly paradise by both Buddhists and Daoists.
(BUDDHIST SCROLL.)

that she had been unfaithful to him with the moon. Khosadam is an evil, destructive deity and appears as a devourer of souls.

KHUN K'AN see *THENS*.

KHUN K'ET see *THENS*.

KIMAT see *KADAKLAN*.

KISHIMO-JIN, or Kariteï-Mo, is Japanese mythology's "Goddess Mother of Demons". She is said to eat children and to have destroyed a town in India while Gautama Buddha was living there. When the townspeople begged the Buddha to save them, he hid Kishimo-Jin's son beneath his begging bowl. The demoness was distraught and finally asked the Buddha for help. The Buddha converted her by explaining that the pain she felt at the loss of her son was similar to that she wilfully inflicted on other

KUNLUN, beyond the western limits of the ancient Chinese empire, was home to the "Queen Mother of the West".

people. Kishimo-Jin was thus converted to Buddhism and became a protector of children. She is often represented seated on a chair and holding a child in her arms.

KUAN-TI see *GUAN DI*.

KUAN YIN see *GUAN YIN*.

KUEI see *GUEI*.

K'UN LUN see *KUNLUN*.

KUNLUN, or K'un Lun, is a mountain range in western China that is regarded as a Daoist paradise. It is said to be the home of *XI WANG MU* and the immortals. As well as rising above the ground, it is said to descend underground, thereby connecting the realm of the dead with that of the gods. Xi Wang Mu, the "Queen Mother of the West" is said to grow the peaches of immortality in the garden of her splendid palace on Kunlun.

THE EIGHT IMMORTALS

DAOISM EMERGED AS A philosophical system at about the same time as Confucianism, around the sixth century BC. Later, in response to the growing popularity of Buddhism, it acquired all the trappings of a religion, including a mythology. The "Eight Immortals" were central figures in Daoist myth and Chinese folk religion. They had all gained eternal life through seeking the Daoist "Way", and each set an example of ideal behaviour that could be followed by ordinary people to gain enlightenment. Though they were not gods, their immortality gave them superhuman powers: they practised magic and could fly through the air at great speed. They had many adventures while pursuing their mission to banish evil from the world, and were all cheerfully addicted to wine, so that they were sometimes described as the Jiu-zhong Ba Xian – the "Eight Drunken Immortals".

LI TIEGUAI (far left, above) was the first immortal. His body was prematurely cremated while his soul was visiting a sacred mountain. As his own body was no longer available to him, his soul had to inhabit that of a lame beggar, and he used an iron crutch to support himself. Li later revived his disciple's dead mother with a phial of magic medicine, and came to be regarded as the patron of pharmacists. (RELIEF TILE, QING DYNASTY.)

HE XIANGU (second from right), the patron of unmarried girls, was a young woman herself who acquired immortality when a spirit appeared to her on the mountain where she lived and instructed her to grind and eat a mother-of-pearl stone. The stone made her weightless and able to fly over the mountains. She is usually shown carrying a peach or a lotus blossom. (RELIEF TILE, QING DYNASTY.)

CAO GUOJIU (far left) carried a golden tablet which allowed him admission to the imperial court, because he was the brother of the empress. He left the court to seek the Daoist "Way" but, when he found he had no money to pay a ferryman, he tried to impress him with his court credentials. The ferryman, who was Lu Dongbin in disguise, pointed out his folly, and Cao threw the tablet into the river. As an immortal, Cao Guojiu was the patron of the nobility. (RELIEF TILE, QING DYNASTY.)

SHOU LAO (left) the Daoist god of longevity, was visited by the "Eight Immortals" on one of their journeys together. Originally a stellar deity, the "Old Man of the South Pole", he had evolved into an old man who carried a gourd containing the water of life. He rode on a stag, a symbol of happiness. (CHINESE DISH, C. 1680.)

HAN XIANG (left), Lu Dongbin's disciple, was said to be the great-nephew of a Daoist philosopher. He was a wandering minstrel who played the flute. During the sea voyage of the "Eight Immortals", Ao Bing, son of the "Dragon King of the Eastern Sea", tried to steal the flute and take Han Xiang prisoner. There was a great battle to rescue Han Xiang, in which the immortals were, naturally, victorious. *(IVORY FIGURE, MING DYNASTY.)*

LU DONGBIN's (below) blessing on parents was believed to bestow intelligent children, so Chinese scholars regarded him especially highly, and he was the guardian of ink makers. When the "Eight Immortals" decided to cross the sea, they each threw down an object on which to ride, which each turned into a sea monster. Lu Dongbin used his magic sword. *(LU DONGBIN RIDING ON A KRAKEN, FROM SUPERSTITIONS EN CHINE, 1915.)*

LAN CAIHE (above) was either a girl or an effeminate man. She was the patron of the poor, because she gained her immortality by her kindness in attending to the needs of a filthy beggar, whose wounds she washed and dressed. The beggar turned out to be Li Tieguai, the first of the "Eight Immortals". Lan Caihe was sometimes shown with a basket of flowers, because of her skill in growing marvellous blooms from a small pot of earth. *(FRESCO, QING DYNASTY.)*

ZHANG GUOLAO (above) rode on a white mule, sometimes sitting facing the animal's tail. He was a great necromancer, and his mule had extraordinary powers. It could travel over vast distances but, when no longer required, it could be folded up like a sheet of paper and kept in a bag. Zhang Guolao is often depicted with the bag containing his mule, or hitting a bamboo drum. He granted both happy marriage and the gift of children. *(IVORY AND BRONZE FIGURE, MING DYNASTY.)*

ZHONG-LI QUAN (left) learnt the "Way" of Daoism from Li Tieguai, then disappeared into the clouds on achieving immortality and became the messenger of heaven. Bald, with a long beard, he carried a feather fan and was the patron of soldiers. Zhong-li Quan was sometimes also shown holding a peach. The peaches of Xi Wang Mu, the "Queen Mother of the West" ripened every 3,000 years, when the immortals ate them to renew their immortality. *(IVORY FIGURE, MING DYNASTY.)*

L

KWANNON, or Kannon, according to Japanese Buddhist belief, is the god or goddess of mercy. She is the Japanese form of the Chinese goddess *GUANYIN*, or Kuan Yin, who herself derives from the Indian male bodhisattva Avalokiteshvara. The feminization of Kwannon is relatively modern. Kwannon, as a bosatsu, or bodhisattva, is a "buddha-to-be" who has decided to remain on earth in order to help other people to achieve enlightenment. She is known as the "Lady Giver of Children" and is a very popular deity, the protector of women and children. Kwannon is said to have been born from a ray of light, which emerged from the right of the Buddha Amitabha. There is also a Kwannon with a horse's head and one with numerous arms. According to one

KWANNON (above) lived in a cave in the Iwai Valley. (WOODBLOCK PRINT BY HIROSHIGE, ANDO OR UTAGAWA, 1853.)

KWANNON (right), the Japanese god or goddess of mercy, could assume 33 different forms, including this one with 11 heads. (WOOD SCULPTURE, 12TH CENTURY.)

tradition, Kwannon could assume 33 different forms, which gave rise to a great ritual pilgrimage to 33 sanctuaries dedicated to her.

LAN CAIHE see *BA XIAN*.

LAO CHÜN see *LAO JUN*.

LAO JUN, or Lao Chün, is the name given to the deified form of Laozi, who, by tradition, wrote the Dao-de Jing, the text which forms the basis of Daoism. He is believed to have lived in the sixth century BC; his deification began in the second century BC. Lao Jun became one of the most important Daoist gods and was sometimes said to have arisen from the primordial chaos. According to another legend, he emerged from his mother's side after a gestation of 80 years.

LEI GONG, or Lei Kung, is the god of thunder in China's Daoist pantheon. Known as "My Lord Thunder", or "Thunder Duke", he is depicted as a horribly ugly man with wings, claws, and a blue body. He carries a drum, and in his hands he holds a mallet and a chisel. Lei Gong attacks any human being

THE MYTHS OF EAST ASIA

guilty of an undetected crime or who remains beyond the reach of the earthly law.

One story tells how a fierce storm arose in the middle of a thick forest. A hunter looked up into the trees and saw a child holding a flag. Lei Gong, the thunder god, approached the child but as soon as the child waved the flag, he retreated. Immediately, the hunter realized that the child must be an evil spirit and that the flag must be made of some unclean material, since all deities dislike impure objects. The hunter shot down the flag, and Lei Gong instantly struck the tree in which the child was perched. Unfortunately, being so

LAO JUN (above) is said to have been a contemporary of Confucius and a teacher of the Buddha. (PAINTED SCROLL, 18TH CENTURY.)

LAO JUN (above right), who was reputed to have been born with white hair and the power of speech, lived to a very great age. (PAINTING BY QIAN GU, 16TH CENTURY.)

close to the tree, the hunter was also struck by the thunder. However, when he came round, the hunter found a message on his body saying that his life had been prolonged for 12 years in thanks for having assisted with the work of heaven. At the foot of the tree, the hunter found the body of a vast lizard, the real form of the child.

LEI GONG (above), the winged thunder god, harasses sheep and swine in a storm of thunder clouds and explosive lightning flashes. (WOODBLOCK PRINT, 19TH CENTURY.)

M

LEI KUNG see *LEI GONG*.

LI NAZHA see *NAZHA*.

LI TIEGUAI see *BA XIAN*.

THE LIGHTNING GODDESS is one of the nature deities referred to in early Chinese legends. She is the wife of the god of thunder, *LEI GONG*, and carries a pair of mirrors which she uses to create flashes of lightning and, occasionally, fires. The gods of thunder, lightning, wind and rain were invoked by the people during times of drought.

LING CHIH see *LING ZHI*.

LING ZHI, or Ling Chih, according to Daoist belief, is a plant of immortality. Its name means "magic herb". Ling zhi is believed to be either a type of grass or a mushroom. It grows on the three islands of the immortals, and anyone who eats it is said to gain immortality for at least 500 years.

LONG WANG, or Lung Wang, are "Dragon Kings" according to Chinese mythology. They are the servants either of Yuanshi Tian-Zong, the "Celestial Venerable of the Primordial Beginning", or *YU HUANG*, the "Jade Emperor", who was Yuanshi Tian-Zong's assistant and later came to surpass him in power. According to Daoist belief, there are different varieties of Long Wang: the celestial dragon kings, the dragon kings of the five cardinal points and the dragon kings of the oceans. Each of the dragon kings of the oceans has responsibility for one of the four oceans, helped by an army of sea creatures. The Long Wang bring rain.

LU DONGBIN see *BA XIAN*.

THE LIGHTNING GODDESS
holding her two mirrors, which she flashes to cause lightning.

LUNG WANG see *LONG WANG*.

LUXING see *SAN XING*.

MAHATALA is the supreme god of the Dayak people of Borneo. He rules over the upper regions and lives on Jewel Mountain.

MAIDERE, according to the Altaic people of Siberia, was the saviour whom the great sky god

THE LIGHTNING GODDESS holding her two mirrors, which she flashes to cause lightning.

ULGAN sent to earth in order to protect human beings from the evil ways of the god and first man *ERLIK*. Erlik succeeded in killing Maidere, whereupon the saviour's blood gave rise to vast flames, which leapt up to the skies, destroying Erlik's heaven.

MAIN is a mythical hero of the Evenk people of Siberia. One story tells how a great elk ran to the top of a hill in the upper world and impaled the sun on its antlers. Immediately, human beings, who lived in the middle world, were subjected to continual darkness. The hero Main flew to the upper world on a pair of skis and proceeded to hunt down the elk. He eventually succeeded in shooting

LONG WANG (above), a dragon king, holds court in this modern mural in a mountain temple in Shanxi province in northern China. It is said that the dragon kings live in their own crystal palaces beneath the water.

the animal with an arrow, whereupon sunshine returned to the middle world of human beings. Main remained in the upper world, guarding the sun. According to Evenk tradition, each evening the elk catches the sun and each night, Main pursues the elk and reclaims the sun in order to rise the next morning.

MAMALDI, according to the Amur people of Siberia, created the continent of Asia. She and her husband, Khadau, are regarded either as the first human couple or as the parents of the first shaman. Whereas Khadau created the souls

LONG WANG (left), a celestial dragon king. Because they were the bringers of rain, dragon kings controlled life and death.

of shamans, Mamaldi breathed life into them. She was eventually killed by Khadau.

MANUK MANUK, according to Sumatran mythology, is a fabulous blue chicken, which belonged to the supreme god. One day, the chicken laid three gigantic eggs from which emerged three gods. The gods created the three levels of the universe: the upper world, or heaven; the middle world, or the earth; and the underworld.

MARISHI-TEN is Japanese Buddhism's goddess, or sometimes god, of war and victory. In the Middle Ages, Japanese warriors believed that Marishi-Ten made them invisible. She is depicted either sitting or standing on a boar or herd of boars. She sometimes has as many as eight arms in which she holds numerous weapons.

LING ZHI (right), the fabled mushrooms of immortality, being gathered by a boy.
(DRAWING BY ZHANG LING, 16TH CENTURY.)

MEN SHEN consist of a pair of Chinese gods who look after entrances and doorways. One of the gods is usually represented with a red or black face, the other with a white one. They are armed with weapons and magic symbols, and guard houses as well as palaces. During the New Year festivities, paper images of the gods are stuck on doors to protect those that live within from evil demons.

Although their origins are supposed to lie in the ancient past – when they were said to prevent spirits escaping from hell – one pair of Men Shen was later said to represent two historical generals who heroically guarded the palace of a Tang dynasty emperor against demons. According to one myth, the emperor had promised to look after a dragon king who had made a mistake while distributing the rain and had been condemned to death by the "Jade Emperor", YU HUANG. However, the emperor was unable to keep his promise and the spirit of the dragon king held him responsible for his death. Each night, the dragon king would come and cause a commotion outside the palace gates. Unable to sleep, the emperor fell ill, so his two generals guarded the doors. Eventually, the dragon king was driven away.

MIROKU-BOSATSU is the Japanese form of Maitreya, the future buddha. He currently lives in the Tushita heaven awaiting his future birth as a human being and finally as a buddha.

MOMOTARO is a Japanese hero who was born from a peach and was renowned for conquering demons. An elderly couple, who had been unable to have children, found a peach floating in a stream. When they cut the fruit open, they found a tiny baby boy inside. The baby sat up and ate the peach, whereupon the delighted couple called him Momotaro or "Peach Child". They raised Momotaro to be a brave and noble boy.

When he was 15, he decided to repay his parents and friends for looking after him, and determined to rid a neighbouring island of the ONI, or devils, which were persecuting them. Momotaro pocketed three dumplings, which the old woman had cooked, and set off for the island. He soon encountered a dog, a pheasant and a monkey, each of whom agreed to accompany him on his quest in return for a dumpling. The four adventurers then took a boat and crossed over to the island. There, they found

MEN SHEN (above left), one of a pair of entrance gods, guards a Chinese temple door in Yogjakarta, Java.

MEN SHEN (above), guarding a temple entrance, are sometimes represented as two generals, Heng and Ha, whose weapons include poisonous breath and fire.

numerous girls who had been taken prisoner by the oni. Momotaro attacked the castle of the oni and, together with his companions, succeeded in killing all the devils. He then piled his boat high with the treasure that the oni had stolen from the village people, helped the captive girls on board and returned home a hero.

MONJU-BOSATSU is the Japanese form of the bodhisattva, or "buddha-to-be", Manjushri. His name means "he whose beauty

MOYANG KAPIR is a civilizing hero spirit, according to the Ma'Betisek people of Malaysia. He stole the bag that contained the rules of civilized human behaviour from the ferocious spirit *MOYANG MELUR* and then distributed them among his people in order that they might no longer commit murder, cannibalism and incest.

MOYANG MELUR, according to the Ma'Betisek people of Malaysia, is a spirit being who guarded the rules of civilized behaviour. He is said to live on the moon and to be half-human, half-tiger. For a long time, Moyang

charms", and he personifies wisdom, compassion and contemplation. Monju-Bosatsu is often shown accompanied by a lion and is usually seated, holding the sword of intelligence, which cuts through ignorance.

Melur kept the rules of civilized behaviour to himself and, as a result, human beings constantly committed murder, incest and cannibalism.

One night, Moyang Melur was so enthralled by the chaos and destruction that was taking place below him that he leaned right out of the moon in order to take a closer look. However, he leaned too far and fell to earth. There, he met a hunter called *MOYANG KAPIR*. Moyang Melur told Moyang Kapir that unless he was able to return to

MIROKU (left), the future buddha, sits in contemplation, awaiting the time of his coming on earth. (JAPANESE SCULPTURE.)

MONJU-BOSATSU (above right), the Japanese form of Manjushri, with the Buddha (seated in the centre) and the bodhisattva Fugen-Bosatsu. (14TH CENTURY.)

the moon immediately, he would kill every single human being. Moyang Kapir promptly threw a rope to the moon, and they both climbed up it.

Moyang Melur was looking forward to killing and eating Moyang Kapir, but the latter quickly slid back down to earth, taking with him the rules of civilized behaviour, which he had found hidden in a bag under a mat. The hunter then distributed the rules among his people.

SHAMANS OF MONGOLIA

IN MANY TRADITIONAL COMMUNITIES, the shaman is a central figure combining the function of priest and doctor. He or she has the power to control spirits which, though neither good nor evil, may be destructive: to protect the community he or she incorporates them in him or herself. The shaman's ability to make out-of-body journeys to the upper and lower spirit worlds is also part of a protective role in the tribe. In shamanistic myths the world was once peopled by beings who could easily travel between heaven and earth, but after the bridge between the two was broken, most people lost their original wisdom. Eventually only a few – the shamans – were able to reach heaven, and they could do so only in spirit, by separating their souls from their bodies. Shamanistic myths, passed down through successive generations in an oral tradition, tell of a process of decline, from a golden age, when great spirits brought knowledge to the world, to the present, when not even all shamans can fly away from it.

DRUMMING (above) is used to induce a trance state in which the shaman's soul can leave his body. The drum beat excludes other stimuli while its insistent rhythm works on the consciousness. According to Mongolian legend, early shamans could use their drums to call back the souls of the dead. The lord of the dead, fearing that he would lose all his subjects, ordained that the shamans' drums, originally double-headed, should have only a single head to reduce their power.

ANIMALS (left) are used by Siberian Yakut shamans as receptacles for their souls. Each shaman keeps his chosen animal far away from other people, so that its life is protected and his spiritual well-being ensured. However, once a year, when the last snow melts, the animals are said to come down from the mountains and walk into the villages. The most powerful shamans keep their souls in horses, elks, bears, eagles or boars; the weakest keep them in dogs. Sometimes the animals fight, and if one is harmed, its shaman will fall ill or die.

おおくにぬしのみこと
大国主命さまは恋愛良縁の守り神と
して有名です。
因幡の白兎を助けられた
心のやさしい神さまでみんなに幸福を与えて下さいます。

京都 地主神社

ご利益

良縁祈願

恋い愛い結婚

OKUNINUSHI, according to Japanese Shinto mythology, is the god of medicine and magic. His name means "Great Land Master", and he ruled the earth after its creation until *AMATERASU* sent her grandson *NINIGI* to take his place. As god of medicine, he is credited with having invented therapeutic methods of healing.

Okuninushi had 80 brothers, all of whom wanted to marry the beautiful princess *YAKAMI* or Ya-Gami-Hime. While the brothers were on their way to visit the princess, a flayed hare stopped them and asked them for help. The brothers told the hare to wash in the sea and then dry itself in the wind. The hare suffered excruciating pain and distress. The creature then met Okuninushi who, feeling sorry for it, told it to bathe in fresh water and then roll around in the pollen of kama grass. The hare did as Okuninushi advised and imme-diately felt better. In gratitude, the hare, who was really a god, told Okuninushi that the beautiful princess Yakami would be his.

Okuninushi's brothers were furious. They heated a vast rock until it was white-hot and rolled it down a mountain towards their brother. Okuninushi mistook the rock for a boar, caught hold of it and was burned to death. However, with the help of his mother, Kami-Musubi, he was brought back to life. The brothers then crushed Okuninushi to death. This time, Kami-Musubi advised her son to avoid further attacks by taking refuge in the underworld.

There, Okuninushi met the storm god *SUSANO-WO* and his daughter Suseri-Hime. The couple fell in love. When Susano-Wo discovered this, he sent Okuninushi to sleep in a room full of snakes. However, the god was protected by a scarf, which Suseri-Hime had given him. The following night, Susano-Wo sent him to sleep in a room full of centipedes and wasps, but again Okuninushi was pro-tected. Susano-Wo then fired an arrow into the middle of an enor-mous field and told Okuninushi to look for it. When Okuninushi reached the middle of the field, Susano-Wo set fire to the grass. However, a mouse showed Okuninushi a hole in which he could take shelter from the fire and then brought the arrow to him.

By this time, Susano-Wo was beginning to approve of Okuninushi. He asked him to wash his hair and then went to sleep. While Susano-Wo was sleeping, Okuninushi tied the storm god's hair to the rafters of his palace and fled with Suseri-Hime. He took with him Susano-Wo's sword, bow and arrows and his harp, called Koto. As Okuninushi and Suseri-Hime made their escape, the harp brushed against a tree, and the noise of its strings awoke Susano-Wo. The god jumped up and in so doing pulled down his house with his hair.

Okuninushi hurried onwards. Eventually, at the borders of the underworld, Susano-Wo almost caught up with the elopers and called out to them, advising Okuninushi to fight his brothers with Susano-Wo's weapons in order that he might rule the world. It seems that Okuninushi's trickery had finally convinced the storm god that he would make a suitable husband for Suseri-Hime, because he then asked the god to make Suseri-Hime his wife and to build a palace at the foot of Mount Uka. Okuninushi became ruler of the province of Izumo.

OKUNINUSHI is seen here with the white hare of Inaoa, who foretold his success in his quest for the hand of Yakami.

P

OTSHIRVANI, according to Siberian mythology, is a god of light. He was sent by the supreme god to fight Losy, a monstrous serpent who killed all mortal beings by covering the world with poison. Otshirvani took the form of an enormous bird and, seizing Losy in his claws, threw him against the world mountain, killing him.

PA HSIEN see BA XIAN.

PAMALAK BAGOBO, according to the Bagobo people of Mindanao in the Philippines, is the god who created human beings. According to tradition, monkeys once behaved and looked like humans and only acquired their current appearance when Pamalak decided to create humankind as a separate race.

P'AN-KU see PANGU.

PANGU, or P'an-ku, is the cosmic giant of Chinese mythology. He is said to be the child of YIN and

THE ONI are giant horned demons. They are said to have come to Japan from China with the arrival of Buddhism, and Buddhist priests perform annual rites in order to expel them. The oni can be a variety of colours and have three fingers, three toes and sometimes three eyes. They are usually cruel and lecherous, and they are said to sweep down from the sky in order to steal the souls of people who are about to die. One story tells how the diminutive hero MOMOTARO freed numerous young girls whom the oni had captured and raped.

The oni of hell have the heads of oxen or horses; they hunt down sinners and take them away in their chariot of fire to EMMA-O, the ruler of the underworld. Some oni are held responsible for illness and disease, and others are said to have once been mortal women whose jealousy or grief transformed them into demons.

OT, the fire queen of the Mongols, is said to have been born at the beginning of the world, when the earth and sky separated. Her blessing is invoked at weddings and her radiance is said to penetrate throughout all the realms. Ot is believed originally to have been identical with UMAI, mother goddess of the Turkic people of Siberia.

PANGU is the giant who emerged from the cosmic egg when it split to form the earth and sky. He held the two apart to create the world.

PANGU, the cosmic creator and mythological deity, on an altar in a temple in Tainan, in southern Taiwan.

the myth tells how Pangu was born from the five basic elements and formed heaven and earth with a chisel and hammer. Pangu is still worshipped by some of the people of South China. (See also CREATION MYTHS; CHINA'S SACRED PEAKS)

PENG LAI, or P'eng-lai, according to Daoist belief, is an island in the East China Sea inhabited by the immortals or XIAN. The plant of immortality, LING ZHI, grows there. Many explorers have attempted to discover the mythical island, but all expeditions have failed – sometimes, it is said, because the island sinks beneath the waves. Everything on the miraculous island is made of gold and jewels: the trees are made of pearl and coral, and the animals and birds are glittering white.

The two other islands of the immortals are Fangchang and Yingzhou. Originally, there were five islands, but a giant caused two of them to break away from their moorings and sink without trace. Fangchang, lying off the east coast of China, is said to be inhabited by dragons and to boast marvellous palaces made of gold, jade and crystal. Thousands of immortals live there, cultivating the plant of immortality. Yingzhou is also credited with a marvellous appearance and inhabitants.

P'ENG-LAI see PENG LAI.

POLONG, according to Malayan and Indonesian tradition, is a flying demon created from the blood of a murdered man. Whoever owns the Polong can order it to attack his enemies. The victims tear their clothes, go blind and eventually lose consciousness. However, the Polong also feeds on the blood of its owner.

PU LANG SEUNG see THENS.

YANG, the vital forces of the universe. The myth of Pangu's birth tells how, at the very beginning of time, only chaos existed. Chaos took the form of a primordial egg, and eventually Pangu took shape inside its shell. The creature slept and grew inside the egg for 18,000 years until, eventually, he woke up and stretched. The light part of the egg, which was pervaded by yang, rose up to become the sky; the heavy part, pervaded by yin, sank down and became the earth.

Pangu, fearing that the earth and sky might merge together again, stood between them, his head keeping the sky aloft and his feet treading down the earth. For 18,000 years, the distance between heaven and earth increased at a rate of 3 metres (ten feet) a day. Pangu grew at the same rate to continue to hold heaven and earth apart.

Eventually, when Pangu considered that there was no risk of the earth and sky rejoining, he fell asleep and eventually died. The giant's enormous corpse gave rise to all the elements. His breath became the wind and clouds, his voice became the thunder and lightning, his left eye became the sun, and his right eye became the moon. His four limbs and his trunk were transformed into the cardinal directions and the mountains, his blood became the rivers and his veins the roads. His flesh became trees and soil, the hair on his head and his beard became the stars in the sky, and the hairs on his body were transformed into grass and flowers. His teeth and bones became metal and stones, and his sweat produced the dew. Finally, the fleas and parasites on his body became the ancestors of the different races of human beings.

Many later tales elaborate the story of Pangu. According to one, the alternation of night and day occurs when Pangu opens and closes his eyes. Another version of

467

CHINESE DRAGONS

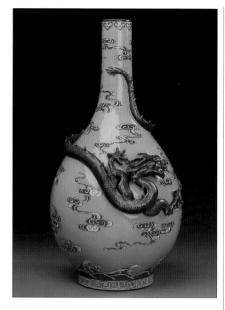

THE CHINESE DRAGON CAME FIRST in the mythical hierarchy of 360 scaly creatures, and was one of the four animals who symbolized the cardinal points. Associated with the east, the dragon stood for sunrise, spring and fertility and was opposed by the white tiger of the west, who represented death. Daoist dragons were benevolent spirits associated with happiness and prosperity, and were kind to humans. However, when Buddhism became popular, their character was modified by the Indian concept of the naga, which was a more menacing creature. In folk religion, the Long Wang were dragon kings who had authority over life and death because they were responsible for rain, without which life could not continue, and funerals. They were gods of rivers, lakes and oceans, and represented wisdom, strength and goodness. Because they had power over the rain, offerings were made to dragons during droughts, but angry Long Wang sent storms, fog and earthquakes. They protected ferrymen and water-carriers, and punished anyone who wasted water.

THE CHINESE DRAGON (above) was a mythical hybrid monster with the "horns of a deer, head of a camel, abdomen of a cockle, scales of a carp, claws of an eagle, feet of a tiger, and ears of an ox." Because dragons represented the yang principle, their images were traditionally accompanied by water or clouds, which were yin. (QIANLONG, FAMILLE ROSE BOTTLE VASE, 18TH CENTURY.)

DRAGON PROCESSIONS (left), which were held all over China in spring, welcomed the annual return of these generous creatures and ensured fertility. Dragons spent the winter underground, emerging on the second day of the second lunar month. Their arrival, announced by claps of thunder, coincided with the beginning of the spring rains, and this was the time to go out into the fields and begin the year's cultivation. As bringers of rain, dragons were coloured blue-green. (HSIE YANG, PROCESSION OF THE BLUE DRAGON.)

IMPERIAL DRAGONS (right) represented the "Sun of Heaven", the emperor of China. The legendary emperor Yu, founder of the Xia dynasty, had originally appeared in the form of a winged dragon who emerged from his father's body when it was slashed open. Each succeeding emperor was said to be a reincarnation of Yu. The emperor's accoutrements, often in imperial yellow, were richly embellished with dragons. (CHINESE DRAGON DISH.)

A DRAGON (above) was often depicted playing with a flaming pearl or ball, which symbolized thunder. It was this heavenly sport which was thought to cause the rain to fall. Only imperial dragons were represented with five claws on each foot. Those with four claws signified the status of a prince, while court officials were allowed only three claws for the dragons embroidered on their robes and other possessions. (CHINESE PILLAR RUG.)

HUI-NENG (right), the Chinese Buddhist patriarch, persuaded a fierce dragon to shrink so small that it would fit into a tiny rice bowl and was thus able to subdue it. The magic powers of dragons included the ability to make themselves invisible at will and change their shape and size. They could shrink to the size of a silkworm or swell to fill all the space between heaven and earth. (ILLUSTRATION FROM SUPERSTITIONS EN CHINE, 1914.)

R

PU-TAI see *PUDAI*.

PUDAI, or Pu-tai, was a Chinese monk who is said to have lived in the tenth century AD and whose original name was Qizi. He is said to have earned his name, which means "Hempen Sack", from his habit of wandering through towns with a beggar's sack on his back. He was believed to be able to predict the weather, and his life was filled with miraculous events. At his death, he revealed himself to be an incarnation of Maitreya, the future Buddha. Pudai is often represented as the "Laughing Buddha", the Chinese style of depicting Maitreya.

PULANG GANA, according to the Iban people of Borneo, is an earth spirit who ensures the abundant growth of rice. According to tradition, a long time ago the Iban began to clear the jungle in order to create the first rice farm. However, when they arose the next morning, they found that all the trees had grown back. The same happened after their next attempt to clear the jungle, and the next. At last, the Iban decided to keep watch during the night in order to try and solve the mystery.

That night, they saw Pulang Gana coax the trees back to life and ensure that they became rooted in the soil once more. They tried to catch the spirit, who explained that he owned the earth and everything that grew in it, and that he alone could ensure that the plants flourished. When the people asked the spirit what they should do before cultivating rice, he told them that they should offer up gifts to him.

QORMUSTA, or Chormusta, according to Mongolian belief, is king of the Tengri, the realms of

heaven. The supreme god, he lives in the centre of the world and is associated with the creation of fire.

RADIN is a mythical hero of the Iban people of Borneo. One tale tells how, after winning a battle, Radin began to be troubled by a hungry ghost. When the ghost introduced smallpox to Radin's tribe, the hero determined to kill it. One night, Radin hid inside a roll of matting, and when the ghost approached, he jumped out and cut it into pieces with his sword. Before falling asleep again, Radin heard something fall to the ground and, when daylight came, he found a carving of a hornbill, a sacred bird, lying on the ground in pieces. Radin realized that this signified that the ghost was far too powerful a being to overcome, so he and his people moved to another area.

THE RAIN SPIRIT is one of the early nature gods who were referred to in Chinese legendary stories. In his struggle with *HUANG DI*, the "Yellow Emperor", *CHIYOU* begged

THE RAIN SPIRIT (left), with his vase of water, sometimes also holds a dragon on a plate, since the dragon is a symbol of rain.

RANGDA (right), the Balinese demon queen, is represented by a terrifying mask.

the "Wind God" and the "Master of Rain" to bring on a major storm, with gales and torrential rains to help him. Along with the *LIGHTNING GODDESS* and the God of Thunder, these nature spirits were invoked during times of drought. The Goddess of Lightning flashes the two mirrors she carries to cause lightning, while thunder is made by the thunder god with his hammer and drums, and has the power to kill. The Master of Rain is said to own a mysterious one-legged bird, which can drink the seas dry.

RANGDA is the terrifying demon queen of Bali. She leads an army of evil witches against *BARONG*, the leader of the forces of good. The evil demon is usually represented as scantily clad, with long hair and with claws in place of fingernails and toenails.

It is sometimes suggested that Rangda derived from an 11th-century Balinese queen who was exiled by the king for practising witchcraft against his second wife. In revenge, Rangda attempted to destroy the kingdom. Half the population died of plague before she was overcome by the superior powers of a holy man. The name Rangda means "widow". (See also *DEMONS*)

ROWANG RIWO is a fabulous creature who, according to the Dayak people of Borneo, appeared during the first epoch of creation with *DIDIS MAHENDERA*. Rowang Riwo had golden saliva and Didis Mahendera had eyes of jewels.

THE SAN QING DAOZU's senior deity is Yuanshi Tian-zong, "Jade Pure", who is invisible and eternal.

THE SAN GUAN DADI, or San Kuan Ta-ti, are the "Three Great Primordial Rulers" and "Controllers of Heaven, Earth and the Waters". Also known as the San Yuan Dadi, they are of mythical origin and are revered as the source of all happiness and forgiveness of sins, able to avert calamities and sickness. Legend has it that *YU HUANG*, the "Jade Emperor", sent them down to earth to govern it, and observe men's good and evil thoughts and deeds.

SAN-HSING see *SAN XING*.

THE SAN QING DAOZU's second deity is Ling-bao Tian-zong, who regulates time and yin and yang.

SAN KUAN TA-TI see *SAN GUAN DADI*.

THE SAN QING DAOZU, or, as they are sometimes known, "The Three Pure Ones", are the supreme deities of the orthodox Daoist pantheon, ruling the entire cosmos from the highest heaven. In the "Doctrine of the Three Pure Ones", they are the symbolic personification of the three life principles: breath, vital essence and spirit. They are prayed to as a group for assistance in coping with the problems of life.

THE SAN QING DAOZU's third deity is Lao Jun. He is the deified form of the legendary founder of Daoism, Laozi.

SAN GUAN DADI, the three great primordial rulers, are transcendent powers who bestow happiness, forgive sins and protect from evil.

The first is the "Perfect One", or "Jade Pure", Yuanshi Tian-zong, the deity of the beginning representing primeval origins. He is in charge of the "Heaven of the Heavenly Ones" and is said to have formulated the heavens and earth and dominated the first phase of creation.

The "Highest Holy One", Ling-bao Tian-zong, the "High Pure", represents energy and activity. He is in charge of the "Heaven of the Perfect Ones", Zhenren, and is said to have devised the rules for calculating time and controlling the interaction of *YIN* and *YANG*, as well as the doctrine for the heavens and earth. He is the guardian of magical writings. Ling-bao dominated the second phase of creation.

The "Greatest Holy One", the "Supreme Pure", *LAO JUN*, representing humankind, is the deified philosopher Laozi who is in charge of the third and lowest heaven, that of the immortals. He is said to have dominated the third phase of the creation of the cosmos, and inspired the formation of religious Daoism at a later stage.

THE SAN XING, or San-hsing, or "Three Stars", are the three Chinese gods of good fortune. They were historical figures who were given divine status in recognition of their special merits. Fuxing or "Lucky Star" is usually depicted alongside a child or as a bat, a symbol of good luck. He is the god of happiness. Luxing or "Star of Honour" is the god of salaries and is often shown as a deer. Shouxing, "Star of Longevity", is shown with the face of an old man, a white beard and eyebrows, a high bald head and holding a knotty staff, a symbol of the immortals.

Fuxing is said to have been a government official called Yang Cheng who lived during the sixth century BC. He came from a village whose inhabitants were all very short in height. Each year, the emperor, who enjoyed surrounding himself with dwarfs, would call a number of the villagers to his court and insist that they remain there. As a result, as time went by, the population of the village began to dwindle. Eventually, Yang Cheng asked the emperor to take pity on the village folk. The emperor was impressed by Yang Cheng's petition and so ceased his demands.

Luxing is sometimes identified with Guo Ziyi, who had many sons, or is said to have been Shi Fei, a servant of the founder of the Han dynasty, who lived at the end of the third century BC.

Shouxing came to be known as *SHOU LAO*, the god of long life and "Old Man of the South Pole". He is said to fix the date of everyone's death, writing it down beforehand. However, although the digits of the appointed date cannot be changed, they can sometimes be juggled.

According to one tale, a child called Zao Yan was told that he had only 19 more years to live. One day, the boy was told to go to a field, taking with him some food and wine. There, he would find two men playing a game of draughts (checkers) under a mulberry tree. Zao Yan was advised to offer the men food and drink but to refuse to answer any of their questions. The boy did as he was told. He gave the two men the food and drink, then waited quietly while they argued over how they should thank him. The men finally decided to reverse the order of the digits of the number of years Zao Yan was to live, thereby decreeing that he should live for a further 91 years. Zao Yan later discovered that one of the men had been Shou Lao.

SEMARA, according to the mythology of the Balinese, is the god of love who lives in the floating sky, one of a series of skies that lies above the layer of water hanging over the earth.

THE SAN XING Luxing and Fuxing are dressed as mandarins, while Shouxing, the god of longevity, holds a sprig of Ling Zhi, the plant of immortality. (JADEITE FIGURES, LATE QING DYNASTY.)

THE SAN XING (above) are usually portrayed as three good-humoured old men, surrounded by symbols of good fortune, longevity and immortality. (PAINTED SILK SCROLL BY WANG CHAO, C. 1500.)

SENGALONG BURONG see *SURONG GUNTING*.

SETESUYARA, according to Balinese mythology, is the goddess who rules over the underworld together with the god *BATARA KALA*.

SHAKA-NYORAI is the Japanese name for the Buddha Shakyamuni Gautama. Although Shaka is worshipped in Japan, the dominant form of Buddhism is the "Pure Land" school, whose followers chiefly venerate the buddha *AMIDA* or Amitabha.

SHANG DI, or Shang Ti, was worshipped as the ancestor of China's Shang dynasty, established around 1500BC. The supreme god, he ruled over heaven and controlled natural phenomena such as

SHAKA-NYORAI, the Japanese buddha, preaching at Ryoj-Usen Mountain. (WALL PAINTING, 8TH CENTURY.)

the thunder, lightning, wind and rain. He was also regarded as the god of agriculture and was believed to determine people's fates. He was sometimes known simply as Di, which means "Lord" or "God".

SHANG TI see *SHANG DI*.

SHEN NONG, or Shen Nung, is an ancient Chinese god of medicine, health, agriculture and forestry. Together with *FU XI* and *HUANG DI*, he was one of the San Huang, or "Three Nobles", legendary emperors of China. He was sometimes referred to as the

"Divine Husbandman", although, as god of the hot winds, he could also bring harm. Shen Nong is said to have invented the plough to improve the lives of the ancient Chinese. He taught them how to grow food and revealed the medicinal properties of plants.

Because he had a transparent stomach, he was able to observe the effect of food and drink on his body. However, while investigating the effect of an unusual piece of grass, he turned black and died.

SHENG MU see *DONGYUE DADI*.

THE SHICHI FUKUJIN are the seven Japanese gods of good fortune or happiness. Their names are *DAIKOKU*, *EBISU*, *BENTEN*,

BISHAMON, *FUKUROKUJU*, *JUROJIN* and *HOTEI*. Among the group are deities from Buddhism, Japanese folklore and Chinese Daoism. The group was assembled in the 17th century by the monk Tenkai, who intended the gods to symbolize the virtues of fortune, magnanimity, candour, dignity, popularity, longevity and amiability. The deities are said to travel together on a treasure ship and are sometimes portrayed thus. (See also *THE SHICHI FUKUJIN*)

SHEN NONG (below left), with Huang Di, another legendary emperor of China.

SHEN NONG (below) is portrayed dressed in green leaves because he is a "primitive" deity and lived before cloth was ever invented.

SHOTEN, or Daisho-Kangiten, is a Japanese form of the Indian elephant-headed god Ganesha, who was adopted by certain Buddhist sects. His cult was introduced to Japan in the ninth century. Shoten both creates obstacles and overcomes them. He is worshipped by esoteric sects, and the god's tremendous power is believed to help people to gain enlightenment.

SHOU LAO is the Daoist god of long life. Originally known as Shouxing, he was one of the SAN XING or Chinese gods of good fortune. In due course, he came to rule over the department of the heavens that decrees the life-span of human beings. The god is usually shown with a large head and carrying a staff as well as a gourd, which holds the water of life. In his other hand, he holds the peach of eternal life. His creature is the white crane, a symbol of immortality. (See also THE EIGHT IMMORTALS)

SHOUXING see SHOU LAO.

SHUN is one of the five legendary emperors, or Wu Di, of Chinese mythology. The emperor YAO chose Shun, rather than his own son, as his successor. Shun was said to be a potter who travelled throughout the four directions and banished all the threatening creatures guarding their entrances. He is said to have lived in the third century BC and to have been succeeded by YU.

SUKU-NA-BIKONA, a dwarf deity, assisted OKUNINUSHI, one of Japan's great mythological heroes. He is regarded as a benevolent deity who is learned in both healing and cultivation.

After Okuninushi had settled in his palace with his wife, Suku-Na-Bikona arrived in a tiny boat on the crest of a wave. Okuninushi put the dwarf in the palm of his hand in order to examine him, whereupon the creature leapt up and bit the hero on his cheek. Okuninushi was

annoyed and told the gods what had happened. One of the gods realized that the dwarf must be his son, a mischievous child who had fallen to earth. The god asked Okuninushi to look after his child, who proceeded to help the hero to establish his rule. Eventually, however, Suku-Na-Bikona disappeared.

SURONG GUNTING is a culture hero of the Iban people of Borneo. He went to visit his grandfather, a spirit called Sengalong Burong and, during his journey, the stars taught him about the agricultural cycle. When he reached his destination, his grandfather taught him about rituals and omens.

SHOU LAO (left) wears the robes and hat of a mandarin in his capacity as the heavenly official who determines human life-spans. (CHINESE PORCELAIN, 18TH CENTURY.)

SHOU LAO (right), the Daoist god of long life, has a large head and carries a staff. (JADE CARVING, 17TH CENTURY.)

In due course Sengalong Burong threw the young man out of his house in punishment for having slept with his aunt, Dara Chempaka Tempurong. According to Sengalong Burong, if people of adjacent generations slept with one another there would be a terrible harvest. Surong Gunting returned to his home and taught his people all that he had learned.

SUSANO-WO is the storm god of Japanese Shinto mythology. He came into being when IZANAGI, the male half of the primal pair, washed his face after returning from the land of the dead. Susano-Wo emerged from Izanagi's nose.

Izanagi divided his kingdom between his three children, the others being the sun goddess AMATERASU and the moon god TSUKIYOMI. To Susano-Wo he allocated rulership of the ocean. Susano-Wo was dismayed with his lot and protested, saying that he wanted to join his mother IZANAMI in the underworld. Izanagi immediately banished Susano-Wo.

Before leaving, Susano-Wo visited his sister Amaterasu. He challenged her to a contest in order to determine which of them was the most powerful. The task was to see who of them could give rise to male deities. Susano-Wo took Amaterasu's fertility beads from her hair and arms and, breaking them with his teeth, blew them out as five male deities. He then pronounced himself victorious. Amaterasu disagreed, saying that the beads belonged to her, and therefore she had won the contest. Susano-Wo ignored his sister's protests and proceeded to celebrate his victory by causing devastation on earth. He finished his riotous activities by throwing a flayed pony through the roof of the sacred weaving hall where Amaterasu sat with her attendants. Amaterasu was so angry that she hid in a cave, thereby bringing darkness to the world. Although Amaterasu was eventually lured out of the cave, the gods decided that Susano-Wo ought to be punished. They ordered him to give them numerous gifts and cut off his beard and the nails of his hands and feet. Finally, the gods threw Susano-Wo out of heaven.

According to another tale, Susano-Wo ordered the food goddess *UKE-MOCHI* to give him something to eat. The goddess responded by pulling food from her nose, mouth and rectum whereupon the disgusted Susano-Wo killed her. From her corpse sprouted all the basic food crops: rice seeds grew from her eyes, millet from her ears, wheat from her genitals, red beans from her nose

and soy beans from her rectum. In some versions of the legend, it is the moon god Tsukiyomi, rather than Susano-Wo, who kills the food goddess.

When Susano-Wo arrived on earth he set out to find some human beings. He soon came across an elderly couple and a beautiful young woman. The couple, weeping, told Susano-Wo that an eight-tailed, eight-headed monster called Yamato-no-Orochi had eaten seven of their eight daughters and was about to take their youngest daughter too. Susano-Wo promised to kill the monster and in return asked to be allowed to marry the daughter.

The couple agreed, whereupon Susano-Wo turned the daughter into a comb, which he fastened in his hair. The god then told the man and woman to place eight large

TAI SUI is surrounded by some of the 60 images which portray the annual Tai Sui. These are all subsidiary deities of the "Lord of Time".

tubs of rice wine on eight platforms and to surround the platforms with a fence containing eight openings. When the monster approached, it began to drink up the wine with its eight heads and soon fell down drunk. The god then chopped up the monster's body with his sword, discovering in the process the famous sword called Kusanagi or "Grass Mower" in its tail. (See also *CREATION MYTHS*)

SUSERI-HIME see *OKUNINUSHI*.

T'AI-I see *TAIYI*.

TAI SUI, the "President of the Celestial Ministry of Time" and "Ruler of the Year", is an arbiter of human destiny worshipped to avert calamities. He rules the cycle of 60 years, each of which is controlled by one of the subsidiary Tai Sui.

Astrology concerns human fortune, and the stellar deity Tai Sui presides over dates and times, auspicious or otherwise. Astrologers match a person's birth date and time with the cycle to provide a guide to auspicious and inauspicious years. Tai Sui was an early

deity honoured at the beginning of spring by the official religion and the official class in imperial China, as well as by Daoists. He is one of the fiercest gods in the pantheon and must be placated whenever ground is disturbed for any reason.

TAIYANG DIJUNG see *YI*.

TAIYI, or T'ai-i, has various meanings within Daoism. Sometimes it is said to be identical with the Dao, but over time it came to be personified as the highest deity within the Daoist pantheon. Taiyi is sometimes said to live in the polar star and to be served by the five mythical emperors.

TAIYI TIANZUN, or T'ai-i T'ientsun, is an early Daoist deity who is the saviour of sufferers and unfortunates. He is one of the more senior and significant of the Daoist gods, and is said to be equal to the "Jade Emperor" in rank.

Before the time of *HUANG DI*, the "Yellow Emperor", Taiyi Tianzun had been regarded as the supreme deity. He became the medical adviser to the "Yellow Emperor".

THE SHICHI FUKUJIN

SEVEN POPULAR JAPANESE DEITIES, the Shichi Fukujin, were considered to bring good luck and happiness. Each one personified a different aspect of good fortune. Although they were included in the Shinto pantheon, only two of them, Daikoku and Ebisu, were indigenous Japanese gods. Others were versions of popular Buddhist gods imported from China, while Benten and Bishamon originated as Hindu deities, and Hotei as a Daoist god. Buddhism was declared the official religion of the Japanese imperial court in AD593, but instead of trying to stamp out the existing faith, Buddhist missionaries in Japan drew parallels between the two faiths and proclaimed the identities of the deities to be the same. Because of this peaceable marriage of the two faiths, it was easy for attractive and popular Buddhist gods, such as those of good fortune, to be assimilated with the innumerable kami of the old religion.

BISHAMON (above) the god of war, came from the Hindu pantheon. He stood for benevolent authority. He was a warrior and always wore full armour, so that he was forever ready for battle. He is always shown carrying a lance and a miniature pagoda to symbolize his dual virtues as a soldier and a missionary. (HERIAN PERIOD FIGURE, 11TH CENTURY.)

THE SEVEN GODS (above left) were often depicted travelling together on their treasure ship Takara-Bune, representing a cargo of all the good luck anyone could ask for in life. The ship carried various magical articles on board, such as a hat which rendered the wearer invisible, and a purse that was always full of money. (HIROSHIGE, TREASURE SHIP WITH SEVEN GODS OF GOOD FORTUNE, WOODBLOCK PRINT, 19TH CENTURY.)

BENTEN (left), the only goddess in the group of seven, was a goddess of love, and was believed to bring good luck in marriage. She rode on a dragon or a sea serpent and was associated with the sea, so her shrines were often located by the sea or on islands. She was a patron of music and played a stringed instrument called a biwa. (GILDED KOMAI BOX, LATE 19TH CENTURY.)

FUKUROKUJU (left), perhaps originally a Daoist sage, was the god of long life, wisdom and popularity. He was a little old man with a short body and legs and a very long, narrow bald head, which indicated his intelligence. His traditional companions were animals associated with longevity: a crane, a stag or a tortoise. (JAPANESE IVORY NETSUKE, 18TH CENTURY.)

HOTEI (left) was a fat, bald monk who carried a large sack and a small screen. His enormous belly was meant to indicate his contentment and serene good nature, rather than greed. He is often depicted seated comfortably on his sack, laughing merrily. (ARITA MODEL, LATE 17TH CENTURY.)

JUROJIN was the godson of Fukurokuju, and also promised long life and a happy old age. He had a long white beard to indicate his great age and was portrayed carrying a staff to which was attached a scroll containing all the wisdom of the world, including the life-span of each individual. (JAPANESE INRO, 19TH CENTURY.)

DAIKOKU was the god of wealth and agriculture. He was portrayed wearing a cap and hunter's clothes, surrounded by the symbols of prosperity. Standing or sitting on a bag of rice, he carried another large sack of rice over his shoulder and a rice mallet in his hand, with which he granted wishes. He was sometimes said to be the father of Ebisu. (SATSUMA MODEL, LATE 19TH CENTURY.)

EBISU was the Shinto god of work. The most popular of the seven gods, he was a fisherman, and was fat and cheerful. He was usually shown holding a large fish. Later, he became associated with profit and could bring good luck to commercial ventures. Ebisu was deaf, so he did not join the other gods for the Shinto festival at Izumo which takes place in October. Instead, his festival was held in his own temple. (SATSUMA MODEL, LATE 19TH CENTURY.)

TARVAA was one of the first shamans of Mongolia. As a young man, he fell ill, and his relatives assumed he was dead. Tarvaa was so displeased at this presumption that his soul left his body and flew up to the spirit world. There, he met the judge of the dead who demanded to know why he had arrived so early. The judge, impressed that the youth possessed the courage to visit his kingdom, offered to give him a present before he returned to the land of the living. Tarvaa, rather than choosing wealth or glory, asked to be given knowledge of all the marvels that he had encountered in the spirit world, together with the gift of eloquence. He then returned to his body. However, he found that in his absence, birds had pecked out his eyes, and so he spent the rest of his days unable to see. He became famous for his wisdom and his tales of the spirit world.

TAWARA-TODA is a hero, possibly of historic origins, who features in the mythology of Japan. He defeated an enormous centipede which had been ravaging the territory of the king of the dragons. In gratitude, the king gave Tawara-Toda several supernatural gifts, including a bag of rice which constantly refilled itself.

THE TENGRI, according to the mythology of the Buriats of Siberia, are a type of spirit being. It is said that 54 good-natured Tengri live in the west, whereas 45 bad-natured Tengri live in the east. The Tengri are also regarded as realms, all of which are interconnected, and which together form a cosmic tree.

THE TENGU are creatures of Japanese mythology who are said to live in trees and mountainous areas. Part human, part bird, they have long noses and are sometimes depicted wearing cloaks of feathers or leaves. Although they play tricks, they are not outrightly evil.

TEVNE, according to traditional Mongolian belief, is a hero who managed to appropriate the yellow book of divination from the king. The king had a beautiful daughter whom he desperately tried to protect by keeping her hidden from the outside world. All the king's servants knew that if they revealed the princess's whereabouts, the yellow book of divination would reveal their guilt. As a result, for many years the princess remained in hiding.

One day, Tevne decided that he would attempt to confuse the book. He dug a deep hole in the ground and trapped one of the princess's servants in it. He then built a fire on top of the hole, placed a kettle over the fire and, taking a piece of iron piping, passed it through the kettle. Then, speaking through the pipe, he asked the woman how he could find the princess. The woman told Tevne how the beautiful girl could be identified, so he released her.

Later, Tevne succeeded in picking out the princess from girls of similar appearance. Although the king was furious, he was forced to allow Tevne to marry her. In order

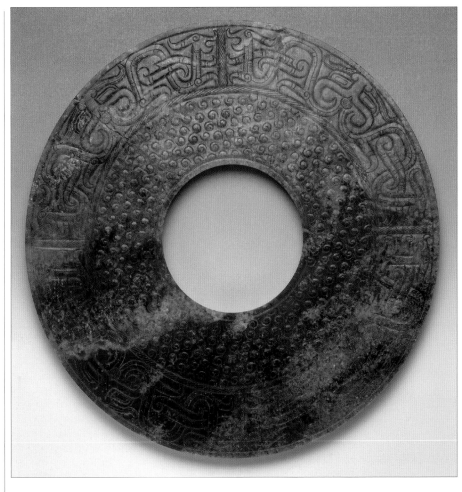

TIAN (above), the sky or heaven, is symbolized by a ceremonial Bi disc. (CHINESE JADE, 3RD–2ND CENTURY BC.)

THE TENGU (left), though wicked, could also be helpful, and rescued the hero Tameto from a giant fish. (WOODBLOCK PRINT BY KUNIYOSHI, 19TH CENTURY.)

to discover who had revealed the secret of his daughter's identity, the king sought advice from his yellow book. The book told him that he had been tricked by a man with earthen buttocks, a body of fire, lungs of water and an iron pipe for vocal cords. The king decided that the book's abilities had deserted it, and so he burned it. Sheep licked up the ashes and thereby acquired divinatory powers.

THE THENS, according to the people of Laos and northern Thailand, are the three divine ancestors who, together with three great men, Pu Lang Seung, Khun K'an and Khun K'et, established human society.

The Thens lived in the upper world, whereas the three great men ruled over the lower world, living by means of fishing and growing rice. A vast bridge joined together the two worlds.

One day, the Thens suddenly announced that all human beings should give them a portion of their food before they sat down to eat a meal. When the people refused, the Thens caused a huge flood to cover the earth. The three great men built a raft on top of which they constructed a house. Taking women and children with them, they travelled over the flood to the upper world in order to seek a reprieve from the chief Then.

The king of the Thens told the travellers to seek shelter in heaven with one of his relatives, Grandfather Then Lo. However, the three great men noticed that the flood was beginning to recede, and they told the king that they would rather return to the lower kingdom, since in heaven they were unable to walk or run because there was no solid ground. The king gave the divine ancestors a buffalo and sent them back down to earth.

Three years passed, after which time the buffalo died. A plant began to grow from its nostrils, and before long gave rise to three gourds. A strange noise issued from the gourds, whereupon one of the great men bored a hole in each of the fruit. Immediately, human beings began to emerge from the plants. The first people to emerge were the aboriginal slaves, followed in due course by the Thai people.

The three great men taught the people how to cultivate fields and how to weave. Later, Then Teng and Then Pitsanukukan descended from the upper world in order to teach the Thais about time as well as how to make tools, weave cotton and silk and prepare food.

Finally, the king of heaven sent the lord of the divine musicians to teach the people how to make and play instruments, and how to sing and dance. When the divine musician had finished his work he returned to heaven, and the bridge that connected the two worlds was destroyed.

TI see *SHANG DI*.

TI TS'ANG WANG see *DIZANG WANG*.

TIAN, or T'ien, is the Chinese word that refers both to the sky, or heaven, and to its personification as a deity. According to Daoism, there are 36 heavens, which are arranged on six levels. Each level is inhabited by different deities. The highest heaven is that of the "Great Web", which is sometimes said to be the home of the "Celestial Venerable of the Primordial Beginning", Yuanshi Tianzun.

From ancient times, Tian, or Tian Di, was regarded as a supreme being who had the power to influence the destiny of human beings, bringing order and calm, or catastrophe and punishment. The Chinese emperor is regarded as the "Son of Heaven", or Tianzi, and is believed to mediate between Tian and humankind.

TIAN DI see *TIAN*.

U

TIAN LONG see *DIYA*.

T'IEN see *TIAN*.

TING-JIAN see *GAO YAO*.

TOKOYO, according to Japanese mythology, was the daughter of a samurai called Oribe Shima who had displeased the emperor and been banished from the kingdom. Oribe Shima set up home on a desolate group of islands known as the Oki Islands.

He was extremely unhappy as he missed his daughter. Tokoyo was also miserable at being separated from her father and determined to find him. She sold all her property and set out for a place called Akasaki on the coast, from where the Oki Islands could just be seen. Although Tokoyo tried to persuade the fishermen to row her out to the islands, they all refused, since it was forbidden to visit anyone who had been sent there.

One night, Tokoyo took a boat and sailed out to the islands alone. She fell asleep on the beach, and the next morning she began to search for her father. The young woman soon encountered a fisherman and asked him if he had seen her father. He replied that he had not, and warned her not to ask anyone where he was as it might cause immense trouble. As a result, Tokoyo wandered all over the islands, listening to what people were saying, but never asking the whereabouts of her father.

One evening, she came to a shrine of the Buddha and after praying to him, fell asleep. She was soon woken by the sound of a girl crying and looking up she saw a young girl and a priest. The priest led the girl to the edge of the cliffs and was about to push her into the sea when Tokoyo ran up and stopped him. The priest confessed that he was forced to carry out the ritual in order to appease the evil god *OKUNINUSHI*. If he were not sent a young girl each year, the god

would become very angry and cause great storms and many fishermen would drown.

Tokoyo offered to take the girl's place, saying that she was so unhappy without her father that the loss of her life meant nothing to her. Then, Tokoyo prayed to the Buddha again and, with a dagger between her teeth, dived into the ocean intending to hunt down the evil god and kill him.

At the bottom of the ocean, Tokoyo spied a marvellous cave. Inside, instead of the evil god, she found a statue of the emperor who had banished her father. She began to destroy the statue, but then thought better of it and, tying it to herself, she began to swim back. Just as she was leaving the cave, Tokoyo found herself confronted by

a serpentine creature. Unafraid, she swam up to it and stabbed it in the eye. Blinded, the creature was unable to gain entrance to the cave, and Tokoyo succeeded in attacking it until finally she killed it.

When Tokoyo arrived at the shore, the priest and the girl carried her to town, and word of her heroic deeds soon spread. The emperor himself, who had suddenly found himself cured of an unknown disease, heard what had happened and realized that Tokoyo must have released him from an evil spell. He ordered the release of Oribe Shima, and the father and daughter returned to their home town.

TOMAM, according to the Ket people of Siberia, is a goddess who looks after migratory birds.

TOKOYO succeeded in killing a monstrous sea serpent and thus freed the emperor from an evil curse. (ILLUSTRATION FROM MYTHS AND LEGENDS OF JAPAN.)

TSAO-CHÜN see *ZAO JUN*.

TS'AO KUO-CHIU see *BA XIAN*.

TSUKIYOMI, in Shinto mythology, is the god of the moon. His name means "Counter of the Months". Tsukiyomi is said to have come into being when *IZANAGI*, the male half of the primal couple, purified himself after visiting the underworld. When he washed his face, Tsukiyomi appeared from Izanagi's right eye, the sun goddess *AMATERASU* from his left eye and the storm god *SUSANO-WO* from his nose. Izanagi divided his kingdom between his three offspring, allocating to Tsukiyomi the realms of the night.

According to one version of the myth relating how the staple crops of Japan were created, Tsukiyomi asked the food goddess *UKE-MOCHI* for a meal, but when she produced the food from her orifices, he was so disgusted that he killed her. The basic foodstuffs then appeared from the corpse of the goddess. When Amaterasu learned what had happened, she was displeased and said that she would never set eyes on her brother again. It is for this reason that the sun and the moon inhabit the sky at different times.

TUNG-YÜEH TA-TI see *DONGYUE DADI*.

UKE-MOCHI, or Ogetsu-No-Hime, is the food goddess, according to the Shinto mythology of Japan. She is married to *INARI*, the god of rice. The storm god *SUSANO-WO* or, in some versions of the story, the moon god *TSUKIYOMI* ordered the food goddess to give him something to eat. The goddess responded by pulling food from her nose, mouth and rectum fire appeared, and the air was filled with flames. On the ground lay a three-legged raven. Yi then shot another arrow at the sky, and another; each time, one of the suns was extinguished and fell to earth as a three-legged raven.

Yao realized that if Yi carried on, no light or warmth whatsoever would be left, so he told one of his courtiers to steal one of Yi's arrows so that he could destroy only nine of the ten suns. When there was only one sun left in the sky, Yi began to kill the wild animals and monsters that were devouring human beings.

Peace returned to the earth, and everyone praised Yi. The divine archer returned to heaven with Zhang E. However, to Yi's surprise, and Zhang E's anger, the god Taiyang Dijun spurned Yi for having killed his sons and ordered him and his wife to leave heaven and live on earth as mortals.

Yi was happy enough, hunting in the forests, but Zhang E grew bored and worried that now, one day, she would die. As a result, Zhang E persuaded Yi to visit the "Queen Mother of the West" and ask her for the elixir of immortality. The Queen Mother agreed to help Yi and Zhang E. She gave them a box containing enough elixir to enable them to live for ever, but said that there was only sufficient elixir for one of them to gain complete immortality.

Zhang E swallowed all of the elixir herself, and was punished by being stranded on the moon. When Yi discovered his wife's treachery, he was dismayed. However, he decided that, since he was to die, he should pass on his skills. He took a pupil, Peng Meng, who soon became an expert archer, although not so proficient as Yi. In time, Peng Meng grew jealous of Yi's superior ability and killed him. Another version tells how Yi was finally forgiven by the gods and returned to heaven.

YIN, according to Daoist belief, originally referred to the mountain slope facing away from the sun. Together with *YANG*, Yin was viewed as one of the two cosmic forces whose interaction produced the universe. Yin represents the female principle – the cold, the dark and softness – and may have originated as an earth deity. (See also *YIN AND YANG*)

YINGZHOU see *PENG LAI*.

YINLUGEN BUD, the ghost of the tree trunk, is an ancient spirit of the Chewong people of Malaysia. He taught the hero *BUJAEGN YED* how to deliver children and instructed him in many other rituals associated with childbirth. He also warned Bujaegn Yed that it was sinful not to share his food when he ate a meal.

YMAI see *UMAI*.

YNAKHSYT see *ITCHITA*.

YOMI is the land of the dead in Japanese Shinto mythology. It is a land of filth rather than of punishment, and it is known as the "Land of Darkness", or the "Land of Roots". *IZANAGI*, the male half of the primal couple, followed his wife *IZANAMI* to Yomi, but failed to secure her release.

YOSHITSUNE, also known as Ushiwaka, is a hero who features in Japanese mythology. He was trained in the art of warfare by the Tengu and then succeeded in

YAO, fourth of the legendary emperors of China, was the pattern of the good ruler. (PAINTING BY MA LIN.)

YOSHITSUNE was trained in sword-play by the Tengu, the bird-like imps of Japanese myth. (WOODBLOCK PRINT BY KUNISADA, C. 1815.)

avenging the defeat of his people, the Minamoto clan. He defeated the giant *BENKEI* in a duel whereupon the giant became his servant.

YU was the hero of the flood in Chinese mythology. He is revered for his dedication to hard work. Yu was sometimes shown as half-dragon, half-human, but eventually he came to be represented as entirely human.

Yu laboured for 13 years to put an end to the flood. He controlled and directed all the waters of the earth by cutting holes through the mountains, creating rivers, springs and estuaries. Eventually, his hands and feet grew callused, and he became so exhausted, he could scarcely walk. However, he struggled on, building an irrigation system in order to drain the flood waters into the sea.

In the course of his mammoth drainage work, he made the land fit for cultivation and connected the nine provinces of China to one another. The ruling emperor was so grateful that he abdicated and gave the throne to Yu, who became the first emperor of the Xia dynasty. Yu is said to have reigned from 2205 to 2197BC. Each succeeding emperor was seen as an incarnation of the dragon Yu.

Another myth tells how, in order to carry out his work, Yu would transform himself into a bear. Each day, when the time came for him to eat, he would beat his drum, and his wife would carry out food for him. One day, when Yu was breaking up rocks, his wife

YU HUANG (above), the "Jade Emperor" or "August Personage of Jade" is the supreme ruler of heaven and earth.

mistook the sound for the beating of his drum. She rushed out with his food, but as soon as she saw the bear she fled. Yu ran after her but, being pregnant, she fell to the ground exhausted and turned to stone. The stone continued to grow and, when the time of the expected birth arrived, Yu split it open, whereupon his son, Qi, was born.

YU DI was another name given to *YU HUANG*, the so-called "Jade Emperor" of Chinese mythology.

YU HUANG, or the "Jade Emperor", came to be regarded as the supreme ruler of heaven in Chinese mythology. He was responsible for determining events both in the heavens and on earth, and he had a vast number of underlings to carry out his commands. Yu Huang's chief assistant was *DONGYUE DADI*, or "Great Emperor of the Eastern Peak". Dongyue Dadi alone had 75 gods to help him in his work.

At the beginning of each year, Yu Huang would summon all the deities to his palace, which was in

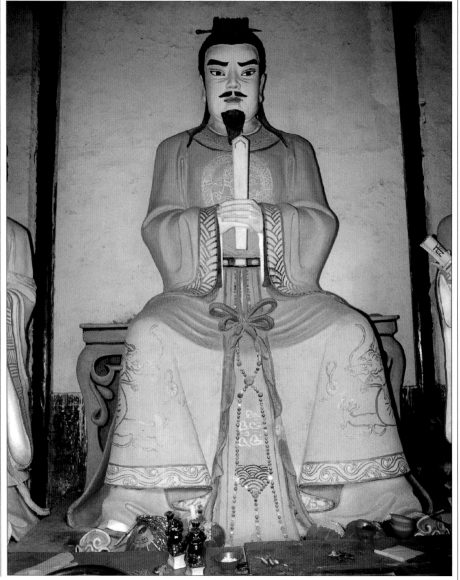

YU (left) the Lord of the Flood, was given the task of controlling and draining the waters that covered the plains of China.

is usually depicted sitting on his throne wearing the ceremonial robes of an emperor, embroidered with dragons.

The "Queen Mother of the West", *XI WANG MU*, who is known by many titles, including Wang Mu Niangniang, was said to be the wife of Yu Huang. He has a large family of sisters, daughters and nephews, and a celestial dog, who helps to protect the heavenly household from evil spirits.

YUANSHI TIAN-ZONG see *SAN QING DAOZU*.

YUQIANG, or Yü-ch'iang, in Chinese mythology, is the god of the sea and of ocean winds. As a

god of the sea, he is represented with the body of a fish and riding two dragons. As a god of the winds, he is represented with the body of a bird and a human face.

According to one tale, Yuqiang was ordered by the king of heaven to anchor the five floating islands of the immortals. Yuqiang succeeded in the task by enlisting the help of 15 giant tortoises. He allocated three of the tortoises to each island and ordered them to take it in turns to carry one of the islands on their backs. Each turn was to last 60,000 years. Unfortunately, a giant caught six of the tortoises, and so two islands were set adrift. They floated away and sank, leaving only three.

QING LONG PA JIANGJUN (left), *the Green Dragon General, guards the entrance to the Jade Emperor Hall.*

YUQIANG (below), *the god of the ocean winds, listens to the Buddhist doctrine.* (PAINTING BY ZHAO BOZHU, SONG DYNASTY.)

the highest of the heavens, and was guarded by the "Transcendental Official". The deities would then be allocated new positions, according to how they had performed their duties during the previous year. The various ministries oversaw everything, from water and time, to war and wealth.

The heavenly administration was a replica of the earthly one. If, for example, there was a flood, the earthly official would warn the heavenly official – the deity – that his work was substandard and, if necessary, he would be fired. New deities would be confirmed by the Daoist priests. The "Jade Emperor" was said to deal directly with the emperor of China, whereas his attendants dealt with less important human beings. In the 11th

century AD, when the emperor of China was losing his power, he attempted to regain support by claiming to be in direct communication with heaven and to have received a letter from Yu Huang.

One myth tells how before Yu Huang was born, his mother dreamt that *LAO JUN*, the deified form of Laozi, the putative founding father of Daoism, handed her a child. The young Yu Huang succeeded his father, the king, to the throne but abdicated after a few days in order to retire to the mountains and study the Dao. He attained perfection and, for the rest of his life, he instructed the sick and poor in the Dao. Eventually, he became an immortal and after millions more years was transformed into the "Jade Emperor". Yu Huang

CHINA'S SACRED PEAKS

THE GREAT CREATOR PANGU lived for 18,000 years, growing every day and filling the space between the earth and the sky. When he died, his body formed the world. In one version of the myth, his head became Tai Shan mountain in the east; his feet, Hua Shan in the west; his right arm, the northern Heng Shan; his left arm, the southern Heng Shan; and his stomach Song Shan, the mountain of the centre. These were the five sacred Daoist mountains of China. They were worshipped as deities in their own right: pilgrims climbed stairways to the summits and made sacrifices to them. In the heavenly bureaucracy of the Chinese pantheon, the "Ministry of the Five Sacred Mountains" was controlled by Tai Shan, the grandson of Yu Huang, the "Jade Emperor".

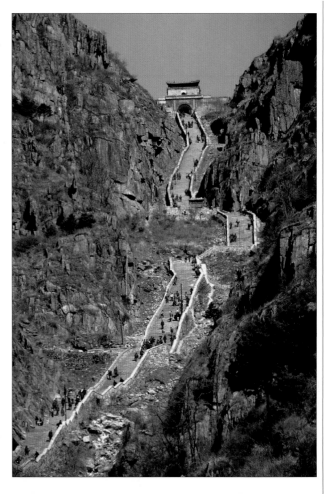

TAI SHAN's (above) summit is reached by climbing the "Stairway to Heaven", which consists of about 7,000 steps lined with shrines and temples. Sacrifices were offered at the top of the mountain by the emperor each spring, but he could not presume to do this unless his reign was a successful one. Successive emperors made ceremonial journeys to the holy mountains that marked the limits of the empire, to assert their claim to their territory.

TAI SHAN (left), the holiest peak, is the sacred mountain of the east. Its presiding deity ("Lord of the Yellow Springs") ruled the earth and regulated birth and death, while his daughter Bixia Shengmu ("Princess of Streaked Clouds") protected women and children. Souls left the mountain at birth and returned there at death. The mountain was granted various noble titles by the Jade Emperor.

A PAGODA (right) *stands at the summit of Mount Song Shan, the mountain of the centre, in the heart of the ancient Chinese empire.*

HUANG DI (below left) *the "Yellow Emperor", was the third and most splendid of the legendary emperors of China, preceded by Fu Xi and Shen Nong. Huang Di ordered roads to be built and mountain passes to be cut throughout his empire. When he journeyed to Tai Shan to make sacrifices, his chariot was drawn by six dragons. Tigers and wolves preceded it, serpents slithered beside it, phoenixes flew overhead and spirits followed behind. The road ahead was cleaned and swept by the gods of wind and rain.*

HUA SHAN (above) *was the sacred mountain of the west. The hero Yu, who controlled the great flood of China, visited the four corners of the world, marked by the sacred peaks. At Hua Shan he found people who drank dew and ate the air, who had three faces each but only one arm. Daoists believed that mountain-tops brought them closest to the Dao and built many of their temples on or near the summits of the sacred mountains.*

HENG SHAN (left) *in Shanxi Province, has a monastery clinging precariously to the sheer rock face. This is the northern Heng Shan, said to have been formed from the right arm of the giant Pangu.*

Z

ZAO JUN, or Tsao-chun, is a Daoist kitchen god, worshipped since at least the second century BC. He is still widely worshipped, and his picture is placed above the kitchen stove. At New Year, his spirit is offered a meal of meat, fruit and wine, and his lips are smeared with honey. The portrait is then burned in order to help the god on his way to heaven. The honey is supposed to keep Zao Jun sweet for when he reports on each family's conduct to YU HUANG.

According to one story, Zao Jun was once a poor man who, because he was unable to support his wife,

or because of a trick she played on him, had to allow her to marry someone else. He wandered far and wide begging. One day, he realized he had come to the home of his former wife and was so ashamed that he tried to hide in the hearth, where he was burned to death.

Another version of the tale tells how, before he became a deity, Zao Jun was a man called Zhang Lang. He was married to a good and faithful woman but left her for a young girl. Things went badly for him. In due course, the young girl became bored with Zhang Lang; he lost his sight and had to beg for food.

One day, Zhang Lang appeared at the door of his former wife. However, being blind, he did not know her. The woman invited Zhang Lang in and gave him his favourite meal. He was reminded of his wife and told the apparent stranger his story. His wife told Zhang Lang to open his eyes, and when he did so, he found he was able to see again. However, Zhang Lang was so ashamed at his former behaviour that he jumped into the hearth and was burned to death. His wife managed to seize one of his legs, which is why the fire poker is described as "Zhang Lang's leg".

ZAO JUN, the kitchen god, is honoured with fire crackers during the New Year celebrations. (CHINESE PAINTING, 19TH CENTURY.)

ZHANG E, or Chang O, according to Chinese mythology, is the wife of the divine archer YI. The lord of heaven, Taiyang Dijun, condemned Yi and Zhang E to live on earth as mortals in punishment for killing nine of his ten sons. Zhang E was furious and persuaded Yi to obtain the elixir of immortality from XI WANG MU, who lived on Mount Kunlun. The myth varies slightly, but, according to one version, the Queen Mother took pity

月宮嫦娥奔月

down a tree. According to one version of the myth, Zhang E did finally regain her human appearance and lived the rest of her life in the palace of the moon. She is often shown wearing regal garments and carrying the disc of the moon in her right hand. She is regarded as a symbol of YIN, the female principle.

ZHANG GUOLAO see BA XIAN.

ZHONG-LI QUAN see BA XIAN.

ZHU RONG, or Chu Jong, according to Chinese mythology, is regent of the southern quarter of heaven and the divine lord of fire. He helped to divide heaven and earth from each other. One myth tells how Zhu Rong and the ferocious monster GONG-GONG decided to fight each other in order to determine which of them was the most powerful. Zhu Rong managed to defeat Gong-gong, who was so ashamed that he tried to kill himself and in the process caused a massive flood.

ZHU RONG (below), the God of Fire, on a temple altar in Taipei, Taiwan.

on Yi and gave him enough elixir to enable two people to live for ever, but only sufficient for one person to gain complete immortality. Yi returned home with the elixir, and Zhang E immediately began to toy with the idea of swallowing all the elixir herself. However, she was worried that the gods might be angry with her if she abandoned her husband, so she consulted an astrologer. The astrologer suggested that Zhang E should travel to the moon where she would be free both from the accusations of the gods and the hardships of life as a mortal. He also promised that Zhang E would be miraculously transformed.

Zhang E was immediately persuaded by the astrologer's suggestion. She stole the elixir of immortality from where it was hidden in the rafters of her house and swallowed it. Immediately, she began to float up to the moon. However, when she tried to call out, she discovered that she could only croak: she had been transformed into a toad.

Zhang E's companions on the moon were a hare and an old man who constantly attempted to chop

FAMILY TREES

Greek and Roman Family Trees

THE CHILDREN OF ZEUS

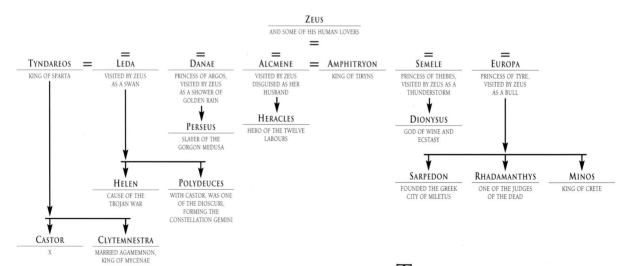

The most powerful of the Greek gods, Zeus was married to Hera, a mother goddess, with whom he had several children. He was also, however, a great lover both of other goddesses and of mortal women, to whom he often appeared in disguise, thereby incurring the anger of Hera. In some cases these unions can be seen as mythological accounts of the union between two cultures, as when Zeus takes the Asiatic Europa to Crete. In others, it appears that particular cities or provinces of Greece have sought to give themselves divine antecedents by tracing the line of their rulers back to the greatest of the gods.

THE HOUSE OF ATREUS

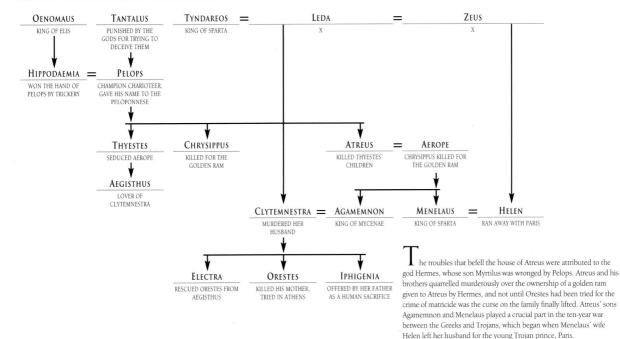

The troubles that befell the house of Atreus were attributed to the god Hermes, whose son Myrtilus was wronged by Pelops. Atreus and his brothers quarrelled murderously over the ownership of a golden ram given to Atreus by Hermes, and not until Orestes had been tried for the crime of matricide was the curse on the family finally lifted. Atreus' sons Agamemnon and Menelaus played a crucial part in the ten-year war between the Greeks and Trojans, which began when Menelaus' wife Helen left her husband for the young Trojan prince, Paris.

THE MINOANS

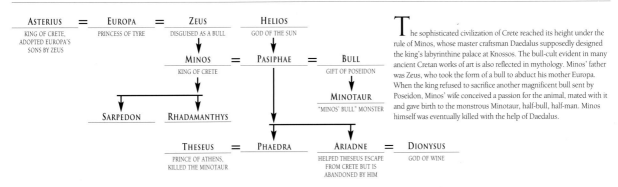

The sophisticated civilization of Crete reached its height under the rule of Minos, whose master craftsman Daedalus supposedly designed the king's labyrinthine palace at Knossos. The bull-cult evident in many ancient Cretan works of art is also reflected in mythology. Minos' father was Zeus, who took the form of a bull to abduct his mother Europa. When the king refused to sacrifice another magnificent bull sent by Poseidon, Minos' wife conceived a passion for the animal, mated with it and gave birth to the monstrous Minotaur, half-bull, half-man. Minos himself was eventually killed with the help of Daedalus.

THE FAMILY OF THESEUS

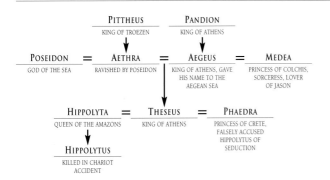

Although a mortal hero, Theseus was said by some to be the son of the god Poseidon. A brave fighter, he was a powerful monarch, uniting the twelve states of Attica into one kingdom with its capital at Athens. It was through Theseus that the two civilizations of island Crete and mainland Greece became closely connected, since he married the Cretan princess Phaedra, having abandoned her sister. Theseus himself died in exile, but his bones were eventually returned to Athens, where the people saw him as a saviour of the city.

497

Celtic Family Trees

THE DAGDA

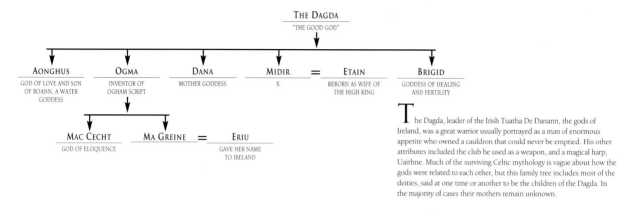

THE DAGDA
"THE GOOD GOD"

AONGHUS
GOD OF LOVE AND SON
OF BOANN, A WATER
GODDESS

OGMA
INVENTOR OF
OGHAM SCRIPT

DANA
MOTHER GODDESS

MIDIR
X

=

ETAIN
REBORN AS WIFE OF
THE HIGH KING

BRIGID
GODDESS OF HEALING
AND FERTILITY

MAC CECHT
GOD OF ELOQUENCE

MA GREINE

=

ERIU
GAVE HER NAME
TO IRELAND

The Dagda, leader of the Irish Tuatha De Danann, the gods of Ireland, was a great warrior usually portrayed as a man of enormous appetite who owned a cauldron that could never be emptied. His other attributes included the club he used as a weapon, and a magical harp, Uaithne. Much of the surviving Celtic mythology is vague about how the gods were related to each other, but this family tree includes most of the deities, said at one time or another to be the children of the Dagda. In the majority of cases their mothers remain unknown.

THE ROYAL HOUSE OF ULSTER

ROTH

CATHBAD
DRUID, ADVISOR TO
CONCHOBHAR

FACHTNA
KING OF ULSTER

=

NESSA

=

FERGUS

SUALTAM

=

DECHTIRE

=

LUGH
SUN GOD

CORMAC
KILLED ON THE ORDERS
OF HIS LOVER'S HUSBAND

CONCHOBHAR
KING OF ULSTER

=

DIERDRE
LOVER OF NAOISE, KILLS
HERSELF WHEN MARRIED
TO CONCHOBHAR

CUCHULAINN
GREAT HERO OF ULSTER

Trained for kingship by his ambitious mother, Conchobhar ruled Ulster at the time of the great hero Cuchulainn, who was said to be the grandson of Conchobhar's advisor, the druid Cathbad. Although otherwise a powerful king, Conchobhar's weakness for the beautiful Deirdre led him into a prolonged war. For, having killed Deirdre's lover so that he might marry her, he found his disgusted step-father Fergus siding against him with the enemies of Ulster. Conchobhar finally perished as the result of a magical sling-shot made by Cuchulainn's foster-brother Conall, which became embedded in the king's skull.

THE FAMILY OF FINN MACCOOL

**MANANNAN
MAC LIR**
SEA GOD

CUMAL
"SKY", CHIEF OF THE
BASCNA, LEADER OF
THE FIANNA

SADB
MISTRESS OF FINN,
SAID TO BE THE
GRANDDAUGHTER OF
THE DAGDA, BEWITCHED
INTO THE FORM
OF A DEER

=

FINN MACCOOL
LEADER OF THE FIANNA

NIAM
"OF THE GOLDEN HAIR"

=

OISIN
"LITTLE FAWN", A
GREAT POET

=

EIBHIR
(POSSIBLY ANOTHER
NAME FOR NIAM)

PLUR NAM BAN
"FLOWER OF WOMAN"

OSCAR
"DEER LOVER", GREAT
WARRIOR

As leader of the Fianna, the warrior bodyguards of the High King of Ireland, Finn can be compared with the British King Arthur. Like Arthur, he was believed to lie asleep for ever in a hillside, waiting until his country needed him. His men, who came mostly from the clan Bascna or the clan Morna, were carefully selected for their physical strength and their skill in battle, and they became involved in various adventures throughout the island. Through Finn's relationship with Sadb, his story also enters the realm of enchantment, a mythical element reinforced in the tales of his son and grandson.

ARTHUR AND THE KNIGHTS OF THE ROUND TABLE

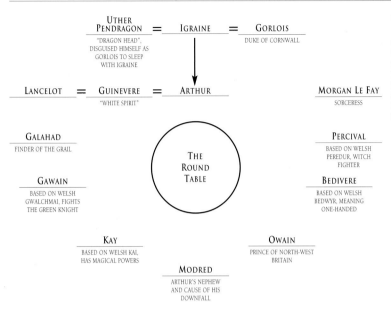

The original Arthur of Welsh and Irish tradition was a warrior king whose band of heroes followed him into a variety of adventures. Medieval legend transformed them into courtly knights and altered many of the Celtic ingredients of the old tales for a Christian audience. The magic cauldrons of inspiration and plenty, for example, became the Holy Grail used at the Last Supper. The concept of rebirth survives in Arthur's title of "Once and Future King". The Round Table, too, was a later addition, but many of those who sat at it were based on characters found in much earlier stories.

THE CHILDREN OF DON

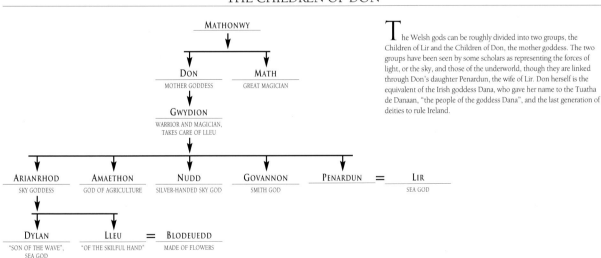

The Welsh gods can be roughly divided into two groups, the Children of Lir and the Children of Don, the mother goddess. The two groups have been seen by some scholars as representing the forces of light, or the sky, and those of the underworld, though they are linked through Don's daughter Penardun, the wife of Lir. Don herself is the equivalent of the Irish goddess Dana, who gave her name to the Tuatha de Danaan, "the people of the goddess Dana", and the last generation of deities to rule Ireland.

THE FAMILY OF PWYLL AND THE CHILDREN OF LIR

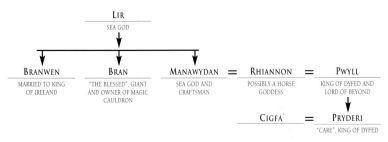

Common to both Welsh and Irish mythical tradition are heroes who are part mortal and part divine. A king of Dyfed, Pwyll is also connected with the otherworld, both through his own adventures there and through his wife Rhiannon, whose magical birds could wake the dead with their song. Indeed, Rhiannon's second husband Manawydan was the son of the Welsh sea god Lir, whose other children Bran and Branwen were similarly seen as humans with supernatural powers. Later Celtic writing absorbed these earlier influences into Arthurian legend, where Pwyll became Pelles, keeper of the Holy Grail.

Norse Family Trees
THE AESIR

The Aesir were the gods and goddesses led by Odin. Predominantly connected with warfare, they lived in Asgard, a mighty stronghold where the souls of the bravest men killed in battle were taken after death by the Valkyries. After settling an early conflict with Vanir, another race of gods, the Aesir turned their attention to fighting the frost giants. Despite their divinity, the Aesir were not immortal. Many of them were fated to die during Ragnarok, the doom of the gods, when Loki and his children united with the giants to attack Asgard. Although Odin was widely rec-

ognized as the father of all gods, there were deities among the Aesir whose parentage was disputed. Tyr, for example, the war god who gave his name to Tuesday, was said by some to be the son of Odin, but by others to be the son of a giant named Humir. Heimdall, the watchman of the gods who stood guard on the rainbow bridge Bifrost, was the son of nine mothers, and himself fathered children in the human world of Midgard. Furthermore, Odin's brothers Vili and Ve, while far less important, were counted among the Aesir.

THE CHILDREN OF LOKI

Since his parents were giants, Loki was not strictly speaking one of the gods, but he lived with them in Asgard. A shape-shifter and a mischief-maker, he was tolerated until he brought about the death of Odin's son Balder, the personification of goodness. Then the gods turned on him and bound him, in an effort to contain the evil he had come to represent. But it was through Loki that the gods were fated to meet their doom, for at the end of the world he would be freed from his prison and join his monstrous children to fight the last battle of Ragnarok.

THE VANIR

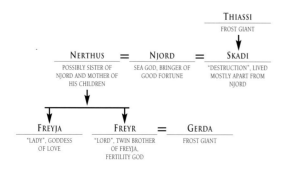

Unlike the warrior Aesir, the Vanir were a race of gods associated with fertility, with wealth and with good weather. They were believed by some to have existed before the Aesir and lived in their own world of Vannaheim. At first the two divine races were hostile to each other and conflict broke out between them. They eventually agreed to live in peace with each other, but the Vanir faded in significance. The best-known of their number were Freyr and Freyja, twins endowed with magical powers, who went to live in the Aesir's home of Asgard.

YGGDRASIL

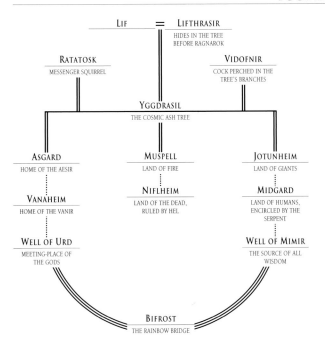

The world picture of Norse myth centred round the sacred tree, Yggdrasil. The branches of this vast ash were believed to hang over the Nine Worlds and its three roots to lead to them. Odin hanged himself from one branch for nine days and then died, in order that he might acquire the wisdom of the dead and bring back from their lands the magic Runes. After Ragnarok, when the Nine Worlds are destroyed, Yggdrasil will survive and the human couple, Lif and Lifthrasir, who took shelter in its branches, will descend to begin a new race of humans.

EXPLANATORY NOTE
The double lines denote the roots of the tree, Yggdrasil. The triple lines denote the link made by Bifrost between Asgard and Midgard, heaven and earth respectively.

THE FAMILY OF SIGURD

The story of the young hero Sigurd (known by the Germans as Siegfried) belongs as much to heroic legend as to myth, though it is connected with the Norse gods through the part played in the tale by Loki and through Sigmund's magic sword, thrust into a tree by Odin. As in many folk traditions, the possession of fabulous treasure brings disaster to the man who acquires it. Even Sigurd, otherwise an innocent figure, is fated to lose Brynhild, the beautiful Valkyrie whom he loves, when he is bewitched into marrying Gudrun.

THOR

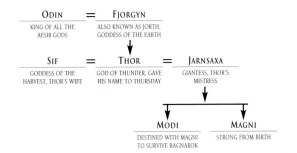

One of the most popular of the Aesir, Thor was renowned as a great warrior. He was enormous, even for a god, and his strength and courage made him a formidable enemy of the giants in many adventures. Although his simple-mindedness laid him open to mockery from the other gods, it endeared him to the ordinary farmers who worshipped him throughout Scandinavia. Thor's chief weapon was Mjollnir, his magic hammer, which created thunder when he flung it down on the earth. The vast hall in Asgard where he lived with Sif was called Bilskirnir, or Lightning.

501

Egypt / Mesopotamia / Iran

THE DESCENDANTS OF RA

The Egyptian creator god Ra and his descendants are known collectively as the Ennead, or "Nine Gods" of Heliopolis, the site of Ra's principal sanctuary. Ra needed no consort, but spat or sneezed out Shu and Tefnut and later, from his own tears, created humanity. The children of Nut were two pairs of twins.

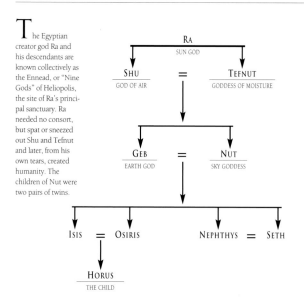

THE SUMERIAN PANTHEON

The Sumerians, living in Mesopotamia in the fourth and third millennia BC, developed a religious framework which was adapted by the Akkadians, Babylonians and other later civilizations in the region. Sumerian deities were organized into a settled pantheon by priests, who inscribed their myths on clay tablets.

THE BABYLONIAN PANTHEON

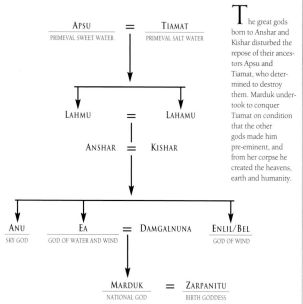

The great gods born to Anshar and Kishar disturbed the repose of their ancestors Apsu and Tiamat, who determined to destroy them. Marduk undertook to conquer Tiamat on condition that the other gods made him pre-eminent, and from her corpse he created the heavens, earth and humanity.

THE ZOROASTRIAN HEAVENLY HIERARCHY

AHURA MAZDA/SPENTA MAINYU
THE WISE LORD

HUMANITY

AMESA SPENTAS
SONS AND DAUGHTERS OF, OR ASPECTS OF, GOD

VOHU MANO	ASHA VAHISHTA	SPENTA ARMAITI	KHSHATHRA VAIRYA	HAURVATAT	AMERETAT
GOOD THOUGHT *animals/cattle*	RIGHTEOUSNESS *fire*	DEVOTION *earth*	DOMINION *sun and heavens*	WHOLENESS *waters*	IMMORTALITY *plants*

YAZATAS
PROTECTIVE SPIRITS

ANAHITA	ATAR	HAOMA	SRAOSHA	RASHNU	MITHRA	TISHTRYA
WATER, FERTILITY	FIRE	HEALING PLANTS	OBEDIENCE, THE HEARER OF PRAYERS	JUDGEMENT	TRUTH	THE DOG-STAR, SOURCE OF RAIN AND FERTILITY

In the Zoroastrian tradition, Ahura Mazda is alone worthy of worship. The Amesa Spentas are his creations and act as intermediaries between Ahura Mazda and his devotees. Many of the Yazatas were ancient Iranian deities who were included in the reformed religion as the servants of Ahura Mazda.

India / Japan

SHIVA'S FAMILY

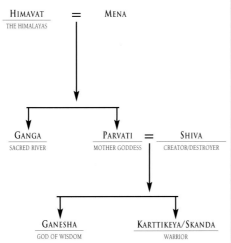

Shiva is both the creator and the destroyer, and Parvati is the gentle aspect of his shakti, or creative energy. She is also an aspect of the great goddess, Devi, and a reincarnation of Shiva's wife Sati, who committed suicide. In her subservience to her husband, Parvati is a model for mortal devotees of Shiva.

HIMAVAT = MENA
THE HIMALAYAS

GANGA
SACRED RIVER

PARVATI = SHIVA
MOTHER GODDESS   CREATOR/DESTROYER

GANESHA
GOD OF WISDOM

KARTTIKEYA/SKANDA
WARRIOR

VEDIC CREATION MYTH

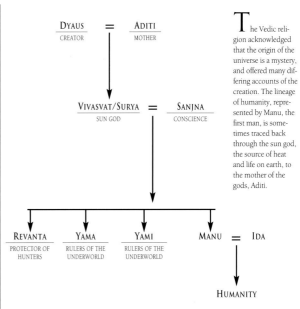

DYAUS = ADITI
CREATOR   MOTHER

VIVASVAT/SURYA = SANJNA
SUN GOD   CONSCIENCE

REVANTA
PROTECTOR OF HUNTERS

YAMA
RULERS OF THE UNDERWORLD

YAMI
RULERS OF THE UNDERWORLD

MANU = IDA

HUMANITY

The Vedic religion acknowledged that the origin of the universe is a mystery, and offered many differing accounts of the creation. The lineage of humanity, represented by Manu, the first man, is sometimes traced back through the sun god, the source of heat and life on earth, to the mother of the gods, Aditi.

HIERARCHY OF VEDIC DEITIES

HEAVEN

DYAUS	VARUNA	MITRA	PUSAN	VISHNU
SKY	RIGHTEOUSNESS	LIGHT	NOURISHER	CREATOR

ATMOSPHERE

INDRA	VAYU	RUDRA	THE MARUTS
RAIN	WIND	DESTRUCTION	STORM

EARTH

SOMA	AGNI	BRHASPATI
PLANTS	FIRE	PRIEST, LORD OF PRAYER

The ancient heavenly deities were endowed with universal power, but were remote figures, whereas Indra and the other gods of the atmosphere exert a more direct influence over human life. Agni is the god of the sacrificial fire, and is therefore an intercessor between the gods and humankind.

SHINTO CREATION MYTH

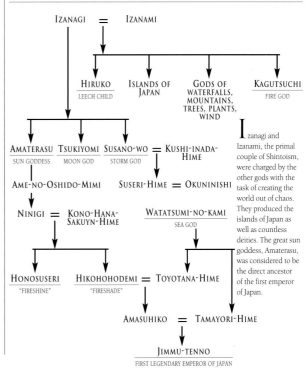

IZANAGI = IZANAMI

HIRUKO
LEECH CHILD

ISLANDS OF JAPAN

GODS OF WATERFALLS, MOUNTAINS, TREES, PLANTS, WIND

KAGUTSUCHI
FIRE GOD

AMATERASU
SUN GODDESS

TSUKIYOMI
MOON GOD

SUSANO-WO = KUSHI-INADA-HIME
STORM GOD

AME-NO-OSHIDO-MIMI

SUSERI-HIME = OKUNINISHI

NINIGI = KONO-HANA-SAKUYN-HIME

WATATSUMI-NO-KAMI
SEA GOD

HONOSUSERI
"FIRESHINE"

HIKOHOHODEMI = TOYOTANA-HIME
"FIRESHADE"

AMASUHIKO = TAMAYORI-HIME

JIMMU-TENNO
FIRST LEGENDARY EMPEROR OF JAPAN

Izanagi and Izanami, the primal couple of Shintoism, were charged by the other gods with the task of creating the world out of chaos. They produced the islands of Japan as well as countless deities. The great sun goddess, Amaterasu, was considered to be the direct ancestor of the first emperor of Japan.

503

Picture Acknowledgements

The Publishers are grateful to the agencies listed below for kind permission to reproduce the following images in this book.

Alan Lee: 44BR, 103, 108T, 109R, 110R, 113B, 127L, 127L, 134R, 139TR, 143TR, 143BR, 145T, 147TL, 148T, 149L, 151TL, 151BR, 152TM, 155R, 158, 159BL, 159BR, 160, 161BR, 163, 164, 166L, 167L, 171T, 172, 173BR, 183T, 185T, 186T, 196T, 197B, 207T, 224TR, 238BL, 239TR, 242, 247MR.

AKG: 14, 15BL, 16B, 17T, 18T, 20L, 21T, 22, 23L, 25, 26, 32, 36BR, 36TR, 37, 38L, 40TR, 41T, 42R, 43T, 43BR,45R, 46TR, 47, 49T, 50TL, 51TL, 52BL, 54TR, 55, 57 58T, 59T, 60BR, 61T, 61B, 62BR, 63TR, 64T, 65T, 66T, 67T, 68T, 68BR, 69T, 70B, 71BR, 72R, 74T, 76TL, 77, 78, 80B, 81B, 82T, 83TM, 84T, 85, 89T, 89B, 90B, 91T, 192B, 267TR, 267BL, 269TL, 271BR, 270BR, 273TR, 274TR, 276BL, 277TR, 278TL, 279R, 281, 285, 295TR, 297B, 301, 303, 304, 306B, 307, 308TL, 309, 310, 311T, 313TR, 313BL, 313BR, 314, 318, 321, 325, 331TL, 335B, 338, 341TR, 342T, 344L, 345R, 360T, 360B, 361TL, 361TR, 361BR, 363T, 366T, 372T, 373T, 373B, 375B, 381, 395BR, 399T, 405TL, 408T, 410, 415B, 441.

Ancient Art and Architecture: 260BL, 262B, 263TL, 264B, 273TL, 275BL, 278BR, 282, 284TL, 288TR, 288BL, 291, 292BL, 293B, 297TR, 298TL, 298B, 300B, 305BL, 316T, 316B, 319B, 324T, 328, 341TL, 350T, 352T, 355T, 357TL, 367, 371TL, 375T, 383BR, 385T, 389TL, 405BR, 405TR, 411B, 415T, 417B, 430, 432B, 438BR, 440TL, 442, 450TL, 453TR, 454R, 459TR, 462TL, 462TR, 464T, 473TL, 473BL, 475T, 476TR, 476M, 478, 487B.

Ancient Egypt Picture Library: 267MR, 269BR, 272BL, 280B, 284TR, 284BL, 287MR, 292BL, 297TL, 300TR, 306T, 311B.

Arnamagnean Institute: 178L, 204BL, 205BR.

Ateneum, Helsinki: 199BL, 205T, 222R, 223TL, 223TR, 243B.

Bildarchiv Foto, Marburg: 451B.

Bildarchiv Preussisher: 226T.

Birmingham Museum and Art Gallery: 103T, 122BR, 137, 143L, 153B, 159T, 169T.

The Bodleian Library: 141TL.

The Bridgeman Art Library: 79B, 86B, 87BL, 87BR, 92, 96BR, 96L, 130R, 140TR, 143L, 157T, 181L, 200BR, 203, 261TL, 268, 272TL, 279, 280T, 289BL, 307, 343B, 346, 353, 356, 363BR, 365T, 366BR, 368T, 377T, 378T, 378BR, 379TR, 379BR, 382T, 383T, 392T 393, 398TL, 398TR, 401T, 402T, 402B, 403B, 406TL, 407BL, 414, 447, 449TL, 454L, 466T, 470BR.

Dundee Art Gallery: 105T, 106B, 109L, 133T, 135T, 138B

E Davison: 121L

The British Museum: 445TL, 455B.

Christie's Art Gallery: 272BR, 287TR, 287BR, 323BL, 23BR, 330TL, 330BR, 331TR, 332, 336, 379MT, 351TR, 364, 370T, 371TR, 379BL, 396BL, 397T, 397BL, 400T, 426, 429, 432T, 436TL, 436TR, 439L, 439TR, 443B, 452B, 453BM, 453BR, 457B, 468T, 469TL, 469TR, 472BL, 476B, 477, 482T, 486TR

Corbis: 261BR, 263BR, 277TL, 294T, 312T, 326, 328, 329R, 330TR, 331BL 333, 335, 343TL, 347B, 351TL, 355B, 387B, 388T, 396BR, 405BL, 409T, 411T, 413BR, 418, 422, 424, 425TL, 435BR, 438TL, 438TR, 444, 451T, 456B, 459B, 461T, 462B, 465, 470T, 472TR, 479, 481, 483, 484B, 485T, 485BR, 485BT, 486TL 488, 491T, 492T 492B, 493TR, 493MR, 493B, 495T

CM Dixon: 264T, 267ML, 283, 302B, 343TR, 350B, 363BL, 416T, 423TL, 440BR, 452T, 453TL, 472TL, 474, 494.

Edimedia: 263LT, 354T, 374.

E.T. Archive: 33TR, 52TR, 53BR, 70T, 87TL, 188T, 215B, 258BL, 265BR, 266T, 266B, 267TL 283, 287MR, 290TR, 292TR, 296 317L, 334, 340, 342B, 344R, 349TR, 351B, 354B, 369, 376T, 380T, 384, 386T, 386B, 391B, 395T 413T, 420, 435TL, 445B, 455TL, 455TR, 468B, 489T, 494.

Fine Art Photographic Library: 76BR, 94, 106T, 104T, 105B, 126BL, 128B, 142R, 144Bl, 168BL, 188T, 245B.

Duncan Baird Publishing: 448.

Glasgow Museums: 117T.

Hutchison Library: 388B, 389B.

Icorec: 466B.

Image Solutions: 390T, 390B, 391TL, 412T.

Images of India: 400B.

Jean Loup Charmet: 199TR, 226B.

King Arthurs Great Hall, Tintagel: 102T, 136TL, 136TR, 139TL, 153TR.

Manchester City Art Galleries: 19B, 54BL, 103B, 194B.

Mary Evans: 277BR, 286T, 286B, 287TL, 287BL, 293T, 294B, 295BL, 295BM, 305T, 320B, 322B, 323TR, 323TL, 327B, 330BL, 331MR, 370B, 423TR, 434B, 435TR, 449BR, 453BL, 461B, 469B, 484R.

Michael Holford: 265TR, 315T, 319T, 322TR, 322ML, 361BL, 404, 434T.

Miranda Gray: 104BL, 130Bl, 146T, 148BL, 170B.

Nasjonalgalleriet, Oslo: 188B, 216B.

National Galleries of Scotland: 101L, 112, 120B, 124T.

National Museum Stockholm: 184T, 192T, 198R, 217T, 232BL.

National Palace Museum, Tapei: 489B, 491B.

Panos Pictures: 312B

Royal Asiatic Society: 359B&T.

Scala Florence: 31TL.

Statens Museum fur Kunst, Copenhagen: 183B, 201T, 247TR, 250B.

K Stevens: 427, 431, 433t, 456t, 457t, 458tr, 458tl, 463r, 463l, 464b, 467, 470bl, 471tr, 471tl, 471br, 471bm, 471bl, 475b, 482b, 487t, 490b, 490t, 495b.

Stuart Littlejohn: 116T, 117BL, 132BR, 170T.

The Tate Gallery: 44T, 136B.

Werner Forman Archive: 176, 177, 212BL, 252TR, 238BR, 191TL, 199TL, 207, 211BL, 215TR, 235, 247TL.

Yvonne Gilbert: 150ML.

INDEX